Quantum Computing

Quantum Computing

The Past, the Present, and the Future

Edited by Sam Goundar,
K. Reddy Madhavi, and J. Avanija

CRC Press
Taylor & Francis Group
Boca Raton London New York

CRC Press is an imprint of the
Taylor & Francis Group, an **informa** business

Designed cover image: Getty Images

First edition published 2026
by CRC Press
2385 NW Executive Center Drive, Suite 320, Boca Raton FL 33431

and by CRC Press
4 Park Square, Milton Park, Abingdon, Oxon, OX14 4RN

CRC Press is an imprint of Taylor & Francis Group, LLC

ISBN: 978-1-032-88656-5 (hbk)
ISBN: 978-1-032-88661-9 (pbk)
ISBN: 978-1-003-53895-0 (ebk)

DOI: 10.1201/9781003538950

Typeset in Times
by Apex CoVantage, LLC

This book is dedicated to our fellow authors who contributed chapters and to our families, friends, colleagues, and mentors. Their patience, understanding, and support have been the foundation for every page we have written. We owe this work to their encouragement and belief in us throughout this journey.

We also dedicate this book to the researchers, students, and practitioners who continue to explore the fascinating world of quantum computing. It is their passion, curiosity, and resilience that inspire us every day and drive this field forward.

Above all, we dedicate this book to you, the readers, who pick it up with a desire to learn, to understand, and to imagine new possibilities. May it serve as a guide, a source of knowledge, and a spark for your own discoveries in the ever-evolving realm of quantum computing.

Sam Goundar, K. Reddy Madhavi, J. Avanija

Contents

PART II The Current (Application)

PART III The Future (Next Generation Applications)

Author/Editor Biographies

Sam Goundar is Senior Lecturer in Information Technology at RMIT University, Australia, and a Visiting Professor of Data Science at SRM University, India. He has over three decades of academic experience across thirteen universities in eleven countries, teaching and researching in areas such as artificial intelligence, cybersecurity, data science, blockchain, cloud computing, and digital transformation. Professor Goundar is the Editor-in-Chief of several international journals, including the *International Journal of Blockchains and Cryptocurrencies*, the *International Journal of Fog Computing*, and the *International Journal of Creative Computing*, and serves on the editorial boards and review panels for numerous prestigious Q1 journals.

He has published extensively, with more than 22 books and numerous peer-reviewed articles focusing on artificial intelligence, cybersecurity, and emergent technologies. Professor Goundar has supervised PhD and master's students across diverse disciplines, including AI for next-generation educational platforms, precision agriculture using AI and IoT, and anti-forensics tactics in cyber-crime investigations. An active contributor to international conferences, he has served as keynote speaker, conference chair, and committee member for events spanning AI, data analytics, and digital innovation. Passionate about making technology inclusive and impactful, Professor Goundar's work aims to foster equity, access, and sustainable growth in an increasingly digital world.

K. Reddy Madhavi received her PhD from JNTU, Anantapur, MTech from JNTU Hyderabad, and BTech from SV University, Tirupati, and is currently working as Professor of AI and ML in the School of Computing, Mohan Babu University, Tirupati. She has filed and published 21 national and international patents and few of them granted too. To her profile, she has more than 100 papers in international journals/conferences indexed in SCI/Scopus/Google Scholar and edited/authored five books. She has undergone a course on design thinking in collaboration with IUCEE EPICS Purdue University, USA. She is also an Innovation Ambassador associated with IIC, MHRD, Government of India. She is the Convener of IEEE and Springer international conferences—ICACT 2025, IC3T 2024, ICATAS 2024, ICCIET 2024, ICIHCNN 2022, ICDIC 2021—and other conferences—NCKITS 2022, NCKITS 2023, and ICATAS 2023. She is acting as a reviewer and program committee member for many international and national conferences and journals. She is acting as Session Chair/Co-chair for many symposia and conferences, delivered expert talks too. She has received the Young Woman

Scientist Award by Dr. Abdul Kalam Educational Trust during the academic year 2019–20, the Young Researcher Award at CHSN 2020 at JNTUK, and the Woman Researcher Award by INSO, International Scientist Award on Engineering, Science, and Medicine, October 2022. She is the senior member of IEEE, a life member of CSI, IETE, ISTE, a member of ACM, and a faculty advisor for the Soft Computing Research Society (SCRS) student chapter.

J. Avanija completed her PhD at Anna University Chennai, India, and is currently working as a Professor in the School of Computing, Mohan Babu University, Andhra Pradesh, Tirupati, India. Her research areas of interest are semantic web mining, machine learning, artificial intelligence, deep learning, big data, and cloud computing. She has 23 years of experience in academia and has 15 patents published and few granted to her credit. She has published more than 75 papers in reputed international journals/conferences indexed in SCI/Scopus (Scopus ID: 55711418900)/Web of Science (Web of Science ID: ABC-1218–2020)/Google Scholar and authored/edited eight books. She has won the Best Woman Researcher Award in 2019. She has been serving as reviewer and editorial board member for various international journals. She is a senior member of IEEE and member of ACM.

Preface

This book is designed to help both seasoned experts and aspiring learners of quantum computing build new skills, deepen their understanding, and save time and energy for the work they are passionate about. Quantum computing is a remarkable blend of quantum mechanics, computer science, and information theory, and it is reshaping how we understand and utilize information. Today, as the world witnesses a surge of exciting advances in this field, it has become more vital than ever to explore the nature of quantum mechanics in depth, gaining a richer understanding of its role in how information is stored, transformed, and retrieved. This book aims to guide readers on this journey, making complex ideas approachable, intriguing, and rewarding.

More than just an introduction, this book covers the evolution, current state, and future directions of quantum computing, making it a truly comprehensive resource. It explores promising application areas such as cryptography, communications, cybersecurity, and teleportation. Its structure is intentionally inclusive, providing foundational knowledge for newcomers through chapters that use simple language and approachable examples, while also addressing the interests of researchers, practitioners, and academics with advanced sections that highlight state-of-the-art technologies, trends, and opportunities for further exploration. In doing so, this book stands apart from many others in the field by offering both breadth and depth, making it an invaluable resource for anyone seeking to understand and shape the future of quantum computing.

This book is designed for a broad and diverse audience that includes junior and senior undergraduate students, graduate students, researchers, academics, and industry professionals. It will be valuable to teaching professionals as well as students pursuing undergraduate, postgraduate, and doctoral degrees across disciplines, such as computer science, engineering, mathematics, and physics. It is ideal for those with a keen interest in quantum computing and a basic understanding of mathematics, making it accessible to readers at many levels of expertise. Its global approach ensures its applicability to readers from every corner of the world, making it a strong resource for university courses and a reliable reference for departments of Computer Science, Mathematics, and Physics.

The book is equally suited to professional and industrial readers, serving as a symbolic and authoritative reference for both public and private sector applications. Its relevance will only continue to grow as quantum computing finds its place in critical fields such as pharmaceuticals, materials science, and beyond. As research institutions and centers of innovation adopt quantum computing for tackling complex and impactful challenges, this book will serve as a trusted guide for students, researchers, and professionals alike, providing a foundation for understanding the theoretical underpinnings, practical applications, and future potential of this revolutionary technology.

Quantum computing is an intriguing field that sits at the crossroads of quantum mechanics, computer science, and information theory. Yet for many, it still feels abstract and elusive. We felt a deep motivation to write this book precisely because the field has advanced far enough that it can no longer be treated as an obscure area of theoretical research. The time is right for a comprehensive resource that makes quantum computing approachable, addressing the knowledge and notation gaps that often separate traditional computing from its quantum counterpart. This book aims to give readers a solid foundation and to illuminate the connections between the theory and its evolving practical implementations.

Although quantum computing has progressed remarkably, it is still very much an active area of exploration. Even experts disagree about which methods and approaches will dominate in the future. We wrote this book to open the door to a broad range of readers, from teaching professionals and university students at every level, to engineers, mathematicians, researchers, and enthusiasts with a basic understanding of math. The text goes beyond theory, highlighting concrete applications that are too often overlooked in introductory materials. We wanted to bridge the gap between abstract concepts and real-world uses, showing how quantum algorithms and protocols can transform industries and redefine computational boundaries.

Today, quantum computing is no longer confined to theoretical papers and academic circles. Leading organizations like IBM and Google already operate quantum machines, making it increasingly relevant for businesses and researchers across disciplines. Yet many still regard this technology as a distant, almost mythical concept. We hope this book changes that perception. By clearly presenting the mechanics and potential of quantum computing, we want to open this field to a wider audience, making it an integral part of both the study of computer science and the ongoing evolution of technology itself.

The book is organized into 21 chapters grouped across three thematic sections that guide readers from foundational knowledge, through current advances, and toward future innovations in quantum computing. The first section, "The Past (Foundation)," explores the evolution and theoretical groundwork of quantum computing. It covers topics such as the basic principles of superposition, entanglement, and interference, foundational hardware, and early advances that shaped the field. Beginning with the Evolution of Quantum Computing and the Fundamentals of Quantum Computing, these chapters guide the reader from theoretical underpinnings to a systematic review of the literature and an examination of how Quantum Computing has evolved into a credible, experimental area of research.

The second section, "The Current (Application)," delves into present-day advances, platforms, and uses of quantum computing across disciplines. Chapters in this section introduce critical frameworks and taxonomies for organizing quantum computing technologies, then move toward real-world deployments and applications. From quantum computing in transportation and agriculture to advances in quantum communication, quantum cryptography, quantum machine learning, and quantum homomorphic encryption for privacy-preserving analytics, these chapters reveal how quantum computing is reshaping industries and fields as diverse as telecommunications, healthcare, and cybersecurity.

The final section, "The Future (Next-Generation Applications)," provides an in-depth examination of the challenges and opportunities that will define quantum computing in the coming years. Here, chapters explore advances in quantum-enhanced

AI, the role of quantum computing in securing 6G and beyond, its interplay with cutting-edge electronics and sensor design, and its ultimate role in a quantum internet. By addressing both the theoretical and experimental dimensions of future quantum computing applications, the book positions itself as an authoritative resource for researchers, educators, and practitioners seeking a roadmap for advances in quantum computing and its transformative potential across disciplines.

The chapters are as follows:

Chapter 1: Evolution of Quantum Computing

Chapter 1 introduces readers to the fundamental concepts of quantum computing and provides a rich historical context that traces its evolution from theoretical beginnings to its present state. It explains the basic ideas of superposition, entanglement, and interference, making it accessible for newcomers while highlighting why these phenomena are central to the field. The chapter presents a robust methodology framed within a three-phase historical classification, making it a valuable entry point for understanding the advances that shaped quantum computing.

Chapter 2: Fundamentals of Quantum Computing

Chapter 2 focuses on the essentials of quantum computing, explaining key concepts such as qubits, gates, error corrections, and entanglement. The chapter emphasizes their role in making quantum computing viable for practical applications. It also provides examples from experimental advances by leading firms in the industry, making this chapter both a theoretical and practical resource for readers.

Chapter 3: Current State of Quantum Computing

In this chapter, readers are introduced to the hardware and software advances making quantum computing a reality. The chapter analyzes the state of the field through comparative analyses using qualitative and quantitative methods such as SWOT, benchmarking, and case studies. It serves as a pivotal chapter for readers to understand the advances and constraints characterizing the state of quantum computing today.

Chapter 4: A Systematic Literature Review of Quantum Computing

Chapter 4 provides a comprehensive review of literature across fields such as physics, computer science, and engineering. It analyzes pivotal breakthroughs like Feynman's conjecture and Shor's algorithm, focusing on advances in hardware, quantum information theory, and machine learning. The chapter is vital for researchers seeking an authoritative review and a roadmap of future directions for the discipline.

Chapter 5: A Framework and Taxonomy for Quantum Computing

Chapter 5 develops an integrative and multidimensional taxonomy for quantum computing that organizes its hardware, algorithms, and application areas. This chapter aims to streamline fragmented terminology and foster multidisciplinary collaboration. Its proposed framework serves as an essential reference point for both researchers and practitioners, aligning academic inquiry with industrial needs.

Chapter 6: Quantum Computing—Real-World Applications and Its Transformative Potential

Chapter 6 explores how quantum computing can optimize industries reliant on massive data processing. From traffic optimization for emergency services to predictive analytics in agriculture and transportation, it provides case studies highlighting quantum advantages. This chapter emphasizes quantum computing's role in making operational environments more efficient, making it a pivotal resource for both researchers and decision-makers.

Chapter 7: Quantum Computing—A Journey Through Time

Chapter 7 takes readers through the milestones in quantum computing's evolution, starting from its theoretical roots in the 1930s, to Feynman's ideas, and the advances shaped by Shor and others. This chapter provides a comprehensive review of how quantum computing emerged from theory to experimental feasibility, making it essential for understanding the discipline's heritage and long-standing impact.

Chapter 8: Quantum Computing—Foundations, Principles, and Modern Applications

Chapter 8 explores the foundational principles of quantum computing, focusing on its mathematical underpinnings and complex problem-solving capabilities. It analyzes advances across disciplines such as optimization, materials design, and cryptography, making it a valuable chapter for readers seeking both theoretical understanding and examples of real-world impacts.

Chapter 9: Evolutionary Algorithms and Quantum Computing—Pioneering the Next Era of Intelligence and Innovation

Chapter 9 analyzes the synergy between quantum computing and evolutionary algorithms, focusing on how this combined approach can revolutionize fields such as financial modeling, bioinformatics, and artificial intelligence. Its case studies highlight the benefits of using quantum computing to optimize complex, multi-variable environments.

Chapter 10: Journey into Quantum Computing—Cryptographic Security and Learning Algorithms

Chapter 10 guides readers from the foundational mathematics of quantum computing, through its cryptographic and machine learning applications. It explores how quantum computing can drive advances in cybersecurity and data analytics, making it a pivotal chapter for researchers and practitioners working in data security and artificial intelligence.

Chapter 11: Next-Gen Quantum Computing—The Fusion of Atoms and Photonic Innovation

Chapter 11 explores the advances in quantum computing brought about by the merging of atomic and photonic technologies. It explains how this synergy can overcome traditional bottlenecks in quantum computing, making it highly relevant for hardware developers and researchers seeking fault-tolerant, scalable quantum platforms.

Chapter 12: Quantum Communication and Secure Channels

Chapter 12 discusses the role of quantum computing in creating secure, tamper-proof communication channels. Covering quantum key distribution and advances in hardware and error correction, this chapter provides readers with a deep understanding of how quantum computing is shaping the future of digital security and privacy.

Chapter 13: Quantum Computing and Teleportation

Chapter 13 provides an in-depth examination of quantum computing's role in information teleportation. It explains the underlying principles of superposition and entanglement and showcases advances like quantum key distribution. This chapter provides valuable context for understanding quantum computing's role in reshaping fields like cryptography, logistics, and artificial intelligence.

Chapter 14: Analysis of Post-Quantum Cryptography Algorithms

Chapter 14 explores the advances and challenges associated with post-quantum cryptography (PQC), focusing on new encryption methods that can remain secure in a quantum computing era. By analyzing isogeny-based, lattice-based, and hash-based methods, it provides an essential resource for cybersecurity researchers and professionals seeking to safeguard data in the age of quantum computing.

Chapter 15: Quantum Computing Paradigms—Bridging Foundational Quantum Mechanics with Contemporary Computational Architectures

Chapter 15 connects theoretical quantum mechanics with practical advances in quantum computing. It covers error correction, coherence stabilization, and quantum phase estimation, making it an essential chapter for physicists, engineers, and technologists focusing on quantum computing hardware and its future potential.

Chapter 16: Revolutionizing Data Science with Quantum Computing—Principles, Applications, and Machine Learning Integration

Chapter 16 explores how quantum computing can transform fields such as data science, AI, and optimization. By focusing on quantum-enhanced machine learning and its integration with traditional approaches, this chapter provides valuable insights for researchers, data scientists, and technologists seeking to utilize quantum computing in their disciplines.

Chapter 17: Advancing AI with Quantum: Quantum Machine Learning Classifiers (QML) and Transfer Learning in Neural Networks

Chapter 17 explains how quantum computing can revolutionize machine learning and AI by leveraging quantum-enhanced neural network transfer learning. It explores case studies across fields such as medical diagnostics and predictive analytics, making it a critical chapter for researchers and practitioners working with high-dimensional data and AI technologies.

Chapter 18: Enhancing Healthcare Data Security using Quantum Homomorphic Encryption

Chapter 18 explores how quantum computing can secure sensitive medical data through quantum homomorphic encryption. By focusing on case studies like diabetes data, this chapter provides actionable knowledge for researchers and healthcare professionals seeking to utilize quantum computing to safeguard patient privacy and data integrity.

Chapter 19: Quantum Communication Systems for Ensuring Secure 6G Network Infrastructure

Chapter 19 analyzes how quantum computing can be embedded within future 6G network infrastructure to create secure, resilient communication environments. It explores quantum key distribution and AI-driven threat detection, making this chapter valuable for technologists working on next-generation telecommunications.

Chapter 20: Superposition in Quantum Computing—Advancements with Google's Willow Chip and IBM's Quantum Systems

Chapter 20 explores the advances in quantum computing hardware that have been made possible by superposition and entanglement, focusing on breakthroughs like Google's Willow chip and IBM's Quantum Systems. The chapter provides case studies highlighting error correction, qubit stability, and improved computational speed, making it a must-read for hardware developers and researchers.

Chapter 21: Quantum Internet and Its Revolutionary Implications for Modern Electronic Devices

Chapter 21 examines the quantum internet's potential to transform electronics, focusing on quantum-enhanced sensors, repeaters, and networking technologies. The chapter highlights the role quantum computing can play in reshaping industries such as telecommunications, electronics design, and cybersecurity, making it a vital resource for researchers and technologists charting the future of quantum computing.

We would like to extend our heartfelt gratitude to the institutions, colleagues, and review teams who have supported the development of this book from its earliest concept to its final form. We acknowledge the vital role played by our respective universities and research centers, whose resources and collaborative environments have inspired and facilitated countless ideas and discussions. We are deeply grateful to our colleagues and friends across disciplines for their valuable insights, constructive feedback, and encouragement throughout the writing process. In particular, we thank the review teams for their meticulous attention and critical suggestions that shaped the book's precision and depth. Their collective efforts have strengthened the work, making it a resource we are proud to present to students, researchers, and professionals across the global quantum computing community.

The editors' vision for this book emerges from the pivotal moment we now witness in the evolution of quantum computing. The world is in the midst of a profound shift, as advances in quantum mechanics, information theory, and computer science converge to redefine how we solve complex problems and harness data. We felt it was vital to create a comprehensive resource that captures this era of exploration and growth, making the concepts and applications of quantum computing accessible to a broad, multidisciplinary audience. At a time when quantum technologies are making their way out of theoretical laboratories and into industries, this book aims to illuminate both the foundations and the frontier, providing readers with the knowledge and context necessary to understand and contribute to this global shift.

More than a compilation of chapters, this book is designed to inspire, educate, and guide its readers. Its impact lies in its ability to bridge disciplines, making quantum computing relevant for students, researchers, educators, and professionals across fields from engineering and computer science to mathematics, physics, and beyond. We hope that it will serve as both a textbook and a reference point, fostering deeper conversations about the role of quantum technologies in shaping a more sustainable, equitable, and innovative future. By capturing this critical moment in the field, we intend for the book to be a catalyst for new ideas, collaborations, and breakthroughs that will define the next generation of computing.

Contributors

Imran Aslan
Bingol University
Bingol, Turkiye

J. Avanija
Mohan Babu University
Tirupati. India

R. Anandan
Vels Institute of Science, Technology and Advanced Studies
Tamil Nadu, India

Akashdeep Bhardwaj
UPES
Dehradun, India

Deepika Bandhana
The University of Fiji
Lautoka, Fiji

M. Bharathi
Mohan Babu University
Andhra Pradesh, India,

Peyyala Balakrishna
VIT-AP University
Andhra Pradesh, India.

Shaik Javid Basha
Santhiram Engineering College
Andhra Pradesh, India

Ganesuni Aasish Chowdary
VIT
Andhra Pradesh, India

Gudditi Chetan
VIT
Andhra Pradesh, India

Madhu G. C.
CMR Institute of Technology
Bengaluru, India.

Nagendra Panini Challa
VIT
Andhra Pradesh, India

Sarvesh Chand
The University of the South Pacific
Suva, Fiji

Akhil Dandamudi
Kalven Technologies
Georgia, USA.

B. Rupa Devi
Annamacharya Institute of Technology and Sciences
Andhra Pradesh, India.

Chandramohan Dhasarathan
Thapar Institute of Engineering and Technology
Punjab, India

Deepak Davala
Aditya Institute of Technology and Management
Andhra Pradesh, India.

Mannipudi Prabhu Das
Mohan Babu University
Andhra Pradesh, India

Vinay Dwivedi
Galgotias University
Uttar Pradesh, India

Anant Shankar E.
Sri Venkateswara College of Engineering
Andhra Pradesh, India.

Manasa Gadiraju
Mohan Babu University
Andhra Pradesh, India.

Sam Goundar
RMIT University
Melbourne, Australia

Sandhya Kumari G.
Siddartha Institute of Science and Technology
Andhra Pradesh, India.

Srinivasa Reddy Gayam
Mohan Babu University
Tirupati, India

S. Hemachandra
Sanskrithi School of Engineering
Puttaparthi, India.

Shaik Jaffar Hussain
Sri Venkateswara Institute of Science and Technology
Andhra Pradesh, India

Vishal Kumar Jaiswal
OPTUM
Virginia, USA

A. Hesanth Kumar
Siddharth Institute of Engineering & Technology
Andhra Pradesh, India.

L. N. C. Prakash K.
CVR College of Engineering
Andhra Pradesh, India.

N. Ashok Kumar
Mohan Babu University
Andhra Pradesh, India.

Shiva Prasad Kaleru
Juniper Networks
California, USA.

Shruthi K.
Siddaganga Institute of Technology
Karnataka, India.

Ushik Shrestha Khwakhali
RMIT University Vietnam
Hanoi, Vietnam.

Vishnu Kumar Kaliappan
KPR Institute of Engineering and Technology
Tamil Nadu, India.

K. Reddy Madhavi
Mohan Babu University
Tirupati, India.

Artor Nuhiu
University of Prishtina
Prishtina, Kosovo.

Beebi Naseeba
VIT
Andhra Pradesh, India

P. Nagarajan
SRM Institute of Science and Technology
Tamil Nadu, India

G. V. L. Narasimha
Aditya Institute of Technology and Management
Andhra Pradesh, India.

K. Neelima
Mohan Babu University
Andhra Pradesh, India

S. Nagini
VNRVJIET
Andhra Pradesh, India.

Ashok Kumar Patel
University of Massachusetts
Massachusetts, USA

N. Padmaja
Mohan Babu Universty
Andhra Pradesh, India.

M. Poornima
Sri Venkateswara College of Engineering
Andhra Pradesh, India.

Ramesh Peramalasetty
Vemu Institute of Technology
Andhra Pradesh, India

S. Praveena
Aditya Institute of Technology and Management
Andhra Pradesh, India.

L. Srinivasa Rao
VNRVJIET
Andhra Pradesh, India.

Nagaraj Ramrao
Mohan Babu University
Andhra Pradesh, India.

R. Roopa
Madanapalle Institute of Technology & Science
Andhra Pradesh, India.

Ch. Sandhya Rani
VNRVJIET
Andhra Pradesh, India.

Sivaranjani Reddi
Raghu Engineering College
Andhra Pradesh, India.

A. Suresh
GRT Institute of Engineering and Technology
Tamil Nadu, India.

Allam Gowri Sankar
Mohan Babu University
Andhra Pradesh, India

G. Sandhyakumari
Siddharth Institute of Engineering & Technology
Andhra Pradesh, India.

G. Suryanarayana
Symbiosis Institute of Technology
Andhra Pradesh, India

Gurram Sunitha
Mohan Babu University
Tirupati, India.

Haranadha Reddy Busireddy Seshakagari
Enterprise Cloud Architect
Pennsylvania, USA.

Jami Venkata Suman
GMR Institute of Technology
Andhra Pradesh, India.

K. Saradhi
Mohan Babu University
Andhra Pradesh, India

M. Sudhakara
Chistats Labs Private Limited,
Maharashtra, India.

P. Sohan Sai
Sree Vidyanikethan Engineering College
Andhra Pradesh, India.

Rajeshwari Sissodia
Galgotias University
Uttar Pradesh, India

Naresh Tangudu
Aditya Institute of Technology and Management
Andhra Pradesh, India.

Saleha Tabassum
Vignan University
Andhra Pradesh, India.

Chinthapatla Pranay Varna
Mohan Babu University
Andhra Pradesh, India

Madhurima V.
Sree Venkateswara College of Engineering
Andhra Pradesh, India.

Pranav Vyas
Charotar University of Science and Technology
Gujarat, India

Mahdieh Zakizadeh
TU Wien University
Vienna, Austria.

N. Padmaja
Mohan Babu Universty
Andhra Pradesh, India.

Part I

The Past (Foundation)

1 Evolution of Quantum Computing

Sam Goundar, Deepika Bandhana, Sarvesh Chand, R. Anandan, and Imran Aslan

1.1 INTRODUCTION TO QUANTUM COMPUTING

The evolution of quantum computing represents a paradigm shift in computational theory, bridging the principles of quantum mechanics and computer science. Traditional computing, grounded in binary logic, is inherently limited in addressing certain complex optimization, cryptography, and simulation problems due to its reliance on deterministic processing. The emergence of quantum computing introduces probabilistic computation models, leveraging the principles of superposition, entanglement, and quantum gates to exponentially enhance processing capabilities.

This chapter aims to provide a systematic analysis of how quantum computing has evolved, from its theoretical foundations in the early 20th century to its modern-day experimental implementations and commercial developments. While several works have reviewed the history of quantum computing, existing literature often lacks a structured framework for understanding its progression across different technological eras. This chapter seeks to address this gap by introducing a historical classification model that categorizes the evolution of quantum computing into three distinct phases:

1. Theoretical Foundations (1900s–1980s): The emergence of quantum mechanics and its implications for computation.
2. Algorithmic Breakthroughs (1980s–2000s): The formalization of quantum computing principles, including quantum algorithms, complexity classes, and computational models.
3. Technological Advancements and Commercialization (2000s–Present): The transition from theoretical models to practical quantum hardware, cloud-based quantum services, and hybrid quantum-classical computing.

In addition, Table 1.1 will make it easier to understand this chapter as it compares the classical and quantum advancements.

This structured approach will provide a clearer perspective on the technological milestones, the key figures and breakthroughs that have shaped the field, and the ongoing challenges that must be addressed for quantum computing to reach its full potential.

DOI: 10.1201/9781003538950-2

TABLE 1.1
Shows Features of Classical Versus Quantum Computer

Feature	Classical Computing	Quantum Computing
Processing unit	Binary	Qubits
Processing method	Sequentially	Operates in multiple states
Computation type	Continuous and deterministic	Discrete and probabilistic
Scalability	Linear	Exponential
Operating phenomena	Classical physics	Quantum mechanics
Error correction	Corrections codes and parity checks	Quantum codes and quantum low-density parity checks
Earliest model	Alan Turing machine	Universal quantum Turing machine
Key theorists	Turing, Von Neumann	Feynman, Deutsch

Moreover, this chapter will not only examine the historical developments but also evaluate the implications of these advancements for modern computing paradigms. By analyzing how quantum computing has progressed from theoretical speculation to a field with real-world applications, this chapter will lay the foundation for deeper discussions on future quantum architectures, scalability challenges, and the ethical considerations of quantum technologies in subsequent sections of this book.

By the end of this chapter, readers will gain a structured understanding of the evolution of quantum computing, allowing them to critically assess its impact on scientific research, cybersecurity, artificial intelligence, and computational complexity.

1.2 BACKGROUND

The field of quantum computing has emerged as a revolutionary advancement in computation, fundamentally challenging the principles of classical computing. Classical computers, based on the Von Neumann architecture, rely on binary logic (bits: 0 and 1) to process and store information. While these systems have powered technological progress for decades, they encounter significant limitations in solving complex problems involving optimization, cryptographic analysis, molecular simulations, and high-dimensional data processing.

Quantum computing, rooted in quantum mechanics, presents an alternative paradigm where information is processed using qubits instead of classical bits. Unlike classical bits, which exist in a single state at a given time, qubits leverage quantum superposition and entanglement, enabling them to exist in multiple states simultaneously. This property allows quantum computers to perform parallel computations exponentially faster than their classical counterparts for certain problem sets.

The motivation for quantum computing arose from the theoretical limits of classical computation, as articulated by Alan Turing and John von Neumann. The foundational shift occurred when Richard Feynman (1982) proposed that quantum mechanical systems could be better simulated using quantum processors rather than classical models. This idea led to the development of key quantum algorithms, such as Shor's algorithm (1994) for factoring large numbers and Grover's algorithm (1996) for unstructured search, demonstrating a clear computational advantage.

Over the years, advancements in quantum hardware and error correction have transformed quantum computing from an abstract theoretical concept into an experimental reality. Companies such as IBM, Google, and D-Wave have developed quantum processors, while governments and research institutions worldwide are investing heavily in quantum research for applications in secure communication, artificial intelligence, and materials science.

Despite these advancements, quantum computing remains an evolving field, with challenges related to scalability, decoherence, quantum error correction, and practical implementation. This chapter provides a structured analysis of the historical development of quantum computing, tracing its evolution from its mathematical foundations to modern-day commercialization efforts.

1.3 THEORETICAL FOUNDATIONS OF QUANTUM COMPUTING

The foundations of quantum computing are deeply rooted in quantum mechanics, a field of physics developed in the early 20th century to explain phenomena that classical physics could not. Unlike classical computing, which operates using deterministic binary logic, quantum computing relies on probabilistic and non-deterministic principles that allow for parallel computation and exponential processing speedups.

The theoretical framework of quantum computing is defined by three fundamental principles.

1.3.1 Quantum Superposition

In classical computing, a bit can exist in one of two states: 0 or 1. In contrast, a qubit (quantum bit) can exist in a superposition of both states simultaneously, allowing quantum computers to process multiple calculations in parallel. Mathematically, a qubit's state is represented as $|\psi\rangle = \alpha|0\rangle + \beta|1\rangle$, where α and β are complex probability amplitudes, and their squared magnitudes sum to 1 (ensuring probabilistic consistency). This property significantly enhances the efficiency of search algorithms, cryptographic analysis, and complex simulations.

1.3.2 Quantum Entanglement

Entanglement is a unique property of quantum mechanics that allows two or more qubits to become correlated in such a way that the state of one qubit is directly dependent on the state of the other, regardless of distance. This enables instantaneous information transfer across entangled qubits, providing a major advantage for secure quantum communication and quantum networking.

For an entangled two-qubit system, the quantum state is represented as $|\psi\rangle = |00\rangle + |11\rangle) / \sqrt{2}$, which means that if one qubit is measured to be 0, the other must also be 0, and if one is 1, the other is 1—even if they are physically separated.

1.3.3 Quantum Interference

Quantum computations rely on wave-like properties of quantum states such as electrons and photons, which allow for constructive and destructive interference. Quantum algorithms exploit this interference to amplify correct solutions while canceling out incorrect ones. For example, Grover's search algorithm leverages interference to enhance the probability of the correct answer, making searches faster than classical algorithms.

1.4 COMPUTATIONAL MODELS OF QUANTUM COMPUTING

The principles of quantum mechanics have led to several computational paradigms that define how quantum computers process information:

- **Quantum Gate Model** (Circuit-Based Computing): Uses quantum gates (Hadamard, CNOT, Toffoli [CCNOT]) to manipulate qubits, similar to classical logic gates but with reversible operations.
- **Quantum Annealing**: A specialized model optimized for solving combinatorial optimization problems using quantum fluctuations (e.g., D-Wave's quantum annealers).
- **Topological Quantum Computing**: Uses non-Abelian anyons and braided particle states to achieve fault-tolerant computation.
- **Measurement-Based (One-Way) Quantum Computing**: Relies on pre-entangled qubits, which are manipulated through quantum measurements to execute computations.

Each of these models plays a role in defining the capabilities and constraints of quantum computing architectures.

These theoretical foundations have shaped the historical development of quantum computing, influencing:

- The formulation of quantum algorithms (Shor's, Grover's).
- The design of quantum hardware architectures (superconducting qubits, trapped ions).
- The emergence of quantum error correction techniques, essential for large-scale quantum computation.

As quantum computing progresses from theoretical models to commercialized implementations, understanding these foundational principles becomes crucial for evaluating its long-term impact on science, technology, and industry.

1.5 WHAT IS QUANTUM COMPUTING?

An article published in the journal *Nature* titled "Ultra strong magnetic light-matter interaction with cavity mode engineering" states that manipulation of weak photons and diploes interaction can bring forth a remarkable outburst of technology improvement that can lead to enhancement of these interactions up to 10^{16}" [1]. Such improvements have been the subject of contemplation since the start of the 20th century, where technologies were slowly automating tasks or bringing miraculous inventions. In 1920, catastrophic crisis of science led to the invention of quantum mechanics, so that the prediction of ultraviolet catastrophe involving infinite energies or electrons spiraling the atom nucleus could be feasible [2]. Now, it is understood that every object either animate or inanimate is made up of atoms, and a single atom is simply the tiniest matter, that has a nucleus at its core and consists of protons, neutrons, and electrons as its outer casing. The electrons are negatively charged and are excitable elements of the atom, whereas the neutrons are neutral in charge and the protons are positively charged.

Transfer of energy and movement is often understood in physics. Physics is the underlying concept of quantum mechanics, which is a set of mathematical frameworks of physical theories. To fully understand quantum mechanics, it is essential to understand what quantum electrodynamics is; to make things simpler, quantum mechanics can be seen as an operating system of a computer, and quantum electrodynamics can be seen as the application software of the computer. The operating system and the application software are both required to serve the purpose of the computer. So, quantum electrodynamics helps us to understand the interaction of electric current with magnetic field accurately. Thus, conceptualizing and collaborating these notions in a machine is called quantum computing.

Quantum computing achieves accuracy, speed, optimization, and complex problem-solving that cannot be offered by classical computing. Classical computers are made up of a hardware that has an operating system in place that runs different applications to perform tasks, and these tasks are performed through commands that are fundamentally called bits. Bits are usually binary in nature and are referred to as 0s and 1s, and this makes it the tiniest information holder, so to store and process information more efficiently, the classical computer often uses a byte, which is a sequence of eight bits [3].

In contrast, the tiniest element of quantum computing is called qubits, a portmanteau of "quantum bits." Qubits are translated data that are stored as 0 or 1, simultaneously, due to a phenomenon called superposition. The phenomenon shows that there are some subatomic properties that are unknown until observed, which in mathematical terms can be expressed that a problem can have two solutions, but it can be approached in the sense of a like mind. In terms of electrodynamics, the same element may exist in different states but have the same properties. This makes quantum computers operate at enormous speed. Another phenomenon that allows quantum computers to have significant power over classical computers is quantum entanglement.

The phenomenon of quantum entanglement shows that qubits can entangle with other subatomic particles in close proximity, and these subatomic particles can be described as independently separate, resulting quantum computers' power increasing exponentially, unlike classical computers, where the power increase is observed linearly. These combined aspects of quantum computer serve an advantage over classical computers to solve problems that classical computers cannot solve. This may lead us to ponder if the current classical computer security is impossible to breach due to its complexity, then it might be possible that a quantum computer can possibly break this complexity and give us another problem to solve.

Since a real quantum computer is on its path of evolution due to the fact that this concept was fully realized in the late 20th century after observing multiple theories and designs of quantum machines. Through these stages of observations and experiments, it was realized that quantum interference is a major setback in the path of quantum evolution. The upcoming sections will highlight what quantum interference is in terms of quantum mechanics.

1.6 UNDERSTANDING THE EVOLUTION?

As mentioned, quantum computer is a great technology that allows us to solve a number of problems and maximize solutions in terms of optimization, risk analysis, and potential enormous speed to break modern cryptography, which basically presents a complex algorithm that can take millions of years to break with classical computers but can be broken or factorized in a minute, especially with a future quantum computer. On the same note, another research area that can be developed with the help of quantum computing advancement is energy. Every task that we perform in this era requires energy, be it electrical cars, smartphones, laptops, or cargo jets. The revolution focuses on maximizing the battery power so that the chemistry of unknown atomic properties could be discovered, leading to the manufacturing of a new-era quantum device to produce batteries with a longer lifetime and better battery power while meeting the cost threshold [4].

Another relevant area that can be transformed with quantum computing is medicine and pharmaceuticals. This was evident during the conception of COVID-19 pandemic, and the world is still susceptible to new and unknown diseases that might impact the human race adversely. Our technologies are still lacking and need significant improvement in terms of simulation and production of drugs that can yield better clinical success. Classical computers are often slow and less accurate in terms of simulation of drugs, especially with protein binding and protein hydration, which determine the success of the drug. Advanced quantum computers will allow the pharmaceutical industry to simulate molecular interactions with precision for efficient drug production, which is currently not possible with classical computers.

In time to come, quantum machine learning will allow the medical industry to study the genetic makeup of each individual, which can allow researchers to uncover insights that might help the drug industry to produce drugs that can better react depending on an individual's genetic makeup. Also, artificial intelligence can be well integrated with quantum computing to produce personalized medicines based on an individual's condition and genetic makeup [5].

Various scientific studies, surveys, and research states the potential of future quantum advancement, but understanding its history properly will provide a better foundation of the field that will revolutionize the world. For instance, understanding the phenomenon of quantum superposition and quantum entanglement will make provisions to enhance the cybersecurity. The classical computer operations are mostly limited to two dimensions most of the time, but with quantum superposition, the data that we are trying to protect in two dimensions can be extended to numerous dimensions that can count up to a thousand.

It will be easier to access the data in a proximity that can be accessed as a group rather than disclosing the exact location or address of this data, enhancing security. In a latter case, if the techniques of separating an atom in a trap to take control of its properties in 1970s was not pioneered or kept a secret, then it would have been difficult to unlock the realm of quantum mechanics. The advancement of this technology is entirely dependent on the knowledge that we possess and what new discoveries can be made by exploiting an atom to harness its usability to our advantage [2].

1.7 METHODOLOGY: A HISTORICAL CLASSIFICATION MODEL

The evolution of quantum computing spans over a century, involving contributions from quantum physics, computational theory, and engineering breakthroughs. To systematically analyze its development, this chapter adopts a historical classification model, segmenting quantum computing advancements into three major phases:

1. **Theoretical Foundations** (1900s–1980s): The emergence of quantum mechanics and the conceptualization of quantum computing.
2. **Algorithmic Breakthroughs** (1980s–2000s): The formulation of quantum algorithms and the first experimental quantum circuits.
3. **Technological Advancements and Commercialization** (2000s–Present): The development of practical quantum hardware and its integration into computing industries.

1.8 HISTORICAL ANALYSIS FRAMEWORK

This methodology is based on a historical analysis framework, which involves:

- Reviewing primary scientific discoveries—examining key papers, theoretical models, and experimental milestones that influenced quantum computing.
- Categorizing breakthroughs into major phases—structuring historical progression into distinct evolutionary periods.
- Comparing classical vs. quantum advancements—highlighting how quantum computing diverged from classical computation over time.

This structured approach ensures that the chapter provides a clear, evidence-based narrative on the scientific, technological, and industrial evolution of quantum computing.

A chronological classification provides a clear timeline for tracking progress. A structured comparative analysis clarifies how quantum computing differs from classical computing.

This framework enables a deeper understanding of the challenges and breakthroughs that have shaped modern quantum computing.

By applying this methodology, the chapter transitions from theoretical discussions to historical analysis, setting the stage for a comprehensive review of quantum computing's evolution from early concepts to real-world applications.

1.9 HISTORICAL FOUNDATIONS

This section highlights the historical evolution of quantum computing into three phases. The first phase elaborates on early quantum theory from the 1900s to the 1980s. The second phase elaborates on theoretical advancements of quantum computing from the 1980s to the 1990s. The third phase discusses the practical developments and emerging technologies from the 2000s till present day. Later these three phases of historical evolution of quantum computing are summarized in a table.

The first section has three subsections discussing quantum mechanics and early theories, the birth of quantum information theory, and the concept of qubits. The first subsection briefly covers the origins of quantum mechanics, including Max Planck's quantum theory, Einstein's photoelectric effect, and Schrödinger's wave function. It discusses how these principles laid the groundwork for quantum computing. Then the second subsection introduces early theoretical developments, Turing machines and computational limits, and Richard Feynman's idea of simulating physics with quantum systems. The third subsection discusses the introduction of qubits by David Deutsch and highlights key differences between qubits and classical bits.

1.9.1 Phase 1: Early Quantum Theory from the 1900s to the 1980s

As already seen, it is known that quantum mechanics and its discovering's are made by exploiting the subatomic properties. According to David Deutsch's *The Fabric of Reality* [6], subatomic elements, such as electrons, neutrons, and protons, have counterparts, the tangible and the shadow. The tangible electron and its shadow electron are traveling together in a space, the tangible electron can be measured and observed by instruments and other means, but the shadow electron remains undetectable and unobserved till its interfering effect is observed with its tangible counterpart. This was elaborated via an experiment that was conducted with a lighting torch to observe the motion of its light and using a lighting torch in a dark room (black room) to imagine scenarios where the light that is shown does not possibly hit a surface and comes back. The experiment is represented in the following figure [6].

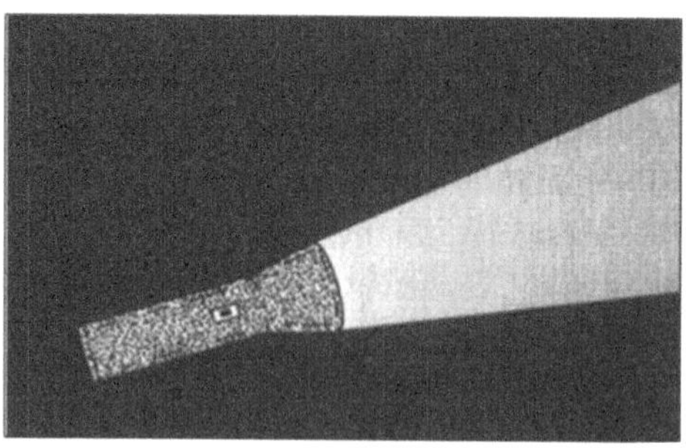

FIGURE 1.1 Light from an electric torch in a dark room from the book *The Fabric of Reality*.

Per the book [6], when a torch is lit up through its filament, two very prominent parts are highlighted, the dark and the light. The dark portion is divided into two phases, which are the umbra and the penumbra. The umbral phase is total darkness, and the penumbral phase is a portion that is less bright than the light portion but extends to a distance as the light phase does. The light portion is observed as a cylindrical cone leaving the filament and extending outward as far as it can reach. The phase of the light that is observed near the torch is brighter than the phase, which is extending to a greater distance. Now, exploiting the subatomic properties of this experiment, the bright particle that leaves the filament is called a photon. The property of a photon is such that there is not a phase where the photon becomes less bright, but it becomes sparse as the distance increases so that the brightness that we observe in the real-time becomes less.

To understand the properties of a photon and its sparsing effect, another experiment was conducted. The light was blocked by a screen to understand what may have caused the blockage at the subatomic level. Also, three screens were used to block the light at a distance, with a hole in each screen to allow the light to pass through this hole. This was to understand that if light has ductile properties. It was noticed that the path of the light leaving the first screen till the edge of the second screen displayed non-ductility, but it was diverging and a little bit lighter when it hit the edge of the first screen. The path display from the second screen to the third screen displayed the same property, but it was much lighter. So, from this, it can be deduced that when the light hit the edge of the screen, though it was a blocking agent, for some instances it behaved and displayed the properties of light.

However, it needed to be understood if a screen with no holes might possess some blocking properties. So far, it is understood that photons have its tangible aspect and shadow aspect. The photon that hits the screen edge is tangible in nature, and per *The Fabric of Reality*, only tangible photons can directly interact with the tangible particles, and not the shadow particles, because the shadow photons are part of a parallel universe and a parallel potential reality. That means every shadow photon of this universe has a tangible photon in the parallel universe or reality.

Consequently, if the tangible photon is interacting with the black screen surface, then the shadow photon must be interacting with shadow aspect of the screen, because the screen must have shadow atoms too, just as it has tangible atoms. From the second scenario of non-ductility, it was observed that when the photon that passed through the first opening, it was deflected due to certain interference and this interference was also observed from the path display to the third screen. So the interference-causing entities must have traveled with the tangible photon. Accordingly, through the quantum mechanical law, it can be stated that the shadow aspect of the photon causes the interferences, and these interferences can only be noticed in rare scenarios where the shadow photon and its tangible photon have separated from their path and remerged. So this proves that there is a set of parallel universes that sort of partitions the counterparts, and these counterparts are the potential interference. Henceforth, it can be asserted that quantum theory is about the correspondence of the reality with the possibility [6].

In addition, in the 19th and the 20th century, a problem of blackbody radiation was noted in classical physics. The classical physics states that any object emitting or absorbing radiation has a direct relationship with its temperature, but this became the cause of ultraviolent catastrophe. This catastrophe is often associated with Lord Rayleigh, who assumed that the energy radiated by the oscillators increased without bounds as it approached the ultraviolent region, but it was the exact opposite. The energy radiation increased as the frequency decreased. To further solve the issue of blackbody radiation, Wilhelm Wien also proposed that the wavelength of the peak blackbody radiation increased as the temperature increased.

This was only correct when the frequencies were high. Note, all these experiments failed because the fundamentals of classical physics were utilized, where the energy of a photon is proportional to its frequency, but this is where Max Planck introduced the concept of quantum mechanics, where the energy of a photon was proportional to its frequency multiplied by the Planck constant ($h = 6.626 \times 10^{-34}$J.s). He stated that the electromagnetic energy absorption and emission occurs in discrete units rather than in a continuous spectrum. The realization of energy absorption and emission is called quanta. The quanta are mathematically represented as the product of the frequency of radiation with the constant [7].

Although Planck's quanta were limited to an atom, later this same concept was extended by Albert Einstein, who introduced the photoelectric effect from quanta to light. Before the discovery of the photoelectric effect, Heinrich Heltz carried out the pioneering experiment by shining ultraviolent beam to metal plate, which produced an emission. Although the display of emission was not bizarre, it was realized that different metals required different minimum frequencies to knock out the electrons from the plate to cause the emission. It was also noted that when the brightness of the light increased, more electrons were emitted but when the frequency of the light wave was increased, then electrons with higher energies were emitted, while the number of electrons that were emitted remained the same.

This was understood by Albert Einstein as the photoelectric effect, while reasoning that light is a particle and a wave too. He stated that light is a beam of particles whose energy is related to the frequency by Planck's formula. As a particle, light carries energy, which is proportional to the frequency of its wave, whereas a wave's frequency can determine the particle's energy [8].

Since the discovery of the photoelectric effect, different wave frequencies can knock out the electrons, and if the wave frequency is increased, then electrons of higher energies were emitted. So in this journey of quantum evolution, a wave function equation was postulated, called the Schrodinger wave function, in 1926 [9]. The Schrodinger wave function equation can calculate the energy levels of electrons in an atom and could provide the probability of finding the location of electrons at a distance from the nucleus [7].

After Schrodinger's discovery of the wave function, another important discovery was made in the world of quantum mechanics that was closely related to the wave function. In 1927, Heisenberg stated that if the position of an electron is known, then it is less likely that the precise position of the electron is known at that particular momentum. This is called the uncertainty principle. He argues that when a photon and an electron collide, the electron suffers recoil, and the momentum is disturbed. So at an instant where the position of the electron is known, the photon is scattered by the electron, and the electron goes through a discontinuous change in the momentum. The change is greater as a smaller wavelength is employed, and this where the determination of the position is more exact [10].

The conception of quantum theory in the 1920s led to the conception of classical theory, or information theory, by Claude Shannon, which defines information mathematically and how this information can be transmitted and received in a noisy channel without being corrupted through error correction, compression, and signal processing. The term "quantum information theory" is a coinage of quantum theory and information theory, which was referenced by Claude Shannon in 1948. In some texts, the term "quantum information theory" is synonymous with "quantum Shannon theory" as a tribute to the scientist.

The essence of this term in quantum mechanics or categorically quantum computing is that it allows to possess knowledge of the quantum state and how quantification can be scrutinized to understand quantum superposition, entanglement, teleportation, interferences, and uncertainty. Though quantum information may appear to be separate branch of study, it is important to note that every physical system has a quantum state, and every quantum state exists in a physical system. So quantum information theory can be seen as an interdisciplinary field that can be associated with any field that can allow us to extract information from matter [10]. Therefore, it is equally important to understand the nature of classical physics its relation to classical computing and how the logic gates work.

Perhaps this was what Alan Turing was contemplating when he was trying to solve the *Entscheidungsproblem*. This led him to invent the Turing machine in 1936, which was running on mathematical algorithms to perform a set of tasks that would be performed by humans. Turing was a codebreaker, and he proposed that any simple machine could mimic the computer algorithms as long as it could read and write in 0s and 1s infinitely. He showed that complex algorithms required complex instructions or states to compute it. He also proposed that the machine has a computation limit and that it cannot solve all the problems mathematically. This was proved with the help of mathematical axioms to show that a statement can be true or false. Also, a number of other scientists have created evolved Turing machines called Z with 7,918 states to solve the decision problem and predict the outcome [11].

In 1946, Alan Turing created a design of an automated computing engine (ACE), which can process, store, and run programs digitally. To further leverage the machine that could perform independently, he delved into philosophy to understand the idea of imitation game by comparing humans to machine outputs, which was called Turing test. This was where modern artificial intelligence was born. To understand the newfound realm further, he explored biology to understand biological patterns in plants and animals, such as spots, stripes, and petals. He anticipated that these biological patterns are a result of chemical interaction and produced a mathematical equation to relate it [12].

After the production of the Turing machine, modern classical computers led to innovations and revolutions, such as smartphones, IoT-based smart homes and cities, and autonomous systems that are running on artificial intelligence. Nonetheless, quantum mechanics was also discovered, and it was realized that this could bring another revolution that is unseen by mankind due to its state of power, speed, and other abilities that are yet to be discovered. So the question is, can classical computers imitate quantum computers so that quantum systems can be simulated well before its production or other possible use? Per Feynman, classical computers do not have the ability to simulate quantum systems. This could be understood by understanding classical physics. It is known that the most important aspect of reality is time. A fraction of time is a fraction of reality, and in a continuous motion, it gives rise to space, thus the physical world.

On the same note, it is also understood that the quantum states exist within the physical systems, but a quantum state can be seen as a realm of lattices, which represents the different states of particles. Therefore, it is impossible to simulate quantum systems in classical computers. Additionally, Richard Feynman's paper [13] also states that a quantum computer can simulate quantum systems that are utilizing boson particles, as these particles have integer spin. It is unclear if quantum computers can simulate a system with Fermi particles as these particles have half integer spin, because a particle can only exist in a state. Boson particles were proved with an experiment that involved passing rays from a calcite, which would display polarization of movement from one direction to the opposite and not to a halfway in any of the two directions. The calcite experiment was conducted with one major calcite, which would intercept the photon and produce an ordinary ray from one point and an extraordinary ray from another. So this proved that quantum systems can be simulated in quantum computers [13].

1.9.2 Phase 1: Early Quantum Theory from the 1900s to the 1980s

The introduction of Planck's constant and the concept of quanta by Max Planck made the world realize that the classical physics cannot solve the problems that cannot be observed arbitrarily, just like the nature of the atom and subatomic particles. The nature of the atoms could be understood more clearly with the conception of Albert Einstein's photoelectric effect, whereby the particle nature of the light was understood. Then Schrodinger's wave function equation highlighted the provisions of electron localization probability from the nucleus and the amount of energy that the electrons contain. Note the Schrodinger wave function utilized fundamentals of 1924 Louis De Broglie, which states that electrons also have wave-like properties. Heisenberg elaborated on the uncertainty principle, concluding that maximum precision needs to be adopted. All this information can assist in the generation of the future quantum computers, which are powerful in a way as the knowledge of the electrons have been extracted to provide power through quantum entanglement and superposition so that this state could be maintained and manipulated to harness more power and efficiency.

The foundation of quantum mechanics revolves around numerous concepts relating to understanding the makeup of atoms and the subatomic properties of electrons and how these electrons are interacting with the photons. Photons possess dual properties of light and particle as well. At the same time, the measurable properties of subatomic elements need to be quantized to create building blocks. In addition, the determination of the momentum and energy level of these subatomic elements are essential, while the attempt to add the principle of uncertainty to make it more precise is exactly the reason that the classical physics will not be able to create quantum transistors and other microelectronic computational units required for quantum computers, as the nature of classical physics is continuous and deterministic, while the nature of quantum mechanics is discontinuous, indeterministic, and probabilistic. This is because in classical physics, if the state of a particular system and the laws governing it are known at a particular point of time, then the future state of that particular system can be precisely predicted at a particular point of time due to its deterministic properties. Also, the continuous nature of classical physics is not challenged as the properties of quantities, such as velocity and position, can be changed smoothly and gradually without any jumps.

Nonetheless, the conception of classical computers was initiated with the Turing machine, which worked on a finite set of instructions.

1.9.3 Phase 2: Theoretical Advancements in Quantum Computation from the 1980s to the 1990s

In 1980, a couple of quantum computing scientists, including David Deutsch, confirmed that a quantum computer can efficiently simulate any physical process. On the same year, Paul Benioff also produced a quantum mechanical theoretical framework for a reversible Turing machine.

Then in 1985, David Deutsch produced the first quantum algorithm that covered speed more than classical computers. The quantum function algorithm could determine if the function was balanced or constant with a probabilistic success of calling only one function as compared to classical computers, which uses two function calls, balanced and constant. The balanced function returns half of each input, while the constant returns all the value inputs [14]. In this same year, David Deutsch produced a model of a quantum Turing machine that could physically simulate procedures in a classical computer. The quantum Turing machine was discrete as it could run all the quantum algorithms with a finite set of qubits. Since this Turing machine was a model of a classical computer that was complex enough to process quanta, the input was accepted in a classical state, which means it could be measured and recreated. In 1989, circuit-based quantum computing initiated the use of logical gates with qubits to implement specific algorithms [16].

The 1992 David-Jozsa algorithm and the 1994 quantum Fourier transform and Shor's algorithm endured exponential speed for quantum computers. Later, in 1995, quantum error-correcting codes were introduced to cancel the noise of the system then in 1997 an error correction scheme was introduced which had primal and logical types of qubits as an associated boundary for defects. In 1988, further discoveries were made to push the evolution boundaries of quantum computing when quantum annealing was proposed to the global minimum of a function using quantum tunneling. Then in 1989, a universal circuit-based quantum computer was introduced which could run any quantum algorithm [14].

1.10 EARLY MODELS OF QUANTUM COMPUTATION

As time and research in quantum computing progressed, different models of quantum computers were developed. Per the Royal Society Publishing, the seven identified models of quantum computers. The following figure shows the seven models of quantum computers with their categories [17].

The circuit model quantum computer is closely related to the classical digital computers. It flips the state of the superposition qubits in which it started using its controlled and uncontrolled gates. It can also flip the state of the next qubit by using the initial qubit's state through the two-qubit quantum gate operation. Additionally, it also consists of two quantum gates: the Hadamard and phase gates. These gates basically transfer the qubit state to superposition to perform quantum computation, it initiates with initializing all qubits in the register to state 0 with one- and two-qubit operation. Then in the final phase, qubits are measured and then interpreted as sequence of 0s and 1s as the output computation. Since these set of gate operations are universal, it is easier to choose any hardware that can perform classical and quantum-based computation. All these properties make this model suitable for quantum computation. However, this model has its limitations too; for example, the quantum state of this model cannot be cloned. The choice of hardware, gate operations, and the environment introduces noise, which is a major detrimental point. Also, this model requires a huge number of physical qubits to contrast a single logical qubit.

Additionally, measurement-based quantum computing model is similar to circuit model but adds features that advantages this model over the latter one. The process begins with initializing the entangled cluster state first, then the measurement is processed in the style of a circuit model with the corresponding gate operations in different phases. This makes the measurement model more efficient as it can speed up the Fourier transform with more qubits, and since the entangled cluster

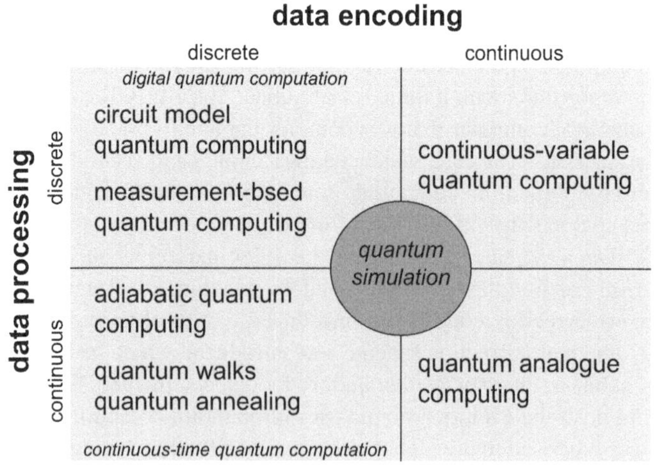

FIGURE 1.2 Seven models of quantum computers against their data encoding and processing method from the Royal Society.

qubits are prepared first, before the measurement, this allows the physical qubits to remain error-free for a fraction of time, as the entire computation adds more errors. Therefore, the error rate is reduced, and the system needs an error correction method if the physical qubits are increased.

Moreover, the third model of quantum computer is quantum analogous model, which by its term corresponds to the analogous computer that represented physical quantized data as voltage and height of water column. This was contrastingly different from the digital computers where data were represented digitally in binary form and had more efficient encoding mechanisms. The analogous computers, on the other hand, had to increase its size to add more volume, which would be easily taken care of in the digital computers with binary powers. Therefore, the biggest drawback of this model is similar to the analogous computer, which processed analogous numbers that proved to be inefficient. In case of quantum analogous computers, the analogous numbers are inefficiently represented as length or frequency, unlike binary qubits. This model of the quantum computer is mostly used for quantum simulation and communication. The advantage of this model is that it can be integrated with continuous variable quantum computing that encodes analogously and processes with discrete gate operations. The implementation of this amalgamated integrated model can be advantageous with a laser light to leverage the laser technology. The limiting factor of this combination is that analogous encoding with be inefficient with large numbers.

The last category of model is continuous-time quantum model. This model can allow its qubit to be encoded in binary, which efficiently combines natural evolution of physical systems continuously with time. Qubits are changed through superposition with Hamiltonian function that can predict the future of the qubit state with conservation laws of energy. This model can be understood with a hydrogen atom as the basis of the quantum computer. The hydrogen atom has one electron and one proton, so the Hamiltonian function of the hydrogen atom is that the energy its electron possesses is bound to the proton. In a confined quantum system, the set of energies are discrete, and the extra energies are noted with the electrons colliding with the photons. This gives rise to unique spectral lines of wavelength that makes the hydrogen atom unique. Although a hydrogen atom is not the most preferred practical choice for quantum computers, the design can be expanded to other designs because the energy-carrying photon may become handy.

Nevertheless, Hamiltonian functions can be used to solve problems of continuous-time quantum model. The Hamiltonian function provides the answer with ground state, which has the lowest energy, and the wrong answer is indicated with high energy. The physical Hamiltonian is realized with classical optimization techniques and other theoretical frameworks that make the continuous-time model equivalent to the circuit model. The continuous-time model employs distinct methods, such as adiabatic quantum computing, quantum annealing, and continuous-time quantum works.

The adiabatic model exploits the quantum system with adiabatic theorem of discrete energy level that allows slow change of the Hamiltonian from the initial stage to the end stage so that the energy level remains the same. That is, the ground state of the Hamiltonian should be transformed to the ground state to encode the answer to a hard problem. The answer is produced when qubits are measured but the drawback of this system is that how slow is slow enough. Quantum computer with limited quantum coherence may not be possible as interactions with the environment can disturb the computation process.

The quantum annealing model cools the system to its ground state. The complication is noted in the non-convex optimization problems where the local minimum can get stuck without reaching the true global minimum, so that system has to perform an extra trick that will ensure that it does not get stuck in the high-energy barrier. This can be achieved by the tunneling process, which can allow the local minimum to pass through the tunnel instead of making a jump to reach the true global minimum. The final model of continuous-time quantum walk is equivalent to classical random processes that combine the unchanging Hamiltonian with spin flip terms that define the problem. This method is useful for universal quantum computers provided that they are encoded with qubits register.

The three models best depend on the hardware; the annealing model and the continuous-time model lack coherence time, so the adiabatic model will be the most suitable choice of practice, but hybrid algorithms can extract the strength of each model with new hardware. The continuous-time model is best suitable to solve optimizable problems. D-Wave has used this model to create a quantum device that consist of 2,000 qubits but loses coherence with the environment.

1.10.1 Phase 3: Practical Development and Emerging Technologies from the 2000s to the Present

In 2003, lattice-based qubits displayed an entangled cluster state where qubits were measured by column rather than with the application of logic gates and circuit models. Recently, in 2021, PsiQuantum ensured fault tolerance by topologically encoding qubits with the cluster state to process information and correct error [14]. On the same note, IBM has produced a 1,121-qubit Condor processor in 2023 and hopes to bridge multiple quantum processing units to produce a 4,000-qubit processor [15].

Subsequently, qubits are a superposition of pure states that are represented as $|0\rangle$ and $|1\rangle$. These are referred to as "ket zero" and "ket one." Correspondingly, classical computer bits are a representation of Boolean variables, which are 0 and 1 [16]. But the bit in classical computers is in two distinct states, where qubits are in $|0\rangle$ state or $|1\rangle$ state or a linear combination of these two states. Classical bits can be measured completely and cannot be changed by any measurement, but qubits are partially measured with a given probability and changed by measurement.

However, classical bits can be copied and erased, whereas qubits cannot be copied or erased. Qubits are exponentially increased by adding a single qubit, this can be represented as 32 qubits to 33 qubits but when this is corresponded with classical bits, it is 34 bits to 64 bits. The quantum computer doubles the power with every qubit unlike classical computers. The superposition allows the qubit to operate in one step whereas classical computers will take 2^n steps to get the result. This is because the quantum computer operates in many states [17].

1.11 THEORETICAL CHALLENGES

So far, we have read about the real and potential advantages that a quantum computer can offer in the near future as this sector is still in its infancy state. In the earlier sections, it was noted that the quantum computer has a difficulty in maintaining its qubit state because of the superposition phenomenon. David Kilai, one of the critics of quantum computing, states that all physical systems are noisy, and the superposition-sensitive qubits will be eventually corrupted by noise when it hits the outside world. According to 2019 US National Academy report, the realization of the true quantum computer is still lagging as the error correction scheme of the quantum computer needs to be further corrected, and if quantum computer production is achieved, then another decade will be needed to replace the existing internet protocol.

The boom in the classical technology was experienced because of the relative demand for these classical technologies relating to the contemporary context. If the quantum computing sector wants to experience the similar boom, then it has to provide similar technological alternatives for contemporary use [18]. The theoretical quantum computer highlights that the qubit can be in one of these two $|0\rangle$, $|1\rangle$ states or it can be simultaneously in both the states. So the probability of the spin state, which can be up ($\uparrow$) or down ($\downarrow$) can have two associated probabilities that needs to be added to one. Therefore, if the probability of the up state is 60%, then the probability that it will be in a down state is 40%; this does not suffice the theory. Experts say that the number of qubits needed to supersede the normal laptop is between 1,000 to 100,000, which means 2^{1000} states at the minimum. This seems like a big number, even combining the subatomic states. Also, these states need to be accounted for on the basis of error correction as well [19].

1.12 FROM THEORY TO EXPERIMENTATION

The previous sections have already highlighted the history of quantum computing and the journey it took to reach thus far. As users of technology, society has experienced all the aspects of classical computing technology in terms of services, but society is yet to experience the theoretical aspects that has been promised of quantum computing. It is noted that the development of quantum computing is carried through either analytics or simulation process [20]. Per this study, quantum simulation is parallel in nature but complex in terms of spatial and temporal, which is a performance hazard. Also, in simulation, the limitation of memory and global access of the quantum state limit qubits and quantum transformation. For this reason, six different simulations were studied to see the results.

On the same note, when it comes to the experimentation or actual implementation of the quantum computer [21], it is essential that the circuits have unitary functions and gates that can make the prototype quantum efficient by possessing the necessary functions such as parallelism, superposition, and irreversibility. This can be achieved with the Unitary Transformation U that can initialize qubits as a base and pass it through the unitary matrix to measure the base state and calculate the amplitude probability. Another important aspect is the error correction which can be reduced by adding redundancy, controlled-NOT (CNOT) and controlled CNOT (CCNOT) logical gates to identify and locate spin flips so that error can be corrected. This paper also mentions the five DiVincenzo criteria for the implementation of quantum computers. These criteria are measurable, universal, scalable, initializable, and coherent (MUSIC).

Furthermore, the physical implementation of a quantum computer is possible if the quantum prototype is structured in a manner where the quantum computer has a quantum processing unit that contains four processing layers—classical processing, digital processing, analog processing, and quantum processing, which must have a running application layer. This strategy has been used by companies such as Google, IBM, and Intel as well. The following figure displays the prototype of a quantum computer [21].

The components have the following tasks to perform to let the quantum computer achieve its functions.

- Application Layer: The application layer is not part of the quantum computer, but it houses the programming environment that allows the operating system to run the quantum-necessary algorithms. The algorithms can be fully quantum or both quantum and classical.

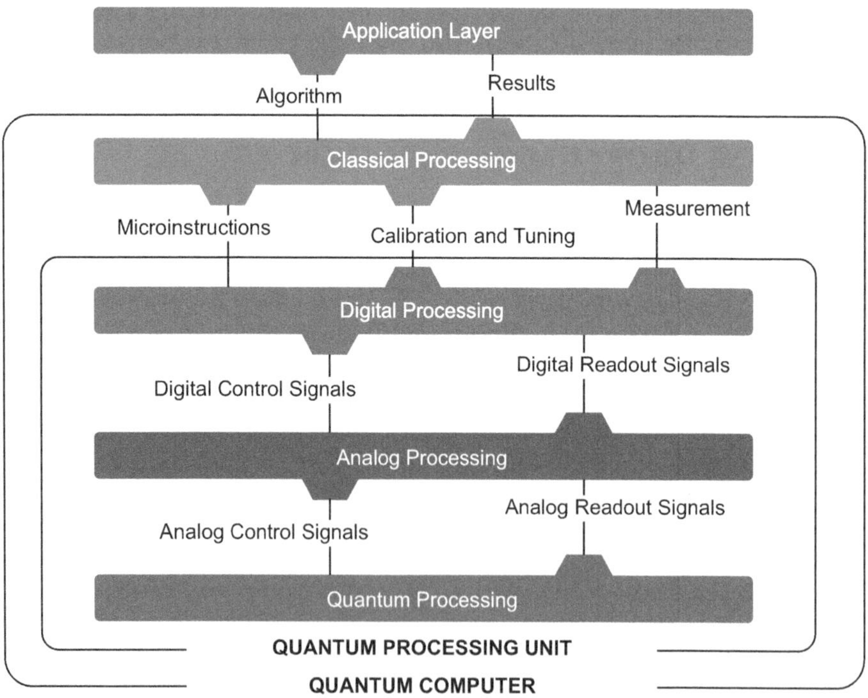

FIGURE 1.3 Components of a quantum computer from the journal article "Towards Physical Implementation of Quantum Computation."

- Classical Processing Layer: The classical processing layers perform three functions:
  - Enhancement of quantum algorithm by assembling its microinstructions.
  - Handling of quantum state measurements of succeeding layers.
  - Calibration and tuning of subsection.
- Digital Processing Layer: This is where the quantum processing is initiated. This layer converts the microinstructions from the classical layer to signals so that it can interact with qubits to perform quantum logic gates.
- Analog Processing Layer: This produces signals that can communicate with the qubits from the quantum processing layer. The signals are mostly the generation of gates, modulation phases, microwave phases, and voltage that will allow the algorithm to interact.
- Quantum Processing Layer: This allows the manipulation of qubits with logic gates and ensures error correction. This operation needs to happen below zero degree Celsius.

Nonetheless, another study proposes that an operational quantum structure needs to operate in four planes. The quantum plane layer holds qubits, logic gates, and the circulatory system The control and measurement plane performs analog and digital processing, and the control processor plane is responsible for sequence execution via algorithm. Finally, the host processor plane hosts the operating system and acts as an interface between the classical computer and the quantum processing unit [21].

The physical manifestation of a quantum computer was observed through the journey of its first predecessors—IBM has been an active participant in quantum development since the presentation of Richard Feynman's of quantum computers at the 1981 IBM and MIT conference. In 1998, IBM achieved its first experimental demonstration of a quantum algorithm on a two-qubit nuclear magnetic resonance (NMR) to solve David Deutsch's problem then, in 2001, the first execution of Shor's algorithm was achieved by factoring number 15 using 1,018 molecules, each with seven active nuclear spins. The following table shows a list of gates that are used by IBM [22].

TABLE 1.2
IBM Processor and Gate Operations

Processor	Gate	Notes
Heron, Eagle, and Falcon	CZ	Two-qubit gate
	RZ	Single-qubit gate
	SX	Single-qubit gate
	X	Single-qubit gate
	ID	Single-qubit gate wait cycle
	Reset	Single-qubit gate, non-unitary
	If-else	Control flow for classical feed-forward
	for loop	Control flow for classical feed-forward
	switch case	Control flow for classical feed-forward
	Measure	***
	Delay	***

The next subsection will explore the different technologies in the advancement of quantum computers.

1.13 ADVANCES IN QUANTUM HARDWARE

As advancement progressed, different approaches of the physical implementation of quantum computers were observed. The approaches include usage of trapped ions, NMR, quantum dots, superconducting qubits, charged qubits, and phase qubits and circuit quantum electrodynamics (QED) [21]. The source states that the trapped-ion method displays the highest precision in the implementation of quantum computers as it uses electromagnetism to trap ions and charged atoms to represent qubits in a confined space. The Penning trap and Paul trap are used with ultra-high vacuum conditions to trap these ions and charged atoms for a long time.

The entanglement is noticed when ions are shared in motion through a quantum bus. The entanglement state is noted with the use of laser interaction and the ions are slowed with Doppler and sideband cooling. The NMR method of quantum computer implementation involves immersing large number of atoms with zero frequency magnetic field and then exposing the atoms to a magnetic field with high and low frequencies resulting in qubit generation. Benefits that can be noted are scalability and long coherence time on the order of nanoscale.

The third method is with the usage of quantum dots, whereby a semiconductor material is used to generate dots with its electron. The dots are in spin up or spin down state, which are captured in a three-dimensional state. It is easy to control the dot size in the fabrication state, as there is a big energy difference when the dot is first excited than the ground state with small dots. The fourth and most relevant method is superconducting qubits because Google and IBM have also used this method to construct their quantum computer. This method is achieved through the property of superconductivity of certain metals, such as aluminum and copper.

These materials have nonexistent electrical resistance at low temperatures. The superconductor generates electrons that are carriers of current and resistance, allowing the superconductivity of degenerate gas for observable coherent quantum computers. This property displays liquid with zero viscosity without any loss of kinetic energy, allowing Bose-Einstein condensation. The following figures show IBM's [23] superconducting processor [4] and Google's [24] superconducting chip called Willow together with its quantum computer.

The fifth method of quantum implementation is using charged qubits, which contain a single Josephson junction with superconducting regions that create a copper pair box with the application of voltage. The electrostatic property of this creation manipulates the quantum system. The final method is phase qubit and circuit QED, which consists of a single Josephson junction and a current source that connects the two electrodes to control the qubit [21]. Another known method of quantum physical implementation is using photons, referred to as photonic quantum computing [25].

This quantum computer does not require any cooling system or vacuum state to retain the quantum state of photons because of its weak interaction with the environment. Due to this reason, photonic quantum computers can operate at room temperatures. Also, photons travel at the speed of light which makes them good

FIGURE 1.4 the IBM's Osprey quantum processor boasts 433 qubits, released in 2022, from the IBM website.

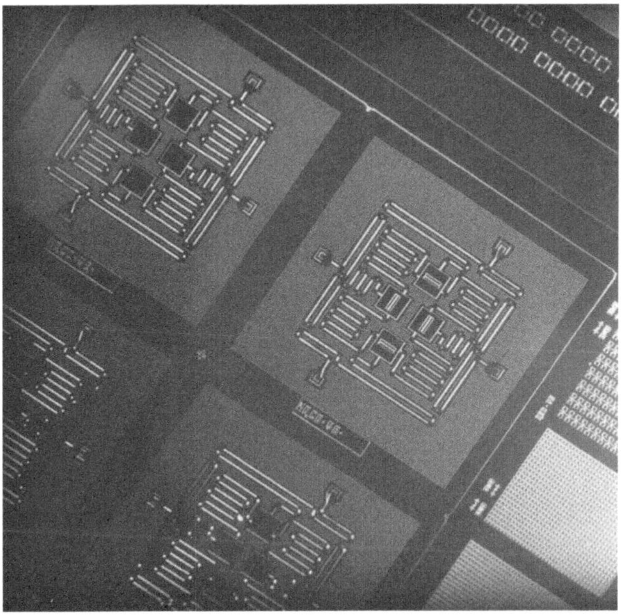

FIGURE 1.5 IBM's four-qubit superconducting quantum computer Layout, in 2015, from the IBM website.

carriers of information and with high data transmission rate. However, due to the nature of photons, it is difficult to implement a qubit entangling gate to capture the entanglement of photons. Another reason that it is not feasible to use photons to implement a quantum computer is because the photons are speedy and do not stay in the same position, so optical gates will have to be arranged and rearranged to process the photons sequentially. Thus, this method of quantum implementation is difficult.

FIGURE 1.6 IBM's Quantum System One, installed at Shin-Kawaski, from the IBM website.

FIGURE 1.7 Google's quantum chip Willow, from the Google website.

1.14 ACHIEVING QUANTUM SUPREMACY

In 2019, Google produced a 53-qubit processor called Sycamore, which claimed quantum supremacy, as the processor was made of programmable superconducting qubits with intermediate noise levels. The processor was operating in a quantum state that could process a sample of the quantum state a million times in 200 seconds; this could take 10,000 years on a corresponding supercomputer [86]. The processor is made of high-fidelity gates that could execute simultaneously in a two-dimensional qubit array. To make this claim, the processor was calibrated as a component and a system, with a tool called cross-entropy benchmarking. This was done to accurately predict the

FIGURE 1.8 Google's QuantumAI, from the Google website.

performance of the system as a component, and it also showed that the whole system synchronizes with quantum information to support large scaling. The processor was constructed with 54 transmon qubits, which were arranged in a rectangular lattice.

Each qubit was coupled with four neighboring qubits and with new adjustable coupler, this coupler could switch to 40 MHz on and off mode. Per the experiment, one qubit was not functioning properly, so the device had 53 working qubits with 86 different adjustable couplers. The processor was made of aluminum and Josephson junctions with indium to connect two silicon wafers. The chip was wired to a superconducting circuit cooled below 20 mK in a dilution refrigerator to reduce the ambient and thermal energy below the qubit energy. The processor is connected through the filters and attenuator to room-temperature electronics to produce signals. The frequency-multiplexing technique is used to read the state of all qubits, while two cycles of cryogenic amplifiers are used to boost the signal which is digitalized and demultiplexed at room temperature.

In total, 277 digital-to-analog converters were orchestrated to complete the quantum processor, which was converting 14 bits per GHz. The processor's single-qubit gate operation was initiated with 25 nm microwave with frequency resonant while the qubit-to-qubit coupling was switched off, the generated pulses were shaped to minimize transition to a higher transmon state. It was stated that the gate performance changes with frequency, leading to a number of issues, such as two-level system defect, stray microwave mode, coupling to control lines and readout resonator, residual stray coupling between qubits, flux noise, and pulse distortions. As a solution, a single-qubit operation is optimized with a cross-entropy benchmark tool to reduce these errors. The following figure shows the quantum processor Sycamore with its rectangular lattice structure [26].

FIGURE 1.9A Quantum processor layout with 54 qubits and 88 adjustable couplers.

FIGURE 1.9B Sycamore chip from the journal article "Quantum supremacy using a programmable superconducting processor."

In 2019, Google claimed that they achieved quantum supremacy with the release of their product. The field of quantum computing experienced tumultuous controversies, and Google was hit back with many clashes as this was accepted by their common rivals, especially MIT and IBM. The researchers at IBM stated that Google has not created anything special and compared how IBM had done better with the production of their 53-qubit processor and their fleet of 14 quantum computers on the cloud to be accessible by its users. IBM also produced a paper that theoretically proves that Google's supercomputer processing of 10,000 years could be reduced to 2.5 days.

E-commerce companies, such as Amazon and Alibaba, expressed concerns relating to the security problem with the introduction of powerful quantum computer that could hack all the commercial encrypted data. Nonetheless, Caltech congratulated Google on the production of their hardware, and Google also promised that they will improve their technology by introducing more qubits. Then in 2024, Google delivered 105-qubit Willow, an upgrade of Sycamore [27]. The following figure displays the system metrics of Willow.

Forbes has confirmed that Willow can solve complex problems in under 5 minutes, which will take the fastest supercomputer 10 septillion years to solve [28].

Even so, claims from competitors like D-Wave have also captured the attention of customers and other stakeholders. In February 2025, D-Wave stated that they have produced their first annealing quantum computer which operates on 5,000 qubits [24] with 15-way connectivity. The 5,000-qubit Advantage™ Quantum Computer is available on-premises and on quantum cloud service through D-Wave Leap™ for businesses and researchers to use it as a high-performance computer or can be combined with supercomputers to achieve one's desired goal. The high-performance computation is expected to compute one quintillion calculations per second, making this the first fastest annealing quantum computer in the world. The Advantage™ is

Random Circuit Sampling (Chip 2)	
Single-qubit gate error[1] (mean, simultaneous)	0.036% ± 0.013%
Two-qubit gate error[1] (mean, simultaneous)	0.14% ± 0.052% (iswap-like)
Measurement error (mean, simultaneous)	0.67% ± 0.51% (terminal, all qubits)
Reset options	Multi-level reset (l1) state and above) Leakage removal (l2) state only)
T_1 time (mean)	98 μs ± 32 μs[2]
Circuit repetitions per second	63,000
Application performance	XEB fidelity depth 40 = 0.1%
Estimated time on Willow vs. classical supercomputer	5 minutes vs. 10^{25} years

FIGURE 1.10 Willow system metric snapshot, from Google's website.

System	D-Wave 2000Q™ QPU	Advantage QPU	Latest Advantage2 QPU Prototype (July 2024)
Better Solutions (Satisfiability problems)	-	Better solution quality than D-Wave 2000Q QPU 81% of the time	Better solution quality than Advantage QPU 87% of the time
Time-To-Solution (3D lattice problems; annealing time)	-	10x faster than D-Wave 2000Q QPU	20x faster than Advantage QPU
Topology	Chimera™ topology	Pegasus™ topology	Zephyr™ topology
Qubits	2000+	5000+	1200+
Couplers	6000+	40,000+	11,000+
Connectivity	6-way	15-way	20-way
Largest embedded 3D lattice	8x8x8	15x15x12	6x6x16
Largest embedded clique	64	180	82

FIGURE 1.11 System matrix of D-Wave's annealing quantum computer, from the D-Wave website.

30 times faster and provides equal and best solution 94% of the time compared to the previous generation [25]. D-Wave has also revealed it roadmap of further improving this current system to Advantage 2™, which will be constructed will more than 7,000 qubits and 20-way connectivity. While their first scalable gate model quantum computer will be improved with practical error correction, hybrid solutions and open source will be also made available [26]. The following figure shows D-Wave's system matrix with it attributes.

1.15 EMERGING PARADIGMS

The contemporary world is still dependent on classical computers, and the future-based full-blown quantum computer is yet to be seen. So the production of quantum computers and its research and exploration are still pretty much dependent on classical computers. According to IonQ, a classical computer and a quantum computer working together to solve a problem is called hybrid quantum computing.

The term "hybrid" corresponds to back-and-forth collaboration from quantum and classical system, where different aspects of a problem is best solved with either a quantum system or a classical system. A useful hybrid algorithm called variational quantum eigensolver (VQE) is used in a variety of chemistry applications to calculate the ground state to achieve the optimal configuration that can ensure that a particular molecule is stable. This process is carried out in a quantum system, but the comparison of each molecule's stability is processed in a classical system [29].

In addition, IBM has also used quantum-classical algorithms in many experiments to approximately describe quantum correlation in many-particle systems. The algorithm illustrates the quantum entanglement method to simulate electronic problems. Some of these experiments are electronic structure of bulk manganese oxide and nickel oxide from coupled cluster theory, finite-temperature correlation functions using the quantum minimally entangled typical thermal states algorithm, variational quantum simulation of the Fermi-Hubbard model, and determining Hamiltonian eigenstates on a quantum computer using quantum imaginary time evolution [30]. The hybrid quantum-classical system provides many advantages where the amalgamation of other technologies, such as artificial intelligence and IoT, can leverage the application to perform complex operations such as [31]:

- Asset management and antifraud
- Pharmaceutical development and medical care
- Security
- Supply chains
- Energy production

Moreover, the single-impurity Anderson model is a hybrid framework that allows the understanding of electron behavior in strongly correlated materials, such as how impurities affect the behavior of electrons in quantum materials. This framework works by utilizing quantum computers to carry out intensive computation, while classical computers rely on its ability to do their best. The Hubbard model was specifically meant to create materials for targeted electrical properties [32].

As new conceptions are unfolding, Quantinuum has advanced and delved in an area of quantum computing, which relies on the spatial ability of the subatomic properties such as quasi effect to eradicate the challenges that quantum computing is facing right now. As stated throughout this chapter, quantum computing utilizes qubits to store and transport information but this particular mechanism utilizes the spatial property to store data, which is referred as topological qubits. The topological qubits store data in patterns of relationship between the system. whereas the arbitrary quantum computing stores data in the system. This property significantly contributes to a fault-tolerant system and is seen as an efficient quantum error correction method.

The topological qubits are implemented on a quantum processor that operates a class of exotic quasiparticles called "non-Abelian anyons" in a topological state—Z_3. The topological state is a qutrit-based Helbert space that stores the quantum information in three quantum states. The quantum defects are taken care of by entangling the non-Abelian anyons principles that can fuse by type and the sequence of combination which makes the topological state a reliable and scalable system. The researchers at Quantinuum stated that 90% of the computational resources are used for error correction in an orthodox quantum system but the non-Abelian anyon principle provides a universal gate set that simplifies these operations.

The experiment was conducted on Quantinuum H2 Ion-trap quantum processor with 56 fully connected qubits that were encoded into qutrits to construct Z_3 lattice. Parafermion and charged conjugation defect [33] were also studied. Per the team, the research pathway is similar to Microsoft's journey of quantum computing, which is also working on topological qubits [34].

Microsoft is creating a topological phase that will ensure speed, stability, and size advantages for a quantum computer. The topological phase is produced through a process that layers semiconducting and superconducting nanowires on a device in a controlled and atomic precise way [35]. A specific amount of magnetic field and voltage charges the semiconducting nanowire to superconducting material which creates the topological phase. The topological phase is a characteristic of the Majorana Zero Mode (MZM)—a one-dimensional non-Abelian quasiparticle that spans from the end of one nanowire to the other. The region in between the wires is called the energy gap as there is no energy, voltage, or quantum mechanical state. The current flows freely through the gap, which makes it possible for the topological gap, noise and interference-resistant [36].

1.16 TAXONOMY OF QUANTUM COMPUTERS

The following table reflects key discoveries of quantum computers and their implications:

TABLE 1.3
Taxonomy of Quantum Computers based on the Era

Era	Key Discovery	Implication for Computing
1982	Feynman proposes a quantum simulation	Lays the foundation for quantum algorithms
1985	David Deutsch's universal quantum Turing machine	Simulation of unitary transformation of a finite number of qubits
1994	Shor's algorithm	Demonstrates quantum superiority in factorization
1995	Quantum error correction code	Cancels the noise of the system
1996	Grover's algorithm	Demonstrates unstructured search operation
1997	Quantum error correction scheme	On primal and logical types of qubits
2003	Application of lattice-based qubits	Displays entangled cluster qubits
2016	First five-qubit quantum computer	Publicly on the cloud
2018	Rigetti quantum cloud services	Made available to the public
2019	Google claims quantum supremacy with Sycamore	First practical demonstration of quantum speedup
	IBM's Q System One	First circuit-based quantum computer
2020	IBM's fleet of 15 quantum computers	Made available to the public
2020	IBM's open-source projects	Made available to the community
	AWS Braket	Available for use
2021	PsiQuantum fault tolerance	Topologically encoded qubits with cluster state to process information and correct error
2023	IBM's 1,121-qubit Condor processor	First superconducting quantum processor
2024	GoogleAI upgrades to Willow	105-qubit superconducting processor
2025	D-Wave announces 5,000-qubit quantum computer	First's commercial annealing model quantum computer

1.17 INITIAL DEVELOPMENTS

This section is divided into three subsections discussing the development of quantum algorithms, academic and government contributions, and theoretical challenges. The first subsection introduces Peter Shor's algorithm for factoring large numbers, transforming cryptography, and explains Grover's algorithm for quantum search. The second subsection mentions early funding and research by institutions like MIT, IBM, and Bell Labs and the role of government initiatives in fostering quantum research. The third subsection explains the initial skepticism about the feasibility of building quantum computers.

1.18 DEVELOPMENT OF QUANTUM ALGORITHMS

In 1994 a computer scientist named Peter Shor developed a polynomial time algorithm for quantum computers to factor large numbers, making it possible to break the current cryptography in adequate time. The algorithm requires the state of classical computers to initiate the steps to determine if the large number (n) is even, prime, or an integer power for prime numbers. Then it will pick an integer of power two such that $n^2 \leq q < 2n^2$, and it will also pick a random integer x that is coprime to n. After this, it will utilize the quantum computer register to create two partitioned superposition states. One register will contain qubits that could represent large integers such as $q-1$. The second partition will contain qubits that are large integers as $n-1$. Then the first register will be loaded with superposition integers weighted 0 to $q-1$, and the second register will be loaded with state 0.

At this point, the memory register will be $\frac{1}{\sqrt{q}}\sum_{a=0}^{q-1} | a,0\rangle$. After this transformation, $x^a \, mod\, n$ will be applied to all the numbers in register 1 and stored in register 2. Due to parallelism of superposition, this will be completed in one step, and at this point, the quantum memory register is $\frac{1}{\sqrt{q}}\sum_{a=0}^{q-1} \left|a, x^a \, mod\, n\right.$. Afterward, a value k needs to be observed in register 2 that has the side effect of collapsing register 1 into equal superposition of value from 0 to $q-1$ such that $x^a \, mod\, n = k$. The next step is performed in a quantum computer such that $\frac{1}{\sqrt{||A||}}\sum_{a=a\epsilon A} |a,k\rangle$ where A is a set of $a's$ such that $x^a \, mod\, n = k$ and $||A||$ is the number of element in a set. Now discrete Fourier transform is applied on register 1 to state $|a\rangle$ such that the state is $|a\rangle = \frac{1}{\sqrt{q}}\sum_{c=0}^{q=1} |c\rangle * e^{2\pi iac/q}$, and this step $\frac{1}{\sqrt{||A||}}\sum_{a=a\epsilon A} \frac{1}{\sqrt{q}}\sum_{c=0}^{q=1} |c,k * e^{2\pi iac/q}$ is performed in quantum computer via parallelism. The state of register 1 is measured to call a value m, and this value is a multiple of $\frac{q}{r}$, where r is the desired period.

Then the post-processing is performed on a classical computer where r is calculated based on the value of m and q. Once the value r is attained, factor n can be determined with $gcd\left(x^{r/2}+1,n\right)$ and $gcd\left(x^{r/2}-1,n\right)$, and if the factor n, is not determined then the process restarts by reloading the two registers. This algorithm can run on quantum computer for $O\left((\log n)^2 * \log log\, n\right)$ and perform $O(\log n)$ steps on classical computer to post-process. In comparison, the closest polynomial algorithm that can factor large number (n) on a classical computer has $\lceil \log n \rceil$ bits and runs for an exponential time $O\left(\left(e^{c(\log n)^{1/3}}\right) * \left((\log log\, n)^{2/3}\right)\right)$. This makes the quantum computer faster than any other classical computer in terms of breaking the cryptography as the encryption security of classical computers are applied on large numbers that will take millions of years to factor [37].

Another such algorithm that can potentially speed up the quantum computer is Grover's algorithm that was introduced in 1996 to sort unsorted large databases where brute force search function cannot be performed due to certain conditions. Per IBM learning, the unstructured Grover search algorithm is feasible for classical computers in comparison with the quantum search function for quantum computers because this technology is still in its infancy. The unstructured search function offers a quadratic improvement, which means Grover's algorithm requires the number of operations on the order of square root of the number of operations needed to solve the unstructured search. The algorithm is designed in such a way that it solves a problem that has no possible structure and for a given function f, which in the case of a structure could be corresponded with the Boolean function and return the particle value of the search. So, to understand the unstructured problem, let $\Sigma = \{0,1\}$ as binary alphabet and suppose $c : \Sigma^n \rightarrow \Sigma$ is a function from a binary string of length n to bits.

Assuming the function is arbitrary and does not have any special structure, the Grover's algorithm search for a string $x \in \Sigma^n \ for \ f(x) = 1$. The string will be considered as the number of counts or the search hit for the function. In case of singular solution, singular search hit is reported and in case of multiple solution, one of the solutions is reported as the answer, and in case of no solution, then no solution is reported. The search function is classically performed through iteration of the strings $x \in \Sigma^n$ to evaluate f for the solution. Assuming that there are N strings in Σ^n, let $\mathrm{N} = 2^n$, taking a Grover's high-probability approach to iterate through all requires $O\left(\sqrt{\mathrm{N}}\right)$ evaluation of f. This evaluation is carried out in superposition with an iterative approach by taking the input strings and interspersing with other effective operations that can create an interfering effect leading to the solution with a high probability after $O\left(\sqrt{\mathrm{N}}\right)$ iterations [23].

1.19 ACADEMIC AND GOVERNMENT CONTRIBUTIONS

After realizing the potential of a quantum computer, several institutions and government bodies have contributed to the research of quantum computers. Mike Lazaridis, a co-founder of Blackberry, contributed 270 million dollars to the Institute of Quantum Computing at the University of Waterloo. This philanthropic effort was to get the best theoretical physicists in Waterloo to create a cluster of quantum computers. Although the vision is bright, the task is difficult, as mentioned by one of the researchers of the university who was trying to sell a photon-creating device for 13,000 dollars in 2013. Per the source, 759 million dollars were contributed for the cause, including 215 million dollars by the Canadian government. The most complex computer was processing with 12 qubits, but keeping the qubits stable was a problem. To further this technological endeavor, Mike Lazaridis donated another 100 million dollars to create the Perimeter Institute for Theoretical Physics in 2000 [38].

IBM labs also contributed to the field as a communalist by uploading their first five-qubit quantum computer publicly on the cloud in 2016 for anyone to experiment with it [39]. In the first week of making the prototype public, 7,000 users were registered, and in the following week, more than 17,000 users joined the community. The community with the team of IBM researchers and technologists produced the first working device after five years in 2021 [40]. Per Futurum, the Australian Commonwealth government and the Queensland government will contribute 940 million Australian dollars for quantum computing project called PsiQuantum. The Japan's National Academic Institute of Science and Technology has been also awarded 41 American dollars by QuEra.

In addition, the US-based Infleqtion received 29 million Australian dollars by Australian Breakthrough Victoria [41]. Other governments have also contributed toward the area of quantum developments in their country. The UK government has contributed 106 million pounds to five quantum research hubs in the country to improve the security of quantum internet and quantum-based position and navigation systems in national security and critical infrastructure. In addition, the UK government has also contributed 45 million pounds to enable the country's quantum-based economy by 2033. Thirty million pounds have been awarded to the UK research institute and the 15 million pounds were awarded to Quantum Catalyst Fund, which is designed to accelerate quantum solutions.

Furthermore, the US government has also allocated funds for quantum development and defense in US dollars since 2020 as listed:

- 2020: 672 million
- 2021: 855 million
- 2022: 1.031 billion
- 2023: 932 million
- 2024: 968 million

The funds were distributed to several government agencies, including NSA, NASA, the Department of Defense, and the Department of Energy, and to support the creation and maintenance of 14 quantum information centers throughout the country. Additionally, the Department of Commerce's Economic Administration and Development contributed 41 million dollars to elevate quantum in the west mountains, which unlocked an additional 77 million dollars, and another 10 million dollars were received as a fund for the movement. The University of Colorado Boulders estimated that another 2 billion dollars will be brought by private stakeholders, which will create tens of thousands job in the quantum sector. Per the 2024 IQM state of Quantum Report, the quantum sector increased by 3% in Europe, the Middle East, and Africa and declined by 80% in the US and 50% worldwide from 2022 to 2023 due to interest notwithstanding [42]. The following figure displays the summary of quantum initiatives worldwide [43].

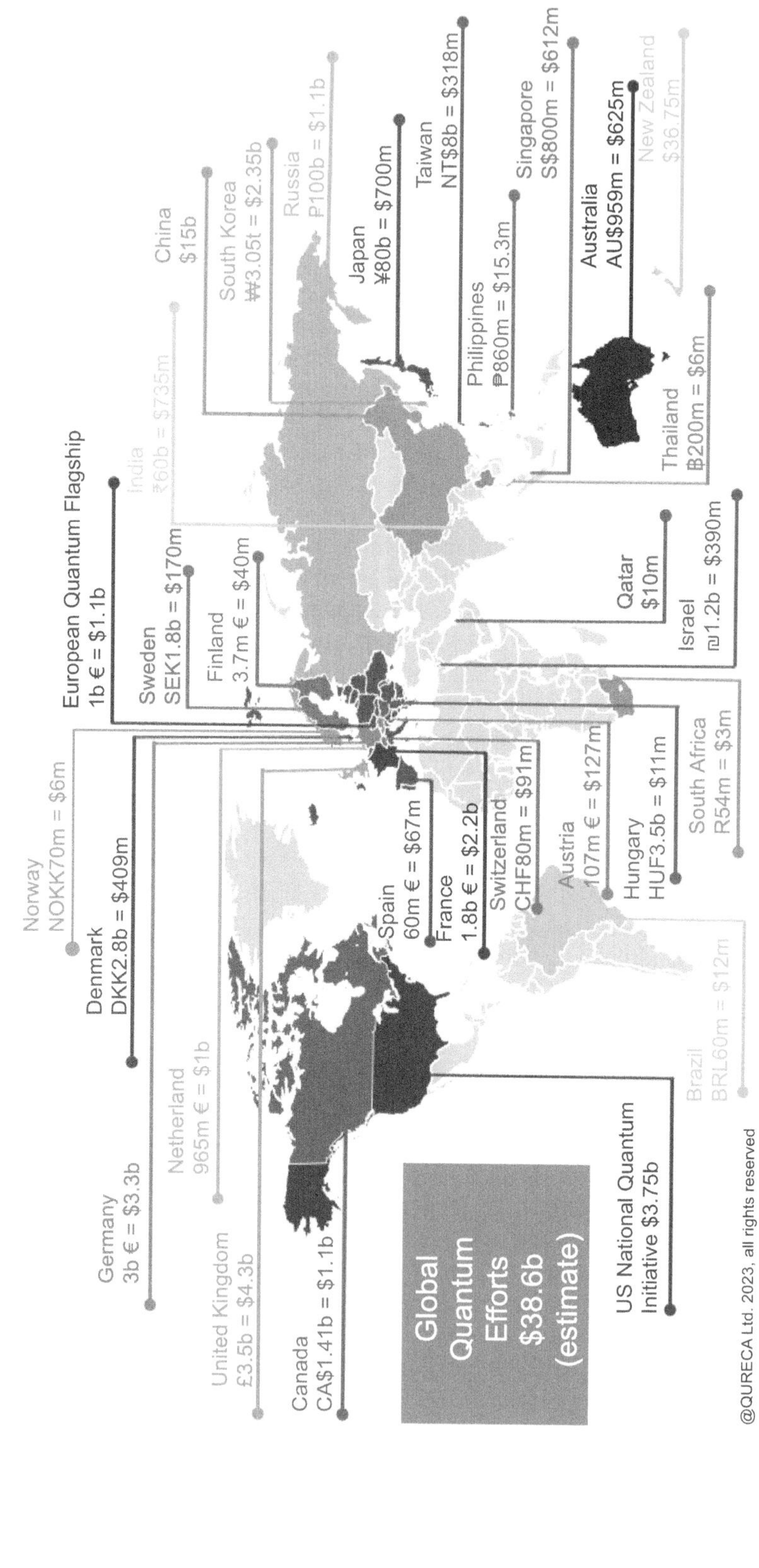

FIGURE 1.12 Summary of Global Quantum Initiative 2024 from Qureca's website [84].

It has been also noted that researchers from Caltech, Google, Fermilab, MIT, and Havard are using Google's Sycamore processor to create and control Einstein–Rosen bridge to reduce space travel time and perhaps teleport [44].

1.20 ERA OF COMMERCIALIZATION

The era of commercialization features corporate investments, quantum computing as a service (QCaaS), and growing ecosystem. Corporate investments shows how companies like IBM, Google, Microsoft, and Amazon have entered the quantum race. Quantum computing as a service (QCaaS) reveals the rise of cloud platforms offering quantum computing. The growing ecosystem involves startups, venture capital funding, and open-source frameworks like Qiskit.

1.21 CORPORATE INVESTMENTS

An article from TechCrunch in 2020 shows the claim of IBM CEO that the company will be producing its first quantum desktop in five years, which will be probably produced in 2025. Articles from TechCrunch also state that in the early days of quantum computer development, everyone was producing or working on it separately or in silos. However, as the time elapsed, third-party, stakeholder, and vendor involvement has led to an ecosystem where people or companies are working in collaboration with each other. It is important that each party realizes its potential in the related area which is part of the ecosystem rather than working on it separately in silos [45]. Although IBM has contributed greatly in the field of science and technology, in the past decades it has been on the decline as it failed to deliver services like cloud computing and other mobile technologies, but with artificial intelligence and quantum computing, it hopes to climb up the leader in the technology market.

IBM's production of its quantum computer in early 2019 called Q System One reassured everyone that IBM is back in the game [46]. In the same year, Google's executive, Sergio Boxio, split its quantum research team into two, which will be based at two different access sites in Southern California [47].

Later in 2020, CNET [48] claimed that big techs such as IBM, Google, Microsoft, Intel, Amazon, IonQ, Quantum Circuits, and Rigetti Computing have joined the competition to deliver quantum computing as a cloud computing service to the public. All these tech heads have joined a multiyear journey to improve their quantum computers by increasing the qubits and processing speed while reducing the error rates. Since quantum computers are expensive, the effort is to make it available through cloud services. It was noted that in 2020, IBM was sort off leading the race by putting their fleet of 15 quantum computers on cloud through IBM Q premium service.

More than 100 companies are paying subscriptions to access this service, while BigBlue, another tech company, has also produced a replica of IBM's 53-qubit quantum computer. It was also noted that Google did not have cloud service of quantum computers at this point of time, but it had announced its intention to do so in the near future while also announcing "quantum supremacy." Amazon has also expressed that they are planning to make their quantum computer available on cloud as a biggest web service on this planet. The services will be accessible by researchers and technologies from D-Wave, IonQ, and Rigetti for experiment and development purposes.

In addition, Microsoft had also announced its Azure quantum cloud service and promised to offer quantum computers through its partners from Honeywell, IonQ, and Rigetti. They also expressed their intention to produce their own quantum hardware. Meanwhile, Rigetti had made its quantum cloud services available in 2018 [48].

In 2024, quantum insiders revealed that big techs have also incorporated artificial intelligence with cloud computing while their technological revolution in the realm of quantum computing made an impression on the market. As of 2024, IBM was the first ranking company, while GoogleAI was in second position, following Microsoft, Amazon Braket, and Alibaba group on the fifth position [49]. However, as of 2025, the list has changed a bit; IBM and GoogleAI are on the same rank, but INTEL has climbed up the ladder to the third rank, following Microsoft and Amazon Braket [50].

1.22 QUANTUM COMPUTING AS A SERVICE (QCAAS)

In 2016, IBM launched its first-ever quantum cloud services with quantum computers to the public, which was called IBM Quantum Experience. Arvind Patel, a senior executive at IBM, stated that the IBM Quantum Experience will give an opportunity to researchers and scientists to accelerate the innovations that are yet to be made with this technology. IBM made sure that the five-qubit system was advanced in terms of technology and electronic control for IBM users, ensuring reliable high-quality performance. The IBM Research ecosystem had created a software that provided an easy user interface for accessing the quantum hardware via cloud [51]. The user interface is called IBM Quantum Composer [4], which contains customizable circuits that allows its users to create, visualize, and run quantum circuits on IBM's quantum hardware. The following figures show how users can access the IBM Quantum Experience with IQM Quantum Composer [52].

In 2020, IBM has also made its open-source project public through OpenQuantumSafe.org by donating its quantum safe algorithm to the public while offering its security

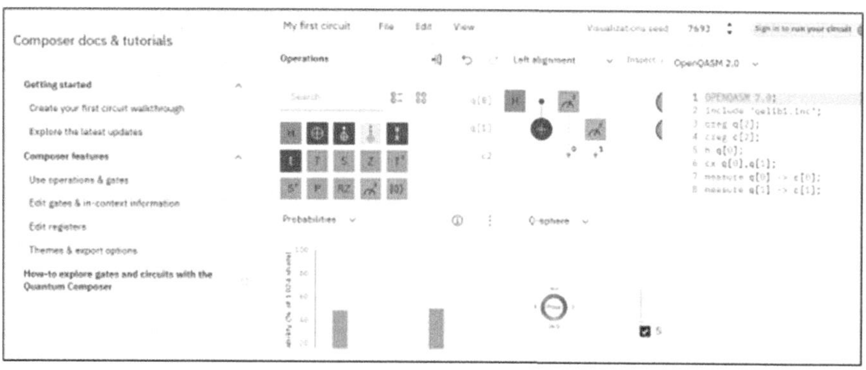

FIGURE 1.13 IQM Quantum Composer from the IBM Quantum Learning website.

services through IBM Quantum Experience, letting users to assess their quantum risk with quantum risk assessment. The algorithm is accessible by the community so that the algorithm is tested by the industry, which will make it interoperable and easily consumable in the common security standards. The security standard is achieved through a mathematical problem of 1980s so-called lattice cryptography suite. The cryptography suite is called CRYSTAL, which stands for Cryptographic Suites for Algebraic Lattices, which is based on two quantum-resistant cryptographic primitives. These two primitives are Kyber and Dilithium. Kyber ensures a secure key encapsulation method, and the latter technique ensures a secure digital signature algorithm. IBM had tested both the security mechanism with AES-256 encryption to ensure the world's first quantum-safe tape drive [53].

On the same note, Microsoft Azure offers cloud services to its users to help perfect user algorithms through its wide range of cloud portfolio [54]. The Azure Quantum Resource Estimator is an open-source tool that allows its user to estimate the quantum resources required to run quantum programs on a fault-tolerant quantum hardware. It calculates the total number of physical and logical qubits, runtime, and details of formula and value for each estimate. This tool compares the hardware characteristics, quantum error correction schemes, and qubit technologies to understand the resources required to run the quantum program. This tool comprises three levels quantum computing stacks, which are the application level, compilation level, and modeling level. The estimator allows its users to customize the parameter at each level and analyze how it impacts the resources. It also comes with an extensible API to model any quantum architecture and modify any assumptions [55].

Furthermore, in 2020 Amazon Web Services (AWS) announced the availability of Amazon Braket to assist its quantum community of developers and researchers with development tools, simulators, and accessibility of diverse quantum hardware. This platform allows its customers to design, test, and troubleshoot its algorithm on a simulated quantum computer running on AWS computing resources for implementation. Once the customers feel ready to implement, they can use Amazon Braket to run their quantum algorithm on their choice of quantum processor technology from IonQ, Rigetti and D-Wave. The simulated and hardware jobs are managed through a unified development experience, and customers are only required to pay for the compute resource [56].

1.23 GROWING ECOSYSTEM

Since the quantum computing ecosystem is growing, research has identified its potential benefits that could allow the world to revolutionize itself manifold. So capitalists, governments, corporate organizations, and individuals have started funding and venturing into projects for quantum computing. Per FasterCapital, Venture Capitalist is offering startup funds to stakeholders who wish to initiate quantum initiatives. They are already working in collaboration with Rigetti Computing, which is focused on building practical quantum computers, and have raised over 150 million dollars from investors such as Andreessen Horowitz and Founders Fund. It also mentions that the US government has allocated 1.2 billion dollars for the next five years through an initiative called the National Quantum Initiative Act. This funding will be given as grants to foster innovation in fields such as cryptography, drug discovery, and problem optimization.

In addition, corporate organizations are also stepping up and taking initiatives to invest in startups to gain a competitive edge. Corporations, such as IBM, have formed strategic partnership with startups to collaborate in research and development through resource and expertise sharing. Nevertheless, angel funding and crowdfunding are also offering initiatives for quantum startups. Angel funding is a process where high-net-worth individuals or investors offer startup funds in exchange for equity, whereas crowdfunding receives small funds from individuals through a platform who believes in the quantum initiative and support the revolutionary idea of an interested area [57].

Moreover, open-source frameworks such as Qiskit are also an invaluable resource for startups through Qiskit tools and the Qiskit community. These two factors are an important force for pushing the quantum community and the quantum computing field forward [58]. This framework is a software development kit (SDK) that has a library as its core component. It contains building blocks to create and work with quantum circuits, quantum operators, functions that are samplers and estimators, and transpilers. The transpiler supports quantum circuit optimization and has a toolbox for the creation of advanced operators [59]. Per IBM, Qiskit is the fastest performing SDK for building and transpiling quantum circuits. The following list shows the key functions of Qiskit [60]:

- Qiskit runtime—executes ISA circuit efficiently in near time environment with managed error suppression and mitigation.
- Qiskit Serverless—runs quantum-centric supercomputing workload in the cloud across QPUs, CPUs, and GPUs.
- AI Tools for Quantum—leverage AI to create Quantum circuits with Qiskit Code Assistant and optimize it for hardware with Qiskit Transpiler Service.
- Addons—Qiskit's Library of Addons enables algorithm discovery.
- Qiskit Ecosystem—the library of community packages can be explored to extend the use of Qiskit.
- Qiskit Functions Catalog—designed to accelerate development workflows.

In the next section, the current landscape of quantum computing will be highlighted.

1.24 CURRENT LANDSCAPE

In this section the current landscape of the quantum computing sector will be reflected based on the reports and news updates of this industry. In the first subsection, the quantum state of art will be highlighted based on the information that has been presented on different forums about the leading quantum institutes and corporations. In the second subsection, the application of quantum computing in the pharmaceutical industry will be underlined, while problem optimization in finance and logistics, cryptography, and post-quantum security will be discussed as well. In the final subsection, the challenge of quantum computing will be elaborated, whereby the issues such as the scalability of quantum computers and the stability of qubits and the quantum state will be reflected together with its high cost and energy requirements.

1.25 STATE OF THE ART

The following table shows the current number qubits achieved by leading quantum computing corporations:

TABLE 1.4
Number of Qubits of the Latest Quantum Computer

Leading Quantum Computing Corporations	The Qubits of Latest Quantum Computer
Atom Computing	1,180 qubits [61]
IBM	1,121 qubits [52]
Google	105 qubits [27]
Microsoft	56 qubits [62], 12 logical qubits [61]
Intel	12 qubits [63]
Rigetti	84 qubits [64]

First, Atom Computing has used neutral atoms instead of electrons, which are in a very excitable state, sensitive to the environment, and error-prone. In contrast, the neutral atom is pretty stable and remains undisturbed because of the quantum property of atom's nucleus spin, which does not interact with the outside world as much as the electron does. A neutral atom's stability prevents the machine's quantum state from collapsing, an attribute that ensures fault tolerance. This is needed for error correction, which in the current machine measures up to one minute in comparison with IBM's Osprey, which had a coherence time of 70–80 microseconds [61].

Simultaneously, IBM is trying to enhance its quantum error correction (QEC) by enhancing its quantum flexibility and low latency. These two are interrelated because quantum flexibility is lacking when it comes to running several operations in the same circuit. While the current latency is minimized by running only a single predefined operation in the setup, flexibility is impacted. This will be corrected through the SurgeryQ project, which enhances the QEC with lattice surgery. This technique operates on logical qubits which are encoded with multiple physical qubits. It allows complex logical operations by merging and reshaping qubit clusters into a two-dimensional lattice. Thus, IBM can execute multiple QEC operations in real time on its superconducting hardware [65].

Moreover, Google introduced an AI-based decoder called AlphaQubit, which identifies quantum error with state-of-the-art accuracy. This led to Google's DeepMind machine learning techniques with Quantum AI error correction that focuses on correcting errors introduced by microscopic hardware defects, cosmic rays, heat, vibration, and electromagnetic interference. The error correction techniques utilizes redundancy by grouping multiple qubits into single logical qubits and regularly performing consistency checks. Therefore, the quantum information is preserved [66].

On the other hand, Microsoft has created a Quantinuum H2 machine with 12 logical qubits that operate in a state of entanglement, reducing error as all these logical qubits are entangled with each other. These 12 logical qubits are entangled in a way that creates the cat state or the Greenberger-Horne-Zeilinger state, which exhibits circuit error rate of 0.0011, which is 22 times faster than corresponding physical qubits that had circuit error rate of 0.024 [67]. This approach is also used by Intel, which is trying to gang up its multiple physical qubits into single larger error-corrected qubits that does not lose the thread of quantum entanglement [68].

Lastly, Rigetti has invested in precise control and flexible gate architecture that will ensure that the error correction requirements are met. Per Rigetti, chip-wide optimization and tuneable coupler frequencies reduce interactions between qubits. The real-time hardware pulse pre-compensation produces gates that will lower incoherent errors. They have also established a robust calibration process for highly expressive square root swap gates that solve some of the compilation challenges. The compilation challenge is solved with practical usage, resulting an nQA-orientated gate set that reduces the error [64].

The next subsection will discuss the application of quantum computing in drug and pharmaceutical industries globally.

1.26 QUANTUM COMPUTING APPLICATIONS

Applications of quantum computing in the pharmaceutical industry, especially drug discovery, is a beneficial integration in the health sector due to the complexity of the chemical nature of drugs. For a drug to be clinically successful, the protein synthesis stage has to be successful, which takes huge amount of time and effort with the current classical technology. However, these challenges can be maximized with quantum computing that has the ability to solve high-dimensional and multi-variable problems. Per the World Economic Forum, quantum computing can reduce time and cost and bring forth innovations that can benefit mankind in situations such as the pandemic that was experienced in 2020. Since then, the health sector has needed a positive technological revolution to reduce health-related threats with services and quality drugs.

Manufacturing and development of drugs are solely dependent on the prediction of drug interaction with the protein, a chain of amino acids in complex three-dimensional shapes. For this process to be effective, ligand binding and protein hydration needs to take place. This process is time-consuming and lacks binding precision. So pharmaceutics such as Pasqal are collaborating into quantum computing to create a hybrid quantum-classical system that can use algorithms of entanglement and superposition phenomena to precisely place water molecules in the right places to ensure protein hydration.

The implementation of the first instance of molecular biology with a hybrid quantum-classical system was seen with Orion, the neutral atom computer. It also states that quantum tools can leverage the accuracy of the binding process efficiently with quantum simulation, allowing faster data generation, which can be fed to machine learning for drug discovery. Pharmaceutics such as Qubit have also integrated into AI so that these models could be used for research and ensure a faster transition of laboratory experiments to preclinical trials [69].

Meanwhile, quantum computing is assisting the finance and logistics sector with problem optimization by reducing the computation time with quantum-optimized models. The optimized models allow easier distribution in real time while avoiding disruptions such as unforeseen circumstances.

It looks for alternate routes and sources during unfortunate events that minimizes the disruptions. On the same note, quantum computers can process and analyze large amounts of data which are needed for demand forecasting, inventory management, and real-time decision-making in the supply [70]. The real application of quantum computing is yet to be experienced, but companies like DHL and Volkswagen are exploring quantum integration, while D-Wave and IBM are actively exploring quantum computing in supply chain optimization. The inclusion of quantum computing with enterprise resource planning (ERP) can add benefits of enhancing the security of ERP with quantum-resistant encryption method by reducing counterfeit goods and cyberattacks, thus elevating the security of the supply chain [71].

Consequently, the most important and feared subject of cryptography and post-quantum security. Updates from various quantum institutes and organizations have reflected that the quantum industry is still at its infancy. Leading corporations are trying to perfect their machines so that they can be used in daily life, but this is a multiyear journey. So it can be said that the real application of quantum cryptography is yet to be experienced, but the theoretical security mechanisms have been developed, and goals have been set, which will be achieved in the future. However, this brings concerns and uncertainties of current security, which will be a threat in the future, when developed quantum computers are in use. The report from the National Institute of Science and Technology, titled "Report on Post-Quantum Cryptography," states that a quantum computer capable of breaking the current 2,000-bit RSA cryptography will be built by 2030 with an estimated budget of a billion US dollars [72].

Subsequently, IBM has ensured that necessary corrective and preventive actions are taken to negate threats of quantum cyberattacks by ensuring quantum-safe cryptography. IBM is offering its three-step quantum-safe crypto-agility framework to the public to ensure that the public are resistant to the attacks. So the framework consists of identifying the three risks of accessing the data, which are through fraudulent authentication, forged signatures, and the possibility of harvesting data now and decrypting it later. So the solution is to discover the cryptography-related artifacts and bring them together as a cryptography bill of material. Then the second step dictates observing the cryptography, which means bringing the dynamic view along with the static view.

It is important to have a full inventory of cryptographic assets from a network and application perspective that includes the key, compliance, and posture requirements. Afterward, the third step is to transform the cryptography by implementing and applying cryptographic safe algorithms, such as encryption algorithms, new certificates, and key lifecycle management that are quantum safe, thus achieving crypto agility through reducing the burden on the development and operational environment of the current to new framework. The new framework security can be accessed by simply making an AI call. IBM's Quantum Safe Explorer can scan all the source codes of the entire enterprise and can create a cryptographic bill of material.

Then IBM's Quantum Safe Advisor can bring together the static and dynamic view of the enterprise asset and ensure the compliance related to it. Finally, IBM's Quantum Safe Remediator allows remediation with quantum-safe algorithms, quantum-safe key management capabilities, certificate management capability, and remediation patterns based on best practices that permit the ultimate crypto agility [73].

1.27 CHALLENGES

So far, the imminent updates and upgrades in the quantum computing world have been noted, and through these updates, it was also noted that the realm is facing some dire challenges as well. One of its major challenges is the scalability and stability of qubits. Through various documentations, increasing physical qubits in current chips and devices seems conveniently feasible, but questions arise if this size increase adds a significant improvement in the quality of quantum computers. Per the researchers, the increase will add a significant advantage if the noise that is added with each increasing qubit is handled. This noise reduces the computing speed, makes the calculations inaccurate, and leads quantum qubits susceptible to instability.

These current noise-susceptible machines are called noise intermediate-scale quantum (NISQ), and the current best one is short by eight orders of magnitude. To deliver the objectives of a quantum computer, it is essential that error rate of one per a trillion operation needs to be met, while the current best machine with tens of qubits delivers an error rate of one per thousand or ten thousand. So an effective quantum computer that can run high-impact applications should have millions of high-quality physical qubits to make the machine fault-tolerant. To ensure that the physical qubits are of high quality, it is essential that these qubits are grouped to form effective logical qubits that can negate the error rate of the overall system, as the logical qubits can have vast superior error rates when compared to the physical qubits.

This means that more physical qubits per the logical bit will reduce the error rate, so it is convenient to use hundreds and more physical qubits per logical qubits. This mechanism of reducing the error of quantum computers is called quantum error correction. It is extremely important that these improvements should be incorporated as soon as possible to create quantum technology that can bring innovation and solve the current global crisis [74]. The following figure shows explanatory hardware benchmarking indicators and engineering challenges to achieve a full-scale fault-tolerant quantum computer [75].

Another big challenge of a feasible quantum computer is its high cost and energy requirements. From the previous sections, it is evident that big corporations like IBM, Google, and others are competing against each other to lead the ultimate quantum race, but in contradiction, small organizations are fighting against the financial constraints of investing in quantum computers. Per the source, investing in research, whether it involves hiring a quantum expert or investing in resources for edge-cutting quantum technology, is extremely expensive [76].

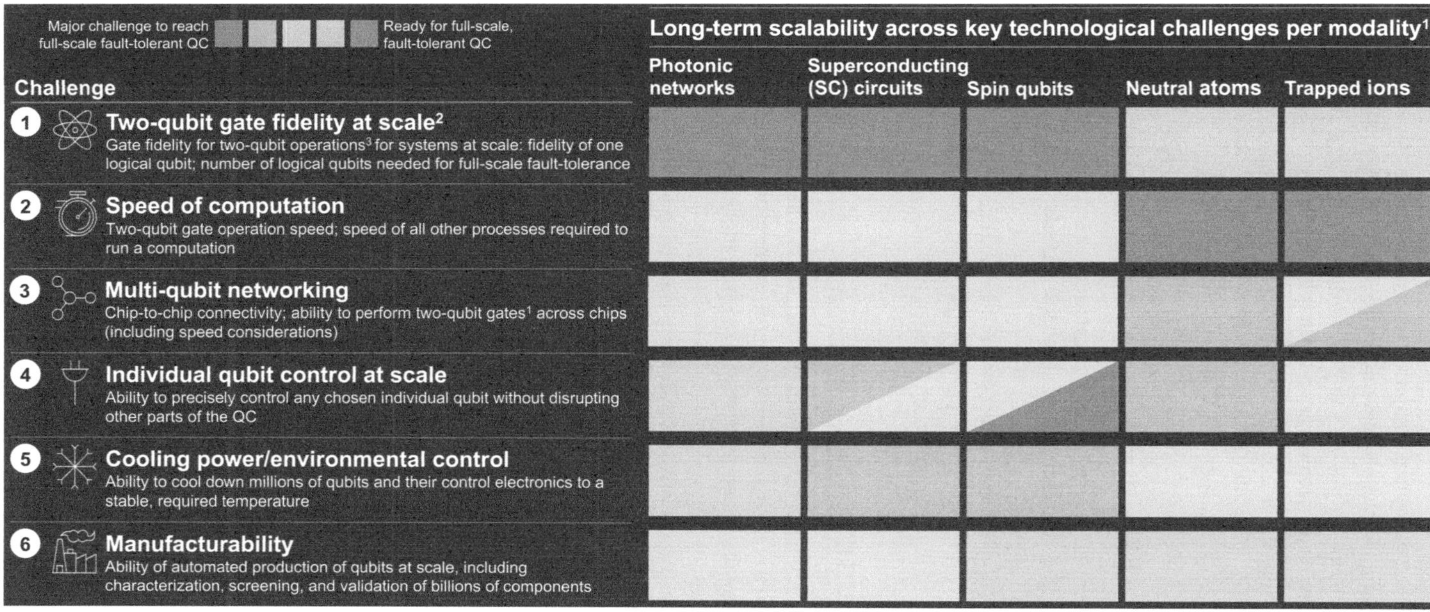

FIGURE 1.14 Hardware benchmarking indicators and engineering challenges to achieve a full-scale fault-tolerant quantum computer from the Quantum Technology Monitor Report.

Simultaneously, the energy requirements of quantum computers have not significantly indicated a red flag when compared with other technologies such as supercomputers or blockchain, but the point is quantum technology is still in its infancy stage. The greener community highlights that quantum computing will reduce the carbon footprints in some cases. However, quantum technologies using superconducting qubits may hike up the energy demands as it needs cryogenic system to supercool the qubits and as the physical qubits increases the energy demand may increase as well [77].

1.28 FUTURE DIRECTIONS

This section focuses on scaling up and the ethical and societal implications of quantum computing. The first subsection discusses goals like fault-tolerant quantum computers and millions of qubits. In the second subsection, topological qubits are explored. The third subsection addresses ethical and societal concerns about quantum-enabled decryption of current cryptographic systems and emphasizes opportunities for solving humanity's grand challenges.

1.29 SCALING UP

Since the challenges have been highlighted, and it was evident that a high-quality fault-tolerant quantum computer is required to solve problems and global crises with science and technology. Therefore, organizations such as IQM Quantum Computers have revealed their development roadmap to produce a fault-tolerant quantum computer by 2030. They have also revealed that they plan to build a scalable processor that can scale up to a million processing qubits. The result is meant to enhance error correction with efficient hardware, while the system will also consist of an open modular software stack for seamless integration with high-performance computing.

The focus is on error reduction and inclusion of low-density parity check codes that will make qubits accurate and less hardware-dependent at least ten times in comparison to classical computers, while the error rate of the logical qubits will be 10^{-7} less [78]. Deloitte [85] states that for the world to experience firsthand quantum supremacy is to produce a fault-tolerant quantum computer that requires a thousand physical qubits at its fundament to make a single logical qubit. A full-blown quantum computer will need hundreds and thousands of these logical qubits. The source predicts that this will be possible in the 2030s, where a first general-purpose quantum computer will be commercialized [79].

A research article [80] also states that the current Noise Immediate Scalable Quantum runs on 100 physical qubits and to scale this to a fault-tolerant quantum computer, 10^7 physical qubits are required to produce 10^4 logical qubits with quantum error correction. Given the scalable size of 10^7 physical or 10^4 logical qubits, ensuring error correction at this stage will be tedious. So it is essential that error correction mechanisms are applied at the intermediate level and appropriate multiscale plans are opted to ensure testing, validation, and benchmarking at each level to ensure error correction is applied and all the challenges are tackled. The multi-scale roadmap must address quantum device design, fabrication, control electronics, calibrations, interconnects, and classes of noise, such as T_1, T_2, single- and two-qubit error, crosstalk, $\frac{1}{f}$ noise, two-level systems defects, the fat tail of error distribution, background radiation, and low-fidelity interconnects. The following table shows challenges at each scale that need to be dealt with to create a fault-tolerant quantum computer [80].

TABLE 1.5
Challenges of Scale-Ups at Each Scale

Scale of Physical Qubits	Challenges of the Scale That Need to Be Dealt With
100–1,000	**Fat Tail Distribution of Errors:** Decoherence mechanisms for superconducting qubits. Mostly coherence time of the best qubit is reported.
	Qubit Fabrication: Better fabrication can improve T_1 tails. Benchmarking and process control needs to be applied especially when fabricating superconducting qubits for cryogenic devices.
	Recalibration: Two-level system defects fluctuate with time, requiring recalibration.
	Catastrophic Error Burst: Impact of cosmic rays on error rates.
	Real-Time Decoding: Real error correction must be applied when logical qubits are formed and speed should be considered as well for error correction.
	Circuit Knitting Overhead: Innovative techniques must be devised to reduce exponential overhead.
	Noise Intermediate Scalable Computing: Algorithms, 2-bit error, and other component level checks.
1,000–10,000	**Wiring and Packaging:** System integration and orchestration challenges relating to packaging and wiring.
	Control Electronics: Production of controlled electronics with quantum fault-tolerant benchmark.
	Near Term Application: Application benchmarked high-performance algorithm.
10,000–100,000	**Fault Tolerance Quantum Computing:** Challenges such as low latency, crosstalk noise error, and two-qubit error need to be addressed.
	Verification, Testing and Debugging
100,000–1,000,000 . . .	**Distributed Fault Tolerance Quantum Computing:** Challenges of two-qubit error rate, compilation of fault tolerance quantum computing algorithms on multi-dilution refrigerator architecture with multiple interconnects.
	Micro Architecture Standardization: Challenges of optimized and modular instruction set architecture.
	Quantum Algorithm Discovery: Challenges of efficient quantum memory block and methods of reading and writing.
	Validation of Quantum Algorithms
	Supply Chain: Reducing the cost of quantum computers.

1.30 ETHICAL AND SOCIETAL IMPLICATIONS

In the previous sections, it was noted that quantum computing is a promising technology that can solve problems instantly in the near future, problems that still take enormous time to be solved. While the advantages are accepted, the disadvantages also need to be highlighted so that individuals, societies, organizations, governments, and nations can prepare for the upcoming threat or find a solution instead. The most feared implication of quantum computer introduction in our society would be the breach of security. The current unbreakable security provided with cryptographic functions such as Rivest-Shamir-Adleman (RSA) and elliptic curve cryptography (ECC) will not be able to stand up to advanced quantum computing.

Since quantum computing is expensive, privileged individuals, societies, governments, and nations will be able to afford and contribute to the ongoing research, which is also expensive in terms of time and resources. This will be seen as inequality and unfairness by the unprivileged ones. Additionally, other technologies such as artificial intelligence, cloud computing, and internet of things have already been integrated with it, and technologies such as blockchain and big data will be integrated soon. The result will be that the workforce will be technology-dependent eventually. The highly automated and autonomous workforce will affect the employability rate, and there is a possibility that the lower stream of the employability curve will be left without a source of income; thus, the poverty rate will increase. In addition, the following challenges will be faced [81]:

- Stealing of sensitive data today but decrypted later.
- Rise in quantum attacks.
- Privacy-enhancing technology will be at risk.
- Regulatory challenges.

Moreover, the quantum computing traits such as superposition, entanglement, and decoherence pose ethical problems in data management. It poses threats to identity, privacy, ownership, and traceability [82]. Although these challenges may seem detrimental, the identified gaps will support in finding solutions, and newer emerging technologies will assist in the transition. The challenges that are identified will fuel the technology world to research more so that we might experience more resilient technology in terms of security and service. As a result, cybersecurity will strengthen, data transmission may become more secure, and organization-to-organization collaborative research effort will increase. This has already been noted with IBM, Quantinuum, Google, Rigetti, and IonQ [81]. *Time* also states that its application in the natural and materials sciences will be advantageous to the health and science sector, as it will be easier to predict how drugs interact with human bodies and at the same time how substances perform under corrosion [83]. Thus, this chapter proceeds to conclude in the upcoming section.

1.31 DISCUSSION

The evolution of quantum computing has followed a trajectory shaped by both theoretical breakthroughs and technological advancements. However, despite significant progress, challenges remain in hardware scalability, algorithmic efficiency, and practical implementations. This section critically evaluates the key milestones, obstacles, and future implications of quantum computing's development.

1.32 THE TRANSITION FROM THEORETICAL MODELS TO PRACTICAL SYSTEMS

The transition from mathematical abstractions to working quantum computers has been gradual and complex. Early work by Richard Feynman (1982) and David Deutsch (1985) provided a theoretical blueprint, but the lack of physical quantum processors delayed real-world applications. The development of superconducting qubits (IBM, Google) and trapped-ion quantum computers (IonQ) in the 2000s enabled practical quantum experimentation. Most quantum computers remain in early-stage research, with real-world applications limited by error rates, decoherence, and quantum noise [87].

1.33 THE ROLE OF ALGORITHMIC INNOVATIONS

The formulation of quantum algorithms provided the first tangible proof of quantum advantage. Shor's algorithm (1994) demonstrated exponential speedup for integer factorization, threatening classical cryptographic systems. Grover's algorithm (1996) provided a quadratic speedup for unstructured search problems [91]. Most known quantum algorithms require thousands to millions of qubits to outperform classical computers significantly.

1.34 HARDWARE CHALLENGES AND SCALABILITY CONCERNS

Qubit stability: Quantum states are fragile, and decoherence occurs within microseconds, limiting computational reliability. Quantum Error Correction (QEC): Current error rates require the use of multiple physical qubits to form a single logical qubit, making large-scale quantum computing impractical. While IBM and Google have demonstrated >100-qubit processors, the road to a fault-tolerant, million-qubit system remains a significant engineering challenge.

1.35 COMMERCIALIZATION AND INDUSTRY ADOPTION

Tech Companies & Investment: IBM, Google, Microsoft, and startups like Rigetti and IonQ are developing quantum hardware and cloud-accessible quantum computing services. Government initiatives (the EU's Quantum Flagship, China's Quantum Supremacy Project, the US's National Quantum Initiative) highlight the global race for quantum dominance. Most commercial applications remain experimental, with industries still exploring quantum advantage for real-world problems. Businesses such as Rigetti, Amazon Braket, and D-Wave are commercializing. D-Wave has commercialized its 5,000-qubit annealing quantum computer in February 2025 and has promised to upgrade this in upcoming years.

1.36 ETHICAL, SECURITY, AND FUTURE IMPLICATIONS

Cybersecurity Threats: Once sufficiently powerful, quantum computers could break RSA and ECC encryption, necessitating post-quantum cryptography. The intersection of quantum computing and artificial intelligence remains largely unexplored but could revolutionize data processing capabilities. The monopolization of quantum technologies by a few dominant corporations raises concerns about access, security, and equitable technological progress [89].

This section highlights the delicate balance between theoretical promise and practical challenges in quantum computing. While fundamental breakthroughs have laid the foundation for future progress, hardware limitations, error rates, and scalability issues remain critical bottlenecks [90]. The next decade will be crucial in determining whether quantum computing can transition from experimental curiosity to widespread technological adoption.

1.37 CONCLUSION

Chapter 1 concludes with a summary of the evolution that reiterates the key historical milestones and achievements from the three phases based on the framework of this chapter. It also underlines Quantum Computing's Transformative Potential and reflects how quantum computing is poised to reshape industries and research fields in the future.

In conclusion, it can be said that the birth of quantum computing was through the initiation of quantum mechanics, which is a branch of physics that makes it possible to understand atoms and their subatomic properties that can be manipulated to harness enormous energy or power to solve problems that were not possible with classical physics. So we must understand the significance and relevance of quantum computing from its birth to present day. The three-phase historical classification highlighted the significant development of classical computers, while abstract theories of quantum computers were slowing realized through practical experiences in the first phase. This phase captured details that will allow the readers of this chapter to understand the evolution of quantum computers from the 1900s to the 1980s so that the fundamentals of quantum computers and how they are different from classical computers are understood. To understand the core of quantum computers' relevant theories and postulates are reflected in Max Planck's work of blackbody radiation and the discovery of Plank's constant, Albert Einstein discovery of the photoelectric effect, Schrodinger's wave function, and Heisenberg's uncertainty principle. These are the underlying principles that make the quantum computer powerful enough to surpass the capabilities of the classical computer.

Additionally, in the second phase, the advancement of the theoretical quantum computer was stressed, as the first model of quantum computer was produced in 1985 by David Deutsch, which was a simulation of a quantum computer on a classical computer. As the second phase focuses on the time era from 1980s–1990s, it was noted that quantum algorithms and quantum error correction codes and schemes were demonstrated. So, as a contribution to the academia, early models of quantum computers were elaborated with their limitations. There are seven types of quantum computer models, and each has its strengths and weakness.

Afterward, in the third phase, key technology breakthroughs were noted from IBM, D-Wave, and Google that showed how the realization of practical quantum computers is becoming a reality. In this phase, a quantum supremacy race began, and leading corporations and organizations are competing and collaborating with each other to achieve excellence in this field. The incorporation of hybrid quantum computers encourages small-scale organizations to join the quantum race, while the use of quantum computers will be maximized with other integrated technologies, such as artificial intelligence and IoT. Based on the research of this chapter, a taxonomy of quantum computers were also tabulated.

The chapter also captures funding and necessary collaboration to highlight that the world is shifting toward quantum computing globally because for now only classical computers are solving global crises involving security, drug discovery, and other materials science concerns. While the promotion is noted, it is necessary to focus on the social and ethical implications of this technology. Future challenges were also stated because challenges of error correction, stability of qubits, and manufacturing of engineered quantum hardware are still an issue. However, multi-year quantum research journey is also on it way. As quantum computing continues to evolve, the interplay between theoretical advancements and practical implementations will shape the next generation of computing paradigms. Future research must explore the balance between quantum hardware innovation and algorithmic breakthroughs to achieve scalable, fault-tolerant quantum computing. Perhaps the world might experience an advanced security with quantum teleportation.

1.38 QUANTUM COMPUTING'S TRANSFORMATIVE POTENTIAL

The realization of quantum computers' potential through theory will assist the world in solving complex problems involving climate change and optimally meeting food production requirements while maintaining balance. Its revolution in the pharmaceutical sector will help the medical industry in boosting drug quality through quantum simulation. Drug production is a time-consuming process, and the result is often reflected by an individual's genome as in how the drug will interact with a particular individual's body. So quantum computing will help us to create quantum systems and produce drugs that are customizable to a particular individual genome type to boost immunity. This will also increase the success rate of clinical trials [88].

Other notable areas where quantum computing can potentially transform industry are finance and logistics, where an implementation of a quantum supply chain will save time and money and increase the productivity rate by instantly locating alternate vendors, retailers, and services. Current cybersecurity will be susceptible to attacks as the cryptosystem will collapse, but this will provide room to look for solutions via research that will further strengthen current cryptography. Although the potential full-blown quantum computer is not ready yet, it is wise to invest in it so that its full potential can be harvested in the real world, in terms of protection, service, prediction, and much more. This was noted through some of the popular sources, including NIST, the World Economic Forum, *Time*, and the sources cited here.

REFERENCES

[1] D. Englund and H. Choi, "Ultrastrong Magnetic Light-Matter Interaction with Cavity Mode Engineering," *Nature*, p. 9, 2023.

[2] M. A. Nielsen and I. L. Chuang, *Quantum Computation and Quantum Information*, Cambridge: The University Press, 2000.

[3] EDX, "Quantum Computing," 23 January 2025. [Online]. Available: https://www.edx.org/learn/quantum-computing.

[4] IBM Quantum Learning, "Introduction to Quantum Computing," 23 January 2025. [Online]. Available: https://learning.quantum.ibm.com/course/quantum-business-foundations/introduction-to-quantum-computing.

[5] Y. Boger, "How Quantum Computing Is Accelerating Drug Discovery and Development," 23 January 2025. [Online]. Available: https://www.forbes.com/councils/forbesbusinessdevelopmentcouncil/2024/10/15/how-quantum-computing-is-accelerating-drug-discovery-and-development/.

[6] D. Deutsch, *The Fabric of Reality*, Penguin Books, 1998.

[7] Scienceshot, "Scienceshot," 30 January 2025. [Online]. Available: https://scienceshot.com/post/max-plancks-impact-on-the-birth-of-quantum-physics.

[8] American Physical Society 2025, "American Physical Society," 30 January 2025. [Online]. Available: https://www.aps.org/apsnews/2005/01/einstein-photoelectric-effect.

[9] M. Bitbol, *Schrodinger's Philosophy of Quantum Mechanics*, Drodrecht: Kluwers Academic Publishers, 1996.

[10] Stanford, "Stanford Encyclopedia of Philosophy," *Stanford*, 12 July 2016. [Online]. Available: https://plato.stanford.edu/entries/qt-uncertainty/. [Accessed 23 February 2025].

[11] M. M. Wilde, *Quantum Information Theory*, New York: Cambridge University Press, 2013.

[12] J. Aron, "Newscientist," *New Scientist Ltd*, [Online]. Available: https://www.newscientist.com/people/alan-turing/. [Accessed 1 February 2025].

[13] BBC, "BBC," *BBC*, 2025. [Online]. Available: https://www.bbc.co.uk/teach/articles/zhwp7nb. [Accessed 1 February 2025].

[14] R. P. Feynman, "Simulating Physics with Computers," *International Journal of Theoretical Physics*, vol. 21, no. 6, pp. 1–22, 1981.

[15] University of Bristol, "Bristol," *2024 University of Bristol*, 2024. [Online]. Available: https://www.bristol.ac.uk/qet-labs/outreach/quantum-timeline/computation/#:~:text=1985%3A%20Deutsch's%20Algorithm,one%20call%20to%20the%20function. [Accessed 2 February 2025].

[16] D. Deutsch, "Quantum Theory, the Church-Turing Principle and the Universal Quantum Computer," *The Royal Society of London*, pp. 97–117, 1985.

[17] V. Kendon, "Royalsocietypublishing," *The Royal Society*, 20 October 2020. [Online]. Available: https://royalsocietypublishing.org/doi/10.1098/rsfs.2019.0143#:~:text=Like%20classical%20analogue%20computing%2C%20the%20encoding%20of,than%20using%20qubits%20for%20a%20binary%20encoding. [Accessed 24 February 2025].

[18] Google, "Quantumai," *Google*, [Online]. Available: https://quantumai.google/quantum-computer. [Accessed 6 February 2025].

[19] S. Takeda and A. Furusawa, "Toward Large-Scale Fault-Tolerant Universal Photonic Quantum Computing," *APL Photonics*, vol. 4, no. 6, 2019.

[20] K. Arya, D. Bacon, J. C. Bardin, R. Barends, R. Biswas, S. Boixo, F. G. S. L. Brandao, D. A. Buell, B. Burkett, Y. Chen, Z. Chen, B. Chiaro, R. Collins, W. Courtney and F. Arute, "Quantum Supremacy Using a Programmable Superconducting Processor," *Nature*, vol. 574, pp. 505–510, 2019.

[21] H. Neven, "Google Technology," *Googleai*, 9 December 2024. [Online]. Available: https://blog.google/technology/research/google-willow-quantum-chip/. [Accessed 7 February 2025].

[22] T. Bajarin, "Why Google's Quantum Computer Chip Willow Is a Game Changer," *Forbes*, 13 December 2024. [Online]. Available: https://www.forbes.com/sites/timbajarin/2024/12/13/why-googles-quantum-computer-chip-willow-is-a-game-changer/. [Accessed 7 February 2025].
[23] T. Cluzel, C. Mazel and D. R. Hill, "HAL Open Science," 16 September 2022. [Online]. Available: https://uca.hal.science/hal-03778746v1/document. [Accessed 2 February 2025].
[24] P. Alto, "Businesswire," *Businesswire*, 5 February 2025. [Online]. Available: https://www.businesswire.com/news/home/20250205099305/en/D-Wave-Announces-Qubits-2025-Quantum-Computing-User-Conference. [Accessed 25 February 2025].
[25] D-Wave Quantum, "D-Wave Quantum," *D-Wave Quantum Inc*, 2025. [Online]. Available: https://www.dwavequantum.com/solutions-and-products/systems/. [Accessed 25 February 2025].
[26] B. Burnaby, "Dwavesys," *Dwave*, 5 October 2021. [Online]. Available: https://www.dwavesys.com/company/newsroom/press-release/let-s-get-practical-d-wave-details-product-expansion-cross-platform-roadmap/. [Accessed 25 February 2025].
[27] Ionq, "Ionq," *Ionq*, 8 January 2025. [Online]. Available: https://ionq.com/resources/what-is-hybrid-quantum-computing#:~:text=%E2%80%9CHybrid%20quantum%20computing%E2%80%9D%20is%20the,of%20running%20a%20quantum%20computer. [Accessed 14 February 2025].
[28] J. Rice and M. Motta, "IBM," *IBM*, 13 March 2022. [Online]. Available: https://research.ibm.com/publications/emerging-hybrid-quantum-classical-algorithms-for-quantum-chemistry. [Accessed 14 February 2025].
[29] K. Svore, "Microsoft," *Microsoft*, 10 September 2024. [Online]. Available: https://azure.microsoft.com/en-us/blog/quantum/2024/09/10/microsoft-and-quantinuum-create-12-logical-qubits-and-demonstrate-a-hybrid-end-to-end-chemistry-simulation/. [Accessed 10 February 2025].
[30] S. Shankland, "CNET," *CNET*, 21 Septemebr 2023. [Online]. Available: https://www.cnet.com/tech/computing/intel-plans-a-quantum-computing-approach-to-leapfrog-rivals/. [Accessed 10 February 2025].
[31] "Worldeconomicforum," *Worldeconomicforum*, 3 January 2025. [Online]. Available: https://www.weforum.org/stories/2025/01/quantum-computing-drug-development/. [Accessed 11 February 2025].
[32] F. Phillipson, "Quantum Computing in Logistics and Supply Chain Management—an Overview," *arxiv*, pp. 1–41, 2024.
[33] Quantum News, "Quantum Zeitgeist," *Quantum Zeitgeist*, 7 October 2024. [Online]. Available: https://quantumzeitgeist.com/quantum-computing-in-logistics-optimizing-supply-chains/. [Accessed 11 February 2025].
[34] S. Jordan, Y.-K. Liu, D. Moody, R. Peralta, R. Perlner, D. Smith-Tone and L. Chen, "Report on Post-Quantum Security," National Institute of Standards and Technology, Gaithersberg, 2016.
[35] I. Smalley and S. Susnjara, "IBM," *IBM*, 4 September 2024. [Online]. Available: https://www.ibm.com/think/topics/quantum-safe-cryptography. [Accessed 12 February 2025].
[36] Universal Quantum, "Scalability Is the Lifeline of Quantum Computing," *UQ Insight Report*, Universal Quantum, 2024.
[37] M. Law, "Technology Magazine," *Technology Magazine*, 13 April 2023. [Online]. Available: https://technologymagazine.com/articles/ibm-and-the-road-to-delivering-real-world-quantum-benefits. [Accessed 2 February 2025].
[38] S. Liu, "UNC," [Online]. Available: https://help.rc.unc.edu/Assets/New_Course_Material/General_Computing/Introduction_to_Quantum_Computers.pdf. [Accessed 2 February 2025].
[39] M. Y. Vardi, "ACM Digital Library," 2019. [Online]. Available: https://dl.acm.org/doi/fullHtml/10.1145/3322092. [Accessed 4 February 2025].

[40] M. Dyakonov, "IEEE Spectrum," *IEEE Spectrum*, 15 November 2018. [Online]. Available: https://spectrum.ieee.org/the-case-against-quantum-computing. [Accessed 4 February 2025].
[41] A. D. Avila, R. H. Reiser, M. L. Pilla and A. C. Yamin, "State-of-the-Art Quantum Computing Simulators: Features, Optimizations, and Improvements for D-GM," *Science Direct*, vol. 393, pp. 223–233, 2020.
[42] C. Ugwuishiwu and O. Ayegbusi, "Towards Physical Implementation of Quantum Computation," *Research Gate*, vol. 9, no. 5, pp. 7936–7944, 2021.
[43] IBM Quantum Documentation, "IBM Quantum Documentation," *IBM*, [Online]. Available: https://docs.quantum.ibm.com/guides/native-gates. [Accessed 6 February 2025].
[44] IBM Quantum Learning, "IBM Quantum Learning," *IBM*, [Online]. Available: https://learning.quantum.ibm.com/course/fundamentals-of-quantum-algorithms/grovers-algorithm. [Accessed 3 February 2025].
[45] PwC, "PwC," *PwC*, 2025. [Online]. Available: https://www.pwc.com/us/en/tech-effect/emerging-tech/essential-eight-technologies.html. [Accessed 14 February 2025].
[46] C. Choucair, "Quantum Insider," *Quantum Insider*, 2 October 2024. [Online]. Available: https://thequantuminsider.com/2024/10/02/hybrid-quantum-classical-computing-decodes-electron-behavior-in-complex-materials/. [Accessed 15 February 2025].
[47] A. Lyons, C. F. Bowen Lo, N. Tantivasadakarn, J. Dreiling, C. Foltz, T. M. Gatterman, D. Gresh, N. Hewitt, C. A. Holliman, J. Johansen, B. Neyenhuis, Y. Matsuoka, M. Mills, S. A. Moses, P. Siegfried and M. Iqbal, "Qutrit Toric Code and Parafermions in Trapped Ions," *arxiv*, pp. 1–28, 2024.
[48] M. Swayne, "Quantum Insider," *Quantum Insider*, 26 November 2024. [Online]. Available: https://thequantuminsider.com/2024/11/26/research-team-achieves-first-ever-topological-qubit-a-step-along-the-path-toward-fault-tolerant-quantum-computing/#:~:text=Unlike%20traditional%20quantum%20bits%2C%20or,of%20quantum%20computing's%20toughest%20chall. [Accessed 16 February 2025].
[49] J. Langston, "Microsoft," *Microsoft*, 14 March 2022. [Online]. Available: https://news.microsoft.com/source/features/innovation/azure-quantum-majorana-topological-qubit/. [Accessed 16 February 2025].
[50] Azure Quantum, "Azure Quantum," *Microsoft*, [Online]. Available: https://quantum.microsoft.com/en-us/insights/education/concepts/topological-qubits. [Accessed 16 February 2025].
[51] M. Hayward, "Quantum Computing and Shor's Algorithm," 17 February 2005. [Online]. Available: https://citeseerx.ist.psu.edu/document?repid=rep1&type=pdf&doi=c4c3ad4aef68f3970d187fec0f13755471579018. [Accessed 3 February 2025].
[52] M. F. Page, "MIT Technology Review," *Rechnology Review*, 22 July 2013. [Online]. Available: https://www.technologyreview.com/2013/07/22/177278/the-bell-labs-of-quantum-computing/. [Accessed 4 February 2025].
[53] IBM, "IBM," *IBM*, [Online]. Available: https://www.ibm.com/history/research-origins. [Accessed 4 February 2025].
[54] R. Mandelbaum, "IBM," *IBM*, 4 May 2021. [Online]. Available: https://www.ibm.com/quantum/blog/quantum-five-years. [Accessed 4 February 2025].
[55] D. B. Sutor, "Futurum Group," *Futurum*, 8 May 2024. [Online]. Available: https://futurumgroup.com/insights/quantum-in-context-government-money-pours-into-private-firms/. [Accessed 4 February 2025].
[56] M. Shapanka, A. Lev, T. Bond and N. Howard, "Insideglobaltech," *Covington & Burling LLP Logo*, 9 August 2024. [Online]. Available: https://www.insideglobaltech.com/2024/08/09/quantum-computing-developments-in-the-uk-and-us/#:~:text=According%20to%20McKinsey%2C%20as%20of,times%20more%20than%20the%20US. [Accessed 4 February 2025].

[57] Qureca 2025, "Qureca," *Qureca*, 1 April 2024. [Online]. Available: https://www.qureca.com/quantum-initiatives-worldwide/. [Accessed 4 February 2025].
[58] EBMedia, "EITC," *EBMedia*, [Online]. Available: http://www.eitc.org/research-opportunities/high-performance-and-quantum-computing/quantum-computing-technology-and-roadmap/quantum-computing-history. [Accessed 4 February 2025].
[59] F. Lardinois, "Techcrunch," *Yahoo*, 15 September 2020. [Online]. Available: https://techcrunch.com/2020/09/15/ibm-publishes-its-quantum-roadmap-says-it-will-have-a-1000-qubit-machine-in-2023/. [Accessed 8 February 2025].
[60] J. Vincent, "Theverge," *VOX Media*, 9 January 2019. [Online]. Available: https://www.theverge.com/2019/1/8/18171732/ibm-quantum-computer-20-qubit-q-system-one-ces-2019. [Accessed 8 February 2025].
[61] A. Katwala, "Wired," *Wired*, 4 June 2019. [Online]. Available: https://www.wired.com/story/quantum-supremacy-google-microsoft-ibm/. [Accessed 8 February 2025].
[62] C. Reichert, "CNET," *CNET*, 9 April 2020. [Online]. Available: https://www.cnet.com/tech/services-and-software/amazon-ibm-and-microsoft-race-to-bring-global-access-to-quantum-computing/. [Accessed 8 February 2025].
[63] J. Dargan, "The Quantum Insider," *Quantum Insider*, 29 December 2023. [Online]. Available: https://thequantuminsider.com/2023/12/29/quantum-computing-companies/. [Accessed 8 February 2025].
[64] P. Kumar, "Techovedas," *Techovedas*, 1 January 2025. [Online]. Available: https://techovedas.com/top-5-companies-leading-the-race-of-quantum-computing-revolution/. [Accessed 8 February 2025].
[65] Cision US, "IBM Makes Quantum Computing Available on IBM Cloud to Accelerate Innovation," *Cision US*, May 2016. [Online]. Available: https://www.prnewswire.com/news-releases/ibm-makes-quantum-computing-available-on-ibm-cloud-to-accelerate-innovation-300262512.html. [Accessed 9 February 2025].
[66] IBM Quantum Learning, "IBM Quantum Learning," *IBM*, [Online]. Available: https://quantum.ibm.com/composer/files/new. [Accessed 9 February 2025].
[67] Prnewswire, "PR Newswire," *Cision US Inc*, 23 August 2019. [Online]. Available: https://www.prnewswire.com/news-releases/ibm-developing-new-cloud-services-and-technology-to-help-keep-data-secured-from-future-fault-tolerant-quantum-computers-300906184.html. [Accessed 9 February 2025].
[68] Microsoft, "Azure Quantum Cloud Service," *Microsoft*, 2025. [Online]. Available: https://azure.microsoft.com/en-us/products/quantum. [Accessed 9 February 2025].
[69] Microsoft, "Learn," *Microsoft*, 2 July 2024. [Online]. Available: https://learn.microsoft.com/en-us/azure/quantum/intro-to-resource-estimation. [Accessed 9 February 2025].
[70] Amazon, "Amazon," *Amazon*, 13 August 2020. [Online]. Available: https://press.aboutamazon.com/2020/8/aws-announces-general-availability-of-amazon-braket. [Accessed 9 February 2025].
[71] Fastercapital, "Fastercapital," *Fastercapital*, 2024. [Online]. Available: https://fastercapital.com/topics/exploring-the-potential-of-quantum-computing-startups:funding-the-future:-investments-in-quantum-computing-startups.html. [Accessed 10 February 2025].
[72] Qiskit, "Medium," *Qiskit*, 16 February 2023. [Online]. Available: https://medium.com/qiskit/how-startups-can-use-qiskit-to-succeed-in-the-quantum-industry-54d3a3099f5e. [Accessed 10 February 2025].
[73] Github, "Qiskit," *Github*, 2025. [Online]. Available: https://github.com/Qiskit/qiskit. [Accessed 10 February 2025].
[74] A. Wilkins, "Newscientist," *Newscientist*, 24 October 2023. [Online]. Available: https://www.newscientist.com/article/2399246-record-breaking-quantum-computer-has-more-than-1000-qubits/. [Accessed 10 February 2025].

[75] J. Zander, "Microsoft," *Microsoft*, 10 September 2024. [Online]. Available: https://blogs.microsoft.com/blog/2024/09/10/microsoft-announces-the-best-performing-logical-qubits-on-record-and-will-provide-priority-access-to-reliable-quantum-hardware-in-azure-quantum/. [Accessed 12 February 2025].

[76] Microsoft, "Microsoft," *Microsoft*, 2025. [Online]. Available: https://azure.microsoft.com/en-us/blog/quantum/2024/09/10/microsoft-and-quantinuum-create-12-logical-qubits-and-demonstrate-a-hybrid-end-to-end-chemistry-simulation/. [Accessed 10 February 2025].

[77] Intel, "Intel," *Intel*, 15 June 2023. [Online]. Available: https://www.intel.com/content/www/us/en/newsroom/news/quantum-computing-chip-to-advance-research.html#gs.kaaton. [Accessed 10 February 2025].

[78] Rigetti, "Rigetti," *Rigetti*, 2025. [Online]. Available: https://investors.rigetti.com/news-releases/news-release-details/rigetti-computing-launches-84-qubit-ankaatm-3-system-achieves. [Accessed 10 February 2025].

[79] M. Swayne, "Quantuminsider," *Quantuminsider*, 6 February 2025. [Online]. Available: https://thequantuminsider.com/2025/02/06/iqm-riverlane-and-zurich-instruments-join-forces-to-launch-quantum-error-correction-platform/. [Accessed 10 February 2025].

[80] Google, "Google," *Google*, 20 November 2024. [Online]. Available: https://blog.google/technology/google-deepmind/alphaqubit-quantum-error-correction/. [Accessed 10 February 2025].

[81] McKinsey &. Company, "Quantum Technology Monitor," Mickinsey Digital, 2024.

[82] Microtime Computers, "Microtime Computers," *Microtime Computers*, 4 September 2024. [Online]. Available: https://microtime.com/quantum-computing-in-2024-breakthroughs-challenges-and-what-lies-ahead/#:~:text=High%20Costs%20and%20Accessibility,invest%20in%20cutting%2Dedge%20technology. [Accessed 12 February 2025].

[83] Pasqal, "Pasqal," *Pasqal*, 2024. [Online]. Available: https://www.pasqal.com/news/quantum-computing-rethinking-energy-consumption/. [Accessed 12 February 2025].

[84] Global Quantum Intelligence, "Global Quantum Intelligence," *Global Quantum Intelligence*, 13 November 2024. [Online]. Available: https://quantumcomputingreport.com/iqm-quantum-computers-outlines-roadmap-to-ftqc-with-40k-physical-qubits-by-2030-and-scaling-to-1-million-a-few-years-later/. [Accessed 13 February 2025].

[85] Deloitte, "Deloitte," *Deloitte*, 2019. [Online]. Available: https://www.deloitte.co.uk/tmt-predictions2019/predictions/quantum-computing/. [Accessed 13 February 2025].

[86] A. Scherer, K. G. Johnson, O. Wertheim, M. Otten, N. A. Aadit, K. M. Bresniker, K. Yamsari, C. B. Chapman, S. Chatterjee, G. A. Dagnew, A. Esposito, F. Fahim, M. Fiorentino, A. Khalid and M. Mohseni, "How to Build a Quantum Supercomputer: Scaling Challenges and Opportunities," *arxiv*, pp. 1–64, 2024.

[87] T. Callan, "SECTIGO," *SECTIGO*, 23 September 2024. [Online]. Available: https://www.sectigo.com/resource-library/quantum-computing-concerns-positive-impacts. [Accessed 16 February 2025].

[88] L. M. Possati, "Ethics of Quantum Computing: An Outline," *Springer*, vol. 36, no. 48, pp. 1–21, 2023.

[89] C. Campbell, "Time," *Time*, 26 January 2023. [Online]. Available: https://time.com/6249784/quantum-computing-revolution/. [Accessed 16 February 2025].

[90] M. Law, "Technology Magazine," *Technology Magazine*, 15 September 2024. [Online]. Available: https://technologymagazine.com/articles/how-microsoft-is-helping-develop-practical-quantum-computing. [Accessed 2 February 2025].

[91] IBM, "Qiskit," *IBM*, [Online]. Available: https://www.ibm.com/quantum/qiskit. [Accessed 10 February 2025].

2 Fundamentals of Quantum Computing

Vishal Kumar Jaiswal, Sam Goundar, Gurram Sunitha, J. Avanija, Srinivasa Reddy Gayam, and S. Hemachandra

2.1 INTRODUCTION

2.1.1 UNDERSTANDING QUANTUM COMPUTING FUNDAMENTALS

Quantum computing quickly changed computational technology, offering unprecedented capabilities in fields like artificial intelligence and cryptography. Unlike classical computers, which process the information in parallel or sequential order using bits (0 or 1), quantum computers perform operations using qubits, which exist in superposition (0, 1, or 0 and 1 simultaneously) and can be entangled to do complex calculations at an exponentially faster rate [1]. Even though they have better efficiency than classical computers, quantum computers remain largely theoretical, with significant challenges preventing large-scale practical applications. However, using quantum mechanical principles, one can reduce the processing time and improve efficiency while solving real-world problems with less computation power [2]. Understanding the fundamental principles of quantum computing is crucial for academic as well as industry professionals to contribute to its inevitable advancement.

2.1.1.1 This Chapter's Contribution to the Field

Most introductory books mainly focus only on quantum mechanics and quantum computing separately, but this book integrates the fundamental computing principles with real-world computational problems and applications [3]. Here are some real-world examples of physical quantum hardware from the most prominent giants in quantum computing [4]. First, IBM Eagle (127 qubits), released in 2021 [5], marked a milestone in IBM to achieve superconducting quantum processor. Later, they developed IBM Osprey (433 qubits), launched in 2022; it significantly has more qubits than Eagle [4]. Later, IBM released the largest publicly available quantum processor named IBM Condor [5], equipped with 1,121 qubits. After that, IBM Quantum System One was introduced, which is a full-stack quantum computing system, installed in locations like Cleveland clinic and Fraunhofer Institute. Like IBM, Google and IonQ are also working on developing quantum computers.

There are few algorithms that play crucial roles in quantum computing, like quantum Fourier transform (QFT), which is mainly used in quantum signal processing. Variational quantum eigensolver (VQE) came into action to simulate small molecules

DOI: 10.1201/9781003538950-3

like H_2, LiH, and BeH_2. Grover's algorithm quadratically speeds up unstructured search problems. Shor's algorithm is used to factorize the large integers, sufficient for breaking RSA encryption, which is currently in use.

2.2 CLASSICAL VS. QUANTUM COMPUTING

2.2.1 Key Differences Between Classical vs. Quantum Computing

At present, classical computers rely on classical bits (0 or 1), whereas quantum computers use qubits, which can be in a superposition of states. This leads to quantum parallelism, allowing quantum computers to provide multiple solutions simultaneously.

Qubits have the ability to exist in multiple states, which provide computational advantage to the user and reduce the computation time to get accurate results. Likewise, classical logic gates (e.g., AND, OR, XOR) are deterministic in nature, while quantum operations (e.g., Hadamard, CNOT) gates rely on probability amplitudes.

2.2.2 Why Quantum Computing Is Needed

Generally, classical computers struggle to solve complex problems that require exponential time to solve, for example Shor's algorithm where classical cryptographic systems (RSA) rely on factorizing large numbers, which practically takes a lot of computational power and time, but it is feasible with help of quantum computers [6]. Like Moore's law, as transistor miniaturization slows down, we require new methods of computation to sustain computational progress [7].

2.2.3 Comparative Tables for Classical vs. Quantum Computing

TABLE 2.1
Classical vs. Quantum computing

Feature	Classical Computing	Quantum Computing
Data Representation	Bits (0 or 1)	Qubits (0 and 1 simultaneously)
Processing Power	Sequential and parallel computing	Quantum parallelism
Key Algorithms	Sorting, searching, encryption	Shor's, Grover's, quantum Fourier transform
Scalability	Limited by transistor size	Potential for exponential speedup

2.3 BUILDING BLOCKS OF QUANTUM COMPUTING

2.3.1 Physical Representation of Qubits

Quantum computing relies on various physical implementations of qubits, each with unique characteristics and challenges. The following is an expanded overview of three primary qubit technologies, incorporating insights from recent research papers.

2.3.1.1 Superconducting Qubits

Superconducting qubits are the most advanced and used widely in the quantum computing era. They use superconducting circuits that are cooled to cryogenic temperatures to exhibit quantum behavior. These superconducting qubits are used as basic processing units in quantum computers, developed by IBM, Goggle, and Rigetti [6, 8], as well as some others.

These superconducting qubits work through Josephson junctions, which are superconducting materials separated by a thin insulating layer that allows for the creation of discrete quantum energy levels [7, 9]. Superconducting qubits can be manufactured using existing semiconductor manufacturing procedures and techniques, facilitating the creation of larger qubit arrays [10]. Also, they provide fast gate operations, which allow for quick quantum computation nearly in the nanosecond range [11]. But coming to the challenges, superconducting qubits frequently suffer from relatively short coherence times, which leads to potential decoherence during computations. Quantum computers must be controlled and isolated from outside noise to maintain low error rates.

2.3.1.2 Trapped Ions (Honeywell, IonQ)

Trapped-ion qubits are nothing but confined and manipulated ions in electromagnetic fields, which offer advantages in quantum computing. Ions are individually trapped in electromagnetic fields and qubits are the internal electronic states [12]. These trapped-ion qubits are used as a ground-level unit in quantum operations performed by companies like Honeywell [13] and IonQ [12, 14].

To manipulate and entangle qubits, laser pulses are used, these trapped ions have more coherence times, which is beneficial for maintaining quantum information over longer times [15]. They allow for precise qubit control which leads to high-fidelity gate operations.

Scaling these trapped-ion systems to many qubits will arouse engineering challenges due to the complexity of trapping and controlling large number of ions [16]. Gate operations in trapped-ion systems are generally slower compared to superconducting qubits [14, 17].

2.3.1.3 Photon-Based Qubits

Photon-based qubits are basic building blocks of optical based quantum computing which support the quantum properties of light particles, i.e., photons for quantum information processing. Photon-based qubits can be encrypted with various properties such as polarization, phase, and path [5]. To manipulate and measure these qubits we will use optical components like beam splitters, phase shifters, and detectors. These photon-based qubits are using by companies like Xanadu, ORCA Computing, and PsiQuantum to perform quantum operations using photon-based qubits [18].

Photon-based quantum systems can work at room temperature by eliminating the need for cryogenic cooling [12]. Photons are environmentally friendly, leading to inherently low decoherence rates. In optical quantum computing, photon loss and having efficient detection are the most significant challenges. Building scalable photon-based quantum systems require precise control over photon sources and detectors [19].

Each quote has unique advantages and disadvantages, but research is still going on to address these to make practical and scalable quantum computing systems in future.

2.3.2 Superposition and Mathematical Representation

2.3.2.1 A Qubit Exists in Both |0⟩ and |1⟩ States Simultaneously

Superposition is fundamental in quantum mechanics and quantum computing and defines how a system exists in multiple states at same time. In classical computation, the states (bits) are definite, which will be either 0 or 1, but in quantum computing, qubits are represented by superposition of multiple possible paths at same time, i.e., the superposition of 0 and 1.

Figure 2.1 shows that a qubit will not choose one state, but it will exist in a superposition of multiple possible states until it is measured.

For example, if a classical bit is represented by a coin that lands on either heads (0) or tails (1), a qubit in superposition is like a spinning coin that is in both states at once until it is observed [20].

2.3.2.2 Mathematical Representation

The state of a qubit can be written as a vector $|\psi\rangle$ in mathematical notation; it can be expanded as:

$$|\psi\rangle = \alpha|0\rangle + \beta|1\rangle$$

which satisfies:

$$|\alpha|^2 + |\beta|^2 = 1$$

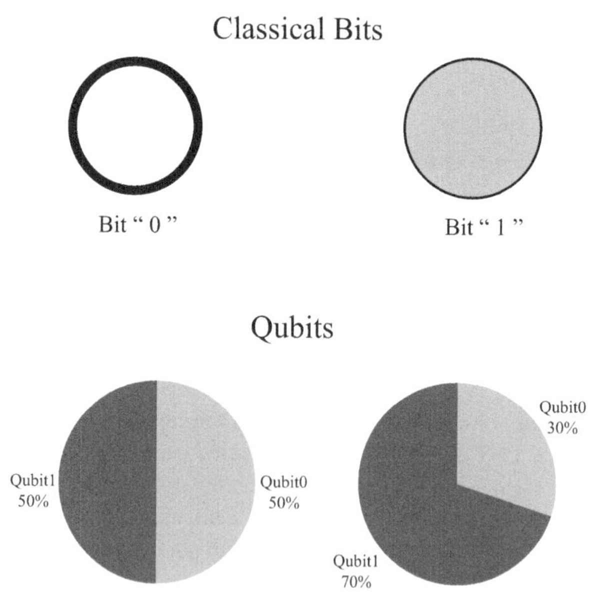

FIGURE 2.1 Graphical representation of classical bits and qubits.

where:

- α and β beta are complex probability amplitudes.
- $|\alpha|^2$ represents the probability of measuring the qubit in the state $|0\rangle$.
- $|\beta|^2$ represents the probability of measuring the qubit in state $|1\rangle$.

The total probability must always be 1, ensuring normalization.

Since α and β are complex numbers, they can encode both magnitude and phase information, which plays a crucial role in quantum interference.

2.3.2.3 Example: Hadamard Gate Applied to $|0\rangle$ Creates Equal Superposition

The Hadamard gate (H) is the one of the simplest and most important gates in quantum computing, generating superposition. When applied to a qubit in the $|0\rangle$ state, it transforms the qubit into an equal superposition of $|0\rangle$ and $|1\rangle$.

$$H|0\rangle = \frac{1}{\sqrt{2}}\left(|0\rangle + |1\rangle\right)$$

Similarly, if applied to $|1\rangle$, the Hadamard gate creates:

$$H|1\rangle = \frac{1}{\sqrt{2}}\left(|0\rangle - |1\rangle\right)$$

The Hadamard gate fixes the probability amplitudes across both basis states equally. The measurement outcome of a qubit in this state is random, with a 50% chance of obtaining state $|0\rangle$ and a 50% chance of obtaining state $|1\rangle$.

2.3.2.4 Practical Applications for Superposition

Superposition allows quantum computers to process multiple possibilities at same time, which speeds up solving certain computational problems exponentially. Superposition plays a crucial role in the following.

Quantum Parallelism

In quantum parallelism, a single qubit in superposition can hold both 0 and 1 states simultaneously. For example, assume with n qubits, a quantum system can represent 2^n states at once.

Quantum Search Algorithms

Superposition is essential for searching algorithms like Grover's algorithm, to speed up unstructured search problems in quantum computation.

2.3.3 Entanglement: Definition and Applications

Quantum entanglement is a quantum mechanical principle. It describes a phenomenon in which two or more qubits become correlated in such a way that the state of one instantly determines the state of the other, regardless of the physical distance of separation between them.

This concept was called a "spooky action at a distance" by Albert Einstein because it seemingly violates classical notions of locality. According to classical physics, information should not be able to travel faster than the speed of light, yet entangled particles appear to "communicate" instantly across vast distances. However, this does not allow for faster-than-light communication, as measuring one qubit's state does not allow control over the outcome of the other; it only reveals the inherent correlation between them [21].

2.3.3.1 Bell States

Bell states are a particular type of two-qubit quantum states that are highly entangled. They are named after physicist John S. Bell, who proposed Bell's theorem to test the validity of quantum mechanics versus classical local realism.

There are four Bell states; each one represents a pair of qubits in a state where the individual qubit outcomes are uncertain, but their joint outcomes are perfectly correlated or anti-correlated.

2.3.3.2 Bell States Mathematical Representation

The four Bell states along with their mathematical representation are:

1. Φ^+ (Phi Plus):

$$|\Phi^+\rangle = \frac{1}{\sqrt{2}}\left(|00\rangle + |11\rangle\right)$$

2. Φ^- (Phi Minus):

$$|\Phi^-\rangle = \frac{1}{\sqrt{2}}\left(|00\rangle - |11\rangle\right)$$

3. Ψ^+ (Psi Plus):

$$|\Psi^+\rangle = \frac{1}{\sqrt{2}}\left(|01\rangle + |10\rangle\right)$$

4. Ψ^- (Psi Minus):

$$|\Psi^-\rangle = \frac{1}{\sqrt{2}}\left(|01\rangle - |10\rangle\right)$$

2.3.3.3 Practical Use Cases of Entanglement

Entanglement is a fundamental resource for many quantum technologies, including:

1. **Quantum Cryptography (BB84 and E91 Protocols)**
    1. The BB84 protocol for secure key exchange we use quantum states.

2. The E91 protocol, based on entanglement, ensures secure communication where any eavesdropping attempt disturbs the entanglement, revealing the intrusion.

2. **Quantum Teleportation**
Entanglement allows for the transfer of quantum information from one qubit to another at a far location without physically sending the qubit itself.
In 2017, researchers successfully teleported quantum states between ground-based stations and satellites over distances exceeding 1,200 km.
3. **Quantum Computing and Error Correction**
Entangled qubits enable quantum gates in quantum circuits.
To detect and correct errors without directly measuring qubit states, quantum error correction codes (QECC) depend on entanglement.
4. **Bell's Theorem and Quantum Nonlocality**
Experimental tests of Bell's inequality have confirmed that entanglement cannot be explained by hidden variables, confirming the fundamental weirdness of quantum mechanics.

2.4 QUANTUM MECHANICS FOR COMPUTING

2.4.1 Key Quantum Mechanics Concepts for Computation

Quantum computing is deeply dependent on the principles of quantum mechanics. To understand the working of quantum computers, one must know several foundational quantum concepts that describe how quantum computers behave. Some of the concepts will be discussed in further.

2.4.1.1 Quantum State Representation

In quantum mechanics and computing, quantum states are represented using Dirac notation, which is popularly known as bra-ket notation, introduced by Paul Dirac.

As per the previous discussion on qubits, a qubit can be in state $|0\rangle, |1\rangle$ or superposition of both. According to the Pauli Dirac, the state of a qubit in quantum system represented as:

$$|\psi\rangle = \alpha|0\rangle + \beta|1\rangle$$

where:

$$|\alpha|^2 + |\beta|^2 = 1$$

$|\psi\rangle$ —Ket represents a column vector describing the state of qubit in a quantum system.

$\langle\psi|$ —Bra is the Hermitian conjugate, i.e., complex conjugate transpose of the ket.

Qubit states are represented in matrix form as:

$$|1\rangle = \begin{bmatrix} 0 \\ 1 \end{bmatrix}$$

$$|0\rangle = \begin{bmatrix} 1 \\ 0 \end{bmatrix}$$

2.4.1.2 State Measurement and Probability Interpretation

When we are measuring a qubit, it collapses from a superposition to one of the basis states (|0⟩ o | 1⟩).

The probability of measuring a qubit in state |0⟩ is $|\alpha|^2$.

The probability of measuring a qubit in state |1⟩ is $|\beta|^2$.

Measurement collapses the wave function and determines the outcome but destroys the original superposition of qubits in the quantum system.

For example, consider:

$$|\Psi\rangle = \frac{1}{\sqrt{2}}\left(|0\rangle + |1\rangle\right)$$

Upon measurement, the outcome is:

1. |0⟩ with 50% probability.
2. |1⟩ with 50% probability.

2.4.1.3 Observables and Measurement Operators

In quantum mechanics, observables are represented by Hermitian operators, also called measurement operators or quantum observables. Observables represent measurable physical quantities, like spin or energy.

If $\hat{O}$ is an observable and |Ψ⟩ is the quantum state, the expected value (average outcome over many measurements) is:

$$\langle\psi|\hat{O}|\psi\rangle$$

Example:

The Pauli-Z operator Z, which measures in the computational basis, is defined as:

$$Z = \begin{bmatrix} 1 & 0 \\ 0 & -1 \end{bmatrix}$$

Applying Z to a qubit state returns eigenvalues +1 for |0⟩ and −1 for |1⟩, corresponding to measurement outcomes.

2.4.2 The Bloch Sphere Representation of Qubits

In a quantum system a qubit is graphically rendered as block sphere. Which is a 3D representation of a single-qubit state to visualize its superposition of states 0 and 1.

The block sphere represented in Figure 2.2 is useful to visualize the pure state of a qubit as a point on the surface of a unit sphere. The north and south poles represent the basis states $|0\rangle$ and $|1\rangle$, respectively.

1. θ is the angle between the vector point to the qubit state on the block sphere and $|0\rangle$ basis state vector.
2. ϕ is the angle between the projection of the qubit state onto the x–y plane and the x-axis of the block sphere.

2.4.2.1 Mathematical Representation Using Rotation Matrices

The process of manipulating the state of qubit around the block sphere by applying unitary operations, i.e., quantum gates like Pauli gates.

$$R_{\vec{n}} = e^{-i\frac{\theta}{2}\vec{n}.\vec{\sigma}}$$

where:

$\vec{n} = (n_x, n_y, n_z)$ is the rotation axis (a unit vector).

θ is the amount of rotation in radians.

$\vec{\sigma} = (X, Y, Z)$ are the Pauli matrices:

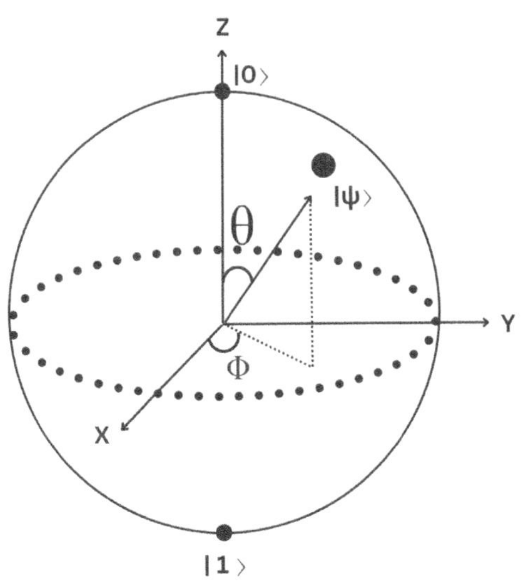

FIGURE 2.2 Block sphere representation of a qubit.

1. Pauli-X flips the qubit.
2. Pauli-Y flips and phases the qubit.
3. Pauli-Z applies a phase flip.

2.4.2.1.1 Rotation Around the X-axis

Rotating the qubit around the X-axis by angle θ is mathematically represented as:

$$R_x(\theta) = e^{-i\frac{\theta}{2}X}$$

On expanding:

$$R_x(\theta) = \cos\frac{\theta}{2} I - i\sin\frac{\theta}{2} X$$

Matrix representation:

$$R_x(\theta) = \begin{bmatrix} \cos\frac{\theta}{2} & -i\sin\frac{\theta}{2} \\ -i\sin\frac{\theta}{2} & \cos\frac{\theta}{2} \end{bmatrix}$$

Similarly, the matrix rotation of qubits along the y- and z-axis using Pauli gates are:

$$R_y(\theta) = \begin{bmatrix} \cos\frac{\theta}{2} & -\sin\frac{\theta}{2} \\ \sin\frac{\theta}{2} & \cos\frac{\theta}{2} \end{bmatrix}$$

$$R_z(\theta) = \begin{bmatrix} e^{-i\frac{\theta}{2}} & 0 \\ 0 & e^{i\frac{\theta}{2}} \end{bmatrix}$$

where:

1. Rotation of the qubit around the y-axis is useful to move states between the north pole, the equator, and the south pole.
2. Rotation around z-axis changes the relative phase between $|0\rangle$ and $|1\rangle$.

2.5 SINGLE QUBITS

In quantum computing, the fundamental unit of information is a qubit. which, unlike a classical bit exists in a superposition of states, i.e., 0 and 1. To manipulate qubits, we use quantum gates' unitary operations that transform the state of a qubit on the Bloch sphere. In general, any single qubit in pure state can be written as:

$$|\Psi\rangle = \cos\frac{\theta}{2}|0\rangle + e^{i\Phi}\sin\frac{\theta}{2}|1\rangle$$

where:

$\theta \in [0,\pi]$ polar angle (from the north pole)
$\Phi \in [0,2\pi]$ azimuthal angle (around the equator)

This section introduces the essential single-qubit gates, which form the building blocks of more complex quantum circuits.

2.5.1 Pauli Gates (X, Y, Z)

The Pauli gates are a set of three fundamental quantum gates that correspond to rotations around the principal axes of the Bloch sphere.

Initially, let's consider basis states as column vectors

1. $|0\rangle = \begin{bmatrix} 1 \\ 0 \end{bmatrix}$
2. $|1\rangle = \begin{bmatrix} 0 \\ 1 \end{bmatrix}$

2.5.1.1 Pauli-X Gate (X)

The Pauli-X gate (X) is also known as the quantum NOT gate, the X gate flips the state of a qubit as it maps $|0\rangle$ to $|1\rangle$ and vice versa. It swaps the amplitudes like a Not gate in classical computing.

The Pauli-X gate works on basis states:

1. $X|0\rangle=|1\rangle$
2. $X|1\rangle=|0\rangle$

Its matrix representation is:

$$X = \begin{bmatrix} 0 & 1 \\ 1 & 0 \end{bmatrix}$$

The Pauli-X gate circuit representation is specified in Figure 2.3.

2.5.1.2 Pauli-Y Gate (Y)

The Pauli-Y gate (Y) gate performs a bit and phase flip, rotating the qubit around the y-axis of the Bloch sphere. In Pauli-Y gate, it flips the qubit state like an X gate, but also introduces a phase shift of ± i, which makes it distinct. The phase shit moves the qubit's state vector from one side of the sphere to the opposite, through a path along the y-axis.

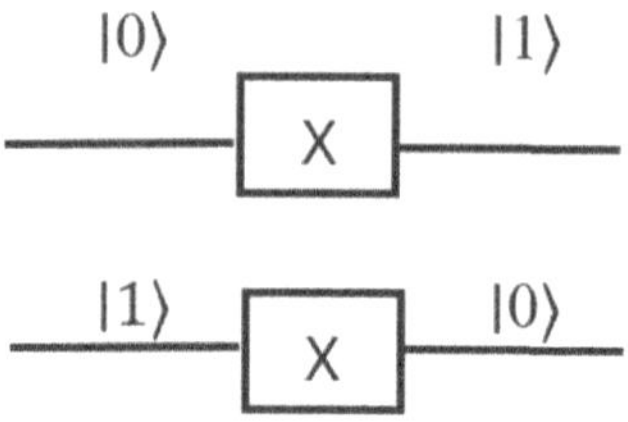

FIGURE 2.3 Pauli-X gate circuit representation.

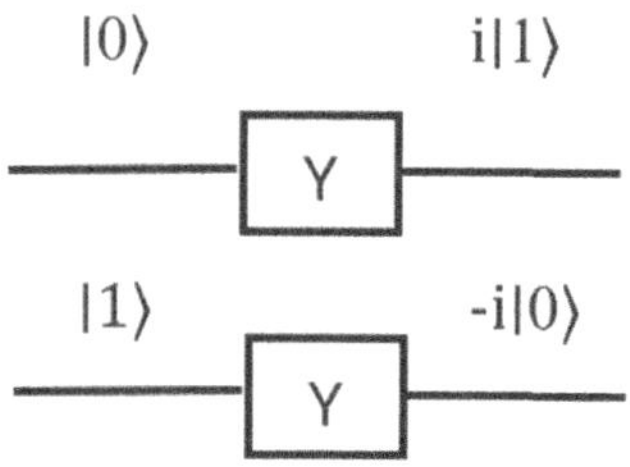

FIGURE 2.4 Pauli-Y gate circuit representation.

Let's see how the Pauli-Y gate works on the basis states:

$$Y|0\rangle = i|1\rangle$$

$$Y|1\rangle = -i|0\rangle$$

Its matrix representation is:

$$Y = \begin{bmatrix} 0 & -i \\ i & 0 \end{bmatrix}$$

The Pauli-Y gate circuit representation is specified in Figure 2.4.

2.5.1.3 Pauli-Z Gate (Z)

The Pauli-Z gate (Z) applies a phase flip. It leaves the $|0\rangle$ state unchanged and flips the phase of the $|1\rangle$ state.

The Pauli-Z gate works on basis states as:

1. $Z|0\rangle = |0\rangle$
2. $Z|1\rangle = -|1\rangle$

Its matrix representation is:

$$Z = \begin{bmatrix} 1 & 0 \\ 0 & -1 \end{bmatrix}$$

The Pauli-Z gate circuit representation is specified in Figure 2.5.

Each of these gates is Hermitian and unitary, making them essential for both quantum operations and quantum error correction.

2.5.2 Hadamard Gate (H)

The Hadamard gate is a key element in quantum algorithms. It creates superpositions by transforming basis states |0⟩ and |1⟩ into equal superpositions:

$$H = \frac{1}{\sqrt{2}}\begin{bmatrix} 1 & 1 \\ 1 & -1 \end{bmatrix}$$

Applying the Hadamard gate to |0⟩ results in:

$$H|0\rangle = \frac{1}{\sqrt{2}}\left(|0\rangle + |1\rangle\right)$$

Similarly, the Hadamard gate to |1⟩ results in:

$$H|1\rangle = \frac{1}{\sqrt{2}}\left(|0\rangle - |1\rangle\right)$$

The Hadamard gate specified in Figure 2.6 is particularly powerful in quantum parallelism and forms the foundation for algorithms like Grover's and Shor's.

A circuit representation of the Hadamard gate:

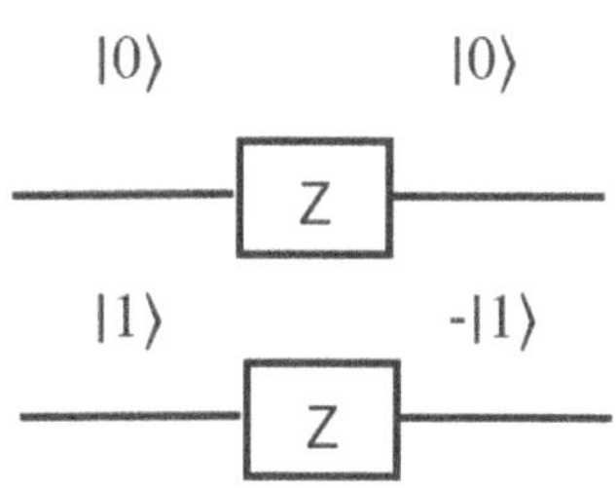

FIGURE 2.5 Pauli-Z gate circuit representation.

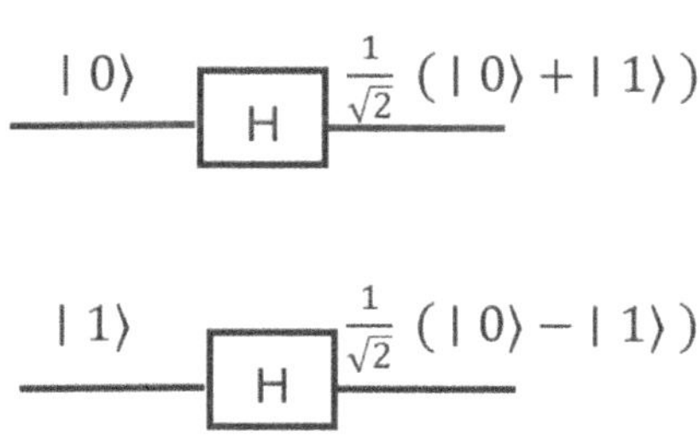

FIGURE 2.6 Hadamard gate circuit representation.

2.5.3 Phase Gates (S, T)

Phase gates introduce a relative phase between the computational basis states. They are vital for constructing arbitrary single-qubit rotations and for achieving universal quantum computation.

2.5.3.1 S Gate (Phase Gate)

It is also known as $\sqrt{Z}$ gate, it introduces a phase of $\frac{\pi}{2}$ to the state $|1\rangle$:

Matrix representation of the S gate:

$$S = \begin{bmatrix} 1 & 0 \\ 0 & i \end{bmatrix}$$

Circuit representation of the S gate is specified in Figure 2.7.

2.5.3.2 T Gate (π/4 Gate)

The T gate introduces a phase of $\frac{\pi}{4}$ and is crucial in approximating arbitrary unitary operations

Matrix representation of the T gate:

$$T = \begin{bmatrix} 1 & 0 \\ 0 & e^{i\frac{\pi}{4}} \end{bmatrix}$$

Circuit representation of the T gate is mentioned in Figure 2.8.

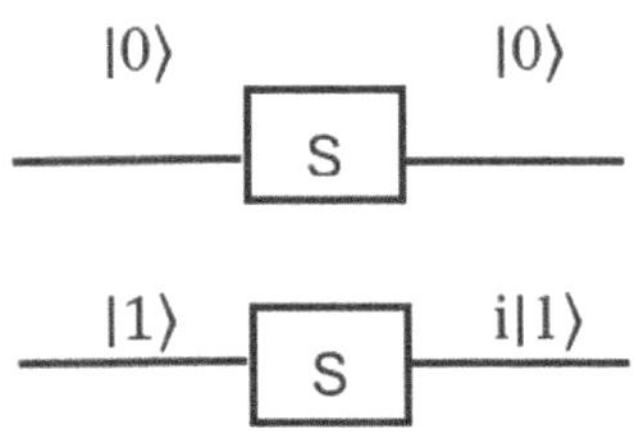

FIGURE 2.7 S gate circuit representation.

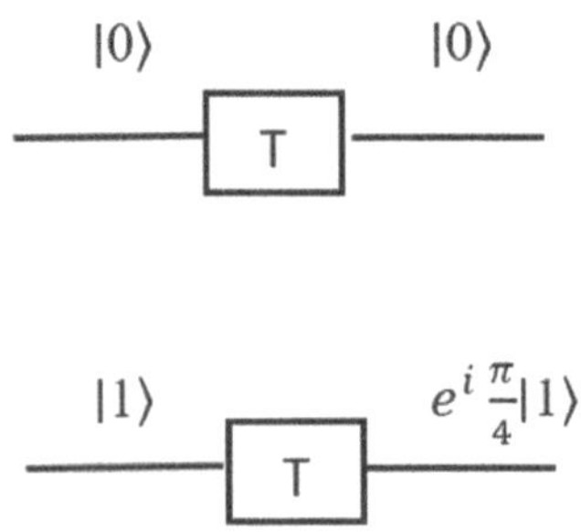

FIGURE 2.8 T gate circuit representation.

These gates are not Hermitian but are unitary, and when used with the Hadamard and Pauli gates, they enable the construction of universal quantum circuits.

Together, these single-qubit gates form the foundational toolkit for manipulating quantum states.

2.6 MULTI-QUBIT GATES

While single-qubit gates allow for basic quantum state manipulation, multi-qubit gates enable qubit interactions, entanglement, and complex operations necessary for universal quantum computation [22]. This section discusses three essential multi-qubit gates: CNOT gate, SWAP gate, and Toffoli gate.

2.6.1 CNOT Gate (Controlled-NOT)

The Controlled-NOT (CNOT) gate is a two-qubit gate that flips the state of the target qubit if and only if the control qubit is in the |1⟩| state. It is a quantum analogue of the classical XOR gate and is crucial for creating entangled states.

The matrix representation of the CNOT gate (with control as the first qubit and target as the second) is:

$$CNOT = \begin{bmatrix} 1 & 0 & 0 & 0 \\ 0 & 1 & 0 & 0 \\ 0 & 0 & 0 & 1 \\ 0 & 0 & 1 & 0 \end{bmatrix}$$

Operation-wise:

$$|00\rangle \rightarrow |00\rangle$$

$$|01\rangle \rightarrow |01\rangle$$

$$|10\rangle \rightarrow |11\rangle$$

$$|11\rangle \rightarrow |10\rangle$$

Circuit representation of the CNOT gate is mentioned in Figure 2.9.

The CNOT gate is instrumental in quantum teleportation, superdense coding, and generating Bell states, a fundamental example of entanglement.

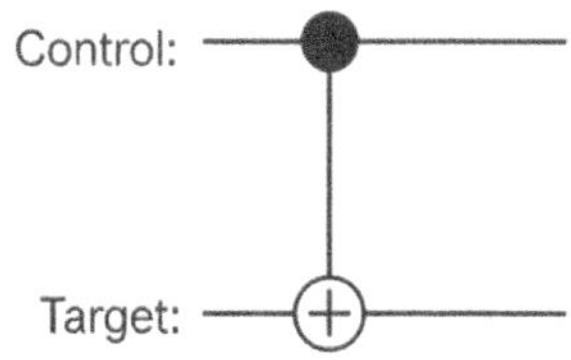

FIGURE 2.9 CNOT gate circuit representation.

2.6.2 SWAP Gate

The SWAP gate is a two-qubit gate that exchanges the states of the two qubits. It is especially useful in circuit optimization and qubit routing when dealing with hardware constraints in quantum processors.

Matrix form of the SWAP gate:

$$SWAP = \begin{bmatrix} 1 & 0 & 0 & 0 \\ 0 & 0 & 1 & 0 \\ 0 & 1 & 0 & 0 \\ 0 & 0 & 0 & 1 \end{bmatrix}$$

This gate performs the following transformations:

$$|00\rangle \rightarrow |00\rangle$$

$$|01\rangle \rightarrow |10\rangle$$

$$|10\rangle \rightarrow |01\rangle$$

$$|11\rangle \rightarrow |11\rangle$$

While SWAP can be constructed using three CNOT gates, having a dedicated SWAP gate can simplify certain hardware implementations.

2.6.3 Toffoli Gate (CCNOT)

The Toffoli gate, also known as the Controlled-Controlled-NOT (CCNOT) gate, is a three-qubit gate. It flips the third (target) qubit if and only if both the first and second (control) qubits are in the $|1\rangle$ state.

It performs the following transformation:

1. If control qubits are $|1\rangle$ and $|1\rangle$, apply an X gate to the target.
2. Otherwise, leave the target unchanged.

The matrix of the Toffoli gate is 8×8, and it acts as an identity matrix except on the last two rows and columns, where it behaves like a CNOT gate.

This gate is significant because:

1. It is reversible and universal for classical computation.
2. It plays a central role in quantum error correction and fault-tolerant quantum computing.
3. It enables the construction of classical logic gates within quantum circuits.

These multi-qubit gates are foundational to quantum logic and circuit design. Their ability to entangle and disentangle qubits underpins the unique power of quantum algorithms, enabling phenomena that have no classical counterparts [22].

2.7 BUILDING QUANTUM CIRCUITS

2.7.1 Implementing a Bell State Generator Circuit

The Bell state represents a two-qubit quantum state that is maximally entangled. One of the most common Bell states is:

$$|\Phi^{+}\rangle = \frac{1}{\sqrt{2}}\left(|00\rangle + |11\rangle\right)$$

To create this state, we perform the following steps:

1. Initialize two qubits in state |0⟩, which is default in most of the cases.
2. Apply a Hadamard gate to the first qubit to create superposition:

$$\mathrm{H}|0\rangle = \frac{1}{\sqrt{2}}\left(|0\rangle + |1\rangle\right)$$

3. Apply a CNOT gate, with the first qubit as control and the second as target. This entangles qubits:

$$\frac{1}{\sqrt{2}}\left(|00\rangle + |11\rangle\right)$$

2.8 QUANTUM ALGORITHMS

Like algorithms, we are using traditional computers to solve problems in step-by-step procedure. So, for quantum computing, there are few algorithms for searching, factoring, and simulation. This section in this book will discuss about few algorithms and their use cases [14].

2.8.1 Searching Algorithms

Classical search algorithms require O(N) time to find a specific item in an unstructured database of N items. This is because, without any structure to exploit, every item might need to be examined. Grover's algorithm, proposed by Lov Grover in 1996, revolutionized this by offering a quadratic speedup, requiring only $O\left(\sqrt{N}\right)$ steps.

For example, let us consider, given a function f(x) that returns 1 for a unique target input X_0 and 0 for all others, find X_0.

Mathematically:

$$f\left(x\right) = \begin{cases} 1, & \textit{if } x = x_0 \\ 0, & \textit{otherwise} \end{cases}$$

In a classical setting, you would need to query f(x) up to N times in the worst case. Grover's algorithm, using quantum parallelism and amplitude amplification, reduces this to approximately $\sqrt{N}$ queries.

Grover's algorithm operates on three key principles:

1. Initialization:
   Start with n qubits in state $|0\rangle$.
   Apply Hadamard gates to place the system into an equal superposition of all possible 2^n states:

$$\frac{1}{\sqrt{N}}\sum_{x=0}^{N-1}|x\rangle$$

2. Oracle Operator:
   A quantum black-box function O_f that marks the correct solution by flipping its phase:

$$O_f = (-1)^{f(x)}|x\rangle$$

   Only the amplitude of the correct solution is negated.
3. Diffusion Operator (Amplitude Amplification):
   A diffusion operator inverts the amplitudes about the average to amplify the probability of measuring the correct state.
   This step is often referred to as the "inversion about the mean."

2.8.1.1 Grover Iteration

The algorithm repeatedly applies to the Grover operator, which is the combination of the oracle and diffusion operators. Each iteration increases the amplitude of the correct solution while decreasing others.

The number of iterations needed is approximately:

$$\left\lfloor \frac{\pi}{4}\sqrt{N} \right\rfloor$$

After sufficient iterations, the probability of measuring the correct solution is very close to 1. It works for any black-box search problem.

2.8.2 Factoring Algorithms

Among the most celebrated achievements in quantum computing is Shor's algorithm, developed by Peter Shor in 1994. It provides an exponential speedup over classical algorithms for factoring large integers, a problem that forms the backbone of many modern cryptographic systems, especially RSA encryption.

Given a large composite number N, find its prime factors. Classically, the best-known algorithms (like the general number field sieve) operate in sub-exponential time, which becomes impractical as N grows large. This computational difficulty underpins the security of RSA.

Shor's quantum algorithm solves the problem in polynomial time:

$$\text{Time complexity:} \qquad O\left((\log N)^3\right)$$

2.8.2.1 Overview

Shor's algorithm cleverly combines quantum period finding with classical number theory. The core idea is to reduce factoring to the problem of finding the period r of a function

$$f(x) = \alpha^x \bmod N \qquad \text{for all randomly chosen } a<N.$$

2.8.2.2 Algorithm

1. Choose a random $a<N$ and compute gcd(a, N).
2. If gcd(a,N) ≠ 1, a factor is found.
3. Use a quantum subroutine (quantum Fourier transform) to find the period r of $f(x) = a^x \bmod N$.
4. Use classical methods to compute the factor from r.

The period-finding step leverages quantum parallelism and interference, allowing it to discover r exponentially faster than classical methods.

2.8.2.3 Shor's Algorithm Use Case

Shor's algorithm can break RSA encryption, which relies on the difficulty of factoring large semiprime numbers. Once a quantum computer with thousands of fault-tolerant qubits is available, it could decrypt classical messages protected by RSA, threatening the security infrastructure of the internet.

This threat has sparked research into post-quantum cryptography, aiming to develop encryption methods resilient to quantum attacks.

2.8.3 Monte Carlo: Modeling Molecules in Chemistry

Quantum computers are not only about breaking codes, but they also promise breakthroughs in scientific simulation, especially in quantum chemistry and materials science. One such approach is the quantum Monte Carlo (QMC) method, which uses probabilistic techniques to study quantum systems.

Simulating molecular interactions or materials at the quantum level involves solving the Schrodinger equation for many particles, a problem that scales exponentially with system size on classical computers. Traditional Monte Carlo techniques help, but they often suffer from the sign problem, making some simulations infeasible.

2.8.3.1 Quantum Monte Carlo

Quantum Monte Carlo methods adapt Monte Carlo integration for quantum systems. On a quantum computer, these simulations can be enhanced by:

1. Sampling from quantum distributions, naturally handled by quantum states.

2. Reducing the sign problem, especially in fermionic systems.
3. Estimating observables, like ground-state energies, with high accuracy.

Quantum Monte Carlo is particularly useful for:

1. Modeling electron correlation in molecules.
2. Predicting chemical reaction rates.
3. Designing drugs and materials.

By simulating systems like water clusters, nitrogen fixation, or complex organic molecules, quantum-enhanced QMC helps scientists achieve results currently out of reach.

For, Software and Simulation Libraries, such as Qiskit Nature, PennyLane, and OpenFermion, are integrating quantum Monte Carlo techniques for hybrid quantum-classical simulations, enabling researchers to explore:

1. Molecular Hamiltonians.
2. Quantum phase estimation.
3. Variational Monte Carlo methods.

These tools bridge the gap between theory and practice as quantum hardware matures.

2.9 WHY QUANTUM ALGORITHMS PROVIDE A SPEEDUP

One of the most exciting aspects of quantum computing is its ability to outperform classical computers on certain tasks. This speedup arises from fundamental properties of quantum mechanics—superposition, entanglement, and interference—which enable quantum algorithms to process information in ways that are impossible for classical systems [11].

2.9.1 Complexity Analysis: Quantum vs. Classical Speedups

To understand the advantage quantum algorithms, we analyze them through the lens of computational complexity—a measure of how resources like time and space scale with input size.

TABLE 2.2

Complexity Analysis Classical vs. Quantum Computing

Problem	Classical Complexity	Quantum Complexity	Speedup Type
Unstructured Search (Grover)	$O(N)$	$O(\sqrt{N})$	Quadratic
Integer Factoring (Shor)	$O(\exp(n^{\frac{1}{3}}))$	$O(n^3)$	Exponential
Period Finding	$O(2^n)$	$O(n^2)$	Exponential
Deutsch-Jozsa Problem	$O(2^n)$ in worst case	$O(1)$	Exponential

These examples demonstrate asymptotic advantages, meaning that quantum algorithms scale far better as input sizes grow. While quantum speedups vary from quadratic like Grover's algorithm to exponential like Shor's, even small improvements can have significant real-world implications for tasks like optimization, simulation, and cryptography.

2.9.2 Deutsch-Jozsa Algorithm: Solving Problems in One Step vs. Classical O(N)

The Deutsch-Jozsa algorithm was one of the first quantum algorithms to show a clear speedup, albeit for a theoretical problem. It showcases the power of quantum parallelism and interference.

Given a function $f:\{0,1\}^n \rightarrow \{0,1\}$ with the promise that it is either:

Constant means same output for all inputs, or Balanced means outputs 0 for half the inputs, 1 for the other half, To Determine whether f is constant or balanced.

In classical procedure:

1. In the worst case, one must evaluate the function on at least $2^{n-1}+1$ inputs to be certain.
2. Time complexity: $O(2^n)$

2.9.2.1 Deutsch-Jozsa Algorithm

The Deutsch-Jozsa algorithm uses superposition to evaluate all inputs simultaneously and employs quantum interference to extract the answer in just one function call. Whose Time complexity is O(1).

Algorithm:

1. Initialize n input qubits and one auxiliary qubit.
2. Apply Hadamard transforms to create superpositions.
3. Apply the oracle U encoding the function f.
4. Apply Hadamard transforms again.
5. Measure the input qubits:
   All zeros → f is constant
   Anything else → f is balanced

Quantum algorithms provide speedup primarily due to:

1. Superposition: Enables evaluation of multiple inputs at once.
2. Entanglement: Creates correlations that reduce the need for redundant computation.
3. Interference: Cancels out incorrect solutions while amplifying the correct ones.

These features allow quantum computers to explore entire solution spaces simultaneously, rather than step-by-step like classical systems.

Quantum speedup isn't universal; some problems don't benefit from it. But for those that do, quantum computing offers transformative potential, solving in seconds what might take centuries for classical computers.

2.10 WHY QUANTUM COMPUTING IS ERROR-PRONE

Despite its immense potential, quantum computing faces one of the most fundamental challenges in technology, i.e., errors. Unlike classical bits, quantum bits (or qubits) are delicate and susceptible to disturbances from the environment. Even the slightest interaction can collapse the fragile quantum state, leading to incorrect results.

2.10.1 Decoherence and Noise

Decoherence refers to the loss of quantum coherence, where qubits stop behaving as intended due to interactions with their environment. It causes quantum information to decay or leak, essentially destroying superposition and entanglement. Qubits lose information over time because of interactions with heat, stray electromagnetic fields, or vibrations. Decoherence times are very short, often measured in microseconds to milliseconds.

Quantum noise encompasses a variety of errors:

1. **Bit-flip error**: $|0\rangle \leftrightarrow |1\rangle$
2. **Phase-flip error**: $|+\rangle \leftrightarrow |-\rangle$
3. **Depolarizing noise**: Randomizes the qubit state completely

These errors arise due to gate imperfections (imprecise operations), measurement errors, and crosstalk between qubits.

2.10.2 Physical Hardware Limitations

Even with cutting-edge fabrication, qubits are noisy and cannot hold information long. Gate fidelities (accuracy of operations) are far from perfect. Quantum processors have limited qubit connectivity, introducing errors in multi-qubit operations. Scaling qubits while maintaining low error rates remains an unsolved engineering problem.

This makes error correction essential for any practical, large-scale quantum computer.

2.11 ERROR CORRECTION TECHNIQUES

Quantum error correction (QEC) aims to detect and correct errors without directly measuring or disturbing the quantum information.

Unlike classical error correction, we cannot clone qubits (due to the no-cloning theorem), so QEC must work by spreading quantum information across multiple physical qubits.

2.11.1 Quantum Error Detection

1. **Shor Code (9-qubit code):**
    1. First quantum error-correcting code, introduced by Peter Shor.
    2. Encodes 1 logical qubit into 9 physical qubits.
    3. Can detect and correct both bit-flip and phase-flip errors.

4. Combines three layers of encoding:
    a. Superposition encoding for phase-flip protection.
    b. Triple redundancy for bit-flip protection.
    c. Syndrome measurement for error detection and correction.
       By entangling qubits and measuring ancillary qubits (without disturbing the logical state), errors can be identified and corrected.

2. **Surface Codes:**
    1. Most promising quantum error correction codes for real-world quantum computers.
    2. It uses a 2D grid of qubits with only nearest neighbor interactions.
    3. Each logical qubit requires ~1,000 physical qubits for fault tolerance at today's error rates.
    4. Highly scalable and compatible with superconducting and trapped-ion architectures.

Surface codes use stabilizer measurements to continuously check for errors without collapsing the quantum state.

2.11.2 Fault-Tolerant Quantum Computing

Error correction is just the start, fault tolerance ensures that even when errors happen during the correction process, computation continues reliably. Its Logical operations are designed to not propagate errors uncontrollably. Logical gates, i.e., transversal gates, applied independently on each qubit in a code block, reducing error spread. Error correction is done repeatedly throughout the computation.

2.12 THRESHOLD THEOREM

If the physical error rate is below a certain threshold (typically ~10^{-2} to 10^{-4}), quantum computation can be made arbitrarily accurate using error correction.

Quantum error correction is the foundation of building scalable, reliable quantum computers. Without it, even the most powerful quantum algorithms would crumble under noise.

2.12.1 Revisiting Classical vs. Quantum Computing

Quantum computing challenges classical computing by exploiting the intrinsic properties of quantum mechanics. While classical computers excel at many practical tasks, they struggle with certain computationally hard problems such as factoring large integers (critical to RSA encryption) or simulating quantum physical systems with exponential complexity.

Quantum computers, through principles like quantum parallelism (enabled by superposition) and entanglement, can explore vast computational spaces simultaneously. Algorithms such as Shor's and Grover's demonstrate theoretical speedups that are not achievable by classical computing.

However, the promise of a quantum speedup is currently tempered by scalability challenges. Quantum hardware is still in its infancy compared to classical supercomputers, with limited qubit counts, short coherence times, and fragile gate fidelities.

2.12.2 Practical Significance of Quantum Mechanics for Computing

The transition from abstract quantum mechanics to real-world computation marks a transformative milestone. Foundational principles like superposition and interference are not merely theoretical—they form the basis of key quantum algorithms. For instance, Grover's algorithm leverages constructive and destructive interference to achieve quadratic speedup in unstructured search.

Quantum entanglement, another hallmark of quantum physics, powers protocols like quantum key distribution (QKD), enabling provably secure communication.

Furthermore, mathematical tools such as Dirac notation, the Bloch sphere, and matrix mechanics provide a formal language to describe and model quantum computation. These representations are essential for developing, simulating, and optimizing quantum algorithms and circuits.

2.12.3 Practical Significance of Quantum Mechanics for Computing

The transition from abstract quantum mechanics to real-world computation marks a transformative milestone. Foundational principles like superposition and interference are not merely theoretical; they form the basis of key quantum algorithms. For instance, Grover's algorithm leverages constructive and destructive interference to achieve quadratic speedup in unstructured search [22].

Quantum entanglement, another hallmark of quantum physics, powers protocols like quantum key distribution (QKD), enabling provably secure communication.

Furthermore, mathematical tools such as Dirac notation, the Bloch sphere, and matrix mechanics provide a formal language to describe and model quantum computation. These representations are essential for developing, simulating, and optimizing quantum algorithms and circuits.

2.13 CONCLUSION

2.13.1 Recap of Key Concepts

This chapter has taken the reader on a progressive journey through the core foundations and emerging frontiers of quantum computing. We began by exploring the basic building blocks of quantum information—qubits—and then emphasizing their unique properties, such as superposition and entanglement. These phenomena, while deeply rooted in quantum mechanics, are no longer just theoretical curiosities; they are now actively shaping the landscape of computational science.

We delved into quantum gates and circuits, highlighting how quantum operations can be systematically composed to perform complex computations. Unlike classical logic gates, quantum gates manipulate information in fundamentally different ways, enabling simultaneous processing through quantum parallelism and introducing entirely new possibilities for computational logic.

A major focus of the chapter was on quantum algorithms. Through the exploration of Deutsch-Jozsa, Grover's, and Shor's algorithms, we illustrated how quantum principles can be harnessed to outperform classical algorithms in specific domains, such as unstructured search, factorization, and decision problems. These examples served as tangible demonstrations of quantum advantage.

We also addressed the crucial area of quantum error correction. As quantum systems are inherently fragile, maintaining computational fidelity over time requires complex methods to detect and correct the errors. Techniques like the Shor code and surface codes were introduced to underscore the current strategies aimed at achieving fault-tolerant quantum computation.

Altogether, this chapter offers a solid foundation for readers who wish to understand not only the basic theory of quantum computing but also its real-world applications and implications for the future.

2.13.2 Novel Contribution of This Chapter

What sets this chapter apart from traditional quantum computing overviews is its effort to bridge the gap between abstract theoretical constructions and the realities of quantum hardware and software development.

Rather than treating quantum mechanics and computing as two separate spheres, this chapter emphasizes their mutual dependence. Principles like quantum interference, entanglement, and decoherence are presented not just as physical phenomena but as computational tools with clear algorithmic applications. This integrated perspective helps students and researchers see how physics informs computation and vice versa.

Additionally, the chapter features a richer layer of mathematical depth than most introductory texts, offering insights into matrix operations, Dirac notation, and quantum circuit dynamics. This allows advanced readers to engage with the material more rigorously while remaining accessible to newcomers through intuitive explanations and practical examples.

Real-world hardware implementations from IBM's superconducting chips to emerging platforms using trapped ions are referenced to ground the theory in current technological capabilities. Similarly, quantum programming frameworks like Qiskit and PennyLane are introduced to give readers practical tools to experiment with the concepts.

In this way, the chapter serves both as a learning resource and a launchpad for deeper exploration into quantum computing research and development.

2.13.3 Remaining Open Questions

Despite substantial advances, quantum computing remains in its early stages. Many crucial problems remain unresolved, and they will determine the course of quantum research in the years ahead.

Scalability is probably the most significant concern. Current quantum devices have tens or hundreds of noisy qubits. The quantum algorithms we know now sometimes require thousands, if not millions, of high-fidelity logical qubits to function well at scale. Can hardware meet these expectations, and if so, how soon?

The concept of quantum supremacy, or when quantum computers surpass traditional supercomputers at a meaningful activity, is still debated. While there have been demonstrations (such as Google's Sycamore experiment), they remain far from practical use. Can supremacy be achieved in a fashion that solves real-world problems?

Finally, there's the issue of fault tolerance. Most quantum error-correcting approaches are still experimental and have significant overhead. Are we approaching the point where full error correction can be included in functional devices, or will this be a long-term goal?

These open questions not only highlight the limitations of current technology but also point the way toward future innovation and discovery in computing.

2.14 FUTURE OUTLOOK

2.14.1 The Next Evolution of Quantum Hardware

Quantum hardware development is at the forefront of scientific and engineering innovation. Multiple approaches are being pursued in parallel, each with unique strengths and limitations.

Superconducting qubits, as used by companies like IBM and Google, currently lead in scalability and integration with existing infrastructure. However, they are prone to decoherence and require extremely low temperatures to operate. Trapped-ion systems, promoted by IonQ and Honeywell, offer longer coherence times but suffer from slower gate operations. Meanwhile, topological qubits, a newer and still largely theoretical approach championed by Microsoft, promise to be more robust against error by design.

Choosing the dominant hardware approach will depend on advances in materials science, quantum control techniques, and integration with scalable architectures. Recent achievements, such as IBM's 127-qubit Eagle processor and Google's demonstration of time-crystal behavior, suggest that breakthroughs are imminent. However, no single approach has yet emerged as definitively superior.

Solving hardware challenges like decoherence, crosstalk, and gate fidelity remains critical. The next generation of quantum processors will likely need to incorporate both hardware-level improvements and software-level error correction to reach true fault tolerance.

2.14.2 The Role of Quantum Software and Algorithms

As the hardware develops, so the software must stack too. Quantum programming is no longer a fringe skill; it's becoming essential for researchers and developers working in advanced problem-solving in computing.

Frameworks like Qiskit, Cirq, and PennyLane are enabling developers to write, simulate, and run quantum circuits using familiar programming languages like Python. In the near future, we can expect to see the emergence of domain-specific quantum languages, compiler optimizations, and middleware that allows seamless integration with classical systems.

Hybrid quantum classical algorithms are expected to dominate the next decade. Algorithms such as the variational quantum eigensolver (VQE) and quantum approximate optimization algorithm (QAOA) already show promise in solving complex optimization and chemistry problems using near-term devices.

Additionally, the scalability of quantum algorithms is under scrutiny. As hardware evolves, we will likely revisit foundational algorithms like Grover's and Shor's, optimizing them for newer platforms or combining them with classical techniques in innovative ways.

2.14.3 Societal and Industry Impact

The impact of quantum computing will extend far beyond the laboratory. Several industries stand to benefit significantly from quantum computing capabilities.

In finance, quantum algorithms may offer faster risk assessments, improved portfolio optimization, and better fraud detection. Pharmaceutical companies are investing heavily in quantum chemistry to accelerate drug discovery by simulating molecular interactions that are infeasible for classical computers.

Cybersecurity presents both an opportunity and a threat. While quantum key distribution (QKD) can offer unbreakable encryption, Shor's algorithm poses a serious risk to widely used classical encryption systems like RSA. This dual nature underscores the urgency of developing post-quantum cryptographic standards.

Beyond the technical difficulties there are some ethical and policy considerations. Should access to quantum computing power be regulated? Who is responsible for its misuse? As quantum technologies approach maturity, governments and global organizations will need to establish frameworks that promote safe, equitable, and secure use.

In conclusion, quantum computing is poised to reshape our computational landscape. It offers revolutionary capabilities but also presents complex technical, societal, and ethical challenges. By grounding the field in strong theoretical foundations while pushing forward with real-world applications, researchers and practitioners can guide this emerging discipline toward a transformative future.

REFERENCES

[1] Bravyi, S., Dial, O., Gambetta, J. M., Gil, D., & Nazario, Z. (2022, October 28). The Future of Quantum Computing with Superconducting Qubits. *Journal of Applied Physics*, 132 (16), 160902. https://doi.org/10.1063/5.0082975.

[2] Google Quantum AI and Collaborators. (2025). Quantum Error Correction below the Surface Code Threshold. *Nature*, 638, 920–926. https://doi.org/10.1038/s41586-024-08449-y.

[3] Muroya, S., Chatterjee, K., & Henzinger, T. A. (2025). Hardware-Optimal Quantum Algorithms. *Proceedings of the National Academy of Sciences of the USA*, 122(12), e2419273122. https://doi.org/10.1073/pnas.2419273122.

[4] Arute, F., Arya, K., Babbush, R. et al. (2019). Quantum Supremacy Using a Programmable Superconducting Processor. *Nature*, 574, 505–510. https://doi.org/10.1038/s41586-019-1666-5.

[5] AbuGhanem, M. (2025). IBM Quantum Computers: Evolution, performance, and Future Directions. *The Journal of Supercomputing*, 81(5). https://doi.org/10.1007/s11227-025-07047-7.

[6] Gill, S. S., & Buyya, R. (2024). Transforming Research with Quantum Computing. *Journal of Economy and Technology*, ISSN 2949-9488. https://doi.org/10.1016/j.ject.2024.07.001.

[7] Devoret, M. H., & Schoelkopf, R. J. (2013). Superconducting Circuits for Quantum Information: An Outlook. *Science*, 339(6124), 1169–1174. https://doi.org/10.1126/science.1231930.

[8] Kjaergaard, M., Schwartz, M. E., Braumüller, J., Krantz, P., Wang, J. I.-J., Gustavsson, S., & Oliver, W. D. (2020). Superconducting Qubits: Current State of Play. *Annual Review of Condensed Matter Physics*, 11(1), 369–395. https://doi.org/10.1146/annurev-conmatphys-031119-050605.

[9] Zhao, Y., & Liu, D. E. (2025, March). Vulnerability of Fault-Tolerant Topological Quantum Error Correction to Quantum Deviations in Code Space. *PNAS Nexus*, 4(3), pgaf063. https://doi.org/10.1093/pnasnexus/pgaf063.

[10] Rodriguez, P., Robinson, J., Jepsen, P., He, Z., Duckering, C., Zhao, C., Wu, K.-H., Campo, J., Bagnall, K., Kwon, M., Karolyshyn, T., Weinberg, P., Cain, M., Evered, S., Geim, A., Kalinowski, M., Li, S., Manovitz, T., Amato-Grill, J., & Cantu, S. (2024). Experimental Demonstration of Logical Magic State Distillation. https://doi.org/10.48550/arXiv.2412.15165.

[11] Suzuki, Y., Sugiyama, T., Arai, T., Liao, W., Inoue, K., & Tanimoto, T. (2023). Q3DE: A Fault-Tolerant Quantum Computer Architecture for Multi-Bit Burst Errors by Cosmic Rays. In *Proceedings of the 55th Annual IEEE/ACM International Symposium on Microarchitecture (MICRO '22)*. IEEE Press, 1110–1125. https://doi.org/10.1109/MICRO56248.2022.00079.

[12] Wright, K., Beck, K. M., Debnath, S., Amini, J. M., Nam, Y., Grzesiak, N., Chen, J.-S., Pisenti, N. C., Chmielewski, M., Collins, C., Hudek, K. M., Mizrahi, J., Wong-Campos, J. D., Allen, S., Apisdorf, J., Solomon, P., Williams, M., Ducore, A. M., Blinov, A., . . . & Kim, J. (2019). Benchmarking an 11-Qubit Quantum Computer. *Nature Communications*, 10(1). https://doi.org/10.1038/s41467-019-13534-2.

[13] Pino, J. M., Dreiling, J. M., Figgatt, C., Gaebler, J. P., Moses, S. A., Allman, M. S., Baldwin, C. H., Foss-Feig, M., Hayes, D., Mayer, K., Ryan-Anderson, C., & Neyenhuis, B. (2021). Demonstration of the Trapped-Ion Quantum CCD Computer Architecture. *Nature*, 592(7853), 209–213. https://doi.org/10.1038/s41586-021-03318-4.

[14] Monroe, C., Campbell, W. C., Duan, L.-M., Gong, Z.-X., Gorshkov, A. V., Hess, P. W., Islam, R., Kim, K., Linke, N. M., Pagano, G., Richerme, P., Senko, C., & Yao, N. Y. (2021). Programmable Quantum Simulations of Spin Systems with Trapped Ions. *Reviews of Modern Physics*, 93(2). https://doi.org/10.1103/revmodphys.93.025001.

[15] Cai, Z., Babbush, R., Benjamin, S. C., Endo, S., Huggins, W. J., Li, Y., McClean, J. R., & O'Brien, T. E. (2023). Quantum Error Mitigation. *Review of Modern Physics*, 95(4), 045005. https://doi.org/10.1103/RevModPhys.95.045005.

[16] DiVincenzo, D. P., & Loss, D. (1999). Quantum Computers and Quantum Coherence. *Journal of Magnetism and Magnetic Materials*, 200(1–3), 202–218, ISSN 0304-8853. https://doi.org/10.1016/S0304-8853(99)00315-7.

[17] Klimov, P. V., Bengtsson, A., Quintana, C. et al. (2024). Optimizing Quantum Gates towards the Scale of Logical Qubits. *Nature Communications*, 15, 2442. https://doi.org/10.1038/s41467-024-46623-y.

[18] Tsimpoukelli, M., Menick, J., Cabi, S., Eslami, S. M. A., Vinyals, O., & Hill, F. (2021). Multimodal Few-Shot Learning with Frozen Language Models. https://arxiv.org/abs/2106.13884.

[19] Rudolph, T. (2016). Why I Am Optimistic about the Silicon-Photonic Route to Quantum Computing. https://arxiv.org/abs/1607.08535.

[20] Bennett, C. H. (2003). Quantum Information: Qubits and Quantum Error Correction. *International Journal of Theoretical Physics*, 42, 153–176. https://doi.org/10.1023/A:1024439131297.

[21] Ghazi Vakili, M., Gorgulla, C., Snider, J. et al. (2025). Quantum-Computing-Enhanced Algorithm Unveils Potential KRAS Inhibitors. *Nature Biotechnology*. https://doi.org/10.1038/s41587-024-02526-3.

[22] Sinitsyn, N. A., & Yan, B. (2023, August). Topologically Protected Grover's Oracle for the Partition Problem. *Physical Review A*, 108(2). https://doi.org/10.1103/physreva.108.022412.

3 Current State of Quantum Computing

Sam Goundar, Deepika Bandhana, K. Reddy Madhavi, Pranav Vyas, and Mahdieh Zakizadeh

3.1 INTRODUCTION

Google has already claimed quantum supremacy in last half decade by introducing its quantum processor called Sycamore, which could perform computations in a few minutes that would take ten thousand years to compute using the classical supercomputers. It was also noted that the quantum industry has joined a highly competitive race to produce the ultimate quantum computer, but big corporations like IBM, Google, Intel, D-Wave, Amazon, Microsoft, IonQ, and Rigetti have not yet delivered the ultimate quantum technology. Meanwhile, a multiyear roadmap is being followed to reach the goal, and necessary quantum developments are introduced every year or the following years. The reason that the quantum development is such a crucial topic globally because a number of chaotic problems and crisis needs to be solved that cannot be solved right now with current resources and technology due to its limitations. Through the theories of thermodynamics, it has been realized that quantum computers can aid the medical and pharmaceutical industry to predict terminal diseases earlier, while safeguarding that, necessary medical and drugs are produced that will increase the chances of patient survival by ensuring that customized drugs are genetically tailored for individual clients. It has been also noticed that quantum computers can optimize resources and processes too, to reduce wastage while increasing the productivity rate exponentially. All of these changes are directly dependent on the output of the quantum industry, which is why it is essential to investigate the current state of quantum computing. Through previous studies, it was noted that the quantum computing revolution is facing several challenges, such as the scalability of quantum computers, noise and error corrections, quantum algorithms, quantum entanglement, and quantum hardware production. Another reason that quantum computing is a topic of debate is that it will incapacitate the current RSA and ECC securities of classical computers. Thus, the most crucial challenge that is awaiting this technology revolution is the cybersecurity. Therefore, the aim of this chapter is not only to find out about the current state of quantum computers but to follow a robust methodology of systematic comparative analysis that will assist in identifying possible trends and patterns, with the current state of quantum computing data that will be collected to formulate this document and comprehend an effective conclusion.

DOI: 10.1201/9781003538950-4

3.2 PURPOSE

The purpose of this chapter is to find out and understand the current state of quantum computing following its path of evolution. It has been realized that the revolution of quantum computing is erupting multiple paths where different technology is discovered and utilized to build a powerful quantum computer that can prove the theories of quantum dynamics and quantum physics. While the multiple creditable sources are explored and scrutinized to get the information for this chapter, the contributed information will be provided in the discussion section, where information is presented that has been analyzed qualitatively and quantitatively following systematic comparative analysis, that will assist in identifying trends and patterns of information and assist with statements that can be used to form the conclusion.

3.3 SCOPE

The scope of this chapter is to find out the current state of quantum computing in terms of quantum hardware innovations, quantum programming and software, quantum computing platforms, quantum supremacy and achievements, and the challenges and barriers of the current state of quantum computing.

3.4 OBJECTIVE

The objective of this chapter is to find out the current information regarding the current state of quantum computing and formulate it for the academic society while identifying gaps through the data that can be captured from valid sources. To meet the objective, it is essential to note that the current state of quantum computing is still in its infancy stage, and the technological development is not up to par to announce that quantum computing can be commercialized.

Hypothesis Statement: In Chapter 1, "Evolution of Quantum Computing," it was noted that the current quantum computing technology is still in its infancy.

3.5 NOVEL CONTRIBUTION

The novel contribution of this chapter to the academic society is to enlighten the readers about the key essential topics of the current state of quantum computing, such as quantum hardware innovations, quantum programming and software, quantum computing platforms, quantum supremacy and achievements, and challenges and barriers. In addition, as the chapter proceeds, a systematic comparative analysis will be performed to identify patterns, emerging trends, and opportunities. The systematic comparative analysis will be performed using the following tools [1];

1. Qualitative Comparative Analysis: Individual scenarios from case studies will be analyzed and evaluated descriptively. Boolean logic will also be employed to analyze data. The variables in this analysis will be checked in

combination with other variables to observe logical relationships in between the variables.

2. Quantitative Comparative Analysis: In this analysis, data visualizing tools will be used to create charts, graphs, and plots. This technique aids in understanding complex relationships while the data is effectively presented.
3. Case Studies: In-depth examinations of specific instances and cases will help present insights to uncover the current information and identify gaps. In this analysis, narration and contextual understanding will be highlighted.
4. SWOT Analysis: This is where the strategic SWOT tool will be used to analyze the context to understand the strengths and weaknesses of the findings of the current state of quantum computing while the opportunities and threats can be later explored for strategic planning to mitigate risk and address threats and maximize opportunities. Overall, this is an effective tool for continuous improvement.
5. Benchmarking: In this analysis, similar findings will be compared against the industry-leading corporations to identify gaps and dynamic processes that will ensure continuous improvement.

3.6 ROADMAP

The roadmap is an essential tool of this document to ensure that the objective of this chapter is met. The following diagram iterates the flow of this roadmap.

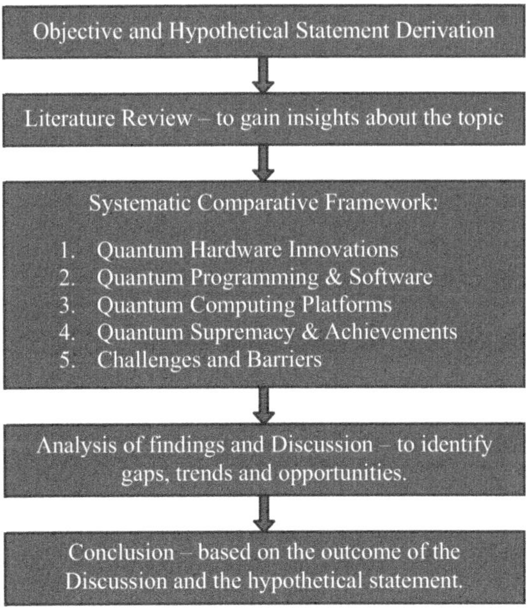

FIGURE 3.1 The roadmap of Chapter 3.

3.7 BACKGROUND

The notion of quantum computing raised from the need to utilize a more powerful computer that is used recently, but its origin traces back to the early 20th century, when the classical physics could not explain certain phenomena, such as blackbody radiation. So quantum physics, or quantum electrodynamics, was discovered. As the field of quantum physics was understood, the field of classical computers boosted and bloomed after Alan Turing's design of the Turing machine, and later Richard Feynman designed a universal Turing machine that borrowed the mechanism of quantum electrodynamics on a classical computer. This computer could mimic the future quantum computer on a classical computer. Since then, scientists have made continuous contributions toward the field of quantum computing, and one such contribution was Shor's algorithm, which could factor large numbers in a finite time, thus posing a potential challenge to the current cybersecurity. Additionally, error correction mechanisms were added to the existing quantum computing architecture, and the plausibility of constructing a physical computer was also explored. Therefore, quantum technologies and subatomic properties were closely scrutinized so that the power of quantum computer could be harnessed in a device. Afterward, the 21st century began, leading corporations, such as IBM and Google, to start contributing toward the evolution of quantum computing. IBM was the first among its competitors to place their fleet of quantum computers on cloud for community use, but it was Google that claimed supremacy in 2019, when they produced their quantum processor called Sycamore. The processing speed of this processor made a significant input toward the refining of a quantum computer running on 53 qubits. Later, Google upgraded its processor that operates on 105 qubits. However, IBM is still triumphing in this field as it has a working superconducting device called Condor, which is running on 1,121 physical qubits. Other big techs have also made necessary contributions toward quantum computing, but with variation in technology. Henceforth, it is important that the key terminology is understood well before specifics are highlighted and scrutinized. The following key terms are the fundaments of this chapter:

1. Quantum Bits (Qubits): Quantum bits are often referred to as qubits. A qubit is the basic unit stores information in a quantum computer. This concept is similar to classical computers, where the basic unit that stores information is called a bit. Bits store data represented as binary numbers, but qubits can store either of the two units, or both units are simultaneously represented due to superposition and entanglement. In quantum computers, these bits are often represented as physical qubits, and tens and hundreds of physical qubits make a logical qubit that is capable of processing at a quantum level.
2. Quantum Entanglement: It is a phenomenon where a group of subatomic particles are in a sharing or an interacting state that is similar to each other despite the distance between them. That means that these particles can be independently described. This phenomenon assists in strengthening the security of the system, as it is not necessary to reveal the exact location of the stored data or information; rather, the location of the cluster could be

shared instead. Thus, parallel speedy processing is conceivable, and Shor's factoring of prime number is also possible.

3. Quantum Superposition: It is a phenomenon where the quantum system can exist in multiple states at the same time without being measured. The superposition phenomenon is possible due to the wave function that uses the probability wave to represent particles in different state, whether it's the energy, spin value, or the location. This serves as an advantage because information can be stored in different states, but the most difficult part of superposition has been maintaining the superposition state to carry out the calculations. This phenomenon can be understood mathematically with the square numbers where the answers can be derived from two possibilities, either the square is positive or negative. So there is a possibility of multiple solution thus machine learning could be elevated.
4. Quantum Decoherence: It is a phenomenon where the quantum system loses its coherence or the quantum behavior due to the interaction with the environment. The properties of quantum entanglement and superposition is lost when it leaks to the environment. So the system loses its quantum capability and becomes more of a classical computing system. The notion is to avoid quantum interaction with the environment. Quantum systems that use a photonic model and topological qubits are not vulnerable to quantum decoherence as interaction is minimized to null.
5. Quantum Gates: They are the most basic building blocks of quantum circuits. These circuits are analogous to the classical logic gates in classical computers. Quantum gates perform the computation in a quantum computer and are the unitary transformation that can control the state of quantum computers to perform complex algorithms. Qubits are also manipulated by the circuits to perform certain functions. Quantum gates are also responsible for preforming the reversible functions that return to the original state of the quantum computer before computation, unlike in the classical computer. In the classical computer scenario, the gates that has been basically used are NOT, OR, AND, EOR, and so on. But in quantum systems, the following quantum gates are used for their specific functions:
   - Hadamard: The gate creates the superposition phenomenon from the definite states of either 1 or 0, so the states can be 1 and 0 simultaneously.
   - CNOT: This two-qubit gate entangles or disentangles qubits. The state of one qubit, or the control qubit, determines whether the next qubit, or the targeted qubit, is flipped. It is used for basic simulation for accuracy, computation, and teleportation.
   - CCNOT, or Toffoli: This gate is similar to the previous one, but this is represented as a three-qubit gate, where two qubits are the control qubits and the last qubit is the target qubit.
   - Pauli X: This is a fundamental NOT quantum gate that flips the state of qubit from one state to the next or the latter to the percussor.
   - Pauli Y: This gate rotates qubits around the y-axis.
   - Pauli Z: This gate introduces a phase shift.

Since the building blocks of a quantum computer have already been highlighted, it is essential that the concepts of quantum mechanics and quantum information theory are briefly captured for ease of understanding and relatability. Quantum mechanics states that matter and radiation display characteristics of light and waves. This means that matter has wave-like properties, and radiation has particle-like properties. This was demonstrated by bypassing monochromatic light into a pair of slits. The emerging light interfered with each other and created a dark and a light band on the screen, reflecting the wave property of light [2]. The field of quantum mechanics took a turn when Max Planck and Albert Einstein stated that quanta are emitted discretely, in contradiction to the classical belief that packets are continuously emitted. As research progressed, quantum mechanics became a solid field, and more theories were developed to explain its unorthodox nature. This was when quantum information theory was introduced. As the nature of quantum mechanics is already understood, it was essential to understand how information was transferred, processed, and stored in the quantum state of superposition and entanglement so that decoherence could be avoided and a powerful practical quantum computer could be produced.

3.8 LITERATURE REVIEW

This literature review was carried out to understand and explore the contributions of the academic society toward the current state of quantum computing in terms of quantum hardware innovations, quantum programming and software, quantum computing platforms, quantum supremacy and achievements, and challenges and barriers. The information will be sought from well-reputed science and technology journals, such as IEEE, Google Scholar, Web of Science, Nature, and other valid sources. The information obtained from these sources will assist in identifying gaps, debates and controversies, and arguments and conflicts that will enable us to judge the current literature on quantum computing. Per the findings, a classical quantum computer assembled with a quantum instrumentation control kit (QICK) that could function with electronics at room temperature and had the capacity for large-scale error correction was assembled on a superconducting architecture. This model utilized the QICK for field programmable gate array (FPGA) implementation with superconducting radiofrequency cavities to control the pulse waveform. The experimentation was conducted on a 3D superconducting qubits architecture that had qubits and cryoelectronic device as the main component that was attached to the single superconducting radiofrequency cavity. It also had four secondary components that were the software blocks that were receiving analog communication from the device and converting it to digital, and then it was forwarded to the processing system and then to the programmable logic, and from there it was transported to the radio frequency (RF) board that interacted with qubits in the fridge via the precisely controlled SMA cable that sent the data back through the communication stack. The QICK ensured that the software block, processing system, programmable logic, and radio frequency board were connected as a system through the FPDA. The software block had four interfaces, and the topmost interface was the user interface that accepted Python commands from the user. The second interface was the application interface, where the application functionalities were carried out. The third interface was allocated as quantum algorithms, and the final interface was the IP core interface that accepted the analog data. The second component of the QICK system was the processing system, which consisted of FPGA-controlled RF system on chip. Similarly, the programmable logic had 16 RF analog-to-digital converters (ADCs), 16 digital-to-analog converter (DACs), and a storage and signal processing unit. Finally, the RF board consisted of 16 ADC and 16 DAC channels. The notion of implementing a quantum system with the QICK is an easy way of implementing a quantum system for individuals who are not experts in electronics, and its Python command makes it much easier for users to interact with the hardware to implement accelerators and custom IP cores. Additionally, the QICK employs a finite impulse response filter that can efficiently shape pulses while avoiding distortion through its control plane that can upsample and downsample so that a high-fidelity pulse for superconducting qubits is generated. The embedded cascade integrator combs (CIC) filter that can mitigate errors introduced by DAC and ADC in the control generation and acquisition process. The CIC filter can be implemented with the same memory space with no additional cost, while this can control pulses without requiring multipliers. This is advantageous in a quantum system as the multiple qubits need to be controlled at a scale of nanoseconds, simultaneously [3].

Another source also states the use of FPGA to assemble a quantum computer that was tested and implemented on a pulsed electron spin resonance spectrometer and an optically detected magnetic resonance spectrometer. Per the test, the superconducting quantum computer had two outstanding modules that performed well in comparison to other experiments that were discovered through literature. These modules were the arbitrary waveform generator (AWG) and the analog-to-digital converter (ADC). It also states that the time for digital converter (TDC) and pulse generator can meet the requirements of signal arrival time measurement and synchronous control of trapped-ions-based systems. As a result, the FPGA hardware platform is flexible and meets the requirements of other quantum applications. The architecture of the experimented hardware had seven components: the AWG, pulse/sequence generator, ADC, TDC, power compartment, resource occupation, and customized software [4]. In addition, hardware such as a systolic accelerator for ring binary learning with errors-based post-quantum cryptography is efficient due to its high performance for light target applications [5].

Moreover, it was noted that there are three additional quantum hardware infrastructures, such as quantum dots, color centers, and topologically protected systems. The two similar quantum hardware, superconducting circuits and trapped Ions, are diagrammatically composed of a Josephson junction, which is $1mm$ in size, in a superconducting circuit, whereas the latter one is $2mm$ in size. Quantum dots are visible even under a microscope, with a size $0.5\,\mu m$, while color centers and topologically protected systems are $1mm$ in size [6]. The superconducting circuits consist of a superconducting transmon qubit, a transmon qubit is an anharmonic microwave resonator created by capacitively shunting a Josephson tunnel junction. The qubit state is controlled by applying a resonant microwave signal. The entire transmon qubit consists of five interfaces: substrate, superconducting metal, oxide, metal-air interface, and metal substrate interface. The function of the transmon qubit is carried out through amorphous oxide, a two-level system, Josephson junction quasiparticle tunneling, dissipation at interfaces, and surface spin that contributes to flux noise. The semiconductor quantum dot spin qubit is an illustration of gate-defined quantum dot spin qubit. The quantum dot spin qubit uses electrostatically confined single-electron or single-hole spin states and exchange coupling between spins for single- and two-qubit operations. Control pulses are superposed with direct current voltages to implement quantum gates. The main layers of the gate structure includes screening, onsite energy control, and interdot tunnel coupling control gates electrically isolated from each other by thin dielectric layers.

The device consists of five interfaces, which are substrate, screen gate, on-site energy control gate, coupling control gate, and dielectric. These five interfaces carry functions that include nuclear spin that introduces noise for spin qubits, the charge trap interface spins, potential fluctuation that introduces electrical noise from the environment that can affect the dot energy detuning and tunnel coupling, and interface inhomogeneity that is introduced because of imperfect interface quality between the substrate and the upper layer.

The color center is achieved from the nitrogen-vacancy center in a diamond qubit device. The nitrogen vacancy can be optically initialized, addressed, and read out. The etching nanostructures in the diamond allows more efficient photon collection. Metal layers from coplanar waveguides for delivering microwave control pulses and electrodes for direct current stark tuning. The device consists of two interfaces, the substrate and metal interface, and carries out functions of the device but produces lattice defects, dangling bonds, nuclear spins, electron traps, surface roughness, and extended defects.

The trapped-ion device consists of surface electrode Paul trap chip for ion qubits. Ions are confined by Coulomb forces from radio frequency and direct current fields resulting from potentials applied to the top electrode layer. Electrodes and potentials are designed to confine ions, typically $\sim 30-100\,\mu m$ in vacuum above the surface. Individual ion qubit coherence is generally not affected by material considerations. Labelled panels indicate material issues relating to sources of noise and drift, affecting multi-qubit operations, as well as components and challenges for scaling.

The ion trap qubit device comprises five interfaces: substrate, direct current metal, radio frequency metal, dielectric, and integrated control. These five interfaces produce stray direct current fields from dielectric, radio frequency dissipation, surface-related E-field noise and integrated photonics and electronics material-related challenge.

Finally, the topological qubit consists of localized Majorana zero modes, that are realized at the end of topological superconductor channels comprising narrow bandgap semiconductor nanowires proximitized by an epitaxially overgrown superconductor shell. The elementary building block is a one-sided hexon. The states of Majorana zero modes are measured by selectively coupling to electrostatically defined quantum dots. The topological qubit device consists of five interfaces as well: substrate, superconducting metal, semiconductor, metal, and dielectric. These interfaces ensure the coupling between semiconductor quantum dots and Majorana zero modes in a nanowire [6].

As the literature review progresses, quantum programming and software highlights will be elaborated. A couple of notable software development kits for quantum computers were noted from a recognized source: Qiskit, PennyLane, Ocean, Microsoft Quantum Development Kit, Intel Quantum Software Development Kit, and Cirq. Qiskit is an open-source quantum computing framework developed by IBM, and PennyLane is a platform that integrates quantum computing with machine learning and provides tools for hybrid quantum classical computing. Ocean is a software development kit developed by D-Wave that consists of open-source Python tools for developing and running quantum algorithms on quantum annealing computers facilitated by D-Wave. Microsoft Quantum Development Kit consists of comprehensive set of tools for quantum programming, such as the Q# language, which is specifically meant to create quantum algorithms. Intel's toolkit is meant to develop quantum applications and interface with their quantum hardware. Cirq is an open-source tool developed by Google for creating, simulating, and running quantum circuits [7].

As more studies were observed, it was noted that the importance is given to the production of quantum circuits rather than to the procedure of creating quantum circuits, whereby the correctness of the software is validated by instantly ensuring its assertiveness. Per this study [8] a design by contract framework was proposed and tested on Hadamard quantum algorithms, against the quantum Fourier transform and quantum phase estimation quantum algorithms. This framework ensured software correctness while building quantum algorithms with different parameters instantly. The framework provides a Python-embedded language to write assertions on input and output states of quantum circuit that is built by a certain procedure. It also ensures the correctness of the procedure to write assertions with a method that can measure the final result of statistical processing. As part of the framework, these assertions are automatically checked with quantum simulator.

The Hadamard test code was constructed with Ugate, which is a representation of unitary gate. The gate was constructed in three parts: the first part was to define the circuit and its decomposing step, the second part was the definition assertion, and the final part was the return of the circuit with its assertion tag. The test runtime showed the accuracy of the gate by printing the estimated time and an assertion error in the latter case. The limitation of this test was that the measurement was not included in the intermediate measurements of the circuit but the last of it. It was noted that this is essential for error correction procedures. The study also expresses that this test will be improved with more examples in the future test cases.

Another study shows that software production line and model-driven engineering method can be used to optimize and maximize the use of software technologies for hybrid quantum classical systems. This model aims to maximize the use of software by reusing software that is common in the entire package of the system. Some of them are domain-specific, and others are processing in memory, coherent Ising machine, and privileged session management specific. The software production line model variability is managed through the feature model, which presents the technicality in a tree node format for clear delineation of commonalities and differences across the spectrum of software products. The feature model provides a structured approach toward variability management that is crucial for addressing challenges while integrating quantum classical algorithms [9].

On the same note, while hybrid classical quantum computers are emerging, the security of these infrastructures are a subject of controversy, so it is essential that strategies and schemes should be considered that can ensure maximum security. Per the National Institute of Standards and Technology, post-quantum cryptography can ensure the security of quantum computers. This technique is implemented with schemes such as binary ring learning with errors using high-level synthesis. Binary ring learning with errors is a lattice-based cryptography that uses binary errors for efficient hardware implementation for lightweight applications. The implementation is done using high-level synthesis that can convert the digital abstraction level to register transfer level using C/C++.

This process is divided into three steps. The first step is where the complier reads the C language and applies the various complier level transformation to the algorithm. In the HLS phase, the finite state machine design is utilized to control and map the scheduling, task allocation, and phase binding of C array to the memory. Then the controller and data path are generated for the third phase, where the back-end phase begins. In this phase, the controller and the data path are synthesized to generate register transfer level (RTL) and testbenches for co-simulation. However, certain challenges were also identified with HLS. It was noted that the HLS cannot synthesis dynamic array, cannot translate certain system functions, and cannot translate pointers and recursion to RTL.

Subsequently, the binary ring learning with error scheme is mostly carried out in three steps: key generation, encryption, and decryption. In this scheme, three parameters are used: a, r_1, r_2, where a is the public parameter; a polynomial with coefficients; and r_1, r_2, binary polynomials, where r_2 is a secret key. The message is *n-bit* binary polynomial to generate the ciphertext after encryption, and n is the security level modulo operation of the polynomial ring $f(x) = x^n + 1$. This scheme is particularly useful for resource-constrained environments such as IoT devices [10].

Since quantum software and programs are widely applicable to the entire quantum ecosystems through hardware and devices, so it is essential to understand the fundamentals of quantum computing platforms. A research article highlighted the concept of distributed quantum computing (DQC), which works at the algorithm and circuit level. The algorithmic distribution ensures task distribution before compiling, allowing different parts of the quantum processing unit to receive distinct parts of the algorithm, whereas the circuit distribution ensures the execution of a quantum algorithm in a distributed manner using circuit and adaptive quantum computing technologies. This is achieved through quantum entanglement and quantum teleportation through the quantum architectures of teledata and telegate.

In the telegate method, a communication qubit in one quantum processing unit is entangled with other communication qubits across different quantum processing units using cat-entangler primitive operation. Thus, the control qubit in one quantum processing unit becomes entangled with the communication qubits from other quantum processing unit, thus enabling nonlocal quantum operations. Also, to ensure operational flexibility, the system employs the cat-disentangler function, which disentangles the control qubits out of control mode and utilizes it for local operation.

The teledata method handles the challenge of transmitting qubit states between the quantum processing unit via quantum teleportation. This happens when the system has a lot of qubits that are not engaged for any computation, so they are teleported to other quantum processing units for usage. Note: teleportation is desired because direct transmission causes decoherence of the system [11].

Quantum computing is still applied on classical computers to achieve an intermediate result of a quantum computer. The resources of the classical computer to run algorithms for a quantum computer on a single node does not match up. So a multi-node computing cluster is required to provide the resources and memory power to operate. Therefore, the message passing interface needs to be utilized to form the multi-cluster platform. The message passing interface has high-performance inter-process communication capabilities that can balance the data transfer between the host. In this way, the quantum computing task can be distributed across the platform to solve the same problem, thus accelerating the process [12].

Nevertheless, platforms such as IBM's Q Experiences allows users to access their quantum hardware and simulators through their cloud platform. Accessing these materials on a cloud platform might seem appealing, but in reality, it becomes difficult to download and modify source codes and libraries. So a docker container needs to be created on a local cloud platform that will ensure that these things can be done with more ease than accessing the IBM Q Experience directly.

Per the source, the docker container can be created with Qiskit on a local system that can access the IBM Q Experience. This container allows single user to develop small project prototype, test it, and implement extreme capability algorithms with agility and flexibility. While the docker container can be scaled to a larger size, there are two limitations that need to be addressed. The first limitation is that the Qiskit IBM Q code compatibility is an issue because Qiskit releases its version several times a year. So, in order to develop a stable docker container, it is essential that Qiskit should stabilize its version source code. The second limitation is the security of this docker system will be neglected. The current prototype users are using root access privilege, but for multi-user access, the root access privileges must be removed [13].

As time progressed, the amalgamation of classical and quantum systems were further advanced to achieve its theoretical benefits and attain quantum supremacy. The term "quantum supremacy" was used in 2019 by Google when Google Gizmo solved a mathematical problem in under three and half minutes, which would take thousands of years for a supercomputer to solve [14]. This source also states that IBM has already produced its 1,121-qubit Condor processor in 2023, while D-Wave has installed a 1,000-qubit quantum artificial lab at NASA. It has also been working on its 5,000-qubit Pegasus P16 installation since 2022.

This source basically elaborates on the quantum phenomenon of superposition and entanglement, which makes the quantum computer so powerful. It also highlights quantum parallelism, which arises due to quantum superposition that is insulated from quantum entanglement of the environment, resulting a classical state or the state of quantum parallelism.

The current IBM superconducting quantum computer is built with cryogenic materials that allows supercooling of qubits' states. The supercooling effect reduces noise in the system while ensuring that qubits are in a state of possible quantum phenomena. The cryogenic quantum controller is connected to the classical computer, which initiates the process, and then the communication is passed through the quantum controller command gates to the quantum registers, which transfers the measurement result after the process. The algorithms that were employed on this device were Shor's algorithm and Grover's algorithm. Shor's algorithm reduces the probability of incorrect answers as the algorithm is repeated. Grover's algorithm was found to be four times faster than other conventional algorithms. The probabilistic algorithm could find the mean and median of the number of entries employed for NP complete problems and collision problems.

The paper also suggests that future quantum computing and artificial intelligence can solve problems of logistics and optimization, weather and climate modeling, customized medicine, space exploration, fundamental science, machine learning, cryptography, and real-time language translation.

Additionally, another source described how IBM is scaling up their quantum processors by coupling multiple processors that work as a module rather than a single, scaled-up processor. This eliminated the collision frequency that arises due to the fabrication process of the sensitive Josephson junction and the readouts and cross-talks of the plane. This reduces the error due to miniaturization, improves device quality and signal delivery, and optimizes other system components as well. This concept was introduced with the IBM Heron processor, where three 133-qubit chips were connected with each other via classical links to ensure quantum parallelism.

This paper also mentions that IBM has produced its 1,386-qubit system by using three 462-qubit Flamingo processors in 2024, and in 2025, this same concept will be used to assemble its three multi-chip 1,386-qubit processors to produce a 4,158-qubit system called Kookaburra in 2025. The roadmap also highlights goals beyond 2026, including error suppression and mitigation, error correction while scaling up to 10,000–100,000 qubits on a classical communication [15].

Subsequently, a source suggests of using quantum deep learning with quantum neural network to further gain benefits of combining artificial intelligence with quantum computing. These two concepts can produce a quantum circuit that works on a quantum convolutional neural network. The quantum circuit that actually utilizes a variational quantum algorithm is a classical quantum hybrid algorithm used by classical computers for optimization and classification.

The quantum convolution neural network works in two steps. The first step is the same as in any quantum neural network, which involves encoding input data to qubit states with rotation operator gates. The convolution layer with quasi-local unitary gate then filters input data to the feature map. The feature map is then downsized with controlled rotation operators in the pooling layer; this process is repeated for a sufficient time till its connected layer acts on the qubit states as classical neural network. In the second step, the measurement of the qubit is decoded into an output data with desired sizes. After each measurement, the circuit parameters are updated with gradient descent optimizer. The challenge with this model is the gradient vanishing of so many quantum levels [16].

Moreover, D-Wave 2000Q model was used to elevate the medical facilities during COVID-19 pandemic, for problems with physician scheduling and nurse-physician scheduling, with its reverse annealing method, and this was achieved with great accuracy. D-Wave was also used to solve logistics problem in Japan in 2020 with other collaborations, where a quantum hybrid solution was adopted by using machine learning to optimize garbage collection and transportation routes for efficiency and reduction of carbon emissions. Quantum computing algorithms have also made contributions to alleviate the security system, especially with its quantum genetic particle filter algorithm, by filtering the target in real time and further improving the real-time tracking with quantum parallelism. The use of quantum computing in smart city construction has been noted where the construction cost of landscapes and trails has been reduced by utilizing the improved hybrid quantum-behaved particle swarm optimization. This algorithm avoids the precocious convergence problem of the particle swarm optimization algorithm, and enhances the global search capability and speeds up the convergence by introducing a natural selection method into the traditional position updating formula [17].

As quantum computing is polishing its attributes, challenges and barriers are experienced where qubits can only be manipulated for a short period of time before stability is lost, and noise is incorporated in the process, and the system faces decoherence. As a result, complex computation is compromised, and real-life problem-solving efficiency is lost. This is due to the fact that superposition cannot be maintained for a long period of time. On the same note, it can be said that scalability is another development issue because qubit coherence and stability need to be maintained as qubits are increased, and challenges of unwanted inter-qubit interaction need to be overcome, while logistics issues of qubit fabrication are another problem. It can be said that transistor miniaturization is another hardware barrier where the quantum effect increases, causing destructive interferences and thus canceling certain outcomes [18].

As more research papers were reviewed, it was also noted that software development engineering for quantum computer is another challenge, especially when producing quantum programs. The first challenge is that the current engineering standards for software production, especially debugging, are classical. The second challenge is that quantum programming utilizes quantum physics, but the current standards of software development comes from the early days of programming, and it focuses on agile development, which means software are rapidly deployed and tested, and the overall software cycle is cheap. This is unlikely with quantum computing, where software deployment and testing require more time, energy, and effort, and the software lifecycle is not cheap.

So, to make things easier, and to fill in the gaps, the quantum computing workflow was identified, with four steps: composing quantum programs, deploying and running these programs, and interpreting quantum execution results. Then the existing software engineering research was mapped to the workflow, and from there, processes were adjusted to suit the needs of the cycle. The quantum software cycle basically consists of three processes: design, deployment, and interpretation. In the last part, data science techniques are suggested to be incorporated to handle the error. However, the source does not present any experiments or results that can prove this strategy [19].

Another prominent issue that can be noticed for quantum computing is that the coherence length is minimal because the system starts interacting with the environment, so superposition is lost, and the system starts entangling, which leads to decoherence. This affects quantum information processing, and the quantum system becomes error-prone. This is where the overall computation of a quantum system can be disrupted because the errors in a quantum system can be continuous and dependent on phases. Also, fabrication is another challenge that is observed for quantum systems, as the components are small and need to be aligned properly, and the temperature needs to be as near as absolute zero as possible to maintain the quantum state [20].

Moreover, algorithms such as Grover's algorithm, Shor's algorithm, variational quantum eigensolver, and quantum algorithm optimizer atomizer are some of the prominent quantum algorithms to solve NP hard problems, even though these algorithms are optimum, but the error increases as the qubit size increases. The experiment results showed that error rate improved while the qubits increased, but only 20 qubits were used in this experiment [21].

Accordingly, the literature review lists a lot of important points about the current state of quantum computing in different sections, so the upcoming methodology section will utilize the various aspects and facts about the current state of quantum computing in a robust way, where a systematic comparative analysis will be used to further evaluate and compare points, which will assist in identifying more gaps, weaknesses, strengths, and opportunities that can bring awareness to the academic society and help us to make a conclusion on the hypothesis.

3.9 METHODOLOGY: SYSTEMATIC COMPARATIVE FRAMEWORK

The goal of this systematic comparative analysis is to compare facts such as quantum hardware innovation, quantum software and programming languages, quantum computing platforms and accessibility, and achievements in quantum supremacy, and it technical and non-technical challenges against various quantum technologies present in the market or at least the ones at experimental stages. The findings about each quantum technology will be compared against the criteria and the comparison factors. The criteria that will be used in this case are recentness, impact, and relevance, and the comparing factors are performance, scalability, industry readiness, accessibility, and governance implications. The criteria and the comparative factors will be explained in detail as follows:

3.10 CRITERIA

Note: the following criteria is for the sources used to get the information for this chapter.

1. Recentness: This criterion refers to the timeline or the up-to-dateness of the facts or the source that presents the information. This criterion ensures that the information that is being utilized for this chapter is also relevant based on the up-to-dateness of the information that will assist in making a valid conclusion after analysis.
2. Impact: This criterion will be used to identify the effectiveness, efficiency, and cohesion of the findings. It will assist in identifying a possible relationship, especially a cause-and-effect relationship based on the intervention that generates a positive or negative effect.

3. Relevance: This criterion refers to the value and worth of the particular finding and how this value or worth meets the objective of this chapter.

3.11 COMPARATIVE FACTORS

The comparative factors, on the other hand, will be utilized to analyze the findings of quantum computing from various techs and manufacturers.

1. Performance: This factor will be utilized to identify the outcomes and the quality of results from the findings of each quantum technology.
2. Scalability: This factor will ensure that the findings reflect the scalability of the systems. The scalability factor will be scrutinized vertically, horizontally, and through hybrid means.
    - Vertical scalability is where resources are applied and added on the existing architecture to enhance the capability of each machine.
    - Horizontal scalability is where machines are added to upgrade the entire system enhancing the system capacity.
    - Hybrid scalability is where the vertical and horizontal approaches are combined to achieve efficiency and effectiveness.
3. Industry: Quantum technology from different industries and sectors will be compared to understand the contributions that quantum computing is adding globally.
4. Readiness: This factor will ensure the current quantum computing state is ready to be utilized commercially and for research purposes to solve a global crisis. This is where instances of quantum technology uses will be checked for practicality.
5. Accessibility: This factor will ensure that the quantum technology is accessible by all. In latter cases, what are the prohibiting factors that is hindering its accessibility?
6. Governance Implications: Governance implications will ensure the risk that is associated with quantum computing is accountable and sustainable.

The information criteria and comparative factors will be weighted with three indicators in three different colors: undesirable, satisfactory, and desirable. The data will be sought from secondary sources, such as journals, academic databases, reports, and online corporate blogs, so that maximum information for the chapter can be analyzed for efficiency and a valid conclusion is made.

■ Undesirable □ Satisfactory ■ Desirable

Subsequently, the systematic comparative analysis that is chosen for this chapter adds contributions based on the criteria and comparative factors that is set up for this chapter to genuinely measure the current state of quantum computing. This measurement will also identify gaps that can be filled with more research and academic scrutiny on quantum computing. As this chapter progresses, the state-of-the-art developments in quantum computing will be elaborated.

3.12 STATE-OF-THE-ART DEVELOPMENTS IN QUANTUM COMPUTING

In this section, different quantum hardware technologies will be analyzed from different business associates, while their weaknesses and strengths will be captured for further analysis and identifying a benchmark for all quantum technologies. Per the findings, there are seven different types of quantum computing hardware innovations present globally: superconducting qubits, trapped ion, photonics and silicon, neutral atoms, quantum dots [22], quantum annealing [23], and topological qubits [24]. However, in this section, importance will be given to superconducting qubits, trapped ions, and photonic and silicon-based qubits.

3.13 QUANTUM HARDWARE INNOVATIONS

3.13.1 Superconducting Qubits

The following table shows quantum innovations from different corporations, with their strengths, weaknesses, technological benchmarks in terms of error rate, and circuit layer operations per second (CLOPS).

3.14 TRAPPED IONS

Trapped-ion quantum computing platforms utilize charged atoms, or ions, that are suspended in either an electric or magnetic field for information processing using technologies such as laser, electric, and magnetic devices. Per Quantum Insider, there are six leading companies that are expanding with trapped ions as their quantum computer platform. These six companies, in their ascending order according to their size, are Quantinuum, IonQ, Quantum Factory, Alpine Quantum Technologies, Oxford Ionics, and eleQtron [34]. Nonetheless, in this subsection, the first two leading companies will be scrutinized in terms of their technology, performance metrics, and industry recognition.

Per the development roadmap of Quantinuum, they produced their first-generation H1 product in 2020, which consisted of 20 physical qubits [35]. The architecture of the H1 product is sort of in a linear structure that supports connectivity to all and all qubits. It has laser-based quantum gates, and the quantum charge-coupled device has five parallel gate zones. The device has more features, including mid-circuit measurement, conditioned circuit branching, and qubit reuse after mid-circuit measurement, and it consists of a high-performing quantum compiler called TKET that optimizes the circuit of this architecture. It also contains sets of native gates, such as single-qubit rotations, two-qubit ZZ gates, arbitrary-angle ZZ gates, and a special unitary entangler for universal computation [36]. The results of this processor show that its quantum volume is up to 2^{20}, single gate fidelity rate is 99.998%, and the two-qubit gate fidelity rate is 99.91% [37].

The H2 product was introduced in 2023 that consisted of 32 to 56 physical qubits as it came out in two versions, H2–1 and H2–2. The H2 processor is mentioned to be fault-tolerant, and it was able to hit three 9 figures in the two-qubit gate fidelity,

TABLE 3.1
Strengths, Weaknesses, and Technological Benchmarks of Superconducting Quantum Hardware

Quantum Hardware	Strength	Weakness	Technological Benchmarks				
			Gates	Location	Error Rate—Best	Error Rate—Layered	CLOPS
Superconducting Qubits							
IBM							
Eagle, 127 qubits	• Successor of 65-qubit Hummingbird • Includes advance 3D packaging techniques • Heavy hexagonal qubit layout • Potential neighboring error rates are reduced • Incorporates readout multiplexing that reduces the electronics and wiring inside dilution refrigerator [25] • Multi-layer wiring that delivers signal in the deep chips and prevents crosstalk • Coherence time of 400 seconds [26]	The weaknesses include perfecting the existing capabilities of this processor: • Complexity • Scalability • Error rates • Decoherence • Crosstalk [26]	ECR, ID, RZ, SX, X	Sherbrooke	2.84e-3	1.36e-2	150K
				Kyiv	3.07e-3	1.55e-2	185K
				Brisbane	3.42e-3	1.82e-2	180K
				Quebec	2.71e-3	2.17e-2	200K
				Kawasaki	3.76e-3	2.26e-2	150K
				Rensselaer	3.61e-3	2.37e-2	200K
				Brussels	3.94e-3	2.43e-2	220K
				Strasbourg	3.21e-3	3.29e-2	220K
Osprey, 433 qubits	• Modular • Computation capability exceeds the classical computer • Multiple quantum unit due to the modular structure • Great connectivity • More Hilbert Space means more states [27]	• Error-prone • Lacks algorithmic depth • Lacks error mitigation [28]	Extends the capabilities of Eagle				

(Continued)

TABLE 3.1 (*Continued*)
Strengths, Weaknesses, and Technological Benchmarks of Superconducting Quantum Hardware

Quantum Hardware	Strength	Weakness	Technological Benchmarks: Gates	Location	Error Rate—Best	Error Rate—Layered	CLOPS
Superconducting Qubits							
Google							
Sycamore, 53 qubits	• Claimed quantum supremacy with the fact that its computation superseded a supercomputer • Computation time taken 200 seconds, which would classically take 10,000 years • Classical spoofing algorithm can be used with strong noise [29]	• The speed is claimed for only certain types and phases of quantum computation • Limited and miniature in terms of qubits [30] • Cost of architecture is high [31]	The fidelity rate is improved with patch cross-entropy benchmarking. The fidelity rate/error limitation is further improved to 0.0001 in 40 cycles [29].				
Rigetti							
Ankaa, 3–84 qubits [32, 33]	• Tunable coupler architecture for better interaction • High fidelity of two-qubit gates	• Scalability • Error correction • Funding	• Single gate (fSim) fidelity—99.5% • Double gate (iSWAP) fidelity—99%				

which was precisely 99.87% and 99.997% for single-qubit gate fidelity. The quantum volume doubled to 2^{21}. The H2 product was introduced in 2023 that consisted of 32 to 56 physical qubits as it came out in two versions, H2–1 and H2–2. The H2 product is mentioned to be fault-tolerant, and it was able to hit three 9 figures in the two-qubit gate fidelity, which was precisely 99.87% and 99.997% for single-qubit gate fidelity. The quantum volume doubled to 2^{21} [38].

Its linear QCCD architecture was further scaled, and the overall performance of the processor demonstrated most reliable logical qubit in the world and after Google's claim in 2019. The result was hundred times better, and for this reason, it was chosen as an entropy benchmark for quantum computers [39].

Moreover, the Quantinuum roadmap also states that Quantum Helios will be released in 2025, which will consist of 96 physical qubits, and the next version, Quantinuum Sols, will be released in 2027, which will be produced with 192 physical qubits and approximately 100 logical qubits. This hardware will be further upgraded to Quantinuum Apollo, which will consist of thousands of physical qubits and hundreds of logical bits [35]. Meanwhile, Quantinuum Helios will be offered as hardware as a service, with better chip architecture that consists of ring design too. This can deliver higher fidelity in the gate functions and faster circuit times with less power consumption [40]. Quantinuum hardware is recognized and accepted by its partners, which are Microsoft Azure, IonQ, and InQuanto.

Subsequently, IonQ utilizes a neutral ytterbium atom and removes one electron with laser technology through a process called ionization, leaving the neutral atom positively charged [41]. So far, IonQ has produced five quantum computers of different generations. The first-generation quantum computer is called Harmony, which consists of 11 qubits arranged in a manner that ensures all and all connectivity. This system has gate fidelity rate of 0.4% for single-qubit gate error and 2.7% for two-qubit gate error. The system is fully configurable, so it can scale up and down as required and has the longest coherence time when compared to superconducting qubits, as it is already in its quantum state, so that stability is maintained throughout. The system experiment shows that it's possible to use 9 qubits out of 11 to run approximately a hundred quantum algorithms. This system consists of five components: operating system, laser system, vacuum chamber, ion trap, and qubit species. The vacuum chamber ensures stability from noise. Note: this system was retired in 2024 [42].

The second-generation quantum computer, Aria, introduced in 2022, fully operates on 25 qubits and has a fidelity rate of 0.06% for single-qubit gate error and 0.6% for two-qubit gate error. Aria has same features as Harmony but is an upgraded version [43].

The third-generation Forte further improves its previous version by operating on 36 qubits fully. The fidelity rate is further improved where the single-qubit gate error is 0.02% and 0.4% for double qubit gate. This system uses acousto-optic-deflector in its laser system for precise control and manipulation of ion qubits. It also uses Iris as the ion trap to allow deeper circuit execution with measurable results [44].

The four-generation Forte Enterprise further expands from Forte, and the fifth-generation Tempo targets 100 physical qubits that can operate on approximately 64 qubits with 95% uptime [45].

Accordingly, IonQ has partnered with Hyundai to use machine-learning quantum computing to produce cars that can improve on computation process, such as road sign image classification, simulation in real-world test environment, and 3D object detection [46]. IonQ has also been named one of the 100 most influential companies by *Time* for solving the world's most pressing problems through innovation [47].

3.15 PHOTONIC AND SILICON-BASED QUANTUM HARDWARE

This quantum device is constructed from photons, single particles of light, using semiconductor manufacturing and packaging with high power cryogenic cooling technology. This can produce a fast, error-corrected quantum computer. In this subsection, two well-known photonic and silicon-based quantum corporations will be highlighted on their current product maturity and relevance with necessary examples.

PsiQuantum hardware are manufactured in small components, then packaged to form the entire quantum system. The process starts with the photonic wafer, then the chip, then the packaging material, and finally the cabinet, and the most important part of this process is the existence of the cryogenic plant required to manufacture the cryostats and cryogenic technology to cool the photons. The miniature component of the photonic and silicon chip is the wafer, which is the photonic source. This wafer consists of single photonic detectors and an ultra-high performance optical switch that is fabricated in a high-volume semiconductor foundry. The production of photonic wafers is constructed with standard materials, making it possible for industry use. More than one thousand of these photonic wafers are tested, and more than one million of these wafer-embedded devices are tested.

The wafer or the photon source are then assembled on a chip with the optical fibers. This assembly ensures entangled states, which is specially designed to implement error-correcting codes, which are, in fact created and measured with a fusion gate. The nondeterministic photon sources and gate operations are made scalable via multiplexing and loss-tolerant error-correcting codes. The chip shows a fidelity rate of 99.99% for a single-qubit gate and 99% for two-qubit gate. This chip is packaged into a manufacturing state by integrating the cryogenic electronics. The package consists of a copper heat sink, circuit board, control chip, photonic chip, and optical fiber.

Note: the cryogenic electronics must be operated at the cryogenic temperature, but due to the fact that copper material and polychloridebipenyl are used, the process is made easier to manufacture on a large scale. This way, the networking and modularization of the phonic chip is easier without transduction. Photons do not need cooling because they cannot experience heat, but the entire system consists of supercooling detectors and cryogenic electronics that needs to be supercooled, so the cabinet houses a heat shield, liquid helium, and optical fiber feed-throughs. The supercooling is achieved with −4K−−10mK refrigeration. PsiQuantum states that with this generation of power, this cabinet is capable of cooling beyond any dilution refrigeration with just 100W of power [48].

Additionally, Xanadu has also recently produced its scalable and possibly fault-tolerant quantum system called Aurora that integrates its previous two generations of quantum computers from the X series and Borealis. The recently produced Aurora is composed of 35 photonic chips in four different 19-inch server racks combined by a 13 km fiber optic wire that processes millions of qubits. The cryogenic component is kept separate from the server racks. The source also states that the previous versions were a cloud-based quantum system with significant computation capabilities, but it could not be fault-tolerant or correct errors. Aurora is produced in such a way that it is scalable and modular and has got good networking capabilities [49]. The hardware is composed of six distinct subsystems: a customized master laser system, source array generator, PNR detection system, array refineries, QPU array, and array of fiber buffer. Thus, subsystems have principal roles [50]:

- Customized Master Laser System: This provides coherent pump and local oscillator beams, as well as reference beams for phase stabilization.
- Source Array Generator: This generates squeezed light and two-mode Gaussian states.
- PNR Detection System: This is used for heralding non-Gaussian states.
- Array Refineries: These are the multiplex's eight inputs to one entangled pair.
- QPU Array: This forms the spatial and temporal connections in the cluster state and performs homodyne measurements on each qubit.
- Array of Fiber Buffer: This provides the appropriate phase and polarization-stabilized delay lines between the sources and refineries, as well as between the refineries and QPUs.

Just like in PsiQuantinum, most operations are carried out at room temperature. The discrete, scalable rack deployed modules components include fiber optic interconnects, 85 squeezers, 36 photon number resolving detectors, and 12 physical qubit modes at each clock cycle. The composition of this system produces a cluster state that is entangled across separate chips with 86 billion modes. It demonstrates error correction and fault tolerance by real-time decoding and foliated distance two-code repetition. Additionally, single temporal-mode non-Gaussian resource states, real-time multiplexing actuated on photon-number-resolving detection, spatiotemporal cluster-state formation with fiber buffers, and adaptive measurements implemented using chip-integrated homodyne detectors with real-time single-clock-cycle feedforward ensure the robustness of the system.

Per the experiment, the germanium photodiodes heterogenous integration of thin-film lithium niobate shows 98.5% quantum efficiency. On the same note, the integration of three to five semiconductor photodiodes with thin-film lithium niobate waveguide can yield an efficiency of 99%, with challenges of heterogenous scheme integration. This can be achieved with high-quality surface integration with deep trench integration with photodiodes, and waveguide cladding. Managing excessive dark current in the photodiodes themselves as their dimensions grow to accommodate near-unity absorption will also require innovative approaches.

Overall, Aurora has a better market, and per Xanadu sources, the company has partnered with powering leading forces like NIST, Google, IBM, Microsoft, Rigetti, IonQ, Harvard University, Toyota, Multiverse, and more [51].

In 2022, Xanadu partnered with Volkswagen on battery simulation simulating key properties of lithium-ion batteries with a fault-tolerant quantum computer using realistic cathode material and dilithium iron silicate [52]. Additionally, it partnered with BMW on a quantum machine learning project that uses tensor-network quantum circuits that emulates the shape and connectivity of tensor networks, such as matrix product states and tree tensor networks [53].

3.16 QUANTUM SOFTWARE AND PROGRAMMING LANGUAGES

In this section, three quantum programming tools from IBM, Google, and Microsoft will be individually and systematically compared. The software development kit from IBM is Qiskit; from Google, Cirq; and from Microsoft, Q#.

IBM's Qiskit was initially introduced in 2017, and this kit is available for cross-platform use. It allows to map problems to quantum circuits and operators, optimizing for target hardware, executing on target hardware, and post-processing results [54].

Cirq is a Python software library for writing, manipulating, and optimizing quantum circuits, and then running them on quantum computers and quantum simulators. Cirq provides useful abstractions for dealing with today's noisy intermediate-scale quantum computers, where details of the hardware are vital to achieving state-of-the-art results [55].

Microsoft's Azure Kit Q language was introduced in 2017 to run quantum algorithms more efficiently. Since then, a lot of progress has been made by Microsoft in the realm of quantum computing using Q.

The following table will show analysis of these three kits in terms of their tools, languages, ease of use, learning curves, community support, and functionality.

After analyzing the top three software development kits, which will be reflected in the discussion, the three languages, and examples of constructing Hadamard, CNOT, and measurement gates, will be elaborated from IBM, Google, and Microsoft. As stated earlier, IBM constructs its circuit in four steps, so a sample of a Hadamard gate will be demonstrated as follows [54].

3.17 CONSTRUCTION OF HADAMARD GATE WITH QISKIT

3.17.1 Step 1: Map the Problem to Quantum Native Format

In this step, the circuit is created with a new circuit object, then instructions are added to it. The following figure shows how an IBM code creates a bell state of qubits that are entangled.

Also, when constructing a circuit, it is important to ensure what type of data should be returned. There are two ways, either obtaining a probability distribution for a set of qubits or obtaining the expectation value of an observable. The following example shows the usage of expectation value from qiskit.quantum_info from its submodule.

TABLE 3.2
Analysis of IBM, Google, and Microsoft in terms of their Tools, Languages, Ease of Use, Learning Curves, Community Support, and Functionality

SDK	Tools	Functionalities	Language	Ease of Use	Learning Curve	Community Support
IBM's Qiskit	1. Circuits and Operators 2. Transpilers 3. Debugging Tools 4. Primitives 5. Execution modes 6. Manage Jobs 7. IBM Quantum Computers 8. Visualization 9. Qiskit Serverless 10. Qiskit Addons 11. Qiskit Code Assistant 12. IBM Cloud services [54]	1. Five distinct circuit functions: a. IBM circuit functions b. Algorithmic tensor network error mitigation c. Q-CTRL performance management d. Qedma QESEM 2. Five distinct application functions: a. Kipu Quantum Iskay Quantum Optimizer b. Multiverse Computing Singularity c. Q-CTRL optimization solver d. QunaSys QURI Chemistry e. Qunova Computing HI-VQE Chemistry [54]	1. Python 2. Open QASM (open quantum assembly language) is a machine-independent programming interface compatible with IBM QPUs. It is an imperative programming language for describing quantum circuits. OpenQASM uses the quantum circuit model to express quantum programs as ordered sequences of parameterized operations (such as gates, measurements, and resets) and real-time classical computation. In addition to quantum algorithms, OpenQASM can describe circuits intended to characterize, validate, or debug quantum processors [56].	1. It's easy to use and get started based on the IBM documentation guide, which is catalogued in order. The two languages that are used are pretty easy to begin with, and in case of QASM, Qiskit SDK provides ways to convert between OpenQASM and the QuantumCircuit class. 2. The information is structured with dropdowns with major headings that can be accessed easily. 3. The Q-CTRL solver optimizer is benchmarked with quantum annealers too, so this means that optimum quantum service is opted.	• Learning path on getting started with Qiskit, understanding quantum information, and scaling toward utility. • Basic and intermediate courses. • Beginners and intermediate tutorials • Tools like Quantum Composer and Labs • Resources on the IBM blog and the Qiskit YouTube channel [58] • >600,000 registered users • >700 Global University users • >550,000 users have built and executed quantum circuits. [59] • Execution of >3 trillion quantum circuits.	1. IBM Cloud Support—paid (Basic, Advanced and Premium) and unpaid 2. IBM Documentation Help—Stack Overflow 3. Qiskit Slack Channel for community engagement 4. GitHub Qiskit Community

(Continued)

TABLE 3.2 (*Continued*)

Analysis of IBM, Google, and Microsoft in terms of their Tools, Languages, Ease of Use, Learning Curves, Community Support, and Functionality

SDK	Tools	Functionalities	Language	Ease of Use	Learning Curve	Community Support
				4. The debugging tool has got build noise model for simulating quantum circuits in the presence of errors. This is useful for emulating noisy quantum processors and for studying the effects of noise on the execution of quantum algorithms [57]. 5. The visual composer is pretty easy to use with simple drag and drop. 6. Qiskit Runtime primitive allows quantum classical computation through samplers and estimators. 7. Qiskit Serverless allows running workloads of quantum-classical resources. 8. Accessibility is simple in terms of free availability, installation, and a large community.	[60] • The user-to-circuit ratio is **1:5,454,545**	

Google's Cirq	1. Quantum Virtual [61] 2. Machine 3. Qualtran 4. Qsim 5. Stim 6. OpenFermion 7. OpenFermion-FQE 8. OpenFermion-PySCF 9. OpenFermion-Psi4 10. TensorFlow Quantum 11. ReCirq [62]	1. Noisy intermediate-scale quantum 2. Flexible gate definition and custom gates 3. Parameterized circuits with symbolic variables 4. Circuit transformation, compilation, and optimization 5. Hardware device modeling 6. Noise modeling 7. Multiple built-in quantum circuit simulators 8. Integration with Qsim for high-performance simulations 9. Interoperability with NumPy and SciPy 10. Cross-platform compatibility [62]	1. Python 2 Jupyter Notebook 3. Type Script 4. Shell 5. Scilab	6. Cirq interface on the following quantum hardware: a. Alpine Quantum Technologies (AQT) b. Azure Quantum c. IonQ d. Pascal e. Rigetti [63] 7. Manage noise when running circuits—noise models and channels and what types of error they replicate 8. Cross-entropy benchmarking (XEB) 9. Visualizing noise—graphing and plotting noise through heat maps [64]	1. 951 users on GitHub 2. 235 contributors on GitHub 3. Algorithms and codes are provided: • Textbook algorithm and workshops • Shor's algorithm • Variational quantum eigensolver • Quantum walks • Fourier checking • Hidden linear function problem • Quantum approximate optimization algorithm • Hartree-Fock VQE • Fermi-Hubbard • Quantum scrambling • Toric code • Kardar-Parisi-Zhang physics • Quantum-classical quantum Monte Carlo [65]	4. GitHub library repository 5. Question and Discussions on Quantum Computing Stack Exchange 6. Documentation tutorial • YouTube • Jupyter Notebook–based tutorials • Text-based tutorial from homepage • Curd stable release • Pre-release • Examples subdirectory • Experiments page • Cirq releases on GitHub [62]

(*Continued*)

TABLE 3.2 (*Continued*)

Analysis of IBM, Google, and Microsoft in terms of their Tools, Languages, Ease of Use, Learning Curves, Community Support, and Functionality

SDK	Tools	Functionalities	Language	Ease of Use	Learning Curve	Community Support
Microsoft's Q#	1. Copilot 2. VS Code 3. Jupyter Notebook 4. Azure Quantum Resource Estimator 5. Quantum Development Kit Simulator 6. Cloud Services	1. Adjoint functor—the applied quantum transformation can be "undone"; that is, it can be inverted. 2. Controlled functor—its execution can be conditioned on the state of other qubits. 3. Immutability—Q# doesn't have a concept of a reference or pointer. Instead, it allows you to reassign a new value to a previously declared variable via an assignment expression. 4. Basic quantum operators 5. Quantum phenomenon—entanglement and superposition 6. Control flow [66]	7. C++ 8. C# 9. DAX 10. Java 11. OData 12. OpenAPI 13. Power Query M 14. VBA 15. Python 16. LLMV 17. Rust 18. TypeScript 19. Qiskit 20. Cirq	1. Can be integrated with broad range of languages 2. Software constructed with these languages can be used on a number of hardware such as IonQ, PASCAL, Rigetti, and Quantinuum 3. Allows user to use preferred environment when constructing quantum codes	1. 187 users on GitHub 2. 45 contributors on GitHub 3. Technical results • Quantum error correction • Azure Quantum Development Kit • Resource estimation challenge • Evaluating cat qubits for fault-tolerant QC using resource estimator • Circuit diagrams with Q# • Defining logical qubits • Shorter qubit circuits • Microsoft Quantum introduces sessions to accelerate research with variational algorithms [67]	4. Training 5. Documentation and Tutorial • Microsoft • GitHub 6. Certification—Microsoft Certified Azure Cosmos DB Developer Specialty 7. Technical blogs 8. Microsoft Tech Community 9. Q learning on Stack overflow

(a)

```
from qiskit import QuantumCircuit
from qiskit.quantum_info import SparsePauliOp
from qiskit.transpiler import generate_preset_pass_manager
from qiskit_ibm_runtime import EstimatorV2 as Estimator

# Create a new circuit with two qubits
qc = QuantumCircuit(2)

# Add a Hadamard gate to qubit 0
qc.h(0)

# Perform a controlled-X gate on qubit 1, controlled by qubit 0
qc.cx(0, 1)

# Return a drawing of the circuit using MatPlotLib ("mpl").
# These guides are written by using Jupyter notebooks, which
# display the output of the last line of each cell.
# If you're running this in a script, use `print(qc.draw())` to
# print a text drawing.
qc.draw("mpl")
```

(b)

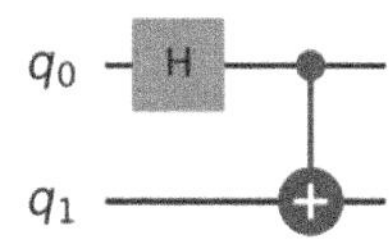

FIGURE 3.2 **a.** Code for Constructing Hadamard Circuit. **b.** Its output. From IBM Quantum Documentation.

```
# Set up six different observables.

observables_labels = ["IZ", "IX", "ZI", "XI", "ZZ", "XX"]
observables = [SparsePauliOp(label) for label in observables_labels]
```

FIGURE 3.3 Example measures expectation values by using the qiskit.quantum_info submodule by using operators. From IBM Quantum Documentation.

3.17.2 Step 2: Optimize the Circuits and Operators

The following code instantiates a real device to submit a job and transforms the circuit and observables to match the backend's instruction set architecture. It ensures that the best results are obtained, and the effects of noise and error are reduced.

```
from qiskit_ibm_runtime import QiskitRuntimeService

service = QiskitRuntimeService()

backend = service.least_busy(simulator=False, operational=True)

# Convert to an ISA circuit and layout-mapped observables.
pm = generate_preset_pass_manager(backend=backend, optimization_level=1)
isa_circuit = pm.run(qc)

isa_circuit.draw("mpl", idle_wires=False)
```

(a)

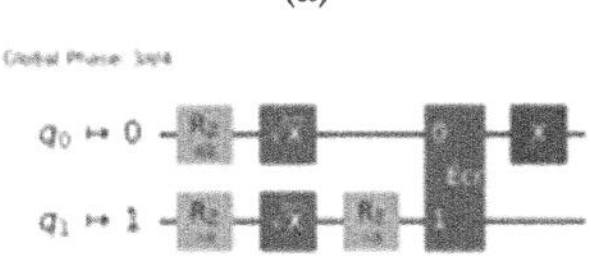

(b)

FIGURE 3.4 **a.** Codes to optimize the circuit and operators in step 1. **b.** Output of the code. From IBM Quantum Documentation.

3.17.3 Step 3: Execute Using Quantum Primitives

In this step, two primitive functions are used, estimators and samplers. The value of observables can be estimated with estimators, and the sampler function can be used to get data from a quantum computer. The run () method returned values from the primitive unified bloc.

After the job is completed, the output must be checked using the job_result () attribute. Alternatively, it can run a simulator.

```
# Construct the Estimator instance.

estimator = Estimator(mode=backend)
estimator.options.resilience_level = 1
estimator.options.default_shots = 5000

mapped_observables = [
    observable.apply_layout(isa_circuit.layout) for observable in observables
]

# One pub, with one circuit to run against five different observables.
job = estimator.run([(isa_circuit, mapped_observables)])

# Use the job ID to retrieve your job data later
print(f">>> Job ID: {job.job_id()}")
```

(a)

```
>>> Job ID: czz0bqerxz8g008f8fkg
```

(b)

FIGURE 3.5 **a.** Codes to construct the estimator. **b.** The output of the codes. From IBM Quantum Documentation.

3.17.4 Step 4: Analyze the Results

This step post-processes the result using a plot graph for measurement error mitigation or zero noise extrapolation. The expectation values and standard deviations for the observables are accessed through the job result's PubResult.data.evs and PubResult.data.stds attributes. To obtain the results from Sampler, use the PubResult.data.meas.get_counts() function, which will return a dict of measurements in the form of bitstrings as keys. The following figure shows codes to plot the result.

```
# Plot the result

from matplotlib import pyplot as plt

values = pub_result.data.evs

errors = pub_result.data.stds

# plotting graph
plt.plot(observables_labels, values, "-o")
plt.xlabel("Observables")
plt.ylabel("Values")
plt.show()
```

(a)

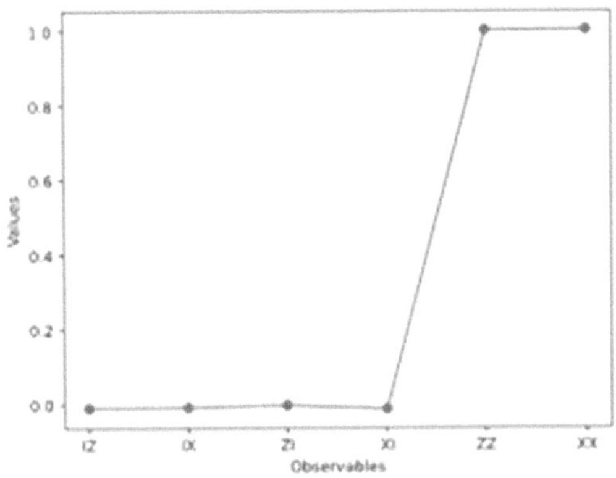

(b)

FIGURE 3.6 **a.** Codes to plot the results. **b.** The output of the results. From IBM Documentation.

3.18 CONSTRUCTION OF CNOT GATE

The next example will demonstrate the CNOT gate from Google [68]

```
class CXPowGate(eigen_gate.EigenGate):
    r"""A gate that applies a controlled power of an X gate.

    When applying CNOT (controlled-not) to qubits, you can either use
    positional arguments CNOT(q1, q2), where q2 is toggled when q1 is on,
    or named arguments CNOT(control=q1, target=q2).
    (Mixing the two is not permitted.)

    The unitary matrix of `cirq.CXPowGate(exponent=t)` is:

    $$
    \begin{bmatrix}
        1 & 0 & 0 & 0 \\
        0 & 1 & 0 & 0 \\
        0 & 0 & g c & -i g s \\
        0 & 0 & -i g s & g c
    \end{bmatrix}
    $$

    where:

    $$
    c = \cos\left(\frac{\pi t}{2}\right)
    $$
    $$
    s = \sin\left(\frac{\pi t}{2}\right)
    $$
    $$
    g = e^{\frac{i \pi t}{2}}
    $$
```

(a)

FIGURE 3.7 **a.** and **b.** Codes to construct a CNOT gate and application with Pauli interaction gate. From Cirq GitHub.

```

    `cirq.CNOT`, the controlled NOT gate, is an instance of this gate at
    `exponent=1`.
    """


    def _num_qubits_(self) -> int:
        return 2

    def _decompose_into_clifford_with_qubits_(self, qubits):
        from cirq.ops.pauli_interaction_gate import PauliInteractionGate

        if self.exponent % 2 == 1:
            return PauliInteractionGate.CNOT.on(*qubits)
        if self.exponent % 2 == 0:
            return []
        return NotImplemented  # pragma: no cover
```

(b)

FIGURE 3.7 (Continued)

3.19 CONSTRUCTION OF A SIMPLE MEASUREMENT GATE

The following figure shows the code for a simple measurement gate using measurement operators with a Hadamard gate from Microsoft Q# [69]:

```
operation GenerateRandomBit() : Result {
    // Allocate a qubit.
    use q = Qubit();

    // Set the qubit into superposition of 0 and 1 using the Hadamard
    H(q);

    // At this point the qubit `q` has 50% chance of being measured in the
    // |0〉 state and 50% chance of being measured in the |1〉 state.
    // Measure the qubit value using the `M` operation, and store the
    // measurement value in the `result` variable.
    let result = M(q);

    // Reset qubit to the |0〉 state.
    // Qubits must be in the |0〉 state by the time they are released.
    Reset(q);

    // Return the result of the measurement.
    return result;
}
```

FIGURE 3.8 Code with M operator to measure the qubit value. From Microsoft Q#.

3.20 QUANTUM COMPUTING PLATFORMS AND ACCESSIBILITY

In this section, four prominent quantum computing platforms, such as IBM Quantum Experience, Microsoft Azure Quantum, Amazon Braket, and Google Quantum AI, will be highlighted and compared against the criteria and comparative factors. The real-world application of these quantum computing platforms will be elaborated in areas of finance, pharmaceuticals, logistics, and cybersecurity. Afterward, the effectiveness, maturity, and adoption levels of these use cases will also be discussed.

Per Quantum Insider, these are the top-tier quantum computing corporations globally as of December 2024. They are also known as the quantum giants due to the advancement made in the quantum hardware and software. The oldest, most recognized quantum corporation is IBM, which was founded in 1911, and since then, IBM has made many contributions, including the advancement of quantum computing. IBM is most notable for offering their fleet of quantum computers online for the community and their publication of journal article in 2023 in *Nature* emphasizing quantum computers that can generate precise outcomes at a magnitude of 100+ qubits, surpassing top classical methods. Then, in 2024, they introduced their 1,121-superconducting-qubit Condor processor, alongside their 133-fixed-frequency-qubit Heron processor, which came with its couplers. This could improve the speed by three to five times.

Additionally, Google's Quantum AI lab was created in 2013 by Google in association with NASA and the Universities Space Research Association. Since then, Cirq Python software libraries for creating circuits, manipulating them are available online, including the libraries for fermion particles and the TensorFlow Quantum for machine learning.

Since its introduction, Quantum AI has claimed supremacy and made contributions to increase physical qubits and produce logical qubits and, at the same time, reduce errors. Microsoft has also notably contributed toward quantum computing in terms of cloud computing, software, and hardware. Its noteworthy contributions include its risk of investing in Majorana zero modes for quantum computing and the introduction of its quantum language Q#.

Finally, Amazon Web Services' Braket is a fully manageable platform for scientific research and software development. It houses hardware and software from prominent quantum computing corporations such as Riggetti, IonQ, D-Wave, Xanadu, and more. It has made contributions such as exploring efficient Bayesian optimization protocols for quantum optimization issues utilizing QuEra's Rydberg quantum computer. In 2024, it announced its inhouse built innovative chip that is capable of reducing bit-flip errors by a factor of 100 through a passive error correction method. Additionally, when combining passive with active error correction techniques, the chip has the potential to perform quantum error correction six times more effectively compared to conventional methods [70]. The following table with systematically compares these platforms against the criteria of accessibility, usability, technological capability, and application readiness. The comparative factors are registration ease, cost, global availability, user experience, tutorials, documentation quality, quantum volume, number of qubits, coherence time, and real-world industry use cases.

TABLE 3.3
Systematic Comparison of Quantum Cloud Platforms from IBM, Google, Microsoft, and Braket Against the Criteria of Accessibility, Usability, Technological Capability, and Application Readiness

Criteria		IBM	Google	Microsoft	Amazon
Accessibility	Registration Case	Simple and user-friendly	Secure registration	Simple and user-friendly	Comprehensive and user-friendly
	Cost	• Free—10 mins/month • Pay as you go—USD 1.60/second • Premium subscription • Dedicated service—exclusive access, price given per request	• Budget-friendly options • Expensive high-performance option	• Free • Pay as you go: —USD 0.000220/1-qubit-gate shot —USD 0.000975/two-qubit-gate shot —Execution program error mitigation—USD 97.50 —Execution program error mitigation off—USD 12.4166 • Aria Plan—USD 25,000/month + infrastructure [71]	• Free tier—1 hour/month • Pay as you go: —On-demand simulator—USD 0.075/min —Gate-based QPU—USD 9.30/10,000 shots —Hybrid job with on demand simulator—USD 1.97/min —Hybrid job with a QPU—USD 45.36/hour —Hybrid job with embedded simulator—USD 0.49/min —Experiment with error mitigation—USD 75.30/2,500 shots • Dedicated service—price given per request [72]
	Global Availability	Yes	No	Yes	Yes
Usability	User Experience	Wildly accessible and user-friendly	Wildly accessible and user-friendly	Wildly accessible and user-friendly	Wildly accessible, extensive, and user-friendly
	Tutorials	• Comprehensive • Detailed	• Comprehensive • Detailed	• Comprehensive • Detailed	• Comprehensive • Detailed

	Documentation Quality	• Clear and concise language. • Content is arranged and properly structured with dropdowns to expand the topic. • Information is provided in terms of text, video, and diagrams, and questions from the community are monitored and answered. • New content is alert is relayed with a notification. • Code library is available for the community on GitHub.	• Clear and concise language. • Content is arranged and properly structured with dropdowns to expand the topic. • Information is provided in terms of text, video, and diagrams. • Community questions are responded on GitHub. • Examples subdirectory. • Multiple code libraries are available for the community on GitHub.	• Clear and concise language. • Content is arranged and properly structured with dropdowns to expand the topic. • Information is provided in terms of text, video, and diagrams. • Community questions are responded on GitHub and Stack Overflow. • Provides certification training. • Code library is available for the community on GitHub.	• Clear and concise language. • Content is arranged and properly structured with dropdowns to expand the topic. • Information is provided in terms of text, video, diagrams, and service guides. • Solutions are arranged per area of interest on the AWS solution library. • Provides certification training. • Code library is available for the community on GitHub.
Technological Capability	Quantum Volume	64	2^{53}	~	$2^5 = 32$
	Number of Qubits	27	53	$1x10^6$ reliable quantum operations per second	5
	Coherence Time	$400\mu s$	200s	10^{-3}	$23\,\mu s$

(Continued)

TABLE 3.3 (*Continued*)
Systematic Comparison of Quantum Cloud Platforms from IBM, Google, Microsoft, and Braket Against the Criteria of Accessibility, Usability, Technological Capability, and Application Readiness

Criteria		IBM	Google	Microsoft	Amazon
Application Readiness	Real-World Industry Use Cases	• Distribution and logistics • Use cases for airlines • Financial services • Health and life sciences • Industrial discrete manufacturing • Industrial process manufacturing • Utilities • Case studies: E.ON, Boeing, CERN, Mercedes-Benz, and ExxonMobil [73]	• Medicine • Batteries • New energy source [74]	• Chemistry • Industry-reliable quantum computers [75]	• Supply chain • Defense • Distribution and logistics • Chemistry [76]

3.21 INDUSTRY-SPECIFIC USE CASES

The potential of quantum computers to solve real-world problems are emphasized, but since this industry is still in its infancy, the application of use cases is yet to be seen in different areas and sectors. On the same note, a number of pioneers who have invested in quantum computing have reaped the benefits. This was seen with the JPMorgan Chase case, where quantum computing was used to optimize its investment portfolio management. The bank replaced traditional Monte Carlo simulations with quantum algorithms, significantly speeding up the process of portfolio optimization. By leveraging quantum computing, JPMorgan Chase aims to improve the accuracy and efficiency of its investment strategies, offering better returns with lower risk. Portfolio management involves selecting a mix of assets that maximizes returns while minimizing risk. This is often challenging with a classical computer as it has to compute with a large number of variables that can take time. So quantum computing algorithms like the quantum approximate optimization algorithm (QAOA) and the quantum Monte Carlo method can dramatically improve the efficiency of portfolio optimization [77]. Additionally, algorithms like the quantum-inspired genetic algorithm (QIGA) with QAOA can maximize returns while minimizing risk. Several universities have shown results of risk management enhancement with quantum computing, but more experiments need to be done to further perfect the algorithms [78].

Moreover, IonQ and General Electric Research have collaborated to explore the impact of quantum computing and IonQ's quantum computers in the fields of risk analysis and are expected to lay the groundwork for risk management across sectors such as finance, government, among others [79]. European banks, such as HSBC, are integrating quantum key distribution (QKD) into FX trading and tokenized gold for future-proof cybersecurity. Intesa Sanpaolo is exploring quantum applications in credit scoring, fraud detection, and derivative pricing. The article also states that 80% of 50 banks tracked by Evidents are engaged in quantum computing, and the results by 2035 will have a massive impact [80].

As the investigation of quantum computing applications in other fields proceeds, the application of quantum computing in the pharmaceutical sector was noted, especially in the processes of drug discovery and protein simulation. A research article highlights how the usage of hybrid quantum computing system has elevated the process of drug discovery. In a research case study, two instances of experiments were carried out on a superconducting quantum device.

In the first case, the Gibbs free energy profile for prodrug activation involving carbon to carbon bond cleavage under solvent conditions were studied. The obtained reaction barrier and Gibbs energy change align well with previous experimental and theoretical studies. In modern drug research, prodrug activation is a very important strategy. It helps turn inactive ingredients into active drugs inside the body. This strategy helps make drugs work better by making sure they only activate at certain places in the body, which lowers the risk of side effects and leads to safer and more effective treatments.

In the second experiment, a covalent inhibitor for KRAS(G12C) using quantum mechanics simulation was investigated. KRAS is a prominent target in cancer therapy due to its significant role in various cancers, and the G12C mutation is its most frequent and consequential mutation. The sotorasib, an innovative covalent inhibitor targeting this mutation, represents a paradigm shift to KRAS-related cancer treatment. The insights gained from this experiment can lay the groundwork for future computations on a quantum computer, promising to enhance the accuracy and speed of our drug discovery processes. However, the current experiment was carried out on a hybrid system, which requires more precision in terms of VQE calculations, and the resources consumed require further improvement [81].

Another dramatic instance of QC's power comes from the pharmaceutical sector itself. In 2023, Forschungszentrum Julich and Lund University researchers utilized D-Wave's quantum annealer to address the protein folding problem. This breakthrough accelerated the discovery of a promising drug candidate and showcased how QC could unlock mysteries previously deemed unsolvable. In addition, IBM, in collaboration with MIT researchers, tackled one of the toughest challenges in quantum chemistry—calculating the ground-state energy of complex molecules. They demonstrated that quantum computers could simulate the electronic structure of molecules with an accuracy unattainable by classical methods. This achievement paves the way for designing novel compounds in record time [82].

Quantum computing in supply chain and logistics is still in its early days, but momentum is building through research initiatives and pilot projects worldwide. Academic studies apply quantum algorithms to logistics problems like vehicle routing, network design, scheduling, and inventory management. Notably, most proposed solutions are hybrid, combining quantum and classical computing, due to the limitations of today's quantum hardware. This underscores that the field is nascent yet progressing; even as current quantum processors remain limited in size and accuracy, researchers are already demonstrating quantum approaches on simplified supply chain models. For instance, small-scale experiments using D-Wave quantum annealers (a type of quantum computer) have tackled the capacitated vehicle routing problem, showing that quantum algorithms can match or sometimes outperform classical heuristics on certain benchmark scenarios.

While a true quantum advantage for logistics hasn't been achieved yet. Major players are forging partnerships with quantum tech firms and research labs to develop proofs of concept. DHL, for example, identified quantum computing as a key trend in its 2020 "Logistics Trend Radar" and has since partnered with a quantum startup to develop quantum-inspired route optimization algorithms. Likewise, Maersk, one of the world's largest shipping companies, has been working with research institutions to explore quantum methods for optimizing supply chain operations. Even automotive companies with logistics needs have jumped in: Volkswagen demonstrated the world's first real-world traffic routing pilot using a quantum computer in Lisbon, calculating optimal routes for city buses in near real time. These collaborations and pilots, though limited in scope, signal serious interest from industry leaders in vetting quantum capabilities [83].

Another useful application quantum computing is in the area of cybersecurity, where quantum computing can improve the encryption of the communication system and the entire network, and threat detection. This can be achieved by utilizing quantum key distribution (QKD), which allows two parties to share encryption keys securely. Parties establish a quantum link between the nodes using principles like quantum entanglement, entangled particles in the node generate secure encryption keys. These keys are distributed and shared between the nodes. The keys are used for communication and to allow the encrypted data to be transmitted securely across the network. Because of the properties of quantum bits, data shared in QKD networks cannot be copied.

In the European Union, the quantum communication infrastructure (EUROQCI 16) counts on the participation of the EU 27 member states. Member states are developing QKD networks inside their territory, and there are already some examples of cross-border communications using quantum networks, but most of the efforts are still within cities and regions. The United States and NATO are only now starting to experiment with quantum networks, leveraging the know-how of their allies and, in the case of the United States, its capacity to mobilize private investments.

Space segments are necessary to overcome the limitations of ground-based links. Space links are necessary to transmit quantum keys for distances beyond 100–200 km. Following the earlier example, in the European Union, this will be done in partnership with the European Space Agency (ESA) through the launch of a constellation of quantum satellites (IRIS2). The first satellite will be launched into low earth orbit in 2025. Accordingly, in 2017, China launched the first quantum satellite in space, Micius, to establish long-distance quantum communications, and in 2023 data showed that ground links exceed 10,000 km in length with commercial services available in cities like Beijing or Shanghai. QKD networks are used nowadays for encrypted calls or security-enhanced financial services [84].

3.22 ACHIEVEMENTS IN QUANTUM SUPREMACY AND INDUSTRY ADVANCEMENTS

In 2019, Google claimed quantum supremacy for its processor called Sycamore, with programmable superconducting qubits to create quantum states on 53 qubits, corresponding to a computational state-space of dimension 2^{53}. The fast-performing chip ensured high-fidelity gate functions, error correction, calibration, and benchmarking at the component and system level through cross-entropy benchmarking.

The benchmarking process begins with comparing the quantum processor against state-of-the-art classical computers to sample the output of a pseudo-random quantum circuit. Random circuits are a suitable choice for benchmarking because they do not possess structure and therefore allow for limited guarantees of computational hardness. The circuits are designed to entangle a set of quantum bits by repeated application of single-qubit and two-qubit logical operations. Sampling the quantum circuit's output produces a set of bitstrings due to quantum interference.

The probability distribution of the bitstrings resembles a speckled intensity pattern produced by light interference in laser scatter, such that some bitstrings are much more likely to occur than others. Classically computing this probability distribution becomes exponentially more difficult as the number of qubits and number of gate cycles grow. The quantum processor is verified through cross-entropy benchmarking, which compares how often each bitstring is observed experimentally with its corresponding ideal probability computed via simulation on a classical computer.

For a given circuit, measured bitstrings $\{x_i\}$ are collected, and linear cross-entropy benchmarking fidelity computed. This is the mean of the simulated probabilities of the bitstrings that is measured $\mathcal{F}_{XEB} = 2^n \langle P(x_i) \rangle_i -$, where n is the number of qubits, $\{x_i\}$ is the probability of bitstring x_i computed for the ideal quantum circuit, and the average is over the observed bitstrings. $\mathcal{F}_{XEB}$ is correlated and when there are no errors in the quantum circuit, the distribution of probabilities is exponential, and sampling from this distribution will produce $\mathcal{F}_{XEB} = 1$.

Similarly, uniform distribution sampling will give $\langle P(x_i) \rangle_i = \frac{1}{2^n}$ and produce $\mathcal{F}_{XEB} = 0$. $\mathcal{F}_{XEB}$ from 0 to 1 corresponds to the probability that no error has occurred while running the circuit. The probabilities $P(x_i)$ must be obtained from classically simulating the quantum circuit, and thus computing $\mathcal{F}_{XEB}$ is difficult.

However, with certain circuit simplifications, quantitative fidelity estimates of a fully operating processor running wide and deep quantum circuits can be obtained. Per the article the goal is to further perfect the program and its execution, while reducing the error rates significantly [85].

In contradiction to Google's claim of supremacy, a couple of corporations have not accepted this simply because the results do not justify the claim. For instance, IBM has debated that their 10,000 years of calculation can be achieved in 2.5 days. Google's main objective was to preserve the qubits' delicate quantum states throughout the process. If they fuzz out, then all outputs become equally likely. But the Google team managed to see the telltale pattern in the generated numbers. To prove the pattern wasn't just noise, researchers compared the results for smaller trials and subgroups of qubits with supercomputer simulations. However, they couldn't do that for the biggest instances of the problem. IBM further criticized this by adding that quantum computers are not "supreme" against classical computers because of a laboratory experiment designed to essentially implement one very specific quantum sampling procedure with no practical applications [86].

Additionally, Intel Labs' director of quantum hardware called Google's update "a notable mile marker." He said that "a commercially viable quantum computer will require" many research and development advancements before becoming a reality. Google indicated that they are one creative algorithm away from valuable near-term applications [87].

Gil Kilai, a prominent critic of quantum computing, also stated that there are some methodological mistakes, and the claim seems like an expectational claim rather than a reality. Per his comments, the "supremacy assertions are flawed estimation of classical running time, the "fidelity" assertions are statistically unreasonable predictions indicating methodological flaws, and the calibration process shows evidence of undocumented global optimization." He also mentioned that IBM computers are more advanced than Google computers in some ways due to IBM's methodological approach [88].

To top all these comments from the industry, an academic paper has also been published to further supplement these arguments. The paper adds three concerns why it does not accept the supremacy claim. The first concern is that the data do not agree with Google's noise model (or any other specific model). The second concern is that a crucial simple formula for a priori estimation of the fidelity seems to involve an unexpected independence assumption, and yet it gives very accurate predictions. The third concern is about the statistical properties of the calibration process [89].

From all these comments, it can be assumed that the claim of quantum supremacy might be bit exaggerated as the results are from experiments rather than real-world applications. Google still needs to prove that their findings can solve a real-world problems in a manner that could not be done by any other technology or corporations. Also, the approximate computation time for a supercomputer is said to be 10,000 years. However, this number is not justified with explanations.

In contrast, an article expresses that another term that is similar to quantum supremacy but not necessarily the same. This new term is called quantum advantage, which reflects the practical difference between a classical computer and a quantum computer through computation performed. In this case, the significant characteristics of a quantum computer is highlighted, which makes the performance of a classical computer seem lagging. It also states that quantum supremacy displays excellence in machine learning, simulation, and optimization. Supremacy is said to be a theoretical concept that shows the power of quantum machines, while advantage focuses on real-world usefulness. Both point toward progress but differ in their focus on practical versus theoretical breakthroughs [90].

Therefore, in order to achieve this, quantum error correction needs to be further improved. Per the updates, IBM has produced its 433-qubit quantum processor, the noise intermediate-scale quantum (NISQ). NISQ devices are often hybrids and use quantum and classical processors with promising applications in specialized machine-learning tasks. Quantum-supervised learning and reinforcement learning demonstrate experimental quantum speedup. However, challenges include classical data representation as quantum states. Quantum advantage may be most evident in applications with inherently quantum data, like quantum chemistry simulations.

Another instance of quantum error correction can be seen with the Sycamore processor, which focuses on surface code error reduction and applies an error suppression technique that can be used on qubits as it scales. This technique ensures that the logical qubit error is lower than the physical qubit error. Surface code refers to two-dimensional lattices of physical qubits that create logical qubits with topological protection. Errors can happen through the lattice without affecting the logical qubit's global state. On the other hand, the stabilizer code detects errors using measurements and applies error correction to corrupted qubits using classical logic. Examples of this class include the Shor code and the Steane code.

Quantum error correction is mostly divided into three categories: bit-flip error correction, phase-flip error correction, and bit-/phase-flip error correction. Bit-flip error is similar to classical computer bit error, where one is switched with the other or vice versa. It is corrected with parity checks and encoding logical qubits across multiple physical qubits. Phase-flip error is unique to quantum computing, where the superposition-like phase changes its state. This error cannot be measured without collapsing the state, so it is corrected by encoding phase information across multiple qubits. The third type of error is a combination of the first two errors, and it is corrected by integrating the mentioned two techniques.

Quantum error correction is a crucial key in achieving quantum supremacy and gain of quantum advantage. Current quantum systems build noise while computing, so computation becomes error-prone and unreliable. This disadvantage can only be counteracted with relevant advancement of quantum software and quantum hardware. This can be accomplished with meeting a high resource requirement of hardware to software, ensuring qubit fragility, error propagation during correction, scalability of a fault-tolerant system, and ensuring a complex implementation of the entire system. Ensuring these steps seems tedious, but it produces results that are promising.

For instance, IBM hopes to achieve quantum advantage by 2026. They are working on improving error correction with heavy-hexagonal lattices, an optimized layout for qubits that reduces crosstalk and improves coherence times. This design makes it possible to surface codes for error detection.

Similarly, NVIDIA contributes to QEC by developing GPU-based quantum emulators, which simulate quantum systems at scale. These emulators are used to test and optimize error correction codes before deploying them on physical quantum hardware.

Intel is pioneering the application of silicon spin qubits, which use existing semiconductor manufacturing technologies for scalable quantum systems. These qubits tend to be smaller and more stable, reducing noise and improving error rates. Intel combines these hardware advancements with machine learning algorithms to optimize error correction protocols.

Another demonstration can be seen with Amazon, which is using its Braket platform to develop hybrid quantum-classical solutions for QEC. By integrating quantum processors with powerful classical systems, Amazon allows for error detection and correction simulations in real time. Microsoft is also trying to improve its topological qubits with necessary QEC.

Companies like BlueQubit is also investing greatly in quantum computing by contributing toward quantum software as a service. The company is breaking down barriers linked with quantum computing, such as high costs, hardware limitations, and, of course, error correction challenges. By integrating emulators, user-friendly tools, and quantum processing units (QPUs), BlueQubit allows businesses and researchers to benefit from quantum computing without the need for infrastructure [91].

All these quantum corporations are majoring in targeting excellence in quantum error correction through research and industrial application so that they can benefit the industries and sectors like health and medicine, energy, transport, and so on. Once quantum advantage is gained at the industrial level, societal adoption will be easy and acceptable due to the advantages.

3.23 CURRENT CHALLENGES AND BARRIERS

There are a lot of challenges and barriers limiting the development of quantum computing, so quantum advantage and quantum supremacy are not yet fully realized. In this section, the current technical and non-technical challenges and barriers will be critically identified and elaborated.

3.24 TECHNICAL CHALLENGES

In this subsection, three prominent technical challenges that were identified through the literature review and further research will be scrutinized. These three technical challenges are quantum scalability, quantum coherence, and quantum error correction. Quantum scalability is a current development issue due to noise, decoherence, hardware complexity, and software and algorithm limitations. The hardware complexity arises from the point of interconnects and control challenges as the system scales. Current qubit architectures, such as those using microwave control lines, require dedicated hardware for each qubit. Scaling this setup to thousands of qubits creates wiring bottlenecks, as cryogenic systems can't support thousands of independent cables. Photonic interconnects or 3D integration might solve this, but these technologies are still experimental. Trapped-ion qubits, which use lasers for control, face similar scaling issues: aligning laser beams across hundreds of ions without crosstalk is nontrivial. Even calibration becomes a hurdle; each qubit's control parameters, such as microwave pulse durations, must be tuned individually, a process that scales poorly with qubit count.

Second, software and algorithm limitations complicate scaling. Today's quantum algorithms assume ideal qubits, but real-world systems require developers to account for noise, connectivity constraints, and hardware-specific quirks. For example, a quantum compiler must map a circuit to a physical qubit layout, avoiding distant qubits that require error-prone SWAP operations. This optimization becomes exponentially harder as qubit count rises. Additionally, classical computers struggle to simulate or verify large quantum systems, making debugging and error analysis slower. Until software tools mature to automate these tasks, scaling will remain labor-intensive and error-prone.

Form factor is another concern, whereby it is essential to ensure that physical miniaturization of large-scale quantum computers for efficient scaling. Therefore, it can be said that the advancement of quantum computers is entirely dependent on advances in hardware stability, control infrastructure, and software tooling while managing the inherent fragility of quantum states [92] and loss of quantum properties, which is normally referred to as decoherence.

Decoherence poses a challenge in quantum computing since, in order to avoid errors, calculations must be completed before decoherence occurs. While increasing the coherence time of a qubit is an important area of research, a popular approach to address it is the development of error-correcting codes. Error-correcting codes become much more challenging in quantum environment than in a classical one because qubits are not replicated in the same way as classical bits due to their complex correction codes [93].

Qubit coherence and error rates become harder to manage as systems scale. Qubits are extremely sensitive to environmental noise, even minor temperature fluctuations or electromagnetic interference can disrupt their quantum states. For example, superconducting qubits, which operate in near absolute zero, require precise cooling systems that become more complex as qubit counts increase. Additionally, quantum operations of gates have inherent error rates. A two-qubit gate might have an error rate of 1%, but in a 1,000-qubit system, these errors multiply, leading to unreliable computations. Error correction techniques, like surface codes, can help, but they require thousands of physical qubits to create a single stable logical qubit, a resource overhead that isn't yet practical [92].

Studies also show that coherent and incoherent errors at logical level could be significant. It was observed that coherent errors can lead to large differences between average-case and worst-case fidelity measures, suggesting that a critical reassessment of commonly used benchmarking measures is necessary. This observation motivates the question of how much coherence is present in the effective logical-level noise experienced by encoded qubits. Depending on whether or not the logical noise is coherent, one may choose different metrics for quantifying the performance of a given fault-tolerant scheme [94].

Another article demonstrates how quantum error correction also provides exponential leverage in reducing logical errors with processor improvements. For example, reducing physical error rates by a factor of 2 would improve the distance to 27 logical performances by four orders of magnitude well into algorithmically relevant error rates. The purpose of this quantum error correction is to enable large-scale quantum algorithms to build a robust memory [95].

As research advances in the area of quantum error correction, the current solutions will be elaborated with their limitation to help the academic readers better understand the current state of quantum computing in terms of excellence. The following table reflects a list of current quantum error correction solutions and their limitations [96–99]

Quantum Error Correction Solutions	Limitations
1. Shor Code (9 Qubit): The first quantum error-correcting code encodes 1 logical qubit in 9 physical qubits. It works by concatenating a 3-qubit repetition code for bit-flips with another 3-qubit repetition code for phase-flips. In essence, it uses 9 qubits arranged as three groups: first, it triples the qubit to protect against bit flips via majority vote, then it uses a clever Hadamard rotation and triples each of those to protect against phase flips. The Shor code can correct any single-qubit error (be it X, Z, or Y) on any one of the 9 qubits. It was a proof-of-concept that quantum redundancy and syndrome measurement can safeguard quantum information.	The 9-qubit Shor code is quite resource-intensive and has high overhead.
2. Steane Code (7-qubit CSS Code): The Steane code is a 7-qubit code invented in 1996 and belongs to the class of Calderbank-Shor-Steane (CSS) codes. It is built from two classical codes: [7, 4, 3] the Hamming code for bit-flips and its dual for phase-flips. The code encodes 1 logical qubit into 7 physical qubits and can correct any single-qubit error with distance d = 3. In stabilizer form, it has 6 stabilizer generators, 3 X-type, and 3 Z-type checks. The Steane code was the first example of a quantum Hamming code. It is more efficient than Shor's using 7 qubits instead of 9 for one logical qubit and is a precursor to many modern codes. Being a CSS code, it separately treats X and Z errors, which simplifies implementation.	Mostly implemented in small-scale experiments.

(Continued)

Quantum Error Correction Solutions	Limitations
3. Surface Code (Topological Code): The surface code is a leading QEC code in today's quantum computing implementations due to its high error threshold and geometric locality. It was introduced by Alexei Kitaev and refined for planar architecture. Qubits in a surface code are arranged on a 2D grid, and stabilizers involve either 4-qubit X operators or 4-qubit Z operators. The code is called "topological" because the logical qubits are encoded in non-local, topologically protected degrees of freedom. The surface code's big advantages are that each stabilizer involves only local qubit interactions and it tolerates relatively high error rates, approximately 1%. In fact, it is below threshold for many current devices, which means increasing the code size is expected to suppress logical errors. Tech companies like Google, IBM, and others have all targeted the surface code or variants of it for their roadmap to scalable quantum computers.	Overhead—it may require hundreds or thousands of physical qubits per logical qubit to reach very low error rates since the distance must be large.
4. Other Stabilizer Codes: Bacon-Shor codes—a variant of Shor's code with fewer stabilizers. Color Codes—another topological code in 2D and 3D with multi-qubit stabilizers. Low-Density Parity Check Codes (LDPCs)—aim to reduce quantum overhead. Used by IBM.	May have lower threshold. The choice of code is often tailored to the hardware and error rates available.
5. Bosonic Qubit Cat Code: In practice, cat qubits exhibit a bias: bit-flip errors become much less frequent than phase-flip errors due to the hardware architecture. One can then apply simpler quantum error correction, like a repetition code to correct the remaining dominant phase errors. Cat codes have been experimentally realized in circuit QED systems, demonstrating the extension of qubit coherence by encoding into cat states. The plus point here is that it converts the physical error into parity change or detectable syndrome.	Relies on the precision of state preparation and maintenance.
6. Bosonic Qubit Gottesman Kitaev Preskill Codes: In principle, correct small arbitrary displacement errors, in both quadratures up to some maximum shift. This directly targets errors like photon loss, jitter, or noise in an oscillator.	These codewords are quite exotic; they require highly squeezed states or approximate finite-energy versions of them, which make them experimentally challenging.
7. Binomial Codes: These are constructed to cancel out errors up to a certain order of photon loss, gain, or dephasing by appropriate choice of codewords. They approximately protect against continuous dynamics like damping. The big appeal of binomial codes is that they can be implemented with finite-energy states that are relatively easier to produce and they can be tailored to the dominant error channel of the oscillator. Binomial codes have been experimentally tested in superconducting cavity setups, showing the extension of qubit lifetime by actively correcting detected photon jumps. They represent a hardware-efficient approach since one oscillatory mode encodes the qubit and only a few ancillary qubits and operations are needed for error syndrome measurement.	Complex and overhead issues in implementation.

(Continued)

(Continued)

Quantum Error Correction Solutions	Limitations
8. Zero-Noise Extrapolation (ZNE): This technique involves purposely varying the noise in the quantum computation and using the results to extrapolate to the zero-noise limit. In practice, one can amplify the noise in a circuit to obtain measurements at higher error rates and then perform a fit extrapolation of the observable's value back to what it should be at zero error. It has been shown to improve the accuracy of computations like variational algorithms.	ZNE is not bias-free as extrapolation assumes a certain noise model. It requires multiple runs of the circuit and classical post-processing but with no extra qubits.
9. Probabilistic Error Cancelation (PEC): This is a more advanced technique where one characterizes the noise on the quantum gates, and then adds a probabilistic mixture of inverse error operations to cancel it out on average. By randomly sampling these operations according to the quasiprobabilities, one can unbias the expectation value of an observable, getting the correct result in expectation.	Sampling overhead: the variance of the results increases with the negativity of the quasiprobabilities, which means you have to sample many more circuit runs to get a high-confidence estimate. PEC has an unbiased estimator of the error-free outcome, unlike ZNE, but if the noise is large, the sampling cost becomes impractical.
10. Dynamical Decoupling: While not a computational post-processing like the previous two, dynamical decoupling (DD) is a pulse control technique used on quantum hardware to suppress certain errors. It involves inserting sequences of pulses on idle qubits to average out low-frequency noise and undesired couplings.	It doesn't correct arbitrary discrete errors but can prolong coherence times.
11. Measurement-Based Error Suppression: These methods involve using additional measurements to detect and reduce errors.	It requires additional circuit runs and are not scalable in the long run since discarding runs is inefficient when error rates are high.
12. Machine-Learning-Assisted Error Correction: Leveraging machine learning algorithms to predict error patterns allows for dynamic and optimized correction strategies, improving system performance under real-world conditions.	Short coherence time.

3.25 NON-TECHNICAL BARRIERS

In this subsection, current non-technical barriers, such as high development and operational costs, infrastructure complexity and investments, talent shortages, and ethical and governance challenges, will be identified and elaborated.

The high costs associated with quantum hardware and infrastructure are significant barriers to the widespread adoption of quantum computing. Building and maintaining quantum computers require substantial financial investment, and the cost of developing the necessary infrastructure is prohibitive for many organizations.

Quantum computers are expensive to build and operate, with costs driven by the need for specialized materials, precision manufacturing, and advanced cryogenic systems. The cost of quantum hardware is a significant barrier for companies and research institutions that want to experiment with quantum computing but cannot afford to invest in the necessary infrastructure [100].

According to SpinQ, the educational and small-scale quantum computer price range initially starts from 50,000 dollars. These quantum computers are designed primarily for educational purposes, quantum learning, and experimentation with quantum algorithms and be less superior in the wide range of quantum computers. Examples are SpinQ's Gemini Mini and Triangulum Mini series are compact, room-temperature quantum computers designed for educational use. They are affordable, portable, easy to maintain, and perfect for introducing students to quantum principles.

Mid-range quantum computer price range begins from 1,000,000 dollars. Mid-range quantum computers offer better performance and can be used for complex quantum research or specialized industry applications. They often come with a larger number of qubits and more sophisticated quantum hardware. The provider of mid-range quantum computer is often SpinQ.

Industrial-grade quantum computer price begins from 10 million dollars. Industrial-grade quantum computers are high-performance, state-of-the-art quantum systems used by large organizations, research institutions, and government agencies. These are typically superconducting quantum computers or ion-trap systems that require massive infrastructure and maintenance, such as cryogenic cooling systems, and involve teams of specialists to run. Their application is seen in high-level quantum simulations, solving complex, large-scale problems in fields such as artificial intelligence (AI), drug discovery, optimization, logistics, cryptography, and financial modeling. The providers are mostly IBM, Google, and SpinQ [101].

In addition to the cost of quantum hardware, maintaining and operating a quantum computer requires specialized infrastructure, including cryogenic systems, vacuum chambers, and electromagnetic shielding. These infrastructure requirements add to the overall cost of quantum computing and make it difficult for smaller organizations to participate in quantum research and development [100]. Additionally, these systems consume a large amount of power, making it impossible to reduce the operational cost [102].

As mentioned, quantum computer facilities are costly in terms of production, operation, and maintenance. This adds more complexity to the quantum infrastructure challenges. Additionally, cryptography plays a role in quantum infrastructure, as quantum algorithm-based cryptography is serving as a bridge from classical computers to quantum computers. Since the perceived quantum computers are yet to be realized and manifested, the gap is bridged with the use of hybrid quantum computers, which are running quantum algorithms on classical computers to harness the potentials of a quantum computer. The true potential of quantum computer is yet to be discovered the path of quantum algorithm complexity will get more complex [103].

Precision engineering is another factor that controls precision mechanisms for qubits creation, such as lasers or microwave pulses. This requires cutting-edge engineering and high precision in fabrication [101].

Since quantum infrastructure complexity is realized through research, more investors are investing in quantum technologies. Per the World Economic Forum, investors have been investing in quantum computers, quantum software, quantum hardware components, and quantum security in the recent years. As of 2024, approximately two billion dollars have been invested in these infrastructures [104]. On the same note, the Quantum Economic Development Consortium's (QED-C) "2025 State of the Global Quantum Industry" report estimates the total global quantum technology market will reach $1.88 billion in 2025, representing a 27.3% increase from $1.48 billion in 2024. Projections indicate the market could reach $4.89 billion by 2029, driven by increased computational power and demand for secure communication [105].

As the market for quantum computing is rising, a talent shortage is noticed, and per McKinsey's research, there is only one qualified quantum candidate available for every three quantum job openings, and by 2025, less than 50% of these job openings will be filled. This will jeopardize and stall the quantum breakthrough, which accounts up to 700 billion dollars. The notable roles includes quantum hardware engineers, quantum software engineers, and quantum translators for strategic planning, governance, and partnership [106]. Forbes states that businesses that wait for the technology to become mainstream before taking action to address the skills gap are setting themselves up to be at a disadvantage to faster-moving competitors [107].

The issue of skill shortage arises as the hard science career path is not prominently visible in the education system due to its novelty, and since this is an emerging technology, the interest of potential candidates can only be captured with awareness. Up till now, quantum physics and quantum mechanics has been major skills that required from the candidates, but it is essential to note that the industry is moving from the theoretical to practical feasibility and engineering. Now, engineers must build cryogenic systems, shielding room, and precision of qubits. This means that a greater knowledge is required [108]. The roles are usually filled with candidates with a background in physics, mathematics, computer science, chemistry, system architecture, application design, database design, AI, machine learning, or development operations engineering [106].

To address the shortage, initiatives like IBM's Quantum Experience program, launched in 2016, and its open-source Qiskit developer kit are enabling programmers to work with quantum computers using basic Python skills. Similarly, the Finnish company IQM Spark is facilitating access to quantum computers for researchers and students, from bachelor's to PhD levels, through its IQM Academy program. Thanks to initiatives like these, a rapid increase is seen in skills using such tools as Qiskit (+129%), PyTorch (+126%) and React.js (+116%) over the past year [109]. The UK has also increased its initiative toward mitigating this shortage, per its National Quantum Strategy Report [110].

Another issue that is slowly creeping up as the realm of quantum technology progresses is the area of ethics and governance. Per Quantum Insider, a Quantum Technologies Policy Primer report outlines the transformative potential of quantum computing, sensing, and communication but warns that inadequate governance could slow progress and deepen global inequalities [111]. Per the OECD report, policies such as support for research and development, and building quantum readiness and resilience through government funding. Other policies include metrics to benchmark quantum technological capabilities, local and international cooperation in research and development, and roles of standardization. The report also highlights some of the challenges that is posing as a regulatory concern; these are international cooperation in terms of dual use, national security risks, and the role of consensus standards and multilateral fora. The second concern is limited and competitive access to skills in the workforce. The third concern is the constraints of the supply chain. The final concern is ensuring access and inclusion to avoid deepening divides in all contexts [112]. The OECD calls for stronger international cooperation, investment in workforce development, and regulatory frameworks that ensure secure and ethical deployment of these technologies [111]. Other ethical issues might arise due to the cyber threat of quantum computers to classical computers, where user rights are violated. As this chapter proceeds toward the discussion section, the findings will be elaborated analytically.

3.26 DISCUSSION

In this section, the major findings of this paper will be analyzed with the comparative analysis framework that will help form the conclusion of this chapter. Five topics will be analyzed in this section using different comparative analysis that was mentioned in this chapter's methodology section: quantum hardware innovation, quantum programming and software, quantum computing platforms, quantum supremacy and achievements, and challenges and barriers of quantum computing. The comparative analyses used are qualitative comparative analysis with Boolean logic, case study, quantitative comparative analysis, benchmarking, and SWOT analysis, accordingly.

3.27 QUANTUM HARDWARE INNOVATIONS

In this subsection, the data obtained from various valid sources on current quantum hardware will be qualitatively analyzed to understand the nature of each architectural type, then Boolean logic will be used to determine any relationship between the variables that are captured in the following table. The architecture type of various quantum hardware will be explored to understand which architecture type is better.

Architecture Type:

1. Heavy Hexagonal Topology [113]: This topology is achieved by reducing a degree 4 node into two degree 3 nodes. The square lattice can be simulated on the heavy hexagonal lattice with constant overhead by introducing swap operations into suitable chosen unit cells. This topology reduces interconnectivity but minimizes qubit frequency collision and spectator qubit collision, which is detrimental for real-world application. This topology also reduces error rate and provides scalability and error correction opportunities. This arrangement is equivalent as well as superior to the square lattice arrangement. The three-qubit repetition code encoding leads to a logical heavy square lattice that corrects the single flip error.

TABLE 3.4
Analysis of Quantum Hardware from Leading Quantum Corporations

Quantum Hardware Type	Quantum Ownership	Number of Physical Qubits	Number of Logical Qubits	Architecture Type	Single-Gate Fidelity	Double-Gate Fidelity
Super-conducting	IBM	127	Undefined	Heavy hexagonal topology	99.5%	99.9%
		433	Undefined	Monolithic heavy hexagonal	Unspecified	Unspecified
	Google	53	Undefined	Transmon coupling	0.2 %	
	Rigetti	84	Undefined	Square lattice—alternating bias assisted annealing	99.5%	99%
Trapped Ion	Quantinuum	20	Undefined	Quantum charge couple device	99.998%,	99.91%
		32–56	Undefined	Quantum charge couple device-non-abelian topology	99.997%	99.87%
	IonQ	11	Undefined	Linear chain individual ions	0.4%	2.7%
		25	25	Reconfigurable multicore architecture—all to all qubit connectivity	0.06%	0.6%
		36	36	Reconfigurable multicore architecture—all to all qubit connectivity	0.02%	0.4%
Photonic and Silicon	PsiQuantum	1,000,000	1000	Fusion network	99.99%	99%
	Xanadu	12	Undefined	Modular photonic architecture	98.5%	

2. Transmon Coupling [114]: For a transmon-based quantum computer, couplings between qubits are realized by just positioning qubits closely so that the coupling capacitance mediates the connection, or by inserting a coupler such as a resonator, represented by a coplanar waveguide or a microwave cavity, or even a transmon. Other transmon systems include a multi-qubit system based on Xmon, where qubits are mediated by a router through tunable switches. Beyond the homogeneous superconducting qubit system, a novel hybrid system has a coupler qubit coupled with multiple neutral atoms or solid-state qubits in cavities for multi-qubit gates. One of the most well-known structures for transmon-based quantum computers is the

transmon-resonator-transmon structure, in which a resonator coupler connects two transmon qubits. This structure enhances the performance and helps in error mitigation, but it has its challenges.

3. Square Lattice [115–117]—Alternating Bias Assisted Annealing: This architecture involves assembling qubits in square lattice with tunable couplers. The Josephson junction used is manufactured with the ABAA technique. The technique requires qubit frequency targeting resulting in improvements in chip performance and allowing for scaling to higher qubit systems with greater control over qubit performance. ABAA manufacturing process shows the cyclic change in junction resistance with a repeated sequence of small and large resistance changes when applying alternating bias bipolar pulses to improve the properties of the material.
4. Quantum Charge Couple Device [118, 119]: This cryogenic surface scalable trap designed parallel interaction zones and fast ion transport into a programmable trapped-ion quantum computer that has a system performance consistent with the low error rates achieved in the individual ion crystals. This architecture makes the crosstalk error negligible and expands the quantum volume that will ensure better performance. The architecture stores quantum information in the internal state of ions that are transported between different processing zones using dynamic electromagnetic fields.
5. Linear Chain Individual Ions [120]: The atoms are arranged in a linear way, which is typical in a radiofrequency ion trap, although this scheme can also apply to other spatial geometries. The spins are coherently manipulated through a pair of counter-propagating laser beams that drive simulated Raman transitions between the spin states, while also coupling off resonantly to the collective motion of the atomic chain. This makes it possible for precise control over quantum states and their interactions, and potential control and manipulation of large qubits.
6. Reconfigurable Multicore Architecture [121]—All-to-All Connectivity: Multiple ion chains are manipulated to dynamically form quantum computing cores, which comprises 12 qubit ions and 4 refrigerant ions. The configuration consists of 4 chains that comprises 12 qubit ions and 4 refrigerant ions each. The configuration begins with assembling the 2 right chains to form a 32 qubit chain, to perform the computation and configuration of the core. After the configuration has been performed, then the 2 middle chains form the 32-qubit core, where reconfiguration and computation are performed. Once this is done, then the trap ion reconfigures, and the 2 left chains are configured to form a core. This way, the reconfiguration processes allows utility of full computation space, which increases the computing power exponentially. In addition to reconfiguring the ion chains into a single quantum computing core at a time, the trap chips can configure the ion chains into multiple simultaneous quantum computing cores, allowing for parallel quantum operations among each of these cores. Moreover, the total number qubits in this particular configuration can be either increased by increasing the number of ions in a chain or by increasing the number of chains.
7. Fusion Network [122]: This architecture allows for the measurement of the entangled state, called fusion measurements, on qubits of small

constant-sized entangled resource states. This framework naturally captures the error structure that arises in certain physical systems for quantum computing, such as photonics. This can offer significant architectural simplifications, enabling hardware made up of many identical modules, requiring an extremely low depth of operations on each physical qubit, and reducing classical processing requirements.

8. Modular Photonic [123]: Modular design provides a pathway to scale quantum systems to thousands of server racks and millions of qubits, positioning it as a potential foundation for future quantum data centers. Additionally, the development is described as evidence in the progress of scaling quantum computing systems toward larger implementations. It can handle quantum computational processes, such as gate operations, real-time error correction, and decoding, all within the practical constraints of quantum clock rates and classical control hardware. The major challenge that is left to be tackled is the challenge of error correction and fault tolerance.

From the table and analysis, it can be deduced that the best architecture for quantum computing would be the Quantinuum-based quantum charge-coupled device and the PsiQuantum fusion network based on the fidelity of single- and double-qubit gates. This may also be applicable in cases where other environmental, state, and crosstalk errors can creep up. Most sources suggest the use of photonics and ions to construct a quantum computer is optimal due to these reasons.

Next, from the previous table, two variables will be taken to construct a Boolean table. These two variables are the number of physical qubits and the number of logical qubits. The Boolean logic that will be used here will be the NOT, OR, and AND gates. The values for known variables will be assigned true, and for unknown variables, they will be false. The reason for choosing Boolean logic is that, from the data that is presented in the table, there may be a possibility that these variables have a relationship in determining the fidelity rate. So, fundamentally, if these variables are known, the fidelity rate will be high. See the following Boolean table for computed logic.

Key: Defined = True, Undefined = False, Physical Qubits Value = True

Physical Qubits	Boolean Value	Logical Gate	NOT Logical Gate	Physical OR Logical	AND
127	True	Undefined	False	True	False
433	True	Undefined	False	True	False
53	True	Undefined	False	True	False
84	True	Undefined	False	True	False
20	True	Undefined	False	True	False
32–56	True	Undefined	False	True	False
11	True	Undefined	False	True	False
25	True	Defined	True	True	True
36	True	Defined	True	True	True
1,000,000	True	Defined	True	True	True
12	True	Undefined	False	True	False

From this Boolean table, it can be deduced that the number of logical qubits characterization is not important for a higher fidelity rate as long as the physical qubits are able to produce a better qubit fidelity rate. However, it may play a role that can contribute toward a higher fidelity rate.

3.28 QUANTUM PROGRAMMING AND SOFTWARE

In this subsection of discussion, the analysis of the cases that were captured in a table under the section of "Quantum Programming and Software" will be scrutinized based on the findings from the perspective of indicators such as the case SDK tools, functionalities, language, ease of use, learning curve, and community support. Based on the three cases from IBM, Google, and Microsoft, it can be deduced that the tools, functionalities, and languages of these three cases were pretty ample. The available tools can come in wide ranges, the functionalities of these three software development kits are optimal, and the language that can be used to construct is mostly Python, which is simple and easy to learn. The exception can be made with Microsoft, which is using its own new language, but in this case as well, a number of other languages can also be used, like C and C++. All three cases show that they are invested in solving the real-world problems. Cases have also reflected collaboration, transport, energy, medicine, and other sectors. The other three indicators—ease of use for users, learning curve, and community support—show that IBM is leading. Several documents, videos, codes, scenarios, code libraries, and fleets of resources are available. This is the largest community of quantum computing as well. Although Google and Microsoft have also shown efforts to make things easy for the community in terms of these indicators, IBM has surpassed them. On the same note, precise data on the learning curve of these kits is not available online, so a clear notion could not be calculated.

3.29 QUANTUM COMPUTING PLATFORMS

In this subsection, the findings of the four platforms, IBM, Google, Microsoft, and Amazon, will be summarized using data visualization tools. The following table summarizes the findings of these platforms using comparative factors. Afterward, the industry-specific use cases will be analyzed using the criteria and data visualization tool, such as a pie chart.

TABLE 3.5
Summary of Quantum Computing Platforms from IBM, Google, Microsoft, and Amazon

Comparative Factors	IBM	Google	Microsoft	Amazon
Performance	Satisfactory	Satisfactory	Satisfactory	Satisfactory
Scalability Vertical	Satisfactory	Satisfactory	Satisfactory	Satisfactory
Scalability Horizontal				Satisfactory
Scalability Hybrid	Satisfactory	Satisfactory		Satisfactory
Industry	Undesirable	Undesirable	Undesirable	Undesirable
Readiness	Undesirable	Undesirable	Undesirable	Undesirable
Accessibility	Desirable	Desirable	Desirable	Desirable

The signs of vertical and hybrid scalability are observed because the quantum computation is still in its developing stages. The following pie chart shows the application of quantum computing in industry-specific use cases. The sources of these use cases are also iterated:

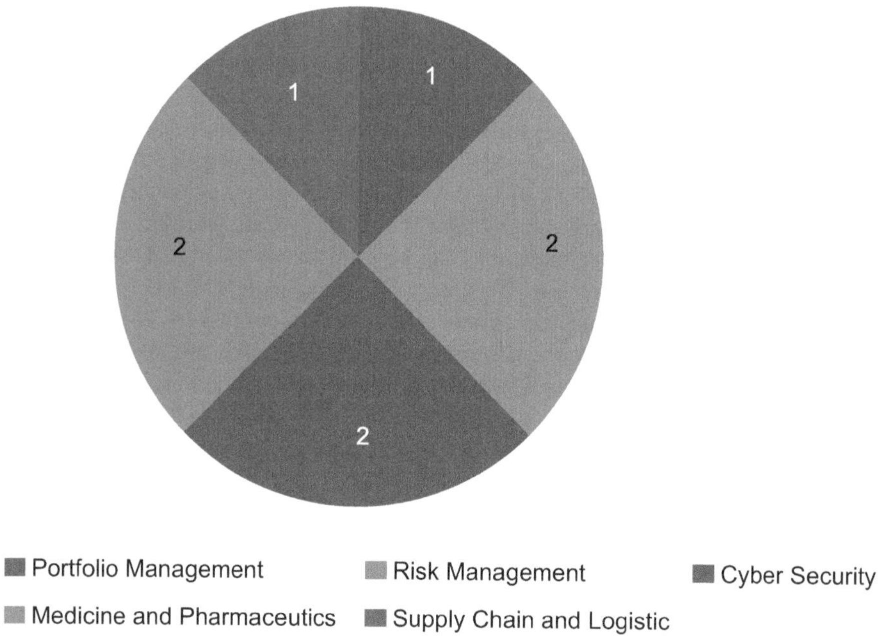

FIGURE 3.9 Industry-specific use cases of quantum computing with their sources.

Industry Specific Use Cases of Quantum Computing	***Source***
Portfolio Management	[77]
Risk Management	[78],[79]
Cyber Security	[80],[84]
Medicine and Pharmaceutics	[81],[82]
Logistics & Supply Chain	[83]

FIGURE 3.10 Pie chart showing the industry-specific use cases of quantum computing.

The industry-specific use cases of quantum computing will be analyzed with criteria of impact, recentness, and relevance.

TABLE 3.6
Analysis of Industry-Specific Use Cases with the Criteria

Criteria	Portfolio Management	Risk Management	Cybersecurity	Medicine and Pharmaceutics	Supply Chain and Logistics
Impact	Positive		Negative	Positive	
Recentness	Lacking, and its initial stages	Lacking, and its initial stages	Lacking, and its initial stages	Lacking, and its initial stages	Lacking, and its initial stages
Relevance	Maximizes resources	Maximizes resources, asset, people and reduces loss	Challenges Current security. Cybersecurity will be strengthened	Improves the drug success rate, fast track the process	Increases productivity of the supply in terms of time, money, and energy

3.30 QUANTUM SUPREMACY AND ACHIEVEMENTS

In this subsection, the cross-entropy benchmark (XEB) will be scrutinized as this is the tool that was used for the Sycamore processor by Google to claim quantum supremacy. The benchmarking tools from IBM will also be scrutinized. The cross-entropy benchmarking has four phases [124]:

1. Cross-Entropy Benchmarking Theory: This uses the properties of random quantum programs to determine the fidelity of a wide variety of circuits. When applied to circuits with many qubits, XEB can characterize the performance of a large device. When applied to deep, two-qubit circuits, it can be used to accurately characterize a two-qubit interaction, potentially leading to better calibration.
2. Cross-Entropy Benchmarking of Coherent and Incoherent Noise: This end-to-end benchmarking compares coherent gate parameter error and incoherent depolarization error. It will mimic a small device graph of cirq.GridQubit pairs and simulate two-qubit XEB benchmarking circuits on them with noise models that introduce coherent and incoherent error before visualizing and comparing the results.
3. Parallel Cross-Entropy Benchmarking: This demonstrates how to use the functionality in cirq.experiments to run parallel XEB end-to-end. "Parallel" means we characterize multiple pairs simultaneously.
4. Cross-Entropy Benchmarking Calibration: Circuits and selected qubits are calibrated.

Note, the process involved in the first phase includes the action of random circuits with noise, possible single-qubit rotations, random circuits, fidelity estimation, circuit execution, definition of observable, and plotting of fit. In the second phase, generation of random circuits, preparation of noise models, mimicking of XEB on real hardware, fidelity data collection of sample circuit, visualizing fidelity using noise model in heatmaps, circuit fidelity by cycle, gate parameter characterization, and visualization of refitted fidelities by noise model. In the third phase, random circuit setup, determination of device topology, setup of combinations, visualization, data take for execution, fidelity benchmarking, and optimization of parameters. In the final phase, setup of calibration by selecting qubits, XEB calibration setup, execution with calibration, and with calibration, results are compared by plotting of graph.

Moreover, the benchmark tool that is opted by IBM is inclusion of a number of software development kits that can build, manipulate, and transpile qubits efficiently. Note in the building and manipulation stage, the quantum SDK has to create and apply transformations to quantum circuits well. In the synthesis and transpiling stage, quantum SDK has to take a circuit as input and translate it into a form that is capable of running on quantum hardware, real and arbitrary.

The benchmarking tool used by IBM is called Benchpress. It is composed of Qiskit, Qiskit Transpiler Service, BQSkit, TKET, Staq, Braket, and Cirq. Benchpress is an open-source tool meant to help industry stakeholders to examine and expand upon this analysis in order to glean meaningful information about various quantum SDKs.

Per the conducted test, it was found out that Braket and Cirq were performing better at circuit building and manipulation, Qiskit Transpiler Service and Staq were better at transpiling circuits, while Qiskit, TKET, and BQSKit could do both. The result showed Qiskit was capable of completing more of the tests than any other SDK. On average, it did so either faster, with fewer two-qubit gates, or both. It was the highest-performing quantum SDK that was tested, 13 times faster at transpiling and producing circuits, with 24% fewer two-qubit gates than TKET, the second highest-performing SDK. On the same note, the latest results shows that Qiskit is 54 times faster at running the Benchpress tests than TKET, with 30% fewer gate operations, for an overall higher fidelity.

Overall, 1,066 tests were conducted on these SDKs, and 22 tests were skipped on all SDKs due to target device size. The following table shows the number of tests that were completed by each SDK and along with other details [125].

The pass rate of the number of tests completed is due to the features of each SDK. It was noted that Staq does not have significant support for circuit manipulation, while Cirq and Braket lack features for circuit synthesis and transpilation. AI transpiler passes delivered a further 24% reduction on average in two-qubit gates, and a 36% reduction on average in circuit depth for utility-scale circuits when transpiling in heavy hexagonal topology. The quality ratio of two-qubit gates needs to be lower for efficient performance, which is reflected by Qiskit. Meanwhile, IBM's quantum optimization benchmarking library [126] is an open-source repository that allows the community to benchmark quantum application optimization. The optimization

TABLE 3.7
Performance Details of Benchpress Suite

SDK	Raw Number of Test Completed	Overall Time to Complete	Build and Manipulate Time	Ratio Quality of 2Q Gates
Braket	10		17.2 seconds	
BQSKit	—			
Cirq	7		17.5 seconds	
Qiskit	10	49 minutes	7.47 seconds	1X
Qiskit Transpiler Service				
Staq	549			2.80X
TKET	957	27 hours	21.3 seconds	1.31X

benchmarking library consists of ten classes problems that will allow the industry to benchmark accordingly [127]:

1. Market Spilt—multidimensional subset-sum
2. LABS—low-autocorrelation binary sequences
3. Minimum Birkhoff decomposition
4. Steneir tree packaging—VLSI design and wire routing
5. Sports tournament scheduling
6. Portfolio optimization—transaction costs and shortselling with multiple periods
7. Maximum independent set—unweighted
8. Network design
9. Vehicle routing—VRP: TSP + time window + knapsack
10. Topology design—graph golf, node-degree-diameter problem

From these details stated, it can be deduced that Benchpress is a better benchmarking tool in comparison with Google's cross-entropy benchmarking for overall quantum computation from creation, manipulation, synthesis, and transpiling of qubits. Also, the XEB majorly concerns itself with eliminating noise for fidelity purposes by ensuring calibration and parallelism.

3.31 CHALLENGES AND BARRIERS

In this section of the discussion, SWOT analysis will be performed on the findings of this section and throughout the course of this chapter. In the findings, technical challenges, such as quantum scalability, quantum coherence, and quantum error correction, will be analyzed using the SWOT tool. The non-technical challenges include talent shortage, ethics and governance implication, high development and operational costs, infrastructure complexity, and investments will also be analyzed.

From the SWOT analysis, it can be deduced that the challenges and barriers are fewer in comparison to the strengths and opportunities of quantum computing.

Strength	Weakness
✓ Accurate, Secure and Complex ✓ Enhanced Optimisation ✓ Exponential Speed ✓ Transformative Impact on Artificial Intelligence and Machine Learning ✓ Revolutisation of Drug Discovery and Material Science ✓ Growing Investment in Quantum Computing	✓ Challenges of Noise, Coherence, Fragility and error correction ✓ Scalability ✓ Cost and Complexity in terms of operation, maintenance and creation ✓ Current limitation on applicability and computation ✓ Security concerns on classical computing ✓ Short of talents in this area of expertise
Opportunities	**Threats**
✓ Industrial Application ✓ Material Science Application ✓ Advancement of Artificial Intelligence and Machine Learning ✓ Research and Development ✓ Technology advancement in terms of precision	✓ Cyber-attacks through use of quantum cyber algorithms ✓ Ethics and Governance will be implicated

FIGURE 3.11 SWOT analysis of the findings.

However, it is important that threats are taken seriously so that strategic plans can be made to eradicate it, especially in the case of ethics and governance, where developing countries or underdeveloped societies might become victims of cyberattacks and other bureaucracies due to the uneven distribution of wealth and assets in terms of quantum computing.

One of the gaps identified were that the quantum hardware is still facing challenges in terms of material and fabrication, which is crucial to support the state of quantum computing. Noise, crosstalk, and environmental error are still an issue. For this, quantum algorithms need to be perfected, either using advanced machine learning or artificial intelligence algorithms. Since the hardware and software gaps were noted, the most prominent quantum computing platforms were also scrutinized, and it was observed that the commercial viability of quantum computer is still lacking in the real world. A number of applications were noted, but these two were mostly in experimental stages. Additionally, it was important to understand the claims of quantum supremacy so that quantum advancement can be achieved at least theoretically, or computationally, regardless of its application in the real world. It was noted that Google might have achieved the computational speed, but algorithm perfection is still needed for its full potential. Later, through the challenges and barriers of quantum computing, it was seen that quantum computing offers more significant advantages than disadvantages. After noting the disadvantages, it is important for society and the government to embrace new technology and find solutions to the threats and weaknesses.

The novel contribution of this chapter is to prove the hypothesis and the systematic comparative framework. Information about important quantum computing topics was analyzed with this framework. The insights that were gained after the analysis are the major contribution of this chapter. The hypothesis is proven correct based on the gaps identified and insights gained from the comparative analysis.

3.32 CONCLUSION

In conclusion, it can be said that while quantum computing has massive potential and its practical advancement toward real-world application has already begun based on the observations of experimental research and development, either academically or commercially. It was noted that its potential has not been reached yet as there are as number technical and nontechnical challenges and barriers that needs to be overcome in order to unlock its true potential. In this chapter, the current state of quantum computing was explored in terms of quantum hardware innovations, quantum programming and software, quantum computing platforms, quantum supremacy and achievements, and challenges and barriers of quantum computing. The insights gained from these findings via research were analyzed with the systematic comparative framework. It was noted that the hypothesis of this chapter is proven to be correct: "*In Chapter 1, 'Evolution of Quantum Computing,' it was noted that the current quantum computing technology is still in its infancy.*"

Also, the possible gaps were also identified as to why the state of quantum computing is lagging. It was noted that quantum hardware is still facing challenges in terms of material and fabrication. Quantum programming and software analysis reflects that quantum algorithms need to be perfected to get rid of errors and ensure maximum fidelity. Quantum computing platforms are also lacking in terms of their application in real-world cases. While the concept of quantum supremacy may be challengeable, it can be said that the pioneering path toward supremacy has already been laid, and more innovation is required in this field. It is also important to note the technical and non-technical challenges of this realm, and through these findings, it was highlighted that quantum computing has more significant advantages than disadvantages, but its threats must not be ignored in terms of cybersecurity, ethics, and governance.

3.33 FUTURE STATE OF QUANTUM COMPUTING

While quantum computing is still in its infancy, advancement is slowly progressing, and a number of developments will be revealed by leading corporations like IBM, Google, and Riggetti, who are trying to improve their superconducting qubits system. Other cooperations, like Microsoft, are running experiments on their topological qubits, and trapped-ion stakeholders, like Quantinuum and IonQ, are also making significant contributions in terms of quantum development and manufacturing. The most reliable hardware option is the use of silicon and photonics, and they are leading in terms of fidelity at the moment, but the near future is unpredictable when it comes to quantum computing. It is important to note that a significant innovation made in any of these technological areas can achieve possible quantum advantage. Meanwhile, it is essential to invest in solving the technical difficulties like noise, computational speed and processes, and state errors that can be handled to consistently achieve the roadmap.

REFERENCES

[1] Appinio Research, "Appinio Research," 30 October 2023. [Online]. Available: https://www.appinio.com/en/blog/market-research/comparative-analysis.
[2] G. L. Squires, "Quantum Mechanics Physics," 1 March 2025. [Online]. Available: https://www.britannica.com/science/quantum-mechanics-physics.
[3] S. Zorzetti, J. Saniie, H. Johnson, "Exploration of Optimizing FPGA-Based Qubit Controller for Experiments on Superconducting Quantum Computing Hardware," in *IEEE International Conference on Electro Information Technology*, Romeoville, 2023.
[4] W. Zhang, L. Wang, Y. Zhao, Y. Tong, X. Rong, J. Du, X. Qin, "An FPGA-Based Hardware Platform for the Control of Spin-Based Quantum Systems," *IEEE Transactions on Instrumentation and Measurement,* vol. 69, no. 4, pp. 1127–1138, 2019.
[5] J. L. Imaña, P. He, J. Xie, T. Bao, "Hardware Accelerator for RBLWE-Based Post-Quantum Cryptography," in *IEEE International Conference on Hardware/Software Codesign and System Synthesis*, Shanghai, 2022.
[6] K. M. Itoh, D. Kim, K. K. Mehta, T. E. Northup, H. Paik, B. S. Palmer, N. Samarth, S. Sangtawesin, D. W. Steuerman, N. P. de Leon, "Materials Challenges and Opportunities for Quantum Computing Hardware," *Science*, vol. 372, no. 6539, 2021.
[7] E. Moguel, J. Garcia-Alonso, T. Mikkonen, J. M. Murillo, M. Haghparast, "Innovative Approaches to Teaching Quantum Computer Programming and Quantum Software Engineering," in *IEEE International Conference on Quantum Computing and Engineering*, Montreal, 2024.
[8] N. Yoshioka, M. Yamaguchi, "Design by Contract Framework for Quantum Software," in *IEEE/ACM 4th International Workshop on Quantum Software Engineering*, Melbourne, 2023.
[9] M. Piattini, R. P. Del Castillo, S. Sepúlveda, "Developing Hybrid Quantum-Classical Software: A Software Product Line Approach," in *IEEE/ACM 5th International Workshop on Quantum Software Engineering*, Lisbon, 2024.
[10] K. Basu, K. Gaj, U. Guin, J. Xie, "Special Session: The Recent Advance in Hardware Implementation of Post-Quantum Cryptography," in *IEEE 38th VLSI Test Symposium*, San Diego, 2020.
[11] A. Singh, U. Stege, S. Kashani, "Towards a Distributed Quantum Computing Platform for Algorithm Experiments," in *IEEE International Conference on Quantum Computing and Engineering*, Montreal, 2024.
[12] L. Qian, D. Cai, Z. Huang, "A Quantum Computing Simulator Scheme Using MPI Technology on Cloud Platform," in *IEEE International Conference on Electrical Engineering, Big Data and Algorithms*, Changchun, 2022.
[13] M. Ramasami, P. Dreher, "Prototype Container-Based Platform for Extreme Quantum Computing Algorithm Development," in *IEEE High Performance Extreme Computing Conference*, Waltham, 2019.
[14] S. Negi, D. Jain, P. Singh, A. K. Sagar, A. K. Sharma, V. Chauhan, "Quantum Computers: A Review on How Quantum Computing Can Boom AI," in *2nd International Conference on Advance Computing and Innovative Technologies in Engineering*, Greater Noida, 2022.
[15] H. Riel, "Quantum Computing Technology and Roadmap," in *IEEE 52nd European Solid-State Device Research Conference*, Milan, 2022.
[16] W. J. Yun, S. Jung, J. Kim, Y. Kwak, "Quantum Neural Networks: Concepts, Applications, and Challenges," in *Twelfth International Conference on Ubiquitous and Future Networks (ICUFN)*, Jeju Island, 2021.
[17] N. Wang, T. Ji, Y. Shi, C. Wang, S. Wang, "Research Progress of Quantum Artificial Intelligence in Smart City," *IEEE*, vol. 5, no. 2, pp. 116–133, 2024.

[18] Y. Kumar, P. Yadav, N. Tripathi, A. Bhargava, A. Rana, A. Singh, "Overcoming Quantum Hardware Challenges: Navigating the Landscape of Quantum Computing," in *International Conference on Communication, Computer Sciences and Engineering*, Gautam Buddha Nagar, 2024.
[19] T. Mikkonen, J. K. Nurminen, V. Stirbu, M. Haghparast, "Quantum Software Engineering Challenges from Developers' Perspective: Mapping Research Challenges to the Proposed Workflow Model," in *IEEE International Conference on Quantum Computing and Engineering*, Bellevue, 2023.
[20] P. Sajwan, N. Jayapandian, Shubham, "Challenges and Opportunities: Quantum Computing in Machine Learning," in *I-SMAC (IoT in Social, Mobile, Analytics and Cloud)*, Palladam, 2019.
[21] A. S. Jamil, A. H. Abdulrazzaq, N. A. Mawla, R. M. Khudhair, Y. Vasiliu, M. M. Younis, "Progress and Challenges in Quantum Computing Algorithms for NP-Hard Problems," in *36th Conference of Open Innovations Association*, Lappeenranta, 2024.
[22] IBM, "IBM Think," *IBM*, 28 February 2024. [Online]. Available: https://www.ibm.com/think/topics/qubit#:~:text=Qubits%20are%20generally%2C%20although%20not%20exclusively%2C%20created,electrons%2C%20trapped%20ions%2C%20superconducting%20circuits%2C%20and%20atoms.&text=Made%20from%20superconducting%20materials%20operati. [Accessed 21 April 2025].
[23] D-Wave, "Quantum Research," *D-Wave*, [Online]. Available: https://docs.dwavequantum.com/en/latest/quantum_research/quantum_annealing_intro.html. [Accessed 21 April 2025].
[24] Microsoft, "Education," *Microsoft*, 2025. [Online]. Available: https://quantum.microsoft.com/en-us/insights/education/concepts/topological-qubits. [Accessed 21 April 2025].
[25] O. Dial, J. Gambetta, J. Chow, "Quantum Research Blog," *IBM*, 16 November 2021. [Online]. Available: https://www.ibm.com/quantum/blog/127-qubit-quantum-processor-eagle. [Accessed 21 April 2025].
[26] O. Dial, "Quantum Research Blog," *IBM*, 23 March 2022. [Online]. Available: https://www.ibm.com/quantum/blog/eagle-quantum-processor-performance. [Accessed 21 April 2025].
[27] IBM, "IBM News," *IBM*, 9 November 2022. [Online]. Available: https://newsroom.ibm.com/2022-11-09-IBM-Unveils-400-Qubit-Plus-Quantum-Processor-and-Next-Generation-IBM-Quantum-System-Two#:~:text='IBM%20Osprey'%20%2D%20IBM's%20new,Wave%20of%20Computing%20to%20Life. [Accessed 21 April 2025].
[28] O. Dial, "Oezratty," 18 March 2024. [Online]. Available: https://www.oezratty.net/wordpress/2022/assessing-ibm-osprey-quantum-computer/?output=pdf. [Accessed 21 April 2025].
[29] A. Morvan, K. Kechedzhi, "Google Research," *Google*, 10 October 2024. [Online]. Available: https://research.google/blog/validating-random-circuit-sampling-as-a-benchmark-for-measuring-quantum-progress/. [Accessed 21 April 2025].
[30] K. Afifi-Sabet, "Technology," *Livescience*, 11 October 2014. [Online]. Available: https://www.livescience.com/technology/computing/googles-sycamore-quantum-computer-chip-can-now-outperform-the-fastest-supercomputers-new-study-suggests. [Accessed 21 April 2025].
[31] B. Tran, "The Cost of Quantum Computing: How Expensive Is It to Run a Quantum System?," *Patentpc*, 13 April 2025. [Online]. Available: https://patentpc.com/blog/the-cost-of-quantum-computing-how-expensive-is-it-to-run-a-quantum-system-stats-inside. [Accessed 21 April 2025].
[32] Rigetti, "Rigetti Systems Ankaa-3 Quantum Processor," *Rigetti*, 2025. [Online]. Available: https://qcs.rigetti.com/qpus. [Accessed 12 May 2025].
[33] Rigetti, "Rigetti Computing Reports Fourth Quarter and Full-Year 2024 Results," *Rigetti*, 5 March 2025. [Online]. Available: https://investors.rigetti.com/news-releases/

news-release-details/rigetti-computing-reports-fourth-quarter-and-full-year-2024#:~:text=84-qubit%20Ankaa-3%20system,major%20enhancements%20to%20key%20technologies. [Accessed 12 May 2025].
[34] J. Dargan, "6 Best Trapped Ion Quantum Computing Companies [2024]," *Quantum Insider*, 19 February 2022. [Online]. Available: https://thequantuminsider.com/2022/02/19/6-quantum-computing-companies-working-with-trapped-ions/#What_Is_Trapped_Ion_Quantum_Computing. [Accessed 22 April 2025].
[35] Quantinuum, "Quantinuum Accelerates the Path to Universal Fully Fault-Tolerant Quantum Computing," *Quantinuum*, 10 September 2024. [Online]. Available: https://www.quantinuum.com/blog/quantinuum-accelerates-the-path-to-universal-fault-tolerant-quantum-computing-supports-microsofts-ai-and-quantum-powered-compute-platform-and-the-path-to-a-quantum-supercomputer. [Accessed 22 April 2025].
[36] Quantinuum, "Quantinuum," 15 October 2024. [Online]. Available: https://docs.quantinuum.com/systems/data_sheets/Quantinuum%20H1%20Product%20Data%20Sheet.pdf. [Accessed 22 April 2025].
[37] Quantinuum, "Quantinuum Systems," *Quantinuum*, 2025. [Online]. Available: https://www.quantinuum.com/products-solutions/quantinuum-systems/system-model-h1. [Accessed 22 April 2025].
[38] Quantinuum, "Quantinuum Systems," *Quantinuum*, 2025. [Online]. Available: https://www.quantinuum.com/products-solutions/quantinuum-systems/system-model-h2. [Accessed 22 April 2025].
[39] Quantinuum, "Quantinuum Launches Industry-First, Trapped-Ion 56-Qubit Quantum Computer, Breaking Key Benchmark Record," *Quantinuum*, 4 June 2024. [Online]. Available: https://www.quantinuum.com/press-releases/quantinuum-launches-industry-first-trapped-ion-56-qubit-quantum-computer-that-challenges-the-worlds-best-supercomputers. [Accessed 22 April 2025].
[40] Quantinuum, "Quantinuum Helios," *Quantinuum*, 2025. [Online]. Available: https://www.quantinuum.com/products-solutions/quantinuum-systems/helios. [Accessed 22 April 2025].
[41] IonQ, "Atoms Makes Better Quantum Computers," *IonQ*, 2025. [Online]. Available: https://ionq.com/technology. [Accessed 22 April 2025].
[42] "IonQ Harmony," *IonQ*, 2025. [Online]. Available: https://ionq.com/quantum-systems/harmony. [Accessed 22 April 2025].
[43] IonQ, "IonQ Aria," *IonQ*, 2025. [Online]. Available: https://ionq.com/quantum-systems/aria. [Accessed 22 April 2025].
[44] IonQ, "IonQ Forte," *IonQ*, 2025. [Online]. Available: https://ionq.com/quantum-systems/forte. [Accessed 22 April 2025].
[45] IonQ, "IonQ Tempo," *IonQ*, 2025. [Online]. Available: https://ionq.com/quantum-systems/tempo. [Accessed 22 April 2025].
[46] Hyundai, "Corporate Information," *Hyundai*, 2025. [Online]. Available: https://www.hyundai.com/worldwide/en/newsroom/detail/ionq-and-hyundai-motor-expand-partnership-to-use-quantum-computing-for-object-detection-0000000050. [Accessed 22 April 2025].
[47] Duke, "IonQ Named as One of TIME's 100 Most Influential Companies," *Duke*, [Online]. Available: https://otc.duke.edu/news/ionq-named-as-one-of-times-100-most-influential-companies/. [Accessed 22 April 2025].
[48] Psiquantum, "Psiquantum Blueprint," *Psiquantum*, 2025. [Online]. Available: https://www.psiquantum.com/blueprint. [Accessed 22 April 2025].
[49] Xanadu, "Xanadu Introduces Aurora: World's First Scalable, Networked and Modular Quantum Computer," *Xanadu*, 22 January 2025. [Online]. Available: https://www.xanadu.ai/press/xanadu-introduces-aurora-worlds-first-scalable-networked-and-modular-quantum-computer. [Accessed 23 April 2025].

[50] T. Ainsworth, R. N. Alexander, B. Altieri, M. F. Askarani, R. Baby, L. Banchi, B. Q. Baragiola, J. E. Bourassa, R. S. Chadwick, I. Charania, H. Chen, M. J. Collins, P. Contu, N. D'Arcy, G. Dauphinais, R. De Prins, D. Deschenes, I. Di Luch, H. A. Rad, "Scaling and Networking a Modular Photonic Quantum Computer," *Nature*, vol. 638, pp. 912–925, 2025.
[51] Xanadu, "Xanadu," *Xanadu*, 2025. [Online]. Available: https://www.xanadu.ai/. [Accessed 23 April 2025].
[52] P. A. M. Casares, R. dos Reis, M. S. Zini, R. Campos, N. Cruz-Hernández, A.-C. Voigt, A. Lowe, S. Jahangiri, M. A. Martin-Delgado, J. E. Mueller, J. M. Arrazola, A. Delgado, "Simulating Key Properties of Lithium-Ion Batteries with a Fault-Tolerant Quantum Computer," *arxiv*, vol. 2, pp. 1–31, 2023.
[53] E. Cruz-Rico, S. Zhang, J. M. Arrazola, D. Guala, "Tensor-Network Quantum Circuits," *Pennylane*, 6 November 2024. [Online]. Available: https://pennylane.ai/qml/demos/tutorial_tn_circuits. [Accessed 23 April 2025].
[54] IBM, "Introduction to Qiskit," *IBM*, 2025. [Online]. Available: https://docs.quantum.ibm.com/guides. [Accessed 24 April 2025].
[55] Quantumai, "Cirq," *Quantumai*, 2025. [Online]. Available: https://quantumai.google/cirq. [Accessed 27 April 2025].
[56] IBM, "Introduction to Open QASM," *IBM*, 2025. [Online]. Available: https://docs.quantum.ibm.com/guides/introduction-to-qasm. [Accessed 24 April 2025].
[57] IBM, "Build Noise Models," *Quantum*, 2025. [Online]. Available: https://quantum.cloud.ibm.com/docs/en/guides/build-noise-models. [Accessed 24 April 2025].
[58] J. Watrous, "IBM Quantum Learning," *IBM*, 2017–2025. [Online]. Available: https://learning.quantum.ibm.com/. [Accessed 25 April 2025].
[59] I. Smalley, J. Schneider, "What Is Quantum Computing?," *IBM*, 5 August 2024. [Online]. Available: https://www.ibm.com/think/topics/quantum-computing#:~:text=of%20quantum%20information.-,Quantum%20software,generative%20AI%20code%2Dassistance%20tools. [Accessed 25 April 2025].
[60] E. Angelini, C. Nay, "IBM Expands Qiskit, World's Most Performant Quantum Software," *IBM*, 15 May 2024. [Online]. Available: https://newsroom.ibm.com/2024-05-15-IBM-Expands-Qiskit,-Worlds-Most-Performant-Quantum-Software#:~:text=Launched%20in%202017%2C%20Qiskit%2C%20as%20a%20software,over%203%20trillion%20quantum%20circuits%20to%20date.&text=%E2%80%9CLaboratory%20researchers%20. [Accessed 25 April 2025].
[61] Google Quantum AI, "Quantum Virtual Machine," *Google Quantum AI*, 2025. [Online]. Available: https://quantumai.google/cirq/simulate/quantum_virtual_machine. [Accessed 27 April 2025].
[62] Github, "Quantum Library Cirq," *Github*, 2025. [Online]. Available: https://github.com/quantumlib/cirq. [Accessed 27 April 2025].
[63] Quantumai, "Hardware," *Quantumai*, 19 April 2025. [Online]. Available: https://quantumai.google/cirq/hardware. [Accessed 27 April 2025].
[64] Quantumai, "Noise," *Quantumai*, 9 April 2025. [Online]. Available: https://quantumai.google/cirq/noise. [Accessed 27 April 2025].
[65] Quantumai, "Experiments," *Quantumai*, 9 April 2025. [Online]. Available: https://quantumai.google/cirq/experiments. [Accessed 27 April 2025].
[66] Microsoft, "Azure Quantum Documentation," *Microsoft*, 2025. [Online]. Available: https://learn.microsoft.com/en-us/azure/quantum/. [Accessed 27 April 2025].
[67] Microsoft, "Q#," *Microsoft*, [Online]. Available: https://quantum.microsoft.com/en-us/insights/blogs/qsharp. [Accessed 27 April 2025].
[68] Cirq, "Common_Gates," *Github*, [Online]. Available: https://github.com/quantumlib/Cirq/blob/v1.5.0/cirq-core/cirq/ops/common_gates.py#L1219-L1416. [Accessed 28 April 2025].

[69] Microsoft Azure, "Tutorial: Implement a Quantum Random Number Generator in Q#," *Microsoft*, 13 January 2025. [Online]. Available: https://learn.microsoft.com/en-us/azure/quantum/tutorial-qdk-quantum-random-number-generator?tabs=tabid-copilot. [Accessed 28 April 2025].

[70] J. Dargan, "Quantum Computing Companies: A Full 2024 List," *Quantum Insider*, 29 December 2023. [Online]. Available: https://thequantuminsider.com/2023/12/29/quantum-computing-companies/#:~:text=The%20Corporate%20Giants%20in%20Quantum,a%20new%20era%20in%20computation. [Accessed 30 April 2025].

[71] Microsoft, "Pricing Plans for Azure Quantum Providers," *Microsoft*, 4 March 2025. [Online]. Available: https://learn.microsoft.com/en-us/azure/quantum/pricing?tabs=tabid-paygo%2Ctabid-paygoPasqal%2Ctabid-H2. [Accessed 30 April 2025].

[72] Amazon, "Amazon Braket Pricing," *Amazon*, 2025. [Online]. Available: https://aws.amazon.com/braket/pricing/. [Accessed 30 March 2025].

[73] IBM, "Case Studies," *IBM*, [Online]. Available: https://www.ibm.com/quantum/case-studies. [Accessed 30 April 2025].

[74] The Quantum AI Team, "3 Real-World Problems That Quantum Computers Could Help Solve," *Google*, 14 April 2025. [Online]. Available: https://blog.google/technology/research/google-quantum-computer-real-world-applications/. [Accessed 30 April 2025].

[75] Microsoft, "Microsoft," *Microsoft*, [Online]. Available: https://quantum.microsoft.com/. [Accessed 30 April 2025].

[76] Quantum Insider, "Quantumchallenge," *Quantum Insider*, [Online]. Available: https://qcc.thequantuminsider.com/#slide-5. [Accessed 30 April 2025].

[77] Spinquanta, "How Quantum Computing Benefits Financial Services [2025]," *Spinquanta*, 2025. [Online]. Available: https://www.spinquanta.com/news-detail/how-quantum-computing-benefits-financial-services20250219023634. [Accessed 1 May 2025].

[78] Quantum News, "Quantum Computing in Finance: Quantum Portfolio Optimization," *Quantumzeitgeist*, 18 September 2024. [Online]. Available: https://quantumzeitgeist.com/quantum-computing-in-finance-quantum-portfolio-optimization/. [Accessed 1 May 2025].

[79] The Quant, "IonQ and GE Kick-Off Initiative in Risk Analysis to Look at Complex Systems," *Quantumzeitgeist*, 21 September 2025. [Online]. Available: https://quantumzeitgeist.com/ionq-and-ge-kick-off-initiative-in-risk-analysis-to-look-at-complex-systems/. [Accessed 1 May 2025].

[80] Finextra, "JPMorgan Leads Quantum Computing Arms Race," *Finextra*, 20 March 2025. [Online]. Available: https://www.finextra.com/newsarticle/45688/jpmorgan-leads-quantum-computing-arms-race. [Accessed 1 May 2025].

[81] Z. Yin, X. Li, D. Ma, S. Yi, Z. Zhang, C. Zou, K. Bu, M. Dai, J. Yue, Y. Chen, X. Zhang, S. Zhang, W. Li, "A Hybrid Quantum Computing Pipeline for Real World Drug Discovery," *Nature*, vol. 14, no. 16942, pp. 1–15, 2024.

[82] S. Singal, "How Quantum Computing Is Revolutionising Drug Development," *DDW*, 8 April 2025. [Online]. Available: https://www.ddw-online.com/how-quantum-computing-is-revolutionising-drug-development-34423-202504/#:~:text=QC%20enables%20precise%20modelling%20of,potential%20therapeutic%20compounds%20more%20effectively. [Accessed 3 May 2025].

[83] M. Ivezic, "Quantum Technology Use Cases in Supply Chain & Logistics," *Postquantum*, 10 June 2023. [Online]. Available: https://postquantum.com/quantum-computing/use-cases-logistics/. [Accessed 3 May 2025].

[84] A. G. Rodriguez, "Cybersecurity Implications of Quantum Computing and Its Combined Use with Artificial Intelligence," *UNISCI*, pp. 137–153, 2025.

[85] Arute, F., Arya, K., Babbush, R., Bacon, D., Bardin, J. C., Barends, R., ... & Martinis, J. M., "Quantum Supremacy Using a Programmable Superconducting Processor," *Nature*, vol. 574, pp. 505–511, 2019.

[86] A. Cho, "IBM Casts Doubt on Google's Claims of Quantum Supremacy," *Science*, 23 October 2019. [Online]. Available: https://www.science.org/content/article/ibm-casts-doubt-googles-claims-quantum-supremacy#:~:text=The%20Google%20group%20reiterates%20its%20claim%20that,Energy%20that%20is%20currently%20the%20world's%20fastest.&text=IBM%20says%20the%20threshold%20for%20qua. [Accessed 5 May 2025].

[87] R. Hackett, "Google Claims 'Quantum Supremacy,' Marking a Major Milestone in Computing," *Fortune*, 20 October 2019. [Online]. Available: https://fortune.com/2019/09/20/google-claims-quantum-supremacy/. [Accessed 5 May 2025].

[88] G. Kilai, "The Case against Google's Claims of 'Quantum Supremacy': A Very Short Introduction," *Gil Kilai's Blog*, 9 December 2024. [Online]. Available: https://gilkalai.wordpress.com/2024/12/09/the-case-against-googles-claims-of-quantum-supremacy-a-very-short-introduction/#:~:text=1)%20Google's%20supremacy%20claims%20(from,even%20with%20tensor%20network%20contraction. [Accessed 5 May 2025].

[89] Y. Rinott, T. Shoham, G. Kalai, "Questions and Concerns about Google's Quantum Supremacy Claim," *Research Gate*, pp. 1–49, 2023.

[90] H. Gharibyan, "Quantum Advantage: Unlocking Potential beyond Limits," *BlueQubit*, 29 January 2025. [Online]. Available: https://www.bluequbit.io/quantum-advantage. [Accessed 6 May 2025].

[91] H. Gahribyan, "What Is Quantum Error Correction: The Key to Quantum Computing," *Bluequbit*, 9 January 2025. [Online]. Available: https://www.bluequbit.io/quantum-error-correction#:~:text=Google%20is%20a%20major%20player,as%20more%20qubits%20are%20added. [Accessed 6 May 2025].

[92] Milvus, "What Are the Challenges of Scaling up Qubit Systems?," *Milvus*, 2025. [Online]. Available: https://milvus.io/ai-quick-reference/what-are-the-challenges-of-scaling-up-qubit-systems. [Accessed 7 May 2025].

[93] Plainconcepts, "Quantum Computing: What Are Its Challenges and Potential for Companies?," *Plainconcepts*, 16 April 2025. [Online]. Available: https://www.plainconcepts.com/quantum-computing-potential-challenges/#Scalability. [Accessed 7 May 2025].

[94] M. Englbrecht, R. König, N. Peard, S. Bravyi, "Correcting Coherent Errors with Surface Codes," *Nature*, vol. 4, no. 55, pp. 1–6, 2018.

[95] Google Quantum AI and Collaborators, "Quantum Error Correction below the Surface Code Threshold," *Nature*, vol. 638, pp. 920–927, 2024.

[96] M. Ivezic, "Quantum Errors and Quantum Error Correction (QEC) Methods," *Postquantum*, 10 May 2023. [Online]. Available: https://postquantum.com/quantum-computing/quantum-error-correction/#categories-of-quantum-error-correction-approaches. [Accessed 7 May 2025].

[97] Schander, "Hardware-Based Advancements in Quantum Error Correction," *Quantumgrad*, 1 December 2024. [Online]. Available: https://www.quantumgrad.com/article/819. [Accessed 7 May 2025].

[98] A. W. Senior, F. J. H. Heras, T. Edlich, A. Davies, M. Newman, C. Jones, K. Satzinger, M. Y. Niu, S. Blackwell, G. Holland, D. Kafri, J. Atalaya, C. Gidney, D. Hassabis, S. Boixo, H. Neven, P. Kohli, J. Bausch, "Learning High-Accuracy Error Decoding for Quantum Processors," *Nature*, vol. 635, pp. 834–861, 2024.

[99] Spinq, "Master Quantum Error Correction: An Essential Guide to QEC," *Spinq*, 12 February 2025. [Online]. Available: https://www.spinquanta.com/news-detail/master-quantum-error-correction-an-essential-guide-to-qec20250212053845. [Accessed 7 May 2025].

[100] A. Adewusi, A. G. Adeleke, L. Akwawa, C. F. Azubuko, O. Oyeniran, "Advancements in Quantum Computing and Their Implications for Software Development," *Computer Science & IT Research Journal*, vol. 4, no. 3, pp. 577–593, 2023.

[101] SpinQ, "Quantum Computer Price Guide: Cost & Options Explained," *SpinQ*, 1 January 2025. [Online]. Available: https://www.spinquanta.com/news-detail/quantum-computer-price-guide-cost-options-explained20250122054717. [Accessed 8 May 2025].

[102] R. Joshi, "Quantum Computing: On the Cusp of Commercial Viability?," *Frontier Enterprise*, 1 June 2023. [Online]. Available: https://www.frontier-enterprise.com/quantum-computing-on-the-cusp-of-commercial-viability/#:~:text=The%20cost%20issue%20is%20complex,establishing%20a%20business%20case%20shifts. [Accessed 8 May 2025].

[103] Cryptomathic, "Quantum Computing and Cryptography Infrastructure Investments," *Cryptomathic*, 9 January 2021. [Online]. Available: https://www.cryptomathic.com/blog/what-is-quantum-computing-and-how-does-it-relate-to-todays-cryptography-infrastructure-investments. [Accessed 8 May 2025].

[104] K. Moskvitch, "What Is 'Quantum Advantage' and How Can Businesses Benefit from It?," *World Economic Forum*, 9 April 2025. [Online]. Available: https://www.weforum.org/stories/2025/04/quantum-computing-benefit-businesses/. [Accessed 8 May 2025].

[105] H. Hall, "Quantum Industry Sees Rapid Growth in 2025, Report Finds," *R&D World*, 25 March 2025. [Online]. Available: https://www.rdworldonline.com/quantum-industry-sees-rapid-growth-in-2025-report-finds/. [Accessed 8 May 2025].

[106] K. Peltz, R. Zemmel, M. Zesko, N. Mohr, "Five Lessons from AI on Closing Quantum's Talent Gap—before It's Too Late," *Mckinsey Digital*, 1 December 2022. [Online]. Available: https://www.mckinsey.com/capabilities/mckinsey-digital/our-insights/five-lessons-from-ai-on-closing-quantums-talent-gap-before-its-too-late. [Accessed 8 May 2025].

[107] B. Marr, "Quantum Talent Wars: The Hidden Crisis Threatening Tech's Next Frontier," *Forbes*, 2 May 2025. [Online]. Available: https://www.forbes.com/sites/bernardmarr/2025/05/02/quantum-talent-wars-the-hidden-crisis-threatening-techs-next-frontier/. [Accessed 8 May 2025].

[108] R. Morrison, "Quantum Computing Has a Looming Skills Gap," *Tech Monitor*, 13 November 2023. [Online]. Available: http://techmonitor.ai/hardware/quantum/quantum-computing-has-a-looming-skills-gap?cf-view. [Accessed 8 May 2025].

[109] Averyfairbank, "Quantum Computing: Skills Shortage Slowing Quantum Revolution," *Averyfairbank*, 18 January 2024. [Online]. Available: https://averyfairbank.com/quantum-computing-skills-shortage-slowing-quantum-revolution/. [Accessed 8 May 2025].

[110] I. &. T. Department for Science, "National Quantum Strategy," Crown Copyright, London, 2023.

[111] M. Swayne, "Governments Face Key Challenges in Quantum Technology Policy, OECD Report Finds," QuantumInsider, 8 February 2025. [Online]. Available: https://thequantuminsider.com/2025/02/08/governments-face-key-challenges-in-quantum-technology-policy-oecd-report-finds/#:~:text=One%20immediate%20challenge%20is%20the,competition%20for%20expertise%20more%20intense. [Accessed 8 May 2025].

[112] O. D. E. Papers, "A Quantum Technologies Policy Primer Report," OECD Publishing, Paris, 2025.

[113] H. Paik, A. Cross, Z. Nazario, P. Nation, "The IBM Quantum Heavy Hex Lattice," *IBM*, 7 July 2021. [Online]. Available: https://www.ibm.com/quantum/blog/heavy-hex-lattice. [Accessed 14 May 2025].

[114] C. Kim, Y. Kim, Y. Kwon, J. Kang, "New Design of Three-Qubit System with Three Transmons and a Single Fixed-Frequency Resonator Coupler," *Nature*, vol. 15, no. 12134, pp. 1–12, 2025.

[115] g. Newswire, "Rigetti Computing Launches 84-Qubit Ankaa™-3 System; Achieves 99.5% Median Two-Qubit Gate Fidelity Milestone," *Rigetti*, 23 December 2024. [Online]. Available: https://investors.rigetti.com/news-releases/news-release-details/rigetti-computing-launches-84-qubit-ankaatm-3-system-achieves#:~:text=Users%20will%20be%20able%20to,increasingly%20higher%20performance%20quantum%20computers. [Accessed 14 May 2025].

[116] Pappas, D. P., Field, M., Kopas, C. J., Howard, J. A., Wang, X., Lachman, E., ... & Mutus, J. Y., "ABAA!—Alternating-Bias Assisted Annealing of Amorphous Oxide Tunnel Junctions," *Springer Nature*, p. all, 2024.

[117] M. Field, C. Kopas, J. A. Howard, X. Wang, E. Lachman, L. Zhou, J. Oh, K. Yadavalli, E. A. Sete, A. Bestwick, M. Kramer, J. Y. Mutus, D. P. Pappas, "Alternating Bias Assisted Annealing of Amorphous Oxide Tunnel Junctions," *arxiv*, pp. 1–7, 2024.

[118] Quantinuum, "Quantum Charge-coupled Device (QCCD)," *Quantinuum*, 2025. [Online]. Available: https://www.quantinuum.com/glossary-item/quantum-charge-coupled-device-qccd. [Accessed 14 May 2025].

[119] J. M. Dreiling, C. Figgatt, J. P. Gaebler, S. A. Moses, M. S. Allman, C. H. Baldwin, M. Foss-Feig, D. Hayes, K. Mayer, C. Ryan-Anderson, B. Neyenhuis, J. M. Pino, "Demonstration of the Trapped-Ion Quantum CCD Computer Architecture," *Nature*, vol. 592, pp. 209–213, 2021.

[120] D. Kafri, W. C. Campbell, R. Islam, E. E. Edwards, Z.-X. Gong, G.-D. Lin, L.-M. Duan, J. Kim, K. Kim, C. Monroe, S. Korenblit, "Quantum Simulation of Spin Models on an Arbitrarylattice with Trapped Ions," *Journal of Physics*, vol. 14, pp. 1–9, 2012.

[121] D. J. Kim, "Reconfigurable Multicore Quantum Architecture," *IonQ*, 8 January 2025. [Online]. Available: https://ionq.com/resources/reconfigurable-multicore-quantum-architecture. [Accessed 15 May 2025].

[122] Psiquantum, "Fusion-Based Quantum Computation (FBQC)," *Psiquantum*, 2021. [Online]. Available: https://www.psiquantum.com/news-import/fusion-based-quantum-computation-fbqc. [Accessed 15 May 2025].

[123] C. Choucair, "Xanadu Introduces Aurora: World's First Scalable, Networked and Modular Quantum Computer," *Quantuminsider*, 22 January 2025. [Online]. Available: https://thequantuminsider.com/2025/01/22/xanadu-announces-aurora-a-universal-photonic-quantum-computer/#:~:text=Insider%20Brief:,racks%20and%20millions%20of%20qubits. [Accessed 15 May 2025].

[124] Google, "Cross Entrophy Benchmarking," *Google*, 9 April 2025. [Online]. Available: https://quantumai.google/cirq/noise/qcvv/xeb_theory. [Accessed 16 May 2025].

[125] D. Kremer, B. Johnson, R. Mandelbaum, P. Nation, "Qiskit Leads Quantum Software Development Kits in Performance, Testing Shows," *IBM*, 16 September 2024. [Online]. Available: https://www.ibm.com/quantum/blog/qiskit-performance. [Accessed 17 May 2025].

[126] S. Woerner, R. Davis, C. Zoufal, "New Quantum Optimization Benchmarking Library Invites Researchers to Put Algorithms to the Test," *IBM*, 14 May 2025. [Online]. Available: https://www.ibm.com/quantum/blog/quantum-optimization-benchmarking. [Accessed 17 May 2025].

[127] M. Schicker, "QOLIB—Quantum Optimisation Library," *Git Zib*, 1 April 2025. [Online]. Available: https://git.zib.de/qopt/qoblib-quantum-optimization-benchmarking-library/. [Accessed 17 May 2025].

4 A Systematic Literature Review of Quantum Computing

Sarvesh Chand, Sam Goundar, Deepika Bandhana, J. Avanija, and Ushik Shrestha Khwakhali

4.1 INTRODUCTION

Over the last decades, quantum computing has really moved into the real world—from a purely theoretical idea into a much more mature area that seems destined to revolutionize the previously unimaginable scope of computing powers (Nielsen & Chuang, 2010). It is more soon than later going out of laboratory into really applicable technology, opening up to impacts really on cryptography, optimization problems, drug discovery, financial modeling, and more with political changes in quantum algorithms, hardware architectures, and quantum error correction protocols (Preskill, 2018). In this case, a systematic literature review provides a formal, critical, and coherent account of the quantum computing research-the reconstruction of internal history, the mapping-out of current developments, and the foreshadowing of future trajectories.

Systematic literature review serves to synthesize knowledge, make trend-spotting, critique methodologies, and evince gaps deserving attention for subsequent explorations (Barenco et al., 1995). Such a review assumes even greater importance in the case of quantum computing since the interdisciplinary field is evolving rapidly (Steane, 1998). Classical computing paradigms are based on classical bits that follow the rules of classical physics; however, quantum computing employs qubits, which use superposition and entanglement-these have no classical comparison anywhere (Nielsen & Chuang, 2010). As a result, the field is not only converged but also opens up many different methodologies and perspectives of research among various disciplines, namely, physics, computer science, mathematics, and engineering. It provides a much deeper systematic scrutiny of the literature, helping one to appreciate significant contributions in different areas and how these come together in current-day quantum computing (Preskill, 2018).

On top of this, the importance of this review statement stems from the conjunction between the fundamental theoretical insights and their types' applications in essentially the real world. Quantum theory promises not only the exponential speedup in algorithms for problems generally viewed as intractable for classical computers (Shor, 1994) but also the advance of the quantum hardware by major technology companies

 DOI: 10.1201/9781003538950-5

and research consortia over the state of qubit coherence times, gate fidelity, and qubit scaling. Google has demonstrated "quantum supremacy" for a particular computational task (Arute et al., 2019; Bremner et al., 2016); IBM has not stopped last year in increasingly investing in superconducting qubit architectures available through cloud-based quantum computing (Booth et al., 2009). Here, an overview, systematically compiled, would be able to set these hardware accomplishments and their theoretical frameworks, but simply offer a little clearer understanding of the pathways to quantum advantage—pragmatically, how quantum devices are expected to solve problems more rapidly, or, at least, more accurately, than best classical algorithms can manage (Harrow & Montanaro, 2017; Boixo et al., 2018; Bremner et al., 2016).

This review in due course offers an overview of quantum computing taking it within a historical panorama context, beginning at its first footing in the 1980s, when Richard Feynman proposed the requirement of devices other than classical ones—such as quantum-mechanical computing devices—to be able to simulate quantum processes efficiently (Feynman, 1982). The literature then proceeds to a comprehensive survey of those pioneering theoretical frameworks, such as Deutsch's universal quantum computer concept (Deutsch, 1985; Jozsa, 1991). Its general development from early works on quantum algorithms, of which the most important are Shor's algorithm for the factorization of integers (Shor, 1994) and Grover's algorithm for database search (Grover, 1997), is also discussed in the literature. This review also points out some important contributions made by quantum information theory to the formalization of concepts, such as quantum entanglement, quantum cryptography, and quantum error correction (Ekert, 1991; Steane, 1996; Dieks, 1982). Organizing this historical trajectory helps one appreciate the transition of quantum computation from that of a small theoretical idea into a multidisciplinary, cutting-edge research area that has caught the eye of not just academia, but also the attention of government agencies, startups, and multinational companies (Preskill, 2018).

The second important thing that this literature review seeks is to evaluate the range of contemporary research on quantum computing to highlight some of the prevailing themes and approaches (Brylinski & Brylinski, 2002). These include challenges in implementing physical qubits, such as superconducting circuits, trapped ions, and topological qubits, all the way toward designing quantum algorithms and beyond (Kjaergaard et al., 2020). Hence, this review includes studies that deal with qubit technology, quantum error correction codes, quantum cryptographic protocols, quantum software developments, and specialized quantum hardware. This review puts into perspective a wide range of undergraduate and graduate research papers, conference proceedings, and industry reports and categorizes and systematizes research landscapes. Moreover, it illustrates how methodological approaches have made some of it increasingly into much diversified methodologies. Indeed, it has gone from being purely theoretical in the very initial research to experimental demonstrations, engineering of quantum devices, and the development of an integrated software and hardware ecosystem (Paler et al., 2017; Laflamme et al., 1998). This spectrum of inquiry necessitates a systematic approach to really capture therein the breadth of ongoing work and emerging directions.

It is advisable to delineate also under this point the criteria prescribed and procedures adopted in guiding the processes of the collection, analysis, and synthesis of the literature (Tranfield et al., 2003). A systematic review pursues stringent methodological approaches with the intention of minimizing bias and ensuring reproducibility, unlike a traditional narrative review, which focuses on a narrower set of topics or adopts an even less structured approach. The review presented in this chapter includes a clear description of the time period targeted, the databases consulted, and the search strings used. Such well-known academic databases for quantum computing literature include underscore such as IEEE Xplore, ACM Digital Library, arXiv, Web of Science, and Scopus, among others (Gomes et al., 2018; Kok et al., 2007). Given the explosive growth of quantum computing research over the last few years, it has been carefully examined from the beginning of the 1990s—when interest was building around quantum algorithms and entanglement—up to the latest discoveries with experimental demonstrations and hardware improvements speeding up (Preskill, 2018). The systematic review makes a replicable approach available with complete record of every procedure that has thus been adopted, besides bringing transparency in data collection.

The next task is to look into trends in quantum computing research after forage scoping and process review. Trends may include changes in the publication growth rate, establishment of cooperative networks, and parallel consumption with moving emphasis from pure theoretical constructions to real-world applications and commercial endeavors (Ladd et al., 2010). Given the harmony that exists between academic, industrial, and government organizations, an important indicator of where the area is going to be manifested by the funding landscape and patent activity. The present research analyzes the trends that sharpen the understanding of the maturation process of quantum computing, directing entrants and veterans to the most promising avenues of research. For example, in the early 2000s, this mostly resided within evidence of quantum gates at small scale in the confines of laboratories. A more recent emphasis is on scaling up the number of qubits in controllable quantum devices and improving error correction protocols to enable fault tolerance (Devitt et al., 2013). In this sense, a systematic literature review reveals the transformations in the evolution of the discipline while providing salience of evidence-based projections for the near future.

This review also investigates the central unresolved challenges with regard to quantum computing. One such challenge is the phenomenon of decoherence; quantum states are perceived to lose coherence extremely rapidly through the environmental noise, eroding the computational advantage of quantum algorithms (Preskill, 2018). Another challenge concerns the development of robust quantum error correction codes that cope with actual qubit imperfections with a feasible overhead in extra qubits and quantum gates (Fowler et al., 2012). From the theory perspective, they still inquire into the sharp boundaries between classical and quantum computational complexities, raising deep questions as to what quantum computing can achieve and what, in principle, it cannot (Aaronson, 2013; Bremner et al., 2016). Further challenge constitutes the design of a standardized quantum software stack that incorporates seamlessly with various quantum hardware backends, especially with the approach of this so-called NISQ era, or the era of noisy intermediate-scale quantum (Preskill, 2018). This is the review that highlights and discusses the identification and categorization of challenges, meaning that while great progress has been made, quantum computing still has to overcome a lot to reach maturity.

Identifying research gaps is as vital for this review. Such gaps may be related to a theoretical models that has been less studied, promising hardware architectures but whose experimental results have yet to reflect its potential or theoretical promising algorithmic approaches that still require more sophisticated error mitigation techniques (Castlevvi, 2017). For example, topological quantum computing, which makes use of anyonic states in specific condensed matter systems, is generating an abundance of theoretical excitement regarding its robustness against local errors (Nayak et al., 2008). Unfortunately, practical implementations are still early, and there is a need for more robust architectures that are experimentally validated. Thus, quantum machine learning now seems to spread wings over a wide possibility of an emerging field which lies at the intersection of quantum computing and artificial intelligence; however, various pertinent issues may arise with respect to realizable speedups and optimal data types for quantum acceleration (Biamonte et al., 2017; Harrow et al., 2009). The review identifies these gaps so that focused research activities can be carried out to answer some of the most fundamental questions and speed up the transition from proof-of-concept experiments to scalable, fault-tolerant quantum systems.

Besides, this systematic review of literature will, later in this chapter, present a comprehensive discussion on future directions based on the earlier noted trends, challenges, and gaps. One of the major future directions is in addressing the internet of quantum computing and already existing computational ecosystems, a case in point is cloud environments and hybrid quantum-classical algorithms (Cleve et al., 1998). As quantum processors scale in terms of qubit count and fidelity, the interaction between these processors and classical high-performance computing resources is expected to open new possibilities in optimization, simulation, and machine learning applications (Biamonte et al., 2017; Barz et al., 2013). Another anticipated area of growth is the synergy that will develop between quantum computing and other dual emerging technologies, such as quantum communication networks and quantum sensors, which may ultimately lead to a complete quantum internet (Wehner et al., 2018). By establishing quantum computing in that wider scope of quantum technological ecosystems, the review stresses the need for multidisciplinary endeavors that will adopt hardware, software, theoretical, and application-oriented approaches simultaneously.

It is high time that this literature review illuminates not only the current state of the field but its real-world meanings to society at large, according to Preskill (2018). Classical cryptographic methods currently securing online transactions threaten new vulnerabilities to quantum attacks, making quantum-safe cryptography a current example (Bernstein et al., 2009). All governments worldwide have made considerable investments to fund quantum research initiatives, which also reflect the national strategic importance of keeping pace with new quantum technologies (Taylor, 2021). Through this review, policymakers, funding bodies, and non-specialists gain a roadmap of quantum computing's trajectory, thereby enabling informed decision-making on resource allocation, risk management, and long-term planning in rapidly evolving technological landscapes.

This systematic literature review of quantum computing is very important for a multitude of reasons. First, it brings together the disparate knowledge from academic fields, industry white papers, and government-sponsored research into a coherent tale of the journey this field has covered—from its theoretical roots to a time of rapid development today. Second, it uses such rigorous methodological framework—it clearly states search databases and time spans, as well as inclusion/exclusion criteria—to guarantee unbiasedness and reproducibility. Third, it provides a detailed analysis of trends and challenges, thereby not only showing the major achievements of the quantum computing community but also the challenges that are still there. Fourth, it maps out the existing research gaps, which, if filled, would trigger a cascade of breakthroughs. Finally, it looks into the future of quantum computing, with great attention to the interaction between academia, industry, and government, as well as the fusion of the quantum computing with other emergent technologies.

Generally, this introductory section seeks to provide the necessary context for both the rationale and relevance of systematic literature reviews, as applied to quantum computing. The next sections of this chapter will familiarize readers with methodologies used to conduct the review, including the mechanisms employed in the formulation of search strings and queries to databases so as to capture the width of quantum computing research. Further, the chapter analyzes the data from both quantitative as well as qualitative findings, thus providing an organized panorama of the field to the reader. At the end of the chapter, one should be able to expect more than a summary of all the happenings regarding quantum computing; one should also have an active vision for where the field most critically needs innovation and discovery to advance. All in all, this review intends to serve as a scholarly resource and at the same time strategic guide for any researcher, policymaker, or technologist engaged in tackling the complicated and ever-changing waters of quantum computing research.

4.2 METHODOLOGY

While this chapter attempts to portray a panoramic view of quantum computing research, anchoring the review in a systematic review methodology—notably the PRISMA (*P*referred *R*eporting *I*tems for *S*ystematic Reviews and *M*eta-Analyses) framework—would indeed ensure rigor, transparency, and reproducibility (Moher et al., 2009). The growth of publications in the fast-evolving fields of quantum computing is indeed intimidating for many conventional narrative reviews. Systematic application of procedural guidelines imparts structure to the process and makes it more reliable (Kitchenham & Charters, 2007; Tranfield et al., 2003). In the next section, we lay out in detail each phase of our methodological approach—selection of an appropriate model all the way to data analysis—so that future researchers are able to replicate or validate this work.

4.3 MODEL/THEORY/FRAMEWORK

Now this review is based on PRISMA modified for engineering and computer science contexts (Moher et al., 2009). From the beginning, PRISMA has been intended for use in medical or healthcare research; however, over the years, it has been adopted to more technical applications in very clear directions on how to identify, screen, assess, and include relevant literature (Kitchenham & Charters, 2007). These stages reduce the risk of missing significant studies or including irrelevant sources by systematic detailing of PRISMA.

4.4 WHY PRISMA FOR QUANTUM COMPUTING?

1. **Multidisciplinary Nature**: The field of quantum computing converges physics, mathematics, and computer engineering. PRISMA has structured coverage to ensure that all possible angles (Tranfield et al., 2003) are captured.
2. **Literature Explosion**: A gradual approach to the ever-increasing publications on quantum hardware and algorithms enable transparency efforts and bias minimization.
3. **Reproducibility**: Legislative documentation of database searches, eligibility and exclusion criteria, and methods of data extraction make PRISMA a viable reproducible template for future reviews.

4.5 LENGTH AND JUSTIFICATION

Adaptation of PRISMA into quantum computing has meant refining the standard checklist that addresses health needs into its engineering version. Kitchenham and Charters (2007), who present guidelines for performing systematic reviews in software engineering, were consulted to include such specificities in the domain. Most importantly, the iterative nature of this adaptation: certain early pilot searches showed quite quickly that research on quantum computing is distributed over several repositories—such as arXiv, a preprint server pertaining to physics, IEEE Xplore, which is more engineering oriented, and other multidisciplinary databases like Scopus. These steps made the standard PRISMA flowchart for systematic reviews prepared by Moher et al. in (2009) a good starting point. We documented each modification clearly (by, for example, adding arXiv preprints with high citation counts as eligible), which better strengthens the review process's credibility and repeatability.

4.6 WHY THIS METHODOLOGY?

Here are some of the reasons that systematic approaches are important:

1. **Transparency**: PRISMA, along with Kitchenham's guidelines (2004), specifies to clearly articulate the search strings, databases used in searches, and all inclusion/exclusion criteria. Such explicitness avoids ambiguity about how the review was made.
2. **Reproducibility**: Filtering of unnecessary research studies must be recorded so that other researchers can reproduce or refine the procedure, which is very important in a constantly improving field.
3. **Least Bias**: The use of a normalized framework makes it easier for reviewers not to be compelled to favor studies that are more familiar or have received more publicity while overlooking those that have fewer citations but are groundbreaking (Kitchenham & Charters, 2007). A systematic protocol helps minimize this inherent bias.
4. **Completeness of Synthesis**: Research in quantum computing cuts across specialized fields (quantum algorithms, hardware, cryptography, among others). Strict adherence to a rigorous approach, therefore, ensures a holistic synthesis of findings rather than fragmented ones.

4.7 STEP-BY-STEP PROCESS

4.7.1 Search Strategy

1. **Databases**: We selected Scopus, IEEE Xplore, SpringerLink, ACM Digital Library, arXiv, and Google Scholar, as shown in Figures 4.1 and 4.2, as data providers. This scope embodies the interdisciplinary character of quantum computing. Physics, computer science, engineering, and mathematics—the interdisciplinary sciences—all compose it.
2. **Search Strings**: Following the identification step guided by PRISMA (Moher et al., 2009), we produced Boolean queries embedding keywords like:
   - "quantum computing" OR "quantum computation"
   - "quantum algorithms" OR "quantum hardware"
   - "qubits" OR "superposition" OR "entanglement"
   - "NISQ" OR "fault-tolerant quantum"
   - "quantum error correction" OR "quantum cryptography"

   We modified the strings accordingly to each of the indexed database because of its indexing system. For example, Scopus allows field-specific queries, while arXiv permits broader text searches.
3. **Cross-Time Period**: As shown in Figure 4.3, the exposure of the publication material constituted time spans from the early 1990s to present to take into consideration the incurring advances in quantum computing since Shor's (1994) and Grover's (1997) substantive works.

4.8 SCREENING AND ELIGIBILITY

Based on the references sourced, we removed any duplicates and underwent a two-step screening process:

1. **Title/Abstract Scanning**: This excludes irrelevant articles that might discuss quantum computing in passing; e.g., "quantum dot solar cells" might be excluded if not specifically mentioned in regard with computation.

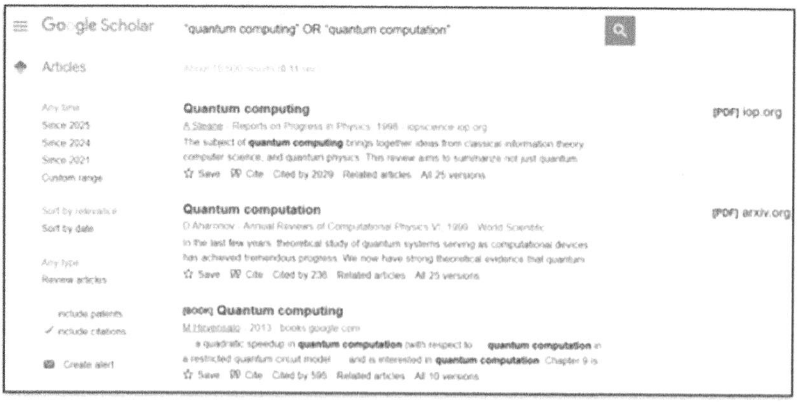

FIGURE 4.1 Google Scholar search.

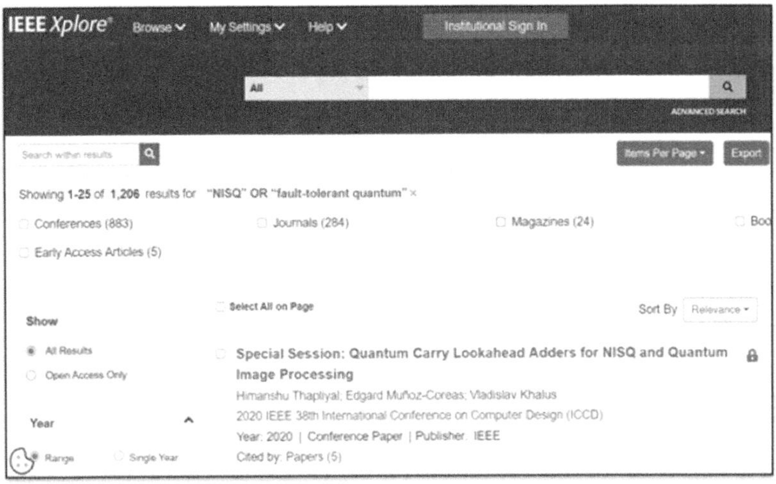

FIGURE 4.2 IEEE Xplore search.

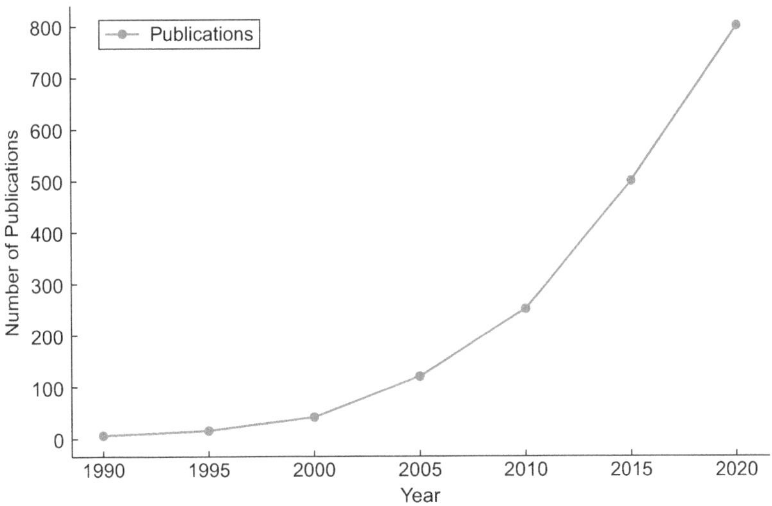

FIGURE 4.3 Publication growth over time in quantum computing.

2. **Full-Text Assessment**: For those articles that passed first screening criteria, full texts were obtained and inclusion/exclusion criteria were applied.
   - **Inclusion Criteria**:
     - Peer-reviewed articles, conference proceedings, key technical reports, or high-impact arXiv preprints.
     - English language.
     - Substantial focus on quantum computing (hardware, algorithms, or applications).

- Publication date within the defined range.
- **Exclusion Criteria**:
  - Non-English works.
  - Editorials, opinion pieces, and abstracts without full text.
  - Studies with minimal relevance in computing, examples of which are purely quantum biology or chemistry without computational modeling.

4.9 DATA EXTRACTION

We utilized a data extraction sheet adapted from Kitchenham's guidelines for each article that passed the eligibility criteria in order to collect information on bibliographic details such as author, title, journal/conference, year, and citation count (if any).

- **Study Type**: Theoretical, experimental, simulation, review, or conceptual.
- **Quantum Focus**: Hardware approach (superconducting, ion trap, photonics), algorithmic scope (e.g., factoring, search, machine learning), cryptography, or foundational theory (e.g., quantum error correction).
- **Key Contributions**: Summary of main findings, challenges identified, future directions suggested.

This standardized form ensured that data are recorded in a consistent manner which allowed comparison across different subfields in quantum computing.

This time around, we collected data from a data extraction sheet adapted from Kitchenham's guidelines (Kitchenham, 2004) for each eligible article in the following aspects:

- Bibliographic Details: Authors, title, journal/conference, year, and citation count(if available).
- Study Type: Theoretical, experimental, simulation, review, or conceptual.
- Quantum Focus: Hardware approach (superconducting, ion trap, photonics), algorithmic scope (e.g., factoring, search, machine learning), cryptography, or foundational theory (e.g., quantum error correction).
- Key Contributions: Summary of main findings, challenges identified, future directions suggested.

This ensured consistency in the manner data were recorded against which comparisons could then be made across the various subfields within quantum computing.

4.10 QUALITY ASSESSMENT

While GRADE is mostly used in SLRs of medicine, we carried out both a relevance- and a citation-based ranking:

- **Citation Metric**: Articles with many citations were signaled for possible relevance to the field. However, we did keep the things in mind that we shouldn't compare citation volume with quality, especially in a newer kind of research.

- **Critique**: We have been given first preference to more reputed journals or conferences, such as *Physical Review Letters*, *Nature*, and *Quantum Information & Computation*. Even though influential arXiv preprints were included, published work should show large endorsement or subsequent citations.
- **Recentness**: The new-age breakthroughs in quantum computing transform at a pace faster than change itself. Hence, we also weighed recent input that might not have as extensive citation records as that of others.

4.11 DATA COLLECTION

This review takes into consideration both qualitative and quantitative meanings of data.

- **Quantitative**: Such data include numbers such as publications, citation counts, word occurrence frequencies (e.g., "quantum supremacy," "topological qubits"), and authorship patterns.
- **Qualitative**: It provides thematic perspectives regarding hardware trends (superconducting vs. trapped-ion qubits), algorithmic advances (quantum machine learning), and numerous challenges (e.g., decoherence).

Each of the sources has been tagged with relevant domain labels—such as hardware, algorithms, cryptography, error correction, or NISQs—to allow for the analysis of trends and the areas of focus in research effort.

4.12 DATA ANALYSIS

Mixed-method analysis tools like thematic codification and bibliometric tools were used to analyze the data:

1. **Thematic Analysis**: We reviewed the data extracted toward the themes being defined and emerged from the categories of findings, for example, scalability challenges and error correction methods, and research on specific applications (such as drug applications through quantum simulation).
2. **Bibliometric Mapping**: Software tools such as VOSviewer (van Eck & Waltman, 2010) and Python libraries (NumPy, Pandas, Matplotlib) enabled the following:
   - **Co-authorship Networks**—to identify existing research clusters or collaboration (for example, between academic labs and industry).
   - **Keyword Co-occurrence**—to find out which quantum topics often intersect with each other (algorithms, hardware, cryptography).
   - **Citation Analysis**—to find seminal papers and trace newer papers that base their models or findings upon them.

This dual approach illuminates both how quantum computing research is evolving and where there might be critical gaps or saturation in the literature. For example, bibliometric data might suggest research has increased in quantum machine learning but is sparse for topological qubits. This would thus determine an exciting research gap for future investigation.

4.13 LITERATURE CATEGORIZATION

A subsequent classification analysis disposed studies in four overall levels according to their forms and the period of impact blurred with notional intervals:

1. **Foundational Works (Before 2005)**: Foundational theories, e.g., Shor's algorithm for factoring (1994) or Deutsch's concept of universal quantum computer (1985). Of these principles, modern quantum computing rests.
2. **Methodological Advances (2005–2015)**: Papers furnishing necessary error-correcting codes, initial scalable hardware proposals and advanced designs for quantum algorithms (e.g., Fowler et al., 2012).
3. **Recent Developments (2015–Present)**: Publications reporting achievements on the milestone of quantum supremacy, further advances in superconducting/ion-trap implementations and applications for the NISQ era (Arute et al., 2019).
4. **Frontiers and Emerging Issues**: Promising investigation topics of the next generation such as topological qubits (Nayak et al., 2008) or hybrid quantum-classical machine learning frameworks (Biamonte et al., 2017).

Not only does this categorization clarify the way the field has evolved, but it also scaffolds the discussion of trends, challenges, and future directions in the subsequent sections of this chapter.

4.14 EVOLUTION OF RESEARCH TRENDS

In this research, the community would present the scenery thus: how the emergence of quantum computing research has come to pass due to a blend of theory, technology, and interdisciplinary collaborations. For about 40 years, quantum computing has gradually changed from an idle thought experiment to a booming field on its own, an intersection between computer science, physics, engineering, and mathematics in their own saying (Nielsen & Chuang, 2010). This section highlights the historical arc of quantum computing's development, showing how foundational theories in the field laid the groundwork for quick technical advances and specialization into subfields. In more detail, we discuss the following issues: the early foundational breakthroughs that made quantum computing a serious avenue of inquiry; technological developments that led directly to creating real-world quantum devices; and finally, the major research areas defining the field today: quantum algorithms; quantum hardware; quantum cryptography; and quantum machine learning.

The future of quantum computing research is colored by the convergence of theoretical findings with technological breakthroughs and interdisciplinary collaborations. Quantum computation has been changed from an idle thought experiment to an unbelievably flourishing branch of study resting in the intersection of computer science, physics, engineering, and mathematics over the last four decades (Nielsen & Chuang, 2010). This section describes the historical arc of quantum computing development, detailing how the foundational theories of the field prepared for rapid technological progress and the emergence of specialized subfields. We would like to discuss (1) the early major breakthroughs that really solidified in the minds of researchers that quantum computing was a line of research, (2) the technological advances that have led to the development of actual devices, and (3) the main areas of research defining this field right now: quantum algorithms, quantum hardware, quantum cryptography, and quantum machine learning.

The initial part of this section focuses on its academic foundations through revisiting the role of Richard Feynman's initial conjectures, David Deutsch's definition of a universal quantum computer, and the subsequent algorithmic milestones. It then surveys how such milestones progressed along a time continuum massively with regard to the developing and increasingly stable qubit platforms contending for breakthroughs in quantum error correction or some considerable hardware demonstrations by academic and industry-led teams like (Arute et al., 2019). Finally, we analyze four major areas into which modern quantum computing research is classified. Quantum algorithms, from Shor's factoring breakthrough to recent hybrid approaches, underscore the capacity of quantum-mechanical principles in solving bottlenecks that classical systems encode. Quantum hardware—or what forms of qubit modalities—tells us about the challenges and triumphs of engineering that brought us closer to practical quantum devices. These bases of research in quantum cryptography derive also from the fundamentals of quantum mechanics but are only adding more and more to the secure communications protocols. Finally, quantum machine learning can be mentioned as a rapidly developing niche in features and is purported to make it happen driven by data through algorithms based on quantum principles (Biamonte et al., 2017). All the while, they exemplify this integrated worldview into the developed theme that builds toward it involving an understanding of how each thing informs the other.

4.15 EARLY FOUNDATIONAL THEORIES AND BREAKTHROUGHS

The theoretical foundations of quantum computing owe much to groundbreaking ideas in the late 1970s and early 1980s, when physicists were preoccupied with the

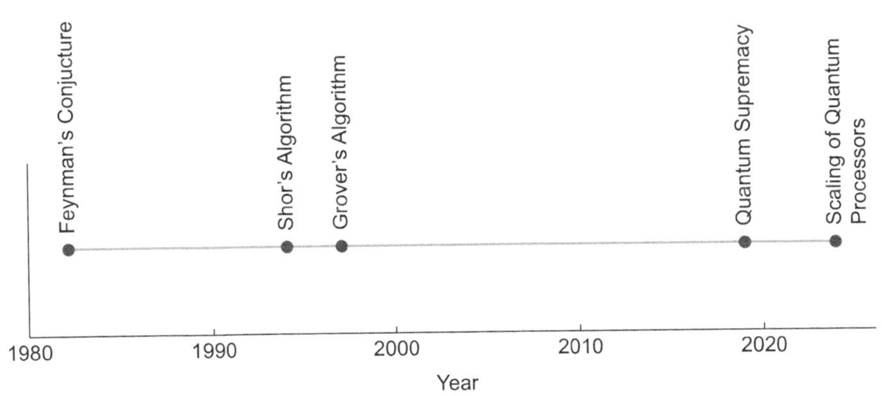

FIGURE 4.4 Evolution of research themes in quantum computing.

question: "Can classical computers efficiently simulate a quantum system?" For example, Feynman (1982) argued that some virtual worlds were inaccessible to a classical machine and that using one would produce an exponential slowdown in the search for the solutions related to this problem, implying that a computationally efficient device taking advantage of quantum mechanics itself would be able to avoid all such inefficiencies. Feynman triggered deeper inquiries into the computational power intrinsic to quantum mechanics and conceived many of the earliest theoretical models of a quantum computer.

These assertions were further developed by David Deutsch to insist on the existence of a universal quantum computer that could simulate any physical system governed by local quantum theories (Deutsch, 1985; Lloyd, 1996). Lee showed that a set of quantum gates could behave as classical logic gates and, in principle, perform any quantum computation. Deutsch's formalism was important not only as a theoretical jump; it also challenged the Church-Turing principle—said to broaden the horizon of what could be computable. This interest soon became the basis for changes initiated by research trends in quantum information theory such as the study of quantum entanglement as a basis for communication and computation (Ekert, 1991; Mattle et al., 1996).

Without doubt, the following two algorithms invented in the mid-1990s gave a big boost to the credibility of quantum computing. One was by Peter Shor (1994), who presented a polynomial-time algorithm for integer factorization on a quantum computer. The moment was defining: integer factorization, which was thought to be hard for classical machines, became feasible in the quantum paradigm. Shor's algorithm propelled quantum computing from being a theoretical curiosity to becoming a powerful competitor that might even break existing cryptography systems like RSA, drawing instant interest from government agencies as well as the entire community of cryptography. Soon after him, Lov Grover (1997) introduced a quantum search algorithm, providing a quadratic speedup stake over classical ones, making it clear that quantum computing would not be limited to factoring performance improvement.

The groundwork that these early thinkers argued has been defined in terms of practical feasibility and importance in relation to quantum error correction (Steane, 1996). Whereas classical bits can be redundantly encoded without introducing large overheads, qubits are subject to decoherence effects and cannot be cloned directly (the no-cloning theorem), and so new approaches to error correction codes and fault-tolerant gate designs thus became central to further intertwining theoretical transformation with experimental realization (Calderbank & Shor, 1996; Steane, 1996; Gottesman, 1997). The 1980s and 1990s were thus marked by intellectual giant strides that gave a twist to shape in quantum computation—that one discovery forced researchers from different quarters into a crucible over what was essentially a budding but potentially thriving field.

4.16 TECHNOLOGICAL ADVANCEMENTS OVER THE DECADES

After laying down the theoretical principles, the next several decades, particularly the late 1990s and early 2000s, would witness efforts directed toward making the emergence of quantum devices as experimental machines. Researchers were able to show how two-qubit or three-qubit gates might work through nuclear magnetic resonance (NMR) systems in limited hardware testbeds (Gershenfeld & Chuang, 1997; Mermin, 2007). Because of the scalability and coherence limitations of NMR techniques, the tests indicated the possibility of controlling a small quantum system in accordance with the logic operations of quantum computation.

As it progressed, however, various qubit platforms competed with each other to become the main game, presenting particular advantages and disadvantages. One of the strong competitors in this case is an ion-trap system—an arrangement applying electromagnetic fields to keep ions quenched into separate points and taking their internal states as qubits (Blatt & Wineland, 2008; Mølmer & Sørensen, 1999; Vandersypen & Chuang, 2005). Ion traps produced highly coherent gate operations and long-lived states. However, they had the engineering issues regarding scaling them into a trap array. Complementary to these would have been the emergence of superconducting circuits as the new stars in the firmament, along with the view as being most compatible with established microfabrication methods and supported rapidly by industry (Clarke & Wilhelm, 2008; Devoret & Schoelkopf, 2013). Improvements in SQUIDs and transmon qubits made way for multi-qubit processors, stretching into larger and more stable chip-based quantum computers by companies, such as IBM and Google (Arute et al., 2019).

The present day saw the initiation of NISQ times, signifying advancements incorporating quantum processors that are up to several dozen in qubit count and nearly as reliable to implement not-so-trivial algorithms (Preskill, 2018). The main part of this era risked almost every near-term quantum application that would be somewhat noiseless or decoherent, such as, for instance, simulations of quantum chemistry, certain optimization procedures, and proving machine-learning concept "works." Besides the development of hardware, there was a refinement of quantum error-correction techniques, such as surface codes, to take care of error syndromes in physically realizable architectures (Fowler et al., 2012). There are other control electronics and fast classical interfaces that engage heavily in using these quantum systems probably the most effective way (Kjaergaard et al., 2020).

Hardware demonstrations have been nothing but extraordinary in the past few years, including Google's "quantum supremacy" result by a dedicated quantum processor outperforming a leading classical supercomputer on a highly contrived sampling task (Arute et al., 2019). The societal significance of this benchmark remains contested; however, it had all the makings of a major troop movement in quantum computing prowess and subsequently brought tech giants and startups rushing into research. Other advances made have been quantum chips integrated into cryogenic control circuitry, exploring topological qubits to minimize decoherence, and developments in photonic quantum computing for network-oriented applications. The result is a complex and lively technology landscape that sets a strong foundation on which to develop unique research topics.

4.17 EMERGENCE OF SPECIFIC RESEARCH AREAS

With its new theoretically and technically supported development, quantum computing research widened into several specialized areas of focus. Although intersecting and informing each other, one can fruitfully consider them separately to understand how they together construct the field.

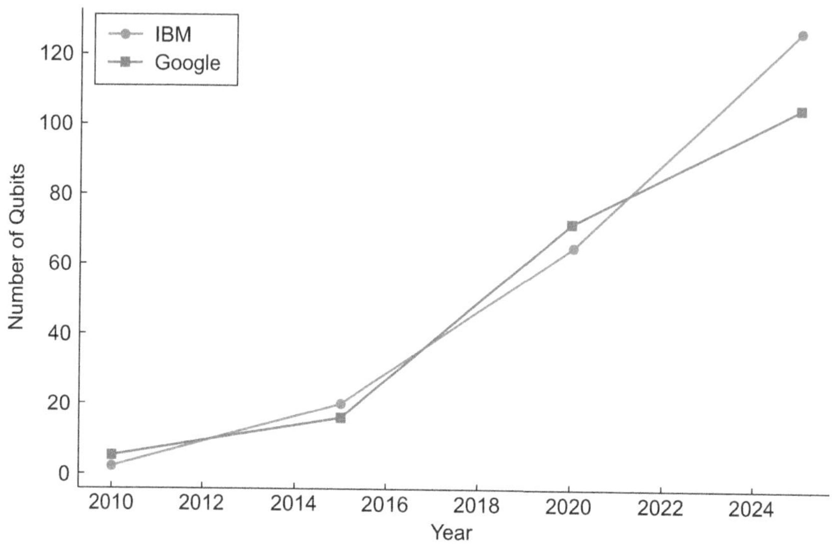

FIGURE 4.5 Qubit count progress over time.

4.18 QUANTUM ALGORITHMS

The study of quantum algorithms has traditionally formed an important part of the vision—theoretical evolution of quantum computing—from Shor's and Grover's early contributions to more modern variations of quantum algorithms (Montanaro, 2016). **Early Milestones:** Shor's (1994) factoring algorithm showed a prospective existential threat to classical cryptography, spurring researchers into motion to find new categories of possible quantum algorithms for cryptanalysis and other computationally intensive tasks. Grover's (1997) search algorithm was designed as an improvement for a class of problems quantum computers could address, unstructured search applications—from database lookups to optimization routines—while it provided less dramatic speedup (quadratic rather than exponential) than Shor's or potentially even Grover's.

After these famous breakthroughs for which lots of historians have gone on writing, it started the era of research about quantum algorithms concerning graph problems, like quantum walks that can outperform classical random walks in traveling and analyzing the architecture of graphs (Venegas-Andraca, 2012). Another sequence discussed is phase estimation, a fundamental component for many quantum algorithms in chemical modeling and Hamiltonian simulation, at the heart of quantum computational chemistry (Aspuru-Guzik et al., 2005; Ambainis, 2003; Jozsa, 1991).

Nearing the NISQ age, more emphasis on algorithms resistant to noise and realizable at qubit-limited devices (Preskill, 2018). Variational quantum algorithms (VQAs), for example, the variational quantum eigensolver (VQE) and the quantum approximate optimization algorithm (QAOA), use a hybrid quantum-classical feedback loop to repeat the process of tuning its parameters in a quantum circuit (Peruzzo

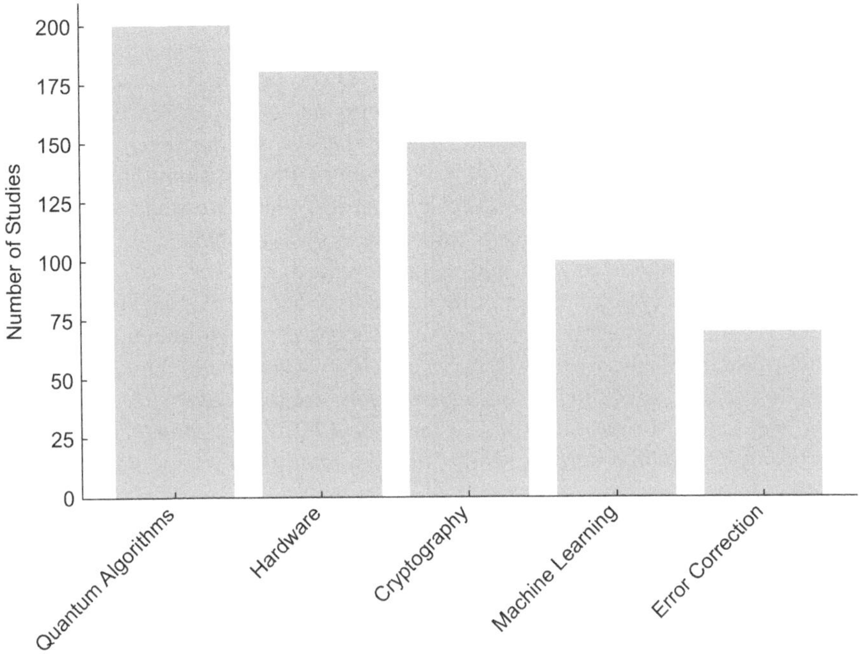

FIGURE 4.6 Quantum computing research focus areas.

et al., 2014). Such algorithms can run on near-term hardware but with very limited fidelity, and they hold promise for applications in the fields of chemistry, materials science, and combinatorial optimization. Most recent expansions of the VQA paradigm incorporate quantum machine learning instantiations such as the quantum neural network (QNN), which optimizes similarly a parameterized quantum circuit through classical optimization routines (Biamonte et al., 2017).

NISQ and Beyond: Researchers continue to explore algorithms that are intended to work in fault-tolerant, large-scale quantum machines. For example, the development of more efficient quantum Fourier transform techniques or new approaches to topological data analysis in quantum systems. These lines of research are the continuation of a long-term quest to identify "killer applications"; those applications are distinguished by their superiority over classical performance. The theoretical horizon remains vast, yet high gates fidelity and qubit coherence remind the community that a large-scale quantum advantage is still a moving target.

Moreover, it has been probable to execute these algorithms on near-term hardware with limited fidelity and results on small-scale applications in chemistry, materials sciences, and combinatorial optimization. Further extensions of the VQA framework are types of quantum machine learning, such as the quantum neural network (QNN), which also optimizes a parameterized quantum circuit via classical optimization routines (Biamonte et al., 2017). Researchers also continue investigating algorithms drafted specifically for fault tolerance and large quantum-scale machines, such as attaining efficient techniques for quantum Fourier transforms or developing new methods of topological data analysis in quantum systems. There remains the very long hunt for "killer applications" that demonstrate performance significantly better through quantum systems than classical ones. Theoretical horizons remain large; practical roadblocks, however, such as gate fidelity and qubit coherence, remind the community that large-scale quantum advantage is still a moving target.

These improvements would enable building more efficient algorithms which are very scalable and possible on these devices. At last, there are some variations of VQAs, including quantum machine learning forms such as QNN.

Researchers continue to look into algorithms meant to work on fault-tolerant, large-scale quantum machines. For example, the development of more efficient quantum Fourier transform techniques or new approaches to topological data analysis in quantum systems. These lines of research are the continuation of a long-term quest to identify "killer applications"; those applications are distinguished by their superiority over classical performance. The theoretical horizon remains vast, but high gates fidelity and qubit coherence remind the community that a large-scale quantum advantage is still a moving target.

NISQ algorithms have turned attention toward algorithm output, where noise-resistant algorithms are generally simulated on devices with limited qubit counts (Preskill, 2018). VQAs, such as VQE and QAOA, were designed with a hybrid quantum-classical feedback loop for iterative improvements on quantum-circuit parameters (Peruzzo et al., 2014). All of these can run on near-term hardware but with very limited fidelity and currently have shown promise for applications.

4.19 QUANTUM HARDWARE

The basis of the entire field, quantum hardware research links fundamental physics experiments to principles in engineering and computer science (Devitt et al., 2013; Gottesman, 1997). Research activity has focused on addressing decoherence, enhancing qubit connectivity, increasing gate fidelity, and investigating new qubit modalities, all as an effort over the last two decades.

Its focus over these last two decades has been on all imaginable attempts to counteract decoherence, enhance qubit connectivity, improve gate fidelity, and investigate new qubit modalities.

Key Architectures

1. **Superconducting Qubits**: The most prominent example of these superconducting circuits is transmon qubits, which realize quantum states in nonlinear resonators built with Josephson junctions (Kjaergaard et al., 2020). These chips usually work at dilution temperatures of a few millikelvins. Advanced improvements in coherence times, coupled with advanced fabrication techniques, finally culminated in commercially available quantum processors from the likes of IBM and Rigetti.
2. **Trapped Ions**: The atom traps are electromagnetic fields that restrict charged atoms in ion-trap systems and are used in laser or microwave-based operations for the gate operation with a high fidelity (Blatt & Wineland, 2008). A latest trend in research is keeping experiments for scale ion-trap

arrays since it becomes very complex to manage in the large size of traps. Nevertheless, ion-trap systems achieved gate fidelities that are as reported best in the range.

3. **Photonic Systems**: Photonic quantum computing employs photons as qubits, typically encoded into combinations of polarization or phase states (O'Brien, 2007). Thus, though it is possible to have photons travel large distances because of an excellent coherence and they are quite seldom bothered by scattering or refraction, developing high-fidelity multi-photon gates remains a daunting task. Integrated photonics platforms seem to be a promising way to scale up the use of photonic qubits.
4. **Topological Qubits**: They are believed to be defect-tolerant in their essential nature as being braiding of non-Abelian anyons that braid about one another in low-dimensional systems. This approach is, however, still essentially at the experimental stage. Major companies such as Microsoft, investing heavily in topological quantum computing initiatives, are considering hardware solutions that can withstand local noise degradation in perfect fidelity.

Challenges and Milestones

- **Scalability**: As quantum devices scale up from tens of qubits to hundreds or thousands, the hardware complexity becomes sharply steeper. The questions of how to achieve high connectivity among qubits without an unacceptable level of noise are formidable barriers.
- **Error Correction Integration**: Fault tolerance relies on complex error-correcting codes, such as surface codes, which demand significant overhead in physical qubits per logical qubit (Fowler et al., 2012). Bridging overheads for such codes and hardware advancement will be paramount in transcending NISQ levels of computing to true quantum fault-tolerance machines.
- **Control Electronics**: Real-time feedback and high-precision control signals are usually needed to execute quantum algorithms. These issues have now become major areas of research focus: cryogenic control systems, cutting-edge FPGA setups, and integrated classical-quantum pipelines.

Basically, quantum hardware research is all about a race among multiple approaches toward achieving reliable, scalable, and cost-effective quantum processors. No single platform has claimed the prize yet; instead, there is an exciting environment where breakthroughs often cross-pollinate among qubit technologies.

4.20 QUANTUM CRYPTOGRAPHY

Quantum cryptography is, along with algorithmic and hardware advances, one of the most advanced areas of application for quantum information science. With its roots deep in the immutability of quantum mechanics—such as the no-cloning theorem and the measurement disturbance principle—quantum cryptography creates methods for an unbreakably communicable protocol safe against classical and quantum computational attacks (Ekert, 1991; Mattle et al., 1996).

Quantum Key Distribution (QKD)

- **BB84 Protocol**: BB84 is a proposed secure unconditionally cryptographic key establishment protocol that relies on single-photon sources employing different polarization bases, introduced by Bennett and Brassard (1984). Any appearance of interference by an eavesdropper would detect anomalies in the measurements, thus alerting rightful parties to such breach of security.
- **E91 Protocol**: In 1991, Ekert used pairs of entangled particles and the testing of Bell's inequalities for guaranteeing security over the shared key distribution. This entangled-based QKD procedure is theoretically said to provide even stronger assurances of the security.

Post-quantum cryptography deals with the design of classical cryptographic systems that resist quantum attacks (Bernstein et al., 2009), while quantum cryptography is the study of creating cryptosystems based only on quantum phenomena. This is distinguished from post-quantum cryptography, which alters classical algorithms to withstand quantum factoring or search.

Beyond QKD, quantum cryptography research has expanded to quantum-safe communication networks, quantum secret sharing, and blind quantum computation, in which a client can outsource computations to a quantum server without revealing private data. All these scintillating developments have hints of a future "quantum internet," joining up quantum communication channels with quantum computing nodes (Wehner et al., 2018; Bose, 2003; Chen et al., 2021). On the other hand, quantum cryptography will influence policy decisions and resources allocated for cybersecurity since their large-scale quantum machines are likely to compromise classical encryption. Research on quantum-resistant classical cryptosystems and quantum key distribution infrastructure continues to be supported by governments and large corporations, expecting a change in cryptographic standards.

4.21 QUANTUM MACHINE LEARNING

Machine learning has blossomed into an incredibly exciting frontier for quantum computing, originally driven by problems such as prime factorization and simulating quantum systems (Schuld et al., 2015). The speed of classical machine learning advancement has transformed and is transforming many aspects of science, commerce, and society. Still, there is often a computational bottleneck related to the deep training of networks or analyzing the data through deep learning. Quantum machine learning claims that quantum algorithms could speed up certain subroutines—such as linear algebra tasks or sampling—in given machine learning workflows (Biamonte et al., 2017).

Core Approaches

1. **Quantum-Enhanced Feature Spaces**: Variational circuits and kernel-based methods employ quantum states to represent the data in higher-dimensional Hilbert spaces, possibly improving the results of classification or clustering (Havlíček et al., 2019; Devoret & Schoelkopf, 2013; Barz et al., 2013).

2. **Quantum Neural Networks (QNNs)**: The neural network metaphor is adapted to quantum gates: QNNs "train" parameterized quantum circuits to approximate functions of interest. The scaling issue continues to be a challenge, but initial results have indicated that even simple tasks can be learned on a small number of parameters using small quantum processors (DiVincenzo, 2000).
3. **Early Proofs-of-Concept**: Proofs-of-concept for qGANs and quantum Boltzmann machines indicate that, under certain conditions, possibilities are opened up for quantum states to more efficiently encode complex probability distributions, though as of now convincing demonstration on NISQ architectures is still scant.

Practical Challenges

- **Data Loading**: Even if an input problem has to transform classical data into a quantum state, it could, in theory, eliminate or negate any speedup recreationally possible, if it has an overhead exponential in the numbers of classical processing steps.
- **Noise and Decoherence**: NISQ devices are considerably error-prone, resulting in executing circuits repeatedly and invoking complex classical error mitigation methods (Preskill, 2018). This environment can restrict the number of quantum machine learning experiments.
- **Benchmarking**: It is often difficult to identify "genuine" quantum advantage in machine learning as versus classical optimizations that simulate or outdo quantum techniques.

These constraints do not prevent big tech companies and major universities from spending millions on quantum machine-learning projects. This is probably for the promise of opening some new doors for making advances in pattern recognition, predictive analytics, and data-driven sciences. This emerging area of machine learning combined with quantum computing has created a larger research ecosystem, including its own conferences, open-source software libraries (for example, PennyLane, Qiskit Machine Learning), and wide-ranging collaborations.

4.22 CONCLUDING PERSPECTIVES ON RESEARCH TRENDS

From the initial kernels of thought on quantum computing in Feynman's musing and Deutsch's theoretical constructs, it has grown into a very diverse discipline, propelled via research all over the globe. The trajectory of research trends indicates a delicate balance among these three components: (1) theories founded on foundational grounds that validate quantum principles for computation purposes and demonstration of their application; (2) technological advances in the mechanisms of qubit design and control; and finally, (3) more focused subfields—from quantum algorithms, hardware, and cryptography to machine learning—demonstrating the degree and spread of the current research under progress.

In the early foundational works of the research, the key breakthroughs were almost wholly theoretical. They posed a direct question—*do quantum computers outperform classical devices?*—and offered hints that such superiority could be achieved through algorithms. The advancement in technology over the decades, beginning with early pioneering experiments coupled with incremental engineering feats, entrenched quantum computing in physical systems, extending the newly established collaboration between physicists and engineers. This synergy paved the way to very high-profile successes, such as partial demonstrations of "quantum supremacy" and the wider expansion of global quantum research initiatives.

At last, specialization research areas have consolidated to transform the field into an inclusive environment. Quantum algorithms continue to push the limits on what is computably feasible, as quantum hardware development races toward stable, large-scale processors. Quantum cryptography, once viewed as a narrowly centered subject, is gaining credence among the masses because of security concerns in future networks. Finally, quantum machine learning may be looked at as relatively nascent, but it might stand out as the next generation where computation enabled through quantum use would interface best with the data-driven revolution of artificial intelligence.

In the future, these research threads are expected to remain tightly coupled. Advances in hardware will inform algorithm design and cryptographic protocols that feed back into new architecture with respect to security at the hardware level. In this light, breakthroughs in quantum error correction, topological qubits, and hybrid quantum-classical models may redesign the mapping of quantum machine learning itself. The challenges of upscaling qubit numbers and ensuring robust fault tolerance, to name a few, are by no means few, but the opportunities are equally enormous, and promise to redefine fields such as optimization, materials science, finance, climate modeling, and beyond.

The following paragraphs will build on this panoramic view of the research trends in quantum computing to examine the current landscape as far as research goes, drill down into the technical and conceptual gaps that remain, and address the ongoing challenges toward scalable quantum computation. Finally, this paper will outline future prospects for this remarkable scientific undertaking.

4.23 CURRENT RESEARCH LANDSCAPE

In the last decade, quantum computing has moved research—from proof-of-concept demonstrations toward operationally challenging prototypes and near-term commercial applications. This shift is made "hot" with the combination of advances in quantum hardware, algorithms, and software platforms—in addition to the private investments and public funding going into the research area (Castlevvi, 2017). Such pioneering research, necessarily, also training new experts through academia, continued to play a fundamental role. Industry behemoths such as IBM, Google, and Microsoft have thrown massive funding behind R&D at very large scales. They are accompanied by numerous emerging themes—such as quantum cloud computing, quantum networks, and hybrid quantum-classical models—in which a new way of thinking is being developed about how practitioners will have quantum technologies built and applied. This section introduces the state of the art in quantum computing, highlights some major breakthroughs from major players, surveys cutting-edge research contributions, and discusses those new frontiers that promise to define quantum computing's future.

4.24 BREAKTHROUGHS FROM ACADEMIC AND INDUSTRY LEADERS

4.24.1 IBM: Expanding the Quantum Ecosystem

Indeed, among corporations, IBM has always been and remains among the front-runners in support of quantum research, thanks to its long history in computer science and high-performance computing. The effort made by IBM in quantum got global visibility with the launch of the IBM Quantum Experience in 2016, which allowed people all over the world to access small-scale quantum processors in the cloud (Gambetta et al., 2017; DiCarlo et al., 2010; Kelly et al., 2015). This action was not simply to democratize experimental research in quantum computing but also to trigger the development of Qiskit—an open-source software development kit (SDK) that simplified the creation, simulation, and execution of quantum circuits.

1. **Advances in Hardware:** IBM's hardware design primarily entails a cryogenic system containing superconducting qubits cooled to millikelvin temperatures in dilution refrigerators, with transmons off integrated circuits (Kjaergaard et al., 2020). Over time, IBM built coherence times and gate fidelities into its design. In its hardware road map as directed, the company envisaged a gradual increase of the number of qubits from tens to hundreds to a number larger than a thousand while incorporating measures aimed at error mitigation and, in the longer term, fault tolerance.
2. **Quantum Volume:** IBM put forth QV, or quantum volume, so that the company could measure its strides into several critical metrics, including gate error, qubit connectivity, and circuit depth. There is a very strong basis for IBM's claims of continuous improvement in quantumizing by demonstrating the consistent growth of QV across generations in quantum processors.
3. **Clouding and Community:** Because it believed in multidisciplinarity in research, IBM nurtures a broad quantum ecosystem via the IBM Quantum Network, including universities, startups, and Fortune 500 firms working on quantum algorithms for problems as diverse as finance and materials science. This community-oriented approach creates strong user bases for IBM's quantum machines and, at the same time, advances the exchange of research ideas and open-source contributions formed in networks.

Thus, IBM is equipped with a general approach wherein its hardware development program is backed up by a broad-based software ecosystem with the accent on education. This multipronged approach has propelled them into the lead in industrial quantum computing for activities like scaling quantum devices among the top players and demonstrating quantum advantage in specific tasks.

4.24.2 Google: The Pursuit of "Quantum Supremacy"

Google's quantum computing research has made a large jump into the headlines around the world in association with its academic partners by announcing that the progress achieved is "quantum supremacy," popularized by John Preskill (2018) and denoting the point at which a quantum device exceeds classical supercomputers at a very clearly defined computational problem (Arute et al., 2019).

1. **Sycamore and Willow Processors:** Google recently presented the Sycamore processor, which was highlighted in its superconducting quantum platform. The processor consists of a two-dimensional grid of transmon qubits with nearest-neighbor couplings and demonstrated a specific sampling task that revealed an enormous performance gap between quantum hardware and classical supercomputers (Arute et al., 2019). In December 2024, Google announced yet another chip called Willow, featuring 105 qubits and showing exponentially reduced error rates. However, while critics still have their reservations over such benchmarks, the refined fabrication process and increased qubit count seem to point toward the strides made by Google in crafting devices that will tend to stability in increasing its scale; thus, error mitigation is as essential as scaling up the qubit networks.
2. **Quantum AI and Open-Source Tools:** Google's quantum research group also encourages open-source developments, such as Cirq—a Python library for tailoring, simulating, and running quantum circuits on hardware configurations envisioned by Google. Besides, Google invests hugely in research studies that connect quantum computing with artificial intelligence, for example, in investigating how quantum hardware can benefit AI training or inference (Biamonte et al., 2017).
3. **Roadmaps and Collaborations:** Like IBM, Google has a roadmap that ultimately involves adding qubits and increasing gate fidelity to allow more general-purpose calculations. For example, the collaborative efforts with academic partners, such as the University of California, Santa Barbara, are greatly responsible for improving the lithographic techniques for the consistent and high-quality qubit chips.

It was certainly a milestone achievement of an specifically defined task performed more efficiently on a quantum processor than on classical systems not necessarily by Google's "quantum supremacy" experiment. It establishes the status of affairs that quantum computing hardware is marching rapidly ahead, even while so much work remains before quantum processors can boast greater fault tolerance and applicability to a much broader class of computational problems.

That is a landmark accomplishment: a task manifestly defined and executed more efficiently on a quantum processor than on classical systems. That only demonstrated how quantum computing hardware is racing down the path. There is still much work to do before quantum processors can claim more fault tolerance and applicability to a much broader class of computational problems.

For an example, not without its controversies, it served as an important benchmark in achieving a very specific task that was completed much more efficiently on a quantum processor than on classical systems. It really drove the case home: Quantum computing hardware is gunning forward fast. So much yet to be done would be necessary before quantum processors could claim to be far more fault-tolerant and applicable to a much wider class of computational problems.

4.24.3 Microsoft: Topological Qubits and Software-Centric Focus

Microsoft isn't banking on the growth and flourishing of vast superconducting qubit arrays like the ones advocated by IBM and Google; rather, the company has built itself a niche on the long-term bet of topological qubits. According to the underlying theory, if quantum states can be encoded in non-Abelian anyons—exotic quasiparticles that appear in some low-dimensional systems—then the topological effects would protect these qubits from many forms of decoherence (Nayak et al., 2008).

1. **Topological Approach:** The entirety of Microsoft strategy hinges on its postulation that once developed, topological qubits would be fault-tolerant in an inherent sense and that this would entail drastically reducing overheads involved in error correction. Research in this direction is technically quite challenging and comes as Microsoft is investing considerably in theoretical and experimental aspects, yet full-conclusive lab demonstrations on well-behaved topological qubits are still works in progress.
2. **Azure Quantum:** Observing the cloud models from IBM and Google, Microsoft has Azure Quantum, which is a cloud-based experimental and development platform for quantum activity. This offers access to quantum hardware installations by partner companies (like IonQ, Quantinuum) and promotes modular methodology to develop quantum solutions in one environment.
3. **Q# and Developer Ecosystem:** This software architecture approach has led to the development of Q#, a domain-specific language for quantum programming. Through bringing together Q# with Visual Studio and Azure Quantum services, Microsoft wants that to be accessible for traditional software developers so that they are encouraged to try out quantum computing while closing the gap between theory of quantum and application in real-world use cases.

Microsoft hasn't demonstrated any massive-scale quantum processors publicly, yet still it is a major player through its advanced research in topological systems, powerful software tools, and cloud platform for third-party quantum hardware in Microsoft's development ecosystem. Such success and failures in research on topological qubits have shown how much uncertainties there are in the search for new qubit modalities, and yet at the same time, their potential benefit in case this approach is a viable one.

Other Notable Contributors: Apart from these three giants in the industry, many other companies and academic laboratories have contributed greatly to the quantum computing landscape. Rigetti Computing and Quantum Circuits Inc. are perfecting their superconducting qubit chips. IonQ and Quantinuum, the latter being a merger of Honeywell Quantum Solutions and Cambridge Quantum, are leaders in trapped-ion technologies (Blatt & Wineland, 2008). Meanwhile, D-Wave Systems is a pioneer of another paradigm, that of quantum annealing, where a quantum-optimal solution is found to optimization problems. The foremost institutions globally are, namely, MIT, Caltech, ETH Zurich, the University of Oxford, the University of Innsbruck, and Tsinghua University, among many others that lead numerous experimental and theoretical breakthroughs. In all their outputs, they propagate diverse ways into the quantum ecosystem, from specific hardware prototypes to very advanced quantum error-correcting codes one finds in research, hence enriching current research by providing different ways and angles through which they can view their results.

4.25 STATE-OF-THE-ART RESEARCH CONTRIBUTIONS AND SOLUTIONS

Research in quantum computing depicts an absolutely developed hardware platform, algorithm, and integration tool. Most breakthroughs come from the industrial R&D laboratories, but basic research continued to provide advanced insights into what could still be possible. This section is focused on reviewing the most important lines of investigation characterizing today's state of the art in quantum computing.

Quantum computing research today is marked by growing maturity in hardware platforms, algorithms, and integrative tools. Advances into which still impinge into the future mostly come from industry R&D laboratories; however, there is still some basic research that delves even deeper. This section is a review of the most significant lines of inquiry with which today's state-of-the-art quantum computing is defined.

4.26 MULTI-QUBIT SCALING AND BEYOND

One of the key indicators when it comes to progress within the processing architecture of qubits is in terms of coherently controlled numbers. Current devices from IBM, Google, and IonQ operate across the tens of qubits to low hundreds. Progressing beyond this range calls for significant advances in:

1. **Fabrication Techniques:** As the number of qubits increases, bringing consistency in the quality of each qubit, uniformity of device parameters, and integration with control electronics becomes exponentially more difficult (Devoret & Schoelkopf, 2013).
2. **Thermal Management:** Superconducting qubit systems are based on dilution refrigerators and have thereby a limited cooling capacity; housing hundreds or thousands of qubits at such extremely low temperatures is going to need new cryogenic engineering solutions.
3. **Crosstalk and Interconnects:** As qubit layouts become denser, electromagnetic crosstalk and undesired coupling pose performance bottlenecks that require refined chip designs and improved packaging.

Scaling is engineering larger and more complex ion-trap arrays on the trapped-ion side. Segmented traps, 2D trap lattices, or shuttling-based architectures are numerous examples that fulfill the mentioned condition. The key underlying success for any qubit modality thus is that of these engineering challenges being cleared while maintaining coherence and high-fidelity gate operations. No one technology has noticeably come to lead yet, but multiple approaches help engender a competitive and cooperative environment to keep the ball rolling.

4.27 ADVANCED QUANTUM ERROR CORRECTION

As quantum devices grow, quantum error correction (QEC) has turned into an inevitable utility to build fault-free quantum computers (Terhal, 2015). QEC codes like the surface code would need several physical qubits to protect a logical qubit against error due to decoherence and operation (Fowler et al., 2012). With dramatic advances in qubit fidelity, it seems that QEC is now nearing practical deployment, but its overhead is still exorbitant—several dozen or even hundreds of physical qubits required per logical one, as the word clearly suggests.

The new style of research is to explore means of reducing overheads or finding more effective codes:

1. **Topological Codes:** Among the major examples are surface codes and color codes. They are 2D- or 3D-structured lattice geometries, which localize error syndromes.
2. **Bosonic Codes:** Another pathway is potential to store quantum information in higher-dimensional Hilbert spaces of harmonic oscillators such as superconducting cavity modes. The logical qubits using these "cat states," or GKP (Gottesman-Kitaev-Preskill) states, show a resilience in the face of certain noise types (Ofek et al., 2016).
3. **Adaptive and Fault-Tolerant:** The protocols focused on creating these higher-performance gate constructions and decoding algorithms revolve around adapting or tolerating higher noise to accompany varying errors or adapting to noise variation in real time.

Indeed, fault tolerance at a broad scale might be an eventual objective, but existing evidence suggests progress in smaller sub-scales. Several research teams engaged have demonstrated, for the first time, a real-time correction where single- or small multi-qubit errors occur, considered initial steps to achieve totally fault-tolerant computers. For example, the fact that repeated quantum error-correction cycles on a small set of qubits demonstrate that the logic can indeed protect quantum states over multiple gate operations (Ristè et al., 2015) confirms that QEC is moving from pure theory to laboratory validation, a crucial milestone along the way toward scalable quantum computing.

4.28 QUANTUM SOFTWARE AND DEVELOPMENT FRAMEWORKS

Thus, while hardware generally holds the limelight, quantum software—from development kits to high-level languages, simulators, and debuggers—is of equal importance. Among the many examples are as follows:

1. **Qiskit (IBM):** A holistic open-source platform containing modules for quantum circuit design, simulation, pulse-level control (Qiskit Pulse), as well as application libraries for chemistry, finance, and machine learning.

2. **Cirq (Google):** As built for controlling and optimizing circuits within its gate for hardware superconductor realizations, Cirq is a specialized high-level API for programming quantum operations in Google's hardware—and is at work getting even its domain-specific optimizations.
3. **Azure Quantum + Q# (Microsoft):** Europe's Microsoft Q# is integrated into cloud-based quantum service with Q#, a unique abstractions for qubit management, operations, and resources, as applied to developers familiar with .NET or Visual Studio environments.

Third-party platforms such as PennyLane and Forest (Rigetti), plus ProjectQ, concentrate on specialized functionality—from quantum machine learning to quantum chemistry—encouraging cross-disciplinary collaboration and lowering the barriers to entry. Together, these software ecosystems emphasize the way strong tooling is very much needed to wield well the quantum hardware and to make it commercially and scientifically valuable products.

4.29 APPLICATION-DRIVEN SOLUTIONS AND COLLABORATIONS

Although quantum hardware is still suffering noise and scaling issues, applied research and development have thrived. Collaborative efforts bring the tech titan, startups, and research institutes to work together and find real-life use cases where near-term quantum processors might have real impact. Some key areas of interest include:

1. **Quantum Chemistry and Materials:** Quantum algorithms, such as variational quantum eigensolver (VQE), extend the horizons of simulations that comprise electronic structures, reaction mechanisms, and molecular properties (Aspuru-Guzik et al., 2005; O'Malley et al., 2016; Reiher et al., 2017). The pharmaceutical and chemical companies such as BASF and Pfizer are sponsoring quantum computing initiatives that envision drug discovery or catalyst design.
2. **Optimization and Finance:** Quantum heuristic algorithms, such as QAOA, perform combinatorial optimization for essential problems associated with supply chains, portfolio optimization, and risk assessments. Joining them are banks like JPMorgan Chase and Goldman Sachs entails forming research alliances with quantum providers to review feasibility and possible early advantages.
3. **Machine Learning:** Industry labs, apart from research alone, have been engaging in quantum-assisted machine learning in tasks like feature mapping, generative modeling, or anomaly detection. Still mostly testing and performing experiments, interest remains alive, especially since artificial intelligence is becoming very crucial in industries driven by data today.

As shown in Figure 4.7, these partnerships, toward a target application, also serve, quite literally. They provide real-world use case scenarios for quantum algorithms and fund and direct hardware and software development as well. Thus, quantum R&D becomes more targeted toward addressing problems, maturity being from theoretical exercises-based solutions to intended but still quite early.

4.30 EMERGING TOPICS: QUANTUM CLOUD COMPUTING, QUANTUM NETWORKS, AND HYBRID MODELS

Apart from hardware scaling, error correction, and quantum software, which are well-known fields of study, new subfields are emerging with a very fast conversion rate. Such things would eventually take quantum computing out of independent laboratory systems and bring it closer to becoming a type of technology along other barrier-free lines with broad user access and integrative capabilities. Among these, three that look especially promising are quantum cloud computing, quantum networks, and hybrid quantum-classical architectures.

4.31 QUANTUM CLOUD COMPUTING

Indeed, as its name suggests, cloud computing is nothing other than a highly classical computing paradigms becoming really possible with remotely located data centers being jammed for demand-based scalability on supply. This progress, in most ways, is a developmental phase similar to what was happening in quantum computer research in that people are now providing such devices over the cloud just as they do for cloud processing to all users. This approach democratizes access, allowing researchers, startups, and students to experience real quantum hardware without the requirement to own and manage expensive cryogenic systems.

1. **Commercial Offerings:**
    - **IBM Quantum:** It offers several superconducting processors with different qubit counts and connectivity features, accessible via an education free tier and paid tiers for professional projects.
    - **Amazon Braket:** This service brings together quantum hardware from companies like Rigetti and IonQ, as well as simulation environments.
    - **Microsoft Azure Quantum:** There are many backend providers that host their services and allow the programming tools of Q# and their quantum hardware to be connected together.
2. **Challenges and Opportunities:**
    - **Latency and Bandwidth:** The operation of quantum circuits in the cloud involves communication delays between the user's local environment and the remote quantum system. Thus, while this does not rule out real-time feedback algorithms or iterative procedures, some design tweaking will have to be performed.
    - **Security and Intellectual Property:** The more common quantum computing becomes, the more urgent the questions on data privacy, encryption standards for quantum circuits, and ownership of results produced by quantum devices will become.

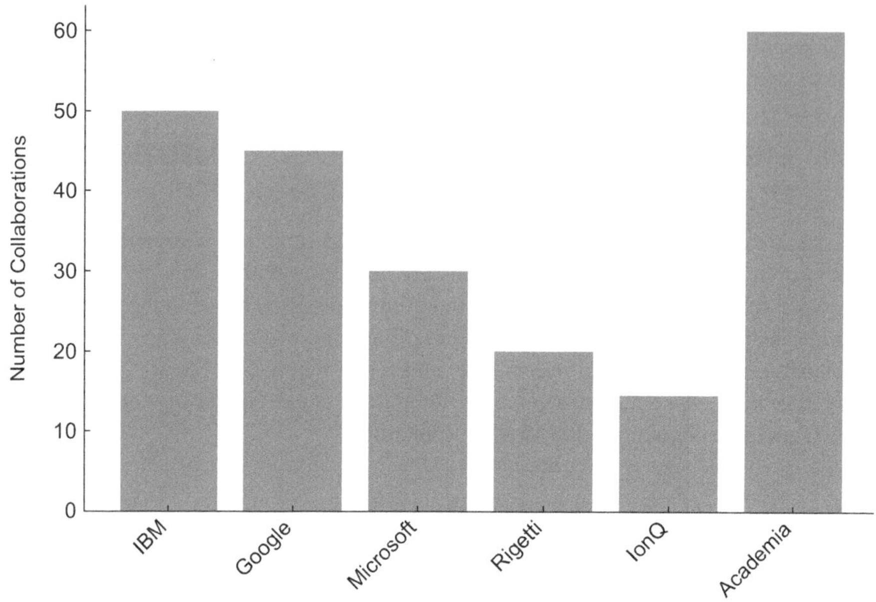

FIGURE 4.7 Collaboration networks in quantum computing.

- **Resource Management:** The scheduling of multi-user devices with quantum resources ready for inauguration presents an interesting problem with respect to optimization, with a character of job scheduling in classical API data centers but within the constraints of qubit decoherence and calibration cycles.

Ultimately, quantum cloud computing is accelerating innovation by democratizing access to quantum hardware for a much larger section of the research community. It also encourages educational initiatives, open-source collaborations, and rapid prototyping of quantum applications across industries.

4.32 QUANTUM NETWORKS

Quantum networks, on the other hand, do not necessarily mean that they connect the quantum systems over very large distances; they could connect a number of quantum systems over short distances as well. These networks will use quantum communication protocols such as entanglement distribution, teleportation, and quantum repeaters to transmit and process quantum information securely (Wehner et al., 2018). Fundamentally, quantum networks can form the basis of some possible future "quantum internet" that will allow collaborating distant quantum devices to solve problems independent of their physical connectivity.

1. **Entanglement Distribution and Repeater Protocols:** The classical repeater works by amplifying signals in order to fight fiber losses, while quantum signals cannot be cloned (the no-cloning theorem). Hence, quantum repeaters generally rely on entanglement swapping and purification as their primary means of extending entanglement over long distances.
2. **Applications:**
   - **Secure Communication:** Once solid enough quantum network infrastructures are established, quantum key distribution (QKD) can fully reach global extension.
   - **Distributed Quantum Computing:** Smaller quantum nodes may pool resources for large-scale computations.
   - **Sensor Networks:** Quantum sensors positioned in a network may help realize unprecedented sensitivity in performing such tasks as gravitational wave detection or probe into deep space.

Apart from this, such research initiatives are US Department of Energy's Quantum Internet Blueprint, which is meant to create testbeds for cutting-edge quantum networking experimentation. Europe is another of the continents that have invested extremely well into such initiatives, with China and other areas also going by that. The technology is still in its infancy, but progress is underway with respect to experiments in large-scale quantum networks demonstrated through quantum entanglement distribution experiments, showing that large-scale quantum networks have indeed come out of the realm of being just a theoretical possibility.

4.33 HYBRID QUANTUM-CLASSICAL MODELS

Even after considerable achievements in hardware and algorithms, quantum processors are still subjected to significant noise and limits in the qubit count. Hybrid quantum-classical models mitigate these issues by performing work on classical coprocessors in applications where they excel and relegating specific SFRs to quantum hardware where potential advantages have been determined (Mitarai et al., 2018). The logic here is more applicable with regard to the NISQ era, for no one has discovered full fault tolerance in quantum computing yet.

1. **Variational Quantum Eigensolvers (VQEs):** One of those is by VQE, in which a quantum circuit parameterized by classical variables is repeatedly run and measured. A classical optimizer then modifies the quantum circuit parameters using the measurement results. This process continues until the circuit state is close to the ground state of a given Hamiltonian.
2. **Quantum Approximate Optimization Algorithm (QAOA):** QAOA also employs a similar quantum-classical feedback loop for combinatorial optimization problems, as with the Max-Cut problem. It starts with the application of parameterized gates on a quantum processor, which is followed by measurements from a classical computer on the outputs and iterative refinements through a classical algorithm on the parameters (Farhi et al., 2014; Childs et al., 2002).

3. **Machine Learning Integrations:** Within quantum machine learning, hybrid models could combine traditional neural networks for data pre-processing or post-processing while using a quantum circuit to perform feature mapping or kernel estimation (Biamonte et al., 2017).

The benefits of practical application:

Heterogeneous architectures might give near-term computational advantage, even if their quantum component is at a small scale. Such methods will not be miracle cures since circuit depth and measurement noise may still limit effectiveness. These, however, offer a more pragmatic path toward the immediate application of quantum resources while more advanced hardware technologies mature toward fault tolerance.

4.34 CONCLUDING REMARKS ON THE CURRENT RESEARCH LANDSCAPE

Today, the quantum computing field is characterized by efforts to translate theoretical promise into real-world solutions. Heavy investment continues by tech giants IBM, Google, and Microsoft in the hardware and software ecosystems—as they're racing into increasing qubit counts and refining qubit modalities. At the same time, a few academic labs and upcoming companies are contributing toward niche expertise—whether alternative hardware platforms like ion traps and photonics (O'Brien, 2007) or specialized quantum algorithms tailored to real-world applications.

It involves state-of-the-art multi-qubit scaling strategies, advanced quantum error correction protocols, and a robust software stack most closely resembling tools found in classical software engineering. The hardware-algorithms-developer-centricing framework has grown by signaling maturity for the industry. From proof-of-concept experiments to quantum chips with more than 100 qubits—and from old ad-hoc code to integrated development environments—it indicates that quantum computing is well past the establishment of an emerging computational paradigm, even though it faces technical and theoretical hurdles.

Emerging issues include quantum cloud platforms, quantum networks, and hybrid quantum-classical approaches, with the last two further diversifying and extending the discipline. Cloud computing services provide quantum computing access to widened democratized research and development and education spending, quantum networks could deter the global reach of secure entangled communications, and quantum components hybrid designs are heralded to obtain performance improvements in the near term.

The future never really holds the promise of strong convergence in terms of such trends. As quantum machines seem to be increasingly opened up in the cloud for access by innovators, experimentation and algorithmic and application-level research will develop further. The improved reliability of hardware will correspondingly accelerate the realization of error correction protocols that could make distributed quantum networks feasible. Meanwhile, hybrid frameworks converge between quantum pure and classically pure architectures for reasonable steps toward large-scale quantum advantage. It is not the complete landscape that could be characterized—in short, it sketches the next stage, in which solutions might be domain-specific in their very meaningful implicature in areas such as pharmaceuticals, materials discovery, finance, and others.

However, as we move through this chapter, we will also explore some of the issues and voids currently present in the work in this area and what remains to be done in future applications of quantum computing. The state of the art today allows us to ascertain important strategic avenues for future research and investment that can help guide the community toward the long-desired goal of fault-tolerant, large-scale quantum computation.

4.35 RESEARCH GAPS AND CHALLENGES

The evolution of quantum computing seems to be at a crucial juncture. After long years of primarily theoretical work and agonizingly slow laboratory demonstrations, the field has recently entered into a prototyping world, global research funding, and an increased public profile. Indeed great strides have been accomplished; however, there is still a long way to go before quantum computing reaches its actual transformative potential—from engineering challenges around scalability and error correction, through algorithmic limits to collaborative gaps between academia and industry. As such, the research field is characterized by so many gaps that should be bridged to move the field forward. The section examines the several dimensions of barriers against quantum computing including technical bottlenecks, algorithm- and hardware-related limitation, and a collaborative divide.

4.36 TECHNICAL CHALLENGES

4.36.1 Scalability

The scalability issue is one of the most intimidating engineering challenges for quantum computing. Proof-of-concept quantum processors can have order tens or even a few hundred qubits (Arute et al., 2019; Kjaergaard et al., 2020), but theory is in agreement that fault-tolerant operation will require thousands—or even millions—of qubits of a particular kind (Devitt et al., 2013; Terhal, 2015). All this has practically severe scaling limits:

1. **Physical Footprint and Fabrication Complexity**
    - Superconducting qubits appear to be gearing up for a very complicated microfabrication process that must ensure uniformity and quality over larger and larger chip areas (Clarke & Wilhelm, 2008; DiCarlo et al., 2010). The presence of minute fabrication defects can adversely affect the coherence times and gate fidelities, thus affecting performance.
    - Trapped-ion systems must now accommodate ever more ions in progressively larger, more complex architectures of traps (Blatt & Wineland, 2008). Ion heating, laser stability, and increasing error rates are but some of the issues that erupt as trap sizes and ion numbers grow.
    - Integration with low loss and high accuracy in multi-photon circuits that are built on chip is very difficult in photonic qubit systems. That is in terms of the beam splitters, phase shifters, and single-photon detectors (O'Brien, 2007).

2. **Cryogenics and Thermal Management**
When qubits are integrated with superconducting circuitry, for example, dilution refrigerators of enormous size are required to bring qubits down to millikelvin temperatures. In addition, when going from a few tens to thousands of qubits, the problems in cryogenic engineering become much more difficult because each additional qubit typically requires more control lines, thermal loads, and wiring (Kjaergaard et al., 2020). Moreover, obtaining the necessary thermal stability for large arrays of qubits poses a significant engineering challenge in itself.
3. **Control Electronics and Crosstalk**
Quotient has its own microwave pulses or laser beams for gate operations. The increasing number of qubits raises the control electronics' requirements beyond simple proportional scaling in signal routing, calibration, and timing synchronization (Gottesman, 1999). As the devices become increasingly densely packed, crosstalk—inadvertent coupling between nearby control lines or between qubits—develops a more and more serious problem, leading to like errors that are difficult to rectify.

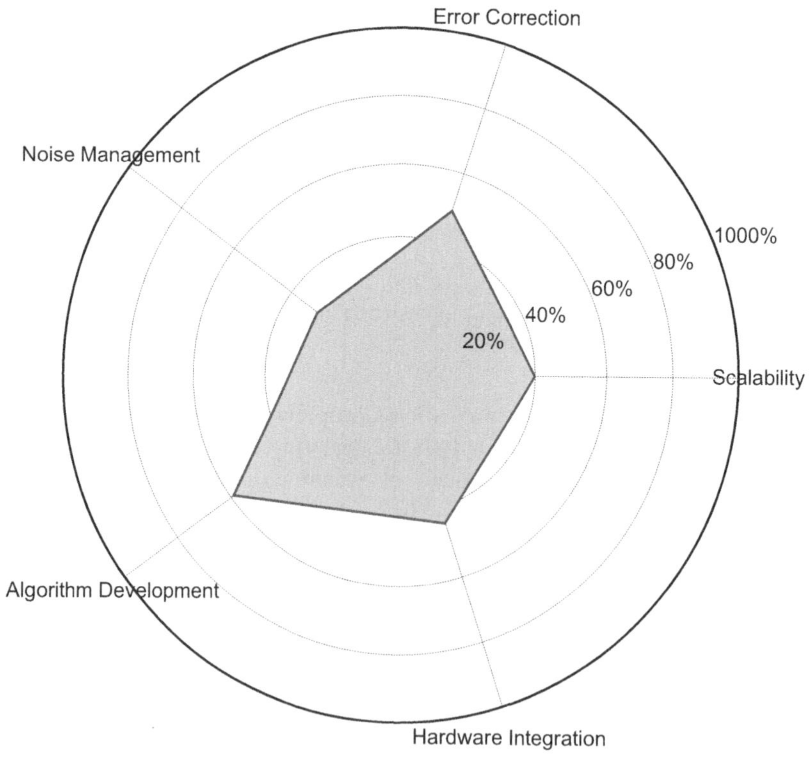

FIGURE 4.8 Research gaps and challenges in quantum computing.

4. **Those Long View Scalability Visions**
   Some grants pave the way for modular or distributed architectures through ganged small quantum processors ("modules") that are entangled with each other through photonic interconnects (Monroe et al., 1995, 2014). Each module might house tens or hundreds of qubits, and coherent communication among modules could, in principle, scale up to thousands or millions of qubits. However, robust entanglement generation across modules is currently very challenging. Even as hardware matures, there is no clear consensus in the field about which will scale gracefully in the future.

Scalability research is messy and open-ended, but it is making little as possible. Every new generation of machines contains slightly more qubits that have better fidelity. Cryogenic control electronics and packaging of sorts might lessen the cross-talk and overhead. But still, closing the gap between today's quantum prototypes and the truly large-scale fault-tolerant machines remains one of the most critical challenges in quantum computing.

4.36.2 Error Correction and Decoherence

The second has to do with the effective correction of the errors and the nevertheless persisting issue of decoherence. Quantum bits are so fragile that every contact with the external environment is likely to lead to the collapse of their delicate superpositions or to destroy entanglement (Preskill, 2018).

1. **High Error Rates**
   Even the best possible quantum gates, however, have error rates in the range of 10^(−3) to 10^(−4), far above the theoretical error threshold for efficient fault-tolerant quantum computing (Fowler et al., 2012). Real physical qubits drift out of coherency on a timescale ranging from microsecond to millisecond and can add errors themselves through gate operations.
2. **Overhead of Quantum Error Correction (QEC)**
   - Surface Codes: One promising proposal, the surface code, would require 1,000 or more physical qubits per logical qubit when overhead for syndrome measurements and ancilla is included (Fowler et al., 2012; Barends et al., 2014; Kelly et al., 2015) in some leading proposals.
   - Topological Qubits: Approaches such as Microsoft's topological qubit are targeted at embedding fault tolerance into the hardware level (Nayak et al., 2008), but have not yet been proven experimentally in larger systems.
   - Bosonic Codes: Some researchers encode quantum information into higher-dimensional states of a superconducting cavity to obtain cat codes or GKP states (Ofek et al., 2016). These are promising but face engineering and scaling challenges.
3. **Noise Modeling**
   The quantum noise environment is often non-Markovian, meaning errors may correlate across qubits as well as evolve in a time-dependent way

(Breuer & Petruccione, 2002). Conventional error models consider uncorrelated, memoryless noise, giving a lower bound in real error probabilities. Thus, noise model identification for specific hardware platforms is imperative for effective QEC protocol design (Devitt et al., 2013).

4. **Near-Term Mitigation Techniques**
   Given the costs from complete QEC, interim strategies are being developed by researchers:
   - Error Mitigation: Post-process measurement data with classical algorithms or calibrate parameters of the noise to reduce the implications of errors without having a fully fault-tolerant overhead on the measurements (Temme et al., 2017).
   - Dynamic Decoupling: Carefully timed sequences of pulses that refocus the qubit states and collapse certain decoherence channels (Viola et al., 1999; Leung, 2002).
   - Pulse-Level Optimization: Fine-tuning analog control signals to reduce gate errors and reduce gate times to outpace decoherence.

These approaches alleviate some of the immediate error burdens. In order to actually reach scalable quantum computing, however, there must be room for heavy-duty QEC. Research remains divided between pushing physical gate fidelities ever closer to thresholds and creating newer error-correcting schemes that need fewer resources. Regardless of the approach, decoherence and errors address one of the fundamental challenges in quantum computing.

4.36.3 Algorithmic and Hardware Limitations

Other non-technical barriers will limit current generations of algorithms and hardware from immediately making use of quantum computing. Even with significant improvements in hardware scaling and error correction, some classes of problems will probably remain hard or impossible for quantum machines to solve.

4.36.4 Algorithmic Bottlenecks

1. **Absence of a Global "Killer App"**
   While Shor's algorithm made an exponential speedup in a mathematically important task (Shor, 1994), its real-world impact completely depends on large-scale fault-tolerant hardware—an achievement still years away from reality. Grover's algorithm brings a quadratic speedup for unstructured search (Grover, 1997); however, most optimization and data-processing problems do not reduce neatly to unstructured searches.
2. **Complexity Theoretic Boundaries**
   The precise frontiers in which a quantum computer outdoes a classical one are still being worked out in theoretical computer science. Some problems in complexity class BQP may turn out not to be as ubiquitous as initially thought (Aaronson, 2013; Montanaro, 2016; Harrow et al., 2009), while the problems outside BQP may still be intractable even at the quantum device

level. Lacking any such clarity between these separation complexities, therefore, researchers must guess judiciously on which problems have the most promise for quantum advantage.

3. **NISQ Algorithms**
   There have been many so-called NISQ algorithms developed within the last few years, like VQE and QAOA (Peruzzo et al., 2014; Farhi et al., 2014; Bremner et al., 2016). Such methods are designed to outperform classical approaches for real-world tasks, but they do not promise *per se* to work in hardware with small qubit counts and large noise. Many also might need many more qubits and a much lower noise environment to show their superiority.
4. **Data Input and Output**
   Quantum speedups often presume that data is already suitably coded in a quantum state. In practice, however, loading a large classical dataset into quantum memory turns out to be a bottleneck that might nullify potential runtime gains (Aaronson, 2015; Ambainis, 2003). Analogously, reading out the results from a quantum circuit (often requiring multiple measurements and post-processing) may impose a throughput limitation for data-hungry applications.

4.36.5 Hardware-Specific Constraints

Each qubit modality—superconducting, trapped-ion, photonic, or topological—has its own constraints that limit certain algorithmic implementations or scale-up strategies:

1. **Connectivity and Gate Layout**
   Most hardware platforms enforce a physical layout that restricts which qubits can directly interact with each other. In 2D superconducting chips, typically only nearest neighbors can perform two-qubit gates (Arute et al., 2019; Boixo et al., 2018). SWAP gates can move information across the chip, but every gate incurs further errors. Limited connectivity thus determines those types of circuits that can be executed efficiently.
2. **Gate Speed and Coherence Time**
   - Although the trapped-ion systems manipulated gates ranging between microseconds to milliseconds, they exhibited excellent coherence times for short circuits. This caused decoherence to be less of a problem for time periods within which short circuits were operated. For long circuits, however, it was compounded when different ions were in an array (Blatt & Wineland, 2008).
   - Superconducting qubits demonstrated greater gate operation speed (nanoseconds to microseconds), while the coherence time measured was usually shorter compared with trapped ions, thus requiring very rapid and accurate control pulses to avoid decoherence during ongoing calculations (Kjaergaard et al., 2020).
3. **Errors and Biases**
   Certain technologies with qubits are endowed with specific error bias. A case is superconducting qubits that have been documented to have

relaxation errors (T1), more to phase errors (T2), or vice versa. Aside from that, trapped-ion systems tend to exhibit motional decoherence more than photonic systems, which would consider photon loss (O'Brien, 2007). Some algorithms require specific gate types or deep circuits but might not be practical unless they've been tuned to the error channels of a given platform.

4. **Applications Resource Requirements**
   Thus, for small-scale molecular simulations, in quantum chemistry, then it must be able to accommodate dozens to hundreds of qubits of high fidelity, particularly as the simulation target moves farther away from simple approximation. Resource assumptions are mind-boggling and thus very hindering at this point for illustrating quantum advantage and thereby revealing where algorithmic theory does not match the reality of hardware (Aspuru-Guzik et al., 2005).

Such hardware constraints means that further the evolutionary journey of quantum bits is dependent on the betterment of hardware as much as algorithmic advancements. Current developments in future applications have to hinge on adapting the available hardware capabilities to algorithmic design. As qubit features become integrated effortlessly into the design, researchers must also create the circuits without compromising the specific errors and connectivity profile of the device, while developers of new quantum chips will address compatibility concerning hardware features such as improved connectivity or qubit reuse blissful with the specific emerging algorithmic needs.

4.36.6 Industry-Academia Collaboration Gaps

Indeed, a significant aspect of contemporary quantum computing is the overwhelming involvement of enterprises and academic institutions. This collaboration results in rapid advancement, but there are also some inevitable gaps in this collaboration that bottleneck the smooth flow of knowledge, resources, and expertise.

4.36.7 Divergent Motivations and Timelines

- Long-term fundamental questions are typically pursued by academic researchers in relation to new modalities of hardware (e.g., topological qubits) or exotic algorithmic frameworks, such as quantum machine learning and quantum chaos. In essence, their reward structures are publication, citation, and breakthrough based.
- Industry, on the other hand, puts most focus on near- or mid-term deliverables, such as showing that there is some quantum advantage through the development of something that could be productized or incorporated into current business lines. Shareholders and their business models want very short-term returns, redirecting the priorities of research (Boon & Wiesner, 2022; Dowling & Milburn, 2003; Castelvecchi, 2017).

Differentially, these divergences could create imbalances in funding for long-term exploratory science compared to those coveting prototypes or products that are immediately sellable. On the other hand, certain industrial efforts might refrain from funding purely fundamental science since these do not yield returns during the short term, thus hindering high-risk, high-reward ventures that would only prove themselves over a longer time span.

4.36.8 Access to Proprietary Knowledge and Tools

Furthermore, it is proprietary advancements that create another obstacle. For instance, IBM and Google have already patented, considered trade secret or proprietary through the design of the hardware that they are unwilling to share fully. While some aspects of quantum computing are open-source, such as software libraries—Qiskit, Cirq—not all of it has to do with critical hardware and manufacturing details, undisclosed though this dynamic can hinder the examining or replicating of cutting-edge claims by academic researchers, impeding thrilling learning across institutions. Most advanced cryogenic hardware and test facilities are hosted in corporate labs where much academic research cannot interface directly with these platforms. Initiatives to bridge those gaps include the IBM Quantum Network and Microsoft Azure Quantum, which partially provide real quantum devices over the internet but do not replace any direct hands-on engineering experience with quantum hardware.

4.36.9 Funding Mechanisms and Intellectual Property (IP)

As quantum computing projects usually occurred at a massive scale and thus required significant grants, mostly based on expensive cryogenic infrastructure, specialized lasers, or large R&D teams, grants and public-private partnerships could be out of the question.

- Government grants typically favor wide-open research and publications but do not match the quick customer-ready cycles demanded by the industry partner.
- Venture capital or commercial R&D funds could seek more market prototype and IP protection and fail to embrace the academic ethos of open science.

Variations in multi-stakeholder consortia raise issues of IP ownership, licensing agreements, and fair distribution of revenues or patent rights. These complexities can, at worse, deter some academics from participating in collaborations or simply slow down the pace of knowledge exchange.

4.37 BRIDGING THE GAP

Some promising models for closing the academic-industry divide include:

1. **Consortia or Hubs:** The Quantum Economic Development Consortium (QED-C) in the United States or the Quantum Flagship in the EU gather together universities, companies, and governmental bodies to set research agendas, funding priorities, and roadmap goals.

2. **Open-Source Ecosystems:** Qiskit (IBM) and Cirq (Google) show how private initiatives can create communities of developers and researchers who work together to improve and extend quantum capabilities by promoting at least partial sharing of their software stacks.
3. **Joint Laboratories and Joint Exchange Programs:** Some multinationals fund laboratories within universities or, when faculty and students come to spend longer periods in corporate R&D facilities, they support activities in such countries. These models enable academic researchers to gain hands-on access to advanced hardware while transferring knowledge directly.

As such, it seems that deeper alignment of purposes—academic curiosity and industrial pragmatism informing each other—is pivotal to moving quantum computing forward. Neither academia nor industry could hope to achieve breakthroughs without collaborative synergy.

4.38 CONCLUDING PERSPECTIVES ON GAPS AND CHALLENGES

The promise of quantum computing is thus extraordinarily large, but the gaps complicating its path toward maturity are equally great. From a technical perspective, researchers face qubit fragility, develop large-scale feasible architectures, and master error correction to unbolt the door to fault-tolerant performance. Algorithmically, the field is plagued by limitations in known quantum speedups, uncertain complexity class separations, and the overhead of preparing and reading out quantum states. Algorithmic constraints due to hardware—connectivity, coherence times, noise bias—restrict the types of algorithms that can be run profitably.

At the system level, cooperation between academia and industry often has different incentives, boundary issues regarding proprietary knowledge, and complicated,

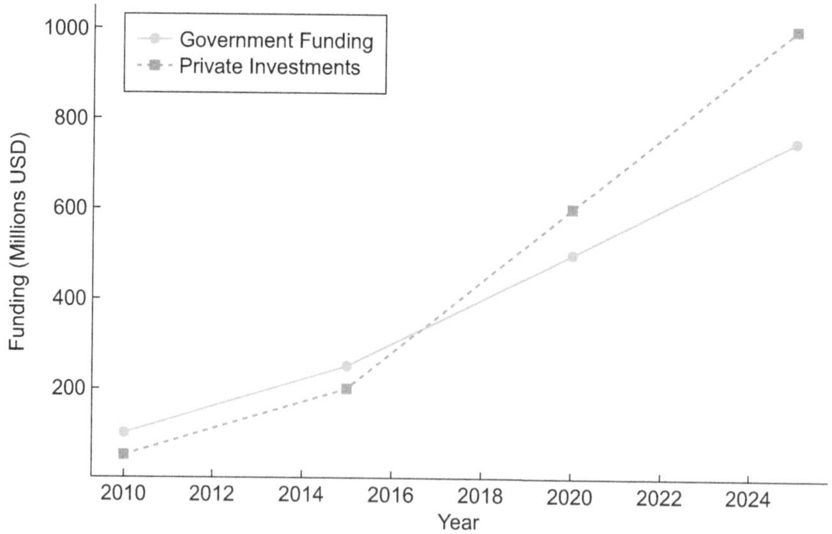

FIGURE 4.9 Funding and investment trends in quantum computing.

often challenging funding mechanisms that can discourage open innovation. And yet it is also the same cooperation that feeds the aggressive program in developing quantum computing, with industry pouring massive investment into scaling devices intended for the near term while universities continue a fundamental research agenda broadening the theoretical underpinnings of the field.

Multipronged approach to date this gap:

1. **Engineering Solution:** The innovating device designs, breakthrough of materials science, and advanced fabrication methods that will increase scalability and qubit performance.
2. **Refined Error-Correction Protocols:** Research that reduces the overhead of QEC, adapts codes to real-world noise characteristics, and pushes physical gate fidelities closer to fault-tolerance thresholds.
3. **Balanced Algorithmic Focus:** Exploring more NISQ era algorithms that can yield partial advantage today while continuing the search for next-generation algorithms that will require more advanced hardware.
4. **Open Collaborations:** Mechanisms through which academia can access cutting-edge hardware while leaving industry able to exploit new theoretical discoveries under fair and transparent IP agreements.

All of these efforts will take quantum computing from being an exciting frontier into a reliable, widely used technology. Stakeholders, such as scientists, engineers, investors, and policymakers, can forge better alignment for beneficial impacts by understanding the depth and complexity of the challenges. Tackling these gaps is not only intellectual exercise but the key driver in advancing quantum computing to its next evolutionary tier.

4.39 RESEARCH DIRECTIONS AND FUTURE SCOPE

With quantum computing moving from lab prototypes to more and more powerful systems, a wide range of opportunities and problems opens up for researchers, engineers, and entrepreneurs alike. The progress of the field as of now shows that advances not only become desirable but must be achieved in hardware, algorithms, error-correction schemes, and collaborative infrastructures to fulfill the technology's transformative potential. This section highlights critical key directions where quantum research is presently expected to grow, as well as how coming areas such as quantum networking and quantum-enhanced artificial intelligence could redefine the technological landscape. In doing so, the future avenues are illuminated while emphasizing multidisciplinary and dynamic character evolution in quantum computing and pointing to clearly defined goals that can help shape the next decade of progress.

4.40 ADVANCING QUANTUM HARDWARE: TOWARD FAULT-TOLERANT AND SCALABLE ARCHITECTURES

4.40.1 Materials Science and Fabrication Techniques

Ongoing optimization of materials science and fabrication processes to improve the performance and scalability of qubits is one area wherein the future research points to. For example, superconducting circuits benefit greatly from thin-film technologies for the reduction of defects at the interfaces between metals and substrates (Kjaergaard et al., 2020). Current work is ongoing on:

1. **Novel Superconductor Compounds:** Some alloys or multilayer structures may show reduced two-level systems (TLS) defects or improved chemical stability. It is thought that this line of innovative materials can provide longer coherence times for devices without radical changes to their designs.
2. **3D Integration and Packaging:** As the qubit array increases, the advanced packaging methods such as 3D stacking and through-silicon vias will allow for encasing qubits at higher densities. Concurrent strands of research focus on cryogenic compatible wiring, where chip-to-chip connectors should perform well at millikelvin temperature operation.

Trapped-ion qubit research relies on further improvements in trap engineering, laser stabilization, and ion transport mechanisms (Blatt & Wineland, 2008). Enhanced microfabrication can shrink trap volume to potentially integrate hundreds or even a thousands of ions in one wafer-scale device. In the interim, photonic-based quantum computing is poised on advancements in nonlinear optical materials and in on-chip integration of detectors and modulators (O'Brien, 2007; Kok et al., 2007). Across all platforms, consistently high-quality manufacture is a bottleneck on future collaborations between quantum physicists, material scientists, and semiconductor engineers moving the field toward the next level of hardware scalability.

4.40.2 Emerging Qubit Modalities

Other viable modalities that could hold promising interest in light of possible future qubit architectures outside of the "mainstream" superconducting or ion-trap circuits have been as follows:

- **Topological Qubits**: This was aimed at developing an intrinsic fault-tolerant computational scheme by encoding information in non-Abelian quasiparticles. Put simply, the hopes are that most of the overhead of error correction will be theoretically reduced (Nayak et al., 2008). Experimental evidence for stable topological quasiparticles has remained elusive until now, but some progress being made in synthesizing certain superconductors or fractional quantum Hall systems may revitalize hopes that topological qubits could actually be built on a largescale.
- **Arrays of Neutral Atoms**: They will be trapped by optical means and can therefore be viewed as scalable qubits, but there are further developments in this branch concerned with controlling interactions between Rydberg excitations. Early experiments on the assembly of 2D arrays of hundreds of atoms are promising, leading toward quantum simulation of spin-lattice models and really interesting phenomena. Future work could make this technology available for general-purpose quantum computation, using high-fidelity gate operations between distant atoms.

- **Color Centers in Diamond (NV and Beyond)**: Solid-state defect centers, such as those of the nitrogen-vacancy (NV) center in diamond, combine optical accessibility with fairly long spin coherence times at room temperature. This opens some good imprints for its use at present in quantum sensing applications. However, it could potentially play much larger roles in quantum information processing with advanced developments in spin initialization, readout, and on-chip integration (Chen et al., 2021).

Exploring diverse qubit technologies mitigates the risk of a singular platform ever becoming blocked in its technological "lock-in" or stagnation. Although each modality has unique advantages and challenges, their coexistence fuels healthy competition and cross-pollination of ideas, collectively advancing the goal of practical, large-scale quantum computing.

4.41 REFINING ERROR CORRECTION AND NOISE MITIGATION STRATEGIES

4.41.1 Toward Practical Fault Tolerance

Great strides have been made in the field of quantum error correction (QEC) codes—such as surface codes, color codes, and bosonic codes (Fowler et al., 2012; Ofek et al., 2016)—but achieving fault tolerance at a large scale with qubit systems remains a great challenge. The following are some future directions on the issue:

1. **Adaptive Error Correction:** Instead of static schedules, they are instead exploring adaptive protocols to modify the syndrome extraction or decoding algorithms based on real-time noise diagnostics, possibly reducing the error threshold by tailoring QEC routines to the hardware condition at the time it encounters that problem (Devitt et al., 2013).
2. **Mixed-Strategy Encoding:** An approach that brings together surface codes for some qubits and bosonic codes for other qubits could yield a better tradeoff between overhead and error resiliency. Some "check qubits" are also dedicated to monitoring correlated noise events: to improve corrections in large arrays, some of the correction circuits may be attached to check qubits.
3. **Hardware-Software Co-Design:** As hardware platforms continue to refine their gate sets and connectivity, QEC codes and decoders must be co-designed to capitalize on that. This co-design paradigm further ensures integration of hardware constraints (e.g., limited nearest-neighbor couplings) into code design, thereby minimizing overhead and gate count.

However, improved realistic fault-tolerance becomes one of the basic landmarks toward quantum computing solutions for real problems—much too large for NISQ devices. Continued research refining the QEC protocols, interface with novel qubit modalities, as well as developing error diagnosis tools will without doubt carry the essential goal forward.

4.41.2 Noise Characterization and Reduction

Indeed, highly advanced noise modeling methods would be applied in concert with QEC developments to the improvement of gate fidelities. Some new approaches include:

- **Machine Learning for Error Identification:** Machine learning techniques are being increasingly applied by researchers to analyze high-dimensional noise data and identify correlations or drifts. Real-time anomaly detection ensures that gates can be rescheduled so as to avoid noise hotspots or calibrate pulses on-the-fly.
- **Quantum Error Mitigation:** The error is partially mitigated through the classical post-processing of acquired measurement results. This eliminates the need to strap on the full costs associated with a complete QEC implementation. Further advanced mitigation schemes could improve NISQ-era computation reliability and possibly enable some early demonstrations of quantum advantage for specific tasks (Temme et al., 2017).
- **Engineering Environmentally Stable Systems:** Intelligent systems designed to give better shielding against electromagnetic interference or vibration and optimized cryostat designs to minimize temperature fluctuations will definitely be furthering the coherence times one tangible step. It is becoming much worse as the multi-qubit systems grow, so that crosstalk or spurious coupling-induced environment decoherence demands innovative engineering solutions.

Thus, the advancement of noise diagnosis, characterization, and mitigation measures would definitely lead to more usability of the existent hardware and backward integration of presently existing noisy processors into future large-scale fault-tolerant quantum computing infrastructures.

4.42 EVOLVING ALGORITHMIC LANDSCAPES AND SOFTWARE INNOVATIONS

4.42.1 Post-NISQ Algorithms and Complexity

Even though NISQ algorithms like QAOA and VQE are still among active research topics in this field, the stage also prepares for giving access to fault-tolerant hardware. More advanced theoretical constructs are being explored by researchers:

1. **Quantum Walks and Graph Algorithms:** Quantum walks can be better in solving certain graph problems than the classical random walk. In future studies that investigate how QEC-friendly quantum walks can carry onto large-scale computing frameworks, real-world graph analytics or secure database queries are the areas that the studies are hoping to focus on (Venegas-Andraca, 2012).
2. **Quantum Simulation Beyond Chemistry:** Quantum simulation was highly concentrated on electronic structure problems in intermolecular systems, but the research field has been extending its application area to high-energy

physics, quantum field theories, and multi particle models significant to the design of materials. Algorithms released by the latest Hamiltonian simulation techniques would lead to new insights into physics and relevant findings to industry sectors such as superconductors and battery chemistries (Aspuru-Guzik et al., 2005).

3. **Quantum Machine Learning Again:** Quantum machine learning (QML), which was once very much in the limelight, suffers from many of its algorithms proposed so far being without any rigorous performance guarantees or based on idealistic hardware assumptions (Biamonte et al., 2017). These newly coming directions seek to keep QML deeply rooted in more robust theoretical frameworks, such as understanding the complexity classes that are relevant to QML tasks, and design QML protocols, which are explicitly tolerant to realistic hardware noise.

An essential factor in delivering theoretical computer science to the domain experts—bench to quantum chemists, physicists, and AI researchers—is expected by maturation of these algorithmic frontiers. More fertile collaboration will help clarify improved problem formulations that are game-aligned with quantum resources through which today's or tomorrow's hardware can do valid work.

4.42.2 Software Ecosystem and Higher-Level Abstractions

At the same time, the quantum software ecosystem should continue evolving with algorithmic advances. While frameworks such as Qiskit by IBM, Cirq by Google, and Q# by Microsoft have lowered the thresholds to entry, further improvements and abstractions will optimize the effort needed to develop:

1. **Domain-Specific Languages and Libraries:** Languages or libraries specializing in quantum machine learning, quantum chemistry, or quantum finance could encapsulate best practices and lessen programming on low-level gates. This would be much like how deep-learning frameworks (such as TensorFlow and PyTorch) dug the road for classical AI research at providing building blocks for complex architectures of neural networks.
2. **Hardware-Agnostic Programming:** This increasingly appears to be the case for quantum developers; very often, they demand that one write code only once and then expect it to run on different backend platforms (superconducting, trapped-ion, or photonic). It can offer improved intermediate representations (IR) and compiler toolchains for cross-platform compatibility and auto-optimization for different hardware topologies.
3. **Debugging and Verification Tools:** Quantum debugging is arguably nontrivial—it boils down to the fact that qubit states once measured directly produce superposition collapses. Circuit-level "breakpoints" wherein an advanced simulation mode allows the discovery of faults in the developer's quantum algorithm might assist such a developer further. Verification protocols such as randomized benchmarking and cross-entropy benchmarking would also see increased accessibility as the software evolved.

In the end, both researchers and industry practitioners will be empowered through a solid and flexible software stack. By hiding some of the intricate hardware details under user-friendly abstractions, software innovations will help quantum computing gain broader acceptance among engineers, data scientists, and domain experts who lack specialized quantum physics backgrounds.

4.43 THE NEXT FRONTIER: QUANTUM INTERNET AND DISTRIBUTED QUANTUM COMPUTING

4.43.1 Laying the Foundation for a Quantum Internet

Unlike the traditional monolithic and singular quantum processors, quantum networks intend to tie various nodes using entangled communication channels. Such newborn "quantum internets" may change the world with secure communications, allow the possibility of distributive quantum algorithms, and pave new paths for fundamental research (Wehner et al., 2018).

1. **Key Enablers:**
   - **Quantum Repeaters**: Because direct amplification of quantum signals is impossible (no-cloning theorem), quantum repeaters use entanglement swapping and purification to extend entanglement over long distances.
   - **Satellite Links**: Initiatives in China and Europe have demonstrated satellite-based quantum key distribution (QKD), bridging hundreds to thousands of kilometers. As more satellites equipped with entangled photon sources are launched, global-scale quantum communication may become a reality.
2. **Potential Applications:**
   - **Secure Communication**: QKD protocols can prove security against classical and quantum eavesdroppers.
   - **Distributed Quantum Computation**: Multiple small-scale quantum processors may collaborate via entangled channels tackling computations beyond the capacity of a single node.
   - **Quantum Sensor Networks**: Entangled sensor arrays are expected to promise ultra-precise measurements in astronomy, geophysics, and navigation.

Creation of strong quantum networks is likely to span over several decades of technological evolution with disruptive advances in photonic integration, quantum memory, and high-rate entanglement distribution. Still, the earlier QKD demonstrations and small-scale entanglement distribution experiments show that now, constructing a quantum internet has gone beyond a speculative level—it's now a burgeoning frontier.

4.43.2 Distributed and Modular Quantum Architectures

The short-range distributed arrangement, joined with a long-distance network, is meant to integrate the multiple quantum "modules" of a data center or laboratory with each module holding tens or hundreds of qubits employing high-bandwidth photonic or ion-based interconnects:

Benefits

- **Scalability**: It is easy to fabricate small modules than a huge chip.
- **Fault Isolation**: Errors can be isolated to the module through communicating using gate teleportation or entanglement swapping to contain noise.
- **Specialization**: Some modules can be specialized for specific tasks like memory storage, error correction, or analog simulation.

Challenges

- **Synchronization**: Timing precisions are a must for entangling modules or transporting qubits.
- **Hardware Complexity**: Adds to the hardware integration complexity since every module has to have its own cryogenic environment or vacuum enclosure as well as additional photonic or microwave link hardware.

Research efforts in this direction include advanced multiplexed photonic circuits, specialized designs of local quantum interconnects, and protocols that minimize entanglement distribution overhead between modules. Future quantum-computing "clusters" will create such a concept of modularity, which will, in principle, scale more conveniently into millions of qubits than by trying to build only one giant, monolithic device.

4.44 QUANTUM AI: CONVERGENCE OF MACHINE LEARNING AND QUANTUM COMPUTING

4.44.1 Hybrid Quantum-Classical Architectures for AI

Machine learning (ML)—from sheer enormous volumes of data to advanced neural architectures—poised for changing industries. Quantum computing, although it is yet under development, may offer ways for speeding up some computations—for instance, the linear algebra subroutine used in all current ML algorithms (Biamonte et al., 2017). One bright prospective area of research, the hybrid approach between quantum and classical approaches, includes:

1. **Variational Quantum Classifiers and Neural Networks:** These use small to medium-sized quantum circuits as network "layers," classically optimizing gate parameters. Preliminary findings indicate that sometimes quantum feature maps can separate data more efficiently in certain higher-dimensional Hilbert spaces.
2. **Sampling and Generative Models:** Quantum systems can realize certain probability distributions that seem to be infeasible to replicate classically. If employed appropriately, these quantum sampling techniques would speed up the training of GANs or Boltzmann machines. Nevertheless, there have not yet been adequate implementations because of hardware noise and qubit counts.

3. **Algorithmic Innovations:** Classical ML optimizations can potentially be employed in the tuning of quantum circuits parameters or for diagnosing hardware drift. Likewise, there are quantum-based schemes such as amplitude amplification that might also enhance classical ML tasks like gradient computation or search. It is pretty much hoped that quantum devices would be useful for some specialized subproblems within a more general classical pipeline.

4.44.2 Longer-Term Vision: Large-Scale Quantum Neural Networks

Continued beyond shimmering near-term hybrids, full quantum neural networks are now quite active theoretical pursuits. It is possible that a quantum neural network would reap the benefits using entanglement for the representation of complicated correlations in "virtual neurons," but further aggressive progress needs to occur in error-corrected hardware and new theoretical breakthroughs about how to go about efficiently training such networks at scale. There are still question marks about data loading, interpretability, and whether quantum entanglement truly gives a competitive advantage over classical deep learning at least for a majority of practical tasks. Yet the lure persists in dynamic fusion between two very fast-track fields—those of quantum computing and AI—as something of unique interdisciplinary malt.

4.45 BROADER ECOSYSTEM: POLICY, STANDARDS, AND WORKFORCE DEVELOPMENT

4.45.1 Policy and Regulatory Considerations

As quantum computing capabilities continue to develop, they will increasingly require consideration from governments and international organizations regarding the implications of policy matters such as:

- **Cryptography Standards:** Governments are currently looking at transitions to post-quantum cryptography that will safeguard classical encryption schemes for the future against these types of threats (Bernstein et al., 2009; Gottesman, 1997; Terhal, 2015; Freedman et al., 2003) along with ongoing efforts to standardize QKD protocols for secure communication in regard to the development of quantum cryptography.
- **Export Controls and Technology Transfer:** The export control and intellectual property rights discussions currently being raged in connection with quantum technologies have emerged as quantum technologies gain increasing strategic importance. Many countries grade some of their quantum technologies as sensitive national assets. Therefore, an even more delicate balance between global partnerships and national security interests will prevail.
- **Ethical and Societal Implications:** The ethical issues related to access equity, data privacy, and the responsible use of modern tools arise as massive-scale quantum computation threatens cybersecurity, financial systems,

and scientific discovery. Policymakers and researchers will probably need to construct an entirely new framework to actually realize the benefits of quantum tools for society.

4.45.2 Standards, Benchmarks, and Certification

Standards and benchmarks will come to be used in assessing the progress of an ecosystem as it develops over time, in addition to helping align expectations:

1. **Performance Metrics:** One such metric is quantum volume (QV), a measure introduced by IBM, which encapsulates processor qubit count, gate fidelity, and connectivity (Gambetta et al., 2017). Additional relevant metrics may need to be established to benchmark specialized tasks such as quantum chemistry calculations or machine-learning performance.
2. **Interoperability Standards:** It could be expected that the emerging community will be able to develop standardized interfaces or data formats, while ensuring cross-compatibility as emerging hardware platforms proliferate and software frameworks diversify. These standards could be overseen by organizations that operate similarly to ISO or IEEE, putting them under the umbrella of global quantum computing ecosystem.
3. **Certification and Compliance:** Just like there are certifications in cybersecurity or even in medical devices, quantum technology would probably be having these compliance standards that verify what the devices may claim or do. It may also have independent labs testing and certifying whether that processor has certain fidelity thresholds or QEC capabilities, thus enhancing user confidence in vendor claims.

4.45.3 Workforce and Education

Robust pipeline networks of workforce sustaining the momentum in quantum computing research are:

- **Interdisciplinary Training:** Quantum computing is physics, computer science, engineering, and mathematics. Universities and research institutes offer increasingly cross-departmental degrees or certificates, or integrated training programs in quantum engineering as Preskill has noted (2018).
- **Industry-Academia Collaboration on Skill Development:** Courses, hackathons, and workshops on quantum computing upskill currently employed professionals, whereas internships and joint labs manned by industry leaders, such as IBM, Google, Microsoft provide students with real-world approaches to R&D, creating a cycle within which new graduates are brought back to academia with cutting-edge knowledge.

- **Public Outreach and Diversity:** Broader outreach can attract underrepresented groups within the STEM field, increase the talent destination pool, and demystify quantum concepts to society. As quantum computing becomes relevant to society, it is also important to maintain equity in educational resource availability.

4.46 CONCLUDING PERSPECTIVES ON THE FUTURE OF QUANTUM COMPUTING

Furthermore, quantum computing will for long be disciplinarily reduced since an interdisciplinary capture of theoretical ingenuity, experimental breakthroughs, industrial entrepreneurship, and policy frameworks exists within the disciplines. There is a need to find a fine balance between those things that seem closer at hand—like, say, the non-adiabatic minor adjustments required for NISQ-era algorithms and scaling to the hundreds of qubits—and in so doing, it demonstrates more serious vision of another eventuality in a nearer possible future, of a stronger quantum internet, of hardware-enabled programming accelerators. Promising research avenues in the scope of pursuing further studies include:

- Hardware Scalability and Material Innovation: New qubit platforms, advanced fabrication, and coherent control methods.
- Algorithmic Exploration: Continuing refinements of present NISQ algorithms along with exploration of next-generation protocols for fault-tolerant devices.
- Quantum Networking: Striking infrastructure capable of covering longer distances and multi-node quantum computation through entanglement distribution.
- Quantum AI: This opens up pathways to merge quantum resources with classical deep learning obtainable with efficient performance in realistic Standards and Ecosystem: Development of measurement standards, interoperability protocols, and a global workforce that can steer many aspects of quantum research-taking applications into a kind of an ecosystem demarcation zone yet.

These streams of innovation create the future on which quantum computing satisfies an historic influence on cryptography, materials science, finance, logistics, climate modeling, and much more. National governments mobilizing multi-billion-dollar initiatives toward assurance of strong capabilities within quantum technology as corporate giants thicken the funding at R&D fronts and create partnerships with academic establishments scale such movements. Such investments should then make certain that quantum research keeps racing upward, forging new capabilities and eventually illuminating the most basic premises about the workability of computation and that of quantum reality.

At the end of the day, the most promising breakthroughs in quantum computing might come from entirely different areas: new qubit modalities that will exceed conventional wisdom, hybrid algorithms invoking classical AI with quantum subroutines, and distributed frameworks utilizing global networks of entanglement. Preparing for these possibilities involves breadth—encouraging cross-disciplinary collaboration—and depth—pursuing specialized, technical rigorous research agendas. Committed to these principles, the quantum community will shape a future in which quantum computing will no longer be a dream but also a transformative tool for science, industry, and society at large.

4.47 SUMMARY AND CONCLUSION

Quantum computing is one of the most interesting and ever-evolving fields in modern science and engineering. It heralds computing systems that exceed the performance of conventional machines. This chapter analyzed all those fascinating aspects of this area systematically from the detailed history of quantum computing through the present research landscape to ongoing gaps and future directions. By interweaving theoretical foundations with methodological approaches and current technology, we intended to crystallize insights and opportunities defining this domain. This final section summarizes the major conclusions of the chapter, outlines the key challenges and gaps, and stresses the many opportunities coming ahead for researchers, practitioners, and policymakers.

Key Findings and Highlights of the Chapter

1. **Historical Arc and Foundational Theories**
   - The first important leap concerning quantum computing was made by Richard Feynman (1982) as he asserted that classical machines would not be able to simulate quantum systems, thus prompting the idea about the capability of a "quantum" machine to carry out those tasks more in the natural way. His proposal paved the way into the more formal conception by David Deutsch (1985), who formulated the very idea of a universal quantum computer.
   - The breakthroughs achieved by Peter Shor (1994), who demonstrated a polynomial-time quantum algorithm for factoring integers, and Lov Grover (1997), who came up with a quadratic speedup for database searches, proved that quantum computers could solve some classes of problems with a more efficient approach than that employed by classical computers. These milestones ushered quantum computing to mainstream attention and effectively whipped content from government agencies, industries, and academic institutions.
   - There is a kernel idea for such algorithm milestones in the realization that entanglement, superposition, and quantum interference will enable people to process information using paradigms that entirely fall outside classical physics. Since then, research has proceeded into the fine mathematics of quantum information theory, directing the path toward powerful quantum error correction codes and the development of early prototype hardware implementations.
2. **Methodological Rigor in Systematic Reviews**
   - Given the cross-disciplinary nature of this field, the chapter adopted systematic review methodology—in its application of frameworks like

PRISMA and guidelines from software engineering—in order to ensure comprehensive, systematic, and reproducible literature searching exercises.
- We talked about the importance of database selection (IEEE Xplore, Scopus, ACM Digital Library, arXiv, etc.), search strategy (Boolean queries involving quantum algorithms, hardware, and applications), and screening protocol (inclusion/exclusion criteria, duplication checks, etc.). This review, then, establishes a transparent procedure that can be replicated or adapted by other researchers in order to keep up with the rapid production of publications in quantum computing.

3. **Evolution of Research Trends**
   - The phases were divided during the early stages of quantum computing, which ranged from 1980 through the late 1990s, into principal theoretical phases. It took place during the time that fundamental questions were asked and addressed on computational complexity and quantum information, providing some scenarios and intellectual foundations for future experimental work.
   - In the past two decades, the focus has shifted toward demonstrating simple quantum logic gates as well as small-scale quantum processors. In fact, it was the emergence of noisy intermediate-scale quantum (NISQ) devices in mid-2010, equipped with around tens of qubits, that ushered in another wave of applications up to very limited implementations due to restrictions by very high error rates and decoherence.
   - Over time, then, four main pillars appeared: quantum algorithms, quantum hardware, quantum cryptography, and quantum machine learning. This captures the breadth of the field: from Shor's and Grover's classical breakthroughs to state-of-the-art NISQ algorithms (e.g., QAOA, VQE); from superconducting and ion-trap hardware to photonics and topological qubits; from quantum key distribution (QKD) to more advanced protocols in secure communication; and from early theoretical proposals in quantum machine learning to today's hybrid quantum-classical schemes.
4. **Current Research Landscape**
   - In fact, industry leaders, including IBM, Google, and Microsoft, have devoted themselves heftily toward quantum computing. Each pursues a different strategic angle: IBM has superconducting qubits and a huge cloud-based ecosystem (IBM Quantum Experience, Qiskit) for itself, Google has been on everyone's lips for its "quantum supremacy" demonstration on their Sycamore chip, and Microsoft is into long-term research on topological qubits, and there's its Azure Quantum platform and Q# language as well.
   - Universities around the globe continue to collaborate to advance application-specific architectures, novel error-correction codes, and new algorithmic frontiers. Smaller startups and research teams (such as Rigetti, IonQ, and Quantinuum) strategize much discussion and technique covering everything from devices for trapped ions to quantum annealers.
   - The state of the art now could have focused on multi-qubit scaling experimentation, continued quantum error correction (more specifically

surface codes), strong software frameworks (such as Qiskit, Cirq, etc.), and application-driven alliances for serious work on quantum chemistry, quantum optimization, and quantum data science. Quantum cloud computing, quantum networks, and hybrid quantum-classical models suggest a brighter horizon in quantum computing beyond that of self-standing laboratory devices.

5. **Research Gaps and Challenges**
   - Even in the face of these achievements, scalability remains the most prominent technical challenge. To construct stable arrays of qubits at very large scales—whether superconducting, ion-trap, or otherwise—new cryogenics, wiring, materials science, and integrated control electronics must be developed. A further aggravation of these concerns is the overhead of quantum error correction and the fragility of qubits in a noisy environment.
   - An algorithmic constraint still operates, as several of these much-ballyhooed quantum algorithms are not yet practically applicable because they require fault-tolerant, large-scale devices before showing an advantage over classical performance in computational tasks. On the other hand, NISQ algorithms are believed to hold promise not letting it out of the doubt whether these algorithms can most assuredly outclass contemporary heuristics for real-world problems.
   - Industry-academia bridges get blocked by proprietary knowledge, different timelines, and even dissimilar reward structures. Closing this gap would be important to accelerate innovation in transparent validation of hardware claims and ensuring that new theoretical advances will help feed into practical demonstrations.
6. **Future Research Directions and Scope**
   - New hardware innovation will probably extend into the topological approaches, populations of neutral atoms, photonic circuits, and further advances in superconducting- or ion-trap systems. Much of the easy development of hardware will be the co-design with error-correcting protocols and advanced cryogenic control systems.
   - Translation into specialized applications, especially in quantum chemistry and optimization, is aided through error-reduction methods and partial error correction making NISQ devices more reliable platforms. Meanwhile, active research into surface codes, bosonic codes, and topological codes aims to enable more complete fault-tolerant computing.
   - The future promises connectivity through all the nodes of an entangled quantum internet that would allow secret communications, distributed quantum computation, and a new computing paradigm where quantum computing and quantum communication technologies are converging.
   - Quantum AI and machine learning are part of the newest frontier in research, determining how quantum hardware might speed up or enrich data-driven workflows. These are highly preliminary efforts that nevertheless demonstrate their synergy with two of the most transformative computational fields of the 21st century.

4.48 RECAP OF GAPS AND OPPORTUNITIES

The examination of quantum computing trends made in this chapter has revealed that the terrain is marked both by phenomenal hopes and considerable obstacles. The following are the salient gaps and opportunities that they open:

1. **Technical Obstacles to Scale and Stability**
   - **Gaps**: Current devices are still far removed from the number of qubits and their fidelities needed to implement large-scale algorithms such as Shor's factoring on nontrivial integers. The overhead for quantum error correction is daunting, and no single architecture of qubit can definitely prove that it can be scaled without trouble.
   - **Opportunities**: There is a broad bandwidth of research areas—from materials science to advanced microelectronics—that can be compatible with research into such scaling issues. Collaboration on 3D chip integration, topological qubits, and cryogenic engineering can result in new opportunities and trigger innovations not only in quantum computing but also in related fields involving superconductors, photonics, and nanofabrication.
2. **Algorithmic Maturity**
   - **Gaps**: Many quantum algorithms, particularly those that have the most promise for exponential speedup, assume fully fault-tolerant hardware; that is, it remains out of reach. Furthermore, the complexity-theoretic boundaries of quantum computing have not been fully mapped, creating uncertainty about how often quantum advantage may be realizable in applying these principles in the real-world situations.
   - **Opportunities**: Gradually improved designs of NISQ algorithms and new post-NISQ frameworks capable of partial error tolerance can pay off quite soon. Hybrid quantum-classical approaches even combine both worlds of strength so that small quantum processors can provide speedups for tasks such as chemical simulations or specific optimization problems.
3. **Collaboration and Ecosystem Development**
   - **Gaps**: Industry-proprietary technologies limit academic validation and knowledge sharing. Funding models, intellectual property (IP) issues, and differences in research timelines continue to impede synergy between fundamental science and product-focused R&D.
   - **Opportunity**: Initiatives like the IBM Quantum Network, Azure Quantum by Microsoft, and consortia supported by the EU or national governments (for example, US National Quantum Initiative) are edges leverageable for multi-stakeholder projects. Such collaborations would sizzle open-source software ecosystems (Qiskit, Cirq, etc.) and establish cross-institutional validation testbeds. The emergence of quantum education programs and specialized quantum labs would guarantee talent in a sustained conveyor belt for diversity and fresh perspectives.
4. **Emerging Fields of Exploration**
   - **Gaps**: Concepts of quantum networking were developed in theory, while practicing and scaling entanglement distribution over large distances—and creating quantum repeaters exhibiting real-world conditions in the

source—are much worse. Also, fully quantum neural networks and generalizable quantum AI solutions are still largely theoretical and are very much constrained within the limits of NISQ-era devices.

- **Opportunities**: A quantum internet, if realized, promises to transform almost completely the distributed computing and cryptographic protocols into just another resource called "anywhere entanglement." Quantum-enhanced AI may tackle computationally demanding challenges that tax classical GPUs or TPUs to failure limits, serving as a testbed for how machine learning can adapt exotic quantum mechanics principles as its foundation. The fields are attractive not only to quantum physicists but also to network engineers, computer scientists, and AI researchers—the drivers of the cultivation of highly productive cross-pollination among ideas.

Societal and Policy Dimensions

- **Gaps**: The enormous large-scale quantum computers for cybersecurity might translate into encryption standards. Accessibility to quantum technology can also intensify the existing inequity globally where only a handful of countries or corporations command the requisite resources.
- **Opportunities**: Governments, standardization bodies, and research consortia are increasingly aware of the need for "quantum readiness." This can be seen in the early adoption of post-quantum cryptographic algorithms, initiatives for a quantum-safe internet, and the search for open and inclusive quantum research frameworks. Clear policy roadmaps balancing national security, economic competitiveness, and global cooperation will be pivotal in ensuring that breakthroughs in quantum technology benefit society broadly and responsibly.

4.49 FINAL REFLECTIONS

At the same time, it is more than captured in this single testament that quantum computing is far from being a settled discipline or even a vibrant, dynamic ecosystem undergoing rapid metamorphosis. At the most fundamental and engineering level, breakthroughs in both disciplines have kicked off not just new scientific knowledge but also an entire industry whose sole commitment is to turn quantum computing into practical reality. Indeed, successes and failures in the domain are also amplified by heavy investments from the world over, international policy interest, and a huge faith that quantum technologies can revolutionize the practices of computation, cryptography, and scientific discovery.

The key points are:

1. **Quantum potential is real but so are their challenges.** While theoretical exponential speedups are made possible, they must contend against some very real-world obstacles that include noise, decoherence, and error correction overhead. With better known qubit coherence, proven error-correcting cycles, or small-scale demonstrations, however, each step closer makes it possible to turn quantum computing into practical reality.

2. **Having a wide spectrum of methods in solving a problem is an advantage.** Each kind of qubit, be it superconducting, ion-trap, photonic, or topological, has its own strengths and weaknesses. And while these myriad solutions may help keep significant industry players, academic pioneers, and innovative startups in check without any single one monopolizing everything, such multiplicity will probably remain necessary, as quantum computing continues to be worked on in many parallel yet independent directions.
3. **A hybrid future is emerging.** Soon, quantum machines will presumably work within classical HPC clusters, and that will lead to hybrid architecture with quantum hardware performing certain niche tasks—curling classical computing toward bulk data processing. The connection already exists in quantum chemistry and materials science and finance applications, and boasts that the "partial" quantum advantage might come well before the fully error-corrected devices.
4. **Collaboration, education, and policy are musts.** To realize fully the promise of quantum computing, stronger links must be established between industry R&D and academic research labs—those creating the policies that help shape economic and regulatory environments. Likewise, robust training programs will develop the capable workforce necessary to grapple with the cross-disciplinary nature of quantum computing, while ethical and policy discussions ensure equitable and responsible deployment of quantum technologies.

Looking ahead, quantum computing will probably continue to be enthralling yet uncertain. The steep technical hurdles confronting this field are competitive with the heights to which it can ascend. From quantum-secure communications to next-generation AI, the stakes and rewards are high. This chapter hopes to lead its readers through the maze that is quantum computing today by mapping out the evolution of research trends, the current technological landscape, pressing gaps, and plausible future directions.

In short, quantum computing is neither simply a brief scientific curiosity nor a mature, fully fledged industry; rather, it is an audacious experiment ongoing at the very frontiers of computation, physics, and engineering, propelled by interdisciplinary collaboration and ever-increasing public visibility. Achieving large-scale, fault-tolerant quantum computers will require sustained global effort as well as innovative thinking and readiness to dovetail results with discovery and setbacks. However, the promise still stands great: a revolution in the paradigms of computation. This remains one of the most alluring prospects in modern science and technology. The tale of quantum computing is still unfolding, with each step—be it theoretical, hardware, or application—marking yet another part of the journey human beings take as they seek to understand what can and cannot be computed or conceptualized.

REFERENCES

Aaronson, S. (2013). *Quantum computing since democritus*. Cambridge University Press.

Aaronson, S. (2015). Read the fine print. *Nature Physics*, *11*, 291–293.

Ambainis, A. (2003). Quantum walk algorithm for element distinctness. *SIAM Journal on Computing*, *37*(1), 210–239.

Arute, F., Arya, K., Babbush, R., Bacon, D., Bardin, J. C., Barends, R., . . . & Martinis, J. M. (2019). Quantum supremacy using a programmable superconducting processor. *Nature*, *574*(7779), 505–510.

Aspuru-Guzik, A., Dutoi, A. D., Love, P. J., & Head-Gordon, M. (2005). Simulated quantum computation of molecular energies. *Science*, *309*(5741), 1704–1707.

Barenco, A., Bennett, C. H., Cleve, R., DiVincenzo, D. P., Margolus, N., Shor, P., . . . & Weinfurter, H. (1995). Elementary gates for quantum computation. *Physical Review A*, *52*(5), 3457–3467.

Barends, R., Kelly, J., Megrant, A., Sank, D., Jeffrey, E., Chen, Y., . . . & Martinis, J. M. (2014). Superconducting quantum circuits at the surface code threshold for fault tolerance. *Nature*, *508*(7497), 500–503.

Barz, S., Kassal, I., Ringbauer, M., Lipp, Y. O., Dakić, B., Aspuru-Guzik, A., & Walther, P. (2013). A two-qubit photonic quantum processor and its application to solving systems of linear equations. *Scientific Reports*, *4*, 6115.

Bennett, C. H., & Brassard, G. (1984). Quantum cryptography: Public key distribution and coin tossing. In *Proceedings of the IEEE International Conference on Computers, Systems and Signal Processing* (pp. 175–179). IEEE.

Bernstein, D. J., Buchmann, J., & Dahmen, E. (Eds.). (2009). *Post-quantum cryptography*. Springer.

Biamonte, J., Wittek, P., Pancotti, N., Rebentrost, P., Wiebe, N., & Lloyd, S. (2017). Quantum machine learning. *Nature*, *549*(7671), 195–202.

Blatt, R., & Wineland, D. (2008). Entangled states of trapped atomic ions. *Nature*, *453*(7198), 1008–1015.

Boixo, S., Isakov, S. V., Smelyanskiy, V. N., Babbush, R., Ding, N., Jiang, Z., . . . & Martinis, J. M. (2018). Characterizing quantum supremacy in near-term devices. *Nature Physics*, *14*, 595–600.

Boon, B., & Wiesner, N. (2022). Governmental initiatives and policies for quantum technologies: A global perspective. *Quantum Policy Journal*, *4*(1), 22–36.

Booth, G. H., Thom, A. J. W., & Alavi, A. (2009). Fermion Monte Carlo without fixed nodes: A game of life, death, and annihilation in slater determinant space. *The Journal of Chemical Physics*, *131*(5), 054106.

Bremner, M. J., Montanaro, A., & Shepherd, D. J. (2016). Achieving quantum supremacy with sparse and noisy commuting quantum computations. *Quantum*, *1*, 8.

Breuer, H.-P., & Petruccione, F. (2002). *The theory of open quantum systems*. Oxford University Press.

Brylinski, J.-L., & Brylinski, R. (2002). Universal quantum gates. In *Mathematics of Quantum Computation* (Chapter 5). Chapman & Hall/CRC.

Calderbank, A. R., & Shor, P. W. (1996). Good quantum error-correcting codes exist. *Physical Review A*, *54*(2), 1098–1105.

Castlevvi, D. (2017). IBM's quantum cloud computer goes commercial. *Nature*, *543*(7644), 159.

Chen, Z., Farahani, H., & Englund, D. (2021). Quantum networks based on color centers in diamond. *Advanced Quantum Technologies*, *4*(5), 2100007.

Childs, A. M., Farhi, E., & Preskill, J. (2002). Robustness of adiabatic quantum computation. *Physical Review A*, *65*(1), 012322.

Clarke, J., & Wilhelm, F. K. (2008). Superconducting quantum bits. *Nature*, *453*(7198), 1031–1042.

Cleve, R., Ekert, A., Macchiavello, C., & Mosca, M. (1998). Quantum algorithms revisited. *Proceedings of the Royal Society of London: Series A*, *454*(1969), 339–354.

Deutsch, D. (1985). Quantum theory, the Church-Turing principle and the universal quantum computer. *Proceedings of the Royal Society of London: Series A*, *400*(1818), 97–117.

Devitt, S. J., Munro, W. J., & Nemoto, K. (2013). Quantum error correction for beginners. *Reports on Progress in Physics*, *76*(7), 076001.

Devoret, M. H., & Schoelkopf, R. J. (2013). Superconducting circuits for quantum information: An outlook. *Science, 339*(6124), 1169–1174.

DiCarlo, L., Reed, M. D., Sun, L., Johnson, B. R., Chow, J. M., Gambetta, J. M., . . . & Schoelkopf, R. J. (2010). Preparation and measurement of three-qubit entanglement in a superconducting circuit. *Nature, 467*(7315), 574–578.

Dieks, D. (1982). Communication by EPR devices. *Physics Letters A, 92*(6), 271–272.

DiVincenzo, D. P. (2000). The physical implementation of quantum computation. *Fortschritte der Physik, 48*(9–11), 771–783.

Ekert, A. K. (1991). Quantum cryptography based on Bell's theorem. *Physical Review Letters, 67*(6), 661–663.

Farhi, E., Goldstone, J., & Gutmann, S. (2014). A quantum approximate optimization algorithm. *arXiv:1411.4028*.

Feynman, R. P. (1982). Simulating physics with computers. *International Journal of Theoretical Physics, 21*(6–7), 467–488.

Fowler, A. G., Mariantoni, M., Martinis, J. M., & Cleland, A. N. (2012). Surface codes: Towards practical large-scale quantum computation. *Physical Review A, 86*(3), 032324.

Freedman, M. H., Kitaev, A., Larsen, M. J., & Wang, Z. (2003). Topological quantum computation. *Bulletin of the American Mathematical Society, 40*(1), 31–38.

Gershenfeld, N. A., & Chuang, I. L. (1997). Bulk spin-resonance quantum computation. *Science, 275*(5298), 350–356.

Gomes, S., Barbosa, E., & Oliveira, L. (2018). Trends in quantum computing research: A systematic literature review. In *Proceedings of the Quantum Information and Computing Conference* (pp. 43–52).

Gottesman, D. (1997). Stabilizer codes and quantum error correction. *arXiv preprint quant-ph/9705052*.

Gottesman, D. (1999). The Heisenberg representation of quantum computers. In S. P. Corney, R. Delbourgo, & P. D. Jarvis (Eds.), *Group22: Proceedings of the XXII international colloquium on group theoretical methods in physics*. International Press.

Grover, L. K. (1997). Quantum mechanics helps in searching for a needle in a haystack. *Physical Review Letters, 79*(2), 325–328.

Harrow, A. W., Hassidim, A., & Lloyd, S. (2009). Quantum algorithm for linear systems of equations. *Physical Review Letters, 103*(15), 150502.

Harrow, A. W., & Montanaro, A. (2017). Quantum computational supremacy. *Nature, 549*(7671), 203–209.

Havlíček, V., Córcoles, A. D., Temme, K., Harńeelk, A., Kandala, A., Chow, J. M., & Gambetta, J. M. (2019). Supervised learning with quantum-enhanced feature spaces. *Nature, 567*(7747), 209–212.

Jozsa, R. (1991). Characterizing classes of functions computable by quantum parallelism. *Proceedings of the Royal Society of London: Series A, 435*(1892), 563–574.

Kelly, J., Barends, R., Fowler, A. G., Megrant, A., Jeffrey, E., White, T. C., . . . & Martinis, J. M. (2015). State preservation by repetitive error detection in a superconducting quantum circuit. *Nature, 519*(7541), 66–69.

Kitchenham, B., & Charters, S. (2007). *Guidelines for performing systematic literature reviews in software engineering* (Technical Report EBSE-2007-01). Keele University & Durham University Joint Report.

Kjaergaard, M., Schwartz, M. E., Braumüller, J., Krantz, P., Wang, J. I., Gustavsson, S., & Oliver, W. D. (2020). Superconducting qubits: Current state of play. *Annual Review of Condensed Matter Physics, 11*, 369–395.

Kok, P., Munro, W. J., & Nemoto, K. (2007). Linear optical quantum computing with photonic qubits. *Reviews of Modern Physics, 79*(1), 135–174.

Ladd, T. D., Jelezko, F., Laflamme, R., Nakamura, Y., Monroe, C., & O'Brien, J. L. (2010). Quantum computers. *Nature, 464*(7285), 45–53.

Laflamme, R., Knill, E., Zurek, W. H., & Catasti, P. (1998). Heat-bath algorithmic cooling. *Philosophical Transactions of the Royal Society A*, *356*(1743), 1941–1948.

Leung, D. W. (2002). Chaining quantum operations: An introduction to quantum error correction. *Journal of Mathematical Physics*, *43*(9), 4454–4455.

Lloyd, S. (1996). Universal quantum simulators. *Science*, *273*(5278), 1073–1078.

Mattle, K., Weinfurter, H., Kwiat, P. G., & Zeilinger, A. (1996). Dense coding in experimental quantum communication. *Physical Review Letters*, *76*(25), 4656–4659.

Mermin, N. D. (2007). *Quantum computer science: An introduction*. Cambridge University Press.

Moher, D., Liberati, A., Tetzlaff, J., & Altman, D. G. (2009). Preferred reporting items for systematic reviews and meta-analyses: The PRISMA statement. *PLoS Medicine*, *6*(7), e1000097.

Mølmer, K., & Sørensen, A. (1999). Multiparticle entanglement of hot trapped ions. *Physical Review Letters*, *82*(9), 1835–1838.

Monroe, C., Meekhof, D. M., King, B. E., & Wineland, D. J. (1995). Demonstration of a fundamental quantum logic gate. *Physical Review Letters*, *75*(25), 4714–4717.

Monroe, C., Raussendorf, R., Ruthven, A., Brown, K. R., Maunz, P., Duan, L. M., & Kim, J. (2014). Large-scale modular quantum-computer architecture with atomic memory and photonic interconnects. *Physical Review A*, *89*(2), 022317.

Nayak, C., Simon, S. H., Stern, A., Freedman, M., & Das Sarma, S. (2008). Non-Abelian anyons and topological quantum computation. *Reviews of Modern Physics*, *80*(3), 1083–1159.

Nielsen, M. A., & Chuang, I. L. (2010). *Quantum computation and quantum information: 10th anniversary edition*. Cambridge University Press.

O'Brien, J. L. (2007). Optical quantum computing. *Science*, *318*(5856), 1567–1570.

Ofek, N., Petrenko, A., Heeres, R., Reinhold, P., Leghtas, Z., Vlastakis, B., . . . & Devoret, M. H. (2016). Extending the lifetime of a quantum bit with error correction in superconducting circuits. *Nature*, *536*(7617), 441–445.

O'Malley, P. J. J., Babbush, R., Kivlichan, I. D., Romero, J., McClean, J., Barends, R., . . . & Martinis, J. M. (2016). Scalable quantum simulation of molecular energies. *Physical Review X*, *6*(3), 031007.

Paler, A., Devitt, S. J., Fowler, A. G., & Wille, R. (2017). Synthesis of topological quantum circuits. *IEEE Transactions on Computer-Aided Design of Integrated Circuits and Systems*, *36*(11), 2030–2043.

Peruzzo, A., McClean, J., Shadbolt, P., Yung, M.-H., Zhou, X.-Q., Love, P. J., . . . & O'Brien, J. L. (2014). A variational eigenvalue solver on a photonic quantum processor. *Nature Communications*, *5*(1), 4213.

Preskill, J. (2018). Quantum computing in the NISQ era and beyond. *Quantum*, *2*, 79.

Reiher, M., Wiebe, N., Svore, K. M., Wecker, D., & Troyer, M. (2017). Elucidating reaction mechanisms on quantum computers. *Proceedings of the National Academy of Sciences*, *114*(29), 7555–7560.

Ristè, D., Poletto, S., Huang, M.-Z., Bruno, A., Vesterinen, V., Saira, O.-P., & DiCarlo, L. (2015). Detecting bit-flip errors in a logical qubit using stabilizer measurements. *Nature Communications*, *6*(1), 6983.

Schuld, M., Sinayskiy, I., & Petruccione, F. (2015). An introduction to quantum machine learning. *Contemporary Physics*, *56*(2), 172–185.

Shor, P. W. (1994). Algorithms for quantum computation: Discrete logarithms and factoring. In *Proceedings of the 35th Annual Symposium on Foundations of Computer Science* (pp. 124–134). IEEE.

Steane, A. (1996). Error correcting codes in quantum theory. *Physical Review Letters*, *77*(5), 793–797.

Steane, A. (1998). Quantum computing. *Reports on Progress in Physics*, *61*(2), 117–173.

Taylor, R. D. (2021, November). *Quantum technology development, policy and governance in the U.S.* Palmer Chair and Professor of Telecommunications Studies and Law Emeritus, Bellisario College of Communications, Penn State University.

Temme, K., Bravyi, S., & Gambetta, J. M. (2017). Error mitigation for short-depth quantum circuits. *Physical Review Letters*, *119*(18), 180509.

Terhal, B. M. (2015). Quantum error correction for quantum memories. *Reviews of Modern Physics*, *87*(2), 307–346.

Tranfield, D., Denyer, D., & Smart, P. (2003). Towards a methodology for developing evidence-informed management knowledge by means of systematic review. *British Journal of Management*, *14*(3), 207–222.

van Eck, N. J., & Waltman, L. (2010). Software survey: VOSviewer, a computer program for bibliometric mapping. *Scientometrics*, *84*(2), 523–538.

Venegas-Andraca, S. E. (2012). Quantum walks: A comprehensive review. *Quantum Information Processing*, *11*, 1015–1106.

Viola, L., Knill, E., & Lloyd, S. (1999). Dynamical decoupling of open quantum systems. *Physical Review Letters*, *82*(12), 2417–2421.

Wehner, S., Elkouss, D., & Hanson, R. (2018). Quantum internet: A vision for the road ahead. *Science*, *362*(6412).

5 A Framework and Taxonomy for Quantum Computing

Artor Nuhiu, Sam Goundar, Shruthi K., Akashdeep Bhardwaj, and Vishnu Kumar Kaliappan

5.1 INTRODUCTION

The development of quantum computing, being a multidisciplinary field, started with a rapid expansion because of its potential to change industries with unprecedented computational power. Its quick evolution, combined with progress in quantum algorithms, hardware architectures, and hybrid quantum-classical systems, created a fragmented environment (Preskill, 2018). Quantum hardware developments, such as IBM's 127-qubit systems and Google's 100-qubit quantum computers, along with new quantum algorithms and applications, have given rise to a dynamic evolution (Devitt, 2022; Gambetta et al., 2017). This rapid progress has led to an explosion of the number of technologies, starting from superconducting and ion trap systems to topological qubits and quantum annealing that do not fit into simple categories. Such an array of techniques introduces many problems for the systematic understanding of these new developments and how to best exploit them, thereby demanding the urgent requirement for an orderly taxonomic structure (Smith, 2020; Wendin, 2017). As researchers are delving into diverse paradigms, such as gate-based quantum circuits, quantum annealing, and photonic quantum systems, the field has become a mosaic of methodologies, with unique principles, applications, and terminology (Núñez-Merino et al., 2024; Feng et al., 2023). While this variety of approaches stimulates the development of innovation, this expansion also poses challenges in the systematic classification and comparison of quantum technologies. A non-unified framework will slow down interdisciplinary collaboration, reduce the obvious technology synergies, and restrict industry adoption. Quick evolution and divergence of quantum technologies have introduced many problems to the classification and standardization processes of newly emerging technologies. The lack of a unified framework makes it impossible for effective research, development, and technology implementation across scientific and industrial communities (Oxford Analytica, 2018). Recognizing these current challenges, we focus on the development of a comprehensive taxonomic and classification scheme tailored for quantum computing.

The chapter presents the development of a new framework that aims to bridge different dimensions (computational models, how the technology is realized in terms

DOI: 10.1201/9781003538950-6

of hardware, algorithms, and area of application) into a single framework to address these taxonomic challenges presented by the domain itself. The most distinguishing aspect of this taxonomic structure compared to other classification or grouping structures is the dynamic and modular characteristics that allow to organization of both well-established technologies, as well as those that are new or emerging such as diamond-based qubits, mobile quantum devices, cloud-based quantum computing. Consequently, the taxonomic structure aims to provide a fluid, adaptable, and comprehensive tool to aid in the field's development and growth and to maintain that development over time. While the taxonomic structure supports our organization of what we now know, it also reveals productive gaps in research allows us to create new ideas/opportunities and contributes to the advancement and development of quantum computing as it moves from a principle- and theory-based field of study to a more practical-based one.

The need for such a framework comes from the urgency of explaining the very complex nature of quantum technologies and making it comprehensible to a wide range of stakeholders including academia, research, and industry. Without a standard framework that organizes various technologies and facilitates their comparisons, the researchers get stuck with the comparison of technological developments, while academia is challenged with curricular organization and industrial actors struggle with the challenge of investments based on sound decisions. This fragmentation, moreover, restricts quantum field cooperation and slows down its translation of theory into application. The fact that there is no standard taxonomy only worsens the problem since this field now lacks a common language and point of reference that it can utilize to cope with its complexity. It seems that the present classifications are more likely to depend on the ad hoc categorizations that arise from some specific type of hardware, some algorithm families, or use cases. This leads to the overlap in definitions and to inconsiderate usage of terminologies, like the difference between NISQ devices and fault-tolerant systems, or between variational quantum algorithms and error-corrected protocols that are not well defined. This unclearness deters knowledge sharing, slows educational efforts, and creates barriers for stakeholders seeking to explore the quantum ecosystem. Academia, industry, and policymakers correspondingly face difficulties in aligning research priorities, benchmarking progress, or identifying scalable commercial applications (Núñez-Merino et al., 2024; Khammassi et al., 2018).

In this chapter, we aim to fill in the gaps with a broad and general taxonomic and classification framework for quantum computing. This classification intends to categorize quantum technologies by their corresponding computation models, hardware implementations, employed algorithms, and domains of applications. Its multidimensional approach differentiates it by being able to include (and expose relationships between) all of quantum computing technologies, which can include new constructs like diamond qubits and mobile quantum systems and infrastructure, and a flexible framework for future development. The framework aims to enhance communication, promote interdisciplinary collaboration, and accelerate innovation through the fusion and clarification of existing paradigms and their relations. This helps researchers in establishing a clearer view of emerging trends, allows teachers to teach how to explain complex concepts, and allows industry players to formulate their views on future technological advancements and market potentials. Objectives of this chapter include:

- Adopting a methodically organized approach to categorize and classify the vast array of technologies that form quantum computing.
- Measuring the benefits from a standardized taxonomy in enhancing knowledge organization, which facilitates easier exploration of the quantum computing field.
- Proposing methodologies that simplify the complexity of quantum technologies, advance better communication, and promote collaborative research and development project.

The present conceptual model provides the basic approach to support academic research and real-world applications related to quantum computing. It aims to develop orderly structures to enable continued developments and evolutions in quantum technologies in other sectors. Taxonomies help simplify the intricacy of a well-built classification system that standardizes terminology, shows gaps in current work, identifies opportunities across domains, and helps in resource allocation. As quantum computing is an inherently interdisciplinary area and thus is developing rapidly, such a framework becomes indispensable. It will make it possible to have better-defined benchmarks for quantum advantages, help build inter-operational standards, and enhance public and private sector participation. In this regard, the chapter aims to create a common language and framework for stakeholders to fully utilize quantum computing potential and exploit its inherent uncertainties.

5.1.1 Background

The advent of quantum computing can be traced back to the early 1980s, when visionary physicists were trying to imagine what would happen in the computation if they would use the concept of quantum mechanics. In his groundbreaking work, Feynman (1982) proposed the possibility of quantum systems being based on quantum-based machines, proposing that classical computers are in general limited in modeling complex quantum phenomena. The idea behind this approach was extended by Deutsch (1985) through the invention of quantum Turing machine that introduced the very theory of universal quantum computing. It has only been through Shor's (1994) algorithm that factoring of large numbers took on exponential speed when compared to classical methods, and that allowed for the application of the quantum search algorithm introduced by Grover (1996). Their research demonstrated that in certain tasks, quantum computing surpasses classical systems. Such important works became the foundation upon which theoretical research developed for decades to follow.

The quantum computer concept, therefore, took a big step forward from abstract conception to real technologies for some fields that came from theoretical bases. Initially, efforts were directed toward physical implementations of qubits, the quantum analogs of classical bits. Development in quantum computing was further supported through superconducting circuits by IBM and Google, trapped ions by IonQ, and optical systems by PsiQuantum (Bartolucci et al., 2021). The breakthroughs of quantum entanglement that Einstein et al. (1935) named "spooky action at a distance" are the core schemes for quantum teleportation and error correction (Bennett et al., 1993). Other works, like surface codes and topological qubits, aimed at mitigating the effect of decoherence and noise while trying to realize the quantum states that form big steps toward building a large and reliable quantum system. Experiments of quantum supremacy by Google in 2019 represent some of the very beginning successes of the development of quantum computing technologies (Arute et al., 2019). Experimental attempts of the late 90s and beginning of 2000s: it was when several milestones, e.g., superconducting qubits at Yale and IBM were born, in terms of the developing and open scalable approach for quantum hardware (Rieffel & Polak, 2011; Martinis et al., 2003; Nakamura et al., 1999). What was initially a simple theory became the basis of quantum information processing through entanglement. Important developments, such as the realization of multi-qubit systems, were accomplished via error correction techniques (surface codes and topological codes) that coped with decoherence as one of the universal challenges of quantum states. The upcoming years will be the era for this field of research with a full push into NISQ by companies such as Google with 100 qubits processors, IBM with 127 qubits processors, etc., which will lead to the applications in cryptography, optimization, and materials science (Sachdeva et al., 2024).

It is a paradox of contrasts that even when quantum computing is making headway, its classification becomes an open puzzle that existing attempts to explain could not catch up to the fast evolution and multidimensional nature of the field. Attempts to classify quantum computing technologies initially were beneficial, as they provided a foundation of classification that categorized quantum hardware, software, and applications. But they could not deal well with finer-grade distinctions between hardware systems, such as differences between ion traps and photonic systems, or with the more recent development of hybrid quantum-classical algorithms and state-of-the-art methods of error mitigation. Previous classifications focused mainly on some hardware types (superconducting vs. photonic qubits) or algorithmic families (Shor-type vs. variational algorithms). Such classifications did not address the interdisciplinary nature of the field, crossing over into physics, computer science, materials engineering, and applications such as cryptography or chemistry (Sete et al., 2016; Nofer et al., 2023; National Academy of Engineering, 2019). Examples of such categorizations ignored, for instance, the hybrid architecture (quantum-classical neural networks) or did not draw the necessary distinctions between heuristic NISQ algorithms and fault-tolerant and error-correcting protocols (Bharti et al., 2022). This fragmentation has been a barrier to consistent terminology within the community, redundant research, and non-alignment of benchmarks across academia and industry (Ukpabi et al., 2023; Smith, 2020). Besides, no standard adaptable classification system leaves researchers and industry professionals in a situation with no common view for evaluation and comparison of technologies, thus hindering collaboration and adoption. Additionally, such a historical background provides relevance to the development of a robust and adaptive taxonomy for quantum computing. The very development from Feynman's (1982) theoretical perspectives up to the modern implementation of practical systems signifies on one side a promise of the field and the growing complexity of this field on the other. Therefore, addressing the weaknesses of previous classification efforts this chapter aims to establish a broad prospective taxonomy providing a clear and focused view of the quantum environment to the scientists, researchers, and industrial partners. Such a taxonomy is not a mere tool of review but a base for future progress ensuring that all possible advantages of quantum computing are put into organized and accessible perspective.

5.1.2 Research Gap and Justification

Despite its exponential growth, the existing classification frameworks of quantum computing remain fragmented and incomplete. Most current taxonomies are more oriented toward isolated features, for instance, qubit types such as superconducting or trapped ions or the classes given to Shor's and Grover's algorithms (Gill et al., 2022). They neglect the global interaction among hardware, software, and applications. They also do not distinguish between the NISQ-period optimized algorithms that are designed for noisy devices and the fault-tolerant protocols that require error-corrected qubits going to mismatched expectations over their performance and scalability. Concurrently, hybrid quantum-classical systems that combine classical machine learning with quantum circuits remain frequently omitted or ambiguous in their labeling, despite being on a rapid rise in their usage for real-world optimization problems. This direction becomes a barrier to cross-disciplinary innovation while also complicating pathways toward quantum advantage. Gill et al. (2022) undertake the first attempt to classify taxonomies, which, although represented in the diagram, provided mapping of related studies identified research gaps, and served as the base understanding of the overall framework for quantum computing. Nonetheless, this taxonomy has failed to detail new hardware types, sophisticated error correction schemes, and novel applications. Moreover, this taxonomy centers on technical aspects, thus ignoring deployment models, such as cloud-based quantum computing, which have gained momentum with the onset of platforms, such as Amazon Braket and IBM Quantum Experience. Thus, new approaches need to capture the current developments for an updated classification scheme. It has, however, been a difficult task to standardize an acceptable taxonomy system that would not leave any field, be it academic, industrial, or governmental, fragmented. In terms of the technical and academic perspective, the classification of quantum annealing is seen as a form of quantum computing; however, in industry perspectives such as that of the financial sector, the latter takes on an altogether separate place for task optimization, and the main cases such as quantum cryptography or material simulation are given preference. In contrast, a classification that is aligned with government policy, national security, or economic and market competitiveness is favored. Such inconsistency is problematic because it can cause confusion during benchmarking, restrict the transformation of research into commercial/practical applications, and render interpretation of terms like "quantum supremacy" or "quantum-ready" difficult across those contexts, risking miscommunication among different stakeholders. No universal standard has thus far been put into use, even though the International Organization for Standardization (ISO) has made efforts in this respect to develop its standard to define terms commonly used in quantum computing but not as detailed taxonomies

(ISO/IEC, 2024). In the meantime, the IEEE Quantum Technical Community and the US Quantum Economic Development Consortium (QED-C) are exploring standardization, though no unified taxonomy has emerged yet (IEEE, 2023; QED-C, 2023). The development of new simulation types is also bringing in new kinds of quantum and classical computing that combine them to solve particular problems, and thus, they do not fit into the currently known classification groups since they mix the lines between hardware and software classification (Khan et al., 2023). Besides that, there are many other noise-resistant qubits, which, by making use of cat qubits for suppressing errors, do not fit into specific classification schemes for the innovation that they provide (Putterman et al., 2025; Xu et al., 2022). Since there is no inclusion of cloud-based quantum computing, which is quantum services done through the internet taxonomy will also be of less significance for use cases about industry needs. Current models might not allow further development of mobile quantum devices and parallel quantum computing, all of which need a flexible framework for growth. This chapter aims to fill the gap of this existing taxonomy gap by providing a structured and adaptive taxonomy to classify quantum computing that unifies them. It is organized into several modern categories that describe several hardware-based systems, software, algorithms, error-correcting techniques, and applications, as well as attempts to cover newer types of technology into hybrid systems and cloud-based computing. Some other benefits of this classification will include facilitating proper knowledge organization from Table 5.1.

This taxonomy will benefit academic research as it will build up a clear teaching model for researchers so they can determine the research gaps, which can then help industry professionals to better evaluate and adopt the technologies. This approach not only clarifies the whole quantum ecosystem but helps the stakeholder identify the synergies and prioritize the resources for a faster transition from theoretical to the practical impact of quantum computing advancements.

TABLE 5.1
Benefits of a Quantum Computing Taxonomy

Benefit	Description
Knowledge organization	Support the future through research and education. Therefore, information management and synthesization of information shall be well developed.
Standardization	Setting up a common terminology will eliminate confusion and build effective communication with the stakeholders.
Simplification	Make the world of quantum computing easy to enter, both for newcomers and even educators.
Research gap identification	Guide future research and innovations with the identification of issues yet in need of further study.
Industry integration	Future investment decisions and development plans should incorporate an understanding of quantum computing so that decision-makers are aware of what has yet to be accomplished, what is being done, and the implications of that work.

5.1.3 Methodology for Developing the Quantum Computing Taxonomy

The development of a taxonomy for quantum computing requires rigorous and thorough analysis to ensure its reliability and relevance. The methodology is based on a systematic literature review, domain analysis, expert consultation, classification criteria, and conceptual modeling. The systematic literature review is the backbone of the process; hence, data sources include, but are not limited to, peer-reviewed articles, conference papers, and industry reports. The review intends to gather all studies published related to quantum computing technologies and their classification. The extraction of data puts special emphasis on the identification of hardware types, software tools, algorithms, and applications, as well as existing taxonomies for comparison. Following this, after a thorough review of the literature, there is a domain analysis carried out to gather in-depth information about the quantum computing field. Getting to know the basic concepts of these topics involves reading standard textbooks and references that organize and develop such concepts (Usman et al., 2020). Moreover, industry reports and market analyses need to be reviewed that reflect real-world applications and trends for commercial/practical development to incorporate the academic point of view in the taxonomy together with the industry view (Juárez-Ramírez et al., 2023; Maass et al., 2024).

Expert consultation: To validate and improve the taxonomy, feedback should be obtained from world-renowned experts in quantum computing. Experts should be identified based on their significant contribution to the field—as viewed by their publications, patents, and leadership roles in well-established programs like the IEEE Quantum Technical Community, or the Quantum Economic Development Consortium (QED-C). The consultation consists of structured interviews along with two rounds of a Delphi survey. Interviews provide the targeted opportunity for deep exploration of taxonomic components, and the Delphi survey systematically achieves consensus on high-priority classifications and emerging developments. The use of multiple research methods ensures that an array of voices could be developed in the taxonomy and is based on the current state-of-the-art knowledge (Bensoussan et al., 2025). After completion, the taxonomy is expected to be referred to the experts to have their comments and inputs for assuring the proper and precise clear definitions as required for the community. Systematically classified criteria will then be set based on information collected for organizing quantum computing technologies. In such a case, they will be built to achieve a multidimensional view: technical, functional, and application-oriented aspects of quantum computing.

Classification by technology includes categorization of quantum computing according to the technological building blocks by which quantum computing falls under:

- ***Hardware***: Physical implementations of quantum computers, such as superconducting, ion traps, topological, photonic, and diamond-based systems, are considered types of quantum computing systems. The classification is performed based on the number of qubits, error rates, coherence times, etc.

- ***Software:*** We include the software that runs quantum computing applications—such as programming languages, development frameworks, and operating systems, including Qiskit, Cirq, and OpenQASM—into three separate categories, classified based on abstraction levels and their compatibility with different hardware.
- ***Algorithms:*** Specific quantum algorithms are grouped into categories based on their intended applications, such as quantum simulation, optimization, machine learning, and cryptography. Optimization includes algorithms such as the Shor algorithm for factoring, the Grover algorithm for search, and the variational quantum eigensolver (VQE). They will also be classified according to their complexity of computation and their fields of application.

Functional classification is the grouping of quantum computing technologies, categorized in terms of their functional use. In other words, the grouping by functional areas includes the following:

- ***Computation:*** Technologies that can solve computational problems impossible for classical computers; simulating quantum systems, optimizing huge data, etc. General-purpose quantum processing and hybrid classical-quantum workflows will be included.
- ***Cryptography:*** Technologies used for encryption, decryption, and secured communication, including QKD and post-quantum cryptographic protocols.
- ***Communication:*** Technologies that permit quantum teleportation, quantum networking, entanglement distribution and secure data transmission, used in quantum internet initiatives.

Industry application is the classification of quantum computing that puts it into different sectors that use or would be likely to use it:

- ***Finance:*** Quantum algorithms in complex financial modeling for risk analysis, portfolio optimization, and fraud detection.
- ***Artificial intelligence (AI):*** Quantum machine learning or optimization of AI applications such as neural network training and pattern recognition.
- ***Cybersecurity:*** Mainly focused on the use of encryption and secured communication in the protection of data from quantum cyber threats.
- ***Medicine:*** The quantum simulation in molecular modeling would enhance drug discovery, protein folding, and genomics.
- ***Other industries:*** The scope of the application of quantum computing includes areas as varied as battery design (energy), logistics for supply chain optimization, and national security (government).

These criteria guarantee that taxonomy includes technical and applied perspectives of the field of quantum computing, thereby achieving an overall view. Figure 5.1 illustrates a bidirectional interdependence among computational models, the specifications of a hardware setup, specific algorithms to solve the problem, and the application fields themselves. The proposed framework allows adaptation for the evolving innovations without losing clarity and standardization.

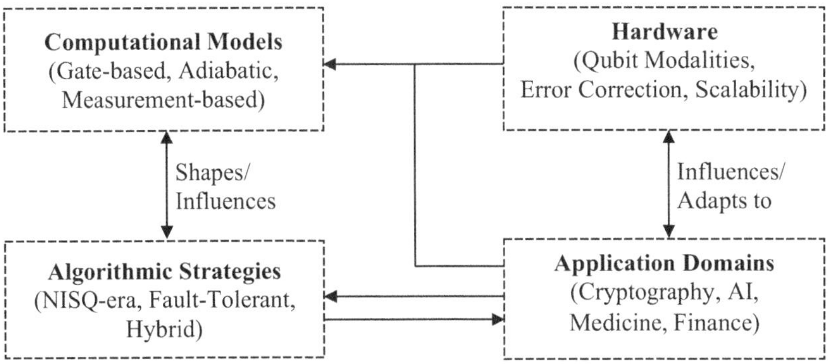

FIGURE 5.1 A four-dimensional taxonomy for quantum computing.

5.1.3.1 Technology Selection and Justification

The chapter characterizes the technologies based on their physical/hardware basis (superconducting, ion traps, topological, photonic, diamond-based systems), software basis (i.e., hardware, software (e.g., Qiskit, Cirq, OpenQASM), algorithm basis (Shor's algorithm, Grover's algorithm, VQE), and application basis (finance, medicine, logistics, cybersecurity). It does not explicitly state in the taxonomy itself that technologies meet any of the criteria. However, the technologies in the proposed taxonomy were specifically included satisfying the following criteria:

1. **Technological maturity:** Only technologies that have moved past theoretical proposal, and have been experimentalized, were included. For example, superconducting qubits were included due to their successful scalable experimental, and operational state, in a system developed by IBM with 127 qubits, and a successful 100-qubit experimental system developed by Google.
2. **Industry adoption:** A preference was given to technologies that are actively developed by prominent companies and research institutes. For example, trapped-ion systems were included because they are in active development by a company called IonQ, while photonic qubits were included given their future potential and capability to connect quantum systems in quantum communication networks.
3. **Expert consensus:** The review of technologies made would be cross-checked with business, university, and consulting experts who consulted to get their thoughts on which technologies are most promising, and which are relevant to current and future adoption applications.
4. **Emergent potential:** To keep the taxonomy relevant, emergent technologies were included, such as diamond-based qubits and photonic systems, which are representative of a future direction in quantum computing in terms of research and development.

These criteria were critical for providing a thorough taxonomy based on established technologies that have the potential for future impact.

5.2 COMPONENTS OF QUANTUM COMPUTING: CONCEPTUAL MODEL

To systematically organize taxonomy, a hierarchical and multidimensional conceptual model will be adopted. This model structures the taxonomy around a framework that begins with general categorizations (technical, functional, and industry applications) and details down into more specific elements (types of quantum algorithms or sector specific application). In developing this model, dynamic modeling is assured, with easy updating whenever new technologies of quantum computing turn up. The taxonomy is structured as follows:

1. ***Quantum hardware:*** Different quantum computing systems based on their physical implementation constitute this category. Subcategories include superconducting systems (transmon qubits, fluxonium qubits), ion trap systems (Penning trap, Paul trap), topological systems, photonic systems, and diamond-based systems. Each of these subcategories are further detailed by specific characteristics, such as qubit count, error rates, and coherence times.
2. ***Quantum software:*** This includes programming languages, development tools, and operating systems that are used in quantum computing. Subcategories include high-level languages (Qiskit and Cirq), low-level languages (OpenQASM), and development frameworks (Amazon Braket and IBM Quantum Experience). Each subcategory can be classified by compatibility with different kinds of hardware and level of abstraction.
3. ***Quantum algorithms:*** This includes algorithms that are classified by their purpose and specific names:
   a. *Types:* Quantum simulation, optimization, machine learning, and cryptograph.
   b. *Specific algorithms:* Factoring with Shor's algorithm, search with Grover's algorithm, optimization with VQE, and combinatorial problems using the QAOA (quantum approximate optimization algorithm). The cost and the fields of application of them are discussed in detail.
4. ***Quantum applications:*** This classification uses categories according to function and industry sector:
   a. *Function:* Solving optimization problems (computation), quantum key distribution (cryptography), and quantum teleportation (communication).
   b. *Industry sector:* Finance (risk analysis and portfolio optimization), AI (quantum machine learning), cybersecurity (secure communication), medicine (drug discovery, genomics), energy (battery design), logistics (supply chain optimization), and government (national security).

This classification hierarchy allows for easy organizing into primary groups with subcategories, split in turn by specific criteria of classification. The subdivision of transmon and fluxonium qubits provides technical descriptions in the branch dedicated to quantum hardware. This feature will permit the technology to be classified based on more than one criterion. One of them is a superconducting quantum computer applied to the fields of cryptography in finance. Table 5.2 presents the potential

TABLE 5.2
The Comparative Advantages of Proposed Taxonomy

Aspect	Proposed Taxonomy	Gill et al. (2022) Taxonomy
Coverage	Includes emerging technologies, such as diamond-based systems	Restricted only to established categories and misses new types
Adaptability	Dynamic, hierarchical, and modular, includes runtime environments and simulators, easy to update	Static, focused on programming languages, less on tools, less flexible for future innovations
Dimensions	Detailed by function: technical, functional, industrial applicability	Mainly technical and application-based, broad categories, less specific examples
Validation	Expert consultation and up-to-date literature review	Based on literature up to 2020, may be outdated

benefits of the proposed taxonomy through comparison with the existing Gill et al. (2022) taxonomy. This draws attention to its prime merits—fluidity and all-encompassing coverage concerning the shortcomings of the prior classifications.

This proposed model is appropriate, as fast and dramatic changes occur in the quantum computing environment. This model hosts bidirectional relations, which influences the design of algorithms due to hardware limitations, and group innovations in a modular way. For instance, photonic quantum computing is initially classified under the hardware category but later may become integrated into communication applications, i.e., quantum networking. New types of hardware or algorithms may be added under their primary categories as a subclass, while new applications could be incorporated into the functional or industry application classifications. This flexibility is an assurance that the proposed taxonomy will be in tune with the changing dynamics of the field of quantum computing.

5.3 CLASSIFYING QUANTUM COMPUTING TECHNOLOGIES

A proper taxonomy of quantum computing should be built on various angles of consideration: functionality, usage, and mechanism of realization. Such grouping can show the variety of capabilities and possible applications of quantum computing technologies in a variety of spheres. This way, it will be able to create a balanced view of current deployments and the new features yet to come in the quantum field.

1. ***Classification by functionality***
   Classification of the functionalities of quantum computing technologies highlights the core operational tasks and what they utilize the quantum principles for, to solve computational problems. In this context, we concentrate on how the technology could be practically utilized. The functional areas may be further distinguished by the specific tasks for which they are designed, with direct influence on design and the focus of operations:
   - *Computation-based quantum computing:* Quantum computing that deals with solving computational problems, leveraging quantum advantage.

The quantum algorithms for factoring large numbers or unstructured search with quantum advantage are, for instance, the Shor algorithm and the Grover algorithm, respectively, exploiting superposition and entanglement to provide exponential or quadratic speedups. This can include *gate-based models* (universal quantum circuits), *quantum annealing* (D-Wave optimization systems), and *measurement-based models* (photonic clusters). These systems can handle problems needing considerable computation by large-scale numerical simulations or optimizing complex systems.

- *Cryptographic applications:* Focusing on enhancing security against classical cryptographic systems. Quantum computers are a threat to classical encryption systems by solving, through efficient ways, problems of integer factorization while, at the same time, enabling quantum-resistant cryptography using lattice-based algorithms. This also includes technologies that support quantum-safe protocols using quantum properties to secure data against future quantum threats—which presents a big issue as it was put under the spotlight by recent trends in cybersecurity.
- *Quantum communication:* Encompasses the technologies that exploit quantum mechanics to enhance security and efficiency in communication and information transfer by quantum teleportation and quantum repeaters. Important here are quantum key distribution (QKD) with BB84 protocols that use quantum entanglement and no-cloning to enable unconditional key exchange as applied in China's Micius satellite-based systems. Quantum teleportation serves as a building block for transferring quantum states over long distances, thus forming the basis for quantum networks and the envisaged quantum internet. Such technologies become relevant in building next-generation communication infrastructures.

2. ***Classification by application area***

   Classification by area of application, the real-world application of quantum computing, with its transformative impact, could be elaborated on from theory to practice. This view correlates theoretical capabilities to real-world use cases for quantum computing:

   - *Optimization:* Quantum computing is utilized for solving optimization problems by finding the best solutions to the different fields of logistics, financial systems, and machine learning that optimize routes, investments, or parameters in neural networks. Using QAOA and quantum annealing techniques developed by D-Wave systems can optimize applications related to supply chain logistics, traffic flow, and financial portfolio management.
   - *Cryptographic security:* This relates the use of quantum computing to creating new cryptographic mechanisms to protect data from confidentiality and integrity in attacks by a quantum adversary. While it goes beyond the task of breaking classical encryption, quantum technology has brought in a new dimension of secured communication with the advent of QKD, which serves as a building block toward the formulation

of post-quantum cryptography standards. Such dual roles put cryptographic security as an important building block, having repercussions for finance, government, and cybersecurity.

- *Material simulations and pharmaceuticals:* Capability to simulate interactions between molecules and atoms at the quantum level with quantum computing. VQE algorithms permit accurate chemical reaction modeling that accelerates the design of new materials (batteries) and pharmaceuticals (protein folding in drug development). The application is especially relevant in materials science and pharmaceuticals as quantum computing would reduce development times for new materials and medicines.

3. ***Classification by realization mechanism***

   Another method to classify quantum computing technologies can be found in their physics implementation of the quantum bits used:

   - *Superconducting qubits* are the basis of superconducting 100-qubit and 127-qubit processors. They employ qubit superconductors made from superconducting materials at temperatures close to absolute zero to create qubits. They are currently being developed, as superconducting qubits may potentially allow scaling and fast operation of gates through microwave frequencies, although such systems are still in their infancy with respect to advanced cryogenic technology, which can counteract any possible noise and decoherence.
   - *Photonic qubits* are those based on the inherent properties of light in the manipulation of photons in polarization, used to perform quantum computations. The main advantage of photonic quantum computing is that it can be readily embedded in currently existing fiber-optic communication networks, which would serve as backbones for quantum communication implementations. Being operated at room temperature with great scalability and compatible with the present optical infrastructure, it is the prospects that have yet to face challenges such as those related to photon loss and detector efficiency.
   - *Trapped ions* utilize electromagnetic fields that store ions that contain internal energy in trapped ions; therefore, these are considered qubits. These trapped ions have long coherence times with high-fidelity quantum operations with precision measurements and scalable quantum processing through lasers. However, their scalability is still much lower than that of superconducting qubits, although their ability to resist noise gives them the lead in the field of quantum simulation and cryptography.

5.3.1 Quantum Computing Hierarchy

Organizing a framework that reflects complex issues of the evolution of quantum computing necessitates a hierarchical structure that effectively categorizes many aspects of advancements in this field. In this section, we present a four-level hierarchy that progresses from basic principles to advanced integrations to systematically simplify the understanding of quantum computing technologies. Every level is built upon another one that create a detailed taxonomy that reflects the theoretical, computational, technical, and practical approaches to these technologies.

Level 1—Basic Concepts and Quantum Principles

This level will focus on the core concepts and principles of quantum mechanics that drive quantum computing. That said, the building block of quantum computing is all based on entanglement. Basic quantum gates, like the Hadamard and the CNOT, as well as the mathematical formalism of quantum states, will be discussed in this section. This will clarify that qubits serve as the basic units of quantum information analogous to the classical bit in conventional computing. The level describes quantum decoherence along with the problem of keeping qubits in a quantum state needed for the development of actual quantum computers.

Level 2—Algorithm Development and Computational Models

This level focuses on the development of quantum algorithms and computational models that use quantum mechanics for efficient problem-solving and practical computations. To provide a quadratic advantage, this category includes Shor and Grover algorithms for integer factorization and unstructured search problem-solving. It also covers quantum circuit computational models and adiabatic quantum computing (used in quantum annealing) as well as the variational quantum eigensolver (VQE) for task optimization and simulation. Qiskit and Cirq will be used as software frameworks for the implementation of these models.

Level 3—Hardware Implementation and Scaling

The focus of this level is physical realization using the specific building blocks for quantum scaling. Such structures consist of quantum computing architectures that integrate superconducting qubits, trapped ions, and photonic qubits, used to realize quantum gates. Considering engineering-related aspects of error correction, cryogenic systems used in superconducting qubits, and laser control in trapped ions, it advances toward realizing a quantum architecture, hence fault-tolerant systems.

Level 4—Hybrid Quantum-Classical Integration

This level will combine quantum and classical computing systems in such a way as to maximize practicality and usage. Such a combination of quantum-classical systems would be capable of handling several computation tasks along with reducing errors. For example, the quantum approximate optimization algorithm (QAOA) will be implemented on NISQ devices with classical infrastructure and cloud-based platforms to give easy access to quantum resources. This level will provide completely integrated quantum-classical workflows in the context of machine learning or material design, as well as the large-scale implementation of quantum technologies.

This four-level dynamic hierarchy would not be something rigid; instead, it is a dynamic progression and evolution of quantum computing. A taxonomy of quantum computing, set within such a hierarchical layer, allows a clear understanding of its constituents involved along with their relationship with theoretical knowledge and practical applications. Not only would this organize the work that has already been completed, but it would also provide a more flexible structure for other projects to be conducted to ensure that it remains a valuable resource going forward with the progression of the quantum computing industry.

5.4 COMPARATIVE ANALYSIS OF EXISTING TAXONOMIES

This section discusses classification models of quantum computing and emphasizes the urgency of developing a unified taxonomy for quantum computing. It performs a comparative study of existing taxonomies and establishes an argument in favor of a taxonomy that can be adapted to the fast-growing quantum computing area. Most existing taxonomies tend to classify quantum computing technologies depending on such criteria as qubit type, target area, or some quantum principles and models. While those taxonomies were useful in some ways, in practice, they generally applied narrow and limited approaches. *Firstly*, the inability to adapt to new challenges and implementations is also a well-known issue when analyzing the Gill et al. (2022) taxonomy. While being based on a static structure, it fails to incorporate later innovations, such as diamond-based qubits that promise to push forward quantum computing to a room-temperature level. Examples include hardware-centric models such as IBM's roadmap that mainly focuses on qubit modalities or scaling metrics and classifies quantum processors according to their coherence times and fidelity for gates. Similarly, although it is practical, Gill et al.'s (2022) model lacks a modular structure that would enable easy future hardware/software updates, thus restricting its longevity.

Second, missing future technologies form an even greater gap. However, the taxonomies primarily developed much earlier than hybrid quantum-classical systems were put in place, such as the case for algorithm-first taxonomies. Other frameworks do not mention cloud-based quantum computing through Amazon Braket and IBM Quantum Experience; it is becoming increasingly important in the industry. Also, mobile quantum devices and parallelized quantum computing are left out. So, they are, therefore, an incomplete view of present and future needs.

Third, fragmentation and little standardization limit the utility of benefits. Gill et al.'s (2022) taxonomy, for example, does not have any subcategories for the emergence of topological codes or quantum machine learning in AI. In some examples, Gill et al.'s (2022) and Hidary's (2021) models fail to standardize terminology in an academic, industrial, and governmental environment, which then becomes problematic in the case of fragmentation.

5.4.1 Justification for the Proposed Taxonomy

The limitation of current taxonomies provides an urgent need to create a new framework. The proposed taxonomy fills the gaps mentioned and contributes to its appropriateness and added value in quantum computing with several improvements:

1. **A flexible and multidimensional approach:** This proposed taxonomy allows easy updates and modifications. The dynamic structure enables the taxonomy

to remain relevant and useful to emerging technologies. It seeks to combine technical (hardware/software/algorithms), functional (computation/cryptography), and application (medicine/finance) hierarchy into a unified structure.

2. **Adaptable to future-oriented technologies:** By employing a multi-level hierarchical approach (see Section 3.1) that covers classifications from basic principles, algorithms, and hardware to hybrid integrations. Unlike the previously static models, this framework is a dynamic and modular design that allows the incorporation of future emerging technologies, such as diamond-based qubits or cloud-based quantum platforms. The dynamic criteria ensure the is an up-to-date transition from NISQ-era algorithms to fault-tolerant protocols.
3. **Standardized classification across various sectors:** The proposed taxonomy offers a classification that intends to be more uniform and standardized across various fields by using a more standardized and consistent terminology to classify quantum technologies. It creates the foundation of a standard framework by taking input from academia, industry, and other regulatory bodies. This model helps promote communication, collaboration, and interoperability within and between sectors and stakeholders.

Table 5.3 presents a comparative analysis between existing quantum computing taxonomies and the proposed framework regarding their strengths and limitations and scope of improvement. This comparative analysis elaborates why an entirely new taxonomy is necessary that fills in the gaps in existing taxonomies but also provides a structure to improve the usage of classification in the field of quantum computing.

An adaptable, inclusive, and unifying taxonomy would allow for better support of the current growing innovation in quantum computing technologies. It also helps in organizing the present status of quantum computing that represents recent improvements such as Google and IBM qubit processors, besides laying the groundwork for future development in this field by fostering collaboration, education, and industry implementation. This will fill the gaps in existing taxonomies so that the new classification system ensures that the quantum computing environment is accessible and

TABLE 5.3
Comparing the Existing and Proposed Taxonomy

Taxonomy Type	Focus	Advantages	Limitations
Hardware-Centric	Qubit types, scalability	Guides engineering R&D	Ignores software/ algorithm requirements
Algorithm-First	Computational power and complexity	Clarifies quantum advantage potential	Overlooks hardware constraints
Application-Driven	Use cases	Aligns with market needs	Fails to link apps to enabling tech
Proposed Taxonomy	**Multidimensional**	**Integrates hardware, algorithms, and applications**	**Requires periodic updates**

actionable and drives progress as the field enters its next phase of development and beyond.

5.5 PROPOSED QUANTUM COMPUTING FRAMEWORK AND TAXONOMY

This section presents a new quantum computing framework and taxonomy developed to overcome the limitations identified in the existing models and create a well-defined classification system for academics, researchers, and industry professionals. The presentation of a diagram that visually represents this framework with categories and subcategories and an explanation of its distinguishing features compared to the previous models show how the proposed taxonomy can contribute to improving the organization, standardization, and applicability of these things in the ever-growing quantum world. Unlike existing models, this framework includes technical, functional, and application layers while focusing on the interdependence among hardware, software, and application of real-world use cases.

5.5.1 Visual Diagram Representing the Taxonomy

The proposed taxonomy's hierarchical structure would ideally be represented as a tree-like diagram with branching categories and subcategories, presented here as a textual representation. Due to text limits, the diagram is represented as follows:

```
[Level 1]—Basic Concepts and Quantum Principles
   ├── Superposition
   ├── Entanglement
   ├── Interference
   └── Quantum Gates (Hadamard, CNOT)

[Level 2]—Algorithm Development and Computational Models
   ├── Quantum Algorithms
   │    ├── Simulation (VQE)
   │    ├── Optimization (QAOA)
   │    ├── Search (Grover algorithm)
   │    └── Cryptography (Shor algorithm)
   └── Computational Models
        ├── Quantum Circuit Model
        ├── Adiabatic Quantum Computing
        └── Topological Quantum Computing

[Level 3]—Hardware Implementation and Scaling
   ├── Superconducting Qubits
   │    ├── Transmon
   │    └── Fluxonium
   ├── Photonic Qubits
   └── Trapped Ions
```

```
├── Diamond-Based Qubits
└── Error Correction
    ├── Surface Codes
    └── Topological Codes
[Level 4]—Hybrid Quantum-Classical Integration
├── Hybrid Algorithms (QAOA with Classical Feedback)
├── Cloud-Based Quantum Computing (IBM Quantum Experience)
└── Application Domains
    ├── Optimization (Logistics)
    ├── Cryptographic Security (QKD)
    ├── Material Simulations (Drug Discovery)
    └── AI/ML (Quantum Neural Networks)
```

This is a four-level hierarchy model of the development of the quantum computer laid out in *Sections 3* and *3.1*, in which each level is divided into specific subcategories, based on a technical, functional, and application-oriented dimension. Level 1 will consist of visualization, using nodes and connectors, to represent entanglement. This will lead to the application of the Shor algorithm (Level 2) on superconducting qubits (Level 3) optimized by hybrid systems (Level 4). In contrast to traditional static models, this taxonomy is dynamic; therefore, it can easily be updated and amended as new quantum technologies and theories appear. This capability would guarantee its relevance and applicability in the future. In this proposed taxonomy, further developments in hybrid systems and scalability solutions could introduce subcategories to ensure a wider and more meaningful picture rather than most other existing taxonomies. To represent its model, it will incorporate input from stakeholders from academia, industry, and governmental regulators. Hence, it considers all relevant aspects of their positions in quantum computing. Thus, it becomes a classification system through which exploration of the labyrinth of quantum computing is possible. It could help in better planning, investing, and cooperation in this area, leading to rapid growth and application of quantum technologies.

5.5.2 Evaluation and Validation of the Taxonomy

To evaluate the flexibility of the proposed taxonomic framework three kinds of validation tests were conducted in order: **comparative benchmarking**, **real-world application testing**, and **expert validation**. This process aims to ensure that the proposed model performs better than existing ones while demonstrating its flexibility for use in academia, industry, and research.

5.5.2.1 Comparative Benchmarking

The taxonomy was tested against four dominant classification frameworks (*see* Table 5.4.). Existing frameworks excel in narrow domains but fail to connect technical capabilities (gate fidelity) to functional outcomes (optimization speed). The proposed taxonomy bridges these gaps by codifying interdependencies.

TABLE 5.4
Comparative Benchmarking of Four Classification Frameworks

Framework	Advantages	Gaps addressed by proposed taxonomy
Hardware-Centric	Explaining qubit scalability	Combining hardware and algorithms, (superconducting qubits that make QAOA possible)
Algorithm-First	Revealing quantum advantage	Relating applications and algorithms, including VQE used for drug discovery
Application-Driven	Putting technology in line with market needs	Matching apps to the appropriate technologies (such as QKD using photonic qubits)
Theoretical	Supported in quantum principles	Practice-based metrics (error rates, time to solution)

5.5.2.2 Flexibility in Real-World Scenarios

The flexibility of proposed taxonomy is tested by applying it to three real-world scenarios, by showing its ability to accommodate in various sectors:

[1] ***Academic Research: Quantum Error Correction***
- **Context**: University team that develops surface codes for trapped-ion qubits.
- **Taxonomy Mapping**:
  - *Hardware*: Trapped ions (high-fidelity gates).
  - *Algorithm*: Fault-tolerant surface codes.
  - *Application*: Secure quantum communication.
  - *Synergy*: The design of code guided by hardware constraints, e.g., ion mobility, which leads to cross-level feedback.

[2] ***Industry: Supply Chain Optimization***
- **Context**: Logistics company that uses a D-Wave quantum annealer.
- **Taxonomy Mapping**:
  - *Hardware*: Quantum annealing (D-Wave Advantage).
  - *Algorithm*: Quadratic Unconstrained Binary Optimization (QUBO).
  - *Application*: Routes for optimizing perishable goods.
  - *Synergy*: Hybrid workflows allowed the incorporation of quantum annealing along with classical solvers to achieve real-time modifications.

[3] ***Research Lab: Photonic Quantum Machine Learning***
- **Context**: Lab that develops photonic circuits for image recognition.
- **Taxonomy Mapping**:
  - *Hardware*: Photonic qubits.
  - *Algorithm*: Quantum neural networks.
  - *Application*: Medical imaging diagnostics.
  - *Synergy*: Low-decoherence photonics made the realization of deeper quantum circuits working with complex data patterns possible.

5.5.2.3 Expert Validation

The taxonomy's practical utility is validated through specific use cases across three sectors, illustrating its value to different stakeholders:

Using this taxonomy in these scenarios and sectors can allow it to be proven effective in flexibility, comprehensiveness, and applicability (see Table 5.5). Such a process would provide an opportunity to enhance the proposed taxonomy and indicate what can still be improved to keep it dynamic and valuable in the quantum computing community.

5.5.3 Discussion

This section considers the evaluation and validation results of the proposed quantum computing taxonomy. It briefly discusses the advantages and disadvantages of this proposed taxonomy, explains which fast-moving fields are being restricted in taxonomy adoption, and proposes what areas need further improvement for classification models.

Strengths of the Framework

- ***Holistic integration***: Some features of the framework are given here. It is based on a four-tier system, with basic concepts (Tier 1) at the lowest end of the hierarchy to hybrid integration (Tier 4) at the other end, thus providing full integration with quantum computing emerging technologies, such as diamond-based qubits and cloud-based platforms. This has an extent wider than previous models since it would always reflect actual trends in technology regarding quantum computing such as IBM 127-qubit processors.
- ***Standardization:*** This model defines standard definitions and criteria of classification that are useful for communication between disciplines dealing with quantum computing, from physics and engineering to computer science and applied mathematics. It creates one terminology to coordinate academia, industry, and policymakers.
- ***Adaptability:*** It is very adaptable in the sense that it allows easy updates such as adding qubit types or new algorithms. It demonstrates the flexibility

TABLE 5.5
Expert Validation of Proposed Taxonomy's Practical Utility

Sector	Feedback Summary	Improvement Implemented
Academia	Explains hardware-algorithm co-design	Incorporated coherence time as a hardware submetric
Industry	Refines ROI analysis for quantum pilots	Matches apps domain to TRL (Technology Readiness Levels)
Government	Sets a standard for policy discussion	Relates post-quantum crypto categories with NIST standards

of this model in real-world situations (*Section 5.1*) in a case study of classifying Google's quantum simulator used in drug discovery. It includes all these emerging technologies in its modules without concerning the current ones.

Weaknesses and Limitations

- ***Complexity:*** The highly complex hierarchy and multidimensional approach could overwhelm newcomers and non-experts alike. Levels 3 and 4 are different (hardware and hybrid integration) and require a proper knowledge of quantum concepts, limiting their access when compared to simple models like the Hidary (2021) framework.
- ***Validation scope:*** The taxonomy's validation has been based on a limited number of examples, such as IBM and QKD. Testing in reality, for example, mobile quantum devices would provide some interesting results about what could be covered and what could not.
- ***Subjectivity in categorization:*** Decisions about subcategory placement, QAOA being classified as an optimization method rather than as a hybrid algorithm, are somewhat arbitrary and might engender discussion among experts about the most optimal classification—a classic subjectivity in taxonomic design but, for our purposes, not fully resolved here.

Challenges in Application

- ***Keeping pace with innovation:*** Keeping up with fast-changing quantum technology has become a big challenge. It may call for numerous and constant modifications and redesigns to embrace the novel technological ideas and conceptualizes that surface.
- ***Interdisciplinary overlap:*** Quantum computing spans physics, computer science, engineering, and other areas like medicine and finance. Combining such perspectives in one taxonomy could lead to either oversimplification or overcomplication, that of cloud platforms that are Level 4 serving several sectors.
- ***Data availability:*** The availability of information is essential in verifying taxonomy, while proprietary technologies such as unreleased Google or IBM innovations or speculative technologies such as mobile quantum devices cannot be sufficiently documented, leading to the inability to adequately test them and hence possibly distort the entire scope of the framework.

The main points to focus on are improving and simplifying the architecture of the updating, increasing the scope of the validation, and combining interdisciplinary harmonization with predictive modeling. The addition of predictive modeling to the framework will considerably increase the potential for it to act as a viable tool for organizing knowledge on the new area of quantum computation. The simplified model or the complementary model for the layman should ease its complex aspects while retaining the basic groups. That is, a tiered representation (basic and advanced views), thus fostering a wider adoption in education and industry compared to Gill et al. (2022) highly specialized technical model. The development of a dynamic updating system, for example, the annual revision done by an expert group (IEEE Quantum Technical Community), to integrate emerging technologies, such as mobile quantum devices or state-of-the-art error-correcting codes, should allow it to sustain flexibility beyond the static bounds imposed by already existing taxonomies. Moreover, inputs from different fields should be considered so that refinement of application domains (Level 4) is enabled and conflicts between disciplines are minimized. Additionally, there is a potential for further standardization of terminology through collaboration with standardization bodies like ISO/IEC. The inclusion of predictive elements, such as trend analysis based on industry reports, would further lengthen the lifetime of the taxonomy by countering the rapid evolution challenges facing the new science of quantum computation.

5.5.4 Relevant Results and Contribution of New Knowledge

The application of the proposed taxonomical framework for quantum computing produces clear and relevant results evidenced by comparative benchmarking and real-world scenarios. These results demonstrate applicability and flexibility across academia, industry, and public policy. However, beyond its observable applicability, the taxonomy produces new knowledge (new learnings) as tangible results of its use, thereby advancing the area of quantum computing in theoretical and practical terms:

- **Academia** may use the taxonomy as a frame of reference for an organized approach to quantum computing-related teaching and research. The taxonomy framework identifies potential collaborative areas between disciplines and highlights the urgent attention needed in certain fields of research. The hierarchical nature of the framework (Level 1 [basic concepts and quantum principles], Level 2 [algorithm development and computational models]) may be useful for curriculum development but will also help highlight potential under-explored research areas in quantum computing, like alternative error correction schemes vs. current leading protocols or the development of other quantum technologies like diamond-based qubits using high-integrity quantum systems.
- **Industry** may use the taxonomy to articulate and connect hardware (superconducting qubits), algorithms (VQE for optimization), and applications (supply chain logistics), clarifying priorities for investment and benchmarking rationales for metrics for planning, facilitation, and standardization of terminology for strategic decision-making about whether or how a quantum solution integrates within other contemporary solutions. For example, the taxonomy was considered in a practice scenario for a logistics company utilizing a D-Wave quantum annealer for optimization, confirming the actual utility the taxonomy could have for practical application.
- **Policymaking** may use the taxonomy and organizational framework to establish and develop standardized policies. The taxonomy serves as an organizational tool in the consideration of the equitable and sustainable use of quantum resources. For instance, quantum computing relies on NIST

TABLE 5.6
The New Key Knowledge Contributions Derived from the Proposed Framework

Sector	Contributions
Academia	—Structured curriculum development
	—Identification of research gaps
	—Enhanced interdisciplinary collaboration
Industry	—Clarified investment priorities
	—Improved technology adoption
	—Standardized terminology for decision-making
Policymaking	—Standardized framework for policy discussion
	—Support for equitable and sustainable utilization
	—Facilitation of inter-sector collaboration

standards for post-quantum cryptography, and the taxonomy could provide an established organizational framework for connecting and aligning these and/or other standards among government and private sectors for policy and practice initiatives, such as developing a sustainable quantum internet.

Table 5.6. presents the new key knowledge contributions of the proposed framework by sector. These new knowledge contributions highlight the benefit of using the taxonomy in merging theory with practice, allowing equitable areas of progress for all stakeholders in the field of quantum computing.

5.6 CONCLUSION

In this chapter, we introduced a taxonomy for quantum computing that aims at structuring a rapidly developing field into a clear and accessible framework. The absence of a unified classification system and the inability of existing taxonomies to cover emerging technologies such as hybrid quantum-classical systems or cloud-based platforms necessitates the development of a relevant and applicable framework and taxonomy for current and future evolution in quantum computing. The proposed taxonomy with its hierarchical structure tends to integrate computational models, hardware implementations, algorithmic strategies, and application domains into a structured lens to develop a feasible quantum ecosystem. The benefits and added value of the proposed taxonomy extend across academia and industry. For researchers it constitutes an important terminology in describing innovation comparison, identification of research gaps, and the decision-making process on interdisciplinary collaborations. Being in a hierarchical structure, this framework provides a tool to address the current issues associated with quantum computing technology. For this purpose, it would offer an industry stakeholder a practical roadmap for checking the existing and upcoming technological improvements that can be correlated with quantum investments and business demands, thus providing a platform to measure business performance with that of its competitors. The contributions of this chapter do not mark the end of development, though, but only the beginning of taxonomy development in quantum computing. Thus, further studies should be performed to determine the possible ways to improve the application potential of the proposed framework. More effort should be made in future studies to design ways of continuously refining taxonomy, responsive to the pace of technological progressions in this field such as automated systems that make use of machine learning. Further studies need to provide information on the various ways taxonomies are used on a global level in different regulatory and cultural environments to meet the needs of a diverse community. The next level of taxonomies should consider the integration of quantum computing into other scientific and technological areas. This understanding will enable one to see the connection between other fields, such as AI and cybersecurity, and how they interact with quantum computing.

REFERENCES

Arute, F., Arya, K., Babbush, R., Bacon, D., Bardin, J. C., Barends, R., Biswas, R., Boixo, S., Brandao, F. G. S. L., Buell, D. A., Burkett, B., Chen, Y., Chen, Z., Chiaro, B., Collins, R., Courtney, W., Dunsworth, A., Farhi, E., Foxen, B., Fowler, A., Gidney, C., Giustina, M., Graff, R., Guerin, K., Habegger, S., Harrigan, M. P., Hartmann, M. J., Ho, A., Hoffmann, M., Huang, T., Humble, T. S., Isakov, S. V., Jeffrey, E., Jiang, Z., Kafri, D., Kechedzhi, K., Kelly, J., Klimov, P. V., Knysh, S., Korotkov, A., Kostritsa, F., Landhuis, D., Lindmark, M., Lucero, E., Lyakh, D., Mandrà, S., McClean, J. R., McEwen, M., Megrant, A., Mi, X., Michielsen, K., Mohseni, M., Mutus, J., Naaman, O., Neeley, M., Neill, C., Niu, M. Y., Ostby, E., Petukhov, A., Platt, J. C., Quintana, C., Rieffel, E. G., Roushan, P., Rubin, N. C., Sank, D., Satzinger, K. J., Smelyanskiy, V., Sung, K. J., Trevithick, M. D., Vainsencher, A., Villalonga, B., White, T., Yao, Z. J., Yeh, P., Zalcman, A., Neven, H., & Martinis, J. M. (2019). Quantum supremacy using a programmable superconducting quantum processor. *Nature*, *574*(7780), 505–510.

Bartolucci, S., Birchall, P. M., Gimeno-Segovia, M., Johnston, E., Kieling, K., Pant, M., Rudolph, T., Smith, J., Sparrow, C., & Vidrighin, M. D. (2021). *Creation of entangled photonic states using linear optics*. arXiv, preprint, 1–18.

Bennett, C. H., Brassard, G., Crépeau, C., Jozsa, R., Peres, A., & Wootters, W. K. (1993). Teleporting an unknown quantum state via dual classical and Einstein-Podolsky-Rosen channels. *Physical Review Letters*, *70*(2), 1895–1899.

Bensoussan, A., Jahangirova, G., & Mousavi, M. R. (2025). *A taxonomy of real faults in hybrid quantum-classical architectures*. arXiv, preprint.

Bharti, K., Cervera-Lierta, A., Kyaw, T. H., Haug, T., Alperin-Lea, S., Anand, A., Degroote, M., Heimonen, H., Kottmann, J. S., Menke, T., Mok, W.-K., Sim, S., Kwek, L.-C., & Aspuru-Guzik, A. (2022). Noisy intermediate-scale quantum algorithms. *Reviews of Modern Physics*, *94*(1).

Deutsch, D. (1985). Quantum theory, the Church-Turing principle and the universal quantum computer. *Proceedings of the Royal Society of London: Series A, Mathematical and Physical Sciences*, *400*(1818), 97–117.

Devitt, S. J. (2022). Blueprint for a scalable photonic fault-tolerant quantum computer. *Quantum Engineering*, *4*(1), 1–20.

Einstein, A., Podolsky, B., & Rosen, N. (1935). Can quantum-mechanical description of physical reality be considered complete? *Physical Review*, *47*(10), 777–780.

Feng, G., Lu, D., Li, J., Xin, T., & Zeng, B. (2023). Quantum computing: Principles and applications. *SPIN*, *13*(3), 1–76.

Feynman, R. P. (1982). Simulating physics with computers. *International Journal of Theoretical Physics*, *21*, 467–488.

Gambetta, J. M., Chow, J. M., & Steffen, M. (2017). Building logical qubits in a superconducting quantum computing system. *NPJ Quantum Information*, *3*(2), 1–12.

Gill, S. S., Kumar, A., Singh, H., Singh, M., Kaur, K., Usman, M., & Buyya, R. (2022). Quantum computing: A taxonomy, systematic review and future directions. *Software—Practice and Experience*, *52*(1), 66–114.

Grover, L. K. (1996). A fast quantum mechanical algorithm for database search. In *Proceedings of the Twenty-Eighth Annual ACM Symposium on Theory of Computing (STOC '96)*, Association for Computing Machinery, 212–219.

Hidary, J. D. (2021). *Quantum computing: An applied approach. quantum computing: An applied approach.* Springer International Publishing.

IEEE. (2023). *Standardization roadmap for quantum technologies.* IEEE Quantum Technical Community.

ISO/IEC. (2024). *ISO/IEC 4879:2024: Quantum computing terminology.* International Organization for Standardization.

Juárez-Ramírez, R., Navarro, C. X., Jiménez, S., Ramírez, A., Tapia-Ibarra, V., Guerra-García, C., Perez-Gonzalez, H. G., & Fernández-y-Fernández, C. (2023). A taxonomic view of the fundamental concepts of quantum computing—a software engineering perspective. *Programming and Computer Software*, *49*(8), 682–704.

Khammassi, N., Ashraf, I., & Bertels, K. (2018). *cQASM v1.0: Towards a common quantum assembly language.* arXiv, preprint.

Khan, A. A., Ahmad, A., Waseem, M., Liang, P., Fahmideh, M., Mikkonen, T., & Abrahamsson, P. (2023). Software architecture for quantum computing systems—a systematic review. *The Journal of Systems & Software*, *201*, 1–29.

Maass, W., Agrawal, A., Ciani, A., & others. (2024). QUASIM: Quantum computing enhanced service ecosystem for simulation in manufacturing. *Künstl Intell*, *38*, 361–370.

Martinis, J. M., Nam, S., Aumentado, J., & Lang, K. M. (2003). Rabi oscillations in a large Josephson-junction qubit. *Physical Review Letters*, *91*(11), 110407.

Nakamura, Y., Pashkin, Y. A., & Tsai, J. S. (1999). Coherent control of macroscopic quantum states in a single-Cooper-pair box. *Nature*, *398*(6732), 786–788.

National Academy of Engineering. (2019). *Frontiers of engineering: Reports on leading-edge engineering from the 2018 symposium.* The National Academies Press.

Nofer, M., Bauer, K., Hinz, O., van der Aalst, W., & Weinhardt, C. (2023). Quantum computing. *Business Information Systems Engineering*, *65*(4), 361–367.

Núñez-Merino, M., Maqueira-Marín, J. M., Moyano-Fuentes, J., & Castaño-Moraga, C. A. (2024). Quantum-inspired computing technology in operations and logistics management. *International Journal of Physical Distribution & Logistics Management*, *54*(3), 247–274.

Oxford Analytica. (2018). *Quantum computing revolution may be decades away.* Expert Briefings.

Preskill, J. (2018). Quantum computing in the NISQ era and beyond. *Quantum*, *2*, 79.

Putterman, H., Noh, K., Hann, C. T., MacCabe, G. S., Aghaeimeibodi, S., Patel, R. N., Lee, M., Jones, W. M., Moradinejad, H., Rodriguez, R., Mahuli, N., Rose, J., Owens, J. C., Levine, H., Rosenfeld, E., Reinhold, P., Moncelsi, L., Alcid, J. A., Alidoust, N., Arrangoiz-Arriola, P., Barnett, J., Bienias, P., Carson, H. A., Chen, C., Chen, L., Chinkezian, H., Chisholm, E. M., Chou, M.-H., Clerk, A., Clifford, A., Cosmic, R., Curiel, A. V., Davis, E., DeLorenzo, L., D'Ewart, J. M., Diky, A., D'Souza, N., Dumitrescu, P. T., Eisenmann, S., Elkhouly, E., Evenbly, G., Fang, M. T., Fang, Y., Fling, M. J., Fon, W., Garcia, G., Gorshkov, A. V., Grant, J. A., Gray, M. J., Grimberg, S., Grimsmo, A. L., Haim, A., Hand, J., He, Y., Hernandez, M., Hover, D., Hung, J. S. C., Hunt, M., Iverson, J., Jarrige, I., Jaskula, J.-C., Jiang, L., Kalaeem, M., Karabalin, R., Karalekas, P. J., Keller, A. J.,

Khalajhedayati, A., Kubica, A., Lee, H., Leroux, C., Lieu, S., Ly, V., Madrigal, K. V., Marcaud, G., McCabe, G., Miles, C., Milsted, A., Minguzzi, J., Mishra, A., Mukherjee, B., Naghiloo, M., Oblepias, E., Ortuno, G., Pagdilao, J., Pancotti, N., Panduro, A., Paquette, JP., Park, M., Peairs, G. A., Perello, D., Peterson, E. C., Ponte, S., Preskill, J., Qiao, J., Refael, G., Resnick, R., Retzker, A., Reyna, O. A., Runyan, M., Ryan, C. A., Sahmoud, A., Sanchez, E., Sanil, R., Sankar, K., Sato, Y., Scaffidi, T., Siavoshi, S., Sivarajah, P., Skogland, T., Su, C.-J., Swenson, L.-J., Teo, S. M., Tomada, A., Torlai, G., Wollack, A. E., Ye, Y., Zerrudom, J. A., Zhang, K., Brandão, F. G. L. S., Matheny, M. H., & Painter, O. (2025). Hardware-efficient quantum error correction via concatenated bosonic qubits. *Nature*, *638*, 927–934.

QED-C. (2023). *Industry benchmarks for quantum technologies*. Quantum Economic Development Consortium.

Rieffel, E., & Polak, W. (2011). *Quantum computing: A gentle introduction*. The MIT Press.

Sachdeva, N., Hartnett, G. S., Maity, S., Marsh, S., Wang, Y., Winick, A., Dougherty, R., Canuto, D., Chong, Y. Q., Hush, M., Mundada, P. S., Bentley, C. D. B., Biercuk, M. J., & Baum, Y. (2024). *Quantum optimization using a 127-qubit gate-model IBM quantum computer can outperform quantum annealers for nontrivial binary optimization problems*. arXiv, preprint.

Sete, E. A., Zeng, W. J., & Rigetti, C. T. (2016). A functional architecture for scalable quantum computing. In *2016 IEEE International Conference on Rebooting Computing (ICRC)*, 1–6.

Shor, P. W. (1994). Algorithms for quantum computation: Discrete logarithms and factoring. In *Proceedings of the 35th Annual Symposium on Foundations of Computer Science*, IEEE, 124–134.

Smith, F. L. (2020). Quantum technology hype and national security. *Security Dialogue*, *51*(5), 499–516.

Ukpabi, D., Karjaluoto, H., Bötticher, A., Nikiforova, A., Petrescu, D., Schindler, P., Valtenbergs, V., & Lehmann, L. (2023). Framework for understanding quantum computing use cases from a multidisciplinary perspective and future research directions. *Futures*, *154*.

Usman, M., Wong, Y. Z., Hill, C. D., & Hollenberg, L. C. L. (2020). Framework for atomic-level characterisation of quantum computer arrays by machine learning. *NPJ Computational Materials*, *6*(1), 1–8.

Wendin, G. (2017). Quantum information processing with superconducting circuits. *Reports on Progress in Physics*, *80*(10), 1–108.

Xu, Q., Putterman, H., Iverson, J. K., Noh, K., Painter, O. J., Brandão, F. G. S. L., & Jiang, L. (2022). Engineering kerr-cat qubits for hardware-efficient quantum error correction. In *Quantum Computing, Communication, and Simulation II* (Vol. 12015, Paper 120150B), SPIE.

6 Quantum Computing—Real-World Applications and Its Transformative Potential

Sam Goundar, Shruthi K., Artor Nuhiu, Chandramohan Dhasarathan, and Akashdeep Bhardwaj

6.1 INTRODUCTION

To date, most intelligent problem-solvers have been developed using conventional computing technologies. In contrast, quantum computing (QC) has emerged as a promising alternative for addressing real-world challenges and optimization problems [1]. QC is increasingly recognized in the scientific community as a pivotal advancement in computational capabilities. Its potential to significantly enhance performance in complex optimization scenarios sets it apart from traditional computing methods [2]. Using qubits as their basic information units, quantum computers use quantum mechanical processes to carry out computations [3]. The restrictions of traditional binary systems are overcome by qubits, which can exist in several states simultaneously in contrast to classical bits, which can only represent a value of either 0 or 1.

Currently, two QC paradigms exist: annealing-based quantum computers and gate-model quantum computers [4, 5]. The former is distinguished by completing a procedure called quantum annealing, which yields the energy function or state of minimal energy of a particular quantum Hamiltonian. The lower energy state in optimization problems is the solution to the problem since the quantum Hamiltonian is specified based on the problem's fitness function [6]. On the other hand, quantum circuits, or operations, called quantum gates, which are comparable to the traditional logic gates found in conventional circuits, are used to differentiate quantum-gate devices. Consequently, quantum gates are used one after the other to control qubit states and get the final answer to the problem [7].

Nevertheless, a closer look at the most well-known databases reveals that the number of scientific research focusing on QC applied to routing issues is constantly increasing. Because the activity is substantial and consistent, it accurately depicts the state of the community today. This body of information creates the perfect

DOI: 10.1201/9781003538950-7

environment for the creation of a reference text that methodically compiles all the previously completed work. The revolutionary topic of QC, which sprang from computer science and quantum mechanics, has generated a lot of attention due to its ability to completely overhaul computation. We start by introducing readers to the basic ideas of qubits, noise, interference, entanglement, superposition, and qubits, then the foundations of QC.

Richard Feynman established the theoretical underpinnings of QC in his paper [8], discussing a computer capable of simulating quantum mechanics. Ignacio Cirac and Peter Zoller then provided their paper's realization of the potential implementation of a quantum computer [9], suggesting that it could be accomplished by trapping cold ions and interacting them with laser beams. Since then, quantum hardware has advanced significantly, and in the upcoming years, a quantum computer with about 1,000 qubits is anticipated. Quantum algorithms have advanced significantly in tandem with the advancements in quantum hardware. Grover's algorithm [10] and Shor's algorithm [11] have already demonstrated the power of quantum algorithms by accelerating search in unstructured databases and solving integer factorization problems, respectively. Only a few quantum algorithms for factorization and searching were created in the early years, but currently, a wide range of quantum algorithm categories, including machine learning, search, approximation, optimization, and algebraic are all developing rapidly. A new discipline known as quantum machine learning (QML) has emerged because of the development of quantum algorithms for machine learning. According to [12], the rapid progress of computational quantum research holds great potential for changing the computing environment. Even though they do similar basic computations, quantum technology is faster than current computing devices, which gives it benefits in a variety of societally beneficial fields. The quantum computing development timeline is shown in Figure 6.1.

6.1.1 Applications of Quantum Computing

Quantum computing applications including pharmacology, drug discovery, astronomy, aerospace, artificial intelligence, and cybersecurity. Certain jobs could be completed by it exponentially more quickly than with traditional computing. Algorithms can be improved, and structures and patterns can be found more effectively with quantum computing. We shall go deeper into the uses of quantum computing in this part. Table 6.1 summarizes applications of quantum computing. Figure 6.2 gives an overview of applications of quantum computing.

6.1.1.1 Medication and Discovery

By mimicking molecular behavior, quantum computers could be utilized to create novel medications and therapies. This might result in the creation of fresh therapies for illnesses like Alzheimer's and cancer.

6.1.1.2 Optimization of the Supply Chain

By effectively managing inventory, demand forecasts, and transportation logistics, it will optimize supply chains. This will improve overall efficiency, cut expenses, and decrease waste [22].

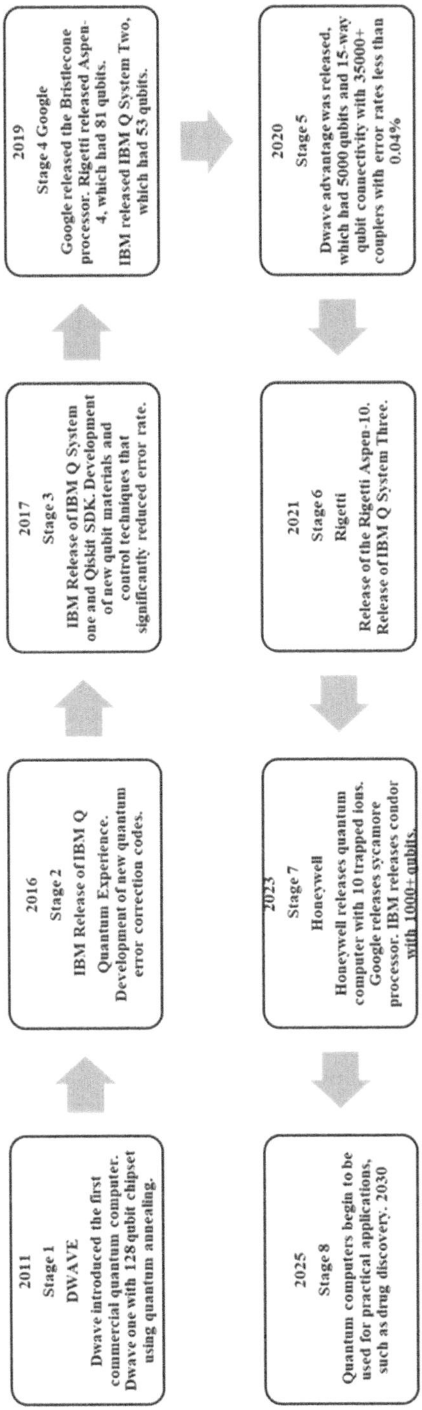

FIGURE 6.1 Quantum computing development timeline.

TABLE 6.1
A Synopsis of Quantum Applications Together with the Model or Technique Employed

Task	Algorithm/Model	Reference	Used for
Secure key distribution	Quantum channels	[13]	Safe communication and eavesdropping detection.
Contrastive learning	Quantum SimCLR Model	[14]	Processing images with the CIFAR-10 dataset.
Image generation	Quantum classical GAN	[15]	MNIST digits and fashion datasets are used to generate high-resolution images.
Dimension reduction	Quantum principal component analysis (QPCA)	[16]	Collection of synthetic financial interest rates.
Classification	Quantum variational classifier	[17]	Sonar, Wisconsin's Breast Cancer (WBC) dataset, and Fisher's Iris.
	Quantum-inspired nearest mean classifier	[18]	Dataset for idiopathic pulmonary fibrosis (IPF).
	Quantum neural network	[19]	Finance and MNIST datasets are used for image categorization.
Reinforcement learning	Hybrid quantum proximal policy optimization	[20]	Using a dataset of several satellites, satellite path planning and task selection are performed.
Regression	Continuous variable–quantum neural network	[21]	Dataset from surface plasmon resonance sensors.

6.1.1.3 Economic Benefits

By precisely forecasting market patterns, optimizing portfolios, and better controlling risk, quantum computers may be able to analyze vast volumes of data and create new financial trading techniques [23].

6.1.1.4 Artificial Intelligence

It can be applied to create new, more potent AI algorithms than those that are already in use. This will result in improvements in robotics, computer vision, and natural language processing [24].

6.1.1.5 Scientific Cryptography

Quantum computers may be able to crack existing encryption algorithms. In future post-quantum future, quantum-resistant cryptography will be essential for protecting private information [25].

6.1.1.6 Prediction of Weather

Weather forecasting could be improved by quantum computers by simulating atmospheric behavior. In this approach, lives and property could be preserved [26].

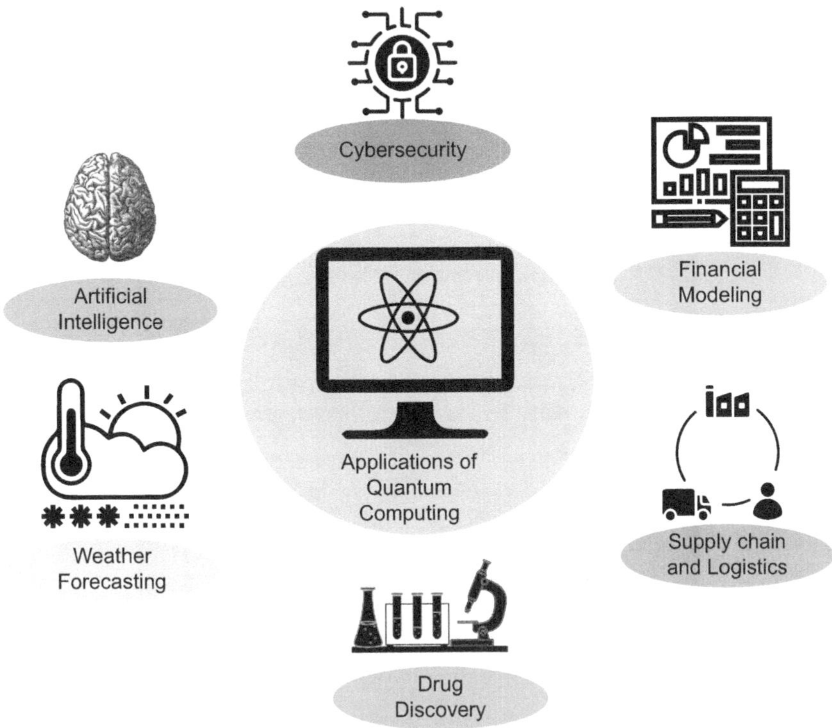

FIGURE 6.2 Applications of quantum computing.

6.1.2 Basics of Quantum Computing

Here we present the basic concepts of quantum physics, which are necessary to comprehend quantum computing. Ideas like entanglement, superposition, and quantum interference, provide insight into the special features of quantum systems. This section looks at the properties of qubits, quantum gates and circuits, quantum algorithms, and qubit technologies. Figure 6.3 depicts a quantum computer's tiered process architecture.

Making use of the ideas of quantum mechanics, quantum computing performs intricate computations at incredibly fast speeds. The behavior of matter and energy at the atomic and subatomic scales is explained by a branch of physics called quantum mechanics. Quantum computing requires an awareness of several quantum mechanical concepts. The two main paradigms of quantum computing currently in use are annealing-based and gate-model systems. Quantum computing leverages unique properties of qubits that distinguish it from classical computing. The principles of entanglement and superposition open exciting possibilities for addressing complex problems. Qubits can inhabit multiple states and become interconnected, independent of distance, due to these quantum phenomena. To protect qubits from noise

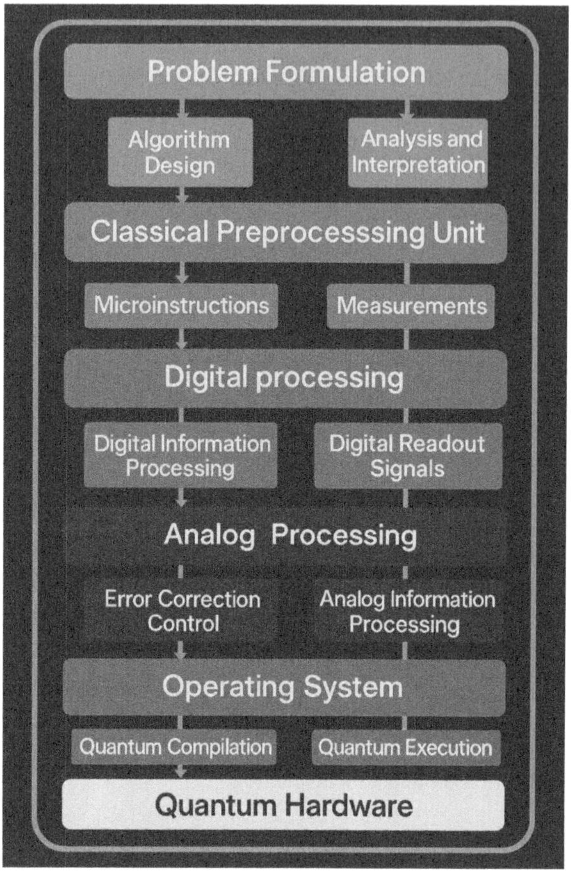

FIGURE 6.3 Processing architecture of a quantum computer.

and quantum error correction is essential to guaranteeing the accuracy of quantum computations. Key concepts from quantum physics relevant to quantum computing include:

1. Superposition: The capacity of a qubit to occupy multiple states simultaneously enables parallel computation.
2. Entanglement: A qubit's capacity to occupy multiple states simultaneously enables parallel computing. This occurs when multiple qubits become correlated, such since one qubit's state is dependent upon another's.
3. Interference: A qubit's capacity to inhabit multiple states simultaneously enables parallel computing. This occurs when multiple qubits establish correlations, causing the state of one qubit to depend on another. In a quantum system, the various potential pathways to a specific state can interfere in ways that are either constructive or destructive, leading to impactful results.

4. Measurement and Collapse: A quantum system has a specific likelihood of transitioning to one of its possible states when observed.
5. No-Cloning Theorem: This theorem posits that a general unknown quantum state cannot be duplicated with exact precision.
6. Heisenberg's Uncertainty Principle: This asserts that measurements are fundamentally limited, as one cannot simultaneously determine a qubit's position and momentum with precision.

6.1.3 Quantum Algorithms

Quantum algorithms are tailored instructions created especially for quantum computing. They facilitate the manipulation of qubits are used to store quantum information through the application of principles derived from quantum gates and circuits. Shor's algorithm effectively resolves the factorization problem. That numerous encryption schemes now in use can be cracked by it has important cryptographic ramifications, and it is an essential algorithm to research in relation to quantum computing.

Grover's technique, which offers a quadratic speedup for searching unsorted databases, is another example. Applications for this approach could be found in several domains, such as data analysis and optimization. The potential of quantum algorithms is being actively explored by researchers who are also looking at how they affect various problem areas. Table 6.2 lists a few instances of quantum algorithms and the kinds of issues they are intended to address.

TABLE 6.2
Quantum Algorithms

Quantum Algorithm	Problem Type	Description	Application
Quantum approximate counting [27]	Computing problems	Counting solutions Approximating the number of solutions to the problem	Statistical analysis, graph theory
Grover's search algorithm [28]	Unstructured search	Speeding up unstructured search in an unsorted list	Database search, molecular simulation, image recognition
Quantum principal component analysis [29]	Data analysis	Extracting principal components from data	Data compression, dimensionality reduction
Quantum support vector machine [30]	Machine learning	Enhancing support vector machines using quantum features	Classification tasks, pattern recognition
Shor's factoring algorithm [31]	Integer factorization	Factoring large numbers into primes	Cryptography, quantum chemistry simulations
Quantum approximate optimization algorithm [32]	Optimization problem	Approximating solutions to optimization problems	Combinatorial optimization, portfolio optimization

6.1.4 Overview of the Potential of Quantum Computing to Address Practical Issues

Superposition, entanglement, and quantum tunneling are just a few of the quantum mechanical concepts that quantum computing can use to tackle real-world issues that are computationally impossible for traditional computers.

- **Optimization Problems**
  Quantum computers can address complex optimization challenges by evaluating multiple solutions simultaneously:
  - **Logistics and Supply Chain:** Optimizing delivery routes and warehouse operations.
  - **Finance:** Option pricing, risk assessment, and portfolio optimization.
  - **Energy:** Energy distribution and smart grid management.
- **Drug Discovery and Healthcare**
  Molecular interactions can be simulated by quantum computing with previously unheard-of accuracy:
  - Finding the ideal molecular structures for novel medications is known as drug development.
  - **Genomics:** Quickening the process of sequencing and analyzing genomes.
  - **Medical diagnostics:** improving predictive models and imaging methods.
- **Materials Science**
  Materials engineering can be revolutionized by simulating atomic and subatomic behaviors:
  - Better energy storage system design is the focus of battery technology.
  - **Semiconductors:** Developing efficient electronic materials.
  - **Environment:** Creating materials for carbon capture and water purification.
- **Cryptography and Security**
  Quantum computing impacts both encryption and decryption:
  - Threatening traditional cryptographic systems (e.g., RSA, ECC).
  - **Post-Quantum Cryptography:** facilitating the creation of algorithms that are resistant to quantum errors.
- **Machine Learning and Artificial Intelligence (AI)**
  Quantum computing can enhance AI by speeding up learning processes and improving data handling:
  - **Pattern Recognition:** Accelerating image and speech recognition.
  - **Optimization:** Solving large-scale problems like neural network training.
  - **Data Clustering:** Analyzing vast datasets faster.
- **Climate Modeling and Environmental Science**
  Quantum systems can handle the complex models required to predict climate changes:
  - **Weather Prediction:** Providing more accurate forecasts.
  - **Carbon Emission Reduction:** Optimizing renewable energy resources.

6.1.5 Industries Benefiting from Quantum Solutions

The anticipated growth of the quantum computing sector over time is depicted in Figure 6.4. Numerous sectors the impact of quantum computing will be significant [33], but there are still a lot of unanswered problems and difficulties. Which issues are amenable to resolution, what is the quantum advantage offered by one of the NISQ quantum devices, and how might this benefit be converted into an influence on business? Here, we provide an examination of quantum applications with significant industry influence. The analysis is based on several workshops, nine bilateral interviews, and a structured survey that was completed by 17 experts from 11 firms in five different industry sectors. Each of the participating businesses has contributed up to three use cases for quantum computing. We discovered several levels, including the problem domain, problem class, model, algorithms, and quantum systems. We recommend using the terms listed in the following definition box to maintain uniformity in discussions on cross-industry applications.

- **Problem Domain:** Applied mathematics and computer science problem fields that share common approaches to solving computational issues (like cryptography, machine learning, simulation, and optimization).
- **Problem Class:** An issue class is a group of use cases that belong to the same computational difficulty class and have a similar mathematical

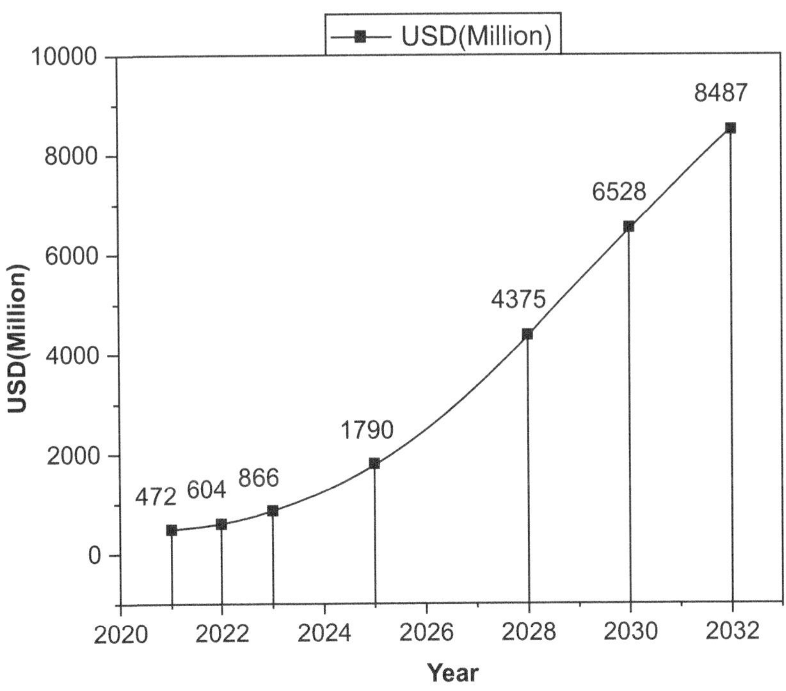

FIGURE 6.4 Industry forecast for quantum computing.

expression. It is distinguished by the typical phrasing of mathematical and business problems (for example, software testing presented as a 3-satisfiability problem).

- **Model:** A mathematical formulation that captures all practically significant aspects of a system is called a model.
- **Algorithm:** A quantum algorithm is a condensed collection of instructions that a quantum computer can use to do computations. Usually, they are employed to determine an approximate solution or a solution to a category of problems with mathematical definitions. A quantum system, sometimes referred to as a quantum computing system, is a computing system that manipulates data directly using quantum-mechanical phenomena like entanglement and superposition. Figure 6.5 provides comprehensive benchmarking that encompasses the entire stack consisting of quantum systems and algorithms.

6.1.5.1 Overview of the Application

Common problem domains among general application challenges in various industrial sectors include simulation, machine learning, and optimization. We highlight specific issues from our chains of value. We concentrate on four value-creation domains: post-quantum security, engineering and design, production and logistics, and materials science. The gathered use cases are compiled in Table 6.3.

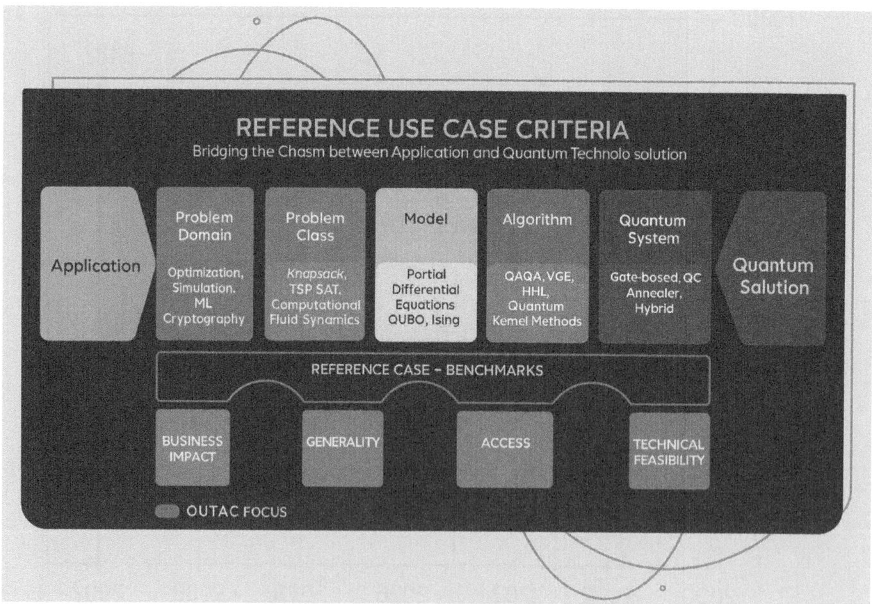

FIGURE 6.5 Comprehensive benchmarking encompassing the full stack, such as quantum systems and algorithms, is made possible by reference use cases.

TABLE 6.3

First-Use Case Portfolio Value chains throughout the German sector face a wide range various problems related to machine learning, simulation, and optimization. Despite the minimal impact over the next five years, several high-impact use cases have been found.

Use Case Based on Application Business Impact and Problem Domain in the Landscape

Numerous value chains stand to gain from quantum computing, including material research, engineering and design, and production and logistics. With almost 50% of all usage, optimization is the most significant problem domain instance. The manufacturing and logistics difficulty is the focus of most optimization use cases. On average, the time-to-maturity is rated as high and the business effect as medium. Numerous components of value chains in various industries will be impacted by quantum computing. Value creation domains and typical problem domains that lend themselves to quantum solutions are depicted in Figure 6.6. Optimization difficulties account for more than half of all use cases, making them the most prevalent problem domain. The manufacturing and logistics difficulty accounts for the majority of optimization use cases. On average, the time-to-maturity is rated as high and the business effect as medium.

Challenge	Problem Domain	Company	Use Case	Impact
Design and engineering	Machine learning	AIRBUS	QC for partial differential equation surrogate modeling	High
	Optimization	AIRBUS	Optimizing wingbox design	High
		Bosch	Testing software and verifying the correctness	Medium
	Simulation	Bosch	Electric drive design optimizations employing finite element and numerical simulation techniques	Medium
		Merck	Finding and managing actionable parameters to stop the spread of disease	Unknown
Materials science	Optimization	Boehringer Ingelheim	Chemical reactivity prediction in molecular quantum chemistry: an overview of quantum chemistry	High
	Simulation	BASF	Quantum chemistry: molecular quantum chemistry's prediction of chemical reactivity	High
		Boehringer Ingelheim	Molecular dynamics: a simulation of molecule dynamics	High
		Merck	Quantum simulations are used in the development of materials and medications	Medium
		Munich Re	Battery cover: vehicle battery performance promises	Medium
		VW	Calculating chemistry for battery research	High

(Continued)

TABLE 6.3 (Continued)

First-Use Case Portfolio Value chains throughout the German sector face a wide range various problems related to machine learning, simulation, and optimization. Despite the minimal impact over the next five years, several high-impact use cases have been found.

Use Case Based on Application Business Impact and Problem Domain in the Landscape

Numerous value chains stand to gain from quantum computing, including material research, engineering and design, and production and logistics. With almost 50% of all usage, optimization is the most significant problem domain instance. The manufacturing and logistics difficulty is the focus of most optimization use cases. On average, the time-to-maturity is rated as high and the business effect as medium. Numerous components of value chains in various industries will be impacted by quantum computing. Value creation domains and typical problem domains that lend themselves to quantum solutions are depicted in Figure 6.6. Optimization difficulties account for more than half of all use cases, making them the most prevalent problem domain. The manufacturing and logistics difficulty accounts for the majority of optimization use cases. On average, the time-to-maturity is rated as high and the business effect as medium.

Challenge	Problem Domain	Company	Use Case	Impact
Post-quantum Security	Cryptography	Munich Re	IoT cyber cover: post-quantum cryptography insurance	Medium
Production and logistics	Machine learning	Siemens	Quantum-assisted reinforcement learning, or QARL, has numerous industrial applications	Medium
	Optimization	BASF	Fleet management: on-site routing and deployment of trucks and machines	Medium
		BMW	Production robot production planning: optimizing production robot paths (e.g., PVC sealing robot)	Medium
		BMW	Testing vehicle features and improving test configuration for vehicle options	Medium
		BMW	Optimizing labor shift assignments through shift scheduling	Medium
		Infineon	Supply chain demand capacity match: choose a production plan based on estimated customer demand	Medium
		Infineon	Enhancing customer-side supply chain operations with Infineon sensors and actuators	Medium
		Munich Re	Transportation coverage: time-critical freight insurance	Medium
		SAP	Logistics: loading trucks	Medium

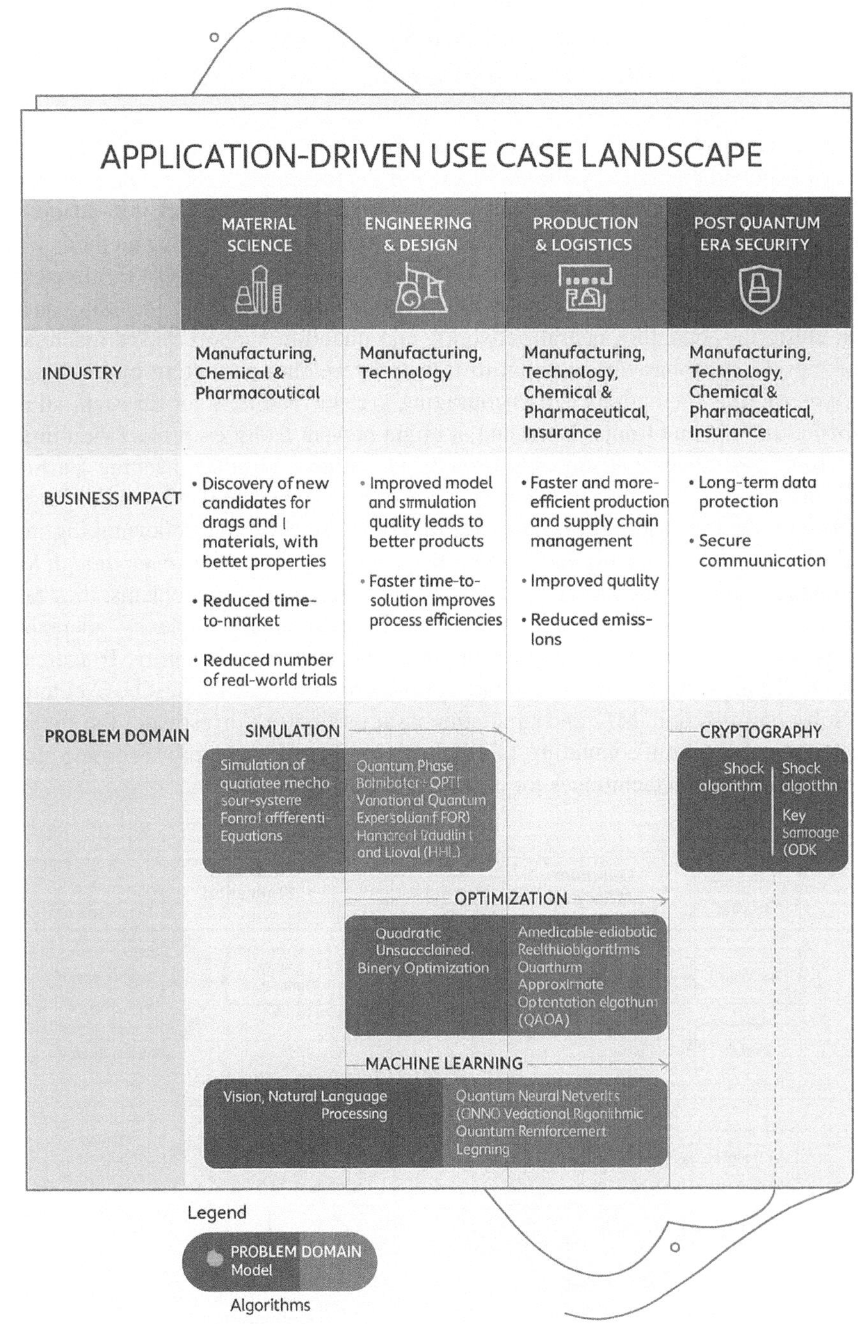

FIGURE 6.6 Application-driven use case.

6.1.5.2 Propose Innovative Frameworks for Applying Quantum Computing in Unexplored Domains

6.1.5.2.1 Sustainability and Climate Modeling

For many businesses, making educated judgments and lessening the impact of extreme weather events depend on weather forecasting. Standard forecasting techniques may be hampered by the intricacy and unpredictability of weather systems, which could result in mistakes and serious risks. The framework for quantum-improved weather forecasting (QWF) combines traditional forecasting methods with quantum machine learning techniques to address these issues. The QWF framework aims to improve forecast accuracy by utilizing quantum algorithms, including quantum clustering, quantum neural networks, and quantum support vector machines. This novel design has the potential to transform weather predicting by increasing the precision of predictions and encouraging greater readiness for disasters, albeit with certain inherent limits. In the end, it might prevent fatalities, protect vital infrastructure, and advance sustainable growth. Quantum and other machine learning (ML) models [34, 35] often function as "black boxes," which makes it challenging to interpret their forecasts. Those involved in climate science and policymaking may find it more difficult to trust and accept this opacity. In conclusion, even though ML techniques have the potential to address climate change-related problems, they face several challenges, including data imbalance, computational complexity, adaptability, hardware limitations, algorithmic optimization, and interpretability. To increase ML's usefulness and efficacy in climate action, several obstacles must be overcome. To solve optimization, ML, and simulation issues, this work investigates the sophisticated use of quantum computing, highlighting its potential to improve climate modeling and mitigation techniques for climate change Figure 6.7.

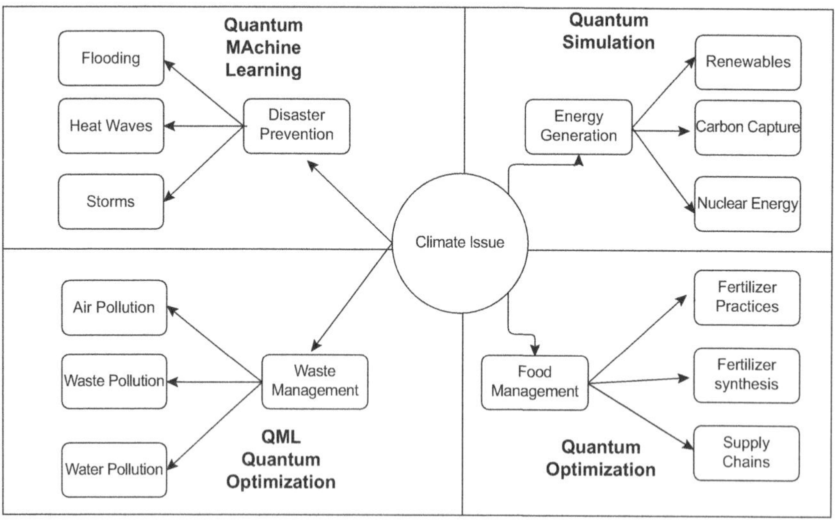

FIGURE 6.7 An overview of the uses of quantum computing in mitigating climate change.

6.1.5.2.2 *Applications of Transportation Systems in Intelligent*

Even though quantum computing is still in its infancy, it offers enormous potential to improve processing efficiency for specific jobs. This advantage stems from unique quantum properties that enable parallel processing, such as entanglement and superposition. The study's goal is to look into the possible uses of quantum computing in many facets of transportation [36].

6.1.5.2.3 *Leveraging Quantum Computing for Traffic Management*

Planning, carrying out, and optimizing the flow of people and products are all included in transportation management. It entails managing every facet of the transportation process, from choosing the best carriers and means of transportation to organizing shipments, keeping an eye on them, and making sure they arrive on schedule. Automatic optimization is often advantageous for transportation management. Quantum algorithms may enhance traffic signal timing and reduce congestion in addition to assessing real-time traffic data, including vehicle density, speed, and road conditions.

Using MEEMD, traffic data is pre-processed to separate its intrinsic mode function (IMF) components. The QNN, which has exceptional nonlinear processing and convergence capabilities, is then used to predict each IMF component. Predicting traffic congestion is as challenging as predicting traffic flow because of dynamic traffic data and complex traffic networks. By constructing a quantum GCN for spatial characteristics and learning the temporal information using a closed-form solution from the Schrödinger approach [36], presented a quantum spatial-temporal graph convolution network (STGCN).

Optimizing traffic signals is a key component in reducing traffic congestion. They created an enhanced Biham, Middleton, and Levine (BML) model to depict urban traffic and used QPSO to improve time scheduling. The first thing they did was map the real road network—which included several two-way multilane roads—into the theoretical lattice space of BML. The proposed upgraded BML provides a better understanding of traffic congestion and phase transition. The optimal regulation of time-dependent traffic lights was converted into a quadratic unconstrained binary optimization (QUBO). Given the hardware constraints of quantum computers, including their tiny qubit count, inter-qubit communication, and significant error rates in D-Wave devices, they proposed a hybrid (quantum-classical) approach. According to [37], studies have looked into using quantum annealing techniques for a QUBO problem to optimize supply chain logistics and traffic flow. This approach aimed to reduce traffic using a D-Wave quantum computing device and the T-drive Beijing Road dataset.

6.1.5.2.4 *Autonomous Vehicle Navigation Assisted by Quantum*

Researchers are looking into how quantum computing might improve traffic management and streamline transit lines, which has greatly increased interest in quantum-assisted autonomous vehicle (QAV) navigation in recent years. By drastically cutting down on traffic and travel time, quantum computing has the potential to completely transform traffic management. According to a study in *Nature Communications*, utilizing quantum algorithms to optimize traffic signal management could result in a 30% decrease in travel time. This is because quantum computing can improve routing efficiency and process big datasets at once.

The quantum approximate optimization algorithm (QAOA) is one of the most promising quantum algorithms in this area. According to research published in *Physical Review X*, QAOA performs better than traditional optimization techniques, especially in circumstances with intricate traffic management. It has been demonstrated that traffic signal optimization using QAOA reduces travel time by 25% and fuel usage by 15%. Furthermore, real-time traffic pattern analysis made possible by quantum computing allows for more intelligent decision-making. Significant progress in the transportation industry is anticipated because of the combination of quantum computing and autonomous vehicle technology. According to a McKinsey & Company analysis, QAOA implementation may result in a 50% reduction in traffic by 2030. Quantum algorithms, which improve routing efficiency, reduce delays, and allow for real-time traffic monitoring, are primarily responsible for this development.

QAV navigation has advantages beyond maximizing traffic flow. According to research in *Science Advances*, quantum computers can improve road safety by detecting high-risk locations and examining traffic patterns, which would result in more precise accident prediction and avoidance. Advanced machine learning algorithms that can process enormous volumes of data in real time are used to do this. Furthermore, quantum computing may improve autonomous cars' energy efficiency. Quantum systems can optimize energy usage by analyzing traffic circumstances and pinpointing opportunities for energy conservation, according to a study published in *Energy & Environmental Science*.

6.1.5.2.5 Industrial Case Studies

The D-Wave 2000Q™ quantum computer is being employed to address complex traffic flow optimization issues in Beijing, leveraging movement data from 418 taxis. Additionally, Volkswagen is creating a hybrid algorithm that integrates both classical and quantum methodologies, which is also applicable to machine learning challenges.

Traffic Data Utilization: The team employed traffic data from here maps to calculate optimal routes, providing real-time updates to bus drivers every two minutes.

Mobile Application Development: Based on their proof-of-concept, Volkswagen created a mobile app that predicts the best routes for buses, which was showcased at the 2019 WebSummit.

Recommendation System: The engineers designed a recommendation system using non-negative/binary matrix factorization to understand customer preferences and help them choose vehicles.

Exploration of Quantum Chemistry: The paper discusses the use of quantum computing as well in quantum chemistry, where the D-Wave system was used to solve basic electronic structure problems.

These methods illustrate Volkswagen's innovative approach to leveraging quantum computing for real-world applications in traffic management and beyond. Volkswagen Group CIO Martin Hofmann posed a question about preventing traffic congestion.

A Quantum Launchpad, the initial quantum project led Volkswagen to explore various applications. Quantum annealing is suitable for optimizing schedules and production logistics.

Current projects include optimizing assembly lines and distribution logistics. A hybrid algorithm combining classical and quantum methods is under development. A recommendation system was created to understand customer preferences for vehicle selection. Quantum chemistry applications are being explored, addressing complex molecular simulations. Future projects may include financial predictions, cybersecurity, and advancements in self-driving technology. Comparing the difficulty of quantum and conventional methods for well-known computer science issues is addressed in [37]. They also discussed the possible future uses of different quantum techniques and solvers and showed how they have been applied to several situations.

6.1.5.2.6 Healthcare: Accelerating Drug Discovery by Simulating Molecular Interactions

Because molecular interactions are so complicated, traditional drug discovery methods face difficulties. Potential medication identification can be optimized and accelerated with quantum computing's assistance. A recent partnership demonstrates how quantum computing might improve important fields including ligand-protein binding research and protein hydration analysis. Drug development is revolutionized by due to quantum computing's ability to manage high-dimensional, multi-variable problems. Quantum computing's use in medication discovery has the potential to significantly alter healthcare systems around the globe. Quantum computing makes it possible to produce novel medicines more quickly and easily by cutting down on the time and expense of research, improving healthcare systems' capacity to satisfy patient requirements.

Quantum Blockchain Framework: The paper [37] introduces a novel quantum blockchain framework specifically designed to protect electronic medical records (EMRs) from quantum computing threats. This framework utilizes post-quantum cryptography techniques and quantum key distribution (QKD) to enhance security and ensure data integrity.

Cost Efficiency: The suggested framework results in a considerable decrease in computational expenses by 30% and a 25% reduction in communication overhead, relative to conventional blockchain systems. This optimization leverages quantum algorithms to improve the efficiency of consensus processes.

6.2 CONCLUSION

Advances in quantum technology, especially the use of quantum computer methods, can solve challenging optimization problems in a variety of fields. Because quantum computing (QC) can aid in mimicking molecular interactions, there is hope for the development of a cure for illnesses like cancer and Alzheimer's. In addition, QC enhances the security of healthcare data by applying quantum-resistant technologies such as entangled quantum medical records (EQMR). Moreover, the use of QC in supply chain management increases efficiency and decreases costs and waste. It also helps improve marketing and portfolio management accuracy. The deployment of QC, however, must accompany the shift to quantum-safe cryptography to handle issues that may arise due to the existing encryption weaknesses. Moreover, QC improves the accuracy of weather prediction, thus enhancing preparation for hazardous conditions via quantum machine learning. Volkswagen's project on optimizing traffic flow in Beijing illustrates its usefulness for improving traffic and transportation systems. The practical use of QC is constrained by several factors, such as the lack of suitable hardware, problems with data encoding, and decoherence. These problems must be solved so that quantum algorithms can be widely applied in practice. In any case, QC is expected to have a far-reaching impact on the healthcare industry, supply chain logistics, and climate science, but further studies are required to mitigate existing limitations.

REFERENCES

[1] A. Steane, "Quantum Computing," Reports Prog. Phys., vol. 61, no. 2, pp. 117–173, 1998, https://doi.org/10.1088/0034-4885/61/2/002.

[2] A. Ajagekar, T. Humble, and F. You, "Quantum Computing Based Hybrid Solution Strategies for Large-Scale Discrete-Continuous Optimization Problems," Comput. Chem. Eng., vol. 132, no. 607, pp. 1–50, 2020, https://doi.org/10.1016/j.compchemeng.2019.106630.

[3] J. D. Prince, "Quantum Computing: An Introduction," J. Electron. Resour. Med. Libr., vol. 11, no. 3, pp. 155–158, 2014, https://doi.org/10.1080/15424065.2014.939462.

[4] Y. Wang, Y. Li, Z. qi Yin, and B. Zeng, "16-Qubit IBM Universal Quantum Computer Can Be Fully Entangled," NPJ Quantum Inf., vol. 4, no. 1, pp. 1–6, 2018, https://doi.org/10.1038/s41534-018-0095-x.

[5] P. Hauke, H. G. Katzgraber, W. Lechner, H. Nishimori, and W. D. Oliver, "Perspectives of Quantum Annealing: Methods and Implementations," Reports Prog. Phys., vol. 83, no. 5, 2020, https://doi.org/10.1088/1361-6633/ab85b8.

[6] L. Gyongyosi and S. Imre, "Quantum Circuit Design for Objective Function Maximization in Gate-Model Quantum Computers," Quantum Inf. Process., vol. 18, no. 7, pp. 1–33, 2019, https://doi.org/10.1007/s11128-019-2326-2.

[7] G. E. Santoro and E. Tosatti, "Optimization Using Quantum Mechanics: Quantum Annealing through Adiabatic Evolution," J. Phys. A. Math. Gen., vol. 39, no. 36, p. R393, Aug. 2006, https://doi.org/10.1088/0305-4470/39/36/R01.

[8] R. P. Feynman, "Simulating Physics with Computers," Int. J. Theor. Phys., vol. 21, no. 6, pp. 467–488, 1982, https://doi.org/10.1007/BF02650179.

[9] J. I. Cirac and P. Zoller, "Quantum Computations with Cold Trapped Ions," Phys. Rev. Lett., vol. 74, no. 20, pp. 4091–4094, May 1995, https://doi.org/10.1103/PhysRevLett.74.4091.

[10] L. K. Grover, "Quantum Computers Can Search Arbitrarily Large Databases by a Single Query," Phys. Rev. Lett., vol. 79, no. 23, pp. 4709–4712, Dec. 1997, https://doi.org/10.1103/PhysRevLett.79.4709.

[11] P. W. Shor, "Polynomial-Time Algorithms for Prime Factorization and Discrete Logarithms on a Quantum Computer," SIAM Rev., vol. 41, no. 2, pp. 303–332, 1999, https://doi.org/10.1137/S0036144598347011.

[12] Asiva Noor Rachmayani, "No 主観的健康感を中心とした在宅高齢者における 健康関連指標に関する共分散構造分析 Title," p. 6, 2015.

[13] H. Rana and N. Verma, "Enhanced Quantum Key Distribution Using Hybrid Channels and Natural Random Numbers," arXiv Prepr. arXiv2007.14298, 2020, [Online]. Available: http://arxiv.org/abs/2007.14298?utm_source=researcher_app&utm_medium=referral&utm_campaign=RESR_MRKT_Researcher_inbound.
[14] B. Jaderberg, L. W. Anderson, W. Xie, S. Albanie, M. Kiffner, and D. Jaksch, "Quantum Self-Supervised Learning," Quantum Sci. Technol., vol. 7, no. 3, pp. 1–13, 2022, https://doi.org/10.1088/2058-9565/ac6825.
[15] S. L. Tsang, M. T. West, S. M. Erfani, and M. Usman, "Hybrid Quantum-Classical Generative Adversarial Network for High-Resolution Image Generation," IEEE Trans. Quantum Eng., vol. 4, pp. 1–19, 2023, https://doi.org/10.1109/TQE.2023.3319319.
[16] E. Dri et al., "Towards an End-to-End Approach for Quantum Principal Component Analysis," Proc.—2023 IEEE Int. Conf. Quantum Comput. Eng. QCE 2023, vol. 2, no. January 2025, pp. 4–9, 2023, https://doi.org/10.1109/QCE57702.2023.10175.
[17] S. Adhikary, S. Dangwal, and D. Bhowmik, "Supervised Learning with a Quantum Classifier Using Multi-Level Systems," Quantum Inf. Process., vol. 19, no. 3, 2020, https://doi.org/10.1007/s11128-020-2587-9.
[18] G. Sergioli et al., "Quantum-Inspired Minimum Distance Classification in a Biomedical Context," Int. J. Quantum Inf., vol. 16, no. 8, pp. 13–16, 2018, https://doi.org/10.1142/S0219749918400117.
[19] G. Hellstem, "Hybrid Quantum Network for classification of finance and MNIST data," Proc.—2021 IEEE 18th Int. Conf. Softw. Archit. Companion, ICSA-C 2021, pp. 106–109, 2021, https://doi.org/10.1109/ICSA-C52384.2021.00027.
[20] S. Rainjonneau et al., "Quantum Algorithms Applied to Satellite Mission Planning for Earth Observation," IEEE J. Sel. Top. Appl. Earth Obs. Remote Sens., vol. 16, pp. 7062–7075, 2023, https://doi.org/10.1109/JSTARS.2023.3287154.
[21] T. Kanimozhi, S. Sridevi, M. Valliammai, J. Mohanraj, N. Vinodhkumar, and A. Sathasivam, "Behavior Prediction of Fiber Optic Temperature Sensor Based on Hybrid Classical Quantum Regression Model," Quantum Mach. Intell., vol. 6, no. 1, pp. 0–19, 2024, https://doi.org/10.1007/s42484-024-00150-7.
[22] S. J. Weinberg, F. Sanches, T. Ide, K. Kamiya, and R. Correll, "Supply Chain Logistics with Quantum and Classical Annealing Algorithms," Sci. Rep., vol. 13, no. 1, pp. 1–18, 2023, https://doi.org/10.1038/s41598-023-31765-8.
[23] D. J. Egger, C. Gambella, J. Marecek, S. Mcfaddin, M. Mevissen, R. Raymond, A. Simonetto, S. Woerner, and E. Yndurain "Quantum Computing for Finance: State-of-the-Art and Future Prospects," IEEE Trans. Quantum Eng., vol. 1, pp. 1–24, 2020, Art no. 3101724, https://doi.org/10.1109/TQE.2020.3030314.
[24] M. Ying, "Quantum Computation, Quantum Theory and AI ☆," Artif. Intell., vol. 174, no. 2, pp. 162–176, 2010, https://doi.org/10.1016/j.artint.2009.11.009.
[25] V. Chamola, A. Jolfaei, V. Chanana, P. Parashari, and V. Hassija, "Information Security in the Post Quantum Era for 5G and beyond Networks: Threats to Existing Cryptography, and Post-Quantum Cryptography," Comput. Commun., vol. 176, no. June, pp. 99–118, 2021, https://doi.org/10.1016/j.comcom.2021.05.019.
[26] F. Tennie, and T. N. Palmer, "Quantum Computers for Weather and Climate Prediction: The Good, the Bad, and the Noisy," Bull. Amer. Meteor. Soc., vol. 104, pp. E488–E500, 2023, https://doi.org/10.1175/BAMS-D-22-0031.1.
[27] L. K. Grover, "Quantum Mechanics Helps in Searching for a Needle in a Haystack," Phys. Rev. Lett., vol. 79, no. 2, pp. 325–328, Jul. 1997, https://doi.org/10.1103/PhysRevLett.79.325.
[28] S. Lloyd, M. Mohseni, and P. Rebentrost, "Quantum Principal Component Analysis," Nat. Phys., vol. 10, no. 9, pp. 631–633, 2014, https://doi.org/10.1038/NPHYS3029.

[29] J. Heredge, C. Hill, L. Hollenberg, and M. Sevior, "Quantum Support Vector Machines for Continuum Suppression in B Meson Decays," Comput. Softw. Big Sci., vol. 5, no. 1, pp. 1–9, 2021, https://doi.org/10.1007/s41781-021-00075-x.
[30] Z. Wang, S. Hadfield, Z. Jiang, and E. G. Rieffel, "Quantum Approximate Optimization Algorithm for MaxCut: A Fermionic View," Phys. Rev. A, vol. 97, no. 2, p. 22304, Feb. 2018, https://doi.org/10.1103/PhysRevA.97.022304.
[31] A. Bayerstadler et al., "Industry Quantum Computing Applications," EPJ Quantum Technol., vol. 8, no. 1, 2021, https://doi.org/10.1140/epjqt/s40507-021-00114-x.
[32] S. Suhas and S. Divya, "Quantum-Improved Weather Forecasting: Integrating Quantum Machine Learning for Precise Prediction and Disaster Mitigation," iQ-CCHESS 2023–2023 IEEE Int. Conf. Quantum Technol. Commun. Comput. Hardw. Embed. Syst. Secur., pp. 1–7, 2023, https://doi.org/10.1109/iQ-CCHESS56596.2023.10391714.
[33] K. A. Cornell, "Assessment of Quantum ML Applicability for Climate Actions: Comparison of the Variational Quantum Classifier and the Quantum Support Vector Classifier with Classical ML Models," 2024 IEEE Int. Conf. Big Data, pp. 4357–4366, 2024, https://doi.org/10.1109/BigData62323.2024.10825181.
[34] K. T. M. Ho et al., "Quantum Computing for Climate Resilience and Sustainability Challenges," 2024 IEEE Int. Conf. Quantum Comput. Eng., vol. 2, pp. 262–267, 2024, https://doi.org/10.1109/QCE60285.2024.10289.
[35] A. Vaezi, A. Movaghar, M. Ghodsi, S. M. H. Kazemi, N. B. Noghrehy, and S. M. Kazemi, "Quantum Complexity vs Classical Complexity: A Survey," 2023, [Online]. Available: http://arxiv.org/abs/2312.14075.
[36] R. Venkatesh and S. Darandale, "Enhancing Healthcare Security with Quantum Blockchain: Electronic Medical Records Protection," 2nd IEEE Int. Conf. Networks, Multimed. Inf. Technol. NMITCON 2024, pp. 1–6, 2024, https://doi.org/10.1109/NMITCON62075.2024.10699120.
[37] A. Balasubramaniam and B. Surendiran, "QUMA: Quantum Unified Medical Architecture Using Blockchain," Informatics, vol. 11, no. 2, 2024, https://doi.org/10.3390/informatics11020033.

Part II

The Current (Application)

7 Quantum Computing—A Journey Through Time

Naresh Tangudu, Deepak Davala, G. V. L. Narasimha, and S. Praveena

7.1 THE DAWN OF QUANTUM MECHANICS (1930S)

The 1930s were regarded as a life-changing era in the field of physics, highlighted by the rise of quantum mechanics. This breakthrough area of science revolutionized the way scientists viewed the fundamental laws governing matter and energy in the quantum realm. Quantum mechanics is unlike classical physics, which relies on predictability and certainty. This introduced a more stochastic approach. This era important discovery included Heisenberg's formulation of the uncertainty principle and Schrödinger's development of wave mechanics.

7.1.1 Foundational Theories

The base of quantum mechanics was built upon two major conceptual approaches: Heisenberg's matrix mechanics and Schrödinger's wave equations. These two mathematical models are used to get powerful insights into the behavior of particles at atomic and subatomic levels. Furthermore, Einstein's work on the photoelectric results highlighted the particle-wave dual nature of light and matter, which further became important in the evolution of quantum computing [1].

7.2 EARLY THOUGHT EXPERIMENTS

Quantum mechanics helps in several thought experiments that proved its strange and non-intuitive principles. One of the most well-known is Schrödinger's cat, a paradox that demonstrates the idea of superposition and the difficulties involved in measuring quantum systems. This experiment also hinted at the future challenges scientists would face in developing quantum-based technologies [2].

7.3 FROM THOUGHT EXPERIMENT TO REALITY: THE BIRTH OF QUANTUM COMPUTING (1980S)

During the 1980s, the evolution of quantum computation from abstract theory to practical exploration occurred. Physics and computer science researchers started

DOI: 10.1201/9781003538950-9

examining how quantum systems have more ability to solve problems that traditional computers couldn't handle efficiently.

7.4 THEORETICAL BREAKTHROUGHS

Richard Feynman introduced the benefits of quantum systems to control other quantum processes [3]—classical computers faced significant limitations in numerous areas. Building on this idea, David Deutsch introduced the concept of a universal quantum computer by formulating the quantum Turing machine [4]. He also discovered how quantum computation could outperform classical approaches for certain tasks.

7.5 TECHNOLOGICAL BEGINNINGS

In the beginning the conceptual work concentrated on developing constructing basic qubit systems and quantum gates. These initial experiments demonstrated how quantum principles could be applied to process information, sparking growing interest in the field of quantum information theory.

7.6 BREAKING CODES: SHOR'S ALGORITHM AND THE POWER OF QUANTUM (1994)

In 1994 Shor's algorithm was introduced and marked a major revolution in the field of quantum computing [5]. Peter Shor demonstrated that quantum computers are used to tackle problems efficiently, such as integer factorization, that are extremely difficult for classical computers to solve.

7.7 CRYPTOGRAPHIC IMPLICATIONS

Shor's algorithm divulges that quantum computers play a key role in RSA encryption to quickly factor large integers [6]. This discovery focuses on quantum attacks, underscoring the need for encryption techniques that can withstand potential security risks in current cryptographic methods.

7.8 EXPERIMENTAL ADVANCEMENTS

After Shor's innovative algorithm came into existence, scientists and researchers began testing it on early quantum processors. These experiments brought attention to the importance of developing robust methods of correcting errors and managing issues like noise and decoherence [7].

7.9 BUILDING THE QUANTUM MACHINE: QUBITS AND BEYOND

Qubits are essential components in quantum computers, used to go beyond classical bits. Whereas classical bits have a value 0 or 1, qubits can have both states at once. This special attribute helps quantum computers manage and process massive amounts of data better than classical machines [8]. The comparison is shown in Figure 7.1.

Types of Qubits:

- Superconducting Qubits: To manage quantum coherence, the circuits are reduced to absolute zero.
- Trapped Ions: By using an electromagnetic field, the charged particles are bound, providing high-fidelity but slower operations.
- Photonic Qubits: They harness photons for fast, room-temperature operations but face challenges in scalability.
- Topological Qubits: This theoretical approach aims to reduce error rates by encoding qubits in topological states.

The upgrades in qubit technology is increasing its limits of scalability, fidelity, and coherence, getting nearer to practical quantum machine.

7.10 ALGORITHMS FOR A QUANTUM AGE: SHOR'S ALGORITHM AND BEYOND

The purpose of quantum computing is to solve problems that are not solvable by classical computers.

Key Algorithms:

- Shor's Algorithm: Efficient prime factorization, crucial for breaking RSA encode.
- Grover's Algorithm: Boosts irregular search problems, offering a quadratic speedup over classical approaches [9].

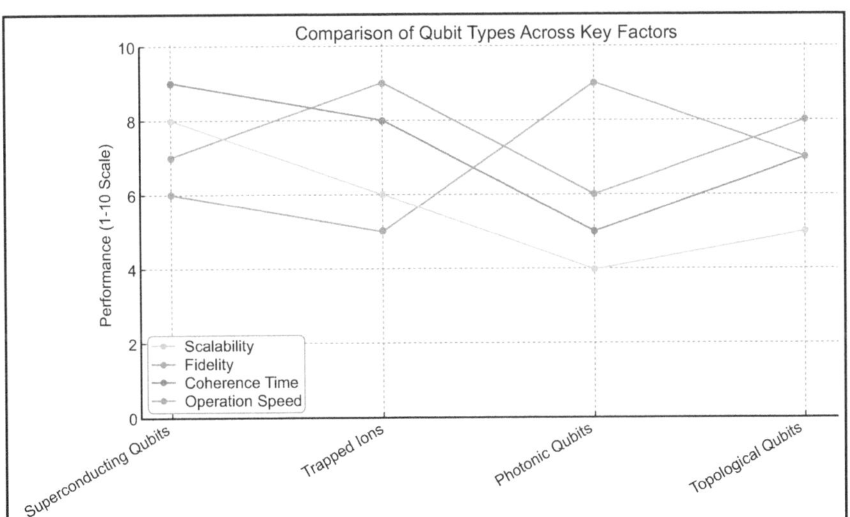

FIGURE 7.1 Comparison of qubit types across key factors.

- Quantum Fourier Transform (QFT): Fundamental to algorithms for solving periodicity-related problems.
- Variational Quantum Algorithms (VQA): Hybrid classical-quantum approaches for optimization and machine learning tasks [10].

These algorithms helps in solving problems in cryptography, chemistry, and other fields.

7.11 THE RACE FOR SUPREMACY: CAN QUANTUM COMPUTERS OUTPERFORM CLASSICAL MACHINES?

Quantum supremacy means quantum computers performing better than the most powerful classical computers [11]. In 2019, Google officially said that it reached a milestone by solving a random circuit sampling calculation in just 200 seconds—whereas the classical supercomputers struggled to solve that in short period.

Challenges to Supremacy:

- Failure Rates: Quantum computations are prone to decoherence and mistakes.
- Scalability: Building machines with millions of error-corrected qubits remains a hurdle.
- Hardware Limitations: Maintaining the extreme conditions required for qubit operation is resource-intensive.

Irrespective of the hurdles, the domination of quantum computing has ruled the competition among major software companies like IBM and Google, as well as new

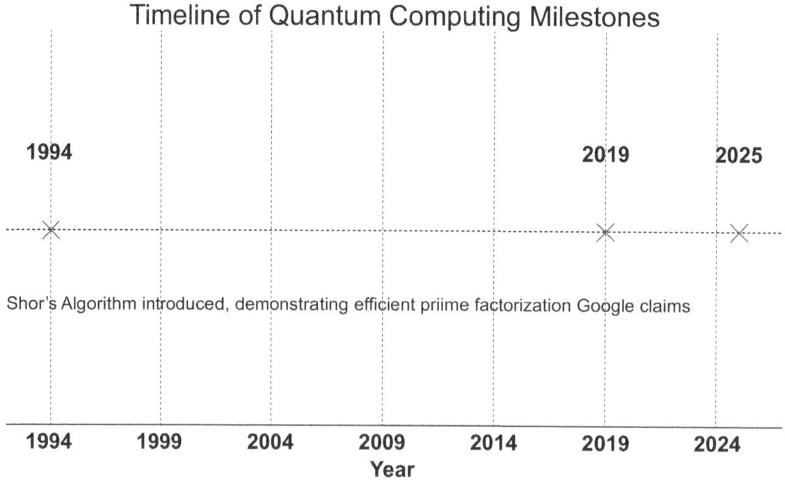

FIGURE 7.2 Timeline of quantum computing.

startups. This fight is speeding up the growth in quantum hardware and algorithm development. The detailed timeline is shown in Figure 7.2 [12].

7.12 TAMING THE NOISE: QUANTUM ERROR CORRECTION AND RELIABLE COMPUTING

Quantum computers are likely to be affected by errors like decoherence and interference in the local environment, interrupting quantum states. Precise quantum computing requires different kinds of error correction strategies that are not similar to classical systems. In a classical system, it can be fixed by duplicating information. It faces an issue caused by the no-cloning theorem, which interrupts the direct copying of data.

Error Correction Techniques:

- Surface Codes: The best approach used for creating multiple physical qubits to generate a single logical qubit, helps in finding errors while running quantum coherence
- Shor Code: One among the initial quantum false rectification schemes that encrypt a logical qubit into nine corporal qubits [13].
- Topological Codes: A fault-tolerant approach to error correction that uses the topology of the qubit system to encode information [14, 15].

Regarding less of significant process, scaling error correlation is still a big challenge in large quantum computers [16].

7.13 DEMOCRATIZING QUANTUM: PROGRAMMING LANGUAGES AND SOFTWARE DEVELOPMENT KITS

Quantum computing is rapidly increasing. In order to support quantum computing, various programming languages and software development kits (SDKs) have been introduced. These are useful to minimize the process of creating and testing quantum algorithms, allowing users to work with quantum systems without having deep knowledge of quantum computing.

Popular Quantum Programming Languages and SDKs:

- Qiskit: Introduced by IBM, this freely available SDK enables end users to build, reproduce, and perform quantum algorithms in IBM's quantum devices [17].
- Cirq: This Google quantum framework supports the creation and simulation of quantum circuits [18].
- Quipper: This is a top-tier, functional programming language designed to simplify to scale the development of quantum algorithms.
- PyQuil: Offered by Rigetti, this Python-based SDK provides tools for constructing and managing quantum circuits.

These platforms help a wide range of audience—from academic researchers to software developers—in quantum algorithm development and experimentation.

7.14 QUANTUM REVOLUTION: APPLICATIONS ACROSS INDUSTRIES

Quantum computing aims to solve the hardest problems by various industries which are not solved by classical computing. Real-world examples include cryptography, optimization, complex system simulation, and machine learning [19].

Industry Applications:

- Medical and Health management: Quantum computing could allow faster drug discovery by identifying molecular combinations at the quantum level.
- Finance: Quantum algorithms also optimize financial models, risk assessment, and portfolio management.
- Logistics and Supply Chain: Quantum computing able to solve difficult optimization issues in a distributed chain, improving efficiency.
- Energy: Quantum simulations can help in materials science by discovering new materials for energy storage and quantum batteries.
- Artificial Intelligence: Quantum machine learning algorithms can accelerate training and enhance the productivity of AI models.

As quantum computing matures, its impact across industries will be transformative, ushering in a new world of creative inventions.

7.15 THE QUANTUM INTERNET: A NETWORKED FUTURE FOR QUANTUM COMPUTATION

The theory of quantum internet means a network where quantum computers, sensors, and other quantum devices communicate and distribute data securely through quantum entanglement and teleportation. This will help in maintaining quantum interaction and quantum key sharing for more-protective data transmission.

Key Components of Quantum Internet:

- Quantum Key Distribution (QKD): By exchanging encryption keys, we can allow a protective interaction between two parties. Certified monitoring cannot interrupt the key without identification.
- Quantum Repeaters: Devices that enlarge the range of quantum communication networks by modifying quantum signals.
- Entanglement Swapping: A procedure that allows the shift of entanglement among distant molecules, forming the backbone of quantum networks.

The quantum internet has the capacity for uprising cybersecurity, communication, and data sharing, offering a highly secure infrastructure for the digital future. You can see a detailed process of quantum computing in Figure 7.3.

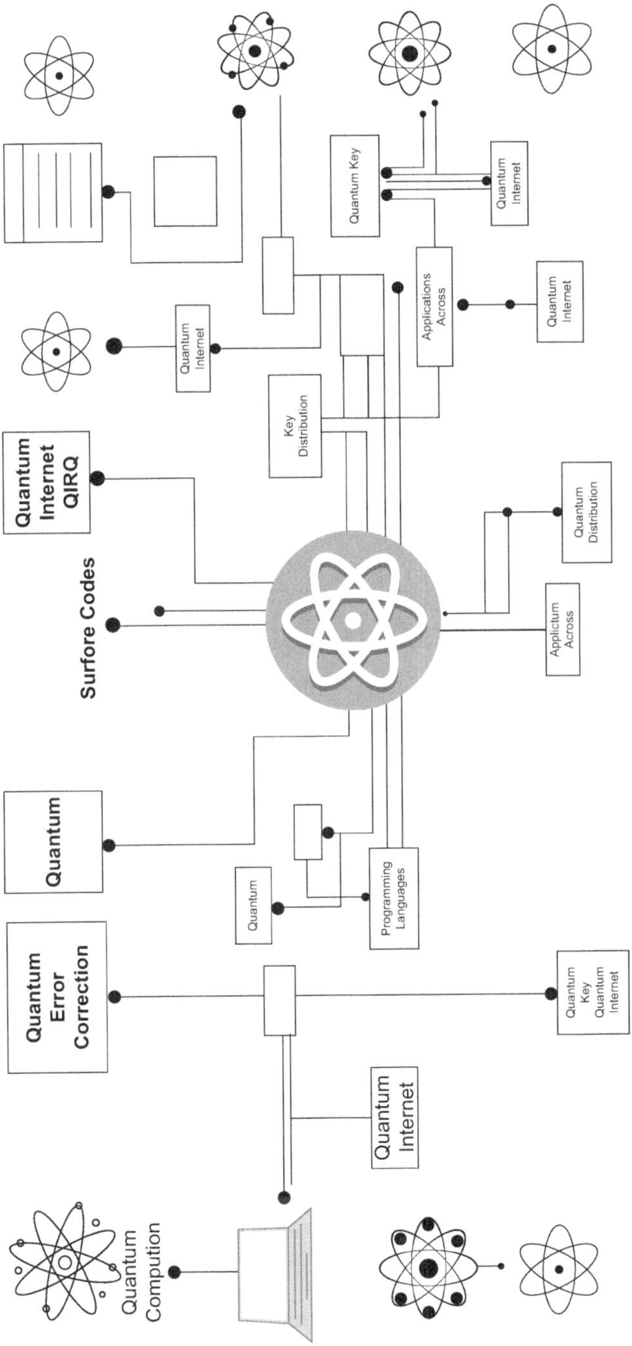

FIGURE 7.3 Mind map.

7.16 SCALING UP: THE HURDLES OF BUILDING MASSIVE-SCALE OF QUANTUM SYSTEMS

The transition from minor-level quantum processors to major-level quantum computers presents significant technical challenges. Quantum decoherence remains a primary obstacle, with error rates increasing exponentially with system size. Recent experiments by IBM demonstrate that maintaining quantum coherence beyond 100 qubits requires sophisticated error correction protocols that themselves demand additional physical qubits [20]. Environmental noise and quantum gate fidelity pose additional scaling challenges. The latest superconducting quantum systems require operating temperatures near absolute zero, making large-scale implementation both technically demanding and resource-intensive.

7.17 QUANTUM FALSE RECTIFICATION

False rectification in quantum systems presents unique challenges compared to classical computing. The no-duplication theorem protects direct cloning of quantum stages, necessitating complex error correction codes. Surface codes have emerged as promising candidates, though they require significant qubit overhead.

7.18 MATERIALS SCIENCE CHALLENGES

The choice of qubit implementation significantly impacts scalability. Current approaches as follows:

- Superconducting qubits
- Trapped ions
- Topological qubits
- Photonic qubits

Every platform represents distinct dominance and limitations for large-scale implementation.

The timeline of post-quantum cryptography standardization and implementation milestones is illustrated in Figure 7.4 [21].

7.19 THE QUANTUM PRICE TAG: COST CONSIDERATIONS IN EXPLORATION AND EXPANSION

The financial implications of quantum computing development are substantial. Current estimates indicate that constructing a false rectifier quantum computer ability to process Shor's algorithm would require investments exceeding $1 billion [22].

7.20 INFRASTRUCTURE REQUIREMENTS

The costs primarily stem from:

- Specialized hardware requirements, including dilution refrigerators and precision control electronics

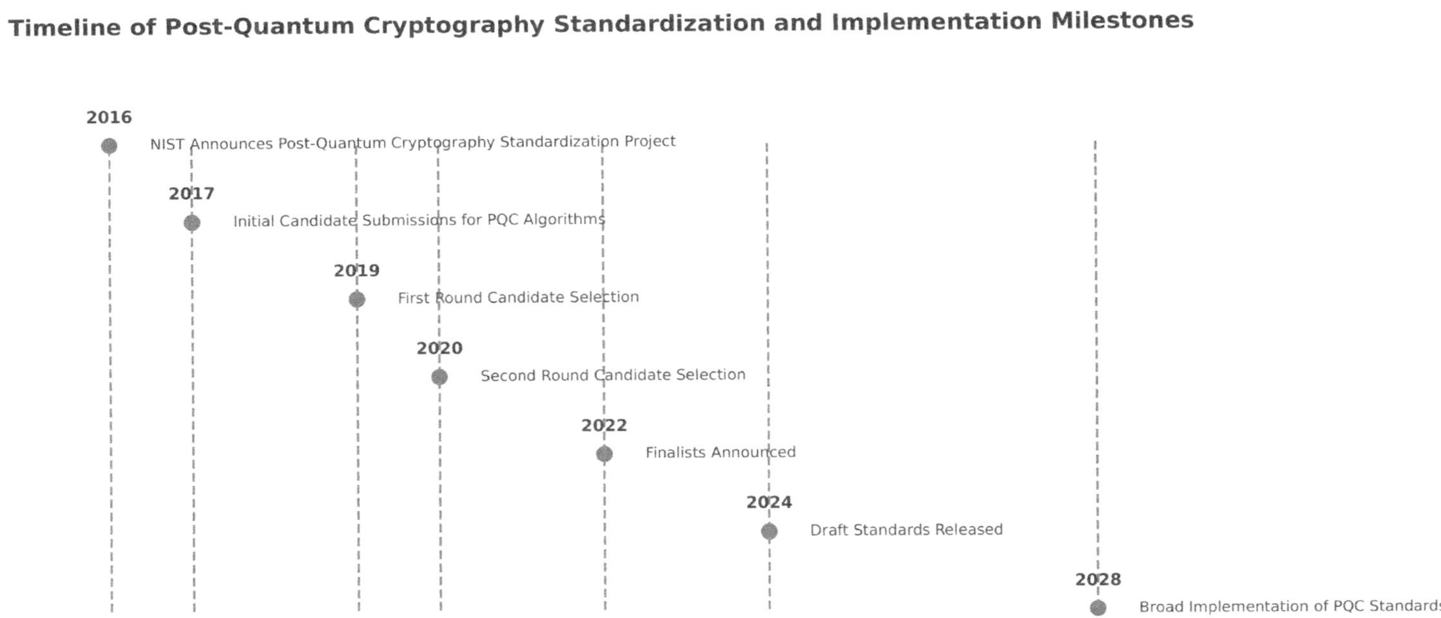

FIGURE 7.4 Timeline of post-quantum cryptography standardization and implementation milestones.

- Development of custom quantum control software
- Maintenance of ultra-low temperature environments
- Skilled workforce requirements

Recent market analysis suggests the quantum computing industry will require sustained investment of $10–15 billion annually through 2030 to achieve practical quantum advantage.

7.21 COMMERCIAL LANDSCAPE

The quantum computing market has attracted significant private investment, with major technology companies and startups competing for dominance. Key market segments include:

- Hardware development
- Software and algorithms
- Consulting services
- Industry-specific applications

7.22 SECURING THE FUTURE: SUPPORT-QUANTUM CRYPTOGRAPHY IN A QUANTUM WORLD

The arrival of large-scale quantum computers causes important problems to present cryptographic systems. Elliptic curve and RSA cryptography, which form the crucial component of modern secure communications, would likely become vulnerable to quantum attacks [23].

7.23 POST-QUANTUM ALGORITHMS

NIST's post-quantum cryptography normalization program has detected several guaranteed quantum-friction algorithms [24, 25]. The CRYSTAL-Kyber protocol has emerged as a leading candidate for key encapsulation, demonstrating strong security against both quantum and traditional attacks.

7.24 IMPLEMENTATION CHALLENGES

Transitioning to post-quantum cryptography shows multiple hurdles:

- Performance overhead of new algorithms
- Integration with existing systems
- Key size management
- Validation and certification requirements (Figure 7.5).

7.25 HYBRID APPROACHES

During the transition period, hybrid classical-quantum cryptographic solutions offer a pragmatic approach to security [26]. These systems combine traditional algorithms with quantum-resistant ones to maintain security against both classical and quantum threats.

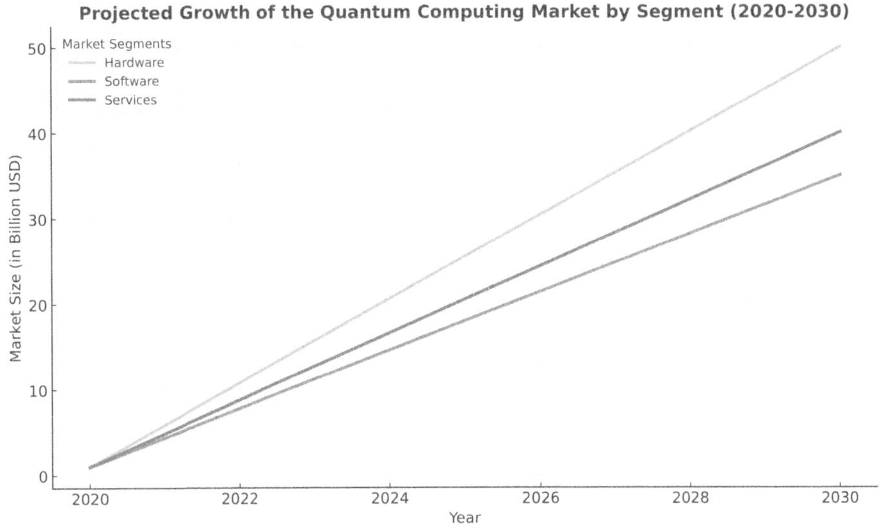

FIGURE 7.5 Projected growth of the quantum computing market by segment (2020–2030).

7.26 CONCLUSION

Quantum computing is a study that combines the relation among physics, computer science, and engineering, with a power to influence quantum mechanics to establish great changes in computation challenges. This chapter is a complete research of its basic principles, hardware advancements, algorithmic development, and correlated challenges, documenting the trajectory of this transformative field.

Chapter 1 presents the general concept of quantum mechanics, which is the foundation of quantum computing. Entanglement, superposition, and quantum measurement are the most rudimentary concepts of this model, facilitating quantum computers to operate data differently from traditional systems. This change shows a new perspective of computation.

Chapter 2 goes through the quantum hardware, which examines the different types of qubits, such as superconducting, trapped-ion, photonic, and topological qubits. Each type of qubits has its own benefits and drawbacks, highlight the inter-processing between materials science and system engineering to achieve scalability and reliability. Challenges like coherence maintenance and noise reduction are mentioned.

Chapter 3 discusses the transformative potential of quantum algorithms, describing their efficient problem-solving ability compared to traditional algorithms. Shor's algorithm, which improved Grover's algorithm, enhances data search, and these improvements spotlight quantum computing's turbulent capacity. Additionally, modified quantum classical algorithms describe the adaptability of quantum systems in addressing current computational challenges.

Chapter 4 points out the obstacles of scaling quantum systems, the financial investments required, and the suggestions for cybersecurity. Subsections describe error correction, which overcomes quantum decoherence and achieves fault tolerance. To build large-scale quantum systems, the economic demand is high to acquire the specialized architecture and investments. Moreover, the threat due to current cryptographic system boosts the urgency of developing post-quantum cryptography and a hybrid solution.

In conclusion, the future of quantum computing is both inspiring and challenging. Though a large-scale fraud-tolerant quantum system is challenging, it is still possible. This study leads to a new technological progress that can change our perspective regarding computation and its applications.

REFERENCES

1. Heisenberg, W. (1927). The Physical Principles of the Quantum Theory. University of Chicago Press.
2. Schrödinger, E. (1935). Discussion of Probability Relations between Separated Systems. Proceedings of the Cambridge Philosophical Society, 31, 555–563. https://doi.org/10.1017/S0305004100013554
3. Feynman, R. P. (1982). Simulating Physics with Computers. International Journal of Theoretical Physics, 21(6), 467–488. https://doi.org/10.1007/BF02650179
4. Deutsch, D. (1985). Quantum Theory, the Church-Turing Principle, and the Universal Quantum Computer. Proceedings of the Royal Society A, 400(1818), 97–117. https://doi.org/10.1098/rspa.1985.0070
5. Shor, P. W. (1994). Algorithms for Quantum Computation: Discrete Logarithms and Factoring. Proceedings of the 35th Annual Symposium on Foundations of Computer Science. https://doi.org/10.1109/SFCS.1994.365700
6. Bennett, C. H., & DiVincenzo, D. P. (2000). Quantum Information and Computation. Nature, 404(6775), 247–255. https://doi.org/10.1038/35005001
7. Preskill, J. (2012). Quantum Computing and the Entanglement Frontier. arXiv:1203.5813.
8. Monroe, C., & Kim, J. (2013). Scaling the Ion Trap Quantum Processor. Science, 339(6124), 1164–1169. https://doi.org/10.1126/science.1231298
9. Harrow, A. W., Hassidim, A., & Lloyd, S. (2009). Quantum Algorithm for Linear Systems of Equations. Physical Review Letters, 103(15), 150502. https://doi.org/10.1103/PhysRevLett.103.150502
10. Farhi, E., Goldstone, J., & Gutmann, S. (2014). Quantum Adiabatic Evolution Algorithms and Local Minima. arXiv:quant-ph/1411.4028. https://arxiv.org/abs/1411.4028
11. Arute, F., et al. (2019). Quantum Supremacy Using a Programmable Superconducting Processor. Nature, 574(7779), 505–510. https://doi.org/10.1038/s41586-019-1666-5
12. Preskill, J. (2018). Quantum Computing in the NISQ Era and beyond. Quantum, 2, 79. https://doi.org/10.22331/q-2018-08-06-79
13. Shor, P. W. (1995). Scheme for Reducing Decoherence in Quantum Memory. Physical Review A, 52(4), R2493–R2496. https://doi.org/10.1103/PhysRevA.52.R2493
14. Bravyi, S., & Kitaev, A. (1998). Quantum Codes on a Lattice. arXiv:quant-ph/9811052. https://arxiv.org/abs/quant-ph/9811052
15. Gottesman, D. (1997). Stabilizer Codes and Quantum Error Correction. arXiv: quant-ph/9705052. https://arxiv.org/abs/quant-ph/9705052
16. Fowler, A. G., et al. (2012). Surface Codes: Towards Practical Large-Scale Quantum Computation. Physical Review A, 86(3), 032324. https://doi.org/10.1103/PhysRevA.86.032324
17. IBM Qiskit Team. (2020). Qiskit: An Open-Source Quantum Computing Software Development Framework. https://qiskit.org/
18. Google Quantum AI Team. (2020). Cirq: A Python Framework for Developing and Simulating Quantum Circuits. https://quantumai.google/cirq

19. Buhl, J., & Briggs, G. A. D. (2019). A Roadmap for Quantum Internet and Communications. Quantum Science and Technology, 4(2), 020502. https://doi.org/10.1088/2058-9565/ab1337
20. DiVincenzo, D. P. (2000). The Physical Implementation of Quantum Computation. Fortschritte der Physik: Progress of Physics, 48(9–11), 771–783. https://doi.org/10.1002/1521-3978(200009)48:9/11<771::AID-PROP771>3.0.CO;2-E
21. Kjaergaard, M., Schwartz, M. E., & Oliver, W. D. (2020). Superconducting Qubits: Current State of Play. Annual Review of Condensed Matter Physics, 11(1), 369–395. https://doi.org/10.1146/annurev-conmatphys-031119-050605
22. Castelvecchi, D. (2017). The Quantum Gold Rush: The Private Funding Pouring into Quantum Computing. Nature, 543(7644), 159–160. https://doi.org/10.1038/543159a
23. Markov, I. L. (2018). Quantum Technology: A Primer. Communications of the ACM, 61(2), 36–39. https://doi.org/10.1145/3178157
24. Alagic, G., et al. (2020). Status Report on the Second Round of the NIST Post-Quantum Cryptography Standardization Process. NIST. https://csrc.nist.gov/publications/detail/nistir/8309/final
25. Chen, L., et al. (2016). Report on Post-Quantum Cryptography. NIST. https://doi.org/10.6028/NIST.IR.8105
26. Bindel, N., et al. (2020). Hybrid Key Encapsulation Methods. Proceedings of the International Conference on Post-Quantum Cryptography. https://doi.org/10.1007/978-3-030-44223-1_15

8 Quantum Computing—Foundations, Principles, and Modern Applications

M. Bharathi, Madhurima V., Sandhya Kumari G., Saleha Tabassum, N. Ashok Kumar, Neelima K., and N. Padmaja

8.1 INTRODUCTION

Quantum computing [2] could fundamentally use transform technology and problem-solving methods. The use of quantum physics principles allows this new computing method to solve problems beyond the reach of standard processors. This chapter delivers a review of quantum computing by exploring its fundamental philosophies as well as its historical progression in present-day situations. Quantum computing signifies a major evolution in computational knowledge by employing a diverse approach to process information compared to classical computing. The central principles of quantum mechanics, which involve particles like atoms, electrons, and photons, are the basis for quantum computing. Quantum computing embraces the probability to transform technology and problem-solving techniques radically. Quantum physics principles qualify for this computational method to solve glitches outside the competencies of traditional processors. Whereas traditional bits are represented by a single value of 0 or 1, quantum bits, or qubits, can in state where they can be both 0 and 1 for a certain period. Quantum computers can speedily make multiple calculations at once because qubits can have multiple states. Qubits, even at a distance, can also affect each other. This phenomenon is called quantum entanglement. The interaction between elements enables coordinated processing capabilities while increasing the complexity of tasks Quantum algorithms derive their helpfulness from their capacity to manipulate interference patterns, eliminating incorrect answers while strengthening the correct ones. Quantum computing transforms optimization by solving complex problems in logistics, finance, and AI and enabling precise quantum simulations for molecular chemistry, which supports drug discovery and material design by implementing quantum algorithms capable of breaking conventional cryptographic methods through rapid number factorization.

Materials science and chemistry profit from quantum simulations that model molecular and chemical reactions with incomparable precision, which advances drug discovery and material design with optimization. Quantum computers [3] can solve complex logistics, finance, and artificial intelligence problems. Shor's algorithm enables rapid large-number factorization, faster than classical cryptographic methods.

DOI: 10.1201/9781003538950-10

The advancement of quantum computing leads to major obstacles, such as creating quantum computers with consistent qubits in large quantities, developing efficient quantum error correction techniques, and establishing consecutively specialized quantum computation hardware comprising cryogenic systems in order to preserve qubits at ultra-low temperatures. The present state of quantum computing remains nascent as investigational quantum computers with small scales have achieved limited but yet remarkable performances. Key technology firms and scientific research entities collaborate enthusiastically to solve present obstacles by advancing qubit coherence with error correction techniques and increasing new quantum algorithms. Quantum computing represents a fundamental transformation in computational methods that shows a promise to solve complex problems in various fields. Achieving real-world large-scale quantum applications demands nonstop research and growth to expose quantum technology's full potential.

8.2 HISTORICAL BACKGROUND AND EVOLUTION

Scientists promote significant growth in emerging and controlling qubits utilizing different physical stages, such as superconducting circuits, trapped ions, and quantum dots. In 2001, IBM and Stanford University accomplished a substantial breakthrough by successfully implementing Shor's procedure on a basic quantum processor, resulting in a factorization of the number 15. This accomplishment, however little, confirmed the tangible capability of quantum computation. Technological progress rapidly increased in the following years, with notable improvements in increasing the quantity of qubits, improving the duration of qubit coherence, and creating reliable error correction methods. Prominent companies like Google, IBM, and Microsoft, as well as startups like Rigetti and D-Wave, have made substantial investments in quantum computing, actively pushing the limits of what can be achieved in this field. In 2019, Google declared their quantum computer Sycamore has attained quantum supremacy through executing a particular computation more swiftly than the most potent classical supercomputer, highlighting the swift progress in this domain. Currently, quantum computing is a dynamic and swiftly developing field. Scientists and engineers are investigating different structures, mathematical procedures, and uses, with the goal of constructing quantum processors that can lever large volumes of files and continue functioning even in the presence of errors. Both governments and private organizations are rapidly acknowledging the revolutionary capabilities of quantum computing [4], leading to noteworthy savings in R&D. With ongoing advancements, quantum computing is arranged the edge of revolutionizing various fields such as drug discovery, cryptography, and materials research. This will guide a new era of computational opportunities.

8.3 QUANTUM COMPUTING

Quantum computing discusses the progress of computer structures that leverage quantum physics ideologies to perform complex computational tasks faster than classical computers as shown in Figure 8.1.

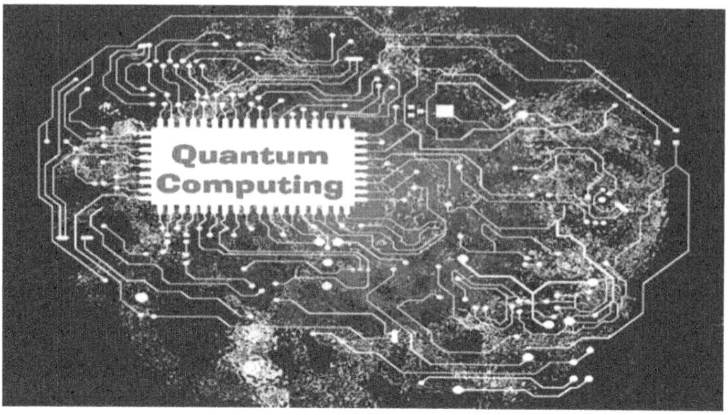

FIGURE 8.1 Visual aid of quantum computing.

(https://indiaai.gov.in/article/quantum-computing-a-road-from-illusion-to-promise)

Quantum computing signifies a novel computational method based on quantum mechanics, which explains atomic and subatomic particle behavior. Quantum computing uses quantum bits, known as qubits, whereas traditional computing uses standard binary bits [5]. Qubits enable progressive information illustration and manipulation methods that exceed classical capabilities.

Definition and Fundamental Concepts

Qubit: A qubit is a straightforward unit of information used in quantum computing structures. A qubit possesses the ability to represent 0 and 1 simultaneously, which differentiates it from conventional bits that operate as either 0 or 1 only. Qubits establish high efficiency in particular computational tasks due to their exclusive ability to accomplish multiple controls at once. This attribute is known as superposition.

Superposition: A qubit in quantum computing displays multiple states simultaneously with the use of superposition. A qubit preserves simultaneous states of 0 and 1, whereas a standard classical bit must select either 0 or 1 only. Quantum processors have the capability to examine numerous solutions to a problem simultaneously, which allow them tackle complex problems.

Entanglement: Entanglement means forming connection between two qubits such that any modification to one qubit promptly affects the other one irrespective of their spatial distance. Quantum interference helps to produce the correct results more quickly by eliminating the incorrect answers. Quantum algorithms resolve definite problems with significantly better speed than traditional algorithms because they exploit interference to elevate computational performance.

Classical Computing and Quantum Computing: In classical computing systems, bits serve as a fundamental information units, which assume one of two possible values of 0 or 1. Qubits, which work in quantum computing [6], dismiss conserve the superposition of 0 and 1 states, as Figure 8.2

demonstrates. Qubits own this special trait that empowers them to process significantly more data simultaneously.

Computational Capacity: Traditional computers have limited processors that achieve calculations through sequential processing/parallel processing. Quantum processors employ superposition and entanglement technologies to have multiple processes instantaneously. With the use of parallelism, quantum processors are capable of solving definite problems exponentially quicker than outdated processors.

Algorithm Efficiency: Quantum processors handle more complex glitches than traditional computers, which are unable to solve them because of inherent complexity.

Shor's method proves exponential factoring capabilities in contrast with the best standard algorithms. The cryptography arena faces major problems due to these developments. Grover's method has four times better performance than that of traditional search algorithms when examining through unsorted datasets.

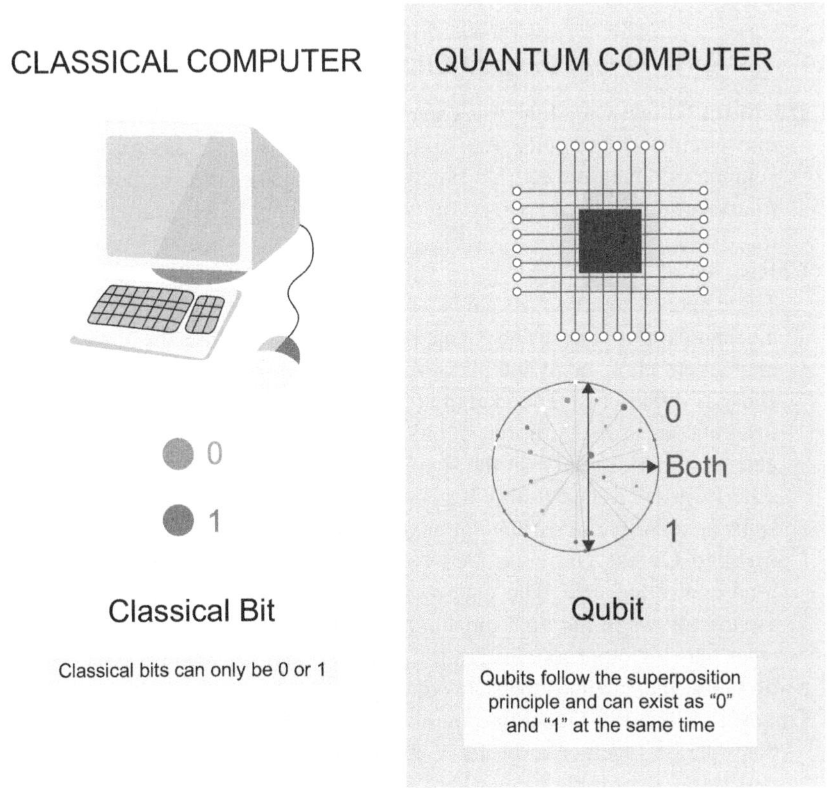

FIGURE 8.2 Classical computing vs. quantum computing.

(https://www.berkeleynucleonics.com/august-23-2024-quantum-computing-vs-classical-computing)

Vulnerability to Errors: Quantum systems show significant sensitivity to environmental issues, which produce mistakes through decoherence along with other noise influences. Research on quantum error correction with fault-tolerant quantum computing has become widespread as experts work to generate trustworthy quantum calculations that solve these current glitches.

In this present computing landscape, classical computing is still widely used, while quantum computing remains in its early development stage. Important challenges comprise maintaining qubit coherence and error correction methods while ensuring an adequate number of qubits for efficient operations. Investigational quantum computers have already outshined traditional computers in certain areas in spite of existing challenges. Quantum computing is a groundbreaking technology that uses quantum mechanics properties in order to process the information with new methods. Quantum computers can elucidate the intricate problems more capably than that of modern computers because they use qubits and with the usage of entanglement, superposition, and quantum intrusion. Quantum computing technology could bring about significant advances within cryptography and materials science as well as optimization techniques [7].

8.4 QUANTUM GATES AND CIRCUITS

Quantum Gates: Quantum gates serve as essential building blocks of quantum circuits in the same way traditional logic gates function in modern computers. Quantum entries function by applying unitary operations that transform qubits while preserving their total probability through reversible transformations.

Categories of Gates: Pauli gates contain the quantum gates X, Y, and Z. These gates resemble classical NOT gates but operate according to quantum mechanical principles. The X gate reverses the qubit state, the Y gate implements both bit reversal and phase reversal together, and the Z gate provides phase reversal only. The Hadamard gate (H) functions as a quantum gate that generates superpositions of quantum states. The action of any quantum gate on a qubit initially in the state $|0\rangle$, transforms it into the superposition state $(|0\rangle+|1\rangle)/2$. The S and T gates together make up phase gates, which apply specific phase shifts to qubit states.

Controlled Gates: The controlled NOT gate stands out as most frequently used controlled gate. The gate modifies the aim of the state of the qubit exclusively when the mechanism qubit maintains the logic state $|1\rangle$. These gates play a vibrant role in creating entanglement between qubits.

Swap Gate: It exchanges the states of two qubits.

Quantum Circuits: Quantum circuits represent measures of quantum gates that operate together to perform specific computational functions. Qubits pass through multiple gates where they receive unitary transformations that convert them into the quantum state that represents the result for the problem at hand.

Construction: When constructing a quantum circuit, we apply gate operations in a particular sequence defined by an algorithm onto qubits. When the quantum circuit completes its operations, measurements occur to excerpt classical data, commencing the final quantum state. The building of a fundamental quantum circuit starts with the use of a Hadamard gate to generate a superposition in a qubit before using a CNOT gate to catch it with another qubit tracked by qubit measurement in order to get the result. Complex algorithms like Shor's algorithm uses factorization method or Grover's unsorted database search method can be processed by erudite quantum circuits. Superposition and entanglement serve as essential assets that permit quantum computational systems to attain extraordinary processing power. Quantum computing methods use complex computations through the application of quantum gates and circuits, which they achieve using entanglement and superposition to solve issues that classical processors cannot address [8].

In summary, quantum gates assist as a fundamental block in quantum circuits that implement reversible unitary processes to convert qubit states via superposition and entanglement. Quantum circuits use Pauli gates (X, Y, Z), the Hadamard gate (H), phase gates (S, T), controlled gates including CNOT, and the swap gate. Quantum circuits use these gates to perform calculations, which make advanced algorithms like Grover's and Shor's possible to distribute computational powers supreme over classical computers.

8.4.1 Complex Numbers in Quantum Computing

Complex numbers are very important in the field of quantum computing. Complex numbers are central in quantum computing for describing the quantum states and operations. Complex numbers are decisive in quantum computing for unfolding quantum states and arrangements. Understanding the complex numbers and their operation in quantum physics is very essential for thoughtful the intricacies of quantum computation [9].

8.4.2 An Overview of Complex Numbers Definition and Representation

A complex number a numerical value that contains a real component and an imaginary component. The illustration of a complex number is expressed as z = a + bi, where a and b are the real numbers and i is the imaginary unit, with i^2 = −1.

Complex Plane: Complex numbers are depicted on the complex plane, with the x-axis representing real numbers and the y-axis representing imaginary numbers.

The magnitude is known as the modulus. A complex number z = a + bi is extracted using the formula |z| = sqrt(a^2 + b^2). The argument or phase of any complex number is the angle θ between the positive real axis and the line on behalf of the complex number. It results into $\theta = \arctan(b/a)$, wherever a and b are real and imaginary parts of a complex number.

8.4.3 Complex Number Operations

Addition of Two Complex Numbers: (a+bi) and (c+di) are calculated by adding their real parts (a & c) and the imaginary parts (b & d).

Multiplication of Two Complex Numbers: (a+bi) and (c+di) are calculated using the formula (ac−bd)+(ad+bc)i.

Complex Conjugate: Complex conjugate denotes the number gained by changing the sign of the imaginary part of a given complex number. The complex number z, represented as z = a + bi, is equal to its complex conjugate characterized as z = a—bi. It reflects z on the real axis. The importance of complex numbers happening quantum states and operations is noteworthy. Quantum states are generally depicted as vectors within a complex Hilbert space. A qubit state can be symbolized as $|\psi\rangle=\alpha\ |0\rangle+\beta\ |1\rangle$, where α and β are the coefficients. α and β are complex numbers that accomplish the normalizing requirement, where an entire value of α squared plus the absolute value of β squared equals 1. The chance of detecting a qubit in the state [0] is identical to an absolute value squared of α, while probability of noting it in the state [1] is equivalent to an absolute value squared of β.

Quantum Superposition: The idea of superposition is created on the usage of complex integers to signify the coefficients of α and β, which holds complex values. Quantum states can be characterized in a more inclusive and adaptable manner compared to predictable probability.

Quantum Operations: Unitary matrices are complex matrices that use the quantum gates and operations. These matrices recollect the mean of quantum states. Applying an unitary operative U to a quantum state |ψ| results in the creation of a new state U|ψ|

Single-qubit gates are usually employed in quantum computing, which includes Pauli gates (X, Y, Z), the Hadamard gate, and phase gates. These gates are signified by intricate matrices.

Quantum Interference: Quantum interference is an essential element in quantum algorithms, emerging from the intricate amplitude of the quantum states. The productive and destructive interference patterns are produced through the relative phases of the complex amplitudes, which amplify or nullify the specific computational pathways [10].

8.4.4 Entanglement and Complex Probability Amplitudes

In entangled states, the complex likelihood amplitudes of the collective system are interconnected. An instance of an entangled state involving two qubits can be expressed as follows: $|\psi\rangle = \alpha\ |00\rangle+\beta\ |01\rangle+\gamma\ |10\rangle+\delta\ |11\rangle$, where α, β, γ, and δ are complex numbers.

Complex numbers are important to the mathematical structure of quantum computing. Quantum states are described using them, quantum processes are facilitated by unitary matrices, and they play a vital part in phenomena such as superposition and entanglement. Comprehending intricate numbers and their characteristics is crucial for anybody engaged in the research or practice of quantum computing.

Quantum Computing Mathematics: Quantum computing largely relies on sophisticated mathematical concepts, including those derived from linear algebra and probability theory. Comprehending these fundamental mathematical ideas is important for comprehending the laws of significant physics and the functioning of quantum computers.

Study of Linear Algebra and Vector Spaces: Any vector space is a precise construct consisting of a fixed vectors that can be combined by addition and scalar multiplication.

Quantum computing represents a state of the quantum system by way of a vector in any complex vector space called a Hilbert space. A qubit is associated with a two-dimensional Hilbert space that is defined by the basis vectors $|0\rangle$ and $|1\rangle$.

Linear Transformations and Matrices: Matrices are used to represent linear transformations in quantum computing. A matrix, when applied to any vector, results in transformation of the vector into another vector within the same space.

Quantum gates are signified by unitary matrices, which implies that they maintain the magnitude of the vector. In other words, the product of the conjugate transpose of a quantum gate U and U itself equals the identity matrix (denoted as I).

Eigenvalues and Eigenvectors: An eigenvector of any matrix A is a vector v that is not equal to 0 and satisfies the equation. The equation $Av = \lambda v$ represents the relationship between the matrix of A, the eigen vector v, and the corresponding eigenvalue λ. In the field of quantum mechanics, when measurements are made, the quantum state is projected onto the eigenvectors of the measurement operator. The probability of every outcome is distinct by the corresponding eigenvalue.

Inner-Product and Mean: The inner-product is often called dot product and is a mathematical operation performed between two vectors. The states $|\psi\rangle$ and $|\phi\rangle$ are represented by the notation $\langle$. The inner-product $\langle\psi|\phi\rangle$ embodies the complex number. The mean of a vector, denoted as $|\psi\rangle$, is equivalent to the square root of the inner-product of the vector itself, $\langle\psi | \psi\rangle$. In the framework of quantum states, a usable vector must have a mean of 1, which is known as the normalization requirement.

Complex numbers are central to quantum computing, which uses quantum states, operations, and occurrences like superposition, interference, and entanglement, with complex probability amplitudes and unitary transformations. Quantum computing mathematics deeply relies on linear algebra concepts, including matrices, vector spaces, eigenvalues, and inner-products. Quantum states are represented as vectors in complex Hilbert spaces, while quantum gates are expressed as unitary matrices that preserve the vector norm. Understanding complex numbers and linear algebra is essential to operate quantum systems [11].

8.5 ALGORITHMS FOR QUANTUM COMPUTING

Quantum computing methods use the principle of quantum physics in order to solve problems with better efficiency than traditional algorithms. Prominent quantum algorithms are Shor's algorithm, Grover's search algorithm, the quantum Fourier transform, and other algorithms with noteworthy implications for search optimization, encryption, and other uses [12].

Shor's algorithm is used to factor large numbers efficiently.

Shor's algorithm was mainly developed to factorize large integers in an efficient way. This has huge usage in cryptography, especially in the usage of encryption methods such as RSA, as shown in Figure 8.3.

Principle

The algorithm employs the principle of quantum parallelism and interloping to predict the period of a task, which is consequently engaged to factorize the given integer.

Steps

1. Start with a quantum state that characterizes the superposition of all believable values.
2. Utilize the quantum Fourier transform to define the periodicity of the given function.
3. Utilize the regular reappearance to ascertain the divisors of the integer.
4. Classical post-processing comprises utilizing the classical computations and converting the quantum consequence into its essential parts.

Impact

Shor's algorithm has the skill to factorize a given integer with n bits by a polynomial function, in comparison to the best-known traditional algorithms that necessitate an exponential time. This advancement poses a significant risk to the security of numerous traditional cryptographic systems. The goal of **Grover's search algorithm** is to capably search through a large database in order to find a specific item or a solution. Grover's algorithm deals a quadratic speeding up for unstructured search concerns as shown in Figure 8.4. This technique efficiently discovers a specific point in an unordered database containing N items by accomplishing this task in O (sqrt of N) time, as opposed to the O (N) time required by out-of-date algorithms.

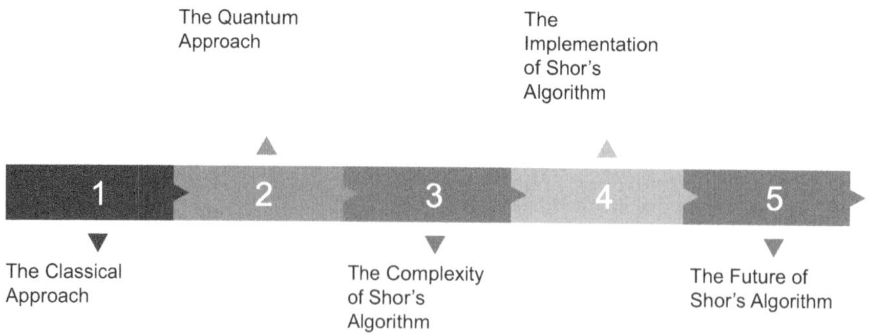

FIGURE 8.3 Shor's algorithm for prime factorization.

(https://fastercapital.com/topics/shors-algorithm-for-prime-factorization.html)

Principle

This method employs amplitude strengthening to improve the probability of finding an answer while decreasing the likelihood of obtaining incorrect ones.

Steps

1. Create a state that is similarly probable to be in any possible state.
2. Utilize an oracle function to reverse the phase of the chosen state.
3. Amplitude strengthening includes application of the Grover dispersion operator to improve the likelihood of the noticeable state.
4. Perform an oracle request and amplitude amplification an entire of O(square root of N) periods.
5. Obtain the designated item with a high likelihood by assessing the status.

Impact

The usage of Grover's approach spreads to various search issues for encompassing the database searches and the perseverance of NP-complete problems, therefore offering a considerable computing benefit.

The purpose of this quantum Fourier transform remains to achieve a mathematical conversion on quantum states. The quantum Fourier transform is the quantum equivalent of traditional discrete Fourier transform and shows a dynamic role in various quantum algorithms, such as Shor's algorithm.

Principle

Quantum Fourier transform is a mathematical operation that converts a quantum state into its essential frequency components. This permits in examination and analysis of periodic designs inside the quantum states.

Steps

1. Set active the quantum state for alteration.

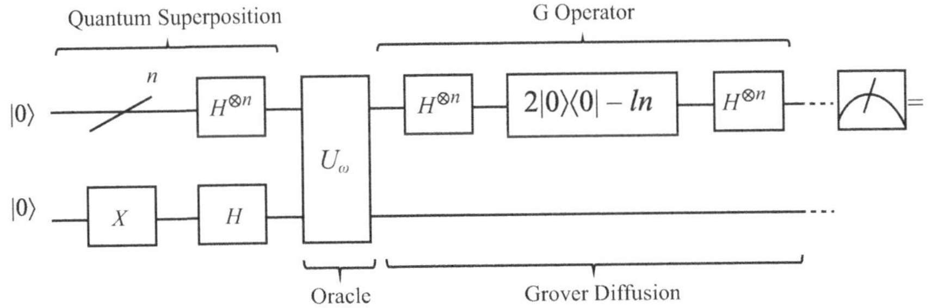

FIGURE 8.4 Quantum circuit for Grover's algorithm.

(https://en.wikipedia.org/wiki/Grover%27s_algorithm)

2. Utilize a sequence of Hadamard gates and controlled phase spins to implement a desired function.
3. In order to thorough the transformation, reverse the order of qubits.

Impact

Quantum field theory exhibits an exponential speedup relative to traditional systems, realizing the alteration in O(n^2) operations for n qubits. This acceleration is crucial for algorithms such as Shor's and for resolving issues in quantum signal processing [13].

Additional Prominent Algorithms

1. **Quantum Phase Estimation:** This algorithm computes the eigenvalue of a unitary operative, an essential component for an algorithm like Shor's algorithm and for solving linear systems of equations. This facilitates the accurate control of eigenvalues, a vital component in numerous quantum algorithms.
2. **Simon's Algorithm:** This algorithm determinates the Simon's problem at an exponential speed compared to any conventional algorithm. This signifies an exponential variation between standard and quantum complexity classes.
3. **Quantum Approximate Optimization Algorithm:** This is a computational algorithm that powers quantum computing to resolve optimization issues. It offers estimated solutions for combinatorial optimization difficulties, such as max-cut and traveling salesman problem. It also provides a confident strategy for resolving NP-hard issues in quantum computers in the future.
4. **VQE:** Variational quantum eigensolver regulates the lowermost energy state of a particle and a crucial factor in quantum chemistry applications. It utilizes a fusion of quantum and conventional computation to tackle challenges in the fields of drug development and materials science.

To recap, quantum computing algorithms use the principles of quantum mechanics in order to give considerable processing benefits in many situations. Shor's algorithm, Grover's search algorithm, and QFT are the fundamental algorithms that allow quantum computing to intensely transform areas such as optimization and encryption and more. Numerous significant algorithms are constantly pushing the bounds of whatever can be achieved computationally, thereby placing the foundation for future progress in the area of quantum technology.

8.6 RECENT APPLICATIONS OF QUANTUM COMPUTING

Quantum computing progresses rapidly while diverse applications demonstrate its superior problem-solving capabilities compared to traditional computing methods. Application of quantum computing extends across multiple essential fields, such as cryptography and optimization, as well as quantum simulations and emerging industries with great future prospects.

Cryptography and Security: Cryptography and security refer to the field where experts study and apply methods that protect information during communication exchanges.

Converting information into a code, or cipher cryptography, safeguards data against unauthorized persons. Encryption methods are used against attacks from quantum processors. Quantum key distribution uses quantum mechanics principle to create secure communication channels. Protocols such as BB84 provide safety by removing physical values to avoid every type of eavesdropping attempt. Researchers develop new cryptographic algorithms that resist attacks through lattice-based problems. These measures are established to protect data against threats from both traditional and quantum opponents.

The quantum approximate optimization is an algorithm that represents a quantum solution approach designed to report combinatorial optimization responsibilities, such as max-cut, the traveling salesman problem, and various NP-hard problems. This approach can produce faster and more precise estimates compared to classical computers. Quantum annealing is an optimization technique that identifies the minimum value of a cost function to solve problems. Quantum annealers developed by D-Wave have demonstrated their usefulness across multiple fields, including logistics planning, financial analysis, and scheduling optimization.

Artificial Intelligence: Quantum machine learning allows quantum algorithms to speed up machine learning training models while improving optimization performance. Current research focuses on the application of quantum maintenance vector machines and quantum neural-networks to resolve large-scale data problem challenges.

Quantum Systems Simulation Quantum Chemistry: Quantum computers enable molecular simulations that accurately represent molecular structures and processes that surpass classical computer capabilities. The development significantly supports the discovery process of new materials and drug compounds. The variational quantum eigensolver determines molecular ground-state energies because this task represents a basic goal in quantum chemistry. Quantum replications reveal atomic-level properties of novel materials that enable progressions in catalysts, superconductors, and nanomaterials.

The exploration of elementary technical views regulates how the matter and energy interact with nature and serves as the groundwork of understanding physical laws. Quantum computers can achieve replications of multifaceted quantum field theories that cannot be computed resourcefully by classical computers. Academics can determine new facts in essential physics with these methods.

Condensed Matter Physics: Firmly correlated electron system simulations, it gives an important identifications of high-temperature superconductivity with numerous quantum spectacles. Quantum algorithms deal with a groundbreaking potential for financial services with enhanced optimization of investment portfolios and additional exact evaluation of risk a with improved pricing of multifaceted financial derivatives. Through the implementation of encryption technologies, quantum computing may improve the finance sector through security measures in transactions and data.

Medical Care and in Finding New Medicines: Quantum computing embraces the power to development and analyze the substantial amounts of genomic data in an effective way, leading to the creation of modified treatment plans on genetic profiles. Quantum simulations can fast-track pharmaceutical discoveries by allowing the microscopic-level modeling of interactions of molecules. The application of this technology achieves significant reduction in time and cost needed for the invention of new drugs. Artificial intelligence (AI) means emerging computer systems that perform tasks that frequently need with human-level intelligence. Quantum-enhanced AI incorporate quantum algorithms to improve performance in natural language processing, pattern recognition, and decision-making. Mainly quantum computing deals with the ability to enrich AI optimization processes, which leads to quicker and more well-organized machine learning algorithms.

Supply Chain and Logistics: Quantum algorithms make a pathway to optimize supply chain management. Algorithms enable both budget savings and quicker delivery by decisive optimum ways and plans.

Active Resource Allocation: Quantum computing allows for sudden resource distribution that adapts to changing supply and demand. Researchers explore how living organisms interact with environments.

Climate Modeling: Quantum simulations provide accurate illustrations of intricate climate systems, addressing the consequences of climate change.

Renewable Energy: Quantum computing delivers many opportunities to increase the performance of energy system through improved renewable energy distribution and storage optimization. Quantum computing holds transformative potential across diverse fields by providing solutions to problems that classical computers cannot address. Advancements in optimization techniques, cryptography, quantum simulations, and application development reveal the vast potential of quantum technology while creating a vital research area that will influence forthcoming innovations. Quantum computing is moving quickly from theoretical research to practical applications across numerous industry sectors. Industries and academic institutions are leveraging quantum capabilities to tackle complex problems that classical computers struggle with, even though the technology is still in its early stages. This analysis explains how it influences logistics processes, financial services, and healthcare to create its practical usage.

8.6.1 Healthcare: Drug Discovery and Personalized Medicine

Case Study: Accelerating Drug Discovery

Company: IBM & Moderna Problem: Traditional drug detection uses too much time computationally, and molecular interfaces also take too much time to find promising medication substitutions.

Quantum Solution: IBM & Moderna work together to effectively simulate chemical interactions and structures by using quantum computing. The time needed to find encouraging medication candidates can be reduced by using quantum processors, which can simulate molecular behaviors on the microscopic level.

Impact:

- Accelerated increase in medications and vaccines.
- Decreased R&D expenses by making more accurate predictions.
- Advances knowledge and addressing intricate proteins, resulting in advances in treatments of disorders.

Future Outlook

- Neurodegenerative diseases like Alzheimer's and cancer may be handled with quantum-enhanced simulations.
- By simulating the interactions between a patient's genetics and specific treatments, tailored medicine could be possible.

8.6.2 Finance: Risk Analysis and Fraud Detection

Case Study: Quantum Risk Analysis in Banking

Company: JPMorgan Chase and Google Quantum AI

Problem: Financial markets involve large volumes of real-time data demanding a sophisticated modeling to detect risk assessment, fraud detection, and portfolio optimization. These goals are too complex for traditional computing.

Quantum Solution: Quantum Monte Carlo and other quantum algorithms have been investigated by JPMorgan Chase to enhance option pricing and risk analysis. The potential for intricate financial modeling has been established by Google's Sycamore CPU, which has shown quantum dominance.

Impact:

- Quicker and more precise risk assessments that reduce monetary losses.
- Better fraud detection by identifying patterns in bank transactions.
- Enhanced investment portfolios by real-time investigation of large datasets.

Future Outlook

Quantum systems might remain castoff by central banks for financial stability studies and economic modeling, while hedge funds and trading companies could utilize them for predictive analytics.

8.6.3 Logistics: Supply Chain Optimization

Case Study: DHL and D-Wave's Quantum Solutions

Company: DHL and D-Wave

Problem: Routes, inventory, and warehouse operations are all optimized as part of logistics and supply chain management. Large-scale supply chain variables are difficult for classical algorithms to handle without a lot of computing power.

Quantum Solution: In order to determine the most effective routes for international shipments, DHL teamed up with D-Wave to investigate how quantum annealing may optimize supply chains. Compared to classical computers, quantum computers provide faster solutions by evaluating several route options at once.

Impact

- Enhanced delivery times as a result of better routing.
- Better warehouse management that minimizes delays in inventory. Lower fuel use and transportation expenses.

Future Outlook

- E-commerce behemoths like Amazon and Alibaba may undergo a revolution thanks to quantum logistics solutions.
- Quantum algorithms may be used by airlines and freight corporations for cost optimization and dynamic scheduling.

8.7 ETHICAL CONCERNS IN QUANTUM COMPUTING

Despite its enormous impact on a number of activities, quantum computing also poses ethical concerns that require consideration. These issues cover a wide range of topics, such as societal effect, fair access, and data privacy.

Cybersecurity and Data Privacy

Cryptographic Vulnerabilities: Existing encryption techniques may be cracked by quantum computers, jeopardizing the confidentiality and privacy of data. This brings up moral questions regarding the protection of private data and the requirement for encryption and resilience against quantum errors.

Data Harvesting and Monitoring: The increased capacity of any quantum computer allows it to process statistics, which may result in previously unheard-of amounts of data breaches, endangering both democratic processes and individual privacy.

Equitable Access and Its Effects on Society

Resource Sharing and Dissimilarity: Only a few countries and businesses can afford this expertise, as substantial resources are required for the development and use of quantum computing, widen socioeconomic gaps worldwide.

Job dislocation: Many jobs are automated by quantum computers, which could cause extensive unemployment and upset society.

Impact on Society and Human Rights

Human Rights Challenges: A significant risk to human rights concerns freedom of expression and non-discrimination, as quantum computing could be used to target specific groups, spread misinformation, and manipulate public opinion.

Global Security and Geopolitics: The goal of quantum dominance may be central to geopolitical pressures and conflicts, highlighting the requirement of moral governance and international assistance.

Accountability and Transparency

Complexity and Non-existence of Clearness: Quantum algorithms are inherently complex; it may be thought-provoking to understand how they make choices, which could weaken accountability and sureness.

Ethical Contexts: Through an emphasis on inclusivity, safekeeping, and transparency, the World Economic Forum and the National Academies of Sciences are generating ethical contexts to direct the accountable development and application of quantum computing. Properly controlling the use of quantum technologies involves constant communication between stakeholders and the creation of strong ethical standards and international collaboration.

8.8 FUTURE DIRECTIONS IN QUANTUM COMPUTING AND DATA SCIENCE

Data science and quantum computing will rock the futures that hold noteworthy potential for innovative developments. The main focus remains on progressing the hardware and scalability parameters of quantum systems. Many scientists are working on large-scale quantum computing projects concentrating to form stable qubits and developing dependable error correction methods to reduce or prevent decoherence. Recent quantum architectures prove to be essential for accessible quantum computing systems to offer cheaper advancement paths and better system approachability. Quantum computing simulations are used in the fields of chemistry and materials research. Quantum processors improve the creation of new resources and treatments with their ability to develop complex chemical interactions precisely. Specialists found that this ability will transform multiple chemistry-related segments to enable the production of improved products, such as advanced sequences and medications. Experts achieve the understanding and precise regulation of molecular interfaces in order to create new materials by using quantum computers to simulate various molecular structures with extraordinary accuracy [14].

Quantum computing provides new possibilities and challenges, especially in the domain of cybersecurity and cryptography. Specialists are creating new cryptographic algorithms resilient to quantum outbreaks because traditional encryption methods might be overwhelmed by quantum computers. Flexible quantum systems shield against data breaches through methods such as secure segment ring barrier and private cloud-based access. Protecting digital infrastructures demand adopting quantum-resistant encryption methods. The combination of machine learning and optimization techniques within quantum computing is an active area of research in this era. Quantum computers can report supply chain management and logistics optimization glitches that conventional computers fail to address. Quantum machine learning progresses the figuring power to undertake noteworthy innovations in pattern recognition and data exploration. These developments will considerably disturb many numerous businesses through their submissions in financial modeling and computational mechanization. The budding applications of data science with quantum computing extend into numerous future uses. Economic institutions could use quantum computing to enhance their capabilities for modeling security behaviors and adjusting collections. The combination of quantum computing with computational methods develops task automation and optimization, especially for complicated datasets. As these technologies advance and reshape entire industries, they also open new avenues for innovative work and technical exploration. The future looks promising for quantum computing and data science, but realizing their full potential depends on ongoing research breakthroughs.

8.9 CONCLUSION

Quantum seems to lead a scientific revolution that promises to modernize computational capabilities in various fields. Quantum computers use superposition and entanglement alongside quantum interference to solve the complex glitches with higher speeds than traditional processors. Two renowned algorithms in quantum computing are Grover's search algorithm and Shor's factoring algorithm, which have a noteworthy impact on encryption and optimization technologies. Though multiple challenges remains, there are the development of scalable quantum hardware, algorithm improvements, and unified integration with present systems. Savings and associations together with imaginative approaches will drive the forthcoming developments in quantum processors. The usage of technology will expand in sectors such as finance, healthcare, and artificial intelligence. Quantum computing boosts financial modeling through improved market pattern predictions, and it will speed up drug discovery through molecular interface simulations and increasing AI capabilities with effective large dataset handling. The enhanced accuracy of climate pattern modeling by quantum computers will benefit in predicting and minimizing climate change consequences. Quantum computing research is emerging in new fields and demands both moral consideration and secure communication approaches. To avoid the socioeconomic gaps from spreading, there is a need to develop encryption methods that minimize quantum errors while stimulating justifiable technology access. The dissemination of quantum technology profits the whole world with appropriate usage and international collaboration. Quantum computing shines brightly due to possible breakthroughs in optimization techniques, machine learning, and cryptographic methods. Quantum key distribution permits the expansion of indestructible encryption with quantum methods and enable us to resolve the optimization problems that modern computers cannot tackle. The continuous development of quantum technologies will alter computational methods and problem-solving strategies, leading to unprecedented breakthroughs in numerous industries. The best way to improve quantum computing and protect societal welfare is integrating technical improvements with ethical values.

Glossary

Qubit: a.k.a. quantum bit; the fundamental unit of quantum information.
Superposition: A quantum state where a qubit can be both 0 and 1 simultaneously.
Entanglement: When two or more qubits become connected in such a way that the state of one qubit cannot be separated from the other.

Quantum Interference: The ability of quantum waves to associate and cancel each other, which is important in performing quantum computing operations.

Shor's Algorithm: An algorithm that uses factoring large numbers exponentially quicker than traditional algorithms, which has noteworthy consequences in cryptography.

Grover's Algorithm: A crucial algorithm for examining an unsorted store of N entries in O(sqrt(N)) time, which is quicker than any classical algorithm.

Swapping: Transfer between two bits that have not ever interacted previously.

Quantum Key Distribution: A method that provides secure communication by using quantum mechanics for encoding and decoding messages.

Quantum Error Correction: One of the techniques used to protect quantum bits from errors, owing to decoherence and other noises.

Quantum Circuit: It is a model for quantum computation where quantum gates are functional sequentially toward qubits in order to perform computations.

Quantum Gate: The quantum correspondence of gates in traditional computing used to manipulate qubits.

Decoherence: Loss of quantum coherence due to interactions with environment, which is a major problem in maintaining stable states.

Quantum Simulation: The usage of quantum systems in order to simulate the complex quantum spectacles that are problematic to model naturally.

Quantum Machine Learning: The integration of quantum computing with machine learning to improve the capabilities of computations mainly in pattern recognition and optimization.

Quantum Supremacy: The point at which a quantum computer can do a calculation that exceeds the capabilities of a traditional computer.

Post-Quantum Cryptography: Cryptographic techniques designed to be safe against the attacks against classical and quantum computers.

Quantum Annealing: A computing technique used for solving with respect to optimization problems by manipulating the quantum channeling in order to find the global smallest of a complex purpose.

Quantum Computing Hardware: A physical system used to create a quantum computer, such as superconducting qubits and ion traps.

Classical Quantum Interface: The combination of quantum computing systems with traditional computing systems to control the strengths of paradigms.

Quantum Information Science: The interdisciplinary arena that incorporates quantum communication, quantum computing, and quantum detecting.

REFERENCES

[1] Ferrari, D., Carretta, S., & Amoretti, M. (2023). A modular quantum compilation framework for distributed quantum computing. *IEEE Transactions on Quantum Engineering, 4*, 1–13. https://doi.org/10.1109/TQE.2023.3303935

[2] Wang, Q., Guan, J., Liu, J., Zhang, Z., & Ying, M. (2024). New quantum algorithms for computing quantum entropies and distances. *IEEE Transactions on Information Theory, 70*(8), 5653–5680.

[3] Pelofske, E., Bärtschi, A., Eidenbenz, S., Garcia, B., & Kiefer, B. (2024). Probing quantum telecloning on superconducting quantum processors. *IEEE Transactions on Quantum Engineering, 5*, 1–19. https://doi.org/10.1109/TQE.2024.3391654

[4] Gaur, B., & Thapliyal, H. (2024). Novel optimized designs of modulo 2n+1 adder for quantum computing. *IEEE Transactions on Very Large Scale Integration (VLSI) Systems, 32*(9), 1759–1763.

[5] Brandhofer, S., Polian, I., & Krsulich, K. (2024). Optimal partitioning of quantum circuits using gate cuts and wire cuts. *IEEE Transactions on Quantum Engineering, 5*, 1–10. https://doi.org/10.1109/TQE.2023.3347106

[6] Pan, D., et al. (2024). The evolution of quantum secure direct communication: On the road to the Qinternet. *IEEE Communications Surveys & Tutorials, 26*(3), 1898–1949. https://doi.org/10.1109/COMST.2024.3367535

[7] Shafique, M. A., Munir, A., & Latif, I. (2024). Quantum computing: Circuits, algorithms, and applications. *IEEE Access, 12*, 22296–22314. https://doi.org/10.1109/ACCESS.2024.3362955

[8] Singh, P., et al. (2024). A survey on available tools and technologies enabling quantum computing. *IEEE Access, 12*, 57974–57991. https://doi.org/10.1109/ACCESS.2024.3388005

[9] AbuGhanem, M., & Eleuch, H. (2024). NISQ computers: A path to quantum supremacy. *IEEE Access, 12*, 102941–102961. https://doi.org/10.1109/ACCESS.2024.3432330

[10] Yang, Z., Zolanvari, M., & Jain, R. (2023). A survey of important issues in quantum computing and communications. *IEEE Communications Surveys & Tutorials, 25*(2), 1059–1094. https://doi.org/10.1109/COMST.2023.3254481

[11] Li, H.-S., Fan, P., Xia, H.-Y., Peng, H., & Song, S. (2019). Quantum implementation circuits of quantum signal representation and type conversion. *IEEE Transactions on Circuits and Systems I: Regular Papers, 66*(1), 341–354. https://doi.org/10.1109/TCSI.2018.2853655

[12] Tsang, S. L., West, M. T., Erfani, S. M., & Usman, M. (2023). Hybrid quantum-classical generative adversarial network for high-resolution image generation. *IEEE Transactions on Quantum Engineering, 4*, 1–19. https://doi.org/10.1109/TQE.2023.3319319

[13] Yang, F., Qiu, D., & Mateus, P. (2023). Continuous-variable quantum secret sharing in fast-fluctuating channels. *IEEE Transactions on Quantum Engineering, 4*, 1–9. https://doi.org/10.1109/TQE.2023.3322171

[14] Djordjevic, I. B. (2016). Integrated optics modules based proposal for quantum information processing, teleportation, QKD, and quantum error correction employing photon angular momentum. *IEEE Photonics Journal, 8*(1), 1–12. https://doi.org/10.1109/JPHOT.2016.2522097

9 Evolutionary Algorithms and Quantum Computing—Pioneering the Next Era of Intelligence and Innovation

A. Suresh, B. Rupa Devi, Roopa R., L. N. C. Prakash K., Anant Shankar E., and M. Sudhakara

9.1 INTRODUCTION

Quantum computing (QC) has appeared as the top transformative innovation of the 21st century, with the ability to transform fields such as computation, cryptography, artificial intelligence, and scientific discovery (Kumar, 2025). QC differs from conventional computing by means of basic quantum physics principles since it operates with binary bits but executes information processing and calculation sequences fast. Using these principles, QC can process massive volumes of data at once, solving issues that traditional computers could not have predicted (Khurana a., 2024). Numerous industries, including materials research, healthcare, and finance, could experience new opportunities (Rana a., 2023). In the early 1980s, physicist Richard Feynman postulated that quantum computers could only accurately model quantum systems, which is where QC started (Silva, 2023). He pointed out that classical computers will have difficulty mimicking quantum occurrences because quantum physics is inherently complex and parallel. Feynman's theory was soon developed by David Deutsch, who proposed the idea of a universal quantum computer that would be more effective than its classical counterpart at any given calculation (Akama, 2015). This was the first instance of QC as a field, and it developed into a science with more study and innovations over time.

Among the notable turning points in the advancement of QC is Shor's algorithm (Shakib, 2025), which presents how quantum computers may take into account large integers effectively and pose a serious risk to the present encryption systems.

DOI: 10.1201/9781003538950-11

Another innovation is the algorithm developed by Grover (Lu a., 2013), which offers a quadratic speedup for searching through unsorted data. The algorithms demonstrate QC's ability to provide outstanding advantages when addressing problems that standard computers cannot solve according to current computational limitations.

In recent years, QC has moved beyond theoretical exploration, with companies such as IBM, Google, and Microsoft making significant advancements in the creation of QC (Singh, 2025). These companies, many startups, and academic research groups work tirelessly to build quantum systems with larger qubit capacities and improved coherence times. Technologies like superconducting qubits, trapped ions, topological qubits, and photonic QC have become central to the race for fault-tolerant quantum computers (Memon, 2024). Despite these improvements, several technical barriers remain in practical QC. Before quantum computers can function dependably on a broad scale, problems including qubit decoherence, quantum noise, and the difficulty of quantum error correction need to be resolved (Gill, 2024). The field of QC is not just confined to theoretical discussions and laboratory research—it is already beginning to make a tangible impact across industries. In cybersecurity, quantum-resistant cryptographic techniques are being constructed to safeguard private information from potential hazards of quantum computers that can defeat current encryption protocols (Sonko a., 2024). Quantum simulations present previously unconsidered insights into molecular interactions and material components in chemistry and materials science, which can lead to improvements in environmental sustainability, material engineering, and medication discovery.

This book extensively examines the applications of QC, its theoretical underpinnings, real-world uses, and possible future advancements. The book gives essential knowledge about quantum gates and circuits and algorithms to help readers grasp the complex nature of quantum computing. The most recent advances in quantum cryptography, hybrid quantum-classical systems, and machine learning are also covered, along with the difficulties industry and researchers have in implementing scalable, error-corrected quantum systems. The book also investigates the real-world uses of QC in industries such as energy, healthcare, and finance for theoretical elements that suggest how quantum computers can deal with challenging adaptation issues, imitate complex systems, and increase artificial intelligence models. Figure 9.1 depicts the taxonomy of the QC technology. By fusing theoretical and practical viewpoints, this work offers a strong basis for anyone interested in comprehending the complete possibilities of QC and its prospective uses.

For professionals, researchers, engineers, and students who want to comprehend and manage the quickly developing quantum technology, this book is a vital resource as QC develops and grows. As quantum computers can transform businesses and spur innovation, incorporating QC into current computational frameworks will fundamentally alter how we approach scientific inquiry, intelligent systems, and problem-solving.

9.1.1 Background

Early in the 1980s, Richard Feynman realized that quantum systems not be effectively simulated by conventional computers, which led to the advancement of QC (Oftelie, 2021). As a result, the field of QC appeared as a separate entity. The idea of

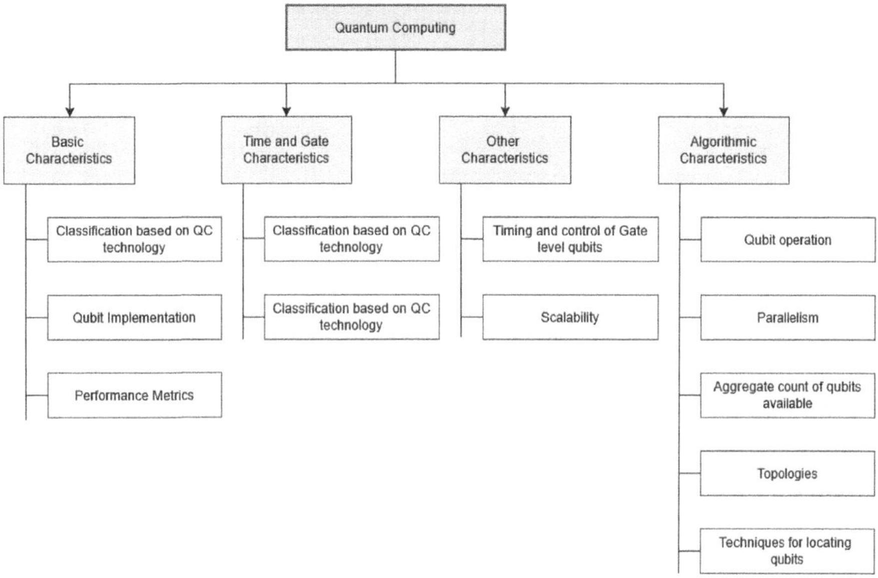

FIGURE 9.1 Taxonomy of the quantum computing technology.

a universal quantum computer was first proposed by David Deutsch, and innovative algorithms such as Grover's (for unstructured search) and Shor's (for integer factorization) demonstrated the potential benefits of QC over classical systems (Sarkar, n.d.). Today, QC has moved beyond theory. Major companies such as IBM, Google, and Microsoft are developing quantum processors, with Google's 2019 quantum supremacy experiment marking a key milestone (Lang, 2021). Quantum technologies like superconducting qubits and trapped ions are advancing, although challenges such as qubit coherence, noise, and error correction remain. Applications in drug development, cryptography, and optimization are growing; two major study topics are quantum-resistant encryption and molecular simulations (Kumar a., 2024).

The future of QC holds transformative potential. As quantum systems become more scalable and error-resistant, they could revolutionize AI, finance, and materials science (Yamini a., 2024). Accelerating machine learning and optimization tasks, hybrid quantum-classical systems have the potential to improve AI and data analytics (Pulicharla, 2023). The technological challenges that remain will not prevent QC from becoming a transformative force that creates several new possibilities while transforming businesses and problem-solving approaches.

9.1.2 Basics of Quantum Computing

Traditional computers use the bit as their base unit of stored information, and it must be present in one of two states: 0 or 1 (Le Bellac, 2006). The quantum bit or qubit functions uniquely in QC due to quantum laws that allow it to occupy multiple states at once. The bit and qubit are shown in Figure 9.2. There are three possible states for a qubit: 0, 1, or a superposition of the two. A qubit is defined mathematically as:

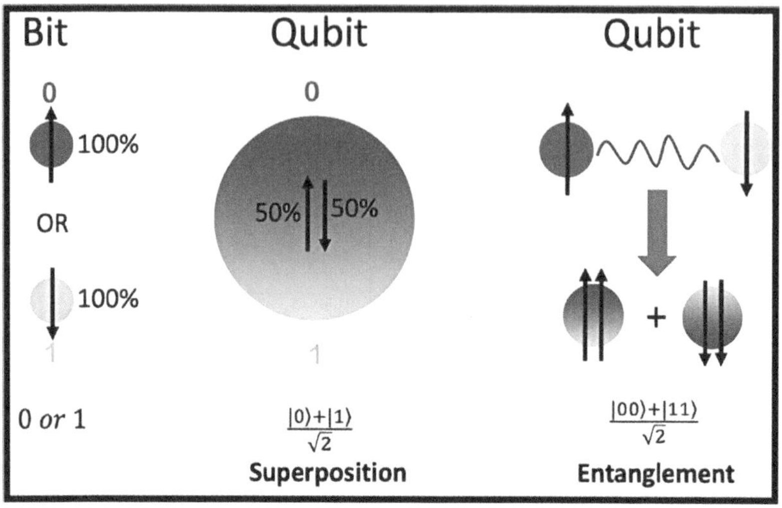

FIGURE 9.2 Representation of a bit and qubit (Gill, 2022).

$$|\psi\rangle = a||0\rangle + b|1\rangle \tag{9.1}$$

The observation probabilities of qubit states $|0\rangle$ and $|1\rangle$ depend on the complicated values a and b. Instead of processing information sequentially like classical computers, quantum computers can simultaneously explore a huge computational area because of their capacity to reside in superposition.

The set {000, 001, 010, 011, 100, 101, 110, 111} has eight potential combinations, of which a conventional 3-bit system can represent just one. In contrast, a three-qubit quantum state may represent all of these possibilities at once. One way to express this situation is:

$$|\psi\rangle = a\,|000\rangle + b|001\rangle + c|010\rangle + d|011\rangle + e|100\rangle + f|101\rangle + g|110\rangle + \mathrm{h}|111\rangle \tag{9.2}$$

This exponential growth in computational space with the addition of each qubit is one of the key advantages of QC. While doubling the number of classical bits doubles the computational capacity, adding a qubit increases it exponentially. For instance, the computational space expands $2^3 = 8$ to $2^4 = 16$ when moving from three to four qubits.

Another crucial quantum property is entanglement (Horodecki a., 2009). Quantum bits differ from conventional bits because they can develop an entangled state which maintains a close connection between the states of separate qubits. The entangled quantum bits remain linked so that measuring one reveals the state of the other at any distance. The spatial effect called "spooky action at a distance," identified by Einstein, represents a crucial factor for quantum communication together with processing methods.

Entanglement makes advanced quantum procedures possible, including dense coding and quantum teleportation (Cacciapuoti, 2020). Entanglement uses the correlations between entangled qubits to "teleport" quantum states between distant sites or, more effectively, transport information.

These steps are commonly applied in the quantum computation procedure:

1. **Superposition Preparation**: The system begins in a superposition state, representing every conceivable result.
2. **Quantum Operations**: Through quantum gates the states of qubits are controlled by implementing both superposition and entanglement principles. The activities direct the system toward reaching its intended solution.
3. **Measurement**: The quantum state calculation leads to the collapse of superposition into one of the possible results that represents the most likely success outcome.

9.1.3 Quantum Mechanics

Quantum mechanics describes the fundamental principles governing physical systems at microscopic scales, mainly focusing on the behavior of particles like electrons and photons (Pang, 2005). One of its key aspects is using Hilbert space *H* to represent quantum states. The group of bounded linear operators on *H* is denoted as *B(H)*, and regarding systems with finite dimensions where $H = c^d$, the corresponding quantum system is called a dd-level system. When d=2d = 2, the system is called a qubit. Quantum states are usually described by positive density matrices, trace-class operators that satisfy the normalization condition tr(ρ)=1. The space of density matrices forms a convex set, where pure states correspond to extreme points.

Mathematically, a density matrix ρ can be defined an orthonormal basis of self-adjoint operators {σj} as:

$$\rho = \frac{1}{d} I + \frac{1}{2} \sum_{j=1}^{d^2} x_j \sigma_j \tag{9.3}$$

where x is a real vector in $R^{d^{2-1}}$. For a qubit (d = 2), the Pauli matrices are commonly used as basis operators, leading to a geometric representation. In this case, the state space forms a unit ball given by

$$S(c^2) = \{x \in R^3 \mid |x| \leq 1\} \tag{9.4}$$

The Bloch sphere presents mixed states within its interior while pure states exist only on its surface where |x| equals 1. The radius of a state space for a d-level system follows the expression:

$$|x| = \sqrt{2(1-1/d} \tag{9.5}$$

showing that as dd increases, the structure of the state space becomes more complex.

9.1.4 Fundamental Concepts of Quantum Information Theory

Quantum information theory fundamentally differs from classical information theory due to the intrinsic properties of quantum mechanics (Fuchs, 2002). In classical systems, information is transmitted using well-defined symbols, such as binary digits (0 and 1), and the medium of transmission, whether electrical signals, optical pulses, or printed text, does not alter the nature of the information itself. Quantum information operates through a vector system that functions in Hilbert space using quantum states, which follow the Schrödinger equation. Quantum states derive from the Hilbert space while following the Schrödinger equation. Qubits serve as the basis of quantum computing because these physical systems maintain dual state existence to which mathematical notation applies:

$$|\psi\rangle=\alpha|0\rangle+\beta|1\rangle \tag{9.6}$$

The complex number values of probabilistic amplitudes α and β exist under the condition $|\alpha|2+|\beta|2=1$. Quantum information distinguishes itself because unitary operator UU cannot achieve perfect duplication according to the no-cloning theorem $U(|\psi\rangle \otimes|0\rangle)=|\psi\rangle \otimes|\psi\rangle$ does not work for all possible states $|\psi\rangle$. Quantum and classical information cannot experience lossless conversion because measurement operations force quantum states to collapse at basis states which irreparably alters them. Additionally, quantum entanglement—where two qubits share a correlated state, such as the Bell state $|\Phi+\rangle=\frac{1}{\sqrt{2}}(|00\rangle+|11\rangle)$—enables unique phenomena like quantum teleportation, but classical teleportation, where information is perfectly transferred from classical to quantum states and back, remains impossible. Quantum measurements create disturbances that prevent obtaining precise measurements of position and momentum pairs because of the Heisenberg uncertainty principle $\Delta x \Delta p \geq \frac{\hbar}{2}$. This fundamental limitation solidifies that quantum information cannot be reduced to classical terms without loss, reinforcing its unique and non-classical nature.

9.2 QUANTUM ALGORITHMS

- **Grover's Algorithm:** Grover's algorithm is a quantum database search algorithm developed to locate a non-ordered list item efficiently (Khurana a., 2023). The primary use of this algorithm focuses on improving brute force key search operations that apply to symmetric key encryption systems that include AES. The search method for unsorted arrays of size N requires O(N) operations through classical algorithms, but Grover's algorithm performs it in $O(\sqrt{N})$ operations.

  The operation of Grover's algorithm relies on placing qubits into a superposition state, which contains all possible ID numbers $\{x = 0, 1, 2, \ldots, N-1\}$ to locate an element xa that satisfies a condition within an unsorted database. In simplified decimal notation, an n-qubit state such as $|1\rangle|0\rangle|0\rangle$ is written as $|4\rangle$. The preliminary state takes the following form:

$$|\psi\rangle = \sum_{x=0}^{N-1} p_x |x\rangle \tag{9.7}$$

- **Shor's Algorithm:** Traditional cryptography techniques like RSA encryption were seriously threatened in 1994 when Peter Shor presented that a quantum computer could factor huge integers in polynomial time (Nkulenu, 2024). RSA encryption operates as one of the standard secure communication protocols although quantum computers could potentially break it.

  RSA encryption operates by making it difficult to factor large numbers. During key generation Alice selects two vast prime numbers (p, q) to create the product $N = p \times q$. The procedure demands the selection of public exponent e that shares no factors with (p−1) (q−1) followed by determining d like as:

$$d=e^{-1} \bmod (p-1)(q-1) \tag{9.8}$$

  Alice possesses the private key d, but her public key consists of (N, e). The following procedure allows Bob to perform encryption of message M:

$$C = M^e \bmod N \tag{9.9}$$

  Alice decrypts it using:

$$M = C^d \bmod N \tag{9.10}$$

9.2.1 Quantum Evolutionary Algorithms

- ***Quantum Genetic Optimization Algorithm (QGOA)*** (Malossini a., 2008)
  The QGOA builds upon traditional genetic algorithms using quantum concepts to improve optimization. It uses quantum fitness evaluation and superposition to apply quantum selection while encoding population states as qubits. Although QGOA provides a polynomial speedup in selection when the fitness function varies, conventional steps, such as crossover, mutation, and replacement, are still present.
- ***Max-Cut Proble*** (Kim a., 2019)
  A graph's vertices are divided into two groups to maximize the number of edges connecting them, a process known as the max-cut issue. The goal function in this instance is as follows for an undirected graph with v vertices and e edges:

$$C(s) = -\sum_{i=1}^{e} C_i(s) \tag{9.11}$$

- where $C_i(s)=1$ if the edge's vertices belong to different sets and 0 otherwise. QGOA optimizes this partitioning using quantum-inspired chromosome encoding.
- ***Implementation of QGOA on a Quantum Computer***

- On noisy intermediate-scale quantum (NISQ) devices, QGOA requires careful circuit design (Ur Rehman a., 2025). Qubit encoding initializes quantum chromosomes, followed by measurement to extract classical bit-strings. The fitness function evaluates solutions, and circuit depth is managed by accumulating rotation angles to optimize performance.
- ***Simulation Results for Max-Cut***
- A 4-vertex, 4-edge graph was simulated using QGOA on the IBM Quantum simulator. The best fitness value of −4 was achieved, confirming accurate partitioning. Increasing the chromosome count improved fitness values due to greater diversity but demanded higher qubit resources, presenting a computational trade-off for NISQ-based implementations.

9.2.2 Quantum-Inspired Meta-Heuristic Algorithms

Due to their low computational complexity and iterative nature, metaheuristic algorithms are widely employed for solving complex and nonlinear optimization problems. Two initial categories can be employed to broadly classify these algorithms: population-based (PB) algorithms and single-solution-based (SSB) algorithms (Sahoo, 2022).

- ***Population-Based Quantum-Inspired Metaheuristic Algorithms (PB-QiMAs):*** Population-based metaheuristic algorithms work on a group of candidate solutions simultaneously (Beheshti a., 2013). The final solution is decided based on the highest gain in the objective function. If the algorithm incorporates evolutionary principles, it is called a quantum-inspired evolutionary algorithm (QiEA) (Fiasch, 2012). One of the most prominent PB-QiMAs is the quantum-inspired genetic algorithm (QiGA), which applies quantum principles to enhance genetic operations such as mutation and crossover. A key mathematical model for PB-QiMAs is the quantum bit (qubit) representation, where each solution is encoded as a probabilistic superposition of states:

$$|\psi\rangle = \alpha_i|0\rangle + \beta_i|1\rangle, where|\alpha_i|^2 + |\beta_i|^2 = 1 \tag{9.12}$$

The update of a quantum population is typically done using rotation gates in a quantum-inspired genetic algorithm:

$$\theta_i^{(t+1)} = \theta_i^{(t)} + \Delta\theta \tag{9.13}$$

where θi represents the rotation angle for adjusting quantum states, and Δθ is an adaptive learning parameter. By leveraging quantum principles, PB-QiMAs improve search diversity, reducing premature convergence while efficiently navigating large search spaces.
- ***Single-Solution-Based Quantum-Inspired Metaheuristic Algorithms (SSB-QiMAs):***

Unlike PB-QiMAs, single-solution-based algorithms focus on iteratively improving a single candidate solution rather than maintaining a population (Shami, 2024). These methods explore the local neighborhood of a solution at each iteration, gradually refining it toward a better result. However, they are more prone to getting trapped in local optima and are highly sensitive to the choice of the initial starting point. One well-known SSB-QiMA is the quantum-inspired Tabu search (QiTS) algorithm, which applies quantum principles to classical local search techniques (Dey a., 2014). Another example is the quantum-inspired simulated annealing (QiSA) algorithm, which incorporates quantum tunneling effects to escape local minima.

Mathematically, the optimization process in an SSB-QiMA can be expressed as:

$$x_{t+1} = x_t + \lambda . \Delta f\left(x_t\right) \tag{9.14}$$

where x_t represents the current solution, $\nabla f(x_t)$ is the gradient of the objective function, and λ is a step-size parameter that adapts based on quantum-inspired principles. The main advantage of SSB-QiMAs is their low computational cost.

9.3 MATHEMATICAL FOUNDATIONS OF QUANTUM COMPUTING

To comprehend QC, one must have a strong quantum physics and linear algebra background. These concepts make it possible to represent and work with quantum states, which are very different from traditional bits.

9.3.1 Linear Algebra and Quantum Mechanics Essentials

At the core of *QC* lies vector spaces, matrices, and complex numbers (Yanofsky, 2008). Quantum states function as vectors within a Hilbert space where Kate's notation establishes quantum state notation for defining their doubles. Operators such as Hermitian and unique matrix control these states' development, ensuring reflection in quantum computation. The law of birth determines the possibilities of measurement, given by:

$$P(x)=|\langle x|\psi\rangle|^{2} \tag{9.15}$$

where P(x) is the probability of measuring state $|x\rangle|$ from $|\psi\rangle$.

9.3.2 Quantum Gates and Circuits

Quantum gates apply unitary transformations as the fundamental control mechanism for qubits just like standard logic gate technologies. Typical gates consist of:

- **Pauli Gates**: X, Y, ZX, Y, Z, representing fundamental single-qubit operations.

- **Hadamard Gate**: Develops superposition by transforming |0⟩ into an equal mix of |0⟩| and |1⟩:

$$H= \frac{1}{\sqrt{2}}[111-1] \tag{9.16}$$

- **CNOT Gate**: A two-qubit gate enabling entanglement crucial for quantum algorithms.

9.3.3 Error Detection and Correction in Quantum Systems

Error correction methods are necessary since quantum bits experience more susceptibility to noise and decoherence than classical bits. Logical qubits are encoded into entangled physical qubits via quantum error correction (QEC) to prevent errors (Paetznick a., 2024). The Shor code represents an early QEC method that uses following encoding scheme to address bit-flip and phase-flip defects:

$$|\psi\rangle=\alpha|0\rangle+\beta|1\rangle\rightarrow\alpha|000\rangle+\beta|111\rangle \tag{9.17}$$

Syndrome measurement detects errors without collapsing quantum information, ensuring fault-tolerant quantum computation.

9.4 QUANTUM CRYPTOGRAPHY

Quantum communication encompasses various technologies, including quantum teleportation, quantum key distribution (QKD), quantum dense coding, and more (Vasani a., 2024). QKD is the most mature in both theoretical research and practical implementation. Two security-related quantum research fields extend further than QKD by incorporating quantum authentication and quantum public key cryptography.

9.4.1 Quantum Key Distribution (QKD)

QKD relies on non-cloning theorem rules for non-orthogonal quantum states to achieve secure key distribution. QKD protocols follow different categories according to:

- **The dimensionality of the source code space**: Continuous-variable (CV) protocols and discrete-variable (DV) protocols.
- **The presence of entanglement**: Entanglement-based (EB) protocols and prepare-and-measure (PM) protocols.

9.4.2 Discrete-Variable QKD (DV-QKD)

DV-QKD protocols utilize a finite-dimensional Hilbert space for encoding quantum states. These protocols are well-developed, with BB84 being the first and most widely studied protocol. DV-QKD methods include:

- **Single-Photon Protocols**
  The encoding and decoding process of key information utilizes single-photon protocols through distinct quantum states of single photons. Key protocols include BB84, B92, the six-state protocol, and SARG04 (Hong, 2016).
- **Entangled-Photon Protocols**
  These protocols leverage quantum entanglement for secure key distribution, relying on correlated photon pairs: E91 and BBM92 (Manju a., 2025).
- **Other DV Protocols**
  Several additional DV protocols enhance security and efficiency:
  - Distributed phase reference (DPR) protocols (Kumar a., 2024)
  - Differential phase shift (DPS) protocol, coherent one-way (COW) protocol (Kumar a., Experimental implementation of distributed phase reference quantum key distribution protocols, 2024)
  - Round-robin differential phase shift (RRDPS) protocol (Murakami a., 2024)
  - Two-way DV protocols (Trinh, 2017)

Currently, DV-QKD systems can gain a maximum transmission distance of 300 km (Oesterling a., 2012).

9.4.3 Continuous-Variable QKD (CV-QKD)

CV-QKD protocols use infinite-dimensional Hilbert spaces to encode information. These protocols can be categorized into:

- Squeezed state protocols (Pezze a., 2020)
- Coherent state protocols (Huttner a., 1995)
- Entangled state protocols (Du a., 2024)

Currently, CV-QKD achieves a maximum transmission distance of 120 km.

9.4.4 Measurement-Device-Independent QKD (MDI-QKD)

While QKD is theoretically secure, practical implementations face vulnerabilities, such as attacks on quantum sources and detectors. However, loophole-free Bell tests (LFBT) limit their efficiency (Chang a., 2020).

To enhance security while maintaining efficiency, several modified DI protocols have been developed:

- One-sided device-independent (1sDI) protocol
- Semi-device-independent (semi-DI) protocol

MDI-QKD effectively counteracts attacks such as:

- Detector time-shift attacks
- Faked-state attacks
- Detector-blinding attacks
- Wavelength-dependent attacks

The MDI-QKD protocol currently holds the record for the longest secure transmission distance of 400 km. Additionally, MDI-QKD has been extended to CV-QKD systems to address detector-based vulnerabilities.

9.4.5 Quantum Public-Key Cryptography (QPKC)

As QC advances, classical public-key cryptography faces security threats (Radanliev, 2023). QPKC research follows two main directions:

1. **Classical Security Approach**—Finding computational problems resistant to quantum attacks.
2. **Quantum Security Approach**—Achieving unconditional security using quantum properties, similar to QKD.

QPKC often incorporates quantum bits (qubits) for enhanced security, unlike classical cryptography.

9.4.6 Quantum Information Encryption

Quantum cryptography enables the secure transmission of classical information using quantum states (Manoharan, n.d.). Conversely, classical encryption techniques can also be applied to protect quantum bits (qubits) during transmission.

9.4.7 Attacks in Quantum Cryptography

Quantum cryptographic attacks are classified into individual, collective, and coherent attacks.

1. **Individual (Incoherent) Attacks:** The eavesdropper (Eve) applies the same quantum operation to each state separately and measures them individually (Datta, 2025). A typical example is the intercept-resend (IR) attack, where Eve intercepts, measures, and resends a modified state to Bob.
2. **Collective Attacks:** Eve maintains all intercepted states before she delays measurement until the protocol finishes. The completion of the protocol grants Eve full access to the intercepted states for subsequent classical post-processing that enables error correction and privacy amplification.
3. **General (Coherent) Attacks:** Eve reaches the highest attack sophistication by performing a collective quantum operation on multiple states before executing a joint measurement. Despite its complexity, security bounds are often similar to those of collective attacks.

9.5 QUANTUM MACHINE LEARNING AND APPLICATIONS

Quantum machine learning (QML) incorporates CQ with traditional ML techniques for more efficient models capable of managing challenges that classic approaches cannot quickly solve (Khurana a., Quantum Machine Learning: Unraveling a New Paradigm in Computational Intelligence, 2024).

9.5.1 Classical Machine Learning Meets Quantum Computing

In classical ML, different algorithms perform computations on data, frequently in matrix operations within high-dimensional vector spaces. Quantum mechanics functions optimally with matrix operations that process vectors across equivalent high-dimensional vector spaces fit for adapting ML protocols.

The main computational elements in QC are quantum states, defined as vectors in a complex Hilbert space. These quantum states evolve through unitary operations, corresponding to matrix operations.

9.5.2 Quantum Support Vector Machines (QSVM)

Quantum support vector machines (SVMs) are an advanced quantum adaptation of conventional SVMs for classification tasks (Orazi a., 2024). In classical SVMs, the motive is to discover the optimal hyperplane that maximally separates two data classes.

A classical SVM formulation requires solving a convex quadratic optimization problem:

$$win\, w, b\ \frac{1}{2} \| w \|^2\ subject\, to\, y_i \left(w^T x_i + b \right) \geq 1, \forall i \tag{9.18}$$

The weight vector w combines with the bias term b to process data points xi while yi represents their corresponding labels.

9.5.3 Deep Quantum Learning

Classical deep neural networks (DNNs) have revolutionized ML, particularly in image recognition, NLP, and other complex tasks (Khan a., 2023). A promising quantum DL model is the quantum Boltzmann machine (QBM), which is a classical Boltzmann machine (Hu a., 2019).

The quantum Boltzmann machine operates under the system's Hamiltonian, which takes the following form:

$$\mathrm{H} = \sum\nolimits_{i,j} J_{ij} s_j s_j - \sum_j h_i s_i \tag{9.19}$$

where J_{ij} represents the coupling constants between spins, s_i represents the spin variables, and h_i represents external fields. Quantum coherence allows the system to thermalize faster, providing quadratic speedups compared to its classical counterpart.

9.5.4 Quantum Machine Learning for Quantum Data

Quantum ML provides uses for quantum data in addition to classical data (Khan, 2020). Quantum ML algorithms can study quantum states, like matter or light, naturally produced by quantum systems.

Using quantum simulators is an intriguing use of quantum machine learning (Krenn a., 2023). These quantum systems are made to mimic the behavior of other quantum systems. QML approaches like approximation Bayesian inference can effectively learn the behavior of the unknown system without requiring lengthy observations by attaching a quantum simulator to a target system and modifying the model to counteract its dynamics.

9.6 REAL-WORLD IMPACT OF QUANTUM COMPUTING ON 5G SECURITY: A CASE STUDY

In our discussion, we assume that users have established a subscription with their home network while their mobile device connects to a serving network. While the home and serving networks may be identical, they are typically distinct entities. This analysis refers to the 5G security framework defined in Release 15 (R15) of the 3GPP 5G security specifications. Although R15 is stable, work has already begun on its successor, Release 16 (R16). However, the security model discussed here remains largely unaffected by the impending changes in R16.

As currently defined, the 5G security model represents an evolution of the security mechanisms found in previous generations, specifically 4G, 3G (UMTS), and 2G (GSM). Notably, three significant differences set 5G apart from 4G:

1. **Authentication Flexibility**: Using the 5G authentication and key agreement (AKA) protocol, the user equipment (UE), usually a mobile device, may authenticate to the host network. The internet's EAP-AKA protocol is used in this protocol, which is a development of the 4G AKA.
2. **Mobile Identity Confidentiality**: Public key encryption significantly improves user privacy by ensuring permanent user identification is never sent over the network in plaintext.
3. **Data Integrity Protection**: The session key generated after authentication is used to generate keys that safeguard data integrity throughout the air interface, including digital speech.

Although a thorough study would also need to take the EAP-AKA protocol into account, we are concentrating on the situation in which the 5G AKA protocol is used, as shown in Figure 9.3. Four main components make up the security architecture:

- **AKA**: The UE and serving network authentication process leads to mutual identification and generates a common session encryption key.
- **Key Derivation**: The method applies a session key which was produced during the AKA procedure to generate specific-purpose keys.
- **Mobile Identity Confidentiality**: This ensures that the UE does not transmit the permanent user identity in cleartext, employing encryption or unlikable temporary identifiers.
- **Session Security**: Derived secret keys protect information sent between the UE and the serving network via the air interface.

A universal subscriber identity module (USIM) card functions as an essential requirement for the user to start these procedures, and it can be either removable or integrated into UE hardware. USIM contains both the authentication key (K) used

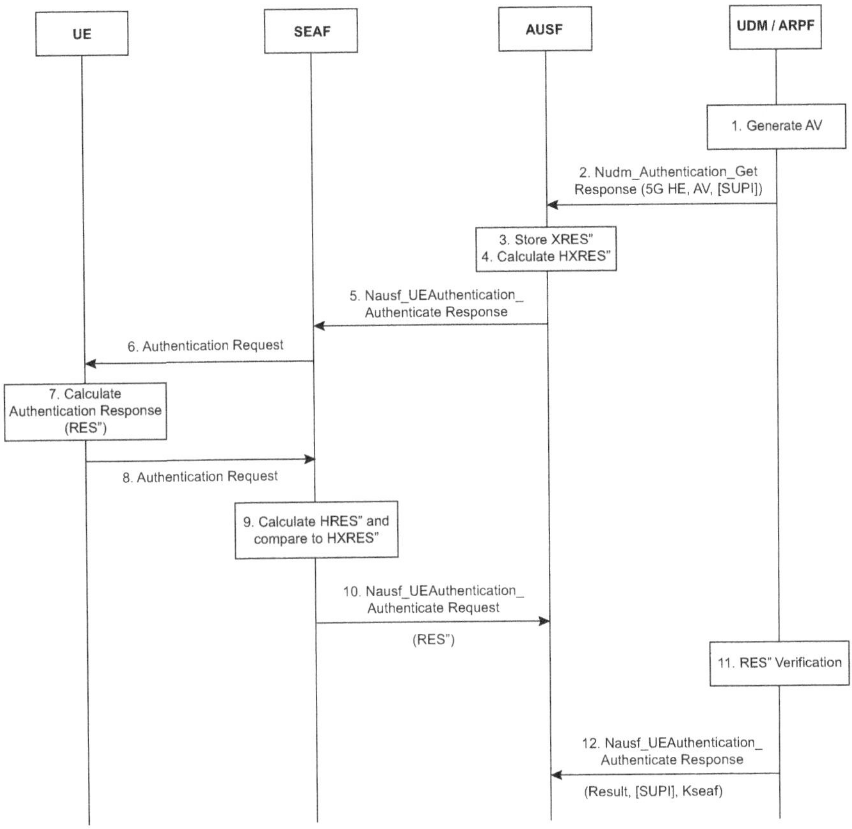

FIGURE 9.3 The procedure of the 5G AKA.

for AKA procedures as well as the public key of the home network for encryption during authentication.

The following analysis will focus on these security components, providing an overview of the authentication and key agreement process unfolding within the 5G system. Notably, we will also touch on the key derivation steps and the handling of session security, which are crucial for ensuring the robustness of 5G's security infrastructure. For simplicity, we will not delve into the extensive security provisions for handovers and roaming, nor will we distinguish the functions of the SEAF from the Access and AMF, as they are co-located within the architecture.

9.6.1 Authentication and Key Agreement

5G security relies on the 5G AKA protocol, which operates similarly to its 4G counterpart yet implements important adjustments. The 5G AKA protocol introduces a new feature which requires serving networks to send proof of successful authentication to home networks. The authentication of UE to the serving network becomes essential for maintaining the integrity of the complete authentication process.

9.6.2 Authentication Vectors

In the 5G architecture, the authentication server function (AUSF) of the serving network requests that the authentication vector (AV) be generated by the home network's authentication credential repository and processing function (ARPF) (Benfarhi, 2024). This process begins with developing a five-value vector (RAND, XRES, CK, IK, AUTN) analogous to the 3G/4G AV generation mechanisms. Specifically:

- RAND is a randomly generated 128-bit value.
- XRES, CK, and IK are 128-bit values derived from RAND and the subscriber's secret key K.
- AUTN is a 128-bit authentication token with the sequence number (SQN), a 48-bit encrypting string, and a message authentication code (MAC) computed from RAND, SQN, and K.

A key function within the process is deriving the 5G authentication vector (5G AV) from this 5-value vector. Notably, this involves combining the original AV components with additional identifiers, like the serving network name, to generate a new key, KAUSF. This 5G AV (RAND, AUTN, XRES, KAUSF) is then transmitted to the serving network's AUSF for further processing (Tang a., 2022).

9.6.3 The AKA Protocol

The 5G AKA protocol begins with the exchange of the 5G AV between the AUSF and the SEAF (Joudah, 2024). The SEAF then sends the RAND and AUTN values to the UE, which checks the message's authenticity through its resident USIM (Mitchell, 2020). If the check is effective, the USIM computes the response (RES) and the keys CK and IK, which are then sent back to the mobile equipment. The equipment computes its response (RES) and derives the KAUSF key.

Upon receiving RES*, the SEAF computes the expected result (HRES*) and compares it with the transmitted HXRES* value (Edris, 2020). If these match, the UE is authenticated, completing the authentication process.

9.6.4 Key Derivation

Post-authentication, the SEAF derives specialized keys from the anchor key (KSEAF), the shared secret established during the AKA protocol (Akman, 2024). These derived keys are used for various purposes, including data integrity protection and encryption for data sent between the UE and the serving network.

This procedure involves several key derivations, each of which provides that distinct keys are employed for different security duties, such as protecting mobile identities or protecting data transmitted over the air interface. This hierarchy of key derivations keeps every component of the connection safe.

Through these processes, 5G achieves a high level of security, providing greater defenses against contemporary issues like user privacy concerns and data integrity threats while addressing more conventional dangers like interception and illegal access.

9.7 CHALLENGES AND FUTURE DIRECTIONS IN QUANTUM COMPUTING

9.7.1 Challenges and Future Directions in Quantum Computing

Several obstacles stand in the way of achieving QC's full potential, yet these obstacles also offer opportunities for groundbreaking developments as shown in Figure 9.4. Technological obstacles must be removed for challenges:

1. **Input Bottleneck:** The advantages of quantum speedups are occasionally overshadowed by the difficulty of encoding classical data into quantum systems, even though quantum algorithms are excellent at processing landed. Input encoding techniques are being optimized as part of ongoing research to lessen this problem.
2. **Output Restrictions:** In many situations, full-state learning is not practicable due to the exponential measurements required to extract whole solutions from quantum calculations. An effective way forward might be

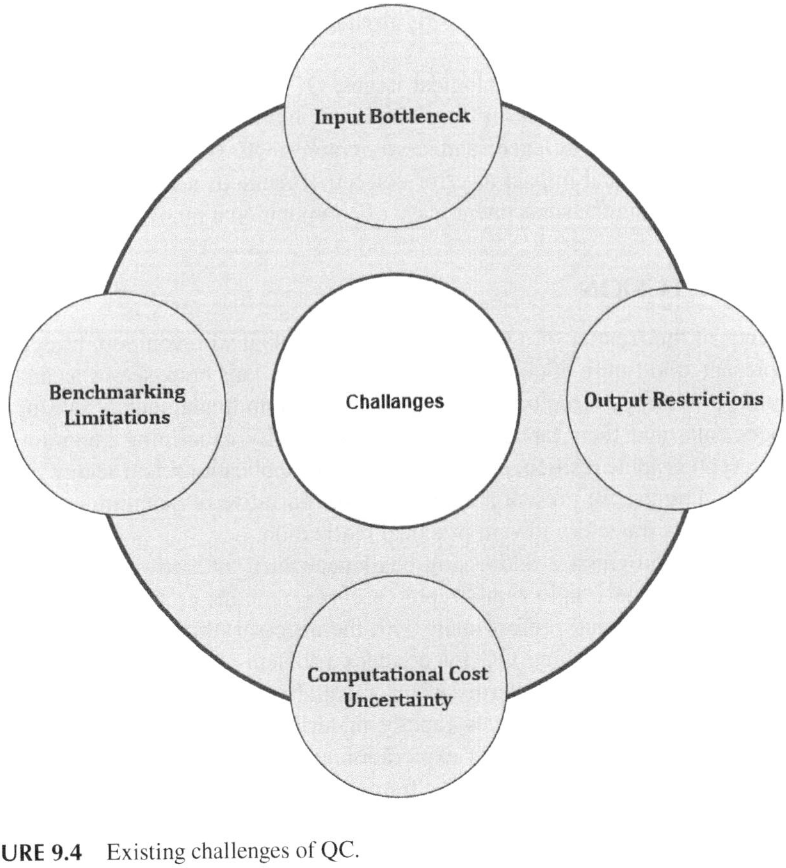

FIGURE 9.4 Existing challenges of QC.

to investigate different strategies, including extracting important statistical features instead of full-state solutions.

3. **Computational Cost Uncertainty:** Despite theoretical advantages, the actual gate complexity of quantum machine learning algorithms remains an open question. Establishing more apparent cost models will be essential to determine when quantum approaches surpass classical counterparts.
4. **Benchmarking Limitations:** Thorough benchmarking against the most advanced heuristics is necessary to show a quantum advantage over classical techniques consistently. The superiority of QC in particular fields will be further established by extending studies on quantum lower limits and empirical validation.

9.7.2 Future Prospects

One promising avenue is the application of quantum ML techniques to quantum data, which makes it easier to optimize and control quantum processors. This self-improving cycle is similar to the evolution of classical computing, where each generation of processors improves the next. There are early indications of this recursive innovation, with classical ML already helping to advance quantum hardware design.

Notwithstanding these technological issues, QC has the prospect of thoroughly transforming some industries by resolving computationally challenging issues in optimization, materials science, and cryptography. QC will move from theoretical promise to practical impact as error correction methods advance and scalability increases, propelling the subsequent wave of computational innovations.

9.8 CONCLUSION

QC stands at the frontier of a transformative technological revolution, bridging the past, present, and future of computational paradigms. This book serves as an essential guide, providing a structured exploration of quantum fundamentals, cutting-edge advancements, and their far-reaching implications. By examining quantum algorithms, cryptographic resilience, machine learning applications, and secure communication techniques, we present a comprehensive narrative of quantum computing's evolution and its trajectory toward practical realization.

As the field progresses, addressing challenges such as hardware development, algorithmic efficiency, and cryptographic security remains crucial. This book not only equips scholars and professionals with the necessary knowledge but also fosters innovation in leveraging QC for complex problem-solving across disciplines. With ongoing research and interdisciplinary collaborations, the vision of QC as a mainstream technological force is rapidly materializing. By contributing to this dialogue, we aim to inspire further exploration and development, ensuring a future where QC reshapes industries, security frameworks, and computational methodologies worldwide.

REFERENCES

Akama, S. (2015). Elements of quantum computing. In *History, Theories and Engineering Applications*. Springer.

Akman, G. (2024). Privacy and mobility aspects in authentication and key agreement protocols.

Beheshti, Z. a. (2013). A review of population-based meta-heuristic algorithms. *International Journal of Advances Soft Computing and Applications*, 1–35.

Benfarhi, Z. (2024). Evaluation of a new authentication and key agreement protocol for 5G network.

Cacciapuoti, A. S. (2020). When entanglement meets classical communications: Quantum teleportation for the quantum internet. *IEEE Transactions on Communications*, 3808–3833.

Chang, Y. a. (2020). Device-independent quantum key distribution protocol based on hyper-entanglement. *Computers Materials & Continua*, 879–896.

Datta, D. (2025). Quantum-key distribution using decoy pulses to combat photon-number splitting by eavesdropper: An event-by-event impairment enumeration approach for performance evaluation and design. *arXiv preprint arXiv:2501.18394.*

Dey, S. a. (2014). Multi-level thresholding using quantum inspired meta-heuristics. *Knowledge-Based Systems*, 373–400.

Du, Z. a. (2024). Mediated semi-quantum key distribution protocol mixing single-state and entangled-state. *Europhysics Letters*, 28001.

Edris, E. K.-K. (2020). Formal verification and analysis of primary authentication based on 5G-AKA protocol. In *2020 Seventh International Conference on Software Defined Systems (SDS)* (pp. 256–261).

Fiasch, M. (2012). A quantum-inspired evolutionary algorithm for optimization numerical problems. In *Neural Information Processing: 19th International Conference, ICONIP 2012, Doha, Qatar, November 12–15, 2012, Proceedings, Part III 19* (pp. 686–693).

Fuchs, C. A. (2002). Quantum mechanics as quantum information (and only a little more). *arXiv preprint quant-ph/0205039.*

Gill, S. S. (2022). Quantum computing: A taxonomy, systematic review and future directions. *Software: Practice and Experience*, 66–114.

Gill, S. S. (2024). Quantum computing: Vision and challenges. *arXiv preprint arXiv:2403.02240.*

Hong, K. W.-M. (2016). Challenges in quantum key distribution: A review. In *Proceedings of the 4th International Conference on Information and Network Security* (pp. 29–33).

Horodecki, R. a. (2009). Quantum entanglement. *Reviews of Modern Physics*, 865–942.

Hu, F. a.-N. (2019). Quantum machine learning with D-wave quantum computer. *Quantum Engineering*, e12.

Huttner, B. a. (1995). Quantum cryptography with coherent states. *Physical Review A*, 1863.

Joudah, R. H. (2024). Implementing of 5G authentication and key agreement protocol: Practical security measures. In *2024 21st International Multi-Conference on Systems, Signals & Devices (SSD)* (pp. 735–744).

Khan, T. M.-K. (2020). Machine learning: Quantum vs classical. *IEEE Access*, 219275–219294.

Khan, W. a. (2023). Exploring the frontiers of deep learning and natural language processing: A comprehensive overview of key challenges and emerging trends. *Natural Language Processing Journal*, 100026.

Khurana, S. a. (2023). Implementation of database search with quantum computing: Grover's algorithm vs linear search. In *2023 International Conference on Ambient Intelligence, Knowledge Informatics and Industrial Electronics (AIKIIE)* (pp. 1–6).

Khurana, S. a. (2024). Quantum machine learning: Unraveling a new paradigm in computational intelligence. *Quantum*, 1.

Kim, Y.-H. a. (2019). A comparison study of harmony search and genetic algorithm for the max-cut problem. *Swarm and Evolutionary Computation*, 130–135.

Krenn, M. a. (2023). Artificial intelligence and machine learning for quantum technologies. *Physical Review A*, 010101.

Kumar, A. (2025). Quantum computing's role in advancing sustainability. In *Digital Transformation for Business Sustainability and Growth in Emerging Markets* (pp. 85–114). Emerald Publishing Limited.

Kumar, G. a. (2024). Recent advances in quantum computing for drug discovery and development. *IEEE Access*, 12, 64491–64509.

Kumar, S. a. (2024). Experimental implementation of distributed phase reference quantum key distribution protocols. *Optical and Quantum Electronics*, 1190.

Lang, V. (2021). Quantum computing. In *Digital Fluency: Understanding the Basics of Artificial Intelligence, Blockchain Technology, Quantum Computing, and Their Applications for Digital Transformation* (pp. 51–111). Springer.

Le Bellac, M. (2006). A short introduction to quantum information and quantum computation.

Lu, X. a. (2013). Workflow of the Grover algorithm simulation incorporating CUDA and GPGPU. *Computer Physics Communications*, 2035–2041.

Malossini, A. a. (2008). Quantum genetic optimization. *IEEE Transactions on Evolutionary Computation*, 231–241.

Manju, A. a. (2025). Quantum key distribution protocols: Survey and analysis. *Advancing Cyber Security through Quantum Cryptography*, 103–136.

Manoharan, A. (n.d.). The rise of quantum cryptography: Securing data beyond classical means.

Memon, Q. A. (2024). Quantum computing: Navigating the future of computation, challenges, and technological breakthroughs. *Quantum Reports*, 627–663.

Mitchell, C. J. (2020). The impact of quantum computing on real-world security: A 5G case study. *Computers & Security*, 101825.

Murakami, Y. a. (2024). Implementation of the RRDPS QKD protocol using time-domain fourier transform via space-time duality. In *APS March Meeting Abstracts* (pp. Q53–011).

Nkulenu, G. (2024). Quantum computing: The impending revolution in cryptographic security.

Oesterling, L. a. (2012). Comparison of commercial and next generation quantum key distribution: Technologies for secure communication of information. In *2012 IEEE Conference on Technologies for Homeland Security (HST)* (pp. 156–161).

Oftelie, L. B. (2021). Simulating quantum materials with digital quantum computers. *Quantum Science and Technology*, 043002.

Orazi, F. a. (2024). Hybrid quantum technologies for quantum support vector machines. *Information*, 72.

Paetznick, A. a.-A.-R. (2024). Demonstration of logical qubits and repeated error correction with better-than-physical error rates. *arXiv preprint arXiv:2404.02280.*

Pang, X.-F. (2005). Quantum mechanics in nonlinear systems.

Pezze, L. a. (2020). Heisenberg-limited noisy atomic clock using a hybrid coherent and squeezed state protocol. *Physical Review Letters*, 210503.

Pulicharla, M. R. (2023). Hybrid quantum-classical machine learning models: Powering the future of AI. *Journal of Science & Technology*, 40–65.

Radanliev, P. (2023). Cyber-attacks on public key cryptography.

Rana, B. a. (2023). Industry 4.0—applications, challenges and opportunities in industries and academia: A review. *Materials Today: Proceedings*, 389–394.

Sahoo, S. K. (2022). A hybrid moth flame optimization algorithm for global optimization. *Journal of Bionic Engineering*, 1522–1543.

Sarkar, A. (n.d.). Quantum algorithms.

Shakib, K. H. (2025). Impersonation attack using quantum Shor's algorithm against blockchain-based vehicular ad-goc network. *IEEE Transactions on Intelligent Transportation Systems.*

Shami, T. M. (2024). Single candidate optimizer: A novel optimization algorithm. *Evolutionary Intelligence*, 863–887.

Silva, V. (2023). Richard feynman, demigod of physics, father of the quantum computer. In *Quantum Computing by Practice: Python Programming in the Cloud with Qiskit and IBM-Q* (pp. 49–85). Springer.

Singh, H. (2025). 9 future directions and challenges, quantum supremacy, and beyond. *Quantum Technology Applications, Impact, and Future Challenges*, 141.

Sonko, S. a. (2024). Quantum cryptography and US digital security: A comprehensive review: Investigating the potential of quantum technologies in creating unbreakable encryption and their future in national security. *Computer Science & IT Research Journal*, 390–414.

Tang, Q. a. (2022). A systematic analysis of 5g networks with a focus on 5g core security. *IEEE Access*, 18298–18319.

Trinh, P. V. (2017). Design and secrecy performance of novel two-way free-space QKD protocol using standard FSO systems. In *2017 IEEE International Conference on Communications (ICC)* (pp. 1–6).

Ur Rehman, J. a.-H. (2025). Evolutionary algorithms and quantum computing: Recent advances, opportunities, and challenges. *IEEE Access*.

Vasani, V. a. (2024). Embracing the quantum frontier: Investigating quantum communication, cryptography, applications and future directions. *Journal of Industrial Information Integration*, 100594.

Yamini, B. a. (2024). Maximizing the revolutionary potential of quantum computing: Challenges, opportunities, and future directions. In *2024 10th International Conference on Communication and Signal Processing (ICCSP)* (pp. 756–761).

Yanofsky, N. S. (2008). Quantum computing for computer scientists.

10 Journey into Quantum Computing—Cryptographic Security and Learning Algorithms

Vishal Kumar Jaiswal, Madhurima V., M. Bharathi, Sandhya Kumari G., Saleha Tabassum, N. Ashok Kumar, and M. Poornima

10.1 INTRODUCTION TO QUANTUM COMPUTING

Quantum computing is a radical new paradigm that employs the principles of quantum mechanics to alter the way information is processed. Conventional computers operate with bits, which carry the value 0 or 1. In contrast, quantum computers employ qubits, which can perform more than one function at the same time. this expansion gives them an almost incomprehensible amount of processing power. Such a potential would certainly have far-reaching repercussions, especially in the area of securing communication. Having stated that, modern cryptography, which is aimed at securing sensitive messages, involves the encryption of data based on the complexity of specific tasks, such as the factorization of integers and the discrete logarithm problem, both of which are the cornerstones of encryption systems like the RSA and ECC. The adoption of quantum algorithms such as Shor's and Grover's presents a worrying outlook, however, as they can complete such tasks at growing speeds many orders faster, making classical encryption potentially defunct as shown in Figure 10.1.

To respond to this challenge, quantum computing also provides robust answers. For example, quantum key distribution (QKD) is based on principles such as superposition or entanglement, in which the key encoding communication is accompanied by glaring sending and interception of the key in a secure manner. Similarly, post-quantum cryptography is emerging as a field focused on algorithms resistant to quantum attacks, ensuring long-term data security. Furthermore, quantum systems can generate true randomness, which can strengthen cryptographic protocols and enhance blockchain security by improving cryptographic techniques and consensus mechanisms.

As promising as these developments appear, there are still problems that need to be addressed for quantum computers, such as the scaling of hardware, the functioning of quantum computers, and the migration to post-quantum-secure frameworks.

 DOI: 10.1201/9781003538950-12

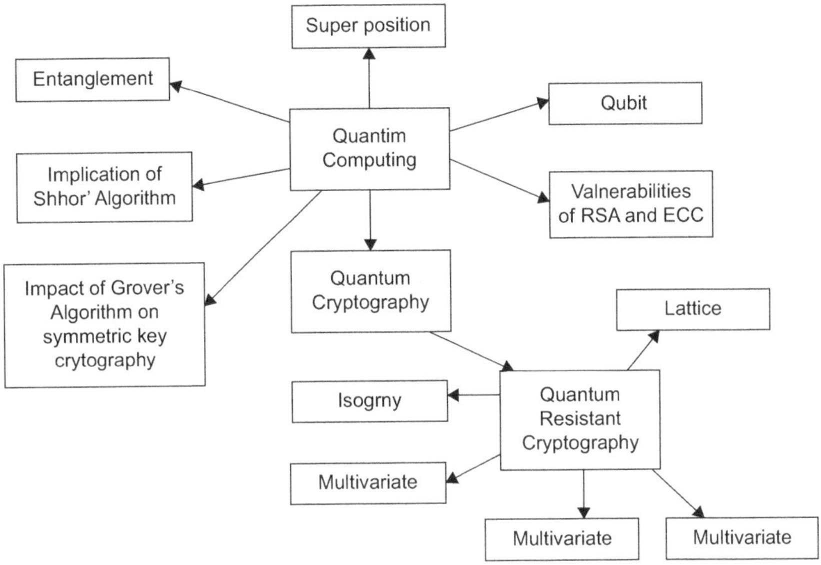

FIGURE 10.1 Overview of quantum computing and cryptography.

(Courtesy of the article "From Bytes to Qubits: The Cybersecurity Implications of Quantum Advancements," [1]

However, its capacity to disrupt as well as enable new delivery systems for secure providers puts it on par with one of the most important factors of change in the secure communication systems. Solving its problems, quantum computing can fundamentally reframe the principles of cryptographic security, allowing us to build up and safeguard the key structures of the future digital landscape.

10.2 QUANTUM CRYPTOGRAPHY AND SECURE COMMUNICATION

Quantum cryptography is an entirely new way of securing communication [2]. In particular, researchers have sought to apply those principles unique to quantum mechanics in order to overcome the problematic nature of classical cryptographic systems. Now that data breaches and cyberattacks are on the rise, information most sensitive and valuable information should be preserved. Classical cryptography relies upon computational complexity to secure information, but quantum cryptography offers security at a more fundamental physical level. It creates systems that use the laws of quantum mechanics such that any attempt at eavesdropping can be detected. This offers an unparalleled degree of assurance in the process of secure communication.

10.2.1 Why Quantum Cryptography Matters

In comparison, quantum cryptography is one of the more robust options since it transfers security issues from mathematical complexity to inherent features of quantum mechanics. However, this is a serious threat to RSA and ECC systems, the bulk of contemporary classical cryptographic systems, where the hardness of factoring large numbers or the discrete logarithm problem is upon which these systems rely, since quantum computers may factor big numbers exponentially faster than such classical algorithms based on Shor's algorithm. Quantum cryptography provides a much stronger alternative because security is now transferred from mathematical complexity to the very properties of quantum mechanics. Even when it is expected that powerful quantum computers would eventually be able to crack these codes, secure communication remains uncompromised. The primary benefit of quantum cryptography is that it detects eavesdropping at once. BB84-type protocols rely on principles of superposition and entanglement to encode the information into quantum states that are then measured or interfered with whenever someone tries to measure or intercept these states. The feature is known as quantum no-cloning, which forbids the eavesdropper from duplicating or retrieving data without detection. The old methods of cryptography rely on an assumption for which quantum computing appears to work: that the adversary does not have enough computing power to break the encryption.

The fact that quantum cryptography itself is future-proof ensures no attack can come from a classical adversary or a quantum adversary. Development on the post-quantum cryptography method tries to harden the systems from all known threats in the quantum arena by categorizing the hardness of computations and also stating claims over the utilization of such problems [3]. Quantum cryptography relies on the known certainties of the laws. This resilience thus places quantum cryptography as the foundation technology for secure communication in this quantum age. Quantum cryptography is already finding applications in important areas such as government communications, financial transactions, and defense systems. Quantum key distribution is one of the most significant applications, enabling secure key exchanges resistant to classical as well as quantum attacks. Indeed, quite a few QKD networks are already in operation nowadays and demonstrate the feasibility and functionality of the whole technology. Once quantum computer development becomes the standard norm, one hopes quantum cryptography will penetrate the stream of quantum applications. Such technology will not only ensure strong protection of tomorrow's digital infrastructure but, due to its immunity toward vulnerabilities affecting current classical systems and an unbreakable security guarantee, quantum cryptography will reshape how sensitive information is protected.

10.2.2 The BB84 Protocol: A Deep Dive

The BB84 protocol is essentially the basis of QKD systems, which were developed in 1984 by Charles Bennett and Gilles Brassard. This protocol uses properties like superposition and uncertainty to share a secret key between two parties, such as Alice and Bob, safely. In the BB84 protocol, the quantum bits (qubits) are transmitted using photons that can be polarized in various states to represent binary values. The protocol ensures that any attempt by an adversary (Eve) to eavesdrop disrupts the quantum states, alerting Alice and Bob to the intrusion, by using a combination of non-orthogonal bases for encoding and decoding these qubits. This particular property allows a robust framework for secure communication [4]. BB84 thus constitutes an important breakthrough in cryptography. The strength of the BB84 protocol lies in the ability to detect eavesdropping through the process of key exchange.

Alice sends a string of qubits to Bob, where every qubit is encoded by Alice with a randomly chosen basis-rectilinear or diagonal. Bob doesn't know the encoding basis used by Alice, and he also measures the incoming qubits using some randomly selected bases. After transmission, Alice and Bob compare their chosen bases through a classical channel and retain only the bits where their bases match and discard the rest. In this way, they obtain an intrinsically secure shared key because any possible interception by Eve would alter the states of qubits, which would result in detectable errors. Thus, Alice and Bob can either produce a secure key or detect any tampering and abort, as shown in Figure 10.2.

Implementing the BB84 protocol in real-world systems is characterized by overcoming several technical difficulties. Quantum communication requires some specific hardware, such as single-photon sources, high-precision detectors, and optical fibers or free-space channels for photon transmission. Environmental factors such as noise, signal loss, and interference may affect the accuracy of quantum states, thus requiring the application of error correction and privacy amplification techniques. The distance over which the quantum signal can be sent reliably within a QKD network further limits its scalability [5].

Recent developments, such as quantum repeaters and satellite-based QKD, are overcoming the challenges to eventually take this technology to many users. A QKD system has both quantum and classical sides. In the quantum side are sources of photons, polarization filters, and detectors, and in the classical side are key reconciliation protocols, error correction, and authentication mechanisms. Strong software must be used for managing key generation, distribution, and monitoring of eavesdropping attempts.

Another very important integration is classical cryptographic methods in authenticating the communication channels, thus securing the system. Hybrid models combining quantum and classical cryptography are emerging as practical solutions in transitional phases where quantum technologies coexist with classical systems.

As quantum computers become stronger, PQC becomes an essential part in securing classical systems against quantum attacks. Unlike QKD, which relies on principles of quantum mechanics, PQC emphasizes the development of algorithms resistant to quantum adversaries. Such algorithms rely on problems such as the hardness of lattice problems, code-based cryptography, and multivariate cryptographic schemes, which remain hard for quantum computers to break. PQC bridges the way to secure communication in the interim before fully quantum systems gain widespread application. Hybrid models that combine QKD with PQC provide an excellent transition by offering instant security against a classical attack while preparing for a quantum future [6].

Quantum cryptographic systems are going to revolutionize secure communication in the digital age by addressing implementation challenges, enhancing hardware and software integration, and adopting hybrid models.

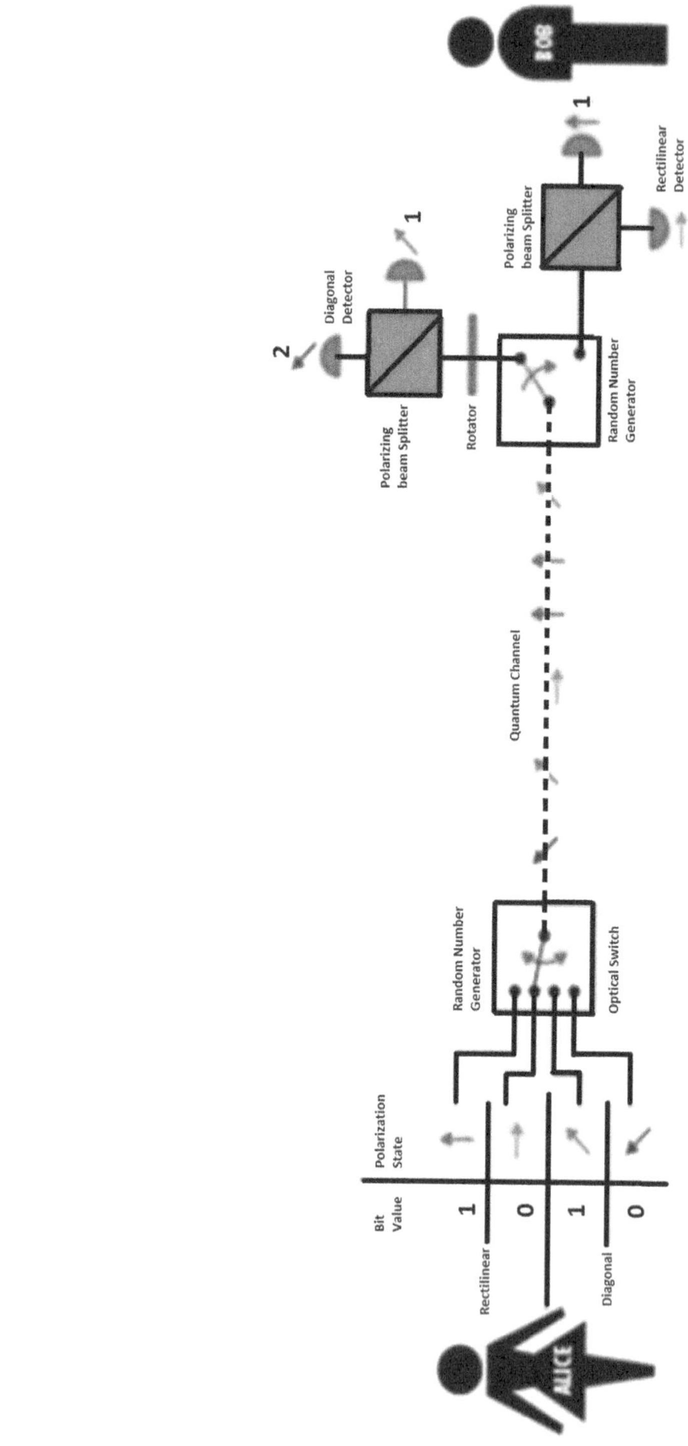

FIGURE 10.2 Working process of the BB84 protocol.
(Courtesy of https://doi.org/10.12694/scpe.v25i1.2152)

10.3 PRACTICAL QUANTUM PROGRAMMING

10.3.1 Getting Started with Qiskit

Qiskit is an open-source framework for quantum computing developed by IBM, in which users are allowed to write, simulate, and execute quantum programs. First, one needs to install Qiskit by using pip, the Python package manager, while setting up an environment, for example, a Jupyter Notebook or preferred integrated development environment. During installation, one has to configure Python and make sure that all modules necessary for the program are installed. Once the environment is set up, you are ready to write your first quantum program. This is generally done by creating a very simple quantum circuit, then applying basic quantum gates, such as Hadamard (H) or CNOT, then running the circuit on either a simulator or real quantum hardware via IBM's Quantum Cloud. This tutorial exercise will give you an initial grasp of Qiskit functionality and the basics of quantum programming.

10.3.2 Quantum Programming with Microsoft Q#

Microsoft Q# is a programming language that was specifically designed for quantum computing and comes with the Quantum Development Kit (QDK). First, you have to install the QDK, which supports Visual Studio, VS Code, and more. Writing a program in Q# is done by defining qubits, applying quantum operations, and executing the program on a simulator. For example, a basic Q# program would be something like the operations that initialize qubits, apply X or Hadamard gates, and measure the results. Compared to Qiskit, Q# is a more abstract level of abstraction because it focuses on the algorithmic aspects of quantum computing rather than circuit-level design. Hence, Q# is the perfect choice for developers who have a preference for programming-centric quantum computing rather than the circuit-oriented methodology used by Qiskit [7].

10.3.3 Building Quantum Circuits: A Hands-On Approach

Building quantum circuits is an important skill in quantum programming that allows developers to construct and run quantum algorithms. Quantum circuit is a sequence of quantum gates applied to qubits to manipulate their states and produce desired outcomes. Learning how to build and test these circuits step by step is, therefore, an important step in really making use of the power of quantum computing. One fundamental part of quantum programming is building quantum circuits. Anyone looking to get into this area will have to do so: create an empty quantum circuit, and iteratively add in quantum gates so you have everything to do whatever operation it needs. Maybe you might come up with a circuit for one qubit, which should be introduced by a Hadamard gate to begin in superposition. You extend the circuit to have a CNOT gate that entangles the qubit. As Qiskit and Q# each have their respective strengths, probably combining the usage of both can be more comprehensive for learning and implementation [8].

10.3.3.1 Advantages of Combining Qiskit and Q#

Qiskit is very powerful for visualizing and building quantum circuits, so it is very intuitive for beginners who focus on hardware-level implementations. Q# focuses more on algorithm development and provides deeper insight into quantum problem-solving. Using both allows users to explore quantum programming from several angles, which generates strong research and real-world application skills. Practical quantum programming becomes even more interesting when used in real-world scenarios and advanced algorithms.

10.3.3.2 Exploring Advanced Quantum Concepts Through Hands-On Projects

With Qiskit, one can build examples; for example, one can implement quantum teleportation or Grover's search algorithm to experience the phenomenon behind these quantum objects. With Q#, it is possible to explore the logical structure and implementation of more complex algorithms, such as quantum phase estimation or Shor's algorithm. The platforms support the step-by-step iteration approach to experimentation, allowing developers to sharpen their skills in this fast-paced world of quantum computing. This would enable the programmers to understand the prospects and limitations of quantum technologies while dealing with these hands-on projects. This would prepare them for the future innovations of that field.

10.3.3.2.1 Step 1: Initializing the Circuit

To create a quantum circuit, initialize the quantum circuit. Using Qiskit, one starts with the importation of required libraries, then the creation of the quantum circuit object. This may start by initializing a circuit using a specific number of qubits and classical bits for measurement:

```
python
Copy code
from qiskit import QuantumCircuit
qc = QuantumCircuit(2, 2) # 2 qubits and 2 classical bits
```

10.3.3.2.2 Step 2: Adding Quantum Gates

Quantum gates are the qubit operations in quantum circuits. Using these gates you can apply, for instance, the Hadamard gate to produce superposition or the Controlled-NOT gate to establish entanglement. For example:

```
python
Copy code
qc.h(0) # Apply Hadamard to the first qubit
qc.cx(0, 1) # Apply CNOT with the first qubit as control and second as target
```

10.3.3.2.3 Step 3: Measuring Qubits

The last step is to run the circuit on a simulator or actual quantum hardware. From Qiskit, you can use simulators from the Aer library or execute the circuit on IBM Quantum devices:

```
python
Copy code
qc.measure([0, 1], [0, 1]) # Measure both qubits into classical bits
```

10.3.3.2.4 Step 4: Visualizing the Circuit

Qiskit offers tools to visualize quantum circuits, giving information of what the operations were and in what sequence. You can see a graph view of your circuit by using the draw() function like this:

```
python
Copy code
print(qc.draw())
```

10.3.3.2.5 Step 5: Running the Circuit

The final step is to run the circuit on a simulator or actual quantum hardware. In Qiskit, you can use simulators from the Aer library or execute the circuit on IBM Quantum devices:

```
python
Copy code
from qiskit import Aer, execute
simulator = Aer.get_backend('qasm_simulator')
result = execute(qc, simulator).result()
print(result.get_counts())
```

10.3.3.3 Testing and Debugging Circuits

Testing circuits requires running the circuits several times and inspecting the output for correctness. The problem arises from the wrong placement of gates, missing measurements, or accidental qubit interactions. Debugging tools like Qiskit's statevector_simulator will display the quantum state of the system before measurement.

10.3.3.4 Advanced Circuit Construction

As you become more competent, you can create increasingly complex circuits. For example, you can develop quantum algorithms like Grover's search and the quantum Fourier transform. Such examples include chaining multiple gates and operations on qubits to accomplish very advanced results.

10.3.3.5 Learning by Doing

Only by experimentation can you learn how to build quantum circuits. Begin with simple circuits and work your way up to complex designs, making use of visualization and debugging tools to get your concepts right. Be it Qiskit or other frameworks like Microsoft Q#, experience will get you ready for the challenges that lie in real-world quantum computing.

10.4 QUANTUM ALGORITHMS

Shor's and Grover's quantum algorithms and quantum simulations are among the greatest breakthroughs of quantum computing, which show how one addresses specific challenges while the others are unachievable classically. Such quantum algorithms prepare a platform for innovative discoveries in cryptography, optimization, and scientific discovery toward the potential of a quantum-computer-driven future for humanity [9].

10.4.1 Shor's Algorithm: Factoring Large Numbers and Implications for Cryptography

Shor's algorithm is a landmark quantum algorithm that demonstrates the fact that quantum computers are computationally more powerful than classical systems for certain problems. It was designed to factor large integers efficiently, an activity exponentially harder for algorithms that are classical and mainly deal with order finding, period finding, and factoring as shown in Figure 10.3. Many modern cryptographic systems, including the widely used RSA system, rely on the hardness of factoring large numbers to keep their sensitive data safe. Shor's algorithm directly threatens this foundation because it reduces the time complexity of factorization from exponential to polynomial.

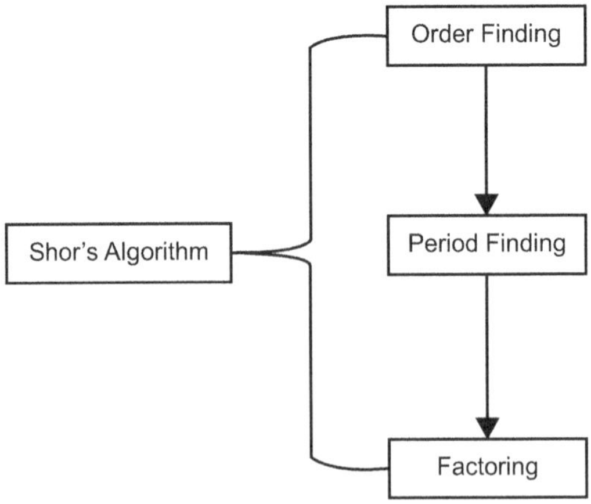

FIGURE 10.3 Shor's algorithm for quantum numbers.

(https://doi.org/10.1109/ACCT.2015.16)

The method exploits two of the most interesting principles of quantum: superposition and QFT. In the running of the algorithm, the factors of a number are encoded into a superposition of states. After that, periodicity about a function, which deals with factors, is known again using the principles of periodicity and modular arithmetic. And then, the QFT is applied to extract this periodicity that, in turn, would determine the factors of that given number.

For example, given a composite number N, Shor's algorithm produces integers p and q such that p×q=N. This is a very serious threat to RSA encryption because the security of RSA relies on the difficulty of factorizing N, which is the product of two large primes [10].

Practical implementation of Shor's algorithm on the existing available quantum hardware is limited, primarily due to noise problems and scalability issues. Improving the hardware would allow one to foresee a time soon when Shor's algorithm would obsolesce all classical approaches to encryption, forcing humanity to migrate toward post-quantum cryptography.

10.4.2 Grover's Algorithm: Quantum Search and Its Applications

Grover's algorithm is a quantum algorithm designed to solve the unstructured search problem, that is, find a specific item in an unsorted database of NNN items. Classically, it requires O(N)) steps on average, but Grover's algorithm achieves a quadratic speedup and solves it in O(square root of N). steps.

This algorithm is amplitude-amplification-based, using a quantum technique to boost the amplitudes to increase the chance of getting the wanted state. The Grover operator, which incorporates the oracle with the diffusion operation, operates iteratively. The oracle marks its desired state with a change of phase; the amplitude amplification, through the diffusion operation, boosts it up. So, after a little more than N iterations, the possibility of measuring the desired state approaches nearly one.

Besides its application in database search, Grover's algorithm has several other applications. It may be used to optimize functions, solve combinatorial problems, and reduce the brute-force search space of the symmetric key encryption systems by improving the cryptographic analysis. For instance, it may reduce the effective key length of a 256-bit symmetric cipher to 128 bits.

Despite Grover's algorithm's flexibility, it does not give an exponential speedup and therefore is not significantly disrupting the applications of Shor's algorithm in cryptography. Its utility in optimization and problem-solving applications certainly underlines the need for quantum computing [11].

10.5 REAL-WORLD APPLICATIONS

Due to their unparalleled computational capacity and security features, quantum computing and cryptography are revolutionizing several industries. Here are some actual instances of how they are used in cybersecurity, healthcare, and finance:

Finance Risk Analysis and Portfolio Optimization: Compared to classical systems, quantum computers are more effective in analyzing market risks and optimizing portfolios. To enhance algorithmic trading and optimize intricate financial systems, for example, JP Morgan is investigating quantum computing. Huaxia Bank subsidiary Longying Zhida has teamed up with SpinQ to create quantum models for digital transformation and ATM removal decisions.

Derivatives Pricing: By calculating complicated derivatives more quickly and accurately, quantum computing might improve trading tactics and risk control. For investment banks trying to replicate different market scenarios and maximize capital allocation, this skill is essential.

Healthcare: Drug discovery and tailored medicine in healthcare can be accelerated by the detailed molecular interaction simulations that quantum computers can provide. In order to better understand diseases like cancer and Alzheimer's, companies like Google and IBM are simulating intricate protein folding using quantum computers.

Genome Assembly: By using quantum computing, genome assembly methods are becoming more efficient and consuming fewer resources. For instance, SpinQ and BGI-Research have partnered to use quantum computing in the biomedical industry.

Cybersecurity: Post-quantum cryptography is becoming more and more necessary as a result of quantum computers' ability to crack some traditional encryption schemes. As quantum computing advances, tech behemoths like Microsoft and IBM are creating quantum-resistant encryption solutions to protect data.

Improved Encryption Techniques: By developing more secure encryption techniques, quantum computing can keep data safe even when it is being used actively. This makes the digital environment safer by providing strong protection for data both in transit and at rest.

These examples show how encryption and quantum computing are being used to improve security and tackle challenging issues in a variety of sectors [12].

Simulating quantum systems is one of the most appealing applications of quantum computing. When the state space explodes with the number of particles, even a simple simulation becomes impossibly computationally expensive. Quantum computers, being bound by the principles of the quantum world, are by construction well adapted to simulate that world.

Quantum simulations can make molecular structures, reaction pathways, and energy states that were impossible to represent in chemistry. The following can be efficiently solved: how to calculate the ground-state energy of molecules, to determine reaction rates, or to study catalytic processes. For example, simulation of the nitrogen-fixation process in ammonia production is so energy-intensive that this process might be made much more efficient, revolutionizing the whole agro-industrial sector.

Quantum simulations allow the design of novel materials with desired properties in materials science. One can predict electronic structure and interactions from the quantum level, which may give the properties of conductivity, magnetism, and strength. This applies in developing superconductors, advanced batteries, and durable materials for space exploration [13].

Hybrid approaches are used to practically implement quantum simulations where a particular subproblem is handled by the quantum computer while a general computation is carried out with a classical computer. Two of the most important algorithms for such simulations are VQE and QAOA. While the current quantum hardware is scaled and noisy, the developments in error correction and qubit fidelity bring us closer to realizing the full potential of quantum simulations. These simulations have promised transformative breakthroughs across fields from pharmaceuticals to renewable energy.

10.5.1 Quantum Machine Learning

It can be considered the backbone of modern artificial intelligence since ML makes it possible for systems to learn through patterns and generate predictions through data. It is primarily at the most basic core of the thing that consists of three prime models. There is a model of supervised learning that uses labeled data to train the models. That, in turn, has found broad application.

Neural Networks (NNs): These are some of the critical components of ML. Modeled on the human brain, they consist of layers of interconnected nodes, known as neurons, which process input data with weights and biases to compute outputs. NNs are great for great for image recognition, natural language processing, and playing games.

Support Vector Machines (SVMs): These classifiers are very robust and have the capability of segregating data into clear categories of separation by searching for a hyperplane where data needs to be located for distinct categorization, which has been very powerful in very small datasets also. Classical ML models are based on iterative optimization; they are based on minimizing errors with algorithms like gradient descent. However, they become inefficient, especially in cases of high-dimensional data or complex optimization problems, due to the computational constraints. That is where quantum computing comes into play.

10.5.2 The Intersection of Quantum Computing and Machine Learning

Quantum computing is combined with machine learning to give birth to quantum machine learning (QML), a field that promises to change the way data-driven problems are addressed. Quantum computing, by allowing information to be processed in superposition and performing parallel computations, brings exponential speedups for specific ML tasks. Key differences between quantum and classical machine learning are found in representation and computation. The former deals with data sequentially; the latter exploits the enormous state space of qubits, natively handling large volumes of data and complex algorithms [14].

Advantages of quantum ML include faster training of models, the ability to handle nonlinear data more effectively, and solving optimization problems that are infeasible for classical systems. For instance, quantum-enhanced kernel methods can improve the performance of SVMs by leveraging quantum states to compute complex decision boundaries. New algorithms, such as quantum principal component analysis, extract key features from data as it comes with quantum power. Thus, QML leads the way for novel solutions along a plethora of industrial branches.

10.5.3 Quantum Support Vector Machines (QSVMs)

The advantages of quantum ML are as follows: they allow for faster model training, do a much better job of handling nonlinear data, and can solve optimization problems that are infeasible for classical systems. For example, quantum-enhanced kernel methods improve the performance of SVMs by using quantum states to compute complex decision boundaries. Training of QSVM includes preparation of qubits to represent data and encoding kernel functions applying quantum circuits, followed by optimization of decision boundaries with measurement outcomes. This methodology is very effective in reducing the time to compute kernels, especially for large structures with high complexity. Deploying QSVMs on real-world data requires integrating quantum algorithms with classical pre-processing and post-processing steps. For instance, financial risk analysis, genomic data classification, and image segmentation can benefit from QSVMs' ability to handle intricate patterns.

Despite their potential, challenges such as noise in quantum systems and scalability limitations must be addressed. Hybrid quantum-classical models, where quantum kernels are computed on quantum hardware while the remaining processes run on classical systems, provide a practical pathway for near-term QSVM deployment [15].

10.5.4 Quantum Neural Networks (QNNs)

Quantum neural networks adapt classical neural network architectures to leverage quantum computing principles. QNNs encode input data into quantum states and apply quantum gates as analogs to activation functions, enabling efficient processing of high-dimensional data.

QNNs adjust classical neural network architectures in the application of quantum computing principles. QNNs encode input data into quantum states and apply quantum gates as analogs to activation functions, allowing efficient processing of high-dimensional data.

In principle, training a QNN is similar to classical gradient-based approaches in that it minimizes a certain cost function over the parameters of quantum circuits. The core element in QNNs is variational quantum circuits (VQCs). These VQCs are flexible models that can represent complex functions.

QNNs have shown promise for tasks such as quantum chemistry simulation, natural language processing, and generative modeling. For instance, qGANs can generate realistic data samples that can aid applications in creative industries and data augmentation [16].

A QNN is far more intuitive compared to classical networks regarding the ability to depict and process nonlinear data relationships. However, scalability and robustness pose challenges, thereby demanding the improvement of quantum hardware and error correction techniques.

10.5.5 Applications of Quantum Machine Learning

Quantum machine learning, or QML, is quickly emerging as the new leader in predictive analytics and beyond. Its application goes to many different fields of human activity, giving new transformations into solving complex data-intensive problems [17].

1. **Predictive Analytics:** Predictive models using QML offer increased accuracy and speed, which is extremely helpful for finance, healthcare, and marketing, such as being able to predict stock market trends and patient outcomes or to optimize marketing strategies.
2. **Optimization:** Optimization is one of the biggest categories of real-world problems that includes supply chain logistics, energy grid management, and portfolio optimization. Quantum optimization algorithms, when integrated with ML, provide faster and more accurate solutions than their classical counterparts.
3. **Natural Sciences:** In chemistry and physics, QML facilitates the discovery of novel materials and drugs by accelerating the simulation of molecular interactions and energy landscapes.
4. **Cybersecurity:** Quantum ML strengthens anomaly detection and threat analysis in cybersecurity, helping organizations respond proactively to potential attacks.
5. **Autonomous Systems:** Applications in robotics and autonomous vehicles benefit from QML's ability to process sensory data and optimize decision-making in real time.

As quantum hardware advances, QML applications will become integrated in multiple sectors in a shape and form that could solve seemingly previously unsolvable challenges. Within a world where the integration of approaches makes room for the advancement of quantum and classical elements side by side, it leaves QML in quite a position at the start of the AI revolution within all those sectors [18].

10.6 ETHICAL CONSIDERATIONS IN QUANTUM TECHNOLOGIES: PRIVACY, SECURITY, AND SOCIETAL IMPACTS

From artificial intelligence to cybersecurity, quantum technologies—in particular, quantum computing and quantum cryptography—have the potential to completely transform several industries. But these developments also bring with them important ethical questions, mostly related to privacy, security, and wider societal effects. To guarantee that quantum technologies be created and used ethically, these ethical issues must be addressed.

10.6.1 Privacy Issues

The effect of quantum technology on digital privacy is among the most serious ethical issues. The enormous processing power of quantum computing directly threatens the security of existing encryption protocols. A sufficiently sophisticated quantum computer may readily crack public key cryptography systems, like RSA and ECC, which protect anything from private communications to financial transactions, by applying Shor's algorithm. The protection of sensitive data, such as business, governmental, and personal information, is called into question by this possible encryption compromise. To counter these dangers, mitigation techniques including quantum-resistant algorithms and post-quantum cryptography (PQC) are presently being developed. Determining who will have access to these technologies and how they will be implemented, however, presents ethical challenges. A major ethical concern is ensuring that quantum-safe encryption is distributed fairly and avoiding abuse by hostile groups or totalitarian governments [19].

10.6.2 Security Difficulties

The security concerns of quantum technologies are also complicated. Although the laws of quantum physics promise impenetrable encryption in quantum cryptography, especially in quantum key distribution (QKD), its use and regulation necessitate rigorous ethical consideration. There is a chance that strong organizations would dominate quantum-secure communication networks, resulting in uneven access to secure communications. Cybercriminals and state-sponsored actors may also take advantage of quantum-enhanced hacking techniques, which could pose serious cybersecurity risks. To create legal frameworks that stop the weaponization of quantum technologies and guarantee their moral application in cybersecurity, governments and international organizations must cooperate.

10.6.3 Broad Effects on Society

Quantum technologies have the power to transform economies, industries, and social structures in addition to privacy and security. Drug development, material research, and optimization issues could all be transformed by quantum computing, which would have enormous positive effects on humanity. These developments could, however, also lead to workforce relocation, which would exacerbate socioeconomic disparities. Policies for worker reskilling and fair access to quantum education and resources must be part of ethical considerations.

The possibility that quantum technology would intensify already-existing geopolitical tensions is another significant social worry. Nations' competition for quantum supremacy may result in technological monopolies, widening power disparities, and escalating instability on a worldwide scale. Instead of escalating divisions, ethical governance must guarantee that quantum improvements are utilized for the benefit of all [20].

10.6.4 Future Aspects and Ethical Governance

Policymakers, technologists, and ethicists must work together to create international guidelines for the advancement and use of quantum technology in order to address these moral dilemmas. Ethical governance frameworks should be centered on research transparency, fair access to quantum innovations, and protections against abuse [21].

10.7 FUTURE TRENDS IN QUANTUM COMPUTING AND CRYPTOGRAPHY

Quantum computing is progressing rapidly, with several key trends shaping its future:

Increased Qubit Stability and Scalability: Current quantum computers struggle with decoherence and error rates. Future advancements in quantum error correction (e.g., surface codes, topological qubits) will enable more stable, fault-tolerant quantum systems.

Quantum Supremacy Expansion: While Google and others have demonstrated quantum supremacy for specific tasks, the next step is achieving practical quantum advantage in real-world applications like optimization, drug discovery, and complex simulations.

Hybrid Quantum-Classical Systems: As fully independent quantum computers remain a distant goal, hybrid models will integrate quantum capabilities with classical supercomputers, accelerating computations in fields like AI and cryptography.

Room-Temperature Quantum Computing: Advancements in materials science, such as photonic and diamond-based qubits, could lead to quantum computers that operate without the need for extreme cooling.

10.7.1 Prospects for Quantum Computing and Cryptography in the Future

Temperature in the Room Quantum Computing: Developments in materials science, including photonic and diamond-based qubits, may result in the development of quantum computers that don't require extremely high cooling.

10.7.2 Cryptography's Prospects in the Quantum Era

Traditional cryptography techniques are seriously challenged by quantum computing, which has resulted in new developments in secure communication:

Post-Quantum Cryptography (PQC): Researchers are creating encryption algorithms that are immune to quantum attacks, a technique known as post-quantum cryptography (PQC). To replace RSA and ECC, the National Institute of Standards and Technology (NIST) is standardizing PQC algorithms such as CRYSTALS-Kyber and CRYSTALS-Dilithium.

Quantum Key Distribution (QKD): By identifying eavesdropping attempts, QKD uses the ideas of quantum mechanics to enable extremely secure communication. Quantum-secure networks are already being implemented by nations and businesses.

Homomorphic and Lattice-Based Encryption: Lattice-based techniques will be the foundation of future cryptographic approaches, enabling computations on encrypted data without the need for decryption and guaranteeing increased security in cloud computing and artificial intelligence applications.

10.8 DIFFICULTIES AND OBSTACLES

Despite these fascinating developments, many challenges still need to be addressed:

Error Rates and Decoherence: Advances in quantum error correction and stability are necessary to address the high error rates that still plague quantum computers.

Scalability Problems: Adding more high-quality qubits without sacrificing coherence is still a difficult technical task.

Global Standardization and Use: Post-quantum cryptography standards will take time to implement, and infrastructure modifications and compatibility issues may prevent broad use.

Ethical and Security Risks: As powerful quantum computers become available, security flaws could arise, making international collaboration necessary for safe transitions [22].

10.9 CASE STUDIES

10.9.1 Case Study 1: Google's Achievement of Quantum Supremacy

Google's Sycamore quantum processor completed a certain calculation in 200 seconds in 2019 that would have taken thousands of years for the most potent supercomputer in the world. This significant achievement paved the way for further optimization and machine learning applications by showcasing the potential of quantum machines to surpass traditional computers in specific tasks.

10.9.2 Case Study 2: Quantum-Secure Communication with China's Micius Satellite

The first quantum communication satellite, the Micius, was launched by China, allowing for secure data transmission using QKD. The first intercontinental QKD-secured video conversation between Beijing and Vienna was successfully demonstrated by China in 2020. This innovation demonstrated that quantum encryption is feasible for use in worldwide cybersecurity applications.

Before becoming widely used, quantum computing must overcome several significant obstacles. Stability requires improvements in quantum error correction because error rates and decoherence are still substantial. Another challenge is scalability because it can be difficult to maintain coherence as the number of qubits increases. It will take time for the industry to adjust to post-quantum cryptography standards without interfering with current systems. Furthermore, the danger posed by quantum computers to conventional encryption raises ethical and security issues as well as cybersecurity issues. Before large-scale quantum attacks become feasible, international cooperation is necessary to create quantum-safe security measures. To fully utilize quantum technology in computing and cryptography [23], several challenges must be resolved.

10.9.3 Case Study 3: Practical Uses of IBM's Quantum Roadmap

With the creation of the first commercially available quantum computer, the IBM Quantum System One, IBM is leading the way in quantum computing. The company works with Daimler to further battery development, especially for electric vehicles, and with ExxonMobil to enhance energy processes. These initiatives show how complicated issues that are beyond the scope of classical computing can be solved by quantum computing, revolutionizing entire sectors. Scaling quantum systems, enhancing error correction, and combining quantum and AI for improved performance are all on IBM's plan. Real-world applications in materials science, logistics, and pharmaceuticals will grow as more industries embrace quantum technology, opening up new avenues for productivity and creativity. IBM's initiatives demonstrate how quantum computing has the potential to soon revolutionize several industries.

10.10 FUTURE QUANTUM COMPUTING DEVELOPMENTS

Many significant trends are influencing the future of quantum computing, which is developing quickly:

Enhanced Qubit Stability and Scalability: Decoherence and error rates are problems for existing quantum computers. More robust, fault-tolerant quantum systems will be made possible by upcoming developments in quantum error correction (such as surface codes and topological qubits). The next stage is to achieve a practical quantum edge in real-world applications like as drug discovery, optimization, and sophisticated simulations, even though Google and others have shown quantum supremacy for particular jobs.

Quantum-Classical Hybrid Systems: Since completely autonomous quantum computers are still a way off, hybrid models will combine quantum and classical supercomputer capabilities to speed up calculations in domains like artificial intelligence and cryptography.

10.10.1 Scaling Quantum Computing

Scaling quantum computing from the very experimental research to fully functional commercial applications is a massive challenge. The bottlenecks are the areas of hardware, software, and infrastructure that need improvements before quantum computing can realize its full potential.

Challenges in Hardware: Quantum systems are very fragile. Qubits are known to be quite noisy and prone to decoherence. Scalable quantum hardware, therefore, would call for innovations in error correction, connectivity between qubits, and cooling systems. One approach is through superconducting qubits, trapped ions, and photonic systems. Increasing the number of qubits, along with good fidelity levels of qubits, is also necessary to achieve computational advantages.

Challenges in Software: Developing robust quantum algorithms and programming environments is important. Quantum software needs to cross the chasm between theoretical algorithms and practical implementation, which usually requires hybrid quantum-classical frameworks. Compilers, debugging tools, and user interfaces must also be improved so that quantum systems can be opened up for much wider access.

Future Prospects for Commercialization: Despite the significant challenges faced while commercializing the process of quantum computing, quite crucial steps have been taken in this regard. Companies like IBM, Google, and Rigetti introduced cloud-based platforms for quantum computing that allowed researchers and developers to perform experiments on a quantum system. Pharmaceuticals, finance, and logistics begin to invest in quantum solutions to real-world problems.

As quantum computing advances further, academia, industry, and governments will have to work together to scale up the technology. The avenues of quantum computing that change industries would include the standardization of protocols, building quantum-ready infrastructure, and addressing gaps in the workforce.

10.10.2 Ethics and the Impact of Quantum Technologies

The transformative potential of quantum computing also brings to the forefront ethical and societal considerations. As quantum technologies mature, their implications on security, privacy, and society must be addressed.

Security and Privacy: Quantum computing attacks current cryptographic systems directly; Shor's algorithm may well break commonly used encryption. Solutions such as QKD exist through quantum cryptography, but there is a vulnerable transition period until post-quantum cryptographic standards are in full use. So safeguarding sensitive information becomes an ethical obligation during this transitional phase.

Societal Implications: Quantum technology will further sharpen extant inequalities by creating a narrow divide between quantum-enabling and nonquantum societies. Quantum-enabled early-access countries or corporations will be poised to enjoy disproportionately larger benefits from innovation, security gains, and advantages in economic development. Equitable access to resources in quantum should thus be ensured in the prevention of such technological disparities.

Preparing for a Quantum-Enabled Future: Prepare society for a quantum-enabled future. Governments, industries, and educational institutions need to collaborate and prepare society for the quantum era. This will include regulations for ethical usage, investment in public awareness, and education programs for building a quantum-literate workforce.

Proactive management of these ethical challenges will enable society to take advantage of the benefits offered by quantum technologies while minimizing their risks.

A quantum future full of promise thus demands careful stewardship so that its impact can be positive, equitable, and sustainable.

10.11 CONCLUSION

Quantum computing is perhaps one of the most important technological advances of the 21st century, representing a combination of the fundamental principles of quantum mechanics and innovative computing. Solving problems that have been deemed by everyone as too big for ordinary computer systems to handle, quantum computing would unlock some incredible applications in cryptography, machine learning, optimization, and scientific discovery, which would unlock unbreakable cryptographic protocols, accelerate drug design, and optimize global logistics.

But with such huge potential comes equal responsibility. The disruption that quantum technologies pose to the current cryptographic systems emphasizes the need for global collaboration in developing post-quantum security standards. Its development and deployment must be guided by ethical considerations, such as equitable access, societal implications, and preventing technological monopolies.

Scalable and robust quantum computing is challenging; today's path involves getting rid of hardware fragility, noise, and software complexity. Yet moving forward is the steady convergence of academia, industry, and government initiatives. Through these efforts, innovation will be fostered, quantum-ready infrastructure will be built, and a quantum-literate workforce will be cultivated, ensuring that humanity enters a future of seamless classical and quantum systems integration.

Quantum computing is a paradigm shift with the potential to address some of the most vital challenges of our time, not just some technological milestone. On the threshold of this new quantum era, its evolution must be done with foresight, inclusivity, and a sense of ethical integrity so that its benefits may be used for the betterment of society and advancement of knowledge.

GLOSSARY

Quantum Computing: A computing paradigm that leverages quantum mechanics to perform computations far beyond classical computers' capabilities.

Qubit: The fundamental unit of quantum information, similar to a classical bit but capable of existing in superposition states.

Quantum Supremacy: The point at which a quantum computer can solve a problem faster than the best classical supercomputers.

Quantum Advantage: The practical application of quantum computing to solve real-world problems more efficiently than classical computing.

Quantum Decoherence: The loss of quantum state information due to interactions with the environment, leading to computation errors.

Quantum Error Correction: Techniques designed to protect quantum information from errors caused by decoherence and other quantum noise.

Post-Quantum Cryptography (PQC): Encryption methods resistant to attacks by quantum computers, developed to replace traditional RSA and ECC cryptography.

Quantum Key Distribution (QKD): A cryptographic method that enables secure communication by detecting eavesdropping attempts using quantum mechanics principles.

Lattice-Based Cryptography: A post-quantum cryptographic approach relying on complex mathematical lattice structures for encryption.

Homomorphic Encryption: A form of encryption that allows computations to be performed on encrypted data without decrypting it first, ensuring privacy and security.

Hybrid Quantum-Classical Systems: Computing models that integrate quantum and classical computing to leverage the strengths of both.

Topological Qubits: A theoretical qubit design that is highly resistant to environmental noise and could lead to more stable quantum computers.

REFERENCES

[1] Ayub, A., S. A. Pereira, M. A. Thayyil and M. Ayub, (2024). "From Bytes to Qubits: The Cybersecurity Implications of Quantum Advancements," in *Interantional Journal of Scientific Research in Engineering and Management*, vol. 8, no. 8.

[2] Bennett, C. H. and P. W. Shor, "Quantum Information Theory," in *IEEE Transactions on Information Theory*, vol. 44, no. 6, pp. 2724–2742, Oct. 1998, https://doi.org/10.1109/18.720553.

[3] Biswas, A., A. Banerji, P. Chandravanshi, R. Kumar and R. P. Singh, "Experimental Side Channel Analysis of BB84 QKD Source," in *IEEE Journal of Quantum Electronics*, vol. 57, no. 6, pp. 1–7, Dec. 2021, Art no. 8000207, https://doi.org/10.1109/JQE.2021.3111332.

[4] Bruscino, C. et al., "High Performance Superconducting Nanowire Single Photon Detectors for QKD Applications," in *IEEE Transactions on Applied Superconductivity*, vol. 34, no. 3, pp. 1–5, May 2024, Art no. 2200205, https://doi.org/10.1109/TASC.2024.3355878.

[5] Coccia, M., S. Roshani and M. Mosleh, "Evolution of Quantum Computing: Theoretical and Innovation Management Implications for Emerging Quantum Industry," in *IEEE Transactions on Engineering Management*, vol. 71, pp. 2270–2280, 2024, https://doi.org/10.1109/TEM.2022.3175633.

[6] Dupuis, F., O. Fawzi and S. Wehner, "Entanglement Sampling and Applications," in *IEEE Transactions on Information Theory*, vol. 61, no. 2, pp. 1093–1112, Feb. 2015, https://doi.org/10.1109/TIT.2014.2371464.

[7] Durr-E-Shahwar, M. I., A. B. Altamimi, W. Khan, S. Hussain and M. Alsaffar, "Quantum Cryptography for Future Networks Security: A Systematic Review," in *IEEE Access*, vol. 12, pp. 180048–180078, 2024, https://doi.org/10.1109/ACCESS.2024.3504815.

[8] Gaur, B. and H. Thapliyal, "Novel Optimized Designs of Modulo 2n+1 Adder for Quantum Computing," in *IEEE Transactions on Very Large Scale Integration (VLSI) Systems*, vol. 32, no. 9, pp. 1759–1763, Sept. 2024, https://doi.org/10.1109/TVLSI.2024.3418930.

[9] Ji, X., B. Wang, F. Hu, C. Wang and H. Zhang, "New Advanced Computing Architecture for Cryptography Design and Analysis by D-Wave Quantum Annealer," in *Tsinghua Science and Technology*, vol. 27, no. 4, pp. 751–759, Aug. 2022, https://doi.org/10.26599/TST.2021.9010022.

[10] Kebapci, B. et al., "FPGA-Based Implementation of an Underwater Quantum Key Distribution System with BB84 Protocol," in *IEEE Photonics Journal*, vol. 15, no. 4, pp. 1–10, Aug. 2023, Art no. 7600210, https://doi.org/10.1109/JPHOT.2023.3287493.

[11] Kumar, A. et al., "Survey of Promising Technologies for Quantum Drones and Networks," in *IEEE Access*, vol. 9, pp. 125868–125911, 2021, https://doi.org/10.1109/ACCESS.2021.3109816.

[12] Li, J. et al., "A Survey on Quantum Cryptography," in *Chinese Journal of Electronics*, vol. 27, no. 2, pp. 223–228, Mar. 2018, https://doi.org/10.1049/cje.2018.01.017.

[13] Munnix, M. C., A. Lochmann, D. Bimberg and V. A. Haisler, "Modeling Highly Efficient RCLED-Type Quantum-Dot-Based Single Photon Emitters," in *IEEE Journal of Quantum Electronics*, vol. 45, no. 9, pp. 1084–1088, Sept. 2009, https://doi.org/10.1109/JQE.2009.2020995.

[14] Nagpal, S. et al., "Quantum Computing Integrated Patterns for Real-Time Cryptography in Assorted Domains," in *IEEE Access*, vol. 12, pp. 132317–132331, 2024, https://doi.org/10.1109/ACCESS.2024.3401162.

[15] Pan, D. et al., "The Evolution of Quantum Secure Direct Communication: On the Road to the Qinternet," in *IEEE Communications Surveys & Tutorials*, vol. 26, no. 3, pp. 1898–1949, Thirdquarter 2024, https://doi.org/10.1109/COMST.2024.3367535.

[16] Putranto, D. S. C., R. W. Wardhani, H. T. Larasati and H. Kim, "Space and Time-Efficient Quantum Multiplier in Post Quantum Cryptography Era," in *IEEE Access*, vol. 11, pp. 21848–21862, 2023, https://doi.org/10.1109/ACCESS.2023.3252504.

[17] Ricci, S., P. Dobias, L. Malina, J. Hajny and P. Jedlicka, "Hybrid Keys in Practice: Combining Classical, Quantum and Post-Quantum Cryptography," in *IEEE Access*, vol. 12, pp. 23206–23219, 2024, https://doi.org/10.1109/ACCESS.2024.3364520.

[18] Shafique, M. A., A. Munir and I. Latif, "Quantum Computing: Circuits, Algorithms, and Applications," in *IEEE Access*, vol. 12, pp. 22296–22314, 2024, https://doi.org/10.1109/ACCESS.2024.3362955.

[19] Shim, K.-S., B. Kim and W. Lee, "Research on Quantum Key, Distribution Key and Post-Quantum Cryptography Key Applied Protocols for Data Science and Web Security," in *Journal of Web Engineering*, vol. 23, no. 6, pp. 813–830, Sept. 2024, https://doi.org/10.13052/jwe1540-9589.2365.

[20] Sutradhar, K. and H. Om, "A Generalized Quantum Protocol for Secure Multiparty Summation," in *IEEE Transactions on Circuits and Systems II: Express Briefs*, vol. 67, no. 12, pp. 2978–2982, Dec. 2020, https://doi.org/10.1109/TCSII.2020.2989447.

[21] Ul Ain, N. et al., "A Novel Approach Based on Quantum Key Distribution Using BB84 and E91 Protocol for Resilient Encryption and Eavesdropper Detection," in *IEEE Access*, vol. 13, pp. 32819–32833, 2025, https://doi.org/10.1109/ACCESS.2025.3539178.

[22] Yang, Z., H. Alfauri, B. Farkiani, R. Jain, R. D. Pietro and A. Erbad, "A Survey and Comparison of Post-Quantum and Quantum Blockchains," in *IEEE Communications Surveys & Tutorials*, vol. 26, no. 2, pp. 967–1002, Secondquarter 2024, https://doi.org/10.1109/COMST.2023.3325761.

[23] Yang, Z., M. Zolanvari and R. Jain, "A Survey of Important Issues in Quantum Computing and Communications," in *IEEE Communications Surveys & Tutorials*, vol. 25, no. 2, pp. 1059–1094, Secondquarter 2023, https://doi.org/10.1109/COMST.2023.3254481.

11 Next-Gen Quantum Computing—The Fusion of Atoms and Photonic Innovation

Ashok Kumar Patel, K. Saradhi, Gudditi Chetan, Ganesuni Aasish Chowdary, Beebi Naseeba, and Nagendra Panini Challa

11.1 INTRODUCTION

Quantum computing is treated as the most technological advancement in history of computer technology. It has witnessed a drastic changes or major improvements in with involvement of ideas from wide variety of technologies, like integrating photonics and atomic systems marks the change of paradigm in quantum computing. Both the quantum system's state and its accuracy can be scaled easily and transmit data at high speed, which creates the perfect, efficient, and scalable quantum systems. To build fault-tolerant, scalable quantum systems, scientists are experimenting and trying find a stable energy which makes this one possible. The application of quantum technologies in the domains like cryptography optimization and materials science can take the domain's technological advancement to a whole new level. This innovative approach of combining theoretical quantum mechanics and real-world applications making it practical and influential. Even though the fusion of atomic accuracy and photonic speeds with current technology needs to overcome the set of drawbacks that include like vulnerability to errors and scaling difficult. This hybrid method takes computing techniques to next level while considering real-life scenarios as challenges, which revolutionize sectors from secure communication networks to sophisticated simulation upon maturation, which leads to new challenges and new domains. This chapter mainly discusses on how the combination of photonic and atomic systems revolutionizes the present existing quantum computing. [1]

11.2 OVERVIEW

Quantum computing exploits the current quantum's state and its entanglement and in comparison, to the traditional systems. Atomic systems, which include the trapping of ions or neutral atoms, are considered viable options for qubits due to their stable

DOI: 10.1201/9781003538950-13

nature and long coherence times. whereas photonics can provide high data transmission speeds and serve as a platform for quantum networks with reduced latency. Synergistic application of these technologies can potentially lead to build highly efficient and accurate quantum computers. Through the physical attributes of the system like speed and scalability, the proposed methods overcome the current limitations and lessen the time required in creation of commercially viable systems. This paper is a detailed discussion of the various elements that make this fusion possible, where it can reshape the computational landscape. This merging of atomic and photonic technologies lies at the core of next-generation quantum systems. Atomic qubits provide highest stability nature, and photonic platforms accommodate fast data communication and scalability. Combined, they provide a resilient platform for distributed computing and quantum networking. This introduction establishes the foundation on which the reader can understand the main technologies involved, their complementary nature, and challenges in developing harmonious hybrid frameworks. The opportunity of this platform is that it can combine speed and precision in a way that will lead to commercially viable quantum solutions. [2]

11.3 FUNDAMENTALS AND CHALLENGES OF ATOMIC QUBITS

Quantum computing is based on qubits, quantum information units, which utilize superposition and entanglement to execute calculations exponentially more rapidly than classical computers. Of the numerous physical systems employed to store qubits, atomic qubits have been one of the most promising because they are intrinsically stable, possess long coherence times, and are precisely controllable. These qubits are implemented in isolated atoms, normally trapped and controlled through electromagnetic fields, with minimal decoherence to ensure. They differ from superconducting qubits, which need to be cooled to cryogenic temperatures. Atomic qubits function at room temperature or modest cooling, minimizing infrastructure expenses. Nonetheless, the integration into scalable quantum systems is still a challenge with the current limitations. It's interaction with light can make it possible to implement photon-mediated quantum gates and quantum networking with interconnectivity among its nodes. This subsection discusses the types of atomic qubits, their coherence characteristics, and the problems involved in their realizations. [3]

11.3.1 Atomic Qubit Mechanics

Atomic qubits, the basic lines of quantum computing, are mostly recognized with two primary methods: trapped ions and neutral atoms. Both methods show the leverage of quantum states of single atoms. They can be controlled with unique level accuracy to store and process them. These systems are among the promising candidates in creating a powerful quantum computer because of their attributes, like stability, coherence times, and capacity to perform quantum operations at high precision. In contrast, of all the strengths and advantages of individual systems, trapped-ion and neutral-atom qubits also possess disadvantages, and hybrid systems that capitalize on the best of both systems are being pursued with very much of high interest to work around these deficiencies and enable large-scale quantum computing.

11.3.1.1 Trapped-Ion Qubits

Trapped-ion qubits are known to be one of the best approaches in using atomic qubits. Here, charged atoms or ions are trapped inside an electromagnetic field inside a vacuum chamber surrounded in linear arrays. The EM traps are designed in a way to shield against external interference to enable precise control of the ions. Laser pulses are used to control the internal energy states of the ions as they essentially carry out quantum operations by moving ions from one energy level to another. These operations are based on precisely controlled laser frequencies, allowing gate operations with high-precision-based settings that are critical for quantum computing. One of the major benefits is high Coulomb interactions of the trapped ions, which can be formed as a result because of the electrostatic forces created between the charged particles. These interactions not only serve but also stabilize the ions while allowing leads to the creation of entanglement—which is considered to be one of the major characteristics of quantum computing that helps in making it possible to create quantum states of qubits. This particular aspect makes trapped-ion qubits well-positioned for applications such as quantum error correction, quantum communication over long distances, and the construction of large-scale quantum networks. The scalability of trapped-ion systems is only to develop large arrays of qubits, but it is also problematic. It becomes increasingly challenging to manage and control the interactions, and technical problems like ion motional heating and complexity of arranging ions in a stable way in large quantities can occur. Despite these challenges, a considerable amount of success has been achieved in scaling ion-trap systems, and ongoing efforts are trying to overcome these constraints, such as through advances in trap design, laser technology, and error-correction methods.

11.3.1.2 Neutral-Atom Qubits

Neutral-atom qubits are based on a distinct method where atoms are trapped and manipulated by optical traps or optical lattices. In an optical lattice, laser beams are crossed where they form a periodic potential, essentially in forming a grid or "trap" in which individual atoms can be placed. These lattices enable the accurate control of the positions of neutral atoms existing, which can subsequently be employed as qubits. The benefit of this method is its scalability: large arrays of neutral atoms can be produced and controlled at once with high accuracy. This renders neutral atom systems a promising candidate for the construction of large-scale quantum computers. The primary difficulty with neutral-atom qubits is the interaction between the atoms. In contrast to trapped ions, which are subject to strong Coulomb interactions because they are electrically charged, neutral-atom interactions are much weaker and so are harder to entangle. To counteract this, many methods such as the Rydberg blockade have been created. In this particular method, very excited atomic states (Rydberg states) are utilized to create strong interactions between neighboring atoms, which allows entanglement and provides a means of quantum gate operations. Laser fields and high-precision engineering prevent deleterious effects, which include decoherence and fidelity loss in quantum operations. Despite having many disadvantages, the neutral-atom method has several advantages. The usage of optical lattices permits the alignment and control of vast numbers of qubits in an accurate and ordered fashion, which simplifies the scalability of a very large number of qubits. Moreover, neutral atoms are less vulnerable to some kinds of noise, like electromagnetic interference, and are much highly controllable using laser. These advantages make neutral-atom qubits promising candidates for future large-scale quantum computing systems. [4]

11.3.1.3 Hybrid Systems

Although both neutral atoms and trapped ions do possess peculiar and unique benefits, they also possess drawbacks that limit the scalability and efficiency of quantum computers. Trapped ions have strong interactions and high-fidelity gate operations but are limited when it comes to scaling up qubit numbers. Neutral atoms always provide a superior scalability and strong control but are hindered again when weaker interactions are made, making it challenging to entangle.

To resolve these problems, scientists are working on hybrid systems that take care of both of the advantages of trapped ions and neutral atoms. These hybrid systems are meant to take advantage of taking great control of largely interacting trapped ions with respect to the scalability of neutral atoms. For an instance, a possible strategy is made to leverage neutral atoms as the primary computational qubits, and trapped ions are considered as a tool for transferring quantum information or the creation of entanglement between widely separated qubits.

Hybrid systems in this configuration may provide a route for breaking the limitations of each technology, resulting in more stable and scalable quantum computers. Besides hybrid systems, there exist some other methods like quantum error correction and developments in quantum communication that have better designs for traps aiding in overcoming the scalability issues of atomic qubits. With more research and development coming, atomic qubits are being developed with trapped ions, neutral atoms, or a combination of both, which is anticipated to dominate quantum computing in the future. Atomic qubits, either realized with trapped ions or neutral atoms, are the cornerstone of contemporary quantum computing.

Qubits utilize the quantum states of single atoms and can be controlled with radical precision through methods such as electromagnetic fields and laser pulses. Trapped-ion qubits tend to be strong because of the Coulomb interactions and high fidelity, for which they are considered to be best suitable for quantum networks and error correction, but they are difficult to scale up. Neutral-atom qubits are also scalable and flexible in controlling big arrays of atoms but also suffer due to weaker interactions. Hybrid systems that utilize both methods are currently being pursued to leverage the strengths of both, providing a promising avenue for more powerful and scalable quantum computing. [5]

11.3.1.4 The Architecture Contains Two Primary Systems

Trapped Ions: The system starts with a vacuum chamber. Here the ions are trapped by using electromagnetic fields. These ions are represented as charged particles (+/–), where these are carefully controlled by laser beams that move the ions between different energy levels. A quantum gate is used to perform these quantum operations on these ions, enabling them to act as qubits. These ions can be linked even in long distances via a qubit link, which is very essential for building quantum networks. In order ensure

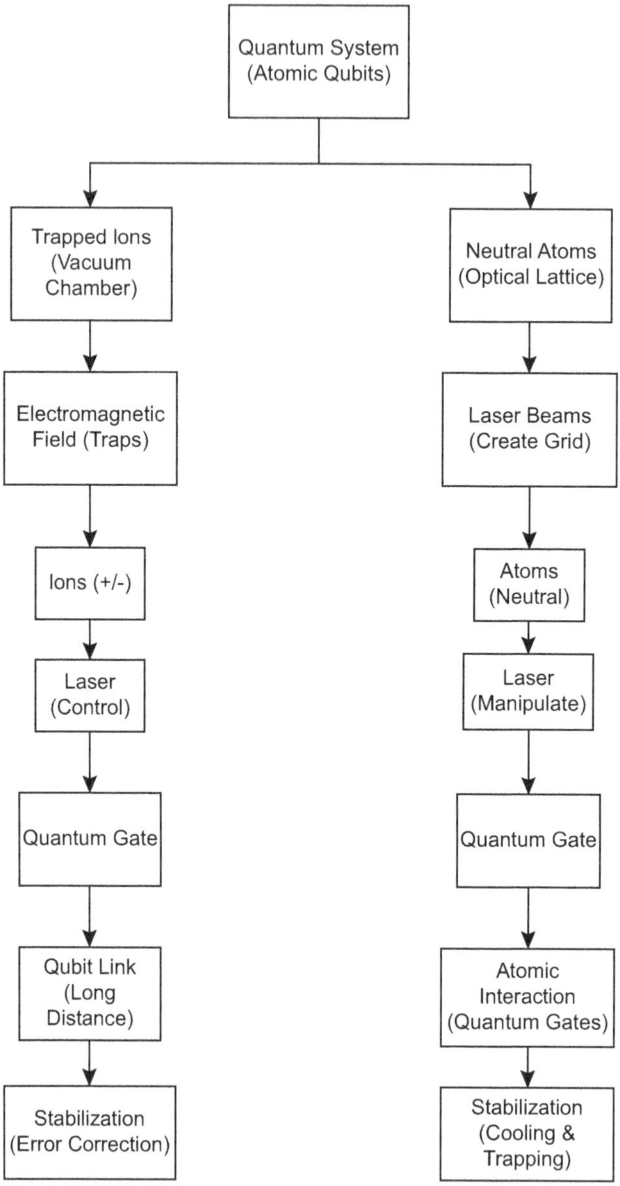

FIGURE 11.1 Architecture of atomic qubits in quantum computing: trapped ions and neutral atoms.

the stability, the system includes error correction methods and stabilization techniques that address environmental noise and external interference, while keeping the quantum states of the ions intact, as shown in Figure 11.1.

Neutral Atoms: In this setup, atoms are trapped in an optical lattice formed by the crossing made by laser beams, creating a grid that confines the atoms.

> Then the neutral atoms interact with one another in the lattice, and they are controlled by the other existing laser beams. Quantum gates are used on these atoms to facilitate quantum operations, which is similar to trapped ions but in the lattice structure. The atomic interactions at the lattice points provide a means of carrying out quantum gates. Similar to that of trapped ions, the system of neutral atoms also involves stabilizing techniques, while including cooling and trapping, safeguarding the delicate quantum states of the atoms. [4]

Still, one of the greatest challenges of atomic qubits is to maintain their superpositions intact. Environmental noise or temperature fluctuations can cause these fragile states to collapse. To avoid or reduce this, scientists are developing more effective error-correcting techniques and more effective trapping schemes that carefully monitor for noise or any kind of fluctuations. They're also attempting to minimize the use of intricate vacuum systems and cooling processes, which would make atomic qubits more suitable for real-world applications. When these challenges are overcome, atomic qubits are likely to be central or most suitable atoms in the development of robust and scalable quantum computers. [5]

Both neutral atoms and trapped ions have their respective advantages and unique traits that make them suitable for different applications in quantum computing. For applications requiring high precision, trapped ions are ideal due to their extended coherence periods and remarkably high gate fidelities. On the other hand, neutral atoms provide a more scalable platform that can support a large number of qubits in a single system. Hybrid methods with advantage for neutral atoms as well as for trapped ions may gain further acceptance with advancing quantum computer technology. Moreover, also newer quantum networking strategies, distribution of entanglement, and correction approaches are explored for the further optimization of efficiency as well as the scalability of systems. Indeed, realizable large-scale future implementation of quantum computers is best envisaged through atomic qubit platforms. [6]

11.3.2 Coherence and Quantum State Stability

A key requirement for any quantum computing system is the coherence time, which determines how long a qubit retains its quantum state before it decoheres due to environmental interactions. Atomic qubits are entirely based on trapped ions and neutral atoms, which exhibit exceptionally long coherence times, and they often surpass those of superconducting qubits. This is mainly because atoms, unlike artificial quantum systems, are naturally identical and do not suffer from material defects. Despite having these advantages, maintaining coherence requires more sophisticated isolation techniques and precise control mechanisms, like magnetic field fluctuations, stray electromagnetic radiation, and atomic motion, which can lead to decoherence, which limits and restricts effective computation time. In order to minimize these issues, researchers have been using vacuum chambers, including active noise cancelation, and using advanced error correction techniques. These efforts ensure that atomic qubits can perform high-fidelity quantum operations, making them ideal for fault-tolerant quantum computing. [7]

11.3.3 Scalability and Error Management

Scalability, which is a primary attribute of but also an issue in quantum computing, represents a major problem in the pursuit of large-scale and multi-qubit systems. Segmented traps have been seen as one of the promising solution to these problems, and they have displayed such a potential in addressing and solving these challenges. The deployment of such traps, however, requires giving the utmost care in maintaining the critical vacuum conditions and also successfully shielding the system from unwanted external noise. This particular highly resource-consuming maintenance highlights the sophistication involved in obtaining the best possible performance and its dependability in quantum systems.

Whenever the system is faced such challenges, it becomes inevitable to design solid error correction algorithms where it reverses the effects of external disturbance and helps in securing the system against tampering and data lose. Recent advances in electromagnetic confinement methodologies have enhanced qubit control efficiency, with potential insights into superior quantum processor efficiency. In addition, technological advancements in segmented ion traps have made a major enhancement in multi-qubit operations capability, with a future where hosting more complex quantum computations is considered to be normal. Although this has occurred, the route toward scalable quantum technology and coherence preservation over longer arrays is a tough technological barrier being tackled actively by researchers. The development of advanced error correction protocols is at the vanguard of such initiatives, which is aimed at countering the negative impact of a host of environmental elements that pose threats to system coherence and stability.

As quantum computing drives the limits of traditional computing techniques and paradigms further, scientists are not only trying to improve hardware designs but also trying to optimize the software and protocols that form the basis of these revolutionary technologies. The pursuit of fault-tolerant quantum processors requires a multi-concept-based approach, which includes all the breakthroughs in hardware engineering, error correction techniques, and theoretical breakthroughs in quantum information processing. By merging all these varied concepts and components, the quantum computing world seeks to realize the full potential of quantum processors, opening the doors to a new age of computational capability and problem-solving ability that can transform a wide range of fields from cryptography to material simulations and many more new domains. In the never-ending quest for technological superiority, the path to scalable quantum computing unwinds with every breakthrough, holding the promise of a future where the limits of computation are rewritten. [8]

11.4 PHOTONICS IN QUANTUM COMPUTING

Photonics has a central place in quantum computing, providing an avenue to quick, scalable, and low-noise quantum information processing. As opposed to matter-based qubits, which experience decoherence resulting from interactions with the environment, photonic qubits utilize the quantum nature of light, for example, polarization, phase, and time-bin encoding, to transport and manipulate quantum information.

Photons move at light speed and exert minimal interaction with their environment, which renders them suitable for entanglement distribution over long distances and quantum communication. Waveguides, beam splitters, and phase shifters can be used for precisely controlling photons, thanks to advancements in integrated photonic circuits. The entangled pairs of photons are also considered the basis for quantum teleportation and cryptography techniques like quantum key distribution (QKD). Nevertheless, despite its benefits, photonic quantum computing can still fall short in terms of implementing the deterministic two-qubit gates and efficiently generating single photons. The principles of photonic qubits, entanglement, and the design of optical quantum circuits for computation will be covered in this section.

11.4.1 Role of Photonics

Photonics does play a key role in the development of efficient, scalable, and quick quantum computers. The process building robust quantum systems that can solve complex problems that are considered to be hard for traditional computer systems to handle requires the ability to process and transport quantum information by using the unique properties of light, which photonic systems enable. Photonics is now becoming an essential enabler for the development of quantum computing and can transform computational power, speed, and efficiency in unexpected ways. Photonic quantum devices are based on integrated waveguides and optical quantum circuits and entangled photon pairs. Integrated waveguides are tiny tunnels that direct light via microchips, which allow for the integration and downsizing of quantum processors. Waveguides allow quantum computers to be smaller, more energy-efficient, and more scalable with precise control directing the path of light. This meticulously controlled photon manipulation, which contains quantum information, is very crucial for efficient quantum computer operation because it removes the need for large, complex setups and saves energy. The integration of photonic components into microchips is a very significant step toward the realization of the vision of small, useful quantum computers.

Photons offer an additional unique advantages for quantum processing in addition to their compactness. One of the best and most beneficial properties of photons is their large-distance quantum coherence. This contrasts sharply with other qubit types, like superconducting qubits or trapped ions, which are required to have careful control of their environment because they are extremely sensitive to noise. But photons have very little decoherence in fiber or free-space networks, which make them an ideal choice for quantum networking and communication applications. Photons are considered a good choice for long-distance, large-scale quantum communication and the development of quantum networks due to their resilience in harsh environments.

Additionally, phonons have a few degrees of freedom as compared to the traditional one that can be used to store quantum information: phase (interference patterns), polarization (horizontal/vertical), and time-bin encoding (earlier/later times). These many degrees of freedom gives photonic qubits a great adaptability for use in a wide range of quantum applications, including quantum sensing, quantum computation, and quantum cryptography. Quantum information can be processed and transmitted efficiently due to the accuracy with which these properties can be processed. [9]

However, photonic qubits present significant challenges to large-scale quantum computing despite their many advantages. One of the primary issues of photons is that they do not naturally interact with one another, unlike atomic or superconducting qubits. This particular lack of interaction makes it difficult to construct deterministic two-qubit gates, which are required to perform many complex quantum operations in a larger scale. Photonic quantum computing circumvents this by deploying linear optics and measurement-induced interactions, which can perform quantum operations without requiring direct photon-photon interactions. These methods require a highly precise light control and advanced error correction techniques for high-fidelity computing.

Moreover, near-optimal single-photon sources and detectors is now a requirement for reliable and efficient quantum processes. High-efficiency detection is very essential to the performance of quantum algorithms since the majority of photonic quantum systems generates entangled photons. Even small reductions in photon detection efficiency can lead to errors and a loss of integrity for quantum activities. Therefore, improving the efficiency and reliability of single-photon sources and detectors is a now a key focused study in photonic quantum computing.

Despite these challenges, current ongoing advancements in integrated photonics and nonlinear optical materials are showing a significant improvement of the scalability and reliability of photonic quantum systems. Researchers are developing new materials, instruments, and techniques in order to improve the performance of photonic qubits. Better detectors, more effective single-photon sources, and innovative techniques for producing and modifying entangled photons are some of the few examples. Specifically, integrated photonics has enormous promise for shrinking photonic devices and incorporating complex quantum circuits into a single chip. This would be consistent with photonic quantum computers, which are useful, scalable, and effective in real-world applications.

Incorporating photonics into quantum computer platforms is thought to accelerate the development of quantum technology. Increased efficiency and scalability is now possible because photonics enable quantum computers to achieve previously unheard-of performance levels. This is especially relevant as we solve problems that are currently beyond the capabilities of conventional computers and push the boundaries of computational problems. It has the ability to perform quantum computations in orders of magnitude faster and with a greater precision that could have revolutionary effects on everything, from materials science and encryption to artificial intelligence and medical research.

In the future, photonics might have an impact on how quantum computing develops. Quantum systems could reach a new high new level and previously unimaginable sizes and also offer previously unimaginable computing power by harnessing the power of light. The development of photonic quantum computing promises the day when quantum computers will be able to the solve complex problems more quickly and effectively as compared to conventional computing systems, opening up a world of revolutionary possibilities currently unattainable with the existing conventional computing systems. Due to its ability to process quantum information at high speeds and with scalability, photonics will be crucial to the future development of quantum technology and its implications. [10]

11.4.2 Single-Photon Emitters

Single-photon emitters, like the color centers in diamonds and quantum dots, produce entangled individual photons. Such entangled photons are essential for secure quantum communication and high-efficiency quantum processing. Without them, many of the intricate characteristics of quantum systems would not be possible. However, the development of dependable single-photon emitters still faces some challenges. One of the key challenges is creating deterministic photon sources, i.e., sources that, when activated, always emit one photon at a time. Another challenge is to minimize signal loss in the optical components that channel and also direct the photons. The large signal loss during the process affects the efficiency and quality of quantum computing and communication, which gives us another crucial concern: ensuring compatibility between atomic and photonic systems. The intricate interactions between photons and atoms are a way for seamlessly integrating the two systems. This would enable more and more potent quantum devices that can simultaneously use atoms and photons.

In order to address the possible difficulties brought about by the intricacy of contemporary technological developments, scientists are working very hard in order to develop new materials and also improve the manufacturing processes for photonic devices. They are dedicated to creating more sophisticated methods for creating high-quality single-photon emitters by reducing optical losses in systems in order to open the door for the potential realization of hybrid quantum systems. These systems integrate a new variety of quantum technologies, such as atomic qubits and photonics that provide a stable and scalable basis for next-generation quantum devices. With these discoveries, researchers not only break through the known existing barriers but also pave the way for a future in which quantum technologies can be seamlessly integrated, which creates a whole new range of possibilities for advanced computing, communication, and scientific applications. The scientific community's collaborative efforts to pursue these initiatives marks the beginning of a new era of innovation and exploration in the development of quantum technology, which is essential to achieving the full potential of quantum devices. Realizing the full potential of quantum devices requires a new age of invention and discovery in the development of quantum technology, which the scientific community is pursuing together through these programs.

11.4.3 Entangled Photon Pairs and Quantum Communication

Entanglement is a strange but powerful quantum property where the particles remain connected even when they are separated. Entangled pairs of photons play key roles in quantum computing for tasks like quantum teleportation, superdense coding, and secure QKD. In quantum technology, the entangled photons are created by using special light-based processes like spontaneous parametric down-conversion (SPDC) and four-wave mixing (FWM), which are also used in advanced tasks like teleporting information, super-fast communication, and ultra-secure encryption. These entangled photons help connect distant quantum devices, laying the foundation for a future quantum internet. While they are advantageous, efficiently producing and distributing entangled photons is still challenging. Optical fiber losses, incomplete detectors, and environmental noise may corrupt entanglement, lessening the credibility of quantum communication. Scientists are making quantum repeaters and entanglement distribution networks with enhanced memory to increase the range and coherence of entanglement-based systems. Furthermore, the incorporation of on-chip entangled photon sources into photonic circuits at the chip level is a turning point toward a practical quantum network. If overcome, entangled photon pairs will transform secure communication and distributed quantum computing. [11]

11.4.4 Optical Quantum Circuits and Integrated Photonic Chips

Optical quantum circuits are the building blocks of photonic quantum computing, allowing photonic qubits to be manipulated with beam splitters, phase shifters, and interferometers. In contrast with classical electronic circuits based on electric charge flow, photonic circuits utilize guided light propagation in waveguides, minimizing heat dissipation and permitting information processing in parallel. The coupling of these elements into silicon photonic chips has made possible quick progress in miniaturized and scalable quantum processors. But universal quantum computing with photonic circuits is still difficult to implement. Existing photonic quantum computers are based on linear optical quantum computing (LOQC) where quantum gates are realized probabilistically through measurement-based models. Despite some advances in deterministic single-photon sources and nonlinear optical materials, the high-efficiency two-qubit gate is still an ongoing field of study. Advances in nanophotonic devices, integrated quantum memory, and atomic-photonic hybrid architectures in the future will play a key role in turning optical quantum circuits from experimental laboratory equipment to functional quantum processors. [12]

11.5 ATOM-PHOTON INTERACTION MECHANISMS

The encounter between atoms and photons is at the core of quantum information processing, supporting quantum gates, entanglement creation, and quantum communication. Atoms are used as robust quantum memories, and photons are used as high-speed and faithful carriers of information, so the interaction between them is central to large-scale quantum computing. The discipline of cavity quantum electrodynamics (CQED) investigates how single atoms interact with confined photons so that quantum states can be controlled with precision. Furthermore, Rydberg atoms, with their high dipole-dipole interaction strengths, enable entanglement between two or more atoms via mediated photon interactions. Such procedures are now the backbone of quantum transduction, where the quantum states are consistently converted between atomic and photonic platforms. Effective quantum gates and long-range entanglement are now feasible due to the advancements in trapped ion-photon coupling, quantum waveguides, and single-photon sources. It is very much related with the basic physics of quantum electrodynamics, light-matter coupling in cavity-based systems, and Rydberg atom collisions, which drive the progress of quantum technology.

11.5.1 Interaction Fundamentals

The theory that explains about how matter and light interact at the quantum level is called quantum electrodynamics, or QED. Because it allows for precise control of atomic qubits through an atom-photon interactions, the interaction is completely the basis for the functioning of quantum computers. Through processes such as absorption, spontaneous emission, and stimulated emission, photons in quantum systems interact with the energy levels of atoms. But in order to carry out quantum operations like quantum gates, quantum teleportation, and photon entanglement, these interactions made it possible to manipulate atomic states.

A few number of factors, such as atomic structure, resonance conditions, and transition dipole moments, affect the intensity and effectiveness of atom-photon interactions. These parameters are very essential to determine the accuracy and dependability of quantum operations because how well they regulate photons can manipulate atomic qubits. Achieving this strong and coherent light-matter coupling in realistic quantum systems is difficult, though. Among the many factors that limit the operation of quantum devices and deteriorate the quality of atom-photon interactions, they spontaneously decay and are prone to decoherence and photon losses.

In order to overcome these limitations, scientists have provided a variety of techniques and instruments that helps in allowing for a better connection between atoms and photons. These include electromagnetically induced transparency (EIT), high-Q optical cavities, and photonic bandgap materials that help enable atom-photon interaction. Because they offer a region where the photons can be stored and interact with atoms for prolonged periods of time, high-Q optical cavities in particular are crucial for enhancing the interaction. This has been accomplished by trapping atoms in cavities that are specifically made to have highly reflective walls. This increases the possibility of the atoms where they will absorb or emit the photons. Limitations like photon loss and spontaneous decay are solved by using this technique but also maximize the photon-atom contact strength while preserving coherence. [13]

The image displays and explains about an atom within a high-fidelity optical cavity (the mirrors). The cavity enhances the interaction between the atom and the photon so that the atom can emit or absorb them. Since the atom can enter or exits the cavity, a photon interacts with it. Cavity quantum electrodynamics, or cavity QED, is one of the fundamental mechanisms that makes this intricate interplay between photons and atoms possible. Cavity QED is utilized in order to improve the atom-photon interaction by confining atoms in superior optical cavities, as represented in Figure 11.2. The design of the cavity is very crucial in ensuring that photons remain inside for an extended period of time and interact with the atom in a very controlled manner. By enhancing the atom-photon coupling in this way, cavity QED makes it possible to fully regulate the quantum states of atoms and photons, which results in more efficient absorption and emission processes. Quantum operations, which enable the extremely precise transport and manipulation of quantum information, are based on this interaction in most systems.

Another notable aspect of cavity QED is its ability to facilitate the transfer of a quantum state from atoms to photons and vice versa. In hybrid quantum systems, the transfer of quantum information from one quantum device to other quantum devices

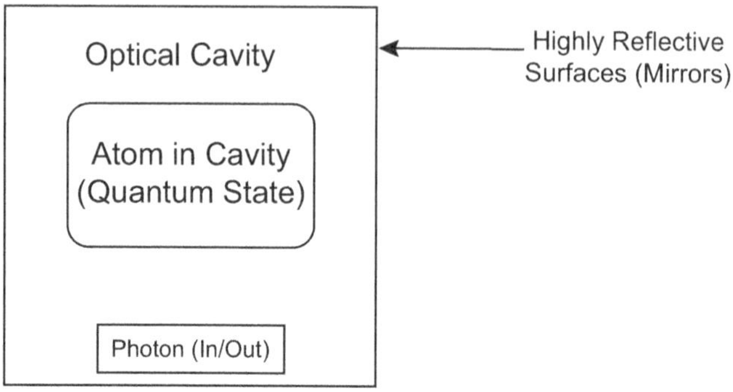

FIGURE 11.2 Cavity QED interaction diagram.

is essential. For example, in quantum networks, photons carry the quantum information between distant stations, while atoms store and process the information. The atom-photon interaction creates entanglement, which is a helpful tool for quantum communication and the usage of error correction codes. Therefore, the production of strong and reliable atom-photon interactions is very essential for the construction of scalable quantum networks and to enable a resilient quantum communication and computation systems.

Another important mechanism that aids in the process of regulating atom-photon interactions is the Raman transition, a two-photon process. In a Raman transition, an atom can interact with two photons simultaneously to change between its quantum states from to another. This technique provides exquisite control over the state of an atom, and it is necessary to achieve quantum gates and other quantum operations for quantum computing. Raman transitions allows qubit states to be manipulated without explicit photon-atom contact, which greatly increases the flexibility and control of quantum operations. [14]

In addition to cavity QED and Raman transitions, researchers are looking into waveguide-based quantum optics as a possible platform for integration of atom-photon interactions on quantum chips. Optical waveguides are devices that can limit and also direct photons, which enables the combination of quantum optics and on-chip quantum computation. By incorporating waveguide-based systems into quantum chips, researchers can create more compact and scalable quantum devices that can leverage the benefits of photonic quantum computing. Waveguide-based systems are open up to new possibilities for building large-scale quantum networks and enable the development of quantum computers that can perform complex tasks effectively and with minimal loss.

By combining cutting-edge techniques like cavity QED, Raman transitions, and waveguide-based quantum optics is proof of constant improving the scalability and reliability of photonic quantum systems is shown, as in Figure 11.3. With each and every development, they hold the potential to overcome the obstacles that have historically hindered the functioning of atom-photon interactions, which results in the development of large-scale, high-fidelity quantum networks. By processing and transferring the quantum information between different devices and locations, the long-term goal is to create stable quantum systems that will form the foundation for new quantum computing and communication technologies.

By refining these methods, scientists are hoping to develop a robust quantum structures that can sustain atom-photon interactions for long periods with high fidelity and a little loss. The entire development of quantum communications networks will depend on the ability of quantum information to travel over extremely long distances without degrading. As quantum optics develops, precise control of the atom-photon interaction will unlock the full potential of quantum communication and computing. Such developments will not only make quantum technologies a disruptive force that will shape computing in the future, but they will also open up new avenues for tackling difficult issues in fields like artificial intelligence, materials science, and encryption.

Lastly, quantum electrodynamics and atom-photon interactions are key components of the recently developed field of quantum computing. The exact control of light-matter interactions is at the heart of quantum processes, and the development of techniques like cavity QED, Raman transitions, and waveguide-based quantum optics will be essential to scaling quantum systems. As they develop, they will be crucial to the creation of scalable, high-performance quantum networks and computers, which will fundamentally alter our understanding of computation and information processing in the quantum era. [15]

11.5.2 Rydberg Atoms and Strong Photon-Matter Coupling

Rydberg atoms, that is, strongly excited states of single atoms, are characterized by unrealistically amplified properties that suit long-range interaction as well as entanglement facilitated by photons. Because Rydberg atoms possess large dipole moments, these atoms strongly experience dipole-dipole or Van der Waals interaction that enables them to affect one another over extended ranges. This effect, referred to as the Rydberg blockade, inhibits simultaneous excitations in a certain area, and it allows deterministic quantum gates and multi-qubit entanglement schemes to be

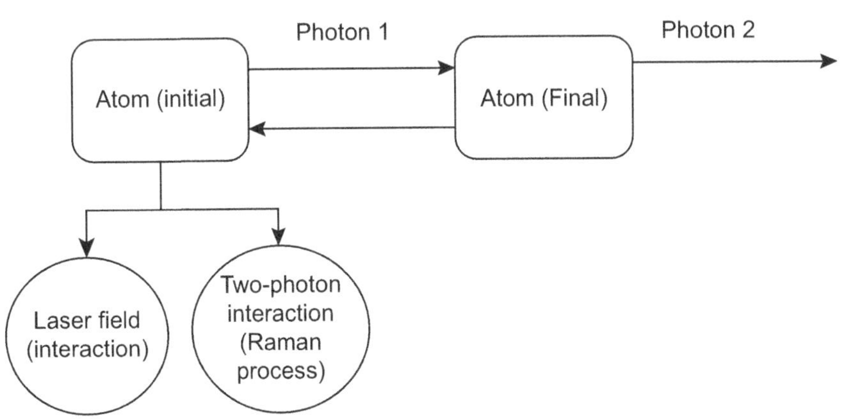

FIGURE 11.3 Raman transition mechanism diagram.

implemented. Such characteristics are very valuable in neutral atom quantum computing, quantum simulation, and hybrid quantum architectures.

Nevertheless, dealing with Rydberg atoms poses some technical issues. Their weakly bound, highly excited states are very sensitive to electric fields, causing decoherence and loss of quantum information. Moreover, laser excitation of the Rydberg states necessitates high-intensity and ultra-high-precision optical control for stable interactions to be maintained. Scientists are responding to these challenges by employing laser cooling, trapping methods, and dynamical decoupling schemes to stabilize Rydberg atom systems. As these methods advance, Rydberg-mediated quantum computing will provide a robust platform for fault-tolerant quantum computation, scalable entanglement distribution, and hybrid atom-photon processors.

11.5.3 Efficiency and Scalability

Rydberg atoms, that is, strongly excited states of single atoms, are characterized by unrealistically amplified properties that suit long-range interaction as well as entanglement facilitated by photons. Because Rydberg atoms possess large dipole moments, these atoms strongly experience dipole-dipole or Van der Waals interaction that enables them to affect one another over extended ranges. This effect, referred to as the Rydberg blockade, inhibits simultaneous excitations in a certain area, and it allows deterministic quantum gates and multi-qubit entanglement schemes to be implemented. Such properties are highly desirable in hybrid quantum architectures, quantum simulation, and neutral atom quantum computing.

However, working with Rydberg atoms presents a number of technical challenges. Decoherence and quantum information loss result from their highly excited, weakly bound state's extreme susceptibility to electric forces. Furthermore, stable atom-to-atom interactions require laser excitation of the Rydberg states, which requires high-intensity and ultra-high-precision optical control. Scientists are using dynamical decoupling protocols, trapping techniques, and laser cooling to stabilize the Rydberg atom systems in order to get past these challenges. Rydberg-mediated quantum computing will offer a solid basis for fault-tolerant quantum computation, scalable entanglement distribution, and hybrid atom-photon processors as these techniques develop. [16]

11.6 INNOVATIONS IN HYBRID QUANTUM ARCHITECTURES

In hybrid quantum architecture, atomic qubits and photonic technologies are combined to optimize both systems' potential for high-fidelity and scalable quantum computing. The atomic qubits tend to offer long coherence durations and dependable quantum memory and photonic qubits enables high-speed communication and efficient quantum information transfer. Hybrid quantum systems can overcome any significant challenges that involves error correction, scalability, and quantum networking by integrating these two platforms. Quantum transducers, which transfer quantum states from photons to atoms, behave and act as a bridge that connects these systems. Moreover, the strong atom-photon interaction enabled by optical cavities and waveguides enables effective quantum gates. Long-range entanglement generation and distributed computing is now possible by atomic and photonic qubit entanglement. Nowadays, quantum interconnects are made possible and scalability is increased, and also feasible fault-tolerant quantum systems are made possible by hybrid architecture.

11.6.1 Interfacing Atomic Qubits with Photonic Networks

One of the primary objectives of hybrid quantum architectures is that the natural integration of these atomic qubits with photonic communication channels which helps in building more efficient and scalable quantum networks. Because of their long and lengthy coherence durations, atomic qubits—in particular and neutral atoms and trapped ions—are highly valued and are supposed to be ideal candidates to be used as quantum memory. The processing and storing of quantum systems depend on these atomic qubits' long-term capacity to store quantum information. However, in order to create massive quantum systems capable of carrying out intricate calculations in multiple locations, these atomic qubits must interface with photons. Photons, which can travel long distances without losing much information, are crucial for transporting quantum data between quantum processors. This coherent transfer of quantum states between atomic and photonic qubits helps in a process known as high-fidelity quantum transduction. These mappings are very much required to link communication channels that can transport from quantum information to quantum networks with quantum information stored in the atoms.

One of the advanced techniques, like cavity quantum electrodynamics (CQED) and waveguide-coupled atomic systems, have been developed in order to make it easier to form a connection between atoms and photons. Because of atoms are positioned inside superior optical cavities in CQED, the photons can couple with the atoms for longer periods of time and strengthening the coupling. Furthermore, waveguide-coupled devices uses either optical fibers or integrated waveguides to couple with atoms and route photons. However, despite all the tremendous progress in these technologies, coupling atoms with photons on a large scale still remains as a challenging task. One of the primary issues is mode mismatch, which tends to happens when atomic transitions and photonic modes aren't precisely aligned, which leads to the loss of quantum information during the conversion process. The reliable transfer of quantum information from atoms to photons is further more complicated by errors caused by spontaneous emission and scattering of photons.

Researchers are now working to overcome these challenges and to optimize the efficiency of atom-photon coupling by creating novel materials and state-of-the-art instruments such as fiber-integrated atomic traps, nanophotonic cavities, and also nonlinear optical materials. By eliminating the mode mismatches and reducing photon scattering, these advancements can easily aim to improve the fidelity of quantum transduction. Long-term goals includes creating efficient and scalable atomic-photonic interfaces, which are very crucial parts of distributed quantum processors and global quantum networks. These networks helps to enable the construction of networks of interconnected quantum systems that can solve difficult and large-scale problems by enabling high-fidelity transmission of quantum information over great distances.

By utilizing the advantages of both atomic and photonic technologies, hybrid quantum systems are now based on this combination. By combining both the stability and coherence of atomic qubits with the efficiency and the speed of photon communication, hybrid designs are now used to create scalable quantum networks. Consequently, an architecture that can disseminate and also alter quantum information from multiple locations where it enables massive quantum computing and networking systems. This helps in achieving the best features of each distinct technology that tend to require these hybrid implementations, which ultimately combine the stability and coherence of the atomic qubit also with the speedy connection and light-loss transmission capabilities of the photon. [17]

Moreover, combining these classical and quantum systems in hybrid architectures is supposed to be a key element in the advancement of quantum computing and communication capabilities. Examples of tasks that a normal and classical computing techniques can perform where the quantum systems cannot include error correction and large-scale data management. By combining the conventional and quantum components, now hybrid systems can more efficiently carry out many complex calculations and communication processes. This hybrid approach advances quantum technology by fusing the best aspects of both computation methods, allowing for the efficient handling of huge amounts of data. It leverages both the unique properties of quantum systems and the benefits of conventional systems. These designs tend to open the door to more reliable and scalable quantum technologies.

Another crucial aspect of hybrid systems is that the maintenance of quantum fidelity. High-fidelity preservation of quantum states is very crucial because even small deviations from the target state would always result in massive errors in quantum computing and communication. The combination of classical and quantum components preserves this error fidelity, which allows for lossless processing, transmission, and storage of quantum data. High-fidelity quantum transduction and error correction techniques are very essential for ensuring the accuracy and dependability of data transmitted via quantum states as well as avoiding errors from accumulating and interfering with the operation of quantum systems. This fidelity preservation is essential for the long-term reliability between communication networks and quantum computers.

Finding a balance between dependability, stability, and speed is a key essential to the success of hybrid quantum systems. In order for quantum computing and communication to coexist with one another, these hybrid systems must strike a delicate balance. By fusing the high accuracy and low latency, which benefits quantum systems with the speed and high-throughput processing power of classical systems, hybrid architectures can always scale to ideal performance levels across a range of applications. When the ability of different components of quantum systems to interact seamlessly is very crucial to realize its full potential, hybrid systems—which combines the best aspects of both classical and quantum technologies—provides a solid basis for the future of quantum technology.

With further development, this hybrid architecture could drive the creation of a distributed quantum computing platforms and massive quantum communication networks also quantum networks. A stable connection for atomic and photonic systems will enable the development of quantum devices capable of performing large-scale, complex calculations and enabling secure and also efficient communication over global quantum networks. These systems tend to enable the next generation of quantum technologies that have the potential to revolutionize domains like materials science, cryptography, artificial intelligence, and drug development. Finally, we can completely change our view on how we manage information, communicate, and compute in the quantum era, thanks to hybrid quantum systems, which will be at the forefront of the push to fully utilize quantum technology.

11.6.2 Quantum Transducers for Efficient Information Transfer

Since enabling the conversion of quantum states between atomic, photonic, and superconducting qubits, quantum transducers are now considered to be essential components of hybrid quantum architectures. They act as a bridge for facilitating efficient communication between quantum systems and disparate physical characteristics. For instance, atomic qubits work in optical frequencies, whereas superconducting qubits work in microwave regimes. Quantum transducers enable this frequency conversion, allowing seamless interoperability among trapped ions, neutral atoms, superconducting circuits, and optical quantum processors. Several strategies, including mechanical resonators, electro-optic modulators, and rare-earth doped crystals, are under investigation to optimize transduction efficiency.

Yet quantum transduction is still an open problem because of inefficiencies in conversion rates and injected noise in state transfer. In order to realize near-deterministic transduction, scientists are working on high-Q optical and microwave cavities, which increase light-matter interaction and reduce losses. Hybrid optomechanical systems involving storage of quantum information in nanomechanical resonator vibrations are also promising for high-fidelity transduction. With further progress, quantum transducers will facilitate the creation of modular quantum computers, in which various qubit modalities coexist in harmony, resulting in more scalable and fault-tolerant quantum systems.

11.6.3 Compact and Efficient Platforms

The hybrid method, which integrates classical and quantum computing methods, allows for the smooth transfer and processing of enormous amounts of information, a key element in the development of the capabilities of quantum computers and communication networks. This approach is a combination of unique properties of quantum systems with the power of classical computing in order to ensure precise and effective execution of complex calculations and communications. In addition to this, collaborative approach is considered to crucial for ensuring quantum fidelity, which guarantees not only the accuracy but also the completeness of data transferred through those states during those processes. This ensures that maintaining quantum fidelity is the foundation in order to ensure that quantum technologies are reliable and trustworthy, but even a slight deviation from the goal state can lead to serious errors in quantum computation and its communication.

This method always provides accurate and efficient execution of intricate computations and communications by fusing the power of traditional computing with the special characteristics of quantum systems. Furthermore, the accuracy and completeness of data which is transferred through these states during those procedures are ensured by quantum fidelity, which is now possible by this cooperative approach. Since even a small departure or miscommunication from the ideal state can result in a significant errors in quantum computation and communication, this should guarantee that maintaining quantum fidelity is to be the cornerstone in ensuring the dependability and credibility of quantum technologies.

11.7 APPLICATIONS IN CRYPTOGRAPHY, OPTIMIZATION, AND MATERIALS SCIENCE

11.7.1 Quantum Cryptography

The combination of atomic and photonic systems has given a whole new dimension, where it leads to a wide range of groundbreaking applications that span almost every essential field. In quantum cryptography, where photon-based QKD is consider to be essential for ensuring accurate and unbreakable encryption, this type of combination is arguably to be one of the most prominent applications. The combination of the best aspects, like atomic and photonic systems for accuracy, speed, and connectivity, enables us to have a secure communication channels and authentication techniques that were previously unattainable. Nowadays, the world is becoming more digital and interconnected, so safeguarding sensitive data from potential cyberattacks and compromises is more crucial and important than ever. One of the important component of this protection is quantum cryptography. This innovative idea not only makes data transit safely but also enables the development of more advanced and highly secure encryption systems that can keep up with the somewhat dynamic nature of digital information sharing. In short, the cross-play between photonic and atomic systems represents the promise of interdisciplinarity in achieving what might be an impossible horizon toward advancing the boundary of secure communication technology. This integration of advanced scientific fields not only helps to enhance the encryption process itself to be stronger and more efficient, but it also highlights that despite all this, there remains a persistent need for innovation and exploration of the discipline of quantum cryptography. Hybrid systems, in the intersection of atomic precision and photonic connectivity, are a leap of giant proportions toward a safer and more secure digital future in which sensitive information can be secured with utmost levels of confidence and trust. [18]

11.7.2 Optimization Problems

Optimization problems occur in numerous applications, including supply chain management, logistics, in which effective solutions are of pivotal significance to ease operation. Quantum hybrid systems emerged as a cutting-edge tool, which can successfully resolve these kinds of issues effectively. Hybrid quantum systems are especially suited to resolving hard combinatorial problems that have been heretofore intractable to classical solvers. In an effective way, hybrid systems can compute very complex decision-making problems with such a remarkable speed and accuracy thanks to the quantum algorithm's computational capacity. Businesses rely heavily on precise resource management and allocation techniques to increase their productivity and also reduce expenses, which benefits most with the speed of the solution.

One of the main and important advantages of hybrid quantum systems is their capacity to process larger amounts of data while simultaneously identifying the best solutions within a small amount of time. This trait is to be considered advantageous to organizations that mainly function in dynamic environments with constantly changing demands and constraints. Furthermore, hybrid quantum systems can be customized and tailored to the industry requirements in a way that it enables different companies to develop original optimization techniques and match those strategies as closely as possible with the operational needs. It helps businesses in a way that solve a variety of issues, which includes inventory control and transportation logistics. Without a doubt, it leads to increased overall efficiency and helps with the profit margins. Hybrid quantum systems are therefore now consider to be "indispensable tools" for companies trying to improve their supply chains and maximize the resource utilization to stay ahead of the competition. The enormous impact of such systems challenges traditional methods of problem-solving, which emphasizes the revolutionary potential of quantum technology across industries.

In summary, hybrid quantum systems are now considered to be the best instruments for rapidly resolving intricate combinatorial issues within a company. This has shown that it would be a useful resource for industries that are seeking to achieve unprecedented levels of efficacy and efficiency in traditional resource management methods. Nowadays, quantum algorithms give businesses wide access to cutting-edge processing power where it allows them to innovate and produce whole new products while responding to unstable consumer needs.

11.7.3 Materials Science

Quantum simulations are consider to be a groundbreaking technique in materials science for unlocking previously undiscovered properties in a wide range of materials. They not only shed light on the behavior of intrinsic matter, but they also open the door to many advance breakthroughs such as in fields like drug development and molecular modeling. Thanks to this beautiful synergy between atomic and photonic systems, scientists can now study the intricate web of molecular interactions with a previously unheard-of level of accuracy and in more detailed way. This groundbreaking capacity to replicate many complex scenarios with unprecedented accuracy not only expands our understanding of basic scientific concepts but also pushes the boundaries of current material innovation. In reality, these diverse applications tend to demonstrate the immense potential of hybrid quantum systems in order to challenge these long-held beliefs and usher a new era of scientific advancement and industrial revolution. We are entering into an era of unparalleled discoveries and accomplishments with the introduction of quantum simulation and the harmonization of heterogeneous systems. We can say these developments are meant to transform entire industries, alter economies, and steer our collective future toward the unprecedented levels of innovation and prosperity. [19]

11.8 CONCLUSION

Quantum computing has reached a whole new level due to the combination of atomic systems and photonic technologies. This is considered to be a big step in the direction of more powerful and efficient computer technology. By using special atomic and photonic properties, researchers address the traditional problems of coherence, error correction, and scalability in quantum computing systems.

This combination of atomic and photonic elements has proved to have potential to revolutionize the field of calculations in the future. These advancements are altering the core principles of computing as a field by influencing its core concepts and providing a groundbreaking method for addressing challenging problems. The possibility that theoretical ideas could form the basis of useful, commercial technologies grows as researchers continue to progress and develop hybrid techniques that seamlessly blend atomic and photonic components.

The field of integrating atomic systems with photonics is so vast and broad that the new frontiers it may bring are unimaginable and will transform conventional approaches to problem-solving, from improved cryptography techniques to new optimization techniques and advanced work in materials science. The intersection of cutting-edge research and technological advancements that have the potential to change the course of quantum computing and beyond is essentially found in atomic systems connected by photonic technologies. A new era of development is being ushered in by the work of the professionals in these domains, where quantum technologies are tangible tools capable of bringing about real change and bringing about previously unheard-of levels of innovation and discovery. [20]

REFERENCES

[1] Awschalom, David, et al. "Development of Quantum Interconnects (Quics) for Next Generation Information Technologies." *Prx Quantum* 2.1 (2021): 017002.

[2] Pelucchi, Emanuele, et al. "The Potential and Hlobal Outlook of Integrated Photonics for Quantum Technologies." *Nature Reviews Physics* 4.3 (2022): 194–208.

[3] Graham, T. M., et al. "Multi-Qubit Entanglement and Algorithms on a Neutral-Atom Quantum Computer." *Nature* 604.7906 (2022): 457–462.

[4] Day, M. L., et al. "Limits on Atomic Qubit Control from Laser Noise." *NPJ Quantum Information* (2022): 72.

[5] Ullah, Md Habib, et al. "Quantum Computing for Smart Grid Applications." *IET Generation, Transmission & Distribution* 16.21 (2022): 4239–4257.

[6] Mangla, Cherry, et al. "Mitigating 5G Security Challenges for Next-Gen Industry Using Quantum Computing." *Journal of King Saud University-Computer and Information Sciences* 35.6 (2023): 101334.

[7] Wang, Yu, et al. "An Atomic-Scale Multi-Qubit Platform." *Science* 382.6666 (2023): 87–92.

[8] Gupta, Rajeev, et al. "Silicon Photonics Interfaced with Microelectronics for Integrated Photonic Quantum Technologies: A New Era in Advanced Quantum Computers and Quantum Communications?" *Nanoscale* 15.10 (2023): 4682–4693.

[9] Sodagari, Shabnam. "Integrating Quantum and Satellites: A New Era of Connectivity." *IEEE Access* 11 (2023): 145101–145110.
[10] Shafique, Muhammad Ali, Arslan Munir, and Imran Latif. "Quantum Computing: Circuits, Algorithms, and Applications." *IEEE Access* 12 (2024): 22296–22314.
[11] Ajani, Samir N., et al. "Frontiers of Computing-Evolutionary Trends and Cutting-Edge Technologies in Computer Science and Next Generation Application." *Journal of Electrical Systems* 20.1s (2024): 28–45.
[12] Shamo, Sebastian Anetey. "The Role of Quantum Computing in the Evolution of Fintech: A Generational Perspective on Gen Z's Influence on Adoption and Growth." Available at SSRN 5070193, 2024.
[13] Alomari, A., and Kumar, S. A. P., "ReLAQA: Reinforcement Learning-Based Autonomous Quantum Agent for Quantum Applications." *IEEE Transactions on Artificial Intelligence* 6(3) (March 2025): 549–558. https://doi.org/10.1109/TAI.2024.3437335.
[14] Ilin, Y., and Arad, I., "Dissipative Variational Quantum Algorithms for Gibbs State Preparation." *IEEE Transactions on Quantum Engineering* 6 (2025): 1–12, Art no. 3100212. https://doi.org/10.1109/TQE.2024.3511419.
[15] Van Huynh, D., Dobre, O. A., and Duong, T. Q., "Optimal Service Placement for 6G Edge Computing with Quantum-Centric Optimization in Real Quantum Hardware." *IEEE Communications Letters* 29(3) (March 2025): 448–452. https://doi.org/10.1109/LCOMM.2024.3523421.
[16] Ur Rehman, J., et al. "Evolutionary Algorithms and Quantum Computing: Recent Advances, Opportunities, and Challenges." *IEEE Access* 13 (2025): 16649–16670. https://doi.org/10.1109/ACCESS.2025.3530952.
[17] Schillo, N., and Sturm, A., "Variational Quantum Algorithms for Differential Equations on a Noisy Quantum Computer." *IEEE Transactions on Quantum Engineering* 6 (2025): 1–16, Art no. 3100416. https://doi.org/10.1109/TQE.2025.3532017.
[18] Rattan, A., Pal, A. Rudra, and Gurusamy, M., "Quantum Computing for Advanced Driver Assistance Systems and Autonomous Vehicles: A Review." *IEEE Access* 13 (2025): 17554–17582. https://doi.org/10.1109/ACCESS.2025.3532958.
[19] Urgelles, Helen, et al. "In-Network Quantum Computing for Future 6G Networks." *Advanced Quantum Technologies* 8.2 (2025): 2300334.
[20] Vasantrao, K. S., and Saxena, A., "Bits to Qubits: An Overview of Quantum Computing." *2025 International Conference on Intelligent Control, Computing and Communications (IC3)*, Mathura, India, 2025, 120–124. https://doi.org/10.1109/IC363308.2025.10956309.

12 Quantum Communication and Secure Channels

Rajeshwari Sissodia and Vinay Dwivedi

12.1 INTRODUCTION

A new field is emerging in quantum communication, using its principles in transferring information securely. Quantum computers threaten classical methods of communication with very powerful computational techniques; hence, quantum communication seems a very promising alternative toward confidentiality and security. Quantum states have properties that enable a system to protect data using hundreds of ways that a classical system cannot.

Familiarization with basic principles of quantum communication is brought forth in this chapter while underlining its prospective applications for secure channels. This is the idea which builds upon the quantum property of phenomena such as superposition, entanglement, and the no-cloning theorem for the security of the communication systems by design. The measurement of quantum states creates a disturbance such that any effort at eavesdropping will eventually be detected as it relates to the confidentiality of the information received.

The basic principles of quantum communication, including quantum key distribution (QKD) protocols such as BB84 and E91, form the theme of this chapter. Such protocols ensure secure quantum communication through the ability of two sides to exchange cryptographic keys in a mutually accessible manner without possible interception by third parties. Information carriers, especially photons, are integrated in quantum communication systems using lighting characteristics and entanglement in a unique way to encode the information and transmit it securely.

On top of that, this chapter discusses the pragmatic development of a quantum cryptographic system, while also talking about the different challenges related to field deployment, hardware needs, and error correction techniques, which are needed to keep fidelity over the channel. The vulnerabilities of quantum communication systems are also studied, especially concerning the threats hence created by the advancement of quantum computing, with potential remedies to safekeep classified information.

12.1.1 Overview of Quantum Communication

Quantum communication involves the use of quantum-mechanical principles, such as superposition and entanglement, for transmitting information in an absolutely

DOI: 10.1201/9781003538950-14

secure manner. In contrast to classical systems that use electromagnetic waves (like radio waves, microwaves, or light) to relay information, communication within a quantum system uses the quantum states of particles, i.e., usually photons, to carry and encode information.

Significant and integral features of quantum communication are that they hold the promise of exploiting basic principles of quantum mechanics to attain phenomenal unprecedented levels of security. In a given quantum communication system, a quantum particle, such as a photon, is manipulated to carry information, such as its polarization. However, observing or measuring a quantum state of a particle unavoidably changes it: this is called the observer effect (or the Heisenberg uncertainty principle). This means that any interception of quantum communication by an eavesdropper would disturb the system, thus revealing the presence of an eavesdropper.

Considerably advanced techniques and protocols are included in quantum communication, and one of the most significant methods among them is QKD (quantum key distribution). This protocol enables the secure sharing of a cryptographic key between two parties over an insecure channel using quantum states without the possibility of copying or interception without being detected.

12.1.2 Importance and Applications of Quantum Communication in Secure Channels

A unique feature of quantum communication is, however, that it promises information security far beyond conventional cryptographic techniques. The security of classical communications is thus often reduced to solving hard mathematical problems (like factorizing very large numbers). In principle, it could be completely broken by sufficiently powerful computers. With the development of quantum computers, many of these classical security systems would become useless. On the contrary, quantum communication depends on the laws of quantum mechanics such that it is completely secure against such a menace.

Key applications of quantum communication include:

- **Quantum Key Distribution (QKD):** As already stated, QKD enables two parties to share a cryptographic key such that they can subsequently communicate using the key. The principle behind the security of QKD is that any eavesdropping of the key exchange creates a disturbance in the quantum state of the information exchanged, thus revealing the presence of an intruder.
- **Quantum Networks:** This means forming a communication backbone to talk to all the quantum states really and completely distant. This indeed is possible through quantum entanglement and teleportation.
- **Quantum Internet:** The secure communicating and sharing of quantum information over larger distances by an incredibly secure network, with capabilities inaccessible to classical networks, is envisioned in theory and future applications within the quantum internet.
- **Secure Government and Military Communications:** The national security aspect of which makes it specifically appealing is secure communication, where confidentiality of sensitive information is most paramount.

Indeed, it promises to ensure complete protection of communications against all conventional and quantum-enabled attacks, thus safeguarding national secrets and critical military operations.

12.1.3 Quantum Mechanics and Its Role in Secure Communication Systems

Such quantum mechanics serve as the backbone of secure communication systems and quantum communication. All classical communication systems relay information through physical means like radio waves or optical fibers, while quantum communication exploits quantum phenomena, which have no analogues in classical systems.

Key quantum principles involved in secure communications are:

- **Superposition:** Superposition permits quantum particles to exist in several states at the same time. For example, a photon can be in a superposition of two polarization states, one of which can be used to encode information; hence, it will allow much richer and more secure forms of communication as compared to classical because the quantum state of the particle can encode it in a manner that classical bits cannot.
- **Entanglement:** Entanglement is the most remarkable of all the various phenomena in quantum mechanics. When two quantum particles (for instance, photons) become entangled with one another, then their properties become correlated irrespective of the separating distance between them. It is the ability of one to determine the instant state of the other that can be used in secure communications. This is a concept common in many protocols including the E91 QKD protocol for secret sharing based on relative remote correlations of entwined particles.
- **Quantum No-Cloning Theorem:** It states that one cannot generate a perfect copy of an unknown quantum state. This principle gives an additional safety dimension to quantum communication systems because an eavesdropper can be prevented from copying or intercepting quantum information unnoticed. Every attempt to measure or clone the quantum state causes disturbance of the quantum state, leaving evidence that measurements or cloning have been attempted.
- **Heisenberg Uncertainty Principle:** This assertion is that certain pairs of physical properties such as position and momentum measurements cannot be taken with arbitrary precision at the same time. In quantum means of communication, it ensures that any attempt at measuring the quantum state of the system shall disturb the same. This becomes very crucial for communication security wherein it guarantees detecting the fact that the channel is under eavesdropping by measurable changes in the system.

It can be inferred that the security of quantum communication systems evolves from the principles of quantum mechanics: entanglement, superposition, and the no-cloning theorem. These are premises that fundamentally embed quantum communication in security; hence, any attempts to intercept or to tamper with the communication can be easily detected and prevented. It is very likely that quantum communication will assume a central role in a future built around secure information transmission as the quantum technologies progressively evolve.

12.1.4 Literature Review

Pan et al. (2019) made significant contributions to the development of quantum-secure direct communication (QSDC). Their work enabled the direct transmission of confidential data via quantum channels without requiring classical communication assistance. By leveraging the phenomenon of quantum entanglement, they ensured end-to-end security, making their system resilient to eavesdropping and quantum computing attacks. This pioneering research laid the groundwork for future quantum networks by demonstrating the feasibility of direct and secure quantum messaging.

Marchetti et al. (2019) focused on incorporating silicon photonics into quantum communication systems. They addressed practical engineering challenges such as signal distortion and optical losses, which are major obstacles to building scalable quantum-secure networks. Their work emphasized the potential of silicon-based platforms to support integrated photonic chips, which are critical for commercializing quantum communication technology due to their compatibility with current semiconductor manufacturing processes.

Brod et al. (2019) explored the use of photon-based quantum systems for boson sampling, proposing this as a method to enhance security in communication protocols. Their study demonstrated how photonic quantum systems could be used to implement complex, secure algorithms resistant to classical computational attacks. They argued that the computational hardness of boson sampling could be harnessed to build quantum communication frameworks with high resilience to data breaches, thus offering a path toward practical encryption systems.

Guccione et al. (2020) advanced the field by developing a hybrid entangled swapping method. This approach enabled interoperability between quantum systems of different architectures, a crucial capability for large-scale quantum networks. Their innovation facilitates the construction of heterogeneous quantum networks—such as those connecting satellite-based systems with ground stations—by ensuring that entanglement can be maintained across diverse platforms.

Schreiber et al. (2022) made strides in the integration of photonic technologies with quantum key distribution (QKD). Their work demonstrated scalable QKD implementations using integrated photonics, reducing the size and complexity of secure communication hardware. This advancement is instrumental in deploying quantum-secure infrastructure across extensive networks, including metropolitan areas.

Pelucchi et al. (2022) concentrated on developing integrated photonic platforms that enhance the usability and reliability of quantum communication. Their research led to the creation of compact, scalable, and energy-efficient devices that can be used for real-world applications of secure quantum channels. This effort significantly contributes to the practical deployment of quantum communication systems.

Silverstone et al. (2023) investigated silicon-based photonic systems for use in quantum communication. They highlighted how such systems can be seamlessly integrated with existing telecommunications infrastructure, which is crucial for transitioning from experimental to commercial deployment. Their work supports the future of quantum-secure communication within mainstream network operations.

Gu et al. (2023) demonstrated a groundbreaking satellite-based QKD system, enabling secure communication over long distances. Their experiment showed that quantum communication is not limited to fiber networks and can overcome geographical limitations. This innovation supports the vision of a global quantum internet that connects continents through space-based quantum channels.

Walmsley et al. (2023) explored light-based quantum technologies in both communication and computing. Their study emphasized the transformative potential of quantum optics in enhancing secure data transfer. By leveraging the unique properties of photons, their work proposes new paradigms for building robust and ultra-secure communication networks.

Cai et al. (2024) addressed a major challenge in continuous-variable quantum communication—maintaining efficiency in noisy environments. Their research focused on optimizing signal fidelity and robustness, which are essential for deploying quantum systems in real-world conditions such as urban environments and industrial settings.

Kim et al. (2024) introduced the application of quantum machine learning (QML) for enhancing secure communication protocols. Their study revealed how machine learning algorithms could predict, adapt, and optimize security settings in quantum communication systems. This fusion of AI and quantum technologies offers a dynamic defense mechanism against evolving cyber threats.

Smith et al. (2024) investigated quantum error correction techniques specifically tailored for secure communication systems. They proposed frameworks to preserve data integrity and reduce transmission errors, ensuring consistent reliability even when operating over noisy or lossy channels. Their contributions are vital to strengthening the robustness of quantum networks.

Huang et al. (2024) designed hybrid frameworks combining classical and quantum protocols, facilitating a smoother transition to quantum-secure communications. Their systems enable interoperability between traditional infrastructure and emerging quantum systems, ensuring backward compatibility and phased integration across networks.

Nguyen et al. (2024) tackled the complex problem of synchronization in quantum networks. They proposed solutions that enhance timing precision across distributed systems, which is essential for maintaining coherence and minimizing data loss during long-distance communication. Their work plays a key role in enabling scalable and synchronized quantum networks.

12.2 QUANTUM COMMUNICATION PRINCIPLES

It purposely set the meaning and transfer of electronic information on space quantum communication. The section describes the principles that underlie quantum communication—from its basic concepts and principles of quantum mechanics to peculiar characteristics of information carriers-photons, which lay the actual development of secure communication systems.

Quantum communication—or in other words, the transfer of information through mathematics of quantum mechanics—uses its basic properties to guarantee an efficient and permanent communication. In this section the principles of quantum communication will be part, from the next ideas to quantum mechanics, through the phenomena of information carriers—photons—causing secure communication systems to be laid.

12.2.1 Fundamental Concepts in Quantum Communication

In actual fact, quantum communication uses quantum states for exchanging information between two people through manipulation and measurement of quantum states, such as superposition with their present look (in which they are able to exist in multiple states at the same time when they are measured) and entanglement (which is the property of one particle to be dependent on another one regardless of distance). All of these are totally different from the above classical communication systems where bits only can exist in two states such as 0 or 1.

The essential quantum principles used in quantum communication involve:

- **Quantum Superposition:** The intrinsic ability of quantum systems whereby they allow for merging of different state possibilities held within the particle and thus allowing such particle to lie in such multiple states. An instance is that of a photon existing in both horizontal and vertical polarization states whereby information can be encoded as more than is the case in classical systems. This mode underlies most of the quantum protocols developed for communication, e.g., QKD.

a. **Entanglement:** If two quantum particles become entangled, their states are currently considered interlinked within themselves, independent from each other as well as the physical distance between them. Therefore, non-local correlations arise from interrelated parts, which can serve the purpose of secure communication, as in the case of E91 for quantum key distribution.
b. **Quantum Interference:** Quantum interference occurs in a way that combines the probability amplitudes of quantum states in such a way that it can amplify or diminish the likelihood of certain results. This holds importance in encoding and decoding quantum information with precision and security.
c. **No-Cloning Theorem:** Although there is a theoretical diagram for it, it is a quantum moral principle that states an arbitrary unknown quantum state cannot be perfectly copied. This serves to further shield the quantum communication systems, believing that an eavesdropper cannot intercept and duplicate the quantum information without someone noticing.

12.2.2 Information Carriers in Quantum Communication: Photons

It's really about quantum communications wherein states of quantum mechanics are superimposed with quantified measurement and manipulation to share information between two parties. Their current manifestations include superpositions (in which they can exist in multiple—albeit simultaneous—states when measured) and entanglement (whereby the properties of one particle are dependent upon the other particle regardless of distance). All that is in sharp contrast with those classical communications systems where bits could only be in two states, 0 or 1.

The fundamental quantum principles that underlie quantum communication are:

Quantum Superposition: This is the intrinsic propensity of quantum systems, so their configuration allows for merging of the alternative state possibilities held in the particle, hence such particle lying in such multiple states. An instance is that of a photon existing in both horizontal and vertical polarization states whereby information can be encoded as more than is the case in classical systems. This mode underlies most of the quantum protocols developed for communication, e.g., QKD.

- **Entanglement:** If two quantum particles become entangled, instead of each other and independent from each one, the states of those quantum particles are together seen as presently interlinked to themselves, irrespective of the distance from each other.
- **Quantum Interference:** It occurs in such an order as to add and subtract the probability amplitudes associated with quantum states thereby increasing or decreasing the chances of a particular outcome; it is very important for precision and security of quantum information encoding as well as decoding.

12.2.3 Key Properties of Photons

Photons possess endowing quantum characteristics that are apt for safe encoding and transmission of quantum information. Among those characteristics are ones like polarization and entanglement, which are usually applied to many quantum communication protocols to ensure secure communications.

12.2.3.1 Polarization

It defines the direction of the oscillation of the electromagnetic field of a photon. While it is clear in classical physics and light waves oscillates in many directions, in quantum mechanics, the polarization of photons could be manipulated and accurately measured.

Encoding Information: Polarization is one of the most widely used methods to encode quantum bits into quantum communication systems. A photon can be in a number of different states of polarization (for example, it can be in horizontal, vertical, or diagonal polarization), which can represent binary information (0 or 1). A quantum communication system may have other means of manipulating photons to secure their information in-transit.

a. **Quantum Key Distribution (QKD):** A typical application of such polarization is represented by BB84 protocol. Here, this kind of usage of polarization prepares the photons in order to exchange secret cryptographic keys between two communicating parties. The advantage of this type of use is that it is easily manipulated with not much disturbance to the photon quantum state that it embodies—thus allowing its communication to remain secret and exclusive.

b. **Security:** Quantum polarization is described as the unique property since any attempt to intercept or measure the photons will disturb their state. That disturbance is detectable and thus indicates whether or not the communication has been intercepted or eavesdropped.

12.2.3.2 Entanglement

It is the most peculiar and promising quality of quantum mechanical entanglement; two photons, when entangled, indicate that the quantum states of one and the other photon become interlinked, meaning that the state of one is instantaneously correlated with that of the other, despite the distance between them.

a. **Secure Communication:** Entangled photons are used in various quantum communication protocols, like the E91 protocol, ensuring secure key distribution; in this specification, the entangled state of the photons affirms that any measuring attempt of the quantum state of one photon will immediately affect the other, exposing the existence of an eavesdropper.
b. **Quantum Teleportation:** Entanglement is another major pillar supporting the principle of quantum teleportation, whereby, instantaneously, the state of a quantum particle, for example, a photon, is passed on to another entangled particle. Thus, the transmission of information becomes secure by reconstructing the same information by the entangled partner without having to pass on the physical photon.
c. **Non-Locality and Security:** Entanglement produces non-local correlations between particles, and these correlations are essential to quantum communication systems. Since entangled particles have their correlations over an infinite distance, it allows one to detect illegal manipulation and maintain secrecy.

Basically, these are the chief characteristics of photons: One is that of polarization, and the other one is entanglement, which enables quantum communication to be secure and efficient at the same time. They permit encoding messages in quantum information, its transmission, and the protection of quantum information through secure communication, even in the presence of presumed eavesdroppers.

12.3 QUANTUM KEY DISTRIBUTION (QKD) PROTOCOLS

Quantum key distribution (QKD) is a key technology enabling two parties to exchange a cryptographic key securely over potentially insecure communications using quantum mechanics. While traditional cryptographic methods rely on the complexity of practical mathematical problems to keep information secure, QKD instead uses fundamental properties of quantum mechanics so that the exchanged keys remain secure. Unlike classical cryptography, security in QKD is founded on features of the universe on principles of quantum mechanics, such as uncertainty principle, superposition, and entanglement that provide inherent protection against eavesdropping.

An introduction to QKD includes exploration of the two most well-known protocols for secure key distribution: BB84 and E91.

12.3.1 Introduction to Quantum Key Distribution

QKD is the transmission of cryptographic keys through quantum mechanics, providing a guarantee that any interception of the transmissions is detectable. It ensures the secure transfer of keys in a way that even if an external entity, validating typically by the name Eve, is attempting to monitor the transmission, the key could still be secure to Alice and Bob, thanks to the no-cloning theorem and the Heisenberg uncertainty principle.

The critical concept of QKD is to use quantum states—such as the polarization of photons—to encode the key. When an eavesdropper attempts to intercept or measure the quantum states during the key exchange, they will disturb the quantum system through measurement and thus produce detectable errors, warning the parties about an intruder. These errors signal the presence of an intruder and allow the parties to discard the compromised key and attempt a new key exchange.

QKD security does not depend on computational difficulty but on the most fundamental properties of quantum physics.

12.3.2 BB84 Protocol

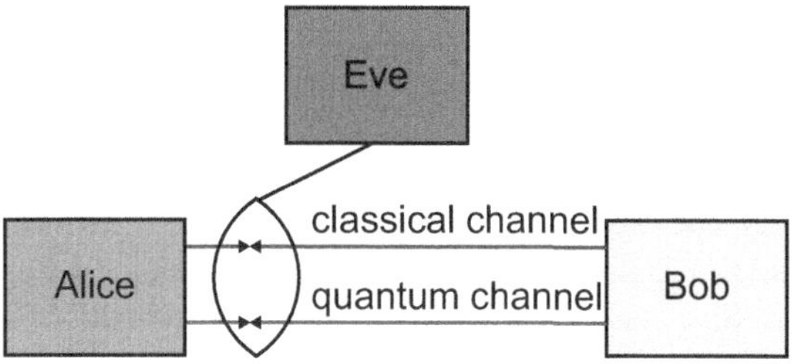

FIGURE 12.1 BB84 KEY distribution protocol.

The following are the functions of the BB84 protocol:

a. Qubit Preparation: Alice sends a series of qubits prepared in one of four possible polarization states. She forms these into two sets as follows: Set 1, rectilinear basis: horizontal (0°) or vertical (90°). Set 2, diagonal basis: +45° or −45° polarization. She randomly chooses one of the two sets for each photon.
b. Transmission: Alice transmits the pre-formed photons to Bob through a quantum channel, not knowing how the photons have been encoded.
c. Measurement: Bob chooses a random measurement basis among the two possible measurement bases (rectilinear or diagonal) for measuring each received photon. The measurements will yield these results: the right value (if Bob chooses the right basis) or a random result (if he chooses the wrong basis).
d. Key Generated: After the transmission, Alice and Bob public bases for the used photon without revealing the measured values. A discarding of cases

with different bases was done and kept for the similar bases' results for both. The leftover bits form the common secret cryptographic key.

e. Error Detection and Spying Detection: If the eavesdropper, Eve, tries to interfere with these photons, she will always disturb their states. These will thus create errors when Bob will compare these with Alice's ones. And from now on, using a small sample of their key bits, Alice and Bob can immediately know whether their communication has been tapped or not. If the error rate is too high, they discard the key and restart the process.

12.3.2.1 Security Assurance Based on Quantum Mechanics

It is the principles of quantum mechanics that ensure security to the BB84 protocol:

Heisenberg Uncertainty Principle: Measure any quantum state of a photon, and the effect is an inevitable disturbance which gives rise to errors in the key shared; thus, any such disturbance will make eavesdropping detectable.

- **No-Cloning Theorem**: Any quantum information is not perfectly clone-able. Thus, Eve will not be able to intercept the photons, copy their quantum state, and learn about the key without any possibility of detection.
- **Randomness of Measurement**: Bob's choice of measurement bases is entirely random, and therefore Eve cannot predict exactly what measurement basis Bob uses to measure the photons. Even if she intercepts the photon, she has no guarantee to measure successfully without inflicting detectable errors.

That is how the BB84 protocol allows for the safe establishment of a cryptographic key that will be used for encrypted communication while ensuring detection of any eavesdropping attempt.

12.3.3 E91 Protocol

The **E91 protocol**, introduced by Artur Ekert in 1991, is another QKD, but it is based on the concept of quantum entanglement rather than the polarization states of individual photons. In the E91 protocol, Alice and Bob share pairs of entangled photons and use the correlations between the photons to generate a shared cryptographic key.

12.3.3.1 Overview and Working

It is the E91 protocol which Artur Ekert gave in the year 1991. This protocol is also a quantum key distribution one but is based on the principle of quantum entanglement rather than on the polarization states of the individual photons. In the E91 protocol, both Alice and Bob possess pairs of entangled photons, and from the correlation found between them will generate a common secret key.

12.3.3.2 Introduction and Working

a. Producing Entangled Photon Pair: Alice has one of the entangled pairs and Bob has one of the other pair. In this way, two entangled photons are generated on both Alice and Bob, which have paired non-local characteristics: their states are instantly correlated regardless of the distance separating this pair of identical photons.

b. Measurement: Alice and Bob measure each of their respective photons using random measurement settings, which mostly involve different polarizers or any other quantum measurement-like "Alice" polarizer. Because they are entangled, their measurement results will be strongly correlated.
c. Key Generation: After taking these measurements, they compare these values publicly so that they can correlate to certain rules given the fact that photons measured are entangled, but individually, they appear in a random way. Thus, it is possible to make a common secret key.
d. Eavesdropping Detection: If Eve attempts to measure the entangled photons using an interception approach, her measurements will disturb the entanglement properties, thereby changing the correlations determined between Alice and Bob with regard to their results. To determine the existence or absence of eavesdropping attempts, Alice and Bob will check the error rates in their common key.

12.3.3.3 Role of Entanglement in Security

The E91 protocol relies heavily on the quantum entanglement established among the photon pairs. The most important contribution to this consideration concerning the security features of entanglement includes, as follows:

- Non-Local Correlation: The disaggregated photons driving these processes exhibit correlations that are surpassingly enhanced to any classical correlation. This means that any interference or eavesdropping shall disturb these correlations in such a way that this disturbance becomes evident at a specific time instant in the future.
- Violation of Bell's Inequality: Furthermore, the E91 protocol relies upon a violation of Bell's inequality, which is one of the fundamental results in quantum mechanics. If Alice and Bob find their correlations to violate Bell's inequality, they can confidently assume that no localized hidden variables (such as classical information) drive their measurements, whereupon they conclude that key generation is secure from classical eavesdropping.
- Eavesdropping Detection: Any attempt made unto interception or measurement by Eve of the entangled photons will destroy their entanglement and give rise to certainly detectable errors in the key generation process: thus making the E91 protocol highly secure, for it is guaranteed that any interference will not go unnoticed.

To summarize, the E91 protocol entangles the entangled photon pairs to build the secure communication channel between two parties. Non-local correlations between entangled photons make it possible for eavesdropping to be detected and form a strong basis for secure key distribution in distributed quantum communication systems.

12.4 QUANTUM CRYPTOGRAPHY SYSTEMS

Quantum cryptography is an advanced technology in modern times that uses the concepts of quantum mechanics to develop secure communication systems that can resist eavesdropping and other forms of interference. Unlike classical cryptographic systems that rely on computational difficulty of certain problems, quantum cryptography guarantees security based on fundamental laws of physics. This section presents the fundamentals of quantum cryptography, the main components of quantum cryptography systems, and the challenges in realizing and deploying such systems in a practical scenario.

12.4.1 Fundamentals of Quantum Cryptography

A field of cryptography known as quantum cryptography deals with securing the transmission of data and key exchange through different phenomena in quantum mechanics. The main advantages it offers over classical conventional cryptographic methods lie in the usage of quantum properties such as superposition, entanglement, and the no-cloning theorem for forming communication channels, which, by virtue of their inherent property, are secure.

The main areas of focus in quantum cryptography are:

- Quantum Key Distribution: Examples include protocols like BB84 and E91 that have already been discussed. Such kinds of protocols empower two parties to exchange cryptographic keys with the certainty that no eavesdropper will ever be successful in catching or measuring the key in their presence without raising detectable disturbances in the two parties—thus alerting both to the potential threat.
- Quantum Entanglement: Entanglement is what covers several protocols of quantum cryptography. The E91 is referred to here as it allows secure key distribution through a system of non-local correlations between two entangled particles. Any disturbance met with entangled photons disturbs the entire system and is thus detectable. The system is very secure.
- No-Cloning Theorem: Yet another powerful fact about quantum cryptography is the no-cloning theorem, which says that any arbitrary quantum state cannot be copied exactly. So that means if one attempts to intercept quantum information, that will disturb that information in turn, making the communicating parties aware of the existence of the one eavesdropping. These intrinsic principles have enabled quantum cryptography to provide levels of security that classical systems cannot even dream of, and thus, this form of cryptography mainly serves applications that are very sensitive: government communications, financial transactions, and secure communications across networks with a possible compromise.

12.4.2 Components of a Quantum Cryptography System

The permission of quantum cryptography is based on many different components for secure communication. The first part of it is a quantum channel. A quantum channel is the means by which different parties communicate quantum information; for example photons are transmitted to either optical fiber or free space. The channel should be designed in such a way that it minimizes loss and interference while transmitting quantum states, such as photons, between communicating parties (e.g., Alice and Bob).

a. Quantum Key Distribution (QKD Protocol): This is the protocol used for cryptographic key exchange between Alice and Bob. The QKD protocol will always ensure detection of any eavesdropping as well as giving an indication of a mechanism for the generation of a shared secret key.
b. Quantum Source: This is the device generating the quantum state (like photons) that encode the information. A typical quantum source in quantum cryptography consists of a laser emitting out single-photon or entangled-photon pairs.
c. Quantum Detectors: These devices measure the quantum states transmitted through the channel. These detectors must be highly sensitive in order to detect and record photon polarization or other quantum properties depending on the QKD protocol being used.
d. Classical Channel: The final key exchange or verification process often requires classical channel, even though quantum states are used for the key distribution in most cases. Classical channels could mean public channels like the internet where Alice and Bob exchange information, such as measurement bases, or examine errors in the key without compromising security.
e. Management Key: Effectively store and manage the key once it is distributed securely. Key management systems ensure the correct usage of cryptographic keys in the encrypting and decrypting processes of messages.

12.4.3 Realization and Implementation of Quantum Cryptography

A quantum cryptography system will require considerable advancement in hardware and infrastructure before it can be said to be effective in practical scenarios. That is the scope of this section in discussing the important aspects about realization or implementation of a quantum cryptographic system.

12.4.3.1 Hardware and Infrastructure

The successful application of quantum cryptography depends on the hardware and infrastructure that have been developed to meet specific demands. The major components include:

1. Photon Sources: The generation of reliable photons or entangled photon pairs is important for quantum cryptography systems, having specific quantum properties, e.g., polarization or phase, and generally with a low error rate in generating these.
2. Quantum Repeaters: Quantum repeaters will be necessary for long-distance quantum communication. They would help in solving the problem of photon loss and decoherence that occur with the distance.

3. Secure Quantum Channels: Optical fiber or free space is the usual media used for the transferring of quantum information. The transmission should have, however, special measures because they face complications such as loss of photons, added noise, and environmental interference. These challenges call for developing extremely efficient optical components and noise-reducing techniques.
4. Quantum-Resistant Classical Infrastructure: While secure exchange of keys is done by quantum systems, classical communication, as in the internet, will still be important to many aspects of the key exchange. So one must think of the hybrid classical-quantum systems that for quantum cryptography are envisaged to be an important component of the existing classical communication networks.
5. Detection Systems: The detection systems are those that will measure the quantum states of the photons through quantum detectors, like avalanche photodiodes or superconducting nanowires, with high sensitivity and accuracy. These systems must operate under cool-temperature conditions and with low error rates for the security of the cryptographic key exchange.

12.4.4 Barriers to Field Deployment

Despite the promising potential of quantum cryptography, several challenges must be addressed to deploy it effectively in the field. These challenges span technical, financial, and practical domains.

12.4.4.1 Technical Challenges

a. Photons Loss and Decoherence: Photon loss is not only transmittance through optical fibers or free space; it is one of the critical issues for which scientists are working through development of quantum repeaters, still remaining active field research. The more distance photons travel, the higher probability of absorption or scattering will happen within them, and eventually leading to loss of information and security.
b. Scalability: Implementation of quantum cryptography is a difficult task to actualize at a larger-scales such as in a nation or even globally. The expensive infrastructure to have quantum communications put over long distances on land is not easy to deploy, especially so in areas that lack high-quality optical fibers.
c. Integration with the Existing Systems: These quantum cryptography systems would also have to live with the already existing classical legacy system. The huge technical issue will lie in merging the classical and quantum communication channels more so when it comes to the issues of key management and error correction.
d. Environmental: Environmental factors can also contribute to various ends in the operation of quantum communication systems. These environmental factors are temperature fluctuation, vibrations, and even atmospheric conditions in the case of free-space communication. The system needs to be made unaffected from such factors and also reliable during deployment in the field.

12.4.4.2 Cost and Practical Constraints

a. Production and Maintenance of Hardware: The specialized equipment required for quantum cryptography, including photon sources, detectors, and quantum repeaters, has become costly to manufacture and maintain. The cost for developing a quantum cryptography system forms a major barrier for large-scale deployment.
b. Scarcity of Infrastructure: Really good-quality optical fibers and free-space communication systems are not found everywhere. Quantum infrastructure for the transmitting quantum information should be developed significantly to achieve worldwide repetition of quantum cryptography that requires huge investments.
c. Competent Personnel and Training: Quantum cryptography is very specialized and requires an advanced understanding of quantum mechanics, optics, and cryptography. As such, the installation, maintenance, and troubleshooting of such systems call for specialized skills that currently exist in limited numbers.
d. Issues of Regulation and Standardization: Quantum cryptography systems are still emerging technologies, and thus, there are no general standards yet, so all the governments and organizations working similarly must create frameworks for standardization and regulation.

12.5 CHANNEL FIDELITY AND ERROR CORRECTION

In quantum communication, channel fidelity refers to the accuracy with which quantum information is transmitted over a communication channel. That has to ensure high fidelity in transmission to verify the integrity and, therefore, confidentiality in quantum communication systems. Because quantum states are fragile and easily disturbed, error correction becomes essential in keeping channel fidelity as it can safeguard information sent from disruption or alteration through noise and interference.

This section discusses quantum channel fidelity and quantum noise effects, along with the error correction techniques deployed for maintaining the fidelity of a quantum communication channel.

12.5.1 Importance of Quantum Channel Fidelity

Quantum channel fidelity indicates the extent to which the quantum state received by the recipient (in particular, a photon's polarization or entanglement state) resembles that state sent by the sender. High channel fidelity becomes critical for several reasons:

a. Information Integrity: In quantum communication, even the tiniest changes in the quantum state—for example, a fluctuation in photon polarization or phase—can cause information loss. Higher channel fidelity prevents change due to perturbations in the quantum channel and accurately preserves transmitted information, thereby preventing it from ever really being corrupted.

b. Security of Quantum Protocols: The security of quantum protocol hinges on secret disturbance detection or the attempt of eavesdropping. Once channel fidelity is out, it becomes harder to trace the eavesdropping and compromise the integrity of exchanged keys or information. If possible, fidelity must be kept so that any interference becomes notable and therefore can be corrected.
c. Reliable Communication over Long Distances: It is because as quantum communication systems are longer deployed, the channel fidelity becomes increasingly difficult because of loss through photons and scattering. It is also important that fidelity be maintained to ensure reliability in the transmission of quantum states over it, albeit for longer distances, especially across the fiber-optic networks or in free-space communication.
d. Error-Free Transmission of Quantum Information: Since quantum systems are highly sensitive, even small nosy errors can disturb the transmission of quantum information. A high-fidelity channel allows the quantum system to operate with little error and thus allows accurate data transmission and safe communication.

12.5.2 Quantum Noise and Its Effects

Quantum noise refers to the disturbances that happen typically in quantum communication channels because of interaction with the environment while the quantum states like photons travel through these agents. Quantum noise influences very much the fidelity of the channel and the integrity of the information received.

The following are examples of quantum noise types:

a. Photon Loss: This is one of the most important contributions to noise that comes into play in quantum communication. As photons are traveling through an optical fiber or just free space, they may be absorbed, scattered, or blocked by an imperfection in the medium they are being transmitted through. Thus, the reduction of photons reaching the receiver leads to a decrease in the efficiency and reliability of the system.
b. Dephasing: Loss of coherence between quantum states is called dephasing. Usually, such noise happens to be caused when the respective quantum states get entangled with their environment, thus losing the ability to interfere from one to another. In quantum communication, dephasing makes it difficult to measure or read the original quantum state, effectively altering it.
c. Bit-Flip and Phase-Flip Errors: These are generalized noises that can happen during quantum transmission. A bit-flip error defines the circuit situation when the state of the quantum bit (qubit) changes from 0 to 1 or vice versa. A phase-flip error can change the relative phase of the quantum states. Both the types of errors give wrong measurement systems and disturb secure key exchange protocols.
d. Thermal Noise: This noise is caused by the random movement of particles present inside the medium through which transmission takes place, such as optical fibers or even detectors. This motion causes fluctuation of states of the photons that have been sent leading to errors in the communication channel.

12.5.3 Error Correction Methods in Quantum Communication

Quantum error correction (QEC) is a critical aspect of quantum communication, as it allows systems to correct errors introduced by noise and other disturbances without directly measuring or collapsing the quantum state. Quantum error correction codes (QECCs) and other strategies help preserve the fidelity of quantum communication systems, ensuring that transmitted information remains secure and accurate.

12.5.3.1 Quantum Error Correction Codes

During transmission of quantum bits over open channels or for communication within light pulses pumped by laser, no innovation or improvement in hardware can do away with environment-induced deflections, or noise. Quantum error correction is the only possible solution to allow a system to correct noise-induced errors into the actual quantum states, without direct measurement, much less breaking the quantum state. Without these precious quantum error correction codes and the constellation of other strategies for the quantum information industry, the fidelity of a quantum communication system transmitting information is purely compromised for security and accuracy stats. Quantum error correction codes are special kinds of algorithms and techniques that encode quantum information in a way that errors caused by noise could be detected and corrected without violation of the no-cloning philosophy. Such sources often work with the use of redundant encoded quantum states into a number of physical qubits in order to identify and fix the errors that would occur.

Some of the examples of important quantum error-correcting codes are:

a. Shor Code: This is among the oldest and the most prominent quantum error correction codes in the quantum communication world. It encodes a single logical qubit into a total of nine physical qubits and is able to correct both bit-flip and phase-flip errors. That is, in order to define the scene where an error occurs, which means something is wrong, the Shor code uses redundancy to distribute the information over many qubits so that errors of a few qubits can be picked up and corrected.
b. Steane Code: The erasure code Steane is the more efficient error-correcting code that encodes one logical qubit into seven physical qubits. The code is based on classical Hamming codes and can correct faults for both bit-flip and phase-flip. The Steane code is efficient compared to the Shor code because less qubits are used for an equal space of strong error correction.
c. Surface Code: Using a two-dimensional lattice of qubits to encode information, surface codes are a subclass of topological quantum error correction codes.
d. Bacon-Shor Code: It is another type of code for protecting against bit-flip and phase-flip error. It creates a subsystem by using a set of qubits that can be checked for errors and corrected without measuring the quantum state directly. It has applications in quantum computing and also quantum communication.
e. Cat Codes: They are the family of quantum error correction codes that use the idea of quantum superposition to create highly redundant states. They can also be used to protect quantum information against decoherence and loss under noise due to the environment. Such codes allow for the detection

and correction of errors in quantum communication systems without compromising the security or general integrity of the communication. However, such codes require a large number of qubits, and there is also overhead by computation which has to be minimized for real experiment purposes.

12.5.3.2 Strategies to Preserve Fidelity in Secure Channels

There are ways to extend quantum error correction beyond quantum error codes, and some strategies can help preserve the integrity of quantum communication channels.

1. Quantum Repeaters: The device is able to extend the distance of a communication system by boosting and regenerating the quantum information traveling through this link. In the operation of these quantum repeaters, it divides the quantum information into small parts and transmits them over great distances. After their travels, these parts are reunited. This highly reduces the photon loss and augments long-distance quantum communication fidelity.
2. Decoherence-Free Subspace (DFS): Decoherence-free subspace refers to those special subspaces in a particular quantum system that do not get affected by specific types of environmental noise such as dephasing. Encoding quantum information in these subspaces helps preserve the coherence and fidelity of the quantum state and reduces noise-related error.
3. Entanglement Purification: Entanglement purification is a process employed to enhance the quality of the entangled quantum states within systems relating to entanglement, like QKD protocol systems. This involves subjecting the entangled particles to local operations and measurements, which upgrade low-quality entangled pairs to high-quality entangled pairs, thereby improving fidelity in quantum key distribution and other quantum communication protocols.
4. Post-selection: Post-selection refers to the fact that results of some of the measurements may be discarded because they are erroneous due to interference or noise. When this is done and only good results are permitted, the fidelity of transmission is increased while the chances of errors occurring during key exchanges or message transmission are reduced.

12.6 VULNERABILITIES AND SECURITY CONCERNS

Quantum communication systems, while offering enhanced security due to the unique properties of quantum mechanics, are not immune to vulnerabilities. As these systems become more widely deployed, understanding the potential threats and how they may impact the security of transmitted information is essential. This section delves into potential threats and eavesdropping mechanisms in quantum communication, as well as the implications of quantum computing on the security of these systems.

12.6.1 Potential Threats and Eavesdropping Mechanisms in Quantum Communication

Quantum communication systems such as QKD use the principles of quantum mechanics to ensure any governments' security. The very basic idea behind quantum security is that any interception or measurement of quantum states would induce a disturbance in those states, which can be detected, thereby alerting both communicating parties of the presence of an unauthorized person. However, inherent indications of such systems into potential threats that could jeopardize quantum communications include:

a. Quantum Eavesdropping: Though the existence of eavesdropping can be detected in a quantum system by the principles of quantum measurement, e.g., Heisenberg's uncertainty principle, sophisticated methods of eavesdropping can impose a threat on it (such as the following examples listed here).
b. Intercept-and-Resend Attacks: In this type of eavesdropping, an attacker intercepts the key exchanged between two parties, measures it, and sends a modified version back to the sender. Although they could be introduced errors, the attacker may attempt to control the noise to evade detection.
c. Quantum Man-in-the-Middle Attack: A malicious actor could put himself between two communicating parties and interfere with the information that is transferred using quantum means. This attack might remain undetectable from the error detection mechanism if the attacker uses advanced techniques to modify quantum states without trigger detection mechanisms.
d. Trojan-Horse Attacks: Here an adversary injects a Trojan horse into the quantum scenario, such as a detector that would influence the quantum channel when turned on. This becomes more important in realistic quantum communication systems that have a complex infrastructure.

12.6.2 The Impact of Quantum Computing on Quantum Communication

Quantum computing, while promising to revolutionize computation by solving problems that are intractable for classical computers, also introduces new challenges to the security of quantum communication systems. Quantum computers are fundamentally different from classical computers in their ability to process and manipulate quantum states, which could have far-reaching implications for cryptographic systems, including quantum communication.

12.6.2.1 New Threats from Quantum Computing

a. However, quantum computing, which promises the possibility of computation at solving otherwise intractable problems by classical computers, introduces new threats into the security of quantum communication systems. Unlike classical computers, quantum computers can process and manipulate quantum states, which has deep implications for cryptographic systems, such as quantum communication.
b. With the implementation of quantum computing, new threats will be brought upon the traditional cryptosystems that the quantum communication aims to protect. Traditional cryptosystems are significantly based on the difficulty of certain mathematical problems, e.g., factoring large numbers (RSA) or

solving discrete logarithms (ECC), for the protection of sensitive data; however, it uses exponential speedups over classical means using algorithms such as Shor's algorithm to solve these problems.

c. Breaking Classical Encryption Schemes: Quantum computers can efficiently break widely used classical encryption protocols, such as RSA and ECC, by leveraging Shor's algorithm. This is a major concern for traditional cryptographic systems that quantum communication systems are intended to protect. Although quantum communication may provide secure key distribution, quantum computers could still be used to break existing encrypted data if they are not secure against quantum algorithms.

12.6.2.2 Potential Impact on QKD Protocols

Protocols such as BB84 and E91 in QKD take advantage of quantum mechanics principles such that they can provide secret communication between two parties using cryptographic keys. Quantum states, for example, photon polarization or entanglement, are measured to sense any disturbance caused by the observance of the measurements on quantum information. Their approaches enable them to catch any eavesdropping by knowing how the key is compromised.

a. Vulnerability to Quantum Computer-Based attacks: QKD means that its security is based on the laws of quantum mechanics and yet not totally free from the impact of quantum computing. The following are how attacks on QKD systems might be performed using quantum computing.
b. Quantum-Hacking Attacks: A highly performing quantum computer may be used to model or break some parts of quantum key exchange. For example, an attacker would be able to bypass some key security features by simulating the errors that would be introduced by an eavesdropper in the implementation of QKD protocols.
c. Post-Quantum Cryptography (PQC): It makes an extremely important transition to post-quantum cryptographic algorithms in the context of quantum computing. These are basically systems meant to secure the classical cryptographic systems ending up under attacks from quantum computers; however, they must be implemented in such a way to integrate them into quantum communication systems to guarantee their long-term security. The future of quantum communication will be to develop cryptographic protocols highly resistant to quantum computational threats.

12.7 REMEDIATION STRATEGIES FOR QUANTUM COMMUNICATION SECURITY

Quantum communication offers groundbreaking security advantages, but it is not impervious to potential threats. To maintain the integrity of these systems, several strategies must be employed to mitigate risks, especially from eavesdropping and the emerging threats posed by quantum computing. This section outlines key remediation strategies for enhancing the security of quantum communication systems.

12.7.1 Techniques to Mitigate Eavesdropping Risks

Quantum communications guarantee revolutionary prospects for security but don't mean that these systems can be declared invulnerable against threats. In fact, one has to bring in a number of strategies to secure these systems from threats, particularly concerning eavesdropping and emerging threats from quantum computing. The section will elaborate on key remedy strategies that can be adopted for the enhancement of the security of quantum communication systems.

12.7.2 Mitigation Against Eavesdropping

Eavesdropping for quantum communication—the most popular form being in QKD—is detectable by disturbance of the quantum states of the involved parties. This, however, is inadequate because of the need for further techniques securing the information:

1. Monitoring of Error Rates: One frequent measure to discover interference is to continually monitor the error rates during the key exchange process. Typically an abnormal error increase indicates interference that is likely caused by an eavesdropper. Once detected, the communication session can be aborted and the key discarded.
2. Photon Authentication: This means authenticating a photon that is being used in quantum communication. If, however, it has not been modified or substituted during transmission, it will be very difficult for a possible eavesdropper to sneak into the grant system unnoticed.
3. Use of Trusted Relays: Trusted relays, which provide support in key-exchanged processes over longer distances, may add to the protection of quantum communication channels. They ensure that the signals sent through are free from interception or tampering during transmission.
4. Adding Randomness to Protocols: Randomness being added on the choosing of the quantum states that will be used under the key generation process adds maximum security. By employing mostly randomly chosen quantum states during key generation, it means that at least some level of guarantee can be given against the eavesdropper termination.

12.7.3 Quantum Entanglement as a Tool for Counteracting Eavesdropping

Entanglement is an important part of quantum mechanics, which constitutes one of the most potent tools for perfect security in quantum communication systems:

a. Agreement with Entanglement: For example, the E91 agreement where entanglement is used for the distribution of quantum keys. Entangled particles correlate the source and destination, thus helping them in detecting third-party interventions. Any eavesdropping on entangled states will disturb the system, revealing the disadvantages.

b. Entanglement Purification. This enhances the quality of entangled pairs to produce stronger and more secure keys. The low-quality entangled states can be thrown away, while maintaining the better security ones by using entanglement purification, so an eavesdropper needs to work hard to obtain the information
c. Quantum Teleportation: Entanglement enables quantum teleportation. In quantum teleportation, qubit states are transferred instantly between distant points in space without being transmitted, physically. Since quantum teleportation is dependent on entanglement, it has a high security feature for incoming sensitive information over vulnerable channels.

12.7.4 Addressing the Challenges Posed by Quantum Computing

At the same time, quantum computing has brought a whole new dimension of security concerns when it comes to QKD and encryption protocols. Possible solutions could include the following:

a. Post-Quantum Cryptography: Post-quantum cryptography is basically creating new cryptographic algorithms that withstand quantum attacks; for example, Shor's algorithm breaks all conventional encryption schemes (like RSA). The quantum-safe encryption algorithms can be integrated into a quantum communication system to protect against threats that may emerge due to the advent of large-scale quantum computers.
b. Quantum Key Recycling: The quantum key recycling process enables the reuse of keys produced through quantum communication for secure communications. The constant recycling and reuse of keys in the system add that "even if the quantum computer were able to crack one, it would have access to a limited amount of information, as new keys would soon replace old ones."
c. Hybrid Systems: Hybrid systems are those in which quantum communication channels are incorporated with classical plus post-quantum cryptography approaches. This will ultimately provide the system with both the quantum mechanical security features and the benefits of quantum-resistant encryption, thereby allowing secure data even when quantum computers become a significant threat to conventional cryptographic techniques.
d. Ongoing Research and Development of Algorithms: The research pursues developing new algorithms and techniques to secure quantum communication against future quantum computers' heaviest computational capabilities and secure quantum key distribution and protocols in general. Quantum communication, like any other, must evolve with time.

12.7.5 Quantum Error Correction for Enhanced Security

The essential role of quantum error correction (QEC) in quantum communication systems, in general, is in security and the reliability of the systems. Error correction maintains quantum information transmission integrity by mitigating the effects of noise and imperfections in quantum channels.

a. Redundancy and Fault Tolerance: Quantum error correction codes encode information redundantly across multiple physical qubits, thereby allowing the detection and correction of errors without the collapse of the quantum state. The Shor code, Steane code, and surface code are some important constructions for fidelity maintenance of a quantum state.
b. Decoherence-Free Subspaces: Decoherence-free subspaces promise a confinement for quantum information against dephasing-noise and other types of noise. They provide complete stability of the quantum states, thus increasing the security of the communication channel and making a much stronger error correction.
c. Error Detecting and Feedback Mechanism: Real-time error detection and feedback mechanism would help in detecting and correcting the errors as they happen, thereby preventing the error accumulation that will lead not only to loss of information in the system but also the compromise of the security of the quantum communication system.

12.8 FUTURE DIRECTIONS IN QUANTUM COMMUNICATION AND SECURE CHANNELS

Quantum communication technology is still in its early stages, and ongoing research is needed to overcome various challenges and unlock its full potential. In this section, we look at emerging trends, the future role of quantum communication, and long-term challenges that must be addressed.

12.8.1 Emerging Trends in Quantum Communication Research

This still has a lot of room for improvement in the very near future because research is underway with an exemplary revolution to solve many problems associated with this new technology. This section describes expected future directions in the development of quantum communication and long-term issues that are likely to arise at that time.

Emerging Trends in Quantum Communication Research

a. Quantum Repeaters and Long-Distance Communication: The work on quantum repeaters will also be taken into account as one of the most exhilarating areas in the world of investigation. Quantum repeaters will transmit quantum information through long distances by taking care of the loss and errors brought on by transmission through a photon. The extension of repeaters into quantum networks is going to be an important step in building a giant-scale, worldwide quantum communication system.
b. Quantum Networking Development: Research on building quantum networks or the so-called "quantum internet" is gradually beginning to gain momentum. These networks aim at integrating quantum computers and quantum devices for secure, instantaneous, and real-time communication at distant points. This will lay the basis of quantum routing, switching, and memory for realizing this network.

c. Integrated Quantum Systems: The push toward integrated quantum systems encompasses coordinated effort to couple quantum communication technologies with other quantum devices, such as quantum sensors and quantum computers, for developing multi-functional quantum networks. This promises communication and computation at the same time.

12.8.2 The Role of Quantum Communication in Future Secure Systems

As quantum communication becomes more widely adopted, its role in securing future systems is becoming increasingly important. Quantum communication will be crucial for safeguarding sensitive information in critical sectors, such as finance, healthcare, and government. Its ability to provide provable security, based on the laws of quantum mechanics, will make it an essential component of next-generation secure communication infrastructures.

12.8.3 Long-Term Challenges and Opportunities for Quantum Cryptography

With the advent of quantum communication, the systems shall be enhanced in the future with their increasing importance. Quantum communication must play a great role in the way secure information is handled in government, healthcare, and finance. In fact, for next-generation secure communication infrastructures, proven security based on laws of quantum mechanics will make it a major element.

a. Scalability of Quantum Systems: Among the very important problems in quantum communication and cryptography is the seamlessness and scalability of quantum systems. The ever-expanding quantum networks will continue to remain centers of attention in research, concentrating on how quantum key distribution and error correction.
b. Hardware and Infrastructure for Quantum Technology: Creating real robust quantum communication infrastructures, including photon detectors, quantum sources, and quantum routers, is another big challenge. Continued advancements in quantum hardware development would be important to facilitate large-scale quantum communications.
c. Legal and Regulatory Aspects: As advances in quantum communication technologies gather pace, the legal and regulatory aspects will assume more significance, such as encryption laws and international standards for quantum security.

12.9 CONCLUSION

Quantum communication is expected to bring a new revolution in secure communication, redefining previously defined levels of security and privacy. There is still quite a long way to go before the existing eavesdropping risks are reduced, facing quantum computing threats, and ensuring that the future scaling of quantum systems is equal to the emerging needs. This chapter has discussed the basic principles of quantum communication, including quantum key distribution (QKD) protocols, quantum cryptography systems, and the role of quantum error correction. Security vulnerabilities and concerns related to quantum communication have been discussed, along with possible strategies against those weaknesses. The future of quantum communication appears very bright, starting from secure data transmission for military and governmental sectors to the bases for quantum networks connecting quantum computing and quantum cryptography. But further research and development will be very much needed to face the challenges that still exist and to unleash the full potential of quantum communication systems.

In a future where quantum communication is gaining more traction in everyday technology use, it is increasingly going to be important for people to ensure that their messages remain secure and private. The continued advancements in quantum technology will soon allow all to have the world's most secure, scalable, and efficient communication system with the use of unique quantum mechanical properties for information safety in the digital age.

REFERENCES

Brod, D. J., Galvão, E. F., Crespi, A., Osellame, R., Spagnolo, N., & Sciarrino, F. (2019). Photonic implementation of boson sampling: A review. Advances in Photonics, 1(1), 1–23. https://doi.org/10.1117/1.ap.1.1.014001

Cai, X., Chen, Y., & Hu, Z. (2024). Continuous variable quantum communication in noisy environments. Journal of Quantum Networks, 2, 101–112. https://doi.org/10.1016/j.jqn.2024.101234

Gu, Z., Zhang, Z., Yin, H., Liang, W., & Ma, X. (2023). Satellite-based quantum communication systems for long-distance QKD. Physical Review Applied, 19, 034011. https://doi.org/10.1103/PhysRevApplied.19.034011

Guccione, G., Darras, T., Jeannic, H. L., Verma, V. B., Nam, S. W., Cavaillès, A., & Laurat, J. (2020). Connecting heterogeneous quantum networks by hybrid entanglement swapping. Science Advances, 6, eaba4508. https://doi.org/10.1126/sciadv.aba4508

Huang, W., Chen, L., & Fang, Y. (2024). Hybrid cryptographic protocols integrating quantum and classical systems. Advances in Cryptographic Research, 12(3), 211–229. https://doi.org/10.1016/j.acr.2024.211229

Kim, H. S., Jang, S., & Lee, H. W. (2024). Machine learning optimization for quantum communication protocols. Quantum Machine Learning Journal, 3, 456–470. https://doi.org/10.1103/QML.2024.456470

Marchetti, R., Lacava, C., Carroll, L., Gradkowski, K., & Minzioni, P. (2019). Coupling strategies for silicon photonics integrated chips. Photonics Research, 7(3), 201–219. https://doi.org/10.1364/prj.7.000201

Nguyen, H. P., & Zhang, S. (2024). Quantum network synchronization for secure communication. Quantum Science and Technology, 9(2), 024010. https://doi.org/10.1088/2058-9565/acb101

Pan, J.-W., Yin, J., Ren, J., Wang, S., Zhang, W., & Peng, C. (2019). Advances in quantum secure direct communication. Physical Review Letters, 122(5), 050502. https://doi.org/10.1103/PhysRevLett.122.050502

Pelucchi, E., Fagas, G., Aharonovich, I., Englund, D., Figueroa, E., Gong, Q., . . . & Matsuda, N. (2022). Integrated photonics for quantum technologies. Nature Reviews Physics, 4, 194–210. https://doi.org/10.1038/s42254-022-00443-5

Schreiber, A., Cassemiro, K. N., Potoček, V., Gábris, A., Mosley, P. J., Andersson, E., . . . & Silberhorn, C. (2022). Advances in integrated photonic quantum technologies. Nature Physics, 4, 194–206. https://doi.org/10.1038/s41567-022-01640-w

Silverstone, J. W., Bonneau, D., O'Brien, J. L., & Thompson, M. G. (2023). Quantum photonics for secure communication systems. Journal of Quantum Engineering, 4, e2022011. https://doi.org/10.1002/qute.2022011

Smith, T. E., & Adams, R. J. (2024). Quantum error correction methods for secure communication networks. Quantum Reports, 7(1), 55–72. https://doi.org/10.3390/qr7010055

Walmsley, I., & Smith, B. J. (2023). Quantum photonics in communication and computing. Optica Quantum, 1, 35–45. https://doi.org/10.1364/oq.1.000035

13 Quantum Computing and Teleportation

Shaik Jaffar Hussain, Haranadha Reddy Busireddy Seshakagari, J. Avanija, Allam Gowri Sankar, and G. Suryanarayana

13.1 THE RISE OF QUANTUM INFORMATION SCIENCE

Quantum information science (QIS) is a rapidly emerging discipline, fusing quantum mechanics with information theory to redefine the processing, transmission, and security of data. The seeds were sown in the 1980s and 1990s when greats such as Richard Feynman and David Deutsch submitted that quantum systems might perform tasks that classical computers never could. This period saw the emergence and blossoming of novel algorithms, such as Shor's factoring algorithm and Grover's search algorithm.

The rise of QIS has matured with the attempts to overcome limitations faced by classical computing, particularly in cryptography, simulations, and optimizations. The deeper the understanding of quantum principles went, the broader the horizon of revolutionary application—intermeshed with quantum teleportation and quantum key distribution, toward even quantum machine learning—was seen. Today, QIS is a multidisciplinary frontier fostering new developments in physics, computer science, and engineering to lay out the possibilities for next-generation technologies with capabilities heretofore unimagined (Arun & Mishra, 2014).

13.2 CLASSICAL VS. QUANTUM COMPUTATION OR QUANTUM PARALLELISM AND INTERFERENCE

In classical computation, the bits represent data that may assume a value 0 or 1 and work deterministically through logic gates, as in Table 13.1. Today's digital gadgets operate on the binary operations that have been firmly established through the years. Yet qubits are in a superposition state, meaning they are at the same time state 0 and state 1. Qubits may also be entangled, creating exceedingly complex correlations that cannot exist among classical bits. Through this, quantum computers can carry out some particular computational tasks, such as factoring huge integers or simulating quantum systems, at speeds exponentially faster than classical computers (Bashar et al., 2009). Classical computation, though, fares well in aspects like scalability and dependability, whereas quantum computing confers brute strength for a niche set of complex problems.

DOI: 10.1201/9781003538950-15

Table 13.1
Comparison Between Classical Bits and Quantum Bits (Qubits)

Concept	Classic bit	Qubit
Values	0 or 1	0, 1, or both
Representations	Binary digit	Vector in 2D complex space
Key features	Deterministic	Superposition and entanglement
Computation	Sequential	Parallel and interferential

13.3 QUANTUM BITS AND ENTANGLEMENT

Qubits are the basic information units of quantum computing. While classical bits can possess either a 0 or 1 state, depending on the measurement, qubits can exist in superpositions of states of 0 and 1 at the same time.

■ Superposition → Qubit = a|0⟩ + b|1⟩ where a and b are probability amplitudes.

This property enables quantum computers to consider equivalently enormous numbers of possibilities, thereby endowing them with huge amounts of parallel computational power. Qubits are often created from quantum systems of electrons, photons, or superconducting circuits, which can be operated on with great precision by means of quantum gates.

Another cornerstone of quantum computing is entanglement, which is a quantum phenomenon whereby two or more qubits become highly correlated such that the state of one immediately determines the state of the other, no matter the distance, as represented in Figure 13.1.

Entanglement means the measurement of one qubit instantly fixes the state of the other qubit.

Thus, entanglement provides the basis for implementation of powerful quantum protocols, such as quantum teleportation, quantum cryptography, and error correction. Moreover, the speedup offered by quantum algorithms is realized because entanglement allows qubits to act in concert in ways that are not possible classically. Through the marvels of superposition and entanglement, the dream of quantum computing sets itself apart from classical computers, thus paving the way to radically new methods of computation, communication, and data security.

13.4 WHAT ARE QUBITS?

In quantum computing, qubits serve as the actual carriers of information. Qubits may be thought of as any two-level quantum system. Unlike classical bits, which are mutually exclusive set either 0 or 1, qubits can be in an intriguing quantum state called superposition, which allows them to be in a combination of both 0 and 1. This property allows quantum computers to analyze extremely complicated data more quickly than their classical counterparts. Qubits can also be entangled, which means the state of one qubit is dependent on the state of another qubit, thereby enabling parallel computations

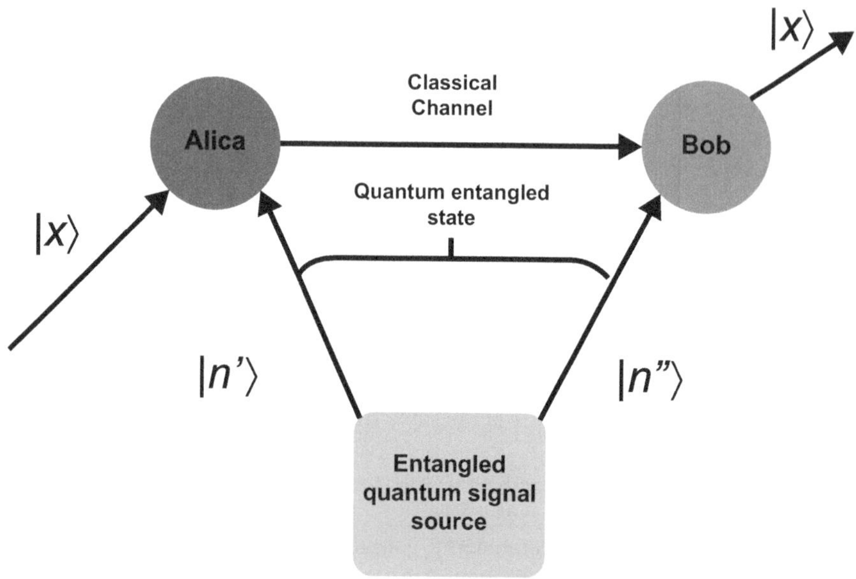

FIGURE 13.1 Quantum entanglement process. This diagram shows the correlation between entangled particles, highlighting instantaneous state determination.

at an unprecedented level of power. When measured, the qubit collapses to either 0 or 1, and the probability to land on each is stipulated by the quantum state. Using mechanisms for quantum mechanical calculations such as superposition, entanglement, and interference, qubits solve tough calculations that are otherwise impractical for a classical machine. A few of the applications for which they are basically being used include quantum cryptography, simulation, and quantum algorithms rewarded for solving some problems that are currently impossible for a classical machine.

13.5 SUPERPOSITION AND MEASUREMENT

Superposition is a basic concept in which a qubit exists in more than one state; here, it is contradictory since the qubit is both 0 and 1 at the same time. Unlike classical bits that are only either 0 or 1, a qubit is in a quantum superposition of states: a probabilistic combination of the two possibilities. Thus, measuring the superposition collapses it to one of the basis states, with the outcome dictated according to probability amplitudes associated with the given state. Thus, a quantum computer explores many possibilities simultaneously, and this is really what gives it computational power.

Measurement in general is an act of observation of the quantum system into a qubit. The qubit in a superposition collapses by measurement into a definite state, either 0 or 1. The probabilities of each of these possibilities depend on what the qubit was in before measurement. Because of this collapse, quantum information is very delicate, and one has to be very cautious about when and how measurements are done in quantum algorithms.

13.6 QUANTUM ENTANGLEMENT EXPLAINED

Quantum entanglement is a phenomenon whereby two or more qubits are correlated such that one qubit's state instantly impacts the state of the other, regardless of the physical distance between the two, as mentioned in Figure 13.2. Once entangled, qubits behave like linked and constrained variables; measuring one immediately gives knowledge of the other's state, even if they are separated by vast distances. This deep linkage violates classical logic, but it plays the most important role in quantum processing in forming interesting correlations and speeding information processing. Entanglement is used in quantum algorithms, teleportation, and the quantum cryptographic method for secure communication. It gives quantum computers the capability of taking entangled qubits, which act in tandem, to tackle problems that classical computers simply cannot solve efficiently, as opposed to tackling them individually.

13.7 QUANTUM GATES AND CIRCUITS

Quantum gates are building blocks of quantum circuits and are similar to classical logic gates, such as AND, OR, and NOT, which function on bits in traditional computers. Quantum gates operate on qubits in accordance with quantum-physical principles: superposition and entanglement, to name two. Unlike classical gates, quantum gates are reversible, whereas their transformations on qubits are represented through unitary matrices (Chou et al., 2018).

Some of the common quantum gates are:

- Hadamard gate (H): It makes superposition by transforming a qubit from a definite state to balanced superposition of 0 and 1.
- Pauli-X: Also called quantum NOT, it flips the qubit state from $|0\rangle$ to $|1\rangle$ or vice versa.
- CNOT (controlled-NOT) gate: It is a two-qubit gate that flips the second qubit only if the first qubit is $|1\rangle$ to establish entanglement.

Quantum circuits are arranged strings of quantum gates working on one or more qubits for the application of computation or an algorithm. A quantum circuit acts on

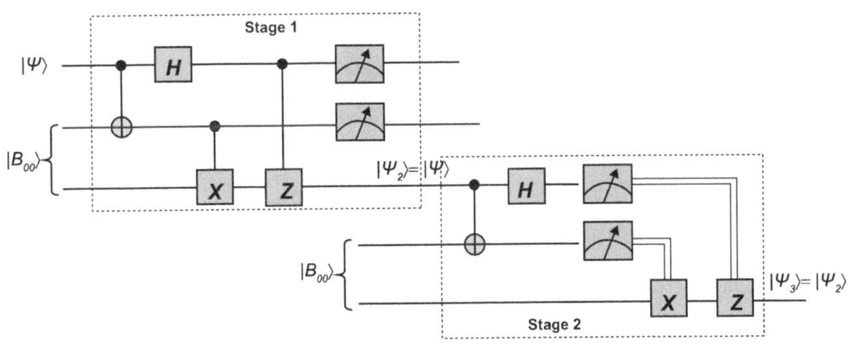

FIGURE 13.2 Detailed step-by-step process of the entanglement process.

qubits, step by step, changing their states using superposition and entanglement to hold information capable of processing in a manner that cannot be possible with classical circuits. Quantum circuits are depicted by circuit diagrams wherein the horizontal lines denote qubits, and symbols show gates applied as a function of time. These circuits are the kernel of quantum algorithms, such as Shor's factoring or Grover's search, giving power to quantum computing.

13.8 SINGLE-QUBIT GATES

Single-qubit gates affect a qubit at a time and are indispensable for any quantum computation, but they rotate and transform the quantum state vector of the qubit over the Bloch sphere, as in Figure 13.3.

Hadamard (H) gate: It creates superposition from $|0\rangle$ or $|1\rangle$ into equal weight.
Pauli-X gate: It flips the qubit state, similar to a classical NOT.
Pauli-Y and Pauli-Z gates: They perform quantum rotations about certain axes.
Phase gates: They alter the phase of the qubit's state and thus affect interference.

Since single-qubit gates are reflective of 2×2 unitary matrices, they are reversible operations working on quantum information.

The mathematical representations of some essential quantum gates are:

- **Hadamard Gate (H):**

H=12[111−1]H = \frac{1}{\sqrt{2}}\begin{bmatrix}1 & 1\\ 1 & −1\ end{bmatrix}H=21[111−1]

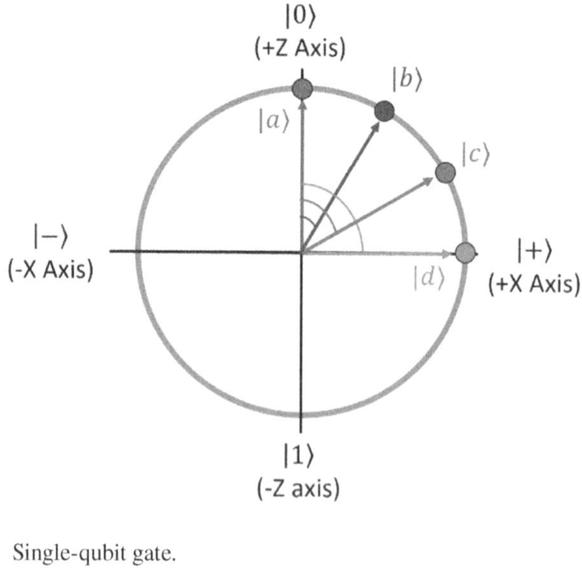

FIGURE 13.3 Single-qubit gate.

- **Pauli-X Gate (NOT gate):**

X=[0110]X = \begin{bmatrix}0 & 1\\ 1 & 0\end{bmatrix}X=[0110]

- **Pauli-Z Gate:**

Z=[100−1]Z = \begin{bmatrix}1 & 0\\ 0 & −1\end{bmatrix}Z=[100−1]

13.9 MULTI-QUBIT GATES AND QUANTUM LOGIC

Multi-qubit gates perform operations on two or more qubits, allowing for more interesting quantum interactions like entanglement or conditioned operations, as specified in Figure 13.4. The most common multi-qubit gate is the CNOT gate: it flips the target qubit's state provided that the control qubit is in state $|1\rangle$. Such gates form the basis of quantum logic: qubits influence each other in their states so as to be transformed jointly (Huang et al., 2004). Multi-qubit gates are crucial in generating entangled states, which are the primary ingredient in quantum algorithms. Along with single-qubit gates, they provide universal quantum computation as they build up quantum circuits that solve anything classical cannot.

13.10 BUILDING A QUANTUM CIRCUIT

A quantum circuit is built by putting together gates that operate on qubits in a predetermined sequence to perform a computation, as represented in Figure 13.5.

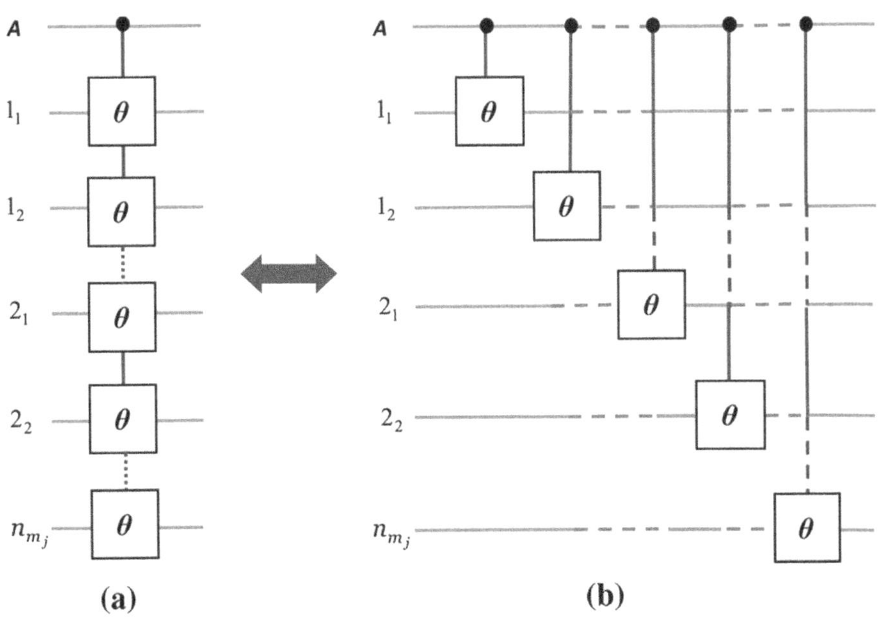

FIGURE 13.4 Multi-qubit gate.

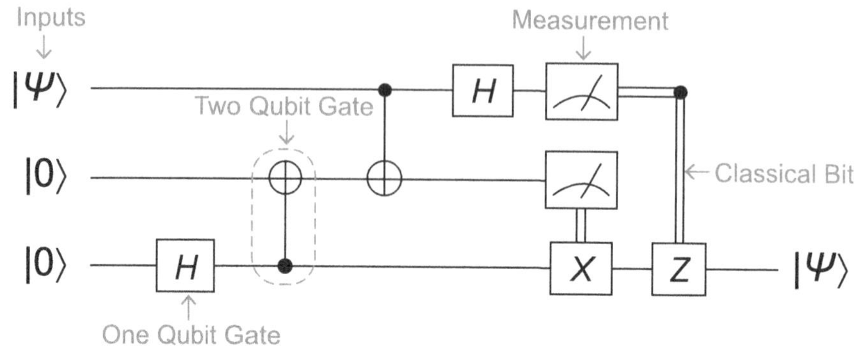

FIGURE 13.5 Quantum circuit diagram.

Each qubit begins the process in some initial state, mostly $|0\rangle$. Single-qubit gates create superpositions and transform the states of individual qubits, while multi-qubit gates such as CNOT entangle qubits to perform more intricate interactions. The circuit is built by factoring in quantum mechanical effects such as interference and entanglement to try to enhance the probability of the correct answer. A picture of quantum circuits would show lines that show the time evolution of the qubit and symbols for gates. Quantum circuits implement algorithms by combining gates in a very precise order, which can outperform classical algorithms for particular tasks. In essence, quantum teleportation transfers the quantum state of a qubit to a remote side without the qubit itself moving. Entanglement and classical communication are essential.

13.11 FOUNDATIONS OF QUANTUM TELEPORTATION

The process begins with two parties, typically named Alice and Bob, sharing a pair of entangled qubits. Alice has an unknown qubit whose state she wants to teleport onto Bob's behalf. She performs a special joint-measurement called a Bell state measurement upon her unknown qubit and her half of the entangled pair. This measurement collapses the system but produces two classical bits of information for Alice to communicate through a classical channel to Bob (Fedortchenko, 2016).

Using the classical bits received, Bob applies the quantum gate from among the four possible ones to his entangled qubit, transforming it into an exact replica of the original state of Alice's qubit. Thus, the teleportation process completes, where states are perfectly transferred without violation of quantum mechanics (Houshmand et al., 2020). Therefore, matter or energy are not transferred in quantum teleportation; instead, quantum information itself is transferred (Liu, 2020). It is one of the essential techniques in quantum communication and is thus the fundamental basis for higher-level protocols like quantum networks and quantum computing error correction (Shih, 2001). Teleportation exploits nonlocality due to entanglement, wherein the combination with classical information allows quantum states to be transmitted securely and instantly over distance (Hu et al., 2023).

13.12 CORE CONCEPTS OF QUANTUM TELEPORTATION

13.12.1 Definition of Quantum Teleportation?

Quantum teleportation is a protocol that allows the transfer of a quantum state from one qubit to another, potentially distant, qubit without physically sending the qubit itself. Unlike science fiction teleportation, it doesn't move particles but transmits the information encoded in the quantum state (Luo et al., 2019). The process demands two major resources: an entangled pair of qubits shared between the sender (Alice) and the receiver (Bob) and a classical communication channel. Alice carries out a joint measurement on her unknown qubit and her half of the entangled pair, which collapses the states and yields classical information. She communicates this information to Bob, who applies a corresponding quantum operation on his entangled qubit, thereby recreating perfectly the original quantum state. Such protocol plays a vital role for distributed quantum computing and quantum communication (Metcalf et al., 2014).

13.12.2 No-Cloning Theorem

According to a lemma formulated in quantum mechanics, the no-cloning theorem states that no one can produce an exact copy of an unknown quantum state. The classical information can be copied without limit, while quantum information remains delicate and cannot be cloned perfectly. This principle preserves the security of the quantum communication system and is the very reason quantum teleportation comes into play: teleportation does not create a copy but rather transfers the state without breaching the no-cloning principle.

Formally, the no-cloning theorem states that it is impossible to construct a unitary operator UUU such that:

U(|ψ⟩⊗|0⟩)=|ψ⟩⊗|ψ⟩U(|\psi⟩ \otimes |0⟩) =
|\psi⟩ \otimes |\psi⟩U(|ψ⟩⊗|0⟩)=|ψ⟩⊗|ψ⟩

for an arbitrary unknown quantum state |ψ⟩|\psi⟩|ψ⟩. This theorem mentioned in Figure 13.6 ensures the uniqueness and security of quantum information transfer.

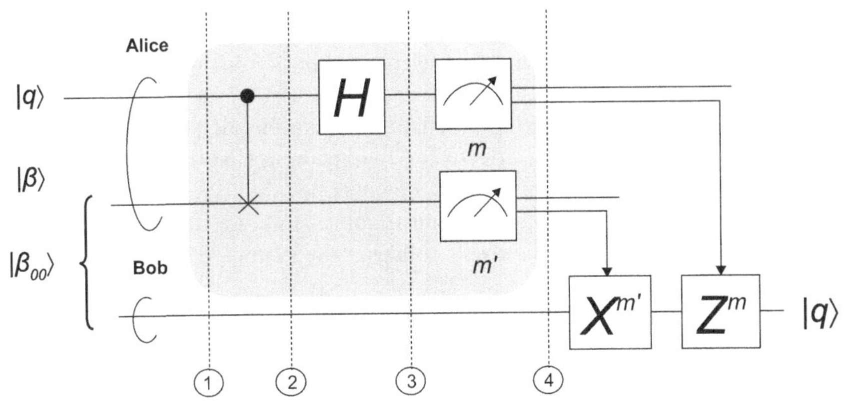

FIGURE 13.6 No-cloning theorem process diagram.

The original quantum state gets destroyed upon measurement to keep any quantum information unique.

13.12.3 Role of Bell States

Bell states are certain maximally entangled two-qubit states on which quantum teleportation is based. There are four Bell states, each indicating a different kind of quantum correlation that can never be classically explained. These states show perfect correlations in their measurements regardless of the distance between qubits, thus exhibiting nonlocality in the quantum realm. Sharing a Bell state between Alice and Bob offers the entanglement resource required to transfer the quantum information during teleportation. Bell states allow quantum entanglement swapping and form the foundation of many quantum communication protocols, thus occupying an important position for the advancement of quantum technologies.

13.12.4 The Teleportation Protocol

The teleportation protocol is a way of quantum communication that allows the exact quantum state of a qubit to be transferred from one side to the other on the basis of entanglement and classical communication (Liu, 2020). It consists of:

1. Entanglement Sharing: Two parties, Alice (sender) and Bob (receiver), share an entangled pair of qubits named a Bell pair. Alice possesses one qubit, while Bob possesses the other;
2. Bell-State Measurement: By its side, Alice desires to teleport a different qubit with an unknown quantum state $|\psi\rangle$ to Bob. For this, she performs a joint measurement on her qubit and her half of the entangled pair, projecting both into one of the four Bell states. This collapses the whole system and produces two bits of classical information, which Alice then sends to Bob via a classical communication channel;
3. State Reconstruction: On receiving these two classical bits, Bob uses them to apply one out of four specific quantum gates {identity, X, Z, or XZ} to his side of the entangled qubit, effectively transforming Bob's qubit into the original state $|\psi\rangle$, thus completing teleportation.

Within the realm of implementing practical quantum circuits, the Bell-state measurement that Alice demands is effectuated by placing a CNOT operation with the unknown qubit acting as the control and the entangled qubit as the target, followed by placing a Hadamard gate on that control qubit. Both are then measured in the computational basis $|0\rangle$, $|1\rangle$. The result collapses the system, effectively generating two classical bits for Bob (Spiller, 2002).

Because the measurement destroys the original state of the qubit, cloning never occurs. The protocol combines the nonlocal correlations owing to quantum entanglement with classical communication for the perfect transfer of quantum information (Wang et al., 2015). Quantum teleportation is a building block for quantum networks, secure communication, and distributed quantum computing (Zeilinger, 2000).

13.12.5 Step-by-Step Protocol

The unknown quantum state gets teleported from Alice to Bob through the following steps:

1. **Entanglement Preparation:** Alice and Bob share an entangled pair of qubits prepared in, say, a Bell state (e.g., |Φ+⟩=12(|00⟩+|11⟩)|\Phi^+\rangle = \frac{1}{\sqrt{2}}(|00\rangle + |11\rangle)). Alice has one qubit; the other is with Bob.
2. **Bell Measurement:** Alice takes the qubit |ψ⟩=α|0⟩+β|1⟩|\psi\rangle = \alpha|0\rangle + \beta|1\rangle she wants to teleport and performs a joint measurement on it along with her entangled qubit, projecting the combined system into one of the four Bell states; this is, in fact, how the unknown qubit gets entangled with her half of the shared pair and yields two classical bits of measurement results.
3. **Classical Communication:** Alice communicates the two classical bits to Bob over a classical channel.
4. **State Reconstruction:** On receiving these bits from Alice, Bob applies the corresponding unitary operation (Identity, X, Z, or XZ) on his qubit, which results in it being in the original state |ψ⟩|\psi\rangle exactly.

13.12.6 The Role of Entanglement and Classical Communication

Entanglement is a strong quantum notion between Alice's qubit and Bob's qubit for transferring the quantum state non-locally. On the other hand, classical communication is necessary to send information of Alice's measurement outcomes to Bob, which guide the correction operations of Bob. Without his receipt of the classical communication, Bob would not stand to recover the state; hence, no faster-than-light information transfer respects causality.

13.12.7 Mathematical Representation of the Process

Initially, the combined system of Alice's unknown state |ψ⟩|\psi\rangle and the entangled pair |Φ+⟩|\Phi^+\rangle is:

|ψ⟩⊗|Φ+⟩=(α|0⟩+β|1⟩)⊗12(|00⟩+|11⟩)|\psi\rangle \otimes |\Phi^+\rangle = \left (\alpha|0\rangle + \beta|1\rangle\right) \otimes \frac{1}{\sqrt{2}} (|00\rangle + |11\rangle)

This can be rewritten as a sum of Bell states on Alice's side and corresponding transformations on Bob's qubit. Alice's Bell measurement projects the system onto one of four Bell states, each associated with a unitary correction Bob applies to recover |ψ⟩|\psi\rangle. This decomposition ensures the original quantum state is perfectly transferred through teleportation.

13.13 EXPERIMENTAL REALIZATIONS

13.13.1 Experimental Realizations of Quantum Teleportation

In principle, teleportation experiments in different materials have been accomplished, opening the way to practical quantum communication technologies.

Due to photons' velocity and their low rate of interaction with an environment, experiments on teleportation mainly use photons. Photon teleportation was first achieved in 1997, transferring the polarization state at very small distances. Since then, teleportation has been realized at larger distances, even including notable satellite experiments, such as the one where the Chinese Micius satellite teleported quantum states further than 1,200 kilometers between space and Earth.

Other possibilities are trapped-ion and atom experiments, which use internal atomic states as qubits. These systems offer precise control and long coherence times, thereby allowing teleportation within ion traps and between ion traps connected by photons.

Solid-state approaches work in superconducting qubits on a chip with cryogenic cooling. Teleportation has been demonstrated between superconducting qubits, which is important for scalable quantum processors.

Due to decoherence and loss, especially in long-distance teleportation, fidelity is still an issue; however, better ways to generate entanglement and correct errors increase it. These experimental achievements have laid the foundation for quantum teleportation to be a key tool for the establishment of quantum networks, secure communication, and distributed quantum computing, bringing it a step closer to realization as the quantum internet.

13.13.2 Emerging Paradigms in Quantum Teleportation

Quantum teleportation has been experimentally certified across diverse platforms. However, its integration into nascent paradigms including quantum satellite constellation, topological qubit, or networked quantum sensing remains less explored. Quantum teleportation linked with topologically protected qubits, for example, would probably mitigate decoherence and enhance fidelity over a long distance. In contrast, the other direction of teleportation in distributed quantum sensing leads to entanglement-enhanced precision measurement of distributed networks. This suggests another interdisciplinary trajectory whereby teleportation builds to much more than a communication protocol, placing it as a foundational ingredient for newer quantum architectures warranting further attention and innovation across fields.

13.13.3 Milestone Experiments in Teleportation

The first experimental setup of quantum teleportation was in 1997 by a group led by Anton Zeilinger, who teleported successfully the polarization state of a photon across a few meters. This experiment verified foundational quantum teleportation principles and inspired the entire world. Subsequently, teleportation was realized between trapped ions, showing it is possible to transfer quantum states within solid-state systems. Increased fidelity, generation of entanglement, and improvements in measurement precision have grown the field over the years to support complex and reliable teleportation protocols.

13.13.4 Teleportation in Photonic Systems

Since photons travel fast and are less vulnerable to decoherence, they seem like good candidates for carrying quantum information (Metcalf et al., 2014). Photonic quantum teleportation thus employs qubits, either polarization- or time-bin-encoded. Nonlinear optical processes such as spontaneous parametric down-conversion generate the entangled photon pairs (Nagy et al., 2021). The sender performs a Bell-state measurement on the unknown photon and one of the entangled photons, then communicates the results classically to the receiver. The receiver performs the correction operations to re-establish the original quantum state's physical realization (Rodrigo et al., 2021). Photonic teleportation has been demonstrated over optical fibers, in free space, and on integrated photonic chips, providing flexibility for quantum communication.

13.13.5 Quantum Teleportation over Long Distances

Long-distance extensions of quantum teleportation are of utmost importance to ever-expanding quantum networks (Pirandola et al., 2025). Among recent milestone experiments is the satellite-based teleportation and time distribution experiments by means of the now-famous Chinese Micius satellite that undertook teleportation beyond 1,200 kilometers between orbit and ground stations. These experiments broke the defense of local realism by proving entanglement distribution and teleportation could triumph over the shackles of atmospheric loss and vast distance (Pirandola et al., 2006). Fiber optic teleportation on the ground, meanwhile, has managed to bypass the hurdle of 100 kilometers. Taken together, these advances will serve as the technological stepping stones toward establishing global-scale quantum communication, enabling infrastructure for secure quantum internet and distributed quantum computation.

13.14 CHALLENGES AND LIMITATIONS

Several problems plague quantum teleportation-the technical and fundamental. A chief among them is decoherence: interaction of qubits with the environment, loss of quantum attributes, and reduced teleportation fidelity. Maintaining entanglement over great distances is censoriously difficult because entangled particles can be subject to loss and noise, especially through optical fibers or through free space. Another limitation arises in the follow-up classic communication channel: it moves at velocity equal to that of light and prevents faster-than-light information transfer.

Due to the no-cloning theorem, quantum teleportation requires the original state to be destroyed upon measurement, which complicates error correction and state verification. On the other hand, generating entangled pairs reliably with a good enough degree of entanglement and performing high-fidelity Bell-state measurements are still an experimental hurdle. Moreover, today's quantum hardware barely scales properly; the error rates prevent integration into practical networks. These drawbacks need to be overcome if one wants to develop large-scale quantum communication systems and the actual quantum internet.

13.14.1 Decoherence and Fidelity

Decoherence is the major hurdle in quantum teleportation. When these qubits interact with the environment around them, they lose their fragile quantum characteristics like the superposition state and the interrelationship with another qubit. This spoiled the teleported state's quality, thereby reducing the state's fidelity—the measure of how well the original state is reconstructed after teleportation. A state of high fidelity is necessary for successful quantum communication and computing. Maintaining coherence along time and distance remains a difficult task, especially given today's noisy channels, such as optical fibers or free atmosphere, wherein photons might get lost or disturbed. Advanced error-correcting and noise reduction techniques will be necessary, but experimental tasks remain challenging.

13.14.2 Scalability Issues

Scaling quantum teleportation for multi-qubit and long-distance networks is a more serious technical matter. Today's quantum hardware and processors usually accommodate only a few qubits with limited coherence times. To entangle and give entanglement across a large quantum network requires a very complicated setup—if only quantum repeaters, which themselves require high-fidelity entanglement swapping, and high-fidelity entanglement storage. Very importantly, scalable and reliable quantum teleportation needs to resolve very important problems related to qubit control, error rates, and integration of different quantum technologies into working systems.

13.14.3 Security and Noise in Quantum Channels

From the theoretical standpoint, teleportation offers security benefits granted by quantum mechanics. However, channels do have noise and imperfections. Noise may cause errors in transmitted qubits or classical bits, lowering the fidelity and security of teleportation. QKD protocols help improve security, but real-life channels incur losses and disturbances, nudging in design elements of error correction and fault tolerance. Moreover, classical communication is limited in speed and could also pose a potential point of infiltration in case of any attack on classic channels. Thus, the main challenge is to ensure security and reliability on noisy, nonideal quantum channels.

13.14.4 Applications of Quantum Teleportation

Quantum teleportation stands as a cornerstone technology of quantum information science and paves the way for several important implementations:

1. Quantum Communication Networks: Teleportation of quantum states across long distances without actually moving qubits is necessary for

building quantum internet and secure communication networks. This functionality further enables QKD protocols to provide encryption that is theoretically unbreakable.

2. Distributed Quantum Computing: By teleporting states between the nodes, teleportation serves distributed quantum computing, whereby quantum processors situated at different locations collaboratively attempt to solve problems so complex that they can no longer be solved by a single quantum computer.
3. Quantum Repeaters: Such devices make use of quantum teleportation techniques to increase the communication distance by mitigating signal loss and decoherence in the transmission channel, constituting an enabling technology for scalable and long-distance quantum networks.

   Quantum repeaters solve one of the major limitations in quantum communication: loss and decoherence over quite a distance. In quantum communication, the particular property of the long-distance link is divided into shorter segments at the quantum repeater node, where entanglement swapping is performed along with storing entangled states in quantum memories.

   Entanglement swapping is when two initially unentangled particles are conditioned to be entangled via joint measurements on particles that are entangled with the former. This process is crucial to extend the distance covered by teleportation, beyond what direct links can achieve.

   Usually, the protocol consists of intermediate stations that perform a Bell-state measurement and then send the classical results forward to apply suitable corrections to the far ends in order to reconstruct entanglement.
4. Quantum Error Correction: Teleportation serves the purpose of helping to carry out error correction, which is an essential safeguard against noise and decoherence for very fragile quantum information in a quantum computer.

   Another meaning of quantum teleportation is that it is used as a fundamental procedure in quantum error correction (QEC). For example, teleportation might be used for gate teleportation, where logical quantum gates are performed by teleportation circuits using ancilla states. This is one method found in fault-tolerant computing, where teleportation circumvents largely error-prone direct gate operations on qubits.

   One instance is in surface codes, where teleporting between logical qubits safeguards the integrity of coherence while minimizing the extent of errors. Hence, teleportation as a modular piece in the quantum computation lays down the road toward scalable and fault-tolerant architectures.

Fundamental Physics Experiments: Quantum teleportation experiments are carried out to test framework assumptions of quantum mechanics, entanglement, and nonlocality, which sheds further light on the quantum world.

Quantum teleportation, capable of reliably transferring quantum information, is at the heart of future secure communication, advanced computing, and fundamental quantum research.

13.14.5 Open Challenges and Future Research Directions

Beyond present-day experimental bounds, there remain some fundamental questions: Is it possible to employ teleportation in multi-party scenarios that involve more than two nodes? How will high-dimensional quantum states (qudits) be limited in fidelity and efficiency when teleported across mixed hardware platforms? Further, can machine learning be used to optimize teleportation gate sequences under noise? Taking these inquiries further could help translate teleportation from a theoretical landmark into a practical tool in scalable quantum infrastructures. As these lines of investigation take shape, other novel use cases for which teleportation could serve will hopefully emerge, where teleportation will be not only an avenue for transferring data but also resource allocation and dynamic routing of qubits across quantum networks.

13.15 FUTURE PROSPECTS

13.15.1 Teleportation of High-Dimensional States

Teleporting higher-dimensional quantum states (qudits) could potentially enable more efficient quantum information encoding. Unlike qubits that encode two levels, qudits (for example, d=3,4 . . .) encode more information per particle, hence increasing channel capacity.

Experimentally, there's progress tracking teleportation of qutrits and above via orbital angular momentum states of photons. However, with dimension scaling, the problems of error correction and decoherence grow really challenging. In the future, we can expect to see qudit teleportation used within quantum machine learning and multivariate encryption protocols.

13.15.2 Quantum Internet and Teleportation

Quantum teleportation serves as a cornerstone technology in the future quantum internet, a worldwide system for secure quantum communication and distributed quantum computing. By reliably teleporting quantum states between remote nodes, teleportation will permit the global and seamless integration of quantum devices. The quantum internet would offer ultra-secure communication, increased data privacy, and new applications such as blind quantum computing users compute on a remote quantum server without revealing sensitive data.

A working model for the quantum internet would employ teleportation-enabled links between regional quantum nodes. Each node maintains entangled memory with several others, using teleportation locally to move logical qubits while preserving their coherence.

These nodes would have:

- Entangled photon sources
- Quantum repeaters
- Quantum routers

For example, a teleportation-assisted multi-node network based on NV centers in diamond and optical fiber links could realize distributed secure quantum computation over metropolitan scales.

13.15.3 Advanced Protocols and Hybrid Systems

Current research pursues the development of teleportation protocols aimed at improving efficiency, fidelity, and error tolerance. Hybrid quantum systems, connecting multiple qubit platforms, will use teleportation to integrate technologies and optimize their potentials. Such integration is crucial if we want scalable quantum networks and functional quantum computers. Newer protocols also consider teleportation of qudits: higher-dimensional quantum states to store richer information and then use it for speedier processing.

13.15.4 Role in Quantum Artificial Intelligence

With QAI rushing ahead, teleportation is not opened just for communication; it serves as a protocol for synchronization and training between distributed quantum neural networks. Consider federated quantum learning models, in which quantum data from various nodes should be aggregated without leaks. In such cases, teleportation will allow transfer of intermediate quantum states from one node to another in a safe and non-destructive way, enabling the nodes to engage in collaborative learning while maintaining privacy and coherence. This marriage between QAI and teleportation could create the frameworks of scalable and secure quantum cognition systems, with teleportation serving as both a computation enabler and a structural status within intelligent quantum ecosystems.

13.16 CONCLUSION

Quantum teleportation stands among the most spectacular achievements of quantum information science—the transfer of an unknown quantum state from one place to another without transferring the particle itself physically. Based on entanglement and quantum measurement, teleportation circumvents basic problems—the no-cloning theorem and the fragility of quantum information. Successful experiments on various platforms such as photons, trapped ions, and superconducting circuits have demonstrated the practical realization of teleportation, thereby setting the stage for its real-world applications.

The technology used for the development of the quantum internet is the enabling quantum-secure communication through long distances. It also enables distributed quantum computing by allowing quantum information to be shared between processors situated far apart, thereby enabling these processors to overcome the limitations of their hardware and hence make scalable quantum architectures. Quantum teleportation is used for quantum error correction, which helps in protecting fragile quantum states from noise and decoherence.

Many challenges continue to face quantum teleportation, including maintaining high fidelity during decoherence, scaling to larger networks, and coping with noise occurring in quantum channels. Such challenges require overcoming through further advances in quantum hardware, error-correcting codes, and hybrid integration of different types of quantum platforms.

Moving into the future, quantum teleportation will realize advanced quantum networks, hybrid quantum systems, and even quantum AI. In a nutshell, as we keep strengthening its robustness and versatility, teleportation is going to lead in the directions of major breakthroughs in communication, computation, and information security, and thus enable the birth of the next generation in science and technology led by the speed of quantum mechanics.

REFERENCES

Arun, G., and Vivekanand Mishra. "A review on quantum computing and communication." In *2014 2nd International Conference on Emerging Technology Trends in Electronics, Communication and Networking*, pp. 1–5. IEEE, 2014.

Bashar, M. A., M. A. Chowdhury, R. Islam, M. S. Rahman, and S. K. Das. "A review and prospects of quantum teleportation." In *2009 International Conference on Computer and Automation Engineering*, pp. 213–217. IEEE, 2009.

Chou, Kevin S., Jacob Z. Blumoff, Christopher S. Wang, Philip C. Reinhold, Christopher J. Axline, Yvonne Y. Gao, Luigi Frunzio, M. H. Devoret, Liang Jiang, and R. J. Schoelkopf. "Deterministic teleportation of a quantum gate between two logical qubits." *Nature* 561, no. 7723 (2018): 368–373.

Fedortchenko, Serguei. "A quantum teleportation experiment for undergraduate students." *arXiv preprint arXiv:1607.02398* (2016).

Houshmand, Mahboobeh, Zahra Mohammadi, Mariam Zomorodi-Moghadam, and Monireh Houshmand. "An evolutionary approach to optimizing teleportation cost in distributed quantum computation." *International Journal of Theoretical Physics* 59, no. 4 (2020): 1315–1329.

Hu, Xiao-Min, Yu Guo, Bi-Heng Liu, Chuan-Feng Li, and Guang-Can Guo. "Progress in quantum teleportation." *Nature Reviews Physics* 5, no. 6 (2023): 339–353.

Huang, Yun-Feng, Xi-Feng Ren, Yong-Sheng Zhang, Lu-Ming Duan, and Guang-Can Guo. "Experimental teleportation of a quantum controlled-NOT gate." *Physical Review Letters* 93, no. 24 (2004): 240501.

Liu, Tao. "The applications and challenges of quantum teleportation." In *Journal of Physics: Conference Series* 1634, no. 1 (2020): 012089. IOP Publishing.

Luo, Yi-Han, Han-Sen Zhong, Manuel Erhard, Xi-Lin Wang, Li-Chao Peng, Mario Krenn, Xiao Jiang, et al. "Quantum teleportation in high dimensions." *Physical Review Letters* 123, no. 7 (2019): 070505.

Metcalf, Benjamin J., Justin B. Spring, Peter C. Humphreys, Nicholas Thomas-Peter, Marco Barbieri, W. Steven Kolthammer, Xian-Min Jin, et al. "Quantum teleportation on a photonic chip." *Nature Photonics* 8, no. 10 (2014): 770–774.

Nagy, Peter, and Peter Tasnádi. "Phantasy and reality-teleportation versus quantum computing." *Journal of Physics: Conference Series* 1929, no. 1 (2021): 012054. IOP Publishing.

Pirandola, Stefano, Jens Eisert, Christian Weedbrook, Akira Furusawa, and Samuel L. Braunstein. "Advances in quantum teleportation." *Nature Photonics* 9, no. 10 (2015): 641–652.

Pirandola, Stefano, and Stefano Mancini. "Quantum teleportation with continuous variables: A survey." *Laser Physics* 16 (2006): 1418–1438.

Rodrigo, Santiago, Sergi Abadal, Carmen G. Almudéver, and Eduard Alarcón. "Modelling short-range quantum teleportation for scalable multi-core quantum computing architectures." In *Proceedings of the Eight Annual ACM International Conference on Nanoscale Computing and Communication*, pp. 1–7, 2021.

Shih, Y. H. "Quantum entanglement and quantum teleportation." *Annalen der Physik* 513, no. 1–2 (2001): 19–34.

Spiller, Timothy P. "Quantum information processing: Cryptography, computation, and teleportation." *Proceedings of the IEEE* 84, no. 12 (2002): 1719–1746.

Wang, Xi-Lin, Xin-Dong Cai, Zu-En Su, Ming-Cheng Chen, Dian Wu, Li Li, Nai-Le Liu, Chao-Yang Lu, and Jian-Wei Pan. "Quantum teleportation of multiple degrees of freedom of a single photon." *Nature* 518, no. 7540 (2015): 516–519.

Zeilinger, Anton. "Quantum teleportation." *Scientific American* 282, no. 4 (2000): 50–59.

14 Analysis of Post-Quantum Cryptography Algorithms

Shiva Prasad Kaleru, N. Ashok kumar, M. Bharathi, G. Sandhyakumari, K. Neelima, P. Nagarajan, and Shaik Javid Basha

14.1 INTRODUCTION

Currently, it is effortless to establish a connection to Wi-Fi networks, and data is consistently transmitted. Ensure their safety. There are numerous methods to ensure that the details are accurate, comprehensive, and confidential in order to accomplish this objective. However, there are instances in which they fail to fulfil their obligations to ensure your safety. Currently, these statements demonstrate the difficulty that quantum computers face in solving a specific mathematical problem [1]. They are not yet sufficiently robust to ensure the security of the information we transmit online. However, in order to ensure our safety, it is imperative that we consider concepts that quantum computers are incapable of comprehending. This is necessary for the new 6G networks in order to ensure safety. In the past, data was safeguarded through the use of ciphers and security methods such as RSA and ECC (1, 2). The safety of these methods has diminished significantly as a result of the significant changes that have occurred. It is currently difficult to halt qubit algorithms such as Grover's and Shor's. A quantum computer has the potential to rapidly circumvent RSA and ECC blocks. This is not a task that can be completed rapidly by PCs that are not particularly potent. Qubit computing has the potential to revolutionize the way in which technology is utilized; however, it also introduces new methods of compromising data security.

The secret steps in this code are beyond the comprehension of quantum computers. This was the primary motivation behind the development of post-quantum cryptography (PQC). When devising novel strategies to safeguard your residence, it is imperative to consider factors beyond the law. It is imperative that this be stated. If you are considering a transition, it is important to be aware of the advantages and disadvantages of both quantum security and post-quantum security. This is crucial for the implementation of 5G and 6G services, as well as for assurance of your protection. It examines the laws, rights, and ideals of the actual world to assist in the selection of the most appropriate security measures for each circumstance [2]. This is done to enable individuals who are involved in safety to identify potential hazards

DOI: 10.1201/9781003538950-16

and avoid them. All of these tasks can be performed by extremely rapid quantum computers. There are quantum organizations in Europe that assist these regions in their development and learning. This is another example of how to ensure our safety following the implementation of quantum computation. Taking these exams can provide you with additional information regarding the subject. Consider the PQ-REACT project for a period of time.

This is a component of the extensive European initiative known as Horizon 2020. At this stage, the primary objectives of the study can be clearly articulated. Develop a method that facilitates the transition from traditional cryptography to the more recent post-quantum cryptography. Please experiment with it and enhance it. That is the objective of this initiative. Numerous safety concepts are currently being evaluated to determine their effectiveness [19]. They are currently being evaluated due to the current state of the planet. NIST is responsible for a significant portion of this transformation. It is designed to enhance security in anticipation of the eventual end of the need for quantum computing. This modification must be implemented. Our objective is to enhance these methodologies in order to facilitate the use of digital fingerprints. That is the primary objective of this research endeavor. Consider the potential benefits of hardware speedups in the context of cryptography in the aftermath of quantum computation [3]. The family, however, has the option of utilizing speedier methods. The objective of this investigation is to identify the challenges and opportunities associated with safeguarding the online safety of our children and descendants. It will be necessary to disregard both the safety measures that are currently in place and those that will be implemented in the absence of quantum computers.

There are numerous methods that post-quantum methods can employ to ensure the security of data. This work demonstrates that they can be employed for digital signatures. In order to ensure the success of this endeavor, it is necessary to establish a method for safeguarding data following quantum computation. This evaluates the functionality of programs and determines whether they can accommodate the power of quantum computers. Numerous individuals safeguard both service and digital IDs to the same extent. That is the only way to ensure that they function properly. Additionally, you should provide instructions on how to implement the methods and provide specifics regarding their efficiency in utilizing time. This item is composed of six distinct components. The objective and scope of the investigation are the subject of this article. It also discusses the utilization of newer forms of cryptography, such as asymmetric ciphers. This is a discussion of the concept of post-quantum cryptography and the possibility that quantum computers could develop a method to circumvent the encryption that is currently in use [4]. It discusses the test platform and the intended use of it. This is the primary focus of the performance study of post-quantum security, which also addresses the issue.

You can evaluate the efficacy of various post-quantum cryptography methods by generating key pairs, signing files, and verifying the accuracy of signatures. A preliminary version of this work may be received. It is more crucial than ever to ensure the security of your information on the internet, as the pace of change is so rapid. This is of the utmost importance, as the majority of our activities are conducted online. There are numerous methods to ensure the confidentiality of confidential information and prevent others from hearing it. However, there are new instruments that can be employed to circumvent these barriers. Different varieties of asymmetric cryptography are currently employed in accordance with the difficulty of the mathematical problems. This is done to prevent direct force from entering. Currently, these methods are not feasible due to the inefficiency of computers. These techniques can still be employed in a safe manner; however, it is also possible to deceive them. Everything is prepared, with the exception of quantum computers that are sufficiently powerful. The current ciphers will soon be insufficient to ensure the safety of a sufficient number of individuals [5]. Quantum computers continue to improve as time progresses.

Computers are safeguarded by contemporary security tools, including RSA. Nevertheless, protected data can be retained, and decoding tools can be employed immediately upon their availability. This is the primary reason that it is imperative to immediately implement encryption that is secure at the quantum level. In the realm of quantum mechanics, there are two optimal methods for transmitting and receiving data. Some of these algorithms are post-quantum, while others are quantum. Quantum physics is employed in the initial selection to impede the ability to listen in and ensure the security of data. This is due to the fact that the quantum state is disrupted when an object is observed. This approach is inadequate due to its incompatibility with certain quantum systems, such as quantum fiber optic lines. This method of transmitting quantum bits is detrimental due to their inconsistent logic. It is impossible to replicate a quantum state that is not comprehended. This is a safety regulation. Due to this concept, there are limited opportunities for your message to be disseminated. Making a quantum repeater is currently impossible. This implies that quantum networks require secure locations to receive and store data as they progress. These sites are referred to as "trusted nodes," and hackers can gain access more readily. This is the second measure you can take to safeguard your data from quantum hazards. It is referred to as post-quantum cryptography [6]. Quantum computers may not be capable of effectively managing these methods, as they necessitate a significant amount of rigorous mathematics. These steps can be completed using any computer or network that is already configured. This is due to the fact that they are more cost-effective and effective in real-world applications than the traditional methods [7].

Before employing new instruments to establish networks, ensure that you possess a comprehensive understanding of their capabilities. It is imperative that you are aware of the methods to ensure the security of your networks. A list of actions that cannot be taken to prevent quantum hazards has been compiled by an organization known as NIST. This will assist individuals in preparing for them. A compendium of all three categories of post-quantum encryption methods was recently made public. Numerous trials have been conducted on these methodologies. In the near future, the government, institutions, healthcare providers, and energy companies will all require systems that function after quantum computation. They are obligated to comply with the new regulations and ensure the safety of their customers [8]. In numerous locations, regulations are being implemented to ensure the security of the transition to post-quantum cryptography [9]. In the EU (GDPR) and other jurisdictions, it is evident that individuals are required to evaluate risks on an ongoing basis. Presently, quantum dangers that may arise in the future are also being examined. It is also probable that companies that handle private data, particularly those that operate with critical infrastructure, will be required to adhere to stringent security protocols in order to ensure the security of data following the implementation of quantum computing [10]. Quantum security regulations will be implemented solely when legally mandated due to changes that occur frequently.

The primary objective of this investigation is to determine the efficacy of various potential post-quantum methods and the extent to which they can be modified to operate with various computer languages. Digital fingerprints are a subject of considerable interest due to their significance in ensuring secure communication between systems that are geographically dispersed [11]. This is the method by which you can verify that the message sender is who they claim to be. They supervise transactions, conversations, and tools to ensure your safety. People must adhere to this regulation on all websites in order to maintain their confidence. It is crucial to ensure the safety of these signals in a manner that is inaccessible to quantum computers, as they are becoming increasingly hazardous. Although post-quantum algorithms will continue to improve in speed and quality as technology advances, the mathematics they employ remains the most critical component of the algorithms. Hash-based cryptography and other forms of encryption may not function effectively on antiquated hardware that lacks sufficient resources. Conversely, this form of security may be more compatible with antiquated technology in general [12]. The objective of the investigation is to determine the efficiency with which a variety of post-quantum digital signature methods allocate time. It provides performance standards and cases for smart infrastructure and automotive applications to demonstrate their functionality in the actual world. This is implemented to guarantee that security requirements are satisfied both immediately and in the future [13].

This chapter also consolidates the most critical concepts in the field of cryptography at the present time. Some of the instruments and methodologies employed in post-quantum security are discussed. When we discussed performance analysis, we deliberated on the location of the assessments and the instruments that were employed. The investigation has concluded that it is feasible to develop a connection between quantum computing and the concepts of quantum physics, as quantum computing processes data in a manner that is not feasible for conventional computers. In the majority of computers, bits represent either a 0 or a 1. In contrast, quantum computers employ qubits, which are also known as quantum bits. Qubits can simultaneously be in both the 0 and 1 states. Quantum computers are capable of performing certain mathematical operations at a significantly quicker pace than conventional computers [14], in addition to coupling and interference. This technology has the potential to revolutionize safety, efficiency, and challenging models, despite the fact that it is still in the process of being fully developed [15].

Shor developed a quantum method that is widely recognized. It is a million times quicker than the previous methods of factoring in large quantities. Based on the difficulty of factoring numbers and solving the discrete logarithm problem, certain encryption methods, such as RSA and ECC, are widely used. This is crucial because it can be employed to circumvent those methods. This ability enables you to perform the task, which is advantageous. Typically, these methods are implemented to safeguard confidential information; however, a quantum computer that implements

Shor's algorithm may be capable of rapidly determining its existence. This would impede the security of data worldwide [16]. It remains a significant technological challenge to ensure that quantum computers capable of executing these methods are accessible to a large number of individuals. In the present day, it is imperative to employ cryptography to ensure the security of your communications and information. A significant portion of the antiquated coding is based on mathematical problems that are beyond the capabilities of computers to solve. Conversely, quantum computers will revolutionize the world. Researchers are currently preparing for this potential outcome on two critical fronts [17]: the potential for the integration of quantum key distribution (QKD) and post-quantum cryptography (PQC). It is important to be aware that these two methods address the quantum hazard in distinct ways.

In order to guarantee the security of key sharing, quantum physics concepts are implemented by QKD. This is not perilous, despite the fact that it is difficult to comprehend. It is secure because quantum objects exhibit a specific behavior. The quantum key cannot be retrieved by an individual who is listening to a conversation. They will always have the capacity to disrupt the quantum state. These individuals will be aware that someone is paying attention when they hear this. QKD can be implemented with existing technology, and individuals have already implemented it. Quantum devices are not required for its functionality. QKD is unable to modify the encryption methods that are currently in use; however, keys may be exchanged [18]. However, PQC is a collection of encryption methods that were designed to be impenetrable by quantum attacks. PQC aims to either eliminate or enhance the current methods of coding in order to ensure the safety of devices, even in the presence of quantum computers. Quantum physics is not as significant in PQC as it is in QHD. Rather, it is predicated on mathematical problems that are challenging to resolve. Certain applications necessitate these quantum-proof methods to ensure their security, such as those that utilize digital signatures, safeguard data, or distribute keys. PQC methods are currently under development; however, they will likely be the sole method of ensuring security once quantum computers are capable of breaching conventional encryption.

Innovative quantum-resistant algorithms are currently under development, which contributes to the continued interest in PQC [19]. The following are a few varieties of encryption: Some of these methods are predicated on issues that quantum computers are not particularly adept at resolving, which is why they are unable to break them. Quantum hazards will no longer be a concern. Consider Grover's approach. The advantage that quantum computers possess over symmetric methods may be diminished if they are employed. This can be accomplished by increasing the size of the key in a stable manner. The National Institute of Standards and Technology (NIST) is responsible for this endeavor. It has made a concerted effort to ensure that all PQC methods adhere to the same standards. In actual life, algorithms are evaluated based on their safety, functionality, and ease of use [20]. New security regulations will be implemented to ensure the security of data and communications, regardless of the utilization of quantum computers. Individuals who successfully navigate this rigorous evaluation will serve as illustrations. Different is cognizant of the fact that the investigation is still incomplete in that it fails to adequately elucidate the diverse computer methodologies.

Different forms of encryption include code-based, isogeny-based, multiple, and lattice-based. Through an in-depth examination of the primary PQC methodologies, this investigation intends to address this deficiency.

The review primarily discusses the shortcomings of the algorithms and their strengths and weaknesses. It also provides instructions on how to apply them in both academic and real-world settings. People can utilize it to identify superior security alternatives that do not necessitate quantum computing [21]. It also ensures that these options function effectively and efficiently. The methods we selected for our study are instrumental in the improvement of particle quality control in numerous significant ways. All of them were implemented as part of the NIST particle quality control's guidelines-setting process. In the past, individuals believed that these methods were crucial for obtaining secure results that quantum computers were unable to comprehend. However, some of them have been either compromised or shut down since that time. We selected them in order to demonstrate the various types of algorithms that are currently being considered and the insights we have gained from examining them. We selected a variety of algorithms, including those that employ braid groups, isogeny, codes, hashes, and multivariate polynomial codes [22]. Additionally, they were selected for their versatility. There are numerous varieties of cryptography that we can discuss.

This demonstrates the judgments and trade-offs that were made during the development of PQC. We are of the opinion that it is crucial to examine both effective and ineffective methodologies in our research. This could assist specialists in not only determining the current location of PQC but also in ensuring that the same errors are not made when they attempt to establish secure security standards again. This can be employed by professionals to attempt to ascertain the current state of PQC. Additionally, we examine the methods by which organizations can transition to the use of PQC. The primary topic of discussion is the ease with which hybrid cryptography can facilitate the transition between conventional systems and those that are not influenced by quantum physics. The article proceeds by examining the current state of standardization and the algorithms that are being standardized by NIST. This is followed by a quantitative comparison and a discussion of potential future directions for quality control. Finally, it concludes with a concise summary of the most significant findings.

14.1.1 Original Contribution to Post-Quantum Cryptography Research

This chapter contributes by providing a comprehensive and practical evaluation of post-quantum cryptographic (PQC) algorithms, specifically Falcon, CRYSTALS-Dilithium, and SPHINCS+, in real-world scenarios. Unlike many theoretical studies, this work empirically benchmarks these algorithms using the liboqs tool on both Linux and Windows platforms, offering insights into their performance regarding computational efficiency, processing time, key size, and signature size. The evaluation is conducted within the context of emerging technologies such as 5G/6G networks and IoT, demonstrating the applicability of PQC in practical environments.

Additionally, this chapter contributes a novel framework for assessing PQC algorithms, which includes custom adaptations for IoT devices like the Raspberry Pi 4. By addressing the scalability and resource constraints of IoT applications, this work provides valuable guidance for the deployment of secure cryptographic systems in future digital infrastructures. The findings of this chapter are crucial for informing the transition to post-quantum cryptography and ensuring the security of communications in a quantum-enabled future.

14.2 MATERIALS AND METHODS

14.2.1 Cryptographic Hash Functions

To create a secure one-time signature method, all that is required is a function that can only be utilized in a single manner. This was demonstrated by Rompel, who demonstrated that digital identification systems require only one method of operation to ensure their security. In this regard, one-time signature schemes are analogous to the fundamental components of digital signature schemes. Individuals are developing security strategies that do not involve quantum or post-quantum computers. Hash functions are a significant component of this. All of these elements must be present in order to digitally sign an item. The safety of these systems is contingent upon the effectiveness of the hash function in managing collisions [23]. It will consistently generate a binary string with length n if you provide it with a binary string whose length is unknown. Information can be stored and retrieved using hash functions. Hash functions are exceedingly prevalent due to their straightforwardness and user-friendliness. With the addition of m characters, the series is at least m characters in length. It also denotes all binary strings that are incapable of being altered in terms of their length. The form employed in the subsequent section is altered when h is invoked.

$$h : \{0,1\}^{*} \rightarrow \{0,1\}^{m}, \tag{14.1}$$

where m is the length of the hash output.

Currently, it is feasible to generate numerous secure hash functions. The "sponge construction" is the most effective and compliant method. A group of cryptographers, led by John Daemen, devised this strategy for the Merkle-Damgård system, which was no longer functional. Raw data that undergoes length changes may be transmitted to data that undergoes length changes. It was initially demonstrated at the 2007 ECRYPT symposium. It was initially released in 2007. The change f is demonstrated by the equation b = r + c when a specific number of bits is present. The frequency is denoted as r, and the quantity is denoted as c. The initial phase of the construction is reminiscent of the Merkle-Damgård plan. It is now lengthier and consists of segments of r bits. The b bits of the state must be set to 0 in order to proceed to the subsequent phase. The process of creating something consists of two distinct stages. The initial stage is referred to as "absorption," and it involves the addition of the message's r-bit blocks to the internal state's initial r-bits. This occurs when the f key is pressed. This concludes each letter block, and that concludes it. The initial r bits of the internal state are subsequently returned to f as output blocks during the "squeezing" phase. Before it can be employed, the cipher sum must exceed this value.

14.2.1.1 Primary Methods of Cryptanalysis of One-Way Hash Functions

A substantial amount of energy is being sent out. If a cryptanalyst is provided with the hash value ($m1$) of a message $m1$, they must continue to experiment until they identify a message $m2$ (where $m1$ is not equal to $m2$) for which ($m1$) is equal to $H(m2)$. This enables them to assert that the hash value was provided for message $m2$ and not $m1$. This method returns n bits for each n steps, which is n times the number of bits as the initial method. This is a straightforward method for identifying hash function conflicts. The term was derived from the birthday paradox, a well-known statistical inquiry. We can determine the duration of time required to locate them once we have determined the number of communications that require examination. Every ₫1–₫22$_e$, you will receive a message from two distinct groups. The code on both the ₫1 and ₫2 lines will be identical. The attack requires 2$_e$2+1 steps if $\boldsymbol{T}1$ is equal to $\boldsymbol{T}2$ and $\boldsymbol{T}2$ is equal to $2\boldsymbol{T}2$. The probability of its successful operation is 0.631. The majority of the data that is saved should undergo significant changes, even if only minor modifications are implemented. This is referred to as the in the field of encryption for block ciphers and hash function methods. This attribute is frequently of paramount significance in the defense sector. This method is employed to determine the appropriate avalanche number by analyzing the avalanche factors.

$$\varepsilon = \left|2k_1 - 1\right|, \tag{14.2}$$

There is a 50% probability that half of the bits in the output will also change when the ith bit in the input series is altered. This is demonstrated by the numerical value. Some parts have been altered, as indicated by the number i.

14.2.2 The Main Properties of the Post-Quantum Signature Scheme

The individuals who manufacture them are unique in that they ensure their safety. There is no secure method of employing evidence in the development of computerized signature systems. This is the reason that not all secure hash functions are applicable in this context. Even if the system was functioning properly, one of these items would be malfunctioning if the plan were to fail. It is important to bear in mind that the components of cryptographic hash functions have been the subject of extensive research for an extended period. However, if it is discovered that a protocol's hash function is not secure, it would be sufficient to replace it with an alternative. The plan would continue to be assembled in the same manner as it is currently. Right now, we are unaware of any quantum methods that could be employed to generate collisions or identify suitable preimages for the first and second preïmage impacts. The following were the most effective cipher functions that were examined: The preimage search method transitions from being d(2i) hard to being d(2i/2) hard. Grover's method simplifies the process. Combining Brassard's method and the impact search method simplifies the process; it transitions from O(2₫) to O(2ƀ3/).

How can I determine the meaning of "signature size" in applications that utilize bits after quantum? It informs you of the number of bits or bytes required to demonstrate that a method can generate a digital signature. Signs can be created using a variety of data structures and mathematical concepts. There are cryptography lattices, hash functions, and other items on this list. What types of credentials are present in these applications? The magnitude of these indicators may be equivalent to or greater than that of those employed in conventional code. The quantity of the signature in post-quantum systems is influenced by a variety of factors. These encompass the selected options, the method and its capabilities, the desired level of security and efficiency, and numerous other factors. Safety features are integrated into post-quantum signature systems, rendering them more secure than quantum signature systems. Changes to security level "b" can be implemented in numerous methods for certain post-quantum systems. Among the items examined are qubit methods, scheme parameters, risk studies, and potential attacks on the scheme. Post-quantum cryptography is "b" secure if it functions effectively in conjunction with conventional security measures. The security level is represented by the "b" bits. We will assert that a method of signing after quantum is secure when it is represented by 128 bits. The same quantity of computer capacity would be required to breach this type of protection as any other.

14.2.3 Proposed Methodology

The KEM method is a method for securing and transmitting a secret key over a public network. Figures 14.1 and 14.2 encrypt a confidential key prior to its transmission to the appropriate recipient. This ensures its security. A second key, also referred to as a, can be employed to decode the first confidential key and retrieve it. This is what they do upon receiving the initial key.

He encased the key. Individuals are not required to generate a secret key that is known to all prior to exchanging keys. The two most critical stages in the key exchange mechanism (KEM) procedure are the creation of a key and the insertion and removal of the key from its envelope.

While the confidential key is being generated by one of the parties, it will be shared by all. Subsequently, there are several alternatives around the confidential key that are visible to all. The key is subsequently transmitted to the other company, which is frequently referred to as the "user" or "receiver." They decrypt the key using their private key, which enables them to view the shared secret key [24]. Math is frequently employed for both encapsulation and packaging. Maintain the security of keys, key exchange modules, or KEMs when transmitting them. They are implemented in numerous defense mechanisms. KEMs are employed in the following critical applications:

- *Two people can use KEMs together to create a secret key that they are both capable of encrypting and decrypting communications. In order to guarantee the safety of contact, KEMs may be implemented in this manner.*
- *This is referred to as a key exchange. KEMs enable two organizations to securely exchange a secret key. This enables them to communicate in a secure manner.*

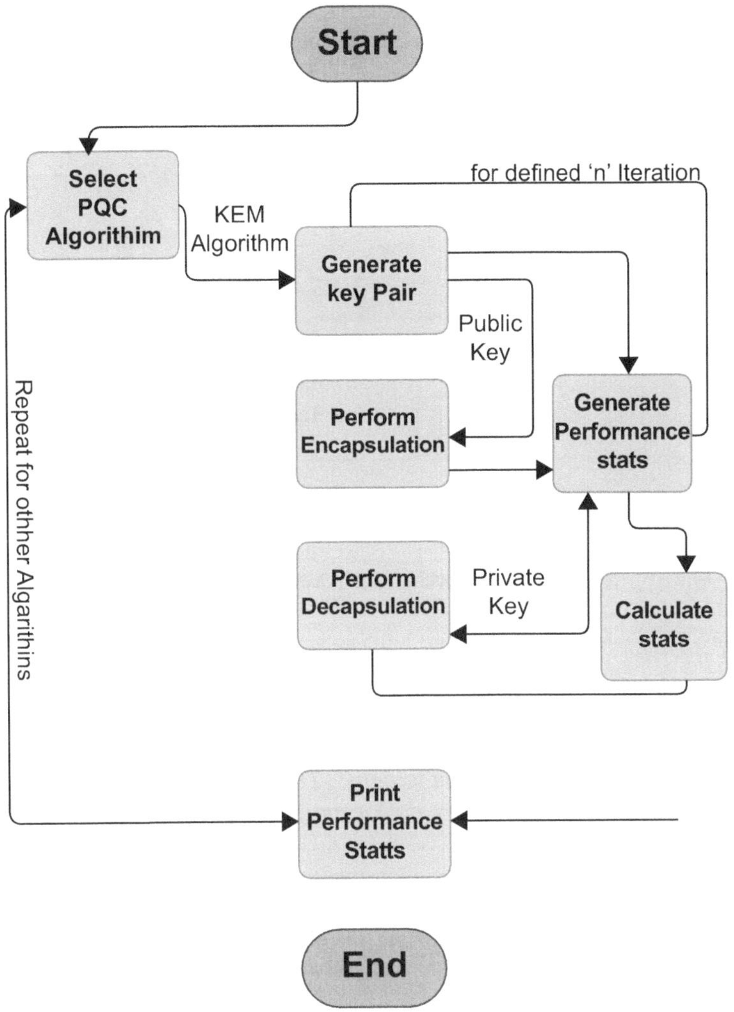

FIGURE 14.1 Overview of the key encapsulation technique.

- *Using KEMs to establish a shared secret key, numerous groups can establish a secure communication channel through key agreement.*
- *Key extraction is the process of generating a secret key from a master key. This is feasible through the utilization of KEMs. After this is completed, you will be able to utilize the secret key to perform tasks such as writing and securing.*
- *Security: Customers and servers can utilize KEMs, which are components of security systems. A common secret key can now be generated. This also serves as evidence that the consumer is who they claim to be. Subsequently, the shared secret key can be employed to verify that the individual is who they claim to be.*

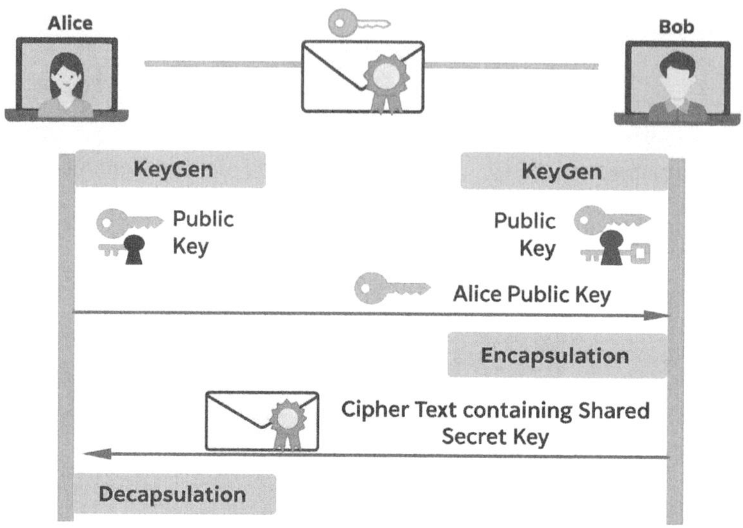

FIGURE 14.2 Information on the mechanism of key encapsulation.

- *In one type of mixed encryption, KEMs are employed to safeguard a symmetric key. This encryption key has the potential to safeguard a significant amount of data. This is the KEM key that is required to encrypt the symmetric encryption key.*
- *This is post-quantum cryptography: This form of cryptography also employs KEMs to safeguard data from potential hazards that quantum computers may pose.*
- *There are numerous methods available to determine the effectiveness of a KEM, including the following:*
- *The key's size is equivalent to the shared secret key generated by KEM. A reduced key size is generally considered to be more effective in terms of security and efficiency.*
- *Key creation, encapsulation, and decapsulation necessitate a specific quantity of processing resources. The computational cost is the term used to describe this. It is generally recognized that increasing efficacy is correlated with a lower computational cost.*
- *The communication cost is the quantity of information that must be conveyed during the encapsulation and decapsulation process. A reduced communication cost is frequently considered to be more advantageous in terms of efficacy.*
- *Security: The KEM's level of security is typically assessed by the number of actions required to penetrate the system. It is generally accepted that a higher level of security is more secure than a lower level of security.*
- *The error rate is the frequency of errors that occur during the key creation, encryption, and decryption processes. An error rate that is less than the average is frequently regarded as more reliable.*

- *Time expenditure: the total time required for the activities of key generation, encapsulation, and decapsulation. It is generally recognized that a higher level of efficacy is indicative of a lower time cost.*

We would like to discuss the potential use of labors to evaluate the efficacy of various KEMs in this study. We evaluate numerous aspects of KEM algorithms, including their safety, execution time, and cost. We developed this concept due to the necessity of a fair and consistent method for testing KEM methods. We were compelled to devise a solution. A study was conducted to evaluate the functionality of the two most widely recognized operating systems. A comprehensive set of review criteria was implemented. Our approach was intended to assist individuals in making informed judgments by demonstrating the effectiveness of KEMs.

Our suggested technique has several distinctive characteristics. These include the following:

- *The processing cost, the magnitude of the key, the number of errors, the level of security, and the time spent were just a few of the factors that were used to evaluate it. Experts can evaluate the effectiveness of KEM algorithms from a variety of perspectives using this comprehensive set of metrics.*
- *In order to obtain more precise measurements, we modified the testing procedure. This approach enabled us to maintain a greater sense of stability and integrity. We were confident that the KEM methods would function consistently and that the measurements would be accurate when we implemented the labors program.*

To find out how well a KEM worked with the labors, the following steps were taken:

- *The KEM method's parameters were identified, and the OQS library was rendered operational. In addition, the scenario was executed. Initially, the selection of the security level was made. This determined the significance of the security claims and the magnitude of the key.*
- *The KEM method was configured to execute multiple times within the loop. The purpose of this was to determine the typical duration of the performance.*
- *Key generation: Within the cycle, a random private key and a public key were generated for the KEM procedure that was being tested.*
- *The CPU's clock was employed to determine the duration of time required to generate the key pairs. Keys that had been previously generated were employed to execute this procedure. Subsequently, the truth that was disclosed was rendered obsolete.*
- *The process was executed a specified number of times to determine the average time required to generate key pairings. Subsequently, the average time required to generate key pairs was determined.*
- *The CPU clock was employed to determine the duration of time required to encapsulate the KEM. A public key and a confidential letter that were generated in advance were implemented.*

- *After conducting the method the required number of times, we determined the average time required for KEM sealing. The KEM layer's typical duration has been determined.*
- *We estimated the duration of time required to obtain the KEM key by utilizing the CPU clock. The process involved the utilization of both the confidential message that had been transmitted and the encryption key that had been generated in advance.*
- *The average time required for KEM decapsulation was determined after the process was executed the appropriate number of times. At present, the average duration required to access the KEM has been determined.*

The screen was presented with critical information. This displayed the standard duration, the CPU's clock speed, the name of the method by which keys were exchanged, and the level of security. In summary, the preceding procedures illustrate our methodology. The following steps were taken to ensure that the method we recommended was effective and that the primary speed benefits of KEM algorithms were obtained. In order to prepare for our subsequent endeavor, we sought to identify novel methods of ratings. Additionally, there will be an increase in the number of activities that are both authentic and fraudulent. This method allows us to observe the effectiveness of KEM algorithms in conjunction with TLS in real-world scenarios. The effectiveness of various KEM algorithms was evaluated and compared using liboqs. An illustration of its utilization is illustrated in Figure 14.3. This is the fabricated code that will be employed to execute the actions as recommended.

Algorithm 1: PQC algorithms for Linux and Windows are evaluated.
Input: PQC KEM algorithm variant, number of iteration
Initialize OQS library, and set parameters for KEM algorithm:;
initialize OQS library;
set the security level;
set the key size;
Set up loop for multiple iterations:;
for i = 1 to desired number of iterations do
    Generate random private and public keys:;
    generate the private key;
    generate the corresponding public key;
    Time the key pair generation method using CPU clock:;
    start CPU clock;
    start_time = clock();
    rim key pair generation method with desired PQC algorithm;
    stop CPU clock;
    end_time = clock();
    Calculate the average time for key pair generation:;
    add elapsed time to total time;
    elapsed_time = (end_time—start_time)/clocks per seconds;
end

calculate average time = total time/number of iterations;
Time the KEM encapsulation method using CPU clock:;
start CPU clock;
rim KEM encapsulation with generated public key and secret message;
stop CPU clock;
Calculate the average time for KEM encapsulation:;
add elapsed time to total time;
calculate average time = total time/number of iterations;
Time the KEM decapsulation method using CPU clock:;
start CPU clock;
run KEM decapsulation with generated private key and cipher secret message;
stop CPU clock;
Calculate the average time for KEM decapsulation:;
add elapsed time to total time;
calculate average time = total time/number of iterations;
Print relevant information to console:;
print name of key exchange method;
print security level;
print average time;
print CPU clock speed;

14.2.4 Proposed Scheme for IoT

14.2.4.1 Architecture Design

The internet of things (IoT) was implemented in Telkom University halls N, O, and P. Figure 14.4 illustrates this approach. These devices are interconnected to transmit the data they have collected to the HPE server, which is also referred to as the distribution, via Wi-Fi, as part of the IoT. Subsequently, the data is transmitted via the MQTT

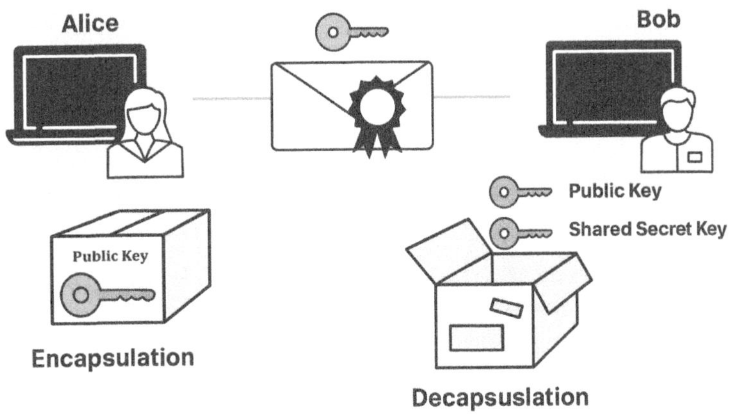

FIGURE 14.3 Workflow of the performance assessment technique.

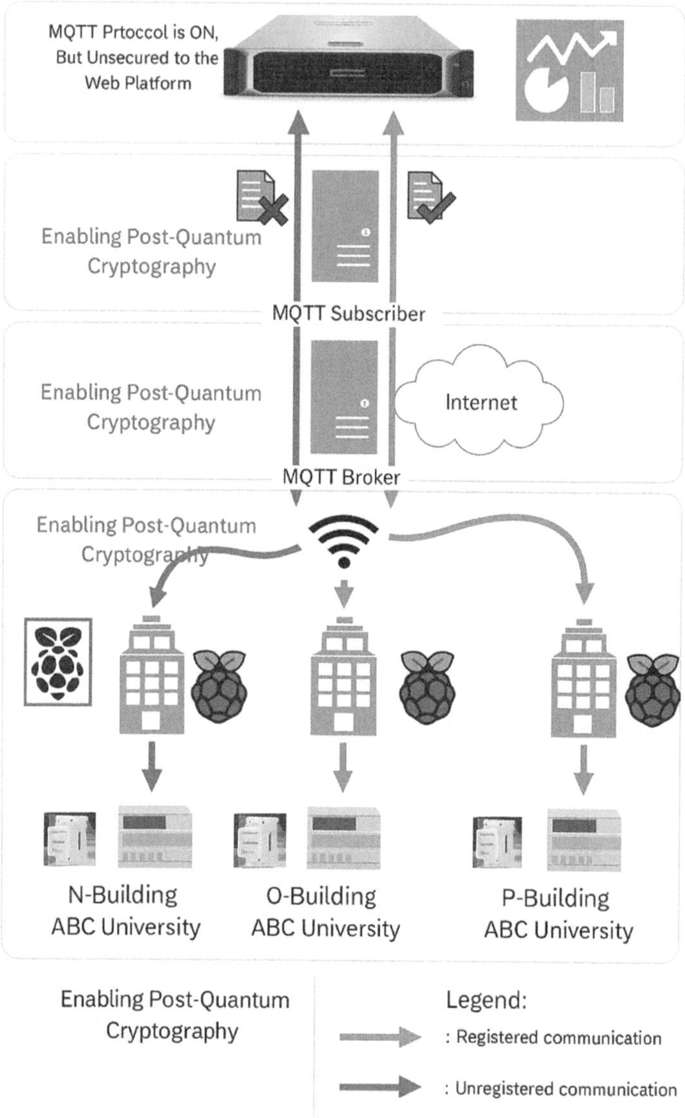

FIGURE 14.4 The adversary's perspective.

protocol. The writer's devices should be equipped with a mechanism to safeguard the messages that are added to them, as indicated by the findings of this investigation. After the writer sends a message to the broker, the broker organizes it into a list and selects the most critical message to send first. Subsequently, the communications are transmitted to a catalog of individuals who chose to receive them [25]. The data is encrypted by this device using the RSA, NTRU, and SABRE protocols. These methods were selected due to their safety and minimal resource requirements. Enemies will be unable to modify the messages that are transmitted as long as this method is employed. Malicious entities may have the ability to ascertain the MQTT topic transmitted by the original authors; however, the broker will not process any messages from these entities due to the lack of proper data.

14.2.4.2 Dealing with Public and Private Keys

The public and private keys are generated on the computer and subsequently transmitted to the Rpi-4. Medium (128 bits) and high (196 bits) were the two security levels. The writer can now retain both the secret key and the public key for RSA, NTRU, and SABRE encryption. Those are the different varieties of public key encryption that are employed, as illustrated in Table 14.1. Table 14.2 contains a comprehensive inventory of all the items that can be utilized in conjunction with the SABRE protection system.

The investigation involved the modification of SABRE and Light SABRE. Afterward, these modifications were approved. The rules demonstrate that the NTRU and SABRE encryption methods do not impose an excessive amount of burden on computers. Conversely, the protected character is restricted to a specific length. For 128-bit security, these two encryption methods are limited to transmitting letters that are 16 bytes in length. For 196-bit protection, they are capable of transmitting letters that are 32 bytes in length. These two are distinct in this regard.

14.2.4.3 Developing RSA on RPi-4

This is a concise examination of the RSA. In 1977, this methodology was introduced. It was named after the three individuals who composed it: Adleman, Shamir, and Rivest. The RSA method is secure due to the difficulty of factoring the products of two large prime numbers. This is referred to as the "factoring problem." There is

TABLE 14.1
Techniques That Use Public-Key Encryption (PKE)

		Make a Plan	
Level of Security	**Plan**	**KPK**	**Sk**
Moderate: 128-bit	RSA 2048	1678	450
	#NTRU401	557	607
	Bright SABRE	1568	672
High: 196-bit	RSA 7680	5972	1404
	NTRU 593	821	891
	SABRE	2304	992

TABLE 14.2
SABRE's Level of Security

Plan	l	n	q	p	T	μμ	Safety	Failure
Bright SABRE	2	256	213213	210210	2323	10	NIST-I	2-1202-120
SABRE	3	256	213213	210210	2424	10	NIST-II	2-1362-136
Fire SABRE	4	256	213213	210210	2626	10	NIST-V	2-1652-165

still no definitive resolution to the question of whether the RSA problem is more difficult or not. The RSA challenge is a method of circumventing the security measures of RSA. According to certain individuals, the method is impenetrable if a suitable key is employed. Ensure that a confidential key is stored securely. It is referred to as the prime key. It is composed of the secret number d. The term "e" and the numerical value "n" comprise the public portion of this key, which collectively denotes "public." Please refrain from disclosing any information regarding p, q, or **d**, as they may be able to assist you in determining d. Nevertheless, they can be discarded once it is established that d is the RSA key. The RSA numbers are detailed in Table 14.3. In Algorithm 3, the MQTT message is safeguarded through the use of RSA encryption (in Algorithm 2) and RSA decode (in Algorithm 2).

Algorithm 2 RSA Encryption

m,$Message$

c=memod$n$

Algorithm 3 RSA Decryption

c,Ci $pher$ $text$

c=cdmod$n$

Algorithm 4 Publisher's Customized RSA

Set up the message m and the public key pk.

Start e, which has the power to encrypt bytes

DO something with publisher_id.

SET UP ***ya***, Ciphertext Array

Start now. RSA.encrypt is the name of the RSA encryption method.

Start base64.encode and base64 Useful for encoding

Startup both MQTT.publish and the MQTT publish function.

x=**S**ength(m)

i=0

while (−(-^mode)+1> do

m'←RSA.efcry(c,pk)

TABLE 14.3
RSA's Parameters

Notation	Definition
p,q p,q	Pick out two different prime numbers
N	The number used for both the public and secret keys
$\phi(n)$ϕ(n)	What is Carmichael's totient function for p and q that are kept secret?
gcdgcd	Finding the largest common divisor (gcd) of two prime numbers
pkpk	The key that has been made public
sksk	The key that only you know will work

12: $ya[i] \leftarrow m'$
13: $_e=_e+1$
14: end
15: MQTT.KvbSi(bas𝔥IF.Encod𝔥($\mathcal{C}b$))

14.2.4.4 NTRU Development on RPi-4

This public-key cryptosystem, which is also referred to as the NTRU cryptosystem, is unique in three respects. This table compiles a comprehensive inventory of the most critical items. One prime number N and one whole number q constitute a ring of convolutional polynomials. Equation (14.3) outlines the process for performing all operations that are possible with numbers in this ring:

$$R_{N,q} = (z / z_q)[X] / [X]^{-1} \tag{14.3}$$

In order for a key to be generated, the entry must contain all four factors (i, j, k, and e). Prior to obtaining the NTRUEncrypt key pair, it is necessary to generate an NTRU key. To the Encryption method, you provide Message M and the public key (x). Then, Algorithm 5 is employed to encrypt Message M and transmit it as ciphertext ($).

Algorithm 5 NTRU Encryption
1: $m \in Rp$
2: $r \in T(d,d)$
3: $c = pr \cdot \text{h} + m(\text{mod}n)$

The recipient of the message must possess a secret key that corresponds to the protected key in order to access it. Algorithm 5 instructs you on how to retrieve message M. Algorithm 6 guarantees the security of the MQTT message through the implementation of NTRU encryption.

Algorithm 6 NTRU Decryption
1: $f \cdot e(\text{mod}q)$
2: $r \in T(d,d)$
3: $c = pr \cdot \text{h} + m(\text{mod}q)$

TABLE 14.4
NTRU's Parameters

Notation	Meaning
ZZ	Numbers
N, qN, q	Species of rings [Equation (1)]
p	Modulus for message space
$d1$, $d2$, $d3$, d1, d2, d3	For product form polynomial words, a constant that is not zero is important
dgdg	A non-zero number is used to count secret key components g
dmdm	Representative of the message limits on Hamming weight

Algorithm 7 Publisher-specific NTRU customization

Set up pk, the public key, and m, the message.
INITIALIZE e, the ability to encrypt bytes
MAKE publisher_id work.
SET UP ***ya***, Ciphertext Array
GET STARTED The NTRU.encrypt method is used for encryption.
Start base64.encode and base64 Function for encoding
Startup MQTT.publish and the MQTT publish function

x=length(m)
i=0
while$x$−($x$mode)e+1>$i$do
m'←NTRU.Encry(c,pk)
$\mathcal{C}a[i]$←m'
i=i+1
end while
MQTT.KvbSi(basђlF.Encodђ($\mathcal{C}b$))

14.2.5 Developing SABER on RPi-4

SABRE is a post-quantum key encoding scheme (KEM) that operates with lattices and can be converted into a secure PKE method, as indicated by this study. There are two types of moduli in SABRE. Their names are q and p, and their bit lengths are $\in_c$ and $\in_c$. The following are illustrated in Algorithms 8 and 9. A 32-byte random number is employed repeatedly when generating the public key X and the secret key X. In addition to functioning as an SSABER, it also performs additional functions. SABRE employs SHAKE-128 to generate a random matrix known as A during the key generation process. In Table 14.5, all of SABRE's factors are illustrated and discussed.

Algorithm 8 SABRE encryption

$m \in M;r$
$pk=(b,seedA)$
$A \leftarrow$gen$(seedA)$
$s' \leftarrow \beta\mu(Rl \times 1q)$
$b'=$bits$(ATs'+h, \in q, \in p) \in Rl \times 1p$
$v'=bT$bits$(s', \in p, \in p) \in Rp$
$cm=$bits$(v'+h1+2\in p-1m, \in p, \in r+1)$
Return $c:=(cm,b')$

Algorithm 9 SABER Decryption

$c=(cm,b')$
$sk=s$
$v=b'T$bits$(s, \in p, \in p) \in Rp$
$m'=(v-2\in p-\in t-1cm+h2, \in p,1) \in R2$
Return m'

TABLE 14.5
SABER's Parameters

Notation	Meaning
p, qp, q	Pick out two different prime numbers
N	The number used for both the public and secret keys
$\phi(n)$ϕ(n)	Carmichael's totient function for p and q that are kept secret
gcdgcd	Finding the largest common divisor (gcd) of two prime numbers
pkpk	The key that has been made public
sksk	The key that only you know will work

Once the encryption is complete, it considers the message $m\in^3$ to be a component of em. M illustrates the message space range in $\boldsymbol{T}\cap 0,1\}n$. In order to generate the ciphertext, one must first generate a matrix, select a binomial, multiply the matrix by a vector, and subsequently generate an additional matrix. In Algorithm 9, a bit transition is employed to determine the optimal method for combining vectors. Encoding is significantly influenced by this. The MQTT message system is safeguarded by SABRE encryption, as demonstrated in Algorithm 10.

Algorithm 10 Publisher-specific SABRE customisation

```
Set up pk, the public key, and m, the message.
INITIALISE e, the ability to encrypt bytes
MAKE publisher_id work.
SET UP ya, Ciphertext Array
Startup SABER.encrypt, the encryption feature of SABRE
Start base64.encode and base64 Function for encoding
Startup MQTT.publish and the MQTT publish function

x=length(m)
i=0
whilex−(xmode)e+1>ido
m′←SABER.encry(c,pk)
Ca[i]←m′
i=i+1
end while
MQTT.Publi(base64.Encode(Ca))
```

14.2.6 Data Specification

Table 14.6 displays the tracking results for a single step, while Table 14.7 displays the results for three cycles. The data was managed according to the regulations outlined in Table 14.8 during a single phase. Table 14.9 contains the regulations for the subsequent three procedures.

14.2.7 Formal Security Proof

We modified the encryption scheme option to facilitate the comparison of Bernstein's lattice-based security proofs. This is done to demonstrate the security of the study's security method.

- Table 14.10 displays the factors G for each PKE.
- Table 14.11 illustrates the process of generating brief elements.
- Table 14.12 illustrates the procedure of generating the difference *Ba-G*.

The key has been produced in its entirety to date.

b and B are generated upon completion of the code. Each item is illustrated in Table 14.11 and Table 14.12. Refer to Table 14.13 to convert D+ to C for Product NTRU. The encoded messages M are illustrated in Table 14.14.

TABLE 14.6
Data Stream from 1-Phase Example

1-Phase Stream Data
"4438ca6fc2a575cfab4fa4f1d4569964", "2022-02-28", "13:59:07", 215.4, 0.03, 3.185766, 5.622129, 6.462, 0.493, 50, 1.49

TABLE 14.7
Data Stream from 3-Phase Example

3-Phase Stream Data
'6cc5dc0059d39c5392784721c78d4bb3', '2022-04-13', '11:22:03', '223.8', '223.8', '0.0', '1.70', '3.50', '0.00', '0.31', '0.63', '0.00', '0.31', '0.07', '0.35', '0.00', '0.42', '0.31', '0.71', '0.00', '0.52', '0.22', '0.50', '0.31', '19265.00', '11065.00', '30331.00', '50.00'

TABLE 14.8
The Specification for 1-Phase Data

The Parameter	An Explanation	The Unit
token	Key for data	—
date	Date for monitoring	—
time	Time for monitoring	—
V	Strength (V)	V
I	Present	A
P	Strength	Watt
Q	Power in reaction (VAr)	VAr
S	Power of appearance (VA)	VA
PF	Power (kWh)	—
F	How often (Hz)	Hz

TABLE 14.9
The 3-Phase Data Specification

The Parameter	An Explanation	Unit of Measurement
token	Token for transmission	—
date	Date for monitoring	—
time	Time for monitoring	—
VaVa	Volts phase R	V
VbVb	Volts phase S	V
VcVc	Phase T of voltage	V
IaIa	Right now phase R	A
IbIb	Present phase S	A
IcIc	Present phase T	A
QaQa	Power on demand R	VAr
QbQb	Changed power S	VAr
QcQc	Reactive power T	VAr
QtQt	Total of reactive power	VAr
PaPa	Active power R	Watt
PbPb	Active power S	Watt
PcPc	Active power T	Watt
PtPt	Total of active power	Watt
SaSa	Power of looks R	VA
SbSb	Power of looks S	VA
ScSc	Power of looks T	VA
StSt	Total power of appearance	VA
PFaPFa	Factor of power R	—
PFbPFb	Factor of power S	—
PFcPFc	Factor of power T	—
EpEp	Power and energy	kWh
FpFp	Forwarded power	kWh
SpSp	Total power	kWh
$Freq$Freq	How often	Hz

TABLE 14.10
Set of Multipliers for Each of the Target PKEs.

System	Parameter Set	Type	Set of Multipliers
NURU	hps2048401	Quotient	(Z/2048)[x]/(x401−1)(Z/2048)[x]/(x401−1)
NURU	hps2048593	Quotient	(Z/2048)[x]/(x593−1)(Z/2048)[x]/(x593−1)
saber	Main	Product	(Z/8192)[x]/(x256+1)2×2(Z/8192)[x]/(x256+1)2×2
saber	Fire	Product	(Z/8192)[x]/(x256+1)3×3(Z/8192)[x]/(x256+1)3×3

TABLE 14.11
The Allocation of Brief Components for Every Target PKE

System	Parameter Set	Short Element
NURU	hps2048401	**Z**[*x*]/(*x*401−1);−1,0,1Z[x]/(x401−1);−1,0,1
NURU	hps2048593	**Z**[*x*]/(*x*593−1);−1,0,1Z[x]/(x593−1);−1,0,1
SABER	main	(**Z**[*x*]/(*x*256+1))3;Σ0≤*i*<8{−0.5,0.5}(Z[x]/(x256+1))3;Σ0≤i<8{−0.5,0.5}
SABER	fire	(**Z**[*x*]/(*x*256+1))4;Σ0≤*i*<6{−0.5,0.5}

TABLE 14.12
An Approximate Key Offset of the NTRU PKEs for the Noisy or Rounded Product

Method	Set of Parameters	Offset of Key
NURU	hps2048401	**Z**[*x*]/(*x*401−1);−1,0,1weight127,127Z[x]/(x401−1);−1,0,1weight127,127
NURU	hps2048593	**Z**[*x*]/(*x*593−1);−1,0,1weight127,127Z[x]/(x593−1);−1,0,1weight127,127
SABER	main	round**Z**/8192to8**Z**roundZ/8192to8Z
SABER	fire	round**Z**/8192to8**Z**

TABLE 14.13
The Noisy or Rounded Product NTRU PKEs Offset Using an Approximation Cipher

System	Set of Parameters	Offset of Ciphertext
NURU	hps2048401	does not apply
NURU	hps2048593	does not apply
SABER	main	round**Z**/8192to512**Z**roundZ/8192to512Z
SABER	fire	round**Z**/8192to128**Z**

TABLE 14.14
A Collection of Encrypted Messages for Every NTRU PKE of the Target Product

System	A Group of Parameters	Set of Encoded Messages
NURU	hps2048401	does not apply
NURU	hps2048593	does not apply
SABER	main	Σ0≤*i*<256{0.4096}*xi*Σ0≤i<256{0.4096}xi
SABER	fire	Σ0≤*i*<256{0.4096}*xi*Σ0≤i<256{0.4096}xi

14.2.7.1 Background

At least one type of public key encryption that NIST intends to evaluate, assess, and establish as official will not be susceptible to breaking by quantum computers. The page titled "Post-Quantum Cryptography Standardisation" contains all the information you require. Macs are incapable of resolving numerous mathematical inquiries due to their excessive complexity. Conversely, qubit devices are capable of accomplishing this. Quantum mechanical events are responsible for the endeavor. Over the past few years, quantum computers have been employed in numerous critical initiatives. The majority of the public key cryptosystems that are currently in use will be rendered unusable by extremely powerful quantum computers. Subsequently, it will be exceedingly challenging to preserve the confidentiality of digital files or notes. Post-quantum cryptography, also known as quantum-resistant encryption, aims to develop encryption systems that are compatible with both conventional and quantum computers. Additionally, these instruments should be capable of connecting to and utilizing existing networks and files.

The date of the construction of a quantum computer that is exceedingly enormous is uncertain. Currently, numerous specialists assert that it is challenging to construct quantum computers that are exceedingly large. The capabilities of these systems were not consistently evident. Some individuals believe that quantum computers will be sufficiently powerful in 20 years to violate nearly all of the current methods of utilizing public keys. The public key system that we employ today was constructed over the course of nearly 20 years. It is uncertain when quantum computing will become prevalent; however, it is imperative that our safety systems are prepared for it immediately.

14.2.7.2 Post-Quantum Cryptography

Prior to commencing the composition of this section, it would be advantageous to ascertain the subject matter. "Post-quantum cryptography" is not concerned with the encryption of data using the next generation of computer processors, regardless of their specifications. After quantum computing, this may transpire. It is untrue. It is unrelated to "quantum cryptography," which is concerned with the development of novel methods for safeguarding information through the application of quantum physics. The majority of the time, computers today employ post-quantum cryptography programs, key sizes, and methods to safeguard data with cryptography that is impenetrable to even quantum computers. You may believe that this is of no significance until quantum computers are developed that are capable of performing tasks beyond determining the prime factors of 21. The most critical consideration in cryptography is the duration of time for which a secret should be maintained. If you wish to conceal a particular piece of data for a period of 20 years, you need not be concerned with the current capabilities of computers.

There is considerable concern regarding the types of devices that will be accessible in the next two decades. Moore's law asserts that the computing capacity of computers doubles every 18 months. If this law remains in effect, a computer that is produced in 20 years will be approximately 10,000 times more potent than the one we currently possess. The objective of cryptography is not to create problems that are difficult to solve. The objective is to create problems that are straightforward to construct but difficult for computers to resolve using the current instruments. One straightforward method to demonstrate this is to multiply two extremely large prime numbers in order to generate a new number that is even larger. Conversely, it is challenging to divide a composite number that is exceedingly large into its prime component numbers. This type of mathematics necessitates an extensive amount of time for codes that are based on counts. In order to implement a cryptographic method that will endure for 20 years, it will be necessary to devise problems that are at least 10,000 times more difficult to solve than the one-step problems currently in use. This is due to the fact that computers double in intelligence every 18 months.

By definition, a "harder" task would necessitate the constant discovery of novel methods for encrypting the message. This would be a challenging endeavor. In the present day, however, we employ a consistent formula and key numbers that continue to increase in size to impede the ability of computers to decipher the encryption. In this instance, the search space for a 31-digit number is approximately ten times larger than that of a 30-digit number. Even today, we address the challenges posed by Moore's law by gradually increasing the smallest key sizes that can be employed in cryptography. Switching to an alternative encryption method with a reduced key size and digital signature will prevent the need to retain an increased amount of the public key and digital signature. However, it is significantly more challenging to devise a novel approach and demonstrate its safety than it is to increase the size of keys. This is the reason we typically adhere to the methods that we are already familiar with. Over the past few decades, we have repeatedly engaged in the same activities.

Many consider the Rivest-Shamir-Adleman (RSA) method to be one of the most effective and widely used asymmetric cryptographic methods for safeguarding data. Ciphertext can be generated rapidly if one of the keys is known; however, it is exceedingly challenging to comprehend without the other key. Know you what I am referring to? The foundation of RSA is the use of extremely large prime numbers to effect numerical changes. This method remains robust due to the necessity of employing sheer force to determine the prime factors of a large composite number. The development of a digital signing method that is based on elliptical curve cryptography (ECC) has been the result of additional research in the field of cryptography. This type of encryption is predicated on the algebraic structure of elliptic curves over finite fields. There is a lack of consensus regarding the safety of Elliptic Curve Cryptography (ECC) in comparison to RSA; however, this is not always the primary advantage. Nevertheless, the most advantageous aspect of ECC is its ability to address complex issues related to digital signatures and key lengths that are significantly shorter. If the keys used in RSA begin to exceed a certain length, ECC may be able to provide assistance. In the present day, secure methods are a combination of various forms of robust security that are user-friendly. A cryptographic task can be completed in a specific number of stages. It is referred to as the "security level." This concept is intended to assist you in determining the strength of various encryption methods and keys. The cryptographic equation will require 2n steps to be solved if the security level is n. Table 14.15 contrasts RSA with a variety of key sizes and ECC methods.

TABLE 14.15
Cryptocurrency Sizes and Levels of Security

Algorithm	Private Key	Public Key	Signature	Security Level (bits)
RSA-1024	1,102	438	259	80
RSA-2048	1,776	620	403	112
RSA-4096	3,312	967	744	140
ECDSA P-256	187	353	146	128
Ed25519	179	300	146	128

14.2.7.3 Algorithm Comparison Analysis

The primary objective was to identify algorithms that are both practical and secure against assaults, including those that are based on quantum mechanics. Some of the primary criteria employed to assess them included security, performance, adaptability, and key/signature size. The following is a summary of the various mathematical methodologies they represented:

Lattice-based cryptography: The difficulties of this problem are rooted in high-dimensional lattices, which are grids of points in multidimensional space. The shortest vector problem (SVP) and learning with errors (LWEs) [26] are two of the most frequently encountered problems. The first one pertains to the difficulty of identifying distinctive lattice points in the presence of chaotic data, while the second one pertains to the difficulty of identifying the nearest point in the presence of vectors that form the lattice's foundation.

Code-based cryptography: It makes use of the challenge of deciphering error-correcting codes that are generated at random. It is quite difficult to decipher the original message from the encrypted codeword without knowing the private key's structure. This method could be a contender as solving generic decoding problems is computationally challenging even for quantum computers [10]. Public and private keys used in code-based cryptography can be massive matrices that go into the hundreds of kilobits in size, which is one of the major limitations of this type of encryption.

Hash-based cryptography: It utilizes one-way hash functions to produce digital signatures. Merkle trees and one-time signatures are implemented in SPHINCS+, which is the most widely recognized example. Hashing functions are a promising option for post-quantum cryptography due to their demonstrated security and simplicity. However, the use of autonomous hash-based techniques may result in the ballooning of document sizes when signed with it.

Another approach, isogeny-based cryptography, was demonstrated to be inadequate in terms of security due to the complexity of identifying isogenies between elliptic curves. The security of the supersingular isogeny key exchange (SIKE) system was compromised in 2022 as a result of an effective assault [17].

A number of algorithms represented the cryptographic approaches previously described; however, only a limited number were deemed secure and resilient enough for widespread application. NIST has recently published a list of approved algorithms:

CRYSTALS-Kyber is a KEM that employs lattice cryptography and the learning-with-errors issue. It enables the secure creation and transmission of a secret key to another individual. Kyber's lattice structure, which offers exceptional security, efficiency, and relatively small key sizes, renders it a promising candidate for practical applications, including secure communication protocols. This investigation is not intended to evaluate this algorithm, as it does not contribute to the public-key encryption system [15].

CRYSTALS-Dilithium is a digital signature algorithm that relies on learning with errors and rounding difficulties and employs lattice-based cryptography. It is distinguished by its efficiency and offers robust security with manageable signature and key sizes. The consistent performance of Dilithium is one of the reasons it is regarded as a leader among post-quantum signature schemes.

SPHINCS+ uses cryptographic hash methods such as SHA-256 to develop a digital signature technique that is dependent on hashes. It is not reliant on maintaining the internal state between signature generations, as it is designed as a stateless signature scheme. To ensure security and resistance to quantum computation, it implements one-time signature techniques and Merkle trees [7].

NIST has already published a list of approved algorithms; however, new algorithms are presently being developed as part of round-4 submissions [17].

Conversely, the MAYO-1's security level is 1, which indicates the lowest level of security, when compared to NIST, Table 14.16 that was previously provided.

14.2.7.4 Methodology

14.2.7.4.1 Quantum Computers

It is commendable that you are of the opinion that computers operate on a "scalar" level. In order to double the number of tasks that can be executed per second, it is necessary to either have twice as many processors or processors that are twice as rapid. There is a significant interest among individuals to develop "quantum" or "quantum computers" in the present day. Information is not a bit with a value of either 1 or 0, and quantum mechanics governs the events that occur in this location. It is a qubit, which is composed of the sum of its two fundamental states. I will refrain from contributing any new information to the subject matter, as there is already a substantial amount of information available. However, it is important to bear in mind that quantum computers are still relatively novel. Many individuals are optimistic that they will improve and be able to resolve significant computer issues within the next few years. They are all exactly the same. It is a device that is capable of performing multiple tasks simultaneously. It is also known as traveling at exponential velocities simultaneously. The production of qubit processors has been exceedingly challenging. A significant amount of effort and money have been expended. It has been completed at last. They are experiencing significant difficulties with their technology. The quantum computer has the potential to resolve certain computer issues if it is sufficiently large.

TABLE 14.16
Attributes of liboqs Algorithms

Algorithm	Claimed NIST Level	Public Key Size (Bytes)	Private Key Size (Bytes)	Signature Size (Bytes)
Dilithium2	2	1312	2528	2420
Dilithium3	3	1952	4000	3293
Dilithium5	5	2592	4864	4595
Falcon-512	1	897	1281	752
Falcon-1024	5	1793	2305	1462
Falcon-padded-512	1	897	1281	666
Falcon-padded-1024	5	1793	2305	1280
MAYO-1	1	1168	24	321
MAYO-2	1	5488	24	180
MAYO-3	3	2656	32	577
MAYO-5	5	5008	40	838
ML-DSA-44-ipd	2	1312	2560	2420
ML-DSA-65-ipd	3	1952	4032	3309
ML-DSA-87-ipd	5	2592	4896	4627
SPHINCS+-SHA2-128f-simple	1	32	64	17,088
SPHINCS+-SHA2-128s-simple	1	32	64	7856
SPHINCS+-SHA2-192f-simple	3	48	96	35,664
SPHINCS+-SHA2-192s-simple	3	48	96	16,224
SPHINCS+-SHA2-256f-simple	5	64	128	49,856
SPHINCS+-SHA2-256s-simple	5	64	128	29,792
SPHINCS+-SHAKE-128f-simple	1	32	64	17,088
SPHINCS+-SHAKE-128s-simple	1	32	64	7856
SPHINCS+-SHAKE-192f-simple	3	48	96	35,664
SPHINCS+-SHAKE-192s-simple	3	48	96	16,224
SPHINCS+-SHAKE-256f-simple	5	64	128	49,856
SPHINCS+-SHAKE-256s-simple	5	64	128	29,792

Many initiatives have been permitted to continue. People who investigate quantum computers believed that they might be capable of performing certain tasks at a significantly quicker pace than conventional computers. The instruments employed in this investigation were antiquated. It was created prior to the advent of quantum computing. People were informed about Peter Shor's method for determining the prime factors of a number in 1994. There is a substantial distinction between this and the optimal method for completing tasks that are not quantum. This has the potential to mark the beginning of a new epoch in the field of code. It is probable that this is a confidential code. RSA and ECC are capable of safeguarding text; however, they will cease to function as soon as quantum computers become sufficiently stable and large. The primary reason for this is that quark computers are capable of performing the task. This computer is also known as a cryptographically relevant quantum computer (CRQC). It is compact and functions efficiently. There is a wide range of opinions regarding the potential occurrence of this.

However, the more rapidly quantum computers are engineered, the more expensive they will be to resolve any technological complications. The year 2030 has been discussed.

There is hope, but it is not a reality that can be achieved. Since it has been 20 years, the confidentiality will be forfeited. It is probable that quantum computers will be employed to attempt to decipher the code in 20 years. If you wish to conceal your message, remember this. In other words, quantum computers that are capable of performing specific tasks have not yet been developed. It is still advisable to employ encryption methods that quantum computers are unable to decipher if safety is a critical concern. At present, the threat is posed by an adversary who is gathering information that they can use to trigger a series of adverse events that will harm all parties. The initial line was not altered, as it is already accurate, as shown in Figure 14.5.

14.2.7.4.2 Algorithms

Six distinct methodologies are employed to investigate post-quantum cryptography. First are secret codes that require your decipherment. The fundamental concept of the work is that you are required to decipher secret codes. Two older forms of encryption are employed with this method: NTRU and GGH. This method also includes

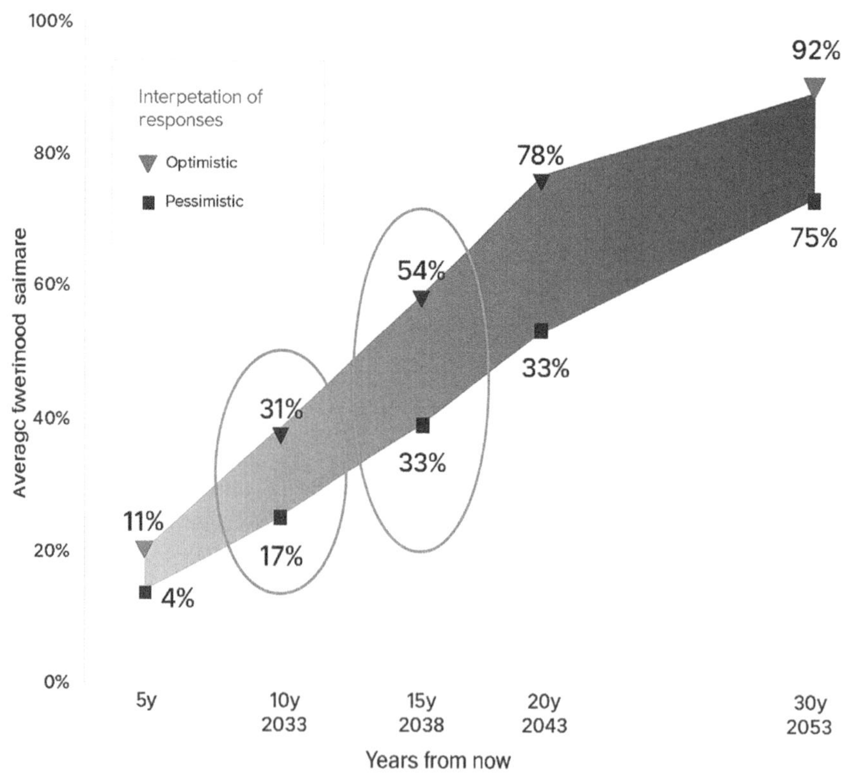

FIGURE 14.5 Expectations of a CRQC timeline ("In-Flight Data Protection in the Quantum Age," Chris Jansen—Nokia, Presentation to NANOG 92).

the NTRU signature and the BLISS signature from a later date. Ring-LWE can be employed to learn from one's errors. Ring-LWE can also be employed to sign items and exchange credentials. Some of these systems, such as NTRU encryption, have been extensively tested; however, no one has been able to successfully decipher them. There are numerous examples that demonstrate that when events go awry, they can become less secure. The Post-Quantum Cryptography Study Group has received funding from the European Commission. According to them, the Stehle-Steinfeld type of NTRU should be investigated more frequently than the NTRU method. NTRU maintained a title at that time. Due to this, the investigation indicates that NTRU may be inherently safer than other lattice-based algorithms.

14.2.7.5 Multivariate Cryptography Main Article: Multivariate Cryptography

Encryption schemes such as the Rainbow (unbalanced oil and vinegar) scheme are one component of this. The concept is derived from the difficulty of resolving groups of intricate problems. This type of plan is illustrated in the following location. Despite numerous attempts, there has yet to be identified a secure method for coding problems that involve numerous variables. On the other hand, in the quantum world, it is possible to create a secure digital signature using Rainbow and other multiple signature methods. A patent has been granted to the Rainbow Signature Scheme.

14.2.7.6 Hash-Based Cryptography Main Article: Hash-Based Cryptography

The WOTS plan is one form of safety that this group utilizes. Signature systems are also known as XMSS, SPHINCS, and Merkle. Ralph Merkle may have created the first digital identities that were based on hashes in the late 1970s. Since that time, number-based digital signatures, such as RSA and DSA, have been investigated and determined to be an advantageous option. A limited number of files can be signed with a public key that is based on a hash. This is the situation in which these methods are not effective. This is due to the fact that a secret key composed of integers can only sign a single file. Before quantum computers were employed to breach security, individuals did not prioritize these indicators. Quantum computers were once again the subject of increased attention when they were employed to breach security. The Merkle signing method is not patentable, as evidenced by a cursory search. Additionally, numerous other hash functions that do not safeguard copies may be implemented. The XMSS stateful hash-based signing method is discussed in RFC 8391. Johannes Buchmann is the leader of a team of scientists who devised this project.

It is important to bear in mind that all of these are either one-time signatures or signatures that are limited in duration. In 1989, Moni Naor and Moti Yung developed the Naor-Yung method and UOWHF hashing. It is possible to sign an item using a hash-based procedure known as the Naor-Yung method. This is the first signature of its kind that does not require any special features, as it can be used multiple times.

14.2.7.7 Code-Based Cryptography

Several signature procedures, including Courtois, Finiasz, and Sendrier, are included in this category. These are compatible with the McEliece and Niederreiter encryption methods. The initial McEliece signature has captivated the attention of all individuals for more than four decades. The goppa numbers were selected at random in order to qualify. However, there are certain hazards associated with the McEliece approach. The objective of these modifications is to arrange the code in a more logical manner, thereby ensuring that the keys are as concise as feasible. We implemented the recommendations of the Post-Quantum Cryptography Study Group. This organization receives funding from the European Commission. There are a few individuals who believe that the McEliece public key encryption method could potentially prevent the development of quantum computers in the future. In order to construct these types of crypt systems, it is necessary to have supersingular isogeny graphs that are capable of interacting with elliptic curves and higher-dimensional abelian varieties over simple fields. This is the method by which secure alternatives can be determined. CSIDH is an acronym that refers to key exchanges, such as Diffie-Hellman. Numerous individuals in this profession possess a wealth of knowledge associated with it.

The Diffie-Hellman and elliptic curve Diffie-Hellman key sharing methods, which are widely recognized, are reliant on quantum physics. However, this method is simpler to comprehend and does not employ it. The SQIsign method is the second type of sign. This concept is derived from the correlation between supersingular elliptic curves and the largest orders in specific types of quaternion algebras. In 2022, SIDH/SIKE, another building that garnered significant attention, ran into some poor fate. However, the exploit is exclusively functional on SIDH/SIKE devices. Another method that is founded on isogeny is incompatible with it. The quantum barrier and the standard key are the two keys. A quantum computer is incapable of breaking certain varieties of encryption, such as AES and SNOW 3G, if the key quantities are sufficiently large. It is also impossible to employ symmetric key cryptography or methods that rely on it in place of public key cryptography on a quantum computer. An example of this is the 3GPP Mobile Network Authentication Structure. Kerberos is an additional option. Public key encryption is the sole form of cryptography. Many individuals believe that one of the most effective methods for improving security in the wake of quantum computation is to increase the use of symmetric key management, such as Kerberos. This is due to the fact that it has been utilized by a significant number of individuals worldwide.

14.2.7.8 A Brief History of Quantum Computers

In the 1980s, Richard Feynman and David Deutsch conducted significant research that inspired the development of quantum computers. However, there have been varying perspectives on quantum mechanics as a physics field since the early 1900s. He [7] was inspired by quantum mechanics to develop the concept of a computer. Additionally, he was aware that quantum events are exceedingly intricate, rendering it challenging for conventional computers to simulate them. This enabled quantum programs to function and expanded the field of quantum computer science. Deutsch ultimately devised the concept of a quantum computer that could establish a connection with any other computer in the world. Additionally, it has the potential to perform a multitude of other tasks. It may be more intelligent than the majority of computers in certain respects. These significant advancements will enhance the capabilities of quantum computers in the years ahead. In 1994, a scientist named Peter Shor made significant news by determining how to operate quantum computers. Every aspect of the game was altered. Shor's method could be employed to rapidly resolve some challenging mathematical inquiries with sufficient capacity. The majority of individuals' devices would require an extended period of time to complete this task. Shor's method was both efficient and straightforward when dealing with large quantities.

Qubit computation was demonstrated to be capable of circumventing the majority of challenges. Quantum computers and security systems that are incompatible with them require significantly more time and money to manufacture. Grover's method is a quantum technique that is of significant importance. In 1996, he executed it. Lov Grover is his given name. A man named Grover devised the scheme. This is a feat that no other computer has ever achieved: the ability to rapidly browse a library. Afterward, the situation will not function in the same manner in real life. Computers that do not employ quantum physics require significantly more time to conduct brute-force searches than those that do. This type of inquiry is designed to identify all keys that could be employed to decrypt the encryption. Quantum computers may not necessitate 100,000 attempts to identify the appropriate key. Occasionally, they may require only 1,000. It has made significant progress since its inception. A greater amount of effort is currently being directed toward the enhancement of quantum computers. Quantum computers have the potential to revolutionize the world in the following ways. In the past few decades, science has made significant progress. According to experts in the field, it is feasible to construct miniature quantum computers. Quantum processes and corrections are more effective, despite the fact that qubits require more time to align. These modifications bring quantum computing one step closer to achieving its stated capabilities.

In 2019, Google announced that it had developed the first Sycamore engine. This was a significant advancement for quantum computers. According to Google, the 53-qubit computer is capable of rapidly solving a mathematical problem. Even the most advanced computer in the world would not have been able to compute the numbers in 10,000 years. IBM had never previously manufactured a quantum processor that was as robust. It was released in November 2022. It contained 433 qubits. In 2021, the organization introduced its Eagle microprocessor, which contains 127 qubits. About three times slower than the Osprey processor. Additionally, it operates at a rate eight times quicker than Google's Sycamore engine. Scientists and technology companies are exerting significant effort to develop quantum computers that are both secure and quickly. Currently, quantum computing is advancing at an accelerated pace. The ability of quantum computers to rectify errors and be of practical use is also improving. This will facilitate their capacity for creativity in numerous respects.

14.2.7.8.1 Test Environment and Methodology

In order to guarantee consistent measurements, a containerized environment was implemented to execute comprehensive performance evaluations of classical and post-quantum cryptography algorithms. The subsequent paragraphs provide descriptions of the instruments employed for visualization and implementation:

liboqs library: The highly optimized variants of the post-quantum algorithms presented in the liboqs (Open Quantum Safe project) [11] library were indispensable to this benchmarking investigation. It is effortless to integrate into a wide variety of projects and applications due to the extensive documentation and numerous example scripts and test cases. In addition to the primary C library, the official interfaces offered by liboqs facilitate the development of alternative languages. We have chosen Golang, Python, and C++. In addition to offering developers in each language intuitive and idiomatic interfaces, these wrappers preserved the original C library's incredible speed.

Docker: We selected this solution as our test platform because it enables us to create distinct, repeatable testing environments for each language. We constructed our own Docker container by utilizing sample Dockerfiles from official repositories for each wrapper. This method enabled us to assess post-quantum algorithms with minimal interference from other programs.

Python: A Python command-line interface (CLI) application was employed to orchestrate test orchestration and data collection across multiple iterations and Docker containers. Python scripts that supervised data visualization and post-processing also enabled the creation of comprehensive performance graphs.

The primary objective of this investigation is to assess the effectiveness of post-quantum algorithms for digital signatures that have been approved by NIST. The efficacy of these algorithms, which were intended to withstand quantum attacks, was compared using a variety of programming languages. To achieve this, we timed each method over 100 iterations to ascertain the time required to generate keys, sign documents, and verify transactions. The selection of the tested algorithms was influenced by the liboqs method for gathering a catalog of supporting signature (SIG) algorithms, which resulted in minimal discrepancies among languages. The same method was employed to evaluate the scaling capabilities of four additional file sizes: 1 KB, 1 MB, 50 MB, and 1 GB. We were able to eradicate variations caused by discrepancies in the input files by using arbitrarily generated information from these files as input for each iteration. It is essential to precisely define variability when conducting measurements across multiple iterations. In this investigation, the standard error of the mean (SEM) of each graph was employed to quantify this variation.

REFERENCES

1. Hegde, S. B., Jamuar, A., & Kulkarni, R. (2023, July 7–8). Post quantum implications on private and public key cryptography. In *Proceedings of the 2023 International Conference on Smart Systems for Applications in Electrical Sciences (ICSSES)* (pp. 1–6), Tumakuru, India.
2. Lopez-Valdivieso, J., & Cumplido, R. (2024). Design and implementation of hardware-software architecture based on hashes for SPHINCS+. *ACM Transactions on Reconfigurable Technology and Systems*, 14, 1–21.
3. Mukil, A., Ashokkumar, N., Lai, N. S., & Lakshmanan, R. (2024, August). Cordic-based, high-performance, and resource-efficient FFT processor: Speech processing application. *AIP Conference Proceedings*, 3161(1), 1–8. AIP Publishing.
4. Zhou, Z., He, D., Liu, Z., Luo, M., & Choo, K. K. R. (2021). A software/hardware co-design of CRYSTALS-Dilithium signature scheme. *ACM Transactions on Reconfigurable Technology and Systems*, 14, 1–21.

5. Bharathi, M., Sandhyakumari, G., Madhurima, V., Tabassum, S., Kumar, N. A., & Neelima, K. (2025). Protecting your digital life from cyber threats and vulnerabilities. In *Convergence of Cybersecurity and Cloud Computing* (pp. 457–472). IGI Global Scientific Publishing.
6. Ananda Mohan, P. V. (2023, September 8–9). Hash-based digital signatures—a tutorial review. In *Proceedings of the 2023 IEEE International Conference on Public Key Infrastructure and Its Applications (PKIA)* (pp. 1–8), Bangalore, India, IEEE.
7. Liang, W., Xie, S., Cai, J., Xu, J., Hu, Y., Xu, Y., & Qiu, M. (2022). Deep neural network security collaborative filtering scheme for service recommendation in intelligent cyber-physical systems. *IEEE Internet of Things Journal*, 9, 22123–22132.
8. Zhao, C., Zhang, N., Wang, H., Yang, B., Zhu, W., Li, Z., Wuxi, M. Z., Yin, S., Wei, S., & Liu, L. (2021). A compact and high-performance hardware architecture for CRYSTALS-Dilithium. *IACR Transactions on Cryptographic Hardware and Embedded Systems*, 2021, 270–295.
9. National Institute of Standards and Technology. (2021). *Advanced Encryption Standard (AES)*. NIST. Available online: https://nvlpubs.nist.gov/nistpubs/FIPS/NIST.FIPS.197-upd1.pdf (accessed on 16 November 2024).
10. Horpenyuk, A., Opirskyy, I., & Vorobets, P. (2023). Analysis of problems and prospects of implementation of post-quantum cryptographic algorithms. In *Proceedings of the CQPC* (pp. 39–49).
11. Ananda Mohan, P. V. (2023, September 8–9). Hash-based digital signatures—a tutorial review. In *Proceedings of the 2023 IEEE International Conference on Public Key Infrastructure and Its Applications (PKIA)* (pp. 1–8), Bangalore, India, IEEE.
12. Nataraj, C., Ashokkumar, N., Mukil, A., & Selvaperumal, S. K. (2024). FPGA architectures for FFT-based 2-D soft decision decoding in the frequency domain for two-dimensional data storage applications. *AIP Conference Proceedings*, 3161(1), 1–8. AIP Publishing.
13. Castryck, W., & Decru, T. (2022). An efficient key recovery attack on SIDH. *Cryptology ePrint Archive*, Paper 2022/975. Available online: https://eprint.iacr.org/2022/975.pdf (accessed on 16 November 2024).
14. Sandhyakumari, G., Bharathi, M., Madhurima, V., Tabassum, S., Neelima, K., & Kumar, N. A. (2025). A dynamic cybersecurity framework for energy-efficient Internet of Things. In *Convergence of Cybersecurity and Cloud Computing* (pp. 165–190). IGI Global Scientific Publishing.
15. Alagic, G., Alagic, G., Apon, D., Cooper, D., Dang, Q., Dang, T., ... & Smith-Tone, D. (2022). Status report on the third round of the NIST post-quantum cryptography standardization process. US Department of Commerce, NIST: Gaithersburg, MD, USA.
16. Nanda, A., Puthal, D., Mohanty, S. P., & Choppali, U. (2018). A computing perspective of quantum cryptography. *IEEE Consumer Electronics Magazine*, 7, 57–59.
17. Kannwischer, M. J., Rijneveld, J., & Schwabe, P. (2019). Faster multiplication in Z_2m[x] on Cortex-M4 to speed up NIST PQC candidates. In *Applied Cryptography and Network Security: ACNS 2019* (pp. 1–16). Lecture Notes in Computer Science, Springer.
18. Dam, D.-T., Tran, T.-H., Hoang, V.-P., Pham, C.-K., & Hoang, T.-T. (2023). A survey of post-quantum cryptography: Start of a new race. *Cryptography*, 7, 40.
19. Ukpabi, D., Karjaluoto, H., Bötticher, A., Nikiforova, A., Petrescu, D., Schindler, P., Valtenbergs, V., & Lehmann, L. (2023). Framework for understanding quantum computing use cases from a multidisciplinary perspective and future research directions. *Futures*, 154, 103277.
20. Liu, Y.-K., & Moody, D. (2024). Post-quantum cryptography and the quantum future of cybersecurity. *Physical Review Applied*, 21, 040501.
21. Imai, H., & Hagiwara, M. (2008). Error-correcting codes and cryptography. *Applied Algebra in Engineering, Communication, and Computing*, 19, 213–228.

22. Algazy, K., Sakan, K., Khompysh, A., & Dyusenbayev, D. (2024). Development of a new post-quantum digital signature algorithm: Syrga-1. *Computers*, 13(1), 26.
23. Roma, C. A., Tai, C. E. A., & Hasan, M. A. (2021). Energy efficiency analysis of post-quantum cryptographic algorithms. *IEEE Access*, 9, 71295–71317.
24. Ashokkumar, N., Thandapani, K., Nagarajan, P., Kabilamani, P., Manimaran, B., & Krishnamurthy, M. (2023). Reconfigurable computer architecture for signal processing applications. In *Intelligent Computing and Control for Engineering and Business Systems (ICCEBS)* (pp. 1–4), Chennai, India.
25. Sajimon, P. C., Jain, K., & Krishnan, P. (2022, May). Analysis of post-quantum cryptography for the Internet of Things. In *2022 6th International Conference on Intelligent Computing and Control Systems (ICICCS)* (pp. 387–394), IEEE.
26. Dziechciarz, D., & Niemiec, M. (2025). Efficiency analysis of NIST-standardized post-quantum cryptographic algorithms for digital signatures in various environments. *Electronics*, 14(1), 70.

Part III

The Future (Next Generation Applications)

15 Quantum Computing Paradigms—Bridging Foundational Quantum Mechanics with Contemporary Computational Architectures

K. Reddy Madhavi, Sam Goundar, K. Saradhi, P. Sohan Sai, and Gudditi Chetan

15.1 INTRODUCTION

Quantum computing is an extremely reengineering of computation beyond classical paradigms which have been built from von Neumann architecture designs and Boolean mathematics. The performance of exponential quantum behavior simulation work is limited in classical computers due to their inability to perform complex calculations related to high-dimensional optimization, molecular simulation, or to process the encryption processes that could provide a cryptographic seal of security (Preskill, 2018). Quantum computers utilize essential quantum mechanical behaviors like superposition, entanglement, and tunneling, which allow them to access information in manners not possible through classical computation (Nielsen & Chuang, 2010). They provide for parallel processing through the storage of quantum states from a blend of qubits, effectively a probability combination of states, and offer way more computation capability in every proposed application domain beyond cybersecurity encryption, such as drug development and artificial intelligence (Arute et al., 2019).

Richard Feynman started the quantum computing advances with his paper in 1982 defining that it was possible to simulate quantum systems themselves by quantum mechanical machines (Feynman, 1982). It then produced more or less further advances in the field that led to essential discoveries in, for example, the quantum

DOI: 10.1201/9781003538950-18

factoring algorithm of Peter Shor in 1994, which established an exponential speedup for integer factorization problems, a fundamental threat to classical cryptography (Shor, 1994). More or less concurrently, Lov Grover developed a quantum search algorithm that yielded quadratic speedups over classical search algorithms (Grover, 1996). Present-day noisy intermediate-scale quantum (NISQ) devices being constructed are from laboratory demonstrations for realizing quantum gates—from superconducting circuits and trapped-ion technology. However, there are some very critical challenges that must be resolved, namely, decoherence, scalability, and error correction (Devoret & Schoelkopf, 2013). Quantum systems require extremely controlled environments at very low temperatures with electromagnetic shielding, and ultrafast operations in order to maintain coherence in multi-qubit regimes (Terhal, 2015). For example, surface codes as well as cat codes are some of the error correction methods which intersperse logical and entangled physical qubits while performing error detection and correction (Campbell et al., 2017). The substantial high-overhead physical qubits needed to acquire fault tolerance also constitute a technical and financial barrier for implementations that involve large scales.

Hybrid quantum-classical algorithms, such as variational quantum eigensolvers, are critical in the age of NISQ in linking quantum computational speedups to classical optimization resources despite the imperfections of current quantum hardware (Peruzzo et al., 2014). The realization of quantum computing as a general-purpose technology will depend ultimately on integrating architectures fault-tolerance, quantum error correction techniques, and further advancements in materials science. The revolution about to happen is capable of transforming fundamental research in physics, redefining chemical concepts, and revolutionizing current understanding of how information is processed.

15.2 QUANTUM MECHANICS FOR COMPUTING

Quantum computing relies on the concept of quantum mechanics and describes the dynamics of very tiny things, i.e., atoms and electrons (Biamonte et al., 2017). These are not rules that we follow in our daily life or in normal computers. The contemporary and classical computers operate on bits. Three sets of possible values of a bit have two values 0 or 1. Quantum computers do utilize quantum bits (qubits). The specialty of the qubit is that it can be in superposition, or it is, otherwise, able to be in both state 0 and state 1 simultaneously. The other property is entanglement. The state of one qubit is proportional to the state of the other qubit when they are separated, irrespective of whether they are entangled. This interaction enables the quantum computers to achieve certain tasks in a comparatively shorter time than their classical counterparts. The third important element is the interference. Interference allows quantum computers to strengthen the chances of finding the right answer while reducing the chances of wrong answers. Due to such properties as superposition, entanglement, and interference, the quantum computers are not just faster models of classical computers. They operate in a totally different way and are capable of solving some issues, which the classical computers will never be in a position to solve (Bharti et al., 2022). To bring the quantum technologies to reality, a clear understanding of what quantum mechanics is and what things that mathematics tells about the behavior of such systems are necessary. It is only based on it that the construction of strong quantum computers in the future can be considered reliable.

15.2.1 Mathematical Underpinnings and Theoretical Basis

Elementary quantum mechanics visualizes states as vectors in Hilbert spaces and represented by linear algebra. The space of quantum systems upon which mathematics is now operating has an abstract concept. The simplest mathematics for setting states of quantum information storage in qubits stems from two-dimensional Hilbert spaces and vector algebra (Bub, 2016). The qubit can be put in a state of superposition by being operated between the two states, both 0 and 1, while classical bits can only take on values of either 0 or 1 only. At any time, it is termed as the working system of superposition. Quantum systems exist in a status of superposition until it is checked; during the act of checking, the outcome probability is calculated from the square amplitude of the particular wave concerned (Ballentine, 2014).

The density matrix describes quantum states wherein not all information about a system can be fully accessed (Bengtsson & Życzkowski, 2006). Vector representation can shine through for single-qubit superpositions, while density matrices properly symbolize mixtures in ensembles of pure states. Dimensional matrices sync superposition theory with classical kinds of uncertainty to describe the physical behavior of quantum systems viewed in conjunction with environmental interference.

From the quantum measurement theory, operations extract information from the quantum measurement operations (Busch et al., 2016). Standard projective measurements will act on a basis formed from eigenstates of an observable, and the system thereafter is irreversibly transformed as a result. Oscillating between the elementary capabilities of measurement, we turn to positive-operator-valued measures, POVMs, which generalize fundamental limits with an added stipulation of state collapse (Heinosaari & Ziman, 2012). In quantum communication networks, implementations of POVM quantum measurements have applications in precise information retrieval without transformation or destruction of entangled states and retaining these states (Wilde, 2017).

From the theoretical viewpoint, quantum mechanics elaborates Figure 15.1 with all the interdependent relationships necessary to elementary mathematics leading to measurement outcomes. Downward from the same top of the structure in Hilbert spaces of mathematics, pure quantum states arise as these abstract mathematical structures interact with one another. The paths of pure states lap over an even higher level in the generalized density matrix formalism monopolizing the center among innumerable quantum phenomena. The density matrix, then, allows branching into the basic features of quantum mechanics: expectation value calculations, emergence of quantum entanglements, and the patterns of decoherence.

Thus, here, the entire edifice proceeds all the way up to measurement theory, including projective measurements, POVMs, and the calculus of probabilities that eventually yield concrete results in the collapse of the state. In a way, then, all of this funnels into measurement theory. This settles the build-up of concepts: abstract mathematical foundations giving rise to observable physical phenomena (Jaeger, 2007).

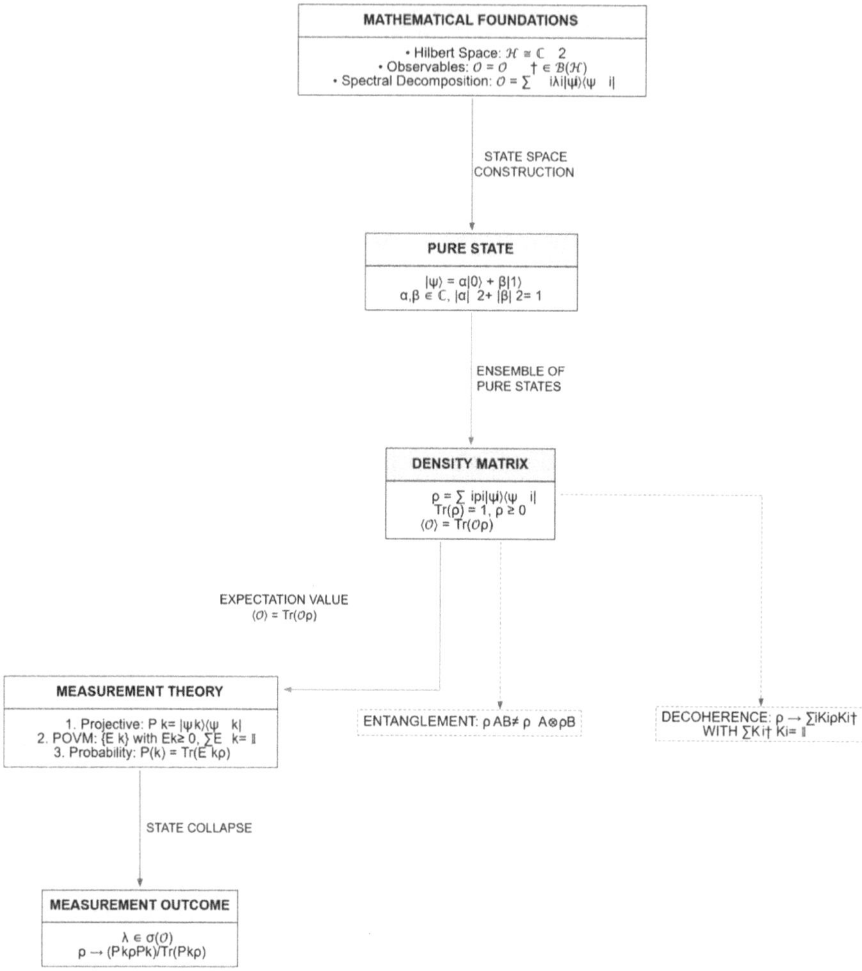

FIGURE 15.1 Hierarchical framework of quantum mechanical foundations and measurement theory.

15.2.2 Key Phenomena

Engineers are creating quantum computer systems with much higher computing abilities than classical systems. Quantum particles have a number of concurrent representation states for all extensive distances, but an entangled particle can change its state instantly when its counterpart does the same. The evolving quantum technology manages the production of Bell state between its two closely located and entangled qubits and prepares GHZ states in its multi-qubit entanglement involving three and more qubit systems. Fundamental capabilities must be provided by states to support engineering quantum teleportation system techniques and the methodologies for error correction operations.

One of the most significant advances in quantum physics thus far seems to be quantum tunneling. It makes it possible for a particle to cross barriers, which is impossible through classical means (Albash & Lidar, 2018). Using quantum tunneling together with adiabatic quantum computers, sophisticated operators create systems, finding their best fit solution by means of quantum jumps between the discrete energy levels of their barriers (Hauke et al., 2020). When, in fact, they have limitations on operational decoherence, the existing protocol conservation prevails because the interactions in that environment naturally decay quantum coherences. The Lindblad master equation shows that, over time, quantum states lose their coherence and gradually become classical statistical mixtures (Breuer & Petruccione, 2007). Decay, in general, is one of the key issues in quantum computer for it destroys valuable quantum operations via quantum entanglement, and thus, probability superposition gives rise quantum speedup benefits.

Quantum computing is modeling a kind of operation that produces result via abstract math combined with the actual physical quantum systems. The mathematical implementations also reveal the quantum systems speedup over classical information processing as their volatility demands considerable engineering ingenuity and error correction techniques.

15.3 QUANTUM COMPUTING ARCHITECTURES

The architectures for quantum computing indeed draw from at least three disparate disciplines, namely, theoretical physics, electrical engineering, and materials engineering, by specification of physical qubits in an architecture which gives relations of quantum equivalents of classical bits, and the management of those relations (Monroe & Kim, 2013). Current implementations of quantum systems are based mainly on superconducting circuits and trapped ions, photonic architectures and topological qubits with special properties (Wendin, 2017). Nonlinearity in the Josephson junctions of superconducting qubits allows transmon and fluxonium differences to operate at cryogenic temperatures with microwave control precision. Transmons achieve long coherence times due to shunting processes that minimize the susceptibility of their junctions to charge noise. Error-resilient operations in fluxonium qubits are performed by flux noise suppression with structures for a superinductor used in obtaining high gate fidelities in quantum operations with ion qubits when trapped ions are positionally integrated within electromagnetic traps, while laser performance renders inner state controls reference to a compatible ion property and long operational times (Blais et al., 2021).

Stability of an ion chain under laser control renders trapped-ion architectures nonscalable beyond the hundred-qubit mark. Photonic qubits encode information in the polarization or orbital angular momentum of a photon, including room temperature operations and compatibility with already-existing infrastructure in fiber optic technologies. Linear optical quantum computation utilizes a beam splitter with a phase shaper for gate operations in its platforms, but involves probabilistic entanglement since it does not have the capability to ensure a deterministic photon coupling. These Majorana fermion-based topological qubits operate through braiding operations among quasiparticles, which carry information using non-local braiding operations with stored information, and theoretical protection gained against localized errors. Microsoft is attempting to build such topological qubits through engineering Majorana zero modes into nanowires made of semiconductor and superconductor under the presence of the long-standing experimental confirmation challenge. Various gate array approaches exist with data coherence versus reliable function scaling challenges with continuous improvement of fabrication materials and protection techniques.

Figure 15.2, showing the layered architecture of a quantum computing system, specifies a hierarchical structure from hardware implementation to application/execution. At the bottom, the physical layer, consisting of several qubit technologies such as superconducting, trapped ions, photonic, and topological qubits, serves as a basis for quantum computation. Above it is the control layer, responsible for qubit manipulation through pulse generation, measurement control, and calibration. Error correction is at the level of the locks necessary to maintain the integrity of the operations performed in computing through surface codes, syndrome detection, and error correction. After this comes the compiler layer, which optimizes quantum circuits, decomposes complex gates, and estimates computational resources for execution (Cross et al., 2019). Lastly, there is the application layer, which grants access to quantum capabilities through quantum algorithms, classical program interfaces, and API interactions in order to be able to portray real-world quantum computing applications.

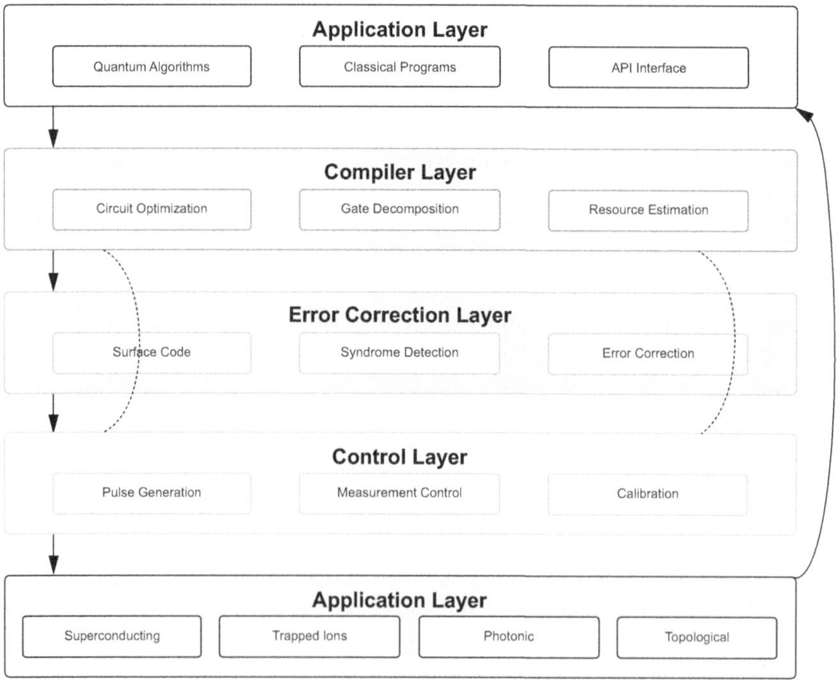

FIGURE 15.2 Quantum computing system architecture.

15.3.1 Scalability Challenges in Practical Implementations

Executing quantum devices entails a lot of daunting technical difficulties. This involves the hardware, the control software, the environment in which the system needs to operate, and most importantly, the very pernicious nature of electromagnetic coupling between qubits (Krantz et al., 2019). As a result, there is degradation in gate infrastructure with regard to superconducting chips, which are most hijacked by microwave pulse errors, and then within the trapped ions, there are errors in laser addressing, resulting in entangled pairs being annihilated. Cancelation of crosstalk will require new solutions in terms of new decoupling sequences and architectural innovations like frequency controllable qubits and 3D integration architectures. Such thermal noise will require that the cooling temperatures be relatively low, in millikelvin, with its thermal management problems. As most of the heat is produced by the qubit number, dilution refrigeration will not perform well with low-power levels of superconducting qubits and much improvement will still be required in cryogenic electronic advancement with wireless controls to reduce generated wiring heat.

Scalability of control electronics would align with scalability of qubit arrays through lines that may number in the thousands and which provide either microwave or laser control with nanosecond precision. Scalability improves with respect to material defects: Scalability of superconducting qubits is hindered through two level systems (TLS) in oxide layers and trapped-ion defects in electrodes and in photonic structures that suffer loss of photons in their optical components (Wang et al., 2020). Silicon spin qubits, when interfaced with superconducting resonators through hybrid approaches, will be able to benefit from dual platform capability. Such integration of disparate systems indeed brings with it its own unique operational complexities. Generally, error correction processes offer two significant problems, as the logical qubits would require a vast amount of resources to become fault-tolerant and thus would need a reeling in of technical specifications and cost. Overcoming this will be through concurrent development between the two hardware platforms with software and error correction processes, together with development in cryogen technology and photonics and quantum materials.

15.3.2 Quantum Networks and Their Role in Communication

Quantum networks shape the future of quantum technology with an objective of linking quantum processors in a distribution for secure computation and communications and enhanced sensing. Quantum networks operate via the transmission of an entangled state over an optical fiber, but transmission over a distance involves solved solutions for photons loss in the optical fibers. The quantum repeater protocol segments the network into short communicational segments for the creation of an entangled state that quantum memories store during an entanglement swap protocol between the links. White crystalline structures with atomic systems and with doping of rare earth are good quantum memory nodes through efficient storing processes with long times of coherence. Hybridization of entanglement purification protocols removes randomness in an entangled pair and creates a strong entanglement for long quantum network communications support. Hybrid quantum classical architectures combine quantum processors with classical computers for the optimization of operations such as variational quantum algorithms through a classical system for parameter optimization and errors suppression and quantum devices for state preparation (Cerezo et al., 2021).

Cloud-based services, such as Amazon Braket and IBM Quantum, are such a model in delivering democratized access to quantum capability and reduction in the complexity dimension in the field of hardware. Small modules combine to form modular quantum architectures that are a scalable architectural option compared to monolithic architectures. Synthetic photonic interconnects stretch between trapped-ion and superconducting quantum modules for partitioning between heterogeneous chips entangled states. Standard quantum internet layers necessitate solution for a myriad of technical problems in consideration of node synchronization as well as quantum entanglement distribution latency mitigation. A quantum network begins components for a global level will incorporate new types of cryptography by means of unbreakable quantum key distribution (QKD) as well as shared computation functionality by means of shared entangled frameworks (Pirandola et al., 2020). End-to-end quantum network deployment is a function of immense breakthrough in quantum memory technology as well as low-loss photonic integration and fault-tolerant network standards to serve as foundation markers for the overall quantum network infrastructure.

15.4 QUANTUM ALGORITHMS AND THEIR REALIZATION

Quantum algorithms embody quantum computer realization in the sense of delivering exponential computational speedups not in traditional ways for specific computational problem-solving. A combination of operation demands, theoretical algorithms, and physical constraints makes the realization pathway challenging. Quantum algorithms utilize quantum mechanical phenomena such as quantum mechanical superposition, quantum mechanical entanglement, and quantum mechanical interference for process efficiency in a manner beyond traditional computation performance limits (Montanaro, 2016). Through quantum Fourier transform, Shor's algorithm factors exponential problem domains to reveal periodic information, which traditional computation takes exponential amounts of times to manage. Unstructured search procedures are re-engineered in Grover's algorithm through state measurement probability amplification, yielding performance enhancement that is quadratic in comparison to other procedures even less spectacular in comparison to Shor's algorithm. Quantum algorithms are utilized by humans daily, but real-world implementation is still undermined through current quantum device limitations. Textbook algorithms must be re-engineered for the NISQ era through quantum machinery consisting of 50–100 qubits but with below fault tolerance requirements.

The theoretical grace of Shor's algorithm demands deep circuits with error-corrected logical qubits beyond contemporary processing powers. Theory and practice's contemporary disconnect compels scientists to move toward the development of hybrid algorithms, such as variational quantum eigensolver (VQE) and quantum approximation optimization algorithm (QAOA) with classical systems for special computations (Youvan, 2024). Such algorithms use successive optimizations for variable parameter quantum circuit architectures in an attempt to generate approximated values, but without guaranteed accuracy for uncertain values. Advances in quantum control and with error mitigation techniques continue to be a demand for quantum algorithm implementations. For the extraction of meaningful information with less-than-ideal hardware, scientists use dynamical decoupling pulse sequences for the cancelation of noise and zero-noise extrapolation, a technique comprising a series of runs with noising in an attempt to generate high-fidelity information. The realization of topological quantum algorithms is an exciting long-term endeavor using non-local data storage architectures designed to inherently protect quantum information from environmental influence. Scientists at Microsoft play with topological qubits in a pursuit of operations resilient to noise, but this experimental realization has not been publicly achieved in contemporary times (Jazaeri et al., 2019). Advances in quantum algorithms await an evolutionary intersection of theoretical approaches and engineering advances for breakthroughs in key error correction schemes, and materials and controls technology will turn quantum speedups into real functional realities.

In Figure 15.3, quantum algorithms exploit basic quantum properties, such as superposition, entanglement, and interference, for computational advantages that cannot be achieved by classical computing. These enable a quantum speedup, allowing exponential or quadratic enhancement over conventional approaches.

Some of the key algorithms embody these improvements: Shor's algorithm gives efficient factorization, Grover's algorithm provides faster unstructured search, and hybrid algorithms, such as VQE and QAOA, were designed for near-term quantum devices. However, practicality poses its own unique challenges-theoretical prowess notwithstanding. In fact, hardware limitations, large error rates, and NISQ power constraints impede its deployment in far-ranging real-life scenarios.

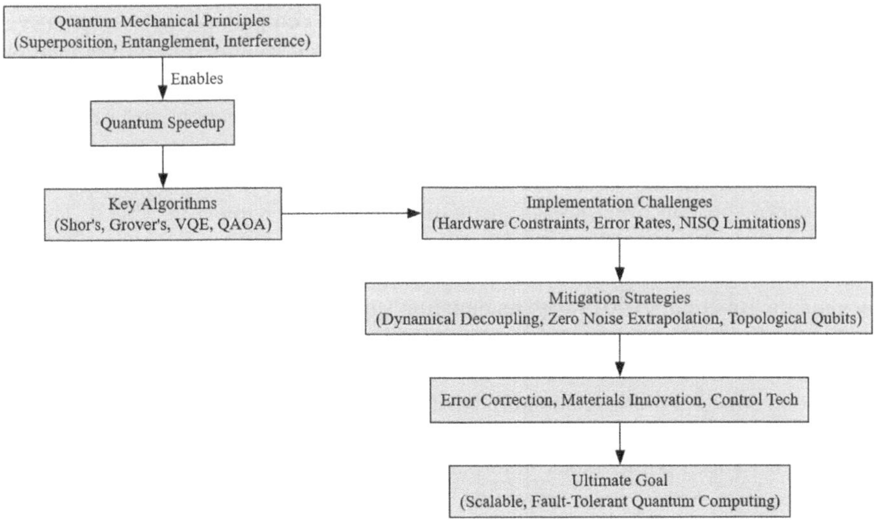

FIGURE 15.3 Architecture of quantum computing algorithms.

To lessen those challenges, different kinds of error mitigations are performed. Generally, dynamical decoupling, zero-noise extrapolation, and studying topological qubits are techniques that reduce noise and extend the coherency time of quantum states. In addition, further development of error correction, materials, and control will be applied to solving problems in quantum computation.

The ultimate goal is a scalable and fault-tolerant quantum computer that can address problems much beyond capability of classical ones. The progress of quantum algorithms depends on the simultaneous desk of theoretical evolution and engineering avenues and will herald great new capabilities in computation.

15.4.1 Conceptual Models and Theoretical Frameworks

Quantum algorithm theoretical models arise from three subjects, computational complexity theory, quantum information science, and linear algebra that specify quantum computational advantage capabilities. Such a model's foundations are quantum circuit model and adiabatic quantum computation. Like digital circuits, modern quantum computation divides operations into discrete minimum blocks (gates) of unitary instruction in discrete units called qubits. With such a model, one can derive language-level design specifications for the evaluation of requirements in terms of resources, like the number of qubits as well as circuit depths and gate fidelity requirements. Quantum circuit issues can formally classify quantum circuits through the use of complexity class BQP (bounded-error quantum polynomial time) to denote its quantum counterpart of P and NP classes for classical computation. Shor's algorithm puts integer factorization in complexity class of BQP but creates a factorization use gap over P class in that nobody has demonstrated its membership in the P-class (Aaronson, 2010). Quantum Hamiltonian complexity solving and quantum simulation of a system require exploration of issues that offer quantum verification of proofs through QMA (quantum Merlin-Arthur) models.

With its continuous-time model, adaptive quantum computing (AQC) maps a system's Hamiltonian in a ground state to a computational solution of an optimization problem. Conversely, though AQC doesn't employ explicit gate-level abstractions of the circuit model, it actually expresses combinatorial optimizations in terms of the Ising model in an effort to minimize spin glass energy landscapes. D-Wave quantum annealers' working model captures continuous-time dynamics but theorists question its extent of speedup over classical heuristic approaches (King et al., 2023). Theory speculates implications of quantum supremacy in determining quantum devices' superiority over classical supercomputers in painstakingly crafted operations. Google hogged the limelight in 2019 with its quantum supremacy demo with pseudo-random quantum circuits, but its methodological contribution as a stepping stone to quantum supremacy was questioned by scientists. Current research needs to surmount pragmatic concerns that produce quantum advantage and yield real-life dividends such as materials discovery through emulated correlated electronic processes and complicated logistics network optimizations. Interplay between theoretical models and physical code execution, such as error correction via surface codes and analog simulation via photonic quantum walks, dictates future algorithm development trends, requiring an evenhanded balancing act between theoretical abstraction and engineering practice.

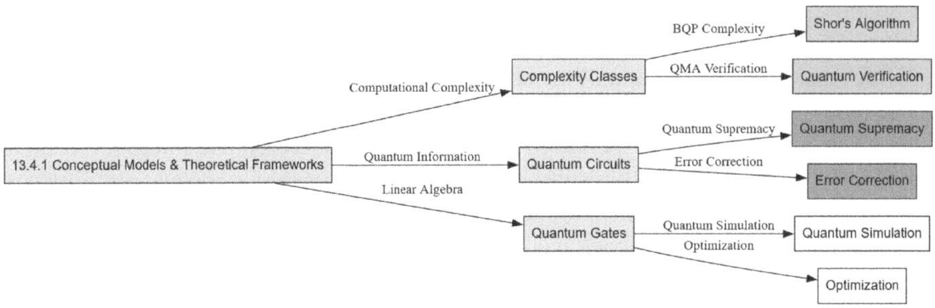

FIGURE 15.4 Quantum computing system architecture

Figure 15.4 illustrates conceptual frameworks of quantum algorithms, breaking their theory into related pieces. The unifying theme underlying is that of quantum information, quantum computational complexity, and linear algebra, all of which together provide basic quantum computational advantages. The structure frames quantum models of computation in terms of such complexity classes as BQP and QMA, defining the problem of quantum means of efficient solution.

Quantum circuits and gates form the building block of quantum computing, serving as working parts for algorithm execution. Shor's algorithm, highlighted in Figure 15.4, also indicates exponential quantum speedup of integer factorization in the BQP complexity class. Quantum supremacy, also partially demonstrated in Google's 2019 experiment, is also a milestone when quantum processors outperform classical supercomputers in specific computational processes. The image also addresses practical challenges such as error correction, to maintain quantum coherence and quantum stability in quantum computations.

Beyond circuits, quantum optimization and quantum simulation, instrumental in tackling complex logistics and physical challenges, meet in Figure 15.4. Quantum simulation allows material discovery through quantum modeling, and optimization approaches apply quantum annealing and combinatorics to large-scale logistics challenges. The tension between practical engineering and theoretical abstraction, displayed in the diagram, is evidence of the challenge of finding a balance between algorithm design and physical realization to provide quantum advantages in reality.

15.4.2 Algorithmic Building Blocks for Problem-Solving

Elementary quantum subroutines provide quantum information processing capability that is not present in classical systems. QFT is a subroutine for a wide range of algorithms and provides an efficient quantum state transformation in the frequency domain. By using periodical analysis of a superposition state, one can construct Shor's algorithm with its factoring and discrete logarithmic function and quantum eigenvalue estimation algorithms for the solution of eigenvalues (Kanamori & Yoo, 2020). QPE is a quantum simulation platform with QFT as a straightforward operation module distinguishing between sharp Hamiltonian eigenvalues for quantum chemistry and condensed matter investigations. Chemically accurate quantum chemical calculation of quantum chemical energy levels in electronic structure investigations of FeMoco molecules requires huge computational powers in normal computers, but QPE can provide useful output for quantum chemical investigations. Grover's algorithm and its generalization amplitude amplification provide quantum processors with two more alternative capabilities with increased runtime speeds for search and integration calculations. Reflections in quantum subspaces iteratively increase target state amplitude in a process providing capabilities for database search and financial model and machine learning but with smaller impact in comparison with exponential speedup possibilities.

Through the variation principle, two computational spaces are merged in one system in a hybrid manner. VQEs enable parameterized quantum circuits to achieve approximated molecular ground states through work by classical optimizers that vary parameters in an effort to approach minimum energy expectations. VQEs' tractability in NISQ-era noise predominates but usefulness is compromised through "barren plateau" problem leading to rapid exponential fall off of gradient magnitudes in parameter spaces. Hardware-efficient circuits and symmetry-preserving architectures introduce new types of ansatz that strive to reduce algorithmic constraints in existing algorithms. But quantum walks, quantum counterparts of classical random walks, enable a rich variety in search in spaces and provide access to information in complex networks along with quantum machine learning prospects (Shafique et al., 2024). Algorithm design at a larger scale involves careful management of blocks in terms of resources, with each subroutine striving toward reaching a decision over circuit depth in addition to qubit requirements. A million physical qubits for a single logical qubit in fault-tolerant versions of Shor's algorithm illustrate a gap between engineering theory and practice. Progress in techniques for error correction through algorithm specific types for codes and the formulation of quantum linear systems algorithm (QLSA) strive toward bridging theoretical gap and enabling incremental progress toward quantum advantage at a scalable level.

The hierarchical structure of quantum algorithmic building blocks is presented in Figure 15.5. The algorithmic building block gives one a starting point at the beginning of the link in the diagram to different basic quantum methods of computation.

The quantum Fourier transform (QFT) introduces a more efficient state conversion. The neighboring state transformation block is a fundamental block in most quantum algorithms, for example, Shor's, in which it is used to check for periodicity in quantum states in favor of integer factorization. The neighboring state transformation block is remarkable in converting quantum states in the frequency domain.

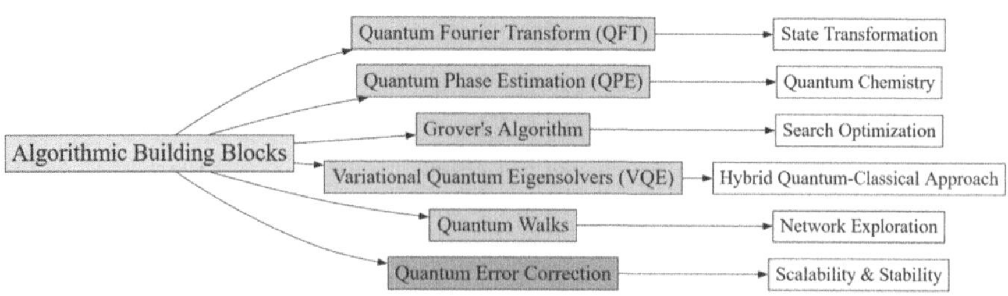

FIGURE 15.5 Quantum algorithmic building blocks and their functional interconnections.

Quantum phase estimation is used to estimate eigenvalues of a unitary operator. Quantum phase estimation is used in quantum chemistry to simulate molecular behavior to estimate electronic structure of large molecules. The quantum chemistry block displays its application in problem-solving in such calculation of energy level in materials science.

Grover's algorithm is applied to enhance optimization of a search in a way that achieves a speedup of unstructured search problems. The quickest way to retrieve specific elements in large data is through Grover's algorithm, and it is applied in many applications, such as machine learning and cryptography. The process of such computer processes is shown in the search optimization block.

VQEs apply a quantum-classical hybrid approach to solve eigenvalue problems. It allows for molecular ground-state approximation, especially in noisy quantum systems, via a quantum circuit combined with a classical optimization process. The process is outlined in the hybrid quantum-classical approach block.

Quantum walks define traversals performed over particular graph problems and over networks of high complexity in quantum computer theory of random walks. Quantum walks also apply to quantum search algorithm or machine learning model construction. Such application is implied in the network exploration block in that it allows unstructured and structured data to be accessed.

Quantum error corrections, in contrast, provide quantum computers their scalability and stability by suppressing decohering effects and noise. Quantum error correction is credited to be responsible for large-scale quantum computations' fault tolerance. The scalability and stability block shows that it is of paramount importance in providing fault tolerance. This is a graphical representation of how these fundamental quantum approaches relate to each other and to their use in developing quantum computing.

15.4.3 NISQ-Era Limitations

Quantum computing has entered its noisy intermediate-scale quantum (NISQ) era when operational fundamental limits necessitate reconsidering theoretical algorithm design and in the interim venture down pragmatic avenues to quantum advantage. NISQ devices can be constructed to function on 100 qubits but possess a per-operation gate error rate of over 0.1% to 1% and thus cannot pursue fault-tolerant computation and sustain deep circuits and extended times of coherence. Quantum computation is faced with a fundamental limitation through depth limitations, which cause errors to build up exponentially with deeper circuits and devastate computational output by orders of magnitude. The implementation of Shor's algorithm to factor a 2048-bit RSA integer far surpasses current hardware capability with a mind-boggling gate count of over a million gates. Shallow circuits must thus remain the priority of algorithm developers with such a hardware limitation and many must make a compromise for algorithm purity at a sacrifice (Brandhofer et al., 2021). Error suppression is a paramount consideration for which reason strategies such as probabilistic canceling out of errors and encoding in a subspace in developing resilience to noise are resorted to in quantum algorithm design. Variational algorithms VQE and QAOA are best suited with a computational heart offloaded to classical optimizers iteratively optimizing quantum circuits to generate an approximation.

Extraction of expectation values from noisy qubits via measurement is still problematic in that it requires repeated runs of a circuit, incurring overall computational run times and with them overall resource usage. The problem of barren plateaus is an effective impediment in training in that randomness in parameter initialization in high dimensional ansatz functions induces decay in gradients with a high exponential dependence with number of qubits and blocks training. Alternative strategies via layer wise training and quantum natural gradients are promising but fail to adequately consider concerns over scalability. Qubit topology is an additional challenge in this respect in that limited communications necessitate long SWAP networks in routing quantum information, deepening quantum circuits and raising error rates. Quantum compilers and transpilers seek to mitigate such a challenge through gate sequence optimizations but whose usefulness in practice is limited in terms of complexity in mapping out qubits. There is still technical challenge in NISQ times with a problem of credibility in that variation in level of operational individual qubits between machines and inhomogeneities in calibration make strong result comparisons between machines impossible. Despite initiatives such as groups such as the Quantum Economic Development Consortium (QED-C) producing benchmark and metric development programs, widespread disagreement over NISQ definitions to use in practice predominates (Pelofske et al., 2022).

The achievement of fault-tolerant quantum computation relies on profound developments of quantum error correction methods like maintaining logical qubits within precise tolerance degrees of error values. Most surface design for the creation of logical qubits requires a thousand of physical ones to achieve a single logical one, something fabrication is not yet able to provide. Error-corrected quantum designs at a larger scale are long term goals irrespective of hybrid approaches with NISQ machines and classical computers through co-processing. In NISQ periods, teams of researchers execute new algorithms in parallel with engineers tackling problems of quantum mechanical computation realization.

15.5 ERROR CORRECTION AND FAULT TOLERANCE

The development of operational large quantum computers with degradation resistance in environments requires quantum fault tolerance and quantum error correction concepts. Quantum information duplication is forbidden in quantum information reproduction by the no-cloning theorem, with additional classical bits having no duplicating nature. Error detection mechanism protection without direct measurement is significant due to measurement of a qubit collapsing superposition states present (Grurl et al., 2023). Fault tolerance promotes reliable quantum system operations through its characteristic of maintaining operational reliability in components with erroneous output. Mathematical treatment through threshold theory confirms error correction methods with error-correcting codes structures effectively removing qubit errors with an error rate below thresholds.

Fault tolerance is achieved through a complex mechanism: Fault detection and correction algorithms in real time use shared logical qubits among a group of a number of physical qubits and require quantum gate operations with no fault chains with catastrophic consequences. 2D physical qubits in surface codes utilize topological features to effect logical qubit encoding through perturbations in checkable lattice parity. Protection against over 1% gate error is created through surface codes but at a cost: With only local interactions with compatibility in present computer technology but with huge overhead: Quantum error correction needs to become hugely developed to function through a thousand constructed physical qubits safeguarding individual logical qubits. Quantum computation through topological error correction using non-Abelian anyons combined with Majorana-based circuits has potential for tolerant-to-error advantage through braiding, but experimental observations on these methods are ambiguous.

Successful fault tolerance integration with error correction is contingent upon fault-tolerant gate operations that suppress error propagation. Clifford gate operations, such as CNOT gates and Hadamards, function effectively through transversal realization in most quantum codes for error correction even when non Clifford gates such as T gates necessitate highly resource-intensive techniques such as magic state distillation technology (Bravyi & Maslov, 2021). Crosstalk and leakage errors and thermal fluctuations and cosmic rays introduce complexity in the system that necessitates specific protocols for minimizing errors. Performance in quantum device scaling necessitates real-time feedback and error decoding through classical control systems, a challenge in terms of intrinsic power consumption and latency constraints. Fault-tolerant quantum computation is a challenging scientific problem in that algorithm and software for error correction and algorithms' achievement and integration with requirements for development in terms of hardware involves balancing between connectivity and qubit quality and additions in computational overloads.

15.5.1 Stabilizing Coherence for More Reliable Operations

Fundamental to quantum computer architectures are coherent quantum states with proper platform environments for computation execution. Environment qubit interaction destroys quantum coherence and induces amplitude degradation and phase damage in qubits. T1 and T2 decoherence times determine quantum circuit depths at the base level through computation processing mechanism processes. Mitigation of decoherence is begun with passive stabilization. Passive stabilization consists of three basic requirements: cryogenic coolings for superconducting qubits and ultra-high vacuum enclosures for trapped ions with quantum dots in requirements for photonic insulation. Superconducting qubits function at extreme cold temperatures below a millionth of a Kelvin for the purpose of excluding thermal excitation events but trapped ions require specific coolings that go down to near ground state through laser processes.

Active stabilization through dynamical decoupling utilizes pulse sequences among idle qubits that permit refocusing phases and thus low frequency noise effect suppression. Periodic π-pulsed CPMG sequence suppresses dephasing of slow environment fluctuations. Quantum error avoidance codes utilize decoherence free subspaces (DFS) by exploiting system Hamiltonian symmetries in creating protective areas for information encoded in them against certain collective errors. Physical qubits constituted by singlet states create a protective shield for collective phases of errors. Bosonic codes utilize a different mechanism by exploiting microwave cavity harmonic oscillator modes (cat codes and Gottesman-Kitaev-Preskill codes) for error detection and correction and achieves infinite dimensional Hilbert space photon function capabilities for the correction of errors (De Micheli et al., 2022).

But longer coherence times also demand breakthroughs in materials science: the application of two-level system (TLS) reductions in superconducting cavities and removal of impurities in diamond nitrogen-vacancy centers and development of ultra-pure silicon for spin qubits are significant breakthroughs in materials science. Hybrid architectures mediating between spin qubits and superconducting cavities attempt to balance between long coherence times with velocity pair gate sequencing. Stabilizing coherence times become increasingly difficult in multi-qubit architectures because locally correlated errors produced through crosstalk and correlated noise, such as global variations in a magnetic field, outstrip local means of correction. Two quantum characterizing techniques, known as tomography and gate set tomography, are significant tools to map out structures in noise and enable developers to devise suitable means of stabilizing them. Developments in quantum technology for memories in the future will have a mechanism for decoupling computational and communicational processes in quantum networks and for facilitating distributed quantum computation. Quantum stability becomes an ongoing dialogue between isolating processes, control techniques, materials engineering, and algorithmic inventive processes in an ongoing effort to successively expand quantum computational horizons.

The control and protection systems alongside the quantum computer stabilization system, as shown in Figure 15.6, are a genuine marvel in achieving stable conditions for the stabilization of quantum processes. The system comprises a combination of passive and active stabilizations, as they could counter decoherence induced by fluctuations in the environment while stabilizing its quantum coherence based on the quantum system's nature. The Hiroshima-type passive stabilization achieves cryogenics to below one-millionths of a Kelvin for superconducting qubits (to avert thermal effects) and ultra-high vacuum systems for trapped ions with photonic isolation to avoid interactions with the environment. The passive way is strong and serves as the very base requirement for quantum processes.

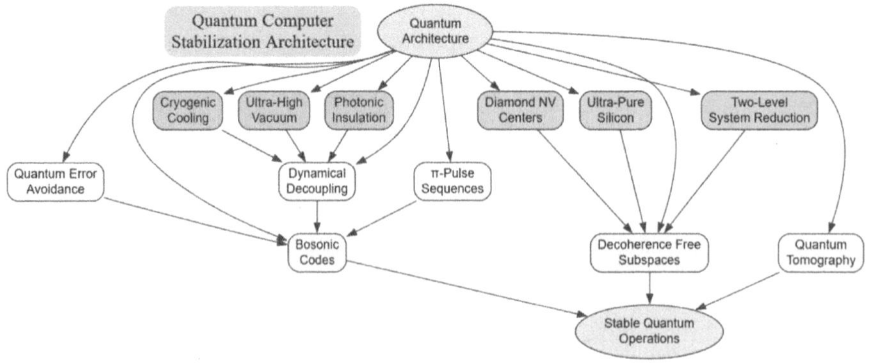

FIGURE 15.6 A multi-layered architectural framework for coherence stabilization.

These dynamic control systems would serve to be active-stabilization in this second layer. Phase nudges on the qubits could also be refocused using a π-pulse sequence through dynamical decoupling to quench low-frequency noises. There are also parallel mechanisms that utilize special encoding strategies but for error avoidance that helps to secure the quantum information. Advanced material engineering would actually play a very important role in overcoming fundamental limits of physics in terms of improving the substrate quality and minimizing two-level system defects in superconducting cavities and in ultra-pure silicon processing for spin qubits. Strong logical qubit formation is equally received from nitrogen-vacancy centers in diamond.

This error-correction layer refers to sophisticated error correction and control processes, which empower the error-free processing. For these, there are included bosonic codes that utilize microwave cavity modes to detect and correct errors, decoherence-free subspaces that protect quantum information using system symmetry, and methods of quantum tomography for the description and projection of the structure of noise. This structure just embodies the multilayered architecture of real quantum computing in that all work not just toward keeping quantum state coherence but toward error-free quantum computation. The actual working of such a system would depend on the performance coordination of all of these components through highly sophisticated control and feedback mechanisms that allow for optimal functioning across various contexts and computation requirements.

15.5.2 Quantum Error-Correcting Codes (QECCs)

Quantum error-correcting codes (QECCs) refer to numerical encoding techniques that protect logical quantum information in physical qubits but maintain quantum laws in quantum processes of quantum error correction. QTCCs rely under a general assumption that discrete cause-independent events, such as a flipping of a bit and a flipping of a phase, can occur in continuous environment interactions. Parity-check syndrome measurement can detect errors through discretized decay in a qubit ensemble probing with no quantum state destruction (Forney et al., 2007). The first quantum model for quantum error correction, a model called the Shor code, showed a single logical qubit could be protected with nine physical qubits through incorporation of three qubit structures for both bit flip and phase flip codes.

The Steane code leveraged CSS code capabilities with conventional linear codes, such as Hamming codes, that distinguished seven physical qubit error correction of bit errors and phase errors. QECCs in practice have prioritized efficiency in addition to usability. 2D lattice topologies stabilize logical qubits with surface codes, converting them with high efficiency and accuracy, with measurements reveal syndromes through defects in terms of string patterns through plaquette operators and vertex operators. These codes map naturally onto planar qubit systems but demand many additional qubits for syndrome extraction. Non-Abelian quasiparticle braiding in Fibonacci anyon-based models enables topological error correction through detectable topology change in the system: theoretical performance is contingent on development of topological superconductors, a challenge with current experimental capabilities: LDPC (low-density parity-check) codes use sparsely connected networks to precisely estimate syndromes of errors and make them strong quantum error correction candidates for photonic and modular architectures: QECCs work through iterative processes: QECC algorithms use state encoding and then stabilizer measurement for syndrome extraction and decode syndrome patterns through minimum weight perfect matching in a classical algorithm and then use recovery protocols. Iterative stabilizer measurement introduces both real-time feedback and processing requirements and introduces complications for cryogenic system controls. A principal weakness in QECCs is the overhead the ratio of physical to logical qubits and can become 1,000; surface codes have a 1 in practice in reduced performance accuracy settings (Devitt et al., 2013).

The added cost arises through encoding information in a redundant form and following through with rarified syndromes in real time. Leakage errors that cause qubits to move out of computational space to require use of Bacon-Shor codes or other leakage reduction units (LRUs). Advances in concatenated codes, hierarchical encoding, and quantum LDPC codes combine to mitigate requirements for overhead through multi-level structuring of codes in spite of quantum LDPC codes' useful asymptotical behavior at a larger scale. Engineered dissipation QECCs (e.g., driven-dissipative cat qubits) introduce passive QECC with a competitor to conventional measurement based QECC. Implementation of QECC comes with intimidating technical requirements through nanosecond accuracy controls that must integrate with high-speed classical processors between high connectivity qubits with minimum interference. Integration of quantum error correction codes with processors remains an objective because it enables fault-tolerant operations that outpace current device noise capabilities.

The architecture of quantum error-correcting codes shown in Figure 15.7 presents a very complex condition for fault tolerance quantum computing through many interconnected error correction and control hierarchies. In fact, at the simplest level thus begins the initiation of the Shor code—the first to afford the nine physical qubits to protect one logical qubit, coupled with the more efficient seven-qubit Steane code built on classical CSS code principles. More intensity is then developed through increasingly sophisticated implementation strategies. This includes surface codes for two-dimensional lattice structures, supplemented with topological codes using non-Abelian anyons, as well as LDPC codes delivering specific optimization for architectural constraints in the error correction scheme.

The error-processing layer introduces that part in between important extraction of syndromes, calculating the perfect matchings in which the correct output for errors comes about, and then reparation protocols putting the final corrections into practice. This whole system runs continuously during quantum computations and finally finalizes into a physical layer in which control systems, as well as measurement and readout mechanisms, are put into place with real-time feedback loops that sustain states in quantum integrity. These theoretical constructions are finally made tangible through the physical implementation layer that comprises a very complex picture between classical control systems and quantum hardware, with associated problems like the ratio of physical qubits to logical qubits or very stringent timing requirements in the protocols for error correction.

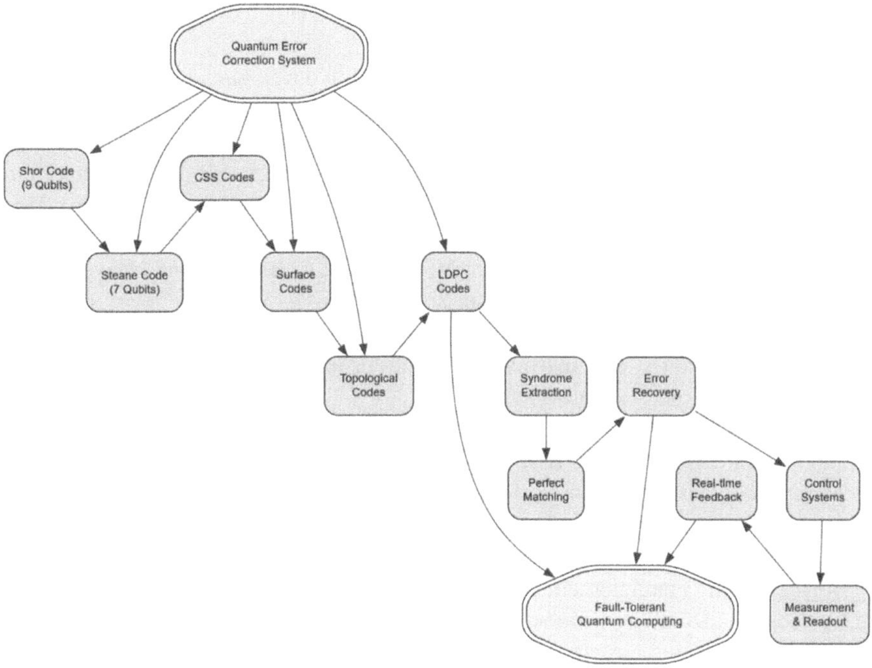

FIGURE 15.7 Quantum error-correcting codes architecture.

Clear indications that the different components have to work together and the information flowing through vertically and horizontally in all levels ultimately meeting at fault-tolerant quantum computing. It supports thereby quantum information throughout an entire computation with every layer bringing significant function either preserving the quantum coherence itself or hiding it. The theoretical underpinnings concerning quantum error correction and the practical points relevant to implementation are superbly represented. Thus, it is good architecture in which to place complementary error correction across different physical quantum computing platforms.

15.5.3 Challenges in Implementation

Identifying practical and large-scale implementations of quantum computers entails a resolution of a variety of complex problems in computer architecture, materials science, physics, engineering. Central quantum computer problems include quantum coherence maintenance under strong controls and accuracy in controlling qubits, in addition to requirements for computation system sizes for utility. Quantum systems suffer susceptibility to environment noise that creates decoherence processes and destroys delicate quantum states on which computation is predicated (Almudever et al., 2017). How long quantum state can be sustained in a qubit (the coherence time) continues to be bounded by defects in materials and thermal fluctuations and electromagnetic interferences in both trapped-ion and superconducting implementations of a qubit.

Superconducting qubit technology is supported in development through improvements in fabrication processes but hindered through two-level system (TLS) defects in insulating materials acting as parasitic resonators that draw energy out of the system. Trapped ions maintain their mark for long times and well characterized gate manipulation processes but suffer in laser system scaling and creating long lasting chains of qubit ions. Photonic qubits have beneficial traits for quantum communications but suffer through photon loss in optoelectronic technology and have challenging deterministic entanglement creation. Solutions will have to arise out of individual platform constraints for each technology but must have error correction processes and control electronics and thermal management function in a shared system platform for all technology types.

Quantum systems face two essential scaling problems in two significant areas: managing functional connectivity among qubits and creating fault tolerance abilities. Current quantum processor architectures face connectivity limitations in terms of IBM's utilization of 433 qubits and Google's utilization of 70 but both architectures limit connectivity among qubits through plane structures. Algorithmic depth performance and entanglement demand appropriate coupling tuning for multi qubit gates but such an activity becomes ever more daunting with a large number of qubits involved. Unintended coupling among qubits in terms of crosstalk generates errors that annihilate valuable independence requirements of quantum error-correcting codes (QECCs) (Golec et al., 2024). With the utilization of superconducting qubits, microwave pulses for a target qubit frequently bump into neighboring qubits and requires high level of calibration methods such as suppression of frequency crowding and dynamic decoupling.

Thermal management worsens these concerns: Dilution fridges suffer a barrier in terms of scaling in that such coolers, when used for cooling down superconducting qubits to near-zero millikelvins, suffer tremendous difficulty in managing heat produced through controlling electronics. Thermal fluctuations and electrical interference concerns have been produced through individually connecting thousands of qubits with microwave controls such that researchers increasingly explore cryogenic CMOS technology in conjunction with wireless controls. Scalability is inhibited through materials science in that substrate defects in silicon wafers and in sapphire introduce decoherence channels and high-fidelity constructions of Josephson junctions and superconducting resonators must be conducted for integration.

The combination of quantum error rates and protocols for error correction make the system complex. QECC breakthroughs in terms of surface codes and bosonic codes have not addressed the daunting count of physical qubits needed per logical qubit. Thousands of committed physical qubits per logical qubit must be drawn in in an attempt to achieve fault-tolerant error thresholds in case of surface codes, but such a level of demand in terms of resources is beyond current fabrication capabilities. Timestamped syndrome detection is challenging in that it entails real-time processing in addition to latency concerns that burden current control infrastructure. Fluctuation in performance character of qubits, such as in terms of resonance frequency drift and gating fidelity degradation, poses a challenge for error correction machinery in that conventional uniformity in errors cannot model real-life variation in practice. Additional circuit parts must be incorporated for repairing leakage errors that occur when qubits leak out of computational subspace through processes such as transmon qubit state transition processes. That creates a demand for additional resources. Interaction between gate velocity and coherence period creates a dangerous balancing act: quantum gates that function at high velocity erode the decoherence effect but demand strong controls in terms of signals that amplify error rates. Hybrid quantum-classical algorithms, such as variational quantum eigensolvers, suffer tension between quantum and classical infrastructure that entails quick feedback interfaces that cause latency strain in a system.

When quantum and conventional systems combine, a variety of impediments in terms of controlling software and hardware co-design methodologies and controlling trapped ions and superconducting qubits in respective temperature environments arise. Conventional systems require nanosecond timing gear specifically designed in controlling trapped ions and superconducting qubits in respective temperature environments. Running such a system involves new thermal anchoring methodologies and sink structures in an effort not to overheat quantum chips even at cryogen temperatures (Sood & Chauhan, 2024). Software stacks including quantum decoders and quantum compilers require redesigns in an effort to port onto many platforms through optimized mapping of qubits and gate sequence depth minimization and crosstalk. Quantization of performance benchmarking is fascinated with no such benchmark in existence, and thus, platform comparison capabilities and overall development velocity slow down. Constructing quantum networks is faced with many impediments with delayed distribution of entanglement between processors and cumbersome maintenance of quantum memories and loss in fiber optics in addition to leveraging reliable quantum communications methodologies. Hybrid quantum processor and machinery architectures must naturally integrate in an effort to serve future environments even when such a system entails heterogeneous controllers for an FPGA with cloud platforms for quantum interfaces management.

Successful implementation of such technology is economically and industrially hindered. Sophisticated infrastructure of cold temperatures is required for quantum systems, and such cannot be maintained in universities, whose great cost to construct and maintain cannot be continued. The lack of professionals with quantum engineering and quantum physics experience causes a talent gap that brings development to a halt. Incompatible intellectual property models of such proprietary processing architectures as IBM's heavy-hex lattice and Google's Sycamore architecture create interfaces of handing over that threaten to hamper cooperation and balkanize discovery paths. Industry and academia are skeptical about "quantum Moore's law" development projections for qubit scaling, with no common long-term design for scaling on the horizon.

The quantum computer realization challenges vary between purely technological to grand-picture frameworks that necessitate heightened dialogue between disciplines. Progress toward fault-tolerant quantum computers rests on three breakthroughs: more robust error-corrected logical qubits and expandable controls and long-coherence materials. Quantum work must navigate lightly between exciting theoretical breakthroughs and engineering pragmatic ones, for with each successive breakthrough, all scientists move one step toward quantum computation revolution.

15.5.4 Inconsistencies in Existing Techniques

Quantum computing will change the world, but current methods are just not practical. This is because quantum computing is fundamentally different than classical computing and the technical challenges of working at the quantum scale.
One of the biggest problems is that quantum algorithms don't play to the strengths of current hardware. Algorithms like Shor's for factoring large numbers and Grover's for database search promise huge speedups but require incredibly stable quantum systems. The problem is that current quantum computers, the so-called NISQ devices, are super error-prone (Awan et al., 2022). They don't have proper error correction, so they can't do the large-scale calculations these algorithms are designed for. Even with error correction techniques like surface codes, the number of physical qubits required per logical qubit is so huge that scaling up quantum systems is a huge problem.

Another problem is the mismatch between quantum and classical information processing. Classical computers store and process information in a straightforward way in bits. Quantum computers, though, use qubits, which can, due to superposition, be in more than one state at the same time. The problem is that classical data can't easily be converted into quantum data (and vice versa). The process is inefficient and error-prone, so it's hard to integrate quantum computers with classical technology. Quantum systems are also super fragile; infinitesimally small interactions with the environment around them cause them to lose their quantum state (a process called decoherence), introducing errors that classical computers aren't immune to.

And then there's the question of whether quantum computers are always better. While they promise applications like cryptography and optimization they're not always going to be better than classical computers. Most practical applications don't yet have a known quantum advantage so we're still figuring out where quantum computing will make the biggest difference. Hybrid approaches like the VQE try to marry quantum and classical computing, but their usefulness largely depends on hardware improvements yet to be realized.

And the hardware to make quantum computing happen is super complicated and expensive. While classical computers can run at room temperature, most quantum processors need to be cooled to near absolute zero. They need advanced shielding to keep out electromagnetic interference and advanced control systems to maintain qubit states. All of these requirements make quantum computers expensive to build and run and are only available to a few research labs and large technology companies.

15.6 APPLICATIONS AND INTERDISCIPLINARY IMPACT

Quantum computers unveil new horizons with unprecedented capabilities in many industries driving scientific breakthrough and industrial revolution (Bhat et al., 2022). Quantum computers reprogrammed cryptography with Shor's algorithm, demolishing encryption protection structures protecting RSA and ECC algorithms and new protocols. Combinations of quantum Fourier transformation with active processing of electrons allow for Shor's algorithm to expose quick factors of integers and discrete logarithmic problem-solving capabilities, demolishing RSA and ECC security in quantum machines tolerant to errors. With quantum attack vulnerabilities undermining future security in encryptions, post-quantum cryptography must develop new modern cryptography with urgency. NIST standardization processes include lattice-based cryptography and hash signatures in sets of multivariate polynomials, best candidates for future post-quantum encryptions standards. Universal quantum technology deployment involves current implementations and regulative frameworks in combination with software frameworks for transforming worldwide. Application of quantum protocols for key transport relies on both no-cloning theory and quantum key distribution (QKD) entanglement for creating unhackable encryptions protocols (Upama et al., 2022). National security and financial assets are aided through critical security dimensions of protocols BB84 and E91, but current implementations have difficulty with the degradation of photons and single-node performance issues.

Materials scientists employ quantum computation to address challenging quantum many-body issues that cannot be addressed with traditional simulations and unlock breakthrough knowledge for high temperature superconductivity and catalysis and topological materials. Condensed matter physics employs the Hubbard model to investigate correlated materials, but traditional simulation methods become unfeasible with increasing system sizes. Simulations of these models in quantum processors will unlock fundamental processes in cuprate superconductivity and transition metal oxide magnetism and will pave the way toward room-temperature superconductivity and effective catalysts for application in energy. Researchers can transform industrial fertilizer production through active site modeling of the nitrogenase enzyme, which performs nitrogen fixation at room temperature.

Both the variational quantum eigensolver (VQE) and quantum phase estimation (QPE) operate on present NISQ hardware to achieve molecular ground state but output accuracy is disrupted by noise. Quantum simulations will grow stronger with hardware advancements that will lead to new advances in materials at a faster rate with aerospace lightweight alloys and solar-energy organic photovoltaic technology following. Materials and quantum computing are uniting physicists, chemists, and engineers in multidisciplinary teams to decode quantum complexity in nature.

The machine learning field sees a quantum revolution with emergent quantum methods to kernels concentrated in creating capabilities in pattern recognition terms. Data undergoes classical methods of kernel-mapping feature spaces to nonlinear pattern discovery but are plagued with heightened computational demands with higher dimensions in datasets. Quantum kernels utilize native quantum dimensions in quantum spaces and quantum circuits in calculating computationally demanding feature maps, in any case, impractically demanding for classical systems. A quantum support vector machine (QSVM) with quantum states for the encoding of feature dimensions of input information can evaluate feature overlap measurements for delivering enhanced performance over classical machines for tasks such as image recognition and drug discovery. Quantum kernels have related performance to feature map capabilities in taking leverage in quantum behavior in contrast to present limitations in regard to quantum device noise and depth limitations in NISQ devices. Quantum neural networks (QNNs) have training quantum circuits with parameters through classical optimizers for financial prediction and genome analysis owing to them being quantum-classical hybrid methods. The question of whether quantum machines provide enhanced ML capabilities is debatable in light of equivalent utilization of resources, with equivalent tensor systems and randomized algorithms managing to outperform or match quantum ones. Quantum machine learning technology development allows for efficient algorithm development, a number of them a number of companies utilize in their supply chains along with drug discovery processes with a number of obstacles still in its way (Sood & Pooja, 2024).

The interdisciplinary worth of quantum computers is in providing developers with an opportunity to calculate best-fit operational frameworks of logistics and platforms of optimization with AI fundamentals. Quantum biology employs quantum computer and simulation software in an attempt to calculate receiver and transfer frameworks to stimulate utilization in studies through long-standing physical methodologies. Societal contribution is profound: the quantum annealing platform bestows laboratory and computer centers with equivalent capabilities in terms of studies through binary options but its reverse contribution in terms of worldwide distribution of assets.

Cooperation among multiple nations is required for research on quantum technology since encryption and decryption require decorous stability (Li et al., 2021). Integration of quantum computers into various disciplines helps in developing a production platform with the potential to solve significant social imperatives such as weather forecasting with personalized medicine. Quantum technology implementation in all disciplines generates general scientific revolution through its potential to allow scientists to collaborate in applying technical quantum theory with computer-based methodology in solving real-world problems.

15.7 FUTURE ARCHITECTURES AND OPEN PROBLEMS

The trajectory of quantum computation is at a crossroads, with theoretical aspirations pitting engineering, material, and algorithmic realities against one another. As quantum computation enters its post-NISQ era, fault-tolerant architectures dominate research agendas, with both hardware and in error correction in need of progress. Surface codes, with high thresholds and two-dimensional (planar) qubit architecture compatibility, are current candidates for near-term fault tolerance, but with a thousandfold (physical to logical) resource burden, they illustrate the chasm between current technology and architectures at a larger, scalable level. Advancement in modular quantum architectures, in which quantum modules of reduced scale are interconnected via microwave and photonic links, is a pragmatic path to scaling. Such modular architectures, drawn analogously from classical distributed computation, could deliver incremental growth through interconnection of superconducting chips via photonic interconnects, for instance, or integration of trapped-ion modules with quantum memories, for instance. High-efficiency quantum repeaters and low-loss photonic channels, however, present a challenging problem, and one in particular for long-term maintenance of long-distance entanglement fidelity. In parallel, topological qubits, such as in Majorana fermions, or in Fibonacci anyons, present the hope for intrinsic tolerance to errors through non-local operations in braiding, circumventing conventional error-correction penalties. Microsoft's quest for Majorana qubits in nanoscale nanowires of hybrid nanoscale semiconductor-superconductor is a brilliant case in point, but experimental demonstration of non-Abelian statistics continues to evade them. Deployment in useful devices of such exotic quasiparticles will depend, in turn, in breakthroughs in materials fabrication, such as in defects in indium antimonide crystals, for instance, or engineered topological superconductors, and these are in infancy in development.

Hybrid quantum-classical architectures bridge NISQ constraints and future fault-tolerant ones. Hybrid frameworks utilize classical computation for real-time control, parameter optimization, and error mitigation and offload specific quantum subroutines to co-processors. Cloud quantum access, embodied in platforms such as Amazon Braket and IBM Quantum, democratizes access but highlights the need for standardized interfaces and middleware to integrate heterogeneous hardware. The creation of quantum compilers, software that optimizes circuits for a specific device constraint, reflects growing software engineering and quantum physics synergy. Yet a lack of a shared programming stack and quantum-native operating systems holds back development, necessitating co-design methodologies to bind algorithm development with device development. Photonic quantum computation, with room-temperature operability and integration with installed telecom infrastructure, is a disruptive path. Scalable quantum processing could be achieved with integrated photonic circuits, leveraging silicon photonics or nonlinear optical materials, but a lack of deterministic photon-photon manipulation and inefficient quantum memories for photonic qubits act as impediments.

Theoretical hurdles are no less challenging, in specific defining and attaining quantum advantage—the sweet spot at which quantum computers can solve real-world problems intractable for traditional machines. Despite quantum supremacy experiments, such as Google's random circuit sampling, with computational performance exceeding classical, such experiments' value is theoretical. Realistic value in real life will demand algorithms leveraging quantum parallelism for industrially useful problem-solving, such as portfolio optimization, quantum machine learning, and quantum simulation for quantum field theory, but development for such quantum algorithms, such as the quantum linear systems algorithm (QLSA), holds out hope for application in such domains, but at a price: a basis in fault-tolerant gates, putting practical realization in the future. Open questions in complexity theory, such as the relation of quantum polynomial (BQP) time to traditional complexity classes, remain to shape the horizon, with implications for cryptography, optimization, and even quantum field theory. Seeking a quantum analogue of Moore's law—a predictable blueprint for scaling in terms of both number and fidelity of qubits—remains unanswered, with breakthroughs in such dependability residing in unpredictable breakthroughs in materials, such as high-temperature superconductors, or ultra-pure silicon spin qubits.

Theoretical challenges are no less daunting, particularly defining and achieving quantum advantage—the sweet spot where quantum computers can be used to solve real-world problems impossible for conventional machines. Despite quantum supremacy experiments, like Google's random circuit sampling, with computational performance eclipsing classical, such experiments are of theoretical value. Real value in real life will demand algorithms leveraging quantum parallelism for industrially relevant problem-solving, e.g., portfolio optimization, quantum machine learning, and quantum simulation for quantum field theory, yet the development for such quantum algorithms, like QLSA, promises applications to such realms, but at a price: a foundation in fault-tolerant gates, assigning practical realization to the future. Open questions in complexity theory, like BQP's relationship to traditional complexity classes, stand to mold the horizon, with ramifications on cryptography, optimization, and even quantum field theory. Searching for a quantum equivalent of Moore's law; a predictable roadmap for scaling in terms of number and fidelity of qubits remains open, with advances in such reliability residing in unpredictable advances in materials, such as high-temperature superconductors, or ultra-pure silicon spin qubits.

Societal and moral factors add a level of complexity to such technological advancement. Democratic access to quantum can expand global inequalities, but infrastructure at present continues to congregate in high-tech nations. Dual-use quantum technology potential, both for enhancing drug discovery and for compromising security via decryption, creates a demand for international governance frameworks to prevent misuse. Staff development is a key bottleneck, with quantum computer demand for an interdisciplinary talent pool speaking to a new generation of quantum physicists, computer programmers, and engineers. Environmental factors, such as high-energy quantum computer data centers' footprint, and quantum AI ethics, make the picture even more complex.

Ultimately, the quantum future will rely on a confluence of multidisciplinary innovation, continued investment, and happy chance. Timeline estimates for fault-tolerant machines vary between a decade and many, but shared determination between academia, industry, and governments worldwide shows a shared will to use quantum mechanics in computational breakthroughs. Today's unsolved problem—from defects in materials to algorithmic scaling—are crucibles in which quantum's future will be determined, not a mere matter of technical wizardry but a reimagining of computation's capabilities.

15.8 CONCLUSION

The journey of quantum computation, from its theoretical foundations to today's noisy intermediate-scale devices and the future goal of fault-tolerant machines, is the most ambitious adventure in this period of science and engineering. Quantum mechanics has a few non-intuitive principles, namely, superposition, entanglement, and interference. Quantum computation promises to expand horizons for computation with exponential acceleration in solving major problems in conventional computers. Through Shor's algorithm, it tries to break conventional cryptography; through Grover's search, it innovates information retrieval in a completely new way. Such abilities of quantum algorithms have led to the competition worldwide to realize scalable, fault-tolerant quantum machines. However, challenges lie within the entire range of sciences and an entire branch of engineering. The unprecedented accuracy in controls, materials science, and error correction are required for the delicate quantum states that are vulnerable to decoherence and errors.

Indeed, NISQ would serve as a benchmark for demonstrating quantum supremacy as well as the enablement of quantum-classical algorithms; however, it would also expose the limitations of the current hardware and create an urgency for breakthroughs in fault tolerance and scalability. The interdisciplinary utilization of quantum computers is beginning to transform such heterogeneous fields as cryptography, materials science, and machine learning. Within the realm of cryptography, the advent of quantum algorithms has led to development of post-quantum encryptions, while quantum key distribution promises the possibility of unbreakable communications in the future. Quantum simulations in materials science reveal high-temperature superconductivity and catalysis and promise revolutionizing energy storage scenarios as well as chemical production. Quantum machine learning is in its infancy, exploring quantum kernel approaches and variational quantum algorithms, which hold great promise in pattern recognition and optimization. Obstacles are, however, in the way of such applications: various NISQ device noise and depth limitations, heavyweight error correction burdens, and lack of benchmark standards hinder development. Bridging theory and engineering with a coordinated transition to move proof-of-concept experiments into useful, scalable implementations will require innovations in qubit technology, in control electronics, and in quantum software.

What does lie ahead in quantum computing seems exciting, but there is no promise of a clear future. The very buildings of future architectures hold promise, even perhaps topological qubits and photonic quantum networks, but its realization will require breakthroughs in materials, fabrication, and error correction. Fault-tolerant machines capable of supporting logical qubits with below-threshold fault tolerance would be the holy grail of quantum computing; however, today's open questions, ranging from quantum advantage to quantum technology's social and ethical implications, remind us that the journey isn't all done yet, even with these incremental steps. As quantum physics, computer science, and engineering increasingly drive innovation, a new era of convergent research will indeed blur even more mainstream disciplinary borders.

REFERENCES

Aaronson, S. (2010). BQP and the polynomial hierarchy. Proceedings of the 42nd ACM Symposium on Theory of Computing, 141–150. Association for Computing Machinery. http://hdl.handle.net/1721.1/54236

Albash, T., & Lidar, D. A. (2018). Adiabatic quantum computation. Reviews of Modern Physics, 90(1), 015002. https://doi.org/10.1103/RevModPhys.90.015002

Almudever, C. G., et al. (2017). The engineering challenges in quantum computing. Design, Automation & Test in Europe Conference & Exhibition (DATE), 836–845. https://doi.org/10.23919/DATE.2017.7927104

Arute, F., Arya, K., Babbush, R., Bacon, D., Bardin, J. C., Barends, R., . . . & Martinis, J. M. (2019). Quantum supremacy using a programmable superconducting processor. Nature, 574(7779), 505–510. https://doi.org/10.1038/s41586-019-1666-5

Awan, U., Hannola, L., Tandon, A., Goyal, R. K., & Dhir, A. (2022). Quantum computing challenges in the software industry: A fuzzy AHP-based approach. Information and Software Technology, 147, 106896. https://doi.org/10.1016/j.infsof.2022.106896

Ballentine, L. E. (2014). Quantum mechanics: A modern development (2nd ed.). World Scientific. https://doi.org/10.1142/9038

Bengtsson, I., & Życzkowski, K. (2006). Geometry of quantum states: An introduction to quantum entanglement (2nd ed.). Cambridge University Press. https://doi.org/10.1017/CBO9780511535048

Bharti, K., Cervera-Lierta, A., Kyaw, T. H., Haug, T., Alperin-Lea, S., Anand, A., . . . & Aspuru-Guzik, A. (2022). Noisy intermediate-scale quantum algorithms. Reviews of Modern Physics, 94(1), 015004. https://doi.org/10.1103/RevModPhys.94.015004

Bhat, H. A., Khanday, F. A., Kaushik, B. K., Bashir, F., & Shah, K. A. (2022). Quantum computing: Fundamentals, implementations, and applications. IEEE Open Journal of Nanotechnology, 3, 61–77. https://doi.org/10.1109/OJNANO.2022.3178545

Biamonte, J., Wittek, P., Pancotti, N., Rebentrost, P., Wiebe, N., & Lloyd, S. (2017). Quantum machine learning. Nature, 549(7671), 195–202. https://doi.org/10.1038/nature23474

Blais, A., Grimsmo, A. L., Girvin, S. M., & Wallraff, A. (2021). Circuit quantum electrodynamics. Reviews of Modern Physics, 93(2), 025005. https://doi.org/10.1103/RevModPhys.93.025005

Brandhofer, S., Devitt, S., Wellens, T., & Polian, I. (2021). Special session: Noisy intermediate-scale quantum (NISQ) computers—how they work, how they fail, how to test them? 2021 IEEE 39th VLSI Test Symposium (VTS), 1–10. https://doi.org/10.1109/VTS50974.2021.9441047

Bravyi, S., & Maslov, D. (2021). Hadamard-free circuits expose the structure of the Clifford group. IEEE Transactions on Information Theory, 67(7), 4546–4563. https://doi.org/10.1109/TIT.2021.3081415

Breuer, H.-P., & Petruccione, F. (2007). The theory of open quantum systems. Oxford University Press. https://doi.org/10.1093/acprof:oso/9780199213900.001.0001

Bub, J. (2016). Bananaworld: Quantum mechanics for primates. Oxford University Press. https://doi.org/10.1093/acprof:oso/9780198718536.001.0001

Busch, P., Lahti, P., Pellonpää, J.-P., & Ylinen, K. (2016). Quantum measurement. Springer. https://doi.org/10.1007/978-3-319-43389-9

Campbell, E. T., Terhal, B. M., & Vuillot, C. (2017). Roads towards fault-tolerant universal quantum computation. Nature, 549(7671), 172–179. https://doi.org/10.1038/nature23460

Cerezo, M., Arrasmith, A., Babbush, R., et al. (2021). Variational quantum algorithms. Nature Reviews Physics 3, 625–644. https://doi.org/10.1038/s42254-021-00348-9

Cross, A. W., Bishop, L. S., Sheldon, S., Nation, P. D., & Gambetta, J. M. (2019). Validating quantum computers using randomized model circuits. Physical Review A, 100(3), 032328. https://doi.org/10.1103/PhysRevA.100.032328

De Micheli, G., Jiang, J.-H. R., Rand, R., Smith, K., & Soeken, M. (2022). Advances in quantum computation and quantum technologies: A design automation perspective. IEEE Journal on Emerging and Selected Topics in Circuits and Systems, 12(3), 584–601. https://doi.org/10.1109/JETCAS.2022.3205174

Devitt, S. J., Munro, W. J., & Nemoto, K. (2013). Quantum error correction for beginners. Reports on Progress in Physics, 76(7), 076001. https://doi.org/10.1088/0034-4885/76/7/076001

Devoret, M. H., & Schoelkopf, R. J. (2013). Superconducting circuits for quantum information: An outlook. Science, 339(6124), 1169–1174. https://doi.org/10.1126/science.1231930

Feynman, R. P. (1982). Simulating physics with computers. International Journal of Theoretical Physics, 21(6/7), 467–488. https://doi.org/10.1007/BF02650179

Forney, G. D., Grassl, M., & Guha, S. (2007). Convolutional and tail-biting quantum error-correcting codes. IEEE Transactions on Information Theory, 53(3), 865–880. https://doi.org/10.1109/TIT.2006.890698

Golec, M., Hatay, E. S., Golec, M., Uyar, M., Golec, M., & Gill, S. S. (2024). Quantum cloud computing: Trends and challenges. Journal of Economy and Technology, 2, 190–199. https://doi.org/10.1016/j.ject.2024.05.001

Grover, L. K. (1996). A fast quantum mechanical algorithm for database search. Proceedings of the 28th Annual ACM Symposium on Theory of Computing, 212–219. https://doi.org/10.1145/237814.237866

Grurl, T., Pichler, C., Fuß, J., & Wille, R. (2023). Automatic implementation and evaluation of error-correcting codes for quantum computing: An open-source framework for quantum error correction. 2023 36th International Conference on VLSI Design and 2023 22nd International Conference on Embedded Systems (VLSID), 301–306. https://doi.org/10.1109/VLSID57277.2023.00068

Hauke, P., Katzgraber, H. G., Lechner, W., Nishimori, H., & Oliver, W. D. (2020). Perspectives of quantum annealing: Methods and implementations. Reports on Progress in Physics, 83(5), 054401. https://doi.org/10.1088/1361-6633/ab85b8

Heinosaari, T., & Ziman, M. (2012). The mathematical language of quantum theory: From uncertainty to entanglement. Cambridge University Press. https://doi.org/10.1017/CBO9781139031103

Jaeger, G. (2007). Quantum information: An overview. Springer. https://doi.org/10.1007/978-0-387-36944-0

Jazaeri, F., Beckers, A., Tajalli, A., & Sallese, J.-M. (2019). A review on quantum computing: From qubits to front-end electronics and cryogenic MOSFET physics. 2019 MIXDES—26th International Conference "Mixed Design of Integrated Circuits and Systems," 15–25. https://doi.org/10.23919/MIXDES.2019.8787164

Kanamori, Y., & Yoo, S.-M. (2020). Quantum computing: Principles and applications. Journal of International Technology and Information Management, 29(2), Article 3. https://doi.org/10.58729/1941-6679.1410

King, A. D., Raymond, J., Lanting, T., et al. (2023). Quantum critical dynamics in a 5,000-qubit programmable spin glass. Nature, 617, 61–66. https://doi.org/10.1038/s41586-023-05867-2

Krantz, P., Kjaergaard, M., Yan, F., Orlando, T. P., Gustavsson, S., & Oliver, W. D. (2019). A quantum engineer's guide to superconducting qubits. Applied Physics Reviews, 6(2), 021318. https://doi.org/10.1063/1.5089550

Li, K., Yan, P.-G., & Cai, Q.-Y. (2021). Quantum computing and the security of public key cryptography. Fundamental Research, 1(1), 85–87. https://doi.org/10.1016/j.fmre.2020.12.001

Monroe, C., & Kim, J. (2013). Scaling the ion trap quantum processor. Science, 339(6124), 1164–1169. https://doi.org/10.1126/science.1231298

Montanaro, A. (2016). Quantum algorithms: An overview. NPJ Quantum Information, 2, 15023. https://doi.org/10.1038/npjqi.2015.23

Nielsen, M. A., & Chuang, I. L. (2010). Quantum computation and quantum information: 10th anniversary edition. Cambridge University Press. https://doi.org/10.1017/CBO9780511976667

Pelofske, E., Bärtschi, A., & Eidenbenz, S. (2022). Quantum volume in practice: What users can expect from NISQ devices. IEEE Transactions on Quantum Engineering, 3, 1–19, Article 3102119. https://doi.org/10.1109/TQE.2022.3184764

Peruzzo, A., McClean, J., Shadbolt, P., Yung, M.-H., Zhou, X.-Q., Love, P. J., . . . & O'Brien, J. L. (2014). A variational eigenvalue solver on a photonic quantum processor. Nature Communications, 5(1), 4213. https://doi.org/10.1038/ncomms5213

Pirandola, S., Andersen, U. L., Banchi, L., Berta, M., Bunandar, D., Colbeck, R., Englund, D., Gehring, T., Lupo, C., Ottaviani, C., Pereira, J. L., Razavi, M., Shaari, J. S., Tomamichel, M., Usenko, V. C., Vallone, G., Villoresi, P., & Wallden, P. (2020). Advances in quantum cryptography. Advances in Optics and Photonics, 12, 1012–1236. https://doi.org/10.1364/AOP.361502

Preskill, J. (2018). Quantum computing in the NISQ era and beyond. Quantum, 2, 79. https://doi.org/10.22331/q-2018-08-06-79

Shafique, M. A., Munir, A., & Latif, I. (2024). Quantum computing: Circuits, algorithms, and applications. IEEE Access, 12, 22296–22314. https://doi.org/10.1109/ACCESS.2024.3362955

Shor, P. W. (1994). Algorithms for quantum computation: Discrete logarithms and factoring. Proceedings of the 35th Annual Symposium on Foundations of Computer Science, 124–134. https://doi.org/10.1109/SFCS.1994.365700

Sood, S. K., & Pooja. (2024). Quantum computing review: A decade of research. IEEE Transactions on Engineering Management, 71, 6662–6676. https://doi.org/10.1109/TEM.2023.3284689

Sood, V., & Chauhan, R. P. (2024). Archives of quantum computing: Research progress and challenges. Archives of Computational Methods in Engineering, 31, 73–91. https://doi.org/10.1007/s11831-023-09973-2

Terhal, B. M. (2015). Quantum error correction for quantum memories. Reviews of Modern Physics, 87(2), 307–346. https://doi.org/10.1103/RevModPhys.87.307

Upama, P. B., et al. (2022). Evolution of quantum computing: A systematic survey on the use of quantum computing tools. 2022 IEEE 46th Annual Computers, Software, and Applications Conference (COMPSAC), 520–529. https://doi.org/10.1109/COMPSAC54236.2022.00096

Wang, J., Sciarrino, F., Laing, A., & Thompson, M. G. (2020). Integrated photonic quantum technologies. Nature Photonics, 14(5), 273–284. https://doi.org/10.1038/s41566-019-0532-1

Wendin, G. (2017). Quantum information processing with superconducting circuits: A review. Reports on Progress in Physics, 80(10), 106001. https://doi.org/10.1088/1361-6633/aa7e1a

Wilde, M. M. (2017). Quantum information theory (2nd ed.). Cambridge University Press. https://doi.org/10.1017/9781316809976

Youvan, D. (2024). Quantum computation and Shor's algorithm: A conceptual framework for advanced problem solving. https://doi.org/10.13140/RG.2.2.21706.34247

16 Revolutionizing Data Science with Quantum Computing—Principles, Applications, and Machine Learning Integration

M. Bharathi, Sandhya Kumari G., Madhurima V., Saleha Tabassum, N. Ashok Kumar, and Madhu G. C.

16.1 INTRODUCTION TO QUANTUM COMPUTING MEETS DATA SCIENCE

In the previous couple of centuries, quantum computing and data science have helped the transformation of finance, healthcare, and cybersecurity independently. On the other hand, the integration of these two disciplines provides us with the opening to rethink the approach to finding solutions for computational problems. This chapter explores quantum computing, highlighting the phenomena of superposition and entanglement, which can enhance traditional data science tools to overcome computational barriers in handling large and complex datasets. Figure 16.1 shows the designs and paradigms involved in classical and quantum approaches. Conventional data science includes precise logic and sufficient repetition, while quantum technology encompasses the use of probabilities in determining new approaches of exploring and analyzing data. Through this lens, we look at what is needed to use a new way of creating algorithms and system designs in a post-classical world and recognize the critical setup, skill, and design innovations required to make quantum science and data science work together successfully.

In addition to providing innovative approaches for exploring high-dimensional data and optimizing processes and predictive capabilities, the incorporation of quantum computing into data science advancements addresses the deficiencies of existing computation techniques. In contrast to conventional computing systems, quantum computers process data through the quantum mechanical phenomena called

DOI: 10.1201/9781003538950-19

FIGURE 16.1 Quantum computing and data science.

(https://www.geeksforgeeks.org/role-of-quantum-computing-in-data-science/)

superposition and entanglement. The capacity of quantum computing [2] to answer some issues more effectively is demonstrated. Quantum computing theories dramatically modify the way decisions are made in data-driven backgrounds.

The relationship between data science and quantum computing will be shown to readers in this chapter, as well as the potential upcoming applications of their combined proficiencies.

It also assesses the impact that quantum algorithms can have in changing the practices of machine learning as well as streamlining methods and giving a better awareness of complicated datasets. It will emphasize practicality. Readers will see in what way data science workflows need to be incorporated into quantum computing paradigms [3] and its related opportunities and challenges. This is an introductory guide to quantum computing and the mandatory skills to work in this arena.

Because of classical computing restrictions in data science, quantum computing is offered as a solution. The area of discussion is to discover both practical implications as well as the capability of quantum computing [4] to alter data science workflows. The groundwork laid at this time empowers readers to get equipped to follow advanced topics that are discussed regarding quantum algorithms, machine learning, and their practical applications.

After finishing this chapter, readers will have an enhanced understanding of how data science capabilities are improved by quantum computing, which paves the way for further investigation into quantum-assisted solutions for data challenges. Through the basic concepts of quantum physics, quantum computing is a revolutionary way of processing data [5]. Quantum computers use qubits, while classical computers use bits, which only use either a 0 or a 1 state.

16.1.1 Fundamentals of Quantum Computing

Quantum computing uses quantum mechanical principles. Figure 16.2 demonstrates that qubits serve as the vital building blocks of quantum information [6]. A qubit functions differently from a classical bit because while a classical bit can merely

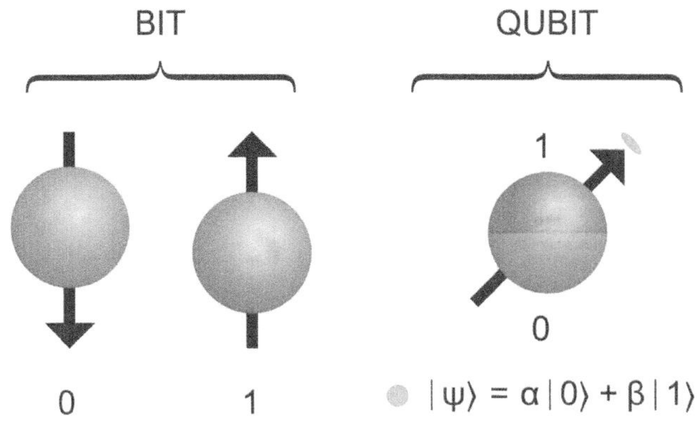

FIGURE 16.2 Qubit information.

(https://www.ensureias.com/blog/current-affairs/new-qubit-circuits)

assume one of the two states (0 or 1), a qubit can have multiple states simultaneously, a combination of $|0\rangle$ and $|1\rangle$. This superposition allows quantum computers to have multiple processes at a time.

1. **Superposition:** Quantum superposition allows qubits to have more than one state at a time. Quantum systems consisting of "n" qubits demonstrate parallelism by representing "n" states simultaneously. Through quantum superposition, these qubits can exist in 2^n possible states, meaning that a single quantum operation is equivalent to 2^n classical operations. Furthermore, quantum entanglement enables more advanced interactions, as a change in one qubit instantly affects its entangled partner [7].
2. **Quantum Entanglement:** This phenomenon means one qubit's state is linked to another's state regardless of the distance between them. As seen in Figure 16.3, the relationships between qubits permit complex computations to be performed efficiently through synchronized operations. Quantum entanglement occurs when a set of particles becomes interconnected through creation or interaction, such that even when the particles are physically separated, their quantum states cannot be independently defined apart from one another (Figure 16.4). The fundamental dissimilarity between classical and quantum physics is quantum entanglement [8]. Entanglement is a central element of quantum mechanics and is not present in classical mechanics.
3. Quantum processes primarily utilize quantum interference to amplify the probabilities of correct outcomes while suppressing incorrect ones during computation, as illustrated in Figure 16.5.

16.2 HISTORICAL EVOLUTION OF QUANTUM COMPUTING

In the early 1980s, Richard Feynman and David Deutsch discovered what is known today as quantum computing, which uses quantum systems to create simulations

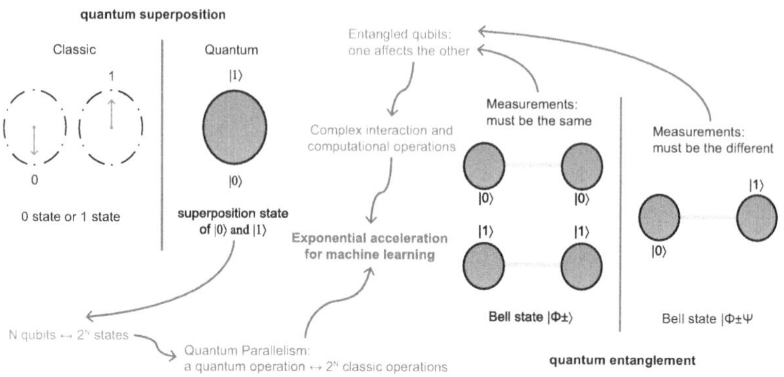

FIGURE 16.3 Diagram of computational speedup based on quantum superposition and quantum entanglement.

(https://www.mdpi.com/2076-3417/15/5/2555)

unattainable through classical means [9]. In 1994, through Peter Shor's integer factorization process, a quantum computer was demonstrated to be capable of explaining problems exponentially more quickly than any existing classical computer. Superconductors and trapped-ion systems signified a central development in the quantum computing hardware, which has empowered practical application more over time.

16.2.1 Computation Advantages Over Traditional Systems

Quantum computing involves many computation supports that enable accurate solutions to issues.

Exponential Speedups: Exponential speedup of factoring large numbers and searching through unsorted data can be done by quantum computers using Shor's and Grover's algorithms, respectively.

Parallelism: By operating simultaneously on multiple states, quantum processors enhance efficiency through the superposition of qubits.

Exceptional Problem-Solving Capabilities: Quantum systems exhibit remarkable synergy when integrated with quantum models and machine learning, addressing the resource constraints and computational delays inherent in classical systems.

Existing Usage of Quantum Computing: Quantum computing applies theoretical concepts into real-world issues. Industry leaders are beginning to take the lead.

IBM Quantum: The quantum information framework serves as a key tool for this organization, alongside Qiskit, which is designed for quantum programming.

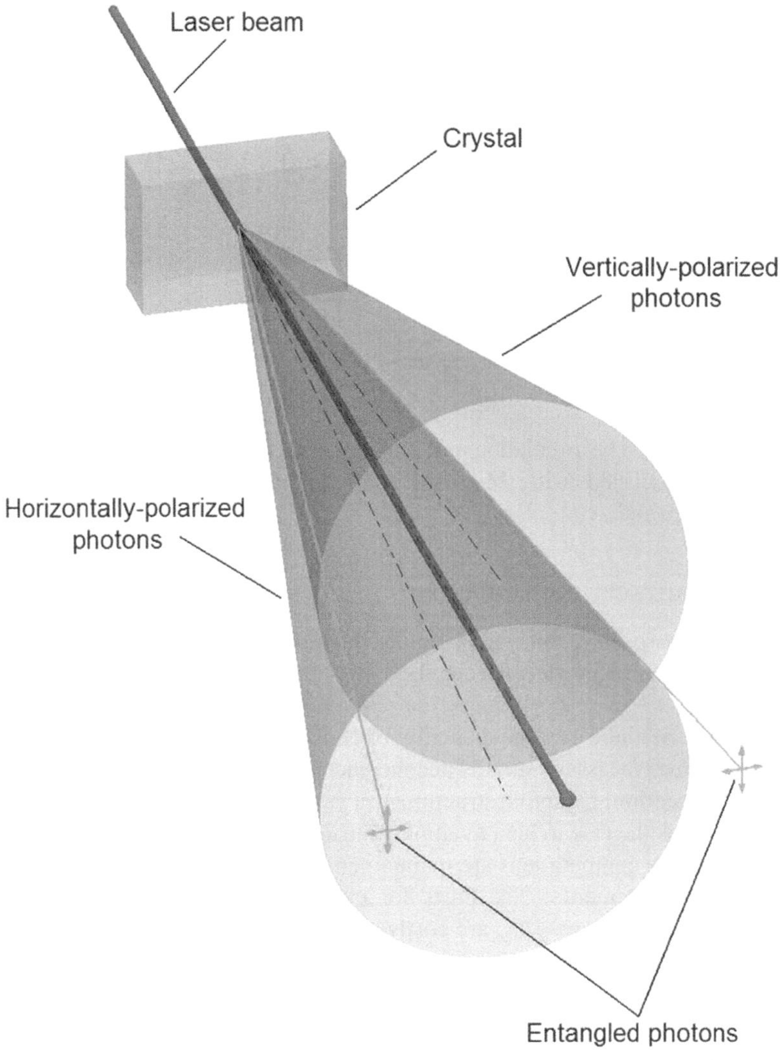

FIGURE 16.4 Quantum entanglement.

(https://en.wikipedia.org/wiki/Quantum_entanglement)

Google: Google claimed quantum supremacy in 2019 when its Sycamore processor solved a problematic job that would have taken traditional processors thousands of years to solve.

Rigetti Calculation: Rigetti's cloud platform allows for the creation of hybrid quantum-classical systems.

D-Wave: Unlike D-Wave, which focuses on quantum annealing for solving optimization problems, gate-based quantum computers.

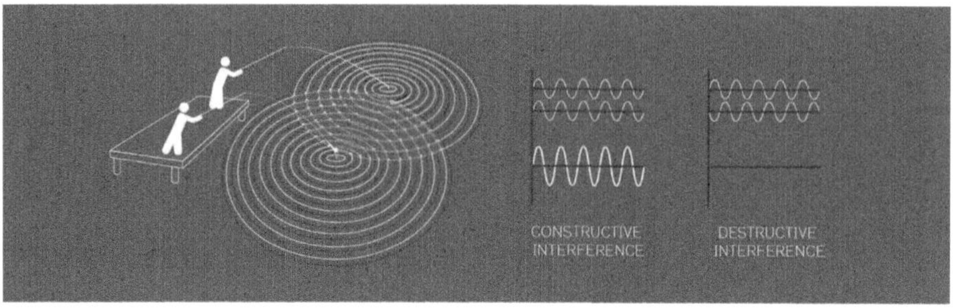

FIGURE 16.5 Quantum interference.

(https://doi.org/10.1103/PhysRevLett.123.080401)

Microsoft Q#: The simulation and implementation of quantum processes can be accomplished using Microsoft's Q# quantum programming language and its specialized toolset.

16.2.2 Challenges and Limitations

Quantum processes have many applications but must overcome a number of difficulties before they can be widely executed.

Hardware Scalability: The difficulty of constructing and maintaining stable qubits involves issues such as decoherence and noise.

Fault Correction: Quantum structures are very sensitive to external noise, and this forces the researchers to employ intricate error correction programs so that precise computations are maintained.

Supply Requirements: The parts for quantum computers, such as those involved in super-cooling, are costly to manufacture.

Algorithm Improvement: Quantum processors demonstrate exceptional performance in specific domains but continue to face numerous challenges, as addressing these obstacles requires entirely new quantum processing approaches.

Practical Applications: There is still a gap between quantum computing theory and its real-world application [10]. Quantum computing entails a paradigm shift in the field of computation, which will seek to elucidate problems that are yet to be determined using outdated methods of computation. Quantum processing is unbeatable in terms of speed and efficiency due to superposition and entanglement principles, but it is hard to be adapted to practical applications due to problems in hardware scaling. The success of quantum computing in the future necessitates not only the improvement in technology but also the joint work of academic establishments, businesses, and governmental institutions as the science progresses.

Quantum computing is rapidly gaining ground as a transformational technology. It has discovered explanations and solutions to problems in various domains. It represents the only future computing platform grounded in quantum mechanics, offering accelerated and efficient computation even for problems that are practically intractable using classical [11].

16.3 CRYPTOGRAPHY AND SECURITY

Quantum computing poses an exceptional threat to current cryptographic systems while also providing innovative security solutions.

- **Quantum Key Distribution (QKD):** QKD and the BB84 protocol are indistinguishable. Quantum mechanics is vital to secure communication via QKD. Because any attempt to intercept the quantum keys during transmission will be detected, the security provided by this encryption method is effective; the protection offered by this encryption technique is potentially indestructible.
- **Post-Quantum Cryptography**: As quantum computing competences grow, the reliability of encryption procedures like RSA and ECC decreases. Lattice-based cryptography a form of post-quantum cryptography that researchers are using to generate algorithms that are resilient to quantum attacks [12].
- **Real-World Applications:** To protect their communications and businesses, financial institutions and administrative organizations are now considering QKD networks. Europe's SECOQC project and China's Micius quantum communication satellite are recent examples of uses of quantum communication knowledge.

16.3.1 Optimization Problems

Practically all industries have profited from quantum technology because it permits vital advancements in resolving the complex optimization problems.

Finance: In the financial area, high-speed data processing can enhance decision-making. In areas where optimization is needed, such as risk assessment, asset sharing, and derivative pricing, quantum algorithms such as QAOA & Grover's search can be used. QKD can be used to hand sensitive transactions. Quantum machine learning can distinguish fraud, predict market developments, and automate economic forecasting. Through quantum optimization and secure communications, the financial sector can control infrastructure-driven developments and technologies that are prompt, robust, and secure.

Supply Chain and Logistics: Quantum computers enhance delivery paths and stock management as well as development tasks, such as in DHL and Volkswagen, to advance operational efficiency.

Industry: Power grid management can be improved with quantum optimization, diminishing harms and promoting grid consistency.

Scientific Research: Quantum computing offers several benefits to science as it allows for a replication of quantum systems that cannot be simulated by classical computers. Applications can be in chemistry, materials science, and drug discovery, where quantum algorithms simulate atomic interactions with extraordinary accuracy. For example, VQE, as well as quantum phase estimation (QPE), can determine molecular ground states and reaction dynamics. In addition to simulations, quantum optimization is an important element of solving NP-hard problems, such as protein folding and molecular docking. Similarly, quantum machine learning is also used in data sorting in the field of genomics and climate modeling, which are usually limited in classical processes. These developments validate the transformational competences of quantum computing, expanding the range of things that can be demonstrated and predicted.

Chemistry: Quantum processes, such as variational quantum eigensolver, enable more rapid drug detection and material design through simulating complex molecular exchanges and response pathways.

Biology: Quantum simulation allows researchers to understand protein folding machineries and enzyme functionalities, expanding our knowledge about diseases.

Machine Learning: Quantum computing can transform machine learning through faster model training and optimization. Quantum-augmented algorithms, like the quantum support vector machine (QSVM) and quantum neural networks (QNNs), exploit superposition and entanglement to search through high-dimensional feature space, which classical algorithms cannot do. Noteworthily, variational quantum circuits support a hybrid quantum-classical system for classification, regression, and pattern recognition tasks.

Neural Networks: Manipulation of neural networks becomes faster in quantum computers. Accelerating processes, such as gradient-based quantum-inspired algorithms, further expand the potential of deep learning applications.

Support Vector Machines (SVMs): Quantum SVMs can achieve more effective classification by enhancing the distinctions that quantum kernels can identify in higher-dimensional spaces.

Clustering and Pattern Recognition: Quantum algorithms of k-means type can detect subtle patterns by processing huge amounts of data faster than classical algorithms.

Applications in Data Science: Quantum computing reshapes data science workflow by doing away with traditional computational restrictions and using formerly unfamiliar approaches.

Faster Data Analysis: Searching and sorting datasets can be done fast due to Grover's search and other quantum algorithms.

Quantum-Assisted Feature Selection: Researchers can detect the essential patterns in data that can imply better performance and accuracy of the model with the help of quantum optimization techniques.

Dimensionality Reduction: Quantum principal component investigation is able to retrieve a valuable data feature while retaining the assembly of a model and resources of its visualization.

In conclusion, quantum computing prepares present opportunities and threats to the field of cryptography. Even although the traditional encryption techniques can be damaged by quantum algorithms, which comprise Shor's algorithms, the advances such as QKD provide practicable alternatives for future-proof security, highlighting the importance of post-quantum cryptographic instruments.

16.4 REAL BENEFITS OF QUANTUM COMPUTING IN VARIOUS INDUSTRIES

Through rapid data analysis, complex system simulation, and optimization, quantum computing [13] drives transformative changes across a wide range of industries. Through quick data analysis, complex system simulation, and optimization, quantum computing [13] origins revolutionary fluctuations in a diversity of industries. This section gives a detailed evaluation how quantum computing affects materials science, cybersecurity, healthcare, and economics.

Financial industry decisions are based on data-driven monitoring, optimization, and risk assessment. With its ability to perform complex tasks at unprecedented speeds, quantum computing has the potential to transform the sector by enhancing financial strategies and reducing delays.

1. **Optimization of the Portfolio:** Quantum computers improve financial portfolios by analyzing large amounts of data and considering the risk factors through return predictions and market trends. Quantum algorithms [14] recognize the best investment possibilities quickly, whereas, regular computers struggle to obtain the vast number of possible asset distributions. This capability allows institutions to accomplish higher risk and value steadiness that lead to financial planning enhancement. Major financial institutions, such as JP Morgan and Goldman Sachs, are leveraging quantum computers to strengthen their portfolio management capabilities. The improvement of investment approaches with the help of algorithms, for example, the quantum approximate optimization algorithm, enables them to accomplish better outcomes.

   Evaluation of Risk: The marketplace and financial unpredictability add further difficulties to the accurate pricing of risks. Quantum processes enhance the preciseness of risk evaluation through simulations. JP Morgan remains a leader in quantum procedures as a way forward of enhancing financial methods as compared to advanced market forecasts and instantaneous appraisal skills.

   Valuation of Spin-offs: Valuing derivatives requires extensive computational resources, as it depends on numerous market parameters and their evolution over time. Quantum computing accelerates Monte Carlo simulations for derivative pricing while substantially reducing computational time and memory requirements [15]. For example, IBM's quantum exploration has improved their computational speed for derivatives estimate, improving its expediency for widespread financial submissions.
2. **Medical Care:** Quantum computing can improve healthcare through advancements in medical inventions, submission procedures, and precise

genetic analysis. Quantum computers can model complex biological processes well, which conventional computers find difficult to do.

Drug Research: Quantum computers' simulation of molecular and atomic reactions [16] will advance the discovery of new medicines and treatments. Pharmaceutical companies can find cures for presently untreatable diseases more quickly. Google and IBM, in cooperation with startups like D-Wave, offer quantum computing methods to create prototypes of proteins that can lead to the creation of new drugs.

Assembly of Genomes: Genomic exploration requires DNA sequences to be gathered, which requires large-scale handling power. Quantum computers can improve genome sequencing by lower the time and financial costs needed for genetic investigation.

3. **Cybersecurity:** Quantum computing uses encryption approaches to create quantum-resistant cryptography, securing data against future internet threats.

   Post-Quantum Encryption and Cryptography: With Shor's algorithm, quantum processors can break present-day encryption approaches such as RSA and ECC [17]. This specific concern led to quantum-resistant cryptography methods. IBM and Microsoft are working to integrate the techniques for quantum-resistant cryptography into the security systems to guard data from post-quantum threats.

   Data Security: The feasibility of quantum computing is supported by QKD (quantum key distribution), which leverages quantum physics to design secure infrastructures. QKD relies on its broadcast technique in confirming encryption for encoded data. ID Quantique creates quantum-safe communication technologies that permit the blocking of unauthorized data access and monitoring.

4. **Materials Science:** Quantum computing promises to bring changes in the field of healthcare through medicine development and application, as well as precise genetic analysis. Quantum processors have a higher capacity to model difficult biological interfaces that the traditional processors cannot do.

   Drug Research: Quantum processors enhance molecular and atomic simulations [16], leading to new medications and treatments, even for previously uncurable diseases. Google and IBM partner with startups such as D-Wave to use quantum protein modeling in creating new drugs.

Quantum computing is an important revolutionary change in numerous industries due to its capability for simulations, data analysis, and optimization. In the business sphere, it helps in the optimization of portfolios, risk assessments, and valuation of derivatives so that institutions can make more knowledgeable and secure choices. In healthcare, quantum computing supports speedy drug discovery and genome sequencing and allows for personalized treatments because of accurate molecular modeling. Quantum-resistant cryptography and quantum key distribution can boost cybersecurity through more robust safeguards [18] despite ever-changing digital pressures. Materials science advances with accurate quantum simulations, improvements in battery technology, and sustainable chemical processes. Quantum computing is gradually becoming less theoretical and more practical in many critical sectors.

16.5 HOW QUANTUM COMPUTING CAN HELP YOU THINK CRITICALLY ABOUT DATA SCIENCE

Quantum technology [19] provides a whole new paradigm aimed at reflective data science procedures. Quantum computing phenomena, such as entanglement, interference, and superposition, allow for computational capacity that was unattainable before, giving data scientists opportunity to solve more complex problems. This section discusses the implications for evolving data science practices, with particular emphasis on selecting appropriate quantum algorithms, enabling quantum-classical collaboration, and evaluating both performance and ethical considerations.

1. **Rethinking Data Science Pipelines for Quantum Integration:** Modern data science techniques can be applied in sequential and iterative processes according to their design, accommodating traditional frameworks that are limited by memory and processing capacity. Integrating quantum computing requires a significant transformation of existing workflows to fully leverage quantum capabilities. This fundamental reimagining of data pipelines results in hybrid workflows, where classical systems continue to benefit from pre-processing and post-processing steps, while quantum processors can perform such operations as optimization and pattern recognition. Quantum structures have to integrate with the data science processes because of the fact that they can substantially build upon the rectilinear algebra processes, which are the fundamentals of machine learning simulations. This is called algorithmic conversion. Organizations should take steps to conduct quantum readiness assessments of their current systems and data assets to evaluate their preparedness for large-scale adoption and identify areas where quantum solutions can deliver substantial advantages. With ceaseless shifting of their intended strategy, businesses will properly reinvent data science pipelines that will fix and create room for improved computation powers and better competences.
2. **Identifying Problems Best Suited for Quantum Solutions:** It is vital to identify the situations in which quantum computing is needed [20]. High-dimensional datasets become challenging for classical systems due to the exponential growth in complexity, whereas quantum computing excels at managing such tasks. The quantum approximate optimization algorithm is significant in handling some NP-hard problems, such as feature collection, gathering, arrangement, and optimization. Since it can efficiently probe massive regions of the combinatorial space, quantum computing is superior compared to combinatorial tests, such as genome sequencing and graph research.
3. **Quantum Algorithms for Large-Scale, High-Dimensional Datasets:** Quantum processes handle massive datasets by utilizing the processing capability of quantum computers. Quantum principal component analysis

(PCA) outperforms conventional PCA techniques in visualizing and model-building by rapidly decreasing the dimensionality of the dataset. Grover's search algorithm achieves a quadratic speedup when navigating through unstructured material, enabling more efficient database queries and evidence retrieval. Quantum k-means clustering evaluates many clusters simultaneously while achieving faster data clustering over quantum superposition. To analyze documents more precisely in high-dimensional spaces, quantum support vector machines (QSVMs) use quantum pips for arranging tasks. Quantum-improved processes offer previously-unheard-of speed and effectiveness for intricate computational tasks that expand the scope of data-processing capabilities.

Quantum computing apparatus is used to alleviate the inadequacies in traditional techniques. Many traditional data science methods produce significant limitations that quantum computing can effectively overcome.

1. ***Exponential Statistics Development:*** Advanced frameworks demonstrate superior performance by leveraging parallelism to process exponential data growth, which traditional methods cannot efficiently handle.
2. ***Difficulty of NP-Hard Anomalies:*** Classical computational frameworks require exponential time to solve problems like the traveling salesman or other large-scale optimization tasks. Quantum approaches provide approximate solutions with significantly higher speed.
3. ***Obscenity of Dimensionality:*** Quantum systems leverage entanglement to maintain efficiency, whereas classical methods encounter significant challenges as dimensionality increases.

16.6 QUANTUM ALGORITHMS AND CLASSICAL MACHINE LEARNING TECHNIQUES EFFORT TOGETHER

Quantum and classical processors, when used together, enhance machine learning abilities. Hybrid techniques utilize both the quantum and classical computers for tasks such as the kernel designs while applying the classical processes for working out and evaluation. Quantum computing [21] provides both the features collection and pre-training procedures that aim to improve the model accuracy and reduce computational problems. Earlier training of the neural networks develops using accelerated methods such as the quantum gradient descent. Quantum schemes are capable of finding a broader space of assumption that hints to better simplification and flexibility that boost the model presentation.

Data science combined with quantum computing enables new advancements in machine learning, improving processing speeds and enhancing pattern recognition compared to traditional methods. Data science and quantum computing enable novel advances in machine learning popular relation to previous handling rates, better pattern finding. The present convergence between quantum computing and data science marks a turning point in computation history that can solve numerous data science problems. This chapter delivers a summary of the important principles that allow for disruptive uses and future-oriented plans for the use of quantum processors in data science. Quantum mechanics and data-driven policymaking deliver approaches to modernize the industry processes, deliver well-organized controls, and solving problems.

With abilities that enhance the development of pattern recognition and composite problem-solving skills and better data analysis jobs, quantum computers are altering data science. Due to entanglement and superposition, quantum computers are proficient in concurrently handling a lot of data, something that steady systems fail to accomplish. As quantum computers carry out massive computational burden, such as kernel computations and feature selections, hybrid quantum-classical machines improve machine learning activities through classical techniques applying training and evaluation processes. Quantum principal component analysis and quantum support vector machines enhance generalization compared to traditional data processing methods while also accelerating model training.

Quantum techniques deliver exceptionally good results for grouping and optimization in high-dimensional numerical processing. The quantum computing will discover essential powers that can completely rewrite current data science workflows. Quantum schemes resort to superposition and entanglement to empirically examine massive resolution spaces at the same time and, consequently, computation processing is hence intensely accelerated and is efficiency and skillfully optimized. State-of-the-art algorithms like Grover's search algorithm, collected by quantum-based machine learning prototypes, deliver superior solutions for complex tasks such as high-dimensional optimization, data analysis, and classification. Quantum computing delivers practical answers to interesting problems in commercial banking and logistics management and in industries seeking cutting-edge problem-solving techniques.

There is a growing interlinking of quantum and classical computing systems in order to further improve machine learning with a combination of the strengths of both procedures. Hybrid models use quantum processors for specific functions, such as kernel computation and feature selection, while classical machinery is used in training and evaluating, which results in increased accuracy and efficiency. Quantum methods like quantum principal component analysis and quantum support vector machines make the processing faster and allow for searching bigger solution spaces, promoting pattern recognition and optimization, and analyzing complicated data. However, real-world implementation involves solving scalability, hardware limitations, and ethical aspects, which necessitates an interdisciplinary and hybrid approach to make quantum computing effectively serve its transformative purpose in the day-to-day life realm of data science problems.

16.7 EXCITING FUTURE RESEARCH DIRECTIONS AND ADVANCEMENTS

The initial stage of combining data science and quantum computing yields great opportunities for creation and discovery.

New Algorithms That Are Quantum-Friendly: Methodology development for quantum-friendly structure design can scale horizontally in many arenas in data science.

Quantum Hardware Scaling: Horizontal evolutions of methods to correct qubit errors and make quantum processors reliable, as well as the incorporation of these methods into powerful streams, will lead to the large-scale use of quantum processors.

Quantum-Augmented Machine Learning: Using AI and quantum computing together, it is possible to develop models that extend the ability of traditional means of pattern recognition and predictive analytics.

Increasing Industry Use Cases: Experts may identify specific use of quantum computing in the areas of community network investigation and pharmaceutical studies.

16.8 CHALLENGES AND FUTURE OUTLOOK

The high potential of widespread quantum computing adoption is accompanied by significant cost-related challenges. With high error rates, quantum decoherence, and gate defects, there is a need for more reliable fault correction mechanisms. The complexity and high maintenance costs of quantum processors are largely determined by hardware limitations, such as the need for ultra-low temperatures and stable qubit control. Scalability remains a central challenge, as current quantum computers have too few qubits to support large-scale computations. Further advancements in quantum hardware—beyond qubit stabilization and error-correction techniques—may lead to future improvements. Emerging technologies, such as alternative quantum computing architectures and topological qubits, aim to develop systems with enhanced computational power and stability. Additionally, the use of hybrid quantum-classical methods offers the potential to bridge current limitations with practical applications. Advances in quantum computing research will necessitate cross-disciplinary partnerships to overcome significant barriers for practical application deployment. Quantum computing has many obstacles to overcome due to errors, hardware constraints, and scalability concerns. Because quantum computing is still in its infancy, it needs to be studied and enhanced. Unfinished connections between qubits in significant processors require further control steps, which will extend the time for management and increase error probability. It is exciting to achieve a unified integration of quantum and classical systems because hybrid approaches are needed in real applications. The significant overhead caused by quantum error correction increases the system's complexity and demands a larger number of qubits. Limitations and high costs of development and conservation limit the obtainability of quantum processors. It is difficult to assess different quantum technologies due to a lack of benchmarks.

Another important issue is the capability of introducing quantum computing into classical systems, especially within the context of machine learning and optimization flows. Classical ML pipelines are very reliant on pre-processing, feature selection, and iterative model refinement, tasks that cannot be translated into quantum processes easily. Converting classical datasets into quantum-readable contexts is challenging due to implanting, quantum kernels, and real-time scalability. On top of that, hybrid models are also exposed to issues of harmonization and communication bottlenecks that result from reiterative traffic among quantum and classical subsystems. The lack of ordinary protocols, middleware platforms, and scalable infrastructure prevents frictionless provision of quantum-enhanced solutions. Solving these major integration hurdles is critical to realize the applied effects of quantum computing.

Quantum processors can break current encryption technologies and consequently require quantum-resistant cryptographic approaches to uphold security. The growth of quantum computing will continue with uninterrupted improvements in quantum hardware and software as well as collaborative efforts across multiple domains.

16.9 PRACTICAL INSIGHTS INTO THE TECHNOLOGY'S PROGRESS

Quantum computing has progressed rapidly in hardware and algorithms, with businesses like Google, IBM, and Rigetti leading in qubit development and error improvement. Google's 2019 quantum supremacy breakthrough and IBM's cloud-accessible quantum platform lead to advancements in research and innovation. Applications span materials science, traffic optimization, drug discovery, and financial modeling. Companies like Pfizer, Roche, and Volkswagen explore quantum resolutions for molecular simulations and logistics. In spite of this progress, problems such as qubit stability, error rates, and scalability remain. Ongoing research about topological qubits and hybrid quantum-classical systems is indispensable for realizing the full practical potential of quantum computing.

Quantum-Enabled Data Science: The purpose of this chapter is to provide the reader with knowledge and motivation to discover the convergence of quantum computing and data science.

1. **Building Confidence:** A solid grasp of quantum computing principles and methodologies facilitates its application in the field of data science.
2. **Encouraging Experimentation:** Real-world technologies that assimilate quantum algorithms into existing workflows allow readers to assess quantum computing techniques within their developments.
3. **Promoting Innovation:** By developing innovative methods, addressing challenges, and creating applications that leverage quantum-enhanced data science, students are encouraged to engage deeply with the field. Data science and quantum computing incorporation is the basis for upcoming innovations and solutions. Merging the ideas of quantum mechanics with conventional data science methods marks the start of a paradigm shift that will be computationally well-organized. Through extraordinary discoveries and inventions, the field, despite its challenges, gives inspiration. Due to limited understanding, the transformative potential of collaboration in advancing energy technologies and scientific innovations that benefit humanity has largely remained untapped

16.10 CONCLUSION

When quantum calculation is applied to data science, it is a groundbreaking paradigm shift in addressing challenging high-dimensional problems that classical machines cannot handle. By using quantum phenomena like entanglement, superposition, and quantum gates, researchers and industries can speed up calculation, develop machine learning, and dramatically alter fields such as finance, healthcare, environmental modeling, and logistics. However, the sustained progress in quantum algorithms, quantum-classical systems, and fault-tolerant hardware are needed to reach the full capacity of quantum computing. But progress must go hand in hand with responsibility, with considerations for privacy, equitable access, societal effects. In this NISQ era, it is essential that scientists and technologists cooperate with the policymakers. The future of quantum-driven data science is not just in technological innovation but also in cooperation between disciplines and a vision that is shared to create responsible change.

REFERENCES

[1] K.-S. Shim, B. Kim and W. Lee, "Research on Quantum Key, Distribution Key and Post-Quantum Cryptography Key Applied Protocols for Data Science and Web Security," in *Journal of Web Engineering*, vol. 23, no. 6, pp. 813–830, September 2024, https://doi.org/10.13052/jwe1540-9589.2365.

[2] N. Garcia-Buendia, A. J. Muñoz-Montoro, R. Cortina, J. M. Maqueira-Marín and J. Moyano-Fuentes, "Mapping the Landscape of Quantum Computing and High Performance Computing Research over the Last Decade," in *IEEE Access*, vol. 12, pp. 106107–106120, 2024, https://doi.org/10.1109/ACCESS.2024.3411307.

[3] R. Huang, X. Tan and Q. Xu, "Quantum Federated Learning with Decentralized Data," in *IEEE Journal of Selected Topics in Quantum Electronics*, vol. 28, no. 4: Mach. Learn. in Photon. Commun. and Meas. Syst., pp. 1–10, July-August 2022, Art no. 6500110, https://doi.org/10.1109/JSTQE.2022.3170150.

[4] S. Wang, Z. Pei, C. Wang and J. Wu, "Shaping the Future of the Application of Quantum Computing in Intelligent Transportation System," in *Intelligent and Converged Networks*, vol. 2, no. 4, pp. 259–276, December 2021, https://doi.org/10.23919/ICN.2021.0019.

[5] K. K. Singamaneni, G. Muhammad and Z. Ali, "A Novel Quantum Hash-Based Attribute-Based Encryption Approach for Secure Data Integrity and Access Control in Mobile Edge Computing-Enabled Customer Behavior Analysis," in *IEEE Access*, vol. 12, pp. 37378–37397, 2024, https://doi.org/10.1109/ACCESS.2024.3373648.

[6] S. K. Sood and Pooja, "Quantum Computing Review: A Decade of Research," in *IEEE Transactions on Engineering Management*, vol. 71, pp. 6662–6676, 2024, https://doi.org/10.1109/TEM.2023.3284689.

[7] X. Ren et al., "Building Resilient Web 3.0 Infrastructure with Quantum Information Technologies and Blockchain: An Ambilateral View," in *Proceedings of the IEEE*, vol. 112, no. 11, pp. 1686–1715, November 2024, https://doi.org/10.1109/JPROC.2024.3520803.

[8] Y. Zhao, Y. Wang, E. Wang, H. Xu, L. Huang and C. Qiao, "An Asynchronous Transport Protocol for Quantum Data Networks," in *IEEE Journal on Selected Areas in Communications*, vol. 42, no. 7, pp. 1885–1899, July 2024, https://doi.org/10.1109/JSAC.2024.3380086.

[9] J. Chung et al., "Design and Implementation of the Illinois Express Quantum Metropolitan Area Network," in *IEEE Transactions on Quantum Engineering*, vol. 3, pp. 1–20, 2022, Art no. 4100920, https://doi.org/10.1109/TQE.2022.3221029.

[10] Y. Ueno et al., "C3-VQA: Cryogenic Counter-Based Coprocessor for Variational Quantum Algorithms," in *IEEE Transactions on Quantum Engineering*, vol. 6, pp. 1–17, 2025, Art no. 3100317, https://doi.org/10.1109/TQE.2024.3521442.

[11] A. O'Dwyer Boyle and R. Nikandish, "A Hybrid Quantum-Classical Generative Adversarial Network for Near-Term Quantum Processors," in *IEEE Access*, vol. 12, pp. 102688–102701, 2024, https://doi.org/10.1109/ACCESS.2024.3433383.

[12] S.-T. Cheng and C.-Y. Wang, "Quantum Switching and Quantum Merge Sorting," in *IEEE Transactions on Circuits and Systems I: Regular Papers*, vol. 53, no. 2, pp. 316–325, February 2006, https://doi.org/10.1109/TCSI.2005.856669.

[13] Kumar et al., "Survey of Promising Technologies for Quantum Drones and Networks," in *IEEE Access*, vol. 9, pp. 125868–125911, 2021, https://doi.org/10.1109/ACCESS.2021.3109816.

[14] Z. Krunic, F. F. Flöther, G. Seegan, N. D. Earnest-Noble and O. Shehab, "Quantum Kernels for Real-World Predictions Based on Electronic Health Records," in *IEEE Transactions on Quantum Engineering*, vol. 3, pp. 1–11, 2022, Art no. 2500311, https://doi.org/10.1109/TQE.2022.3176806.

[15] S. Anwer, A. Younes, I. Elkabani and A. Elsayed, "Preparation of Quantum Superposition Using Partial Negation," in *IEEE Access*, vol. 10, pp. 18944–18954, 2022, https://doi.org/10.1109/ACCESS.2022.3151196.

[16] D. Leung, A. Nayak, A. Shayeghi, D. Touchette, P. Yao and N. Yu, "Capacity Approaching Coding for Low Noise Interactive Quantum Communication Part I: Large Alphabets," in *IEEE Transactions on Information Theory*, vol. 67, no. 8, pp. 5443–5490, August 2021, https://doi.org/10.1109/TIT.2021.3086221.

[17] W.-R. Zhang, "From Equilibrium-Based Business Intelligence to Information Conservational Quantum-Fuzzy Cryptography—a Cellular Transformation of Bipolar Fuzzy Sets to Quantum Intelligence Machinery," in *IEEE Transactions on Fuzzy Systems*, vol. 26, no. 2, pp. 656–669, April 2018, https://doi.org/10.1109/TFUZZ.2017.2687408.

[18] C. Hirche, C. Rouzé and D. S. França, "Quantum Differential Privacy: An Information Theory Perspective," in *IEEE Transactions on Information Theory*, vol. 69, no. 9, pp. 5771–5787, September 2023, https://doi.org/10.1109/TIT.2023.3272904.

[19] W.-L. Chang, J.-C. Chen, W.-Y. Chung, C.-Y. Hsiao, R. Wong and A. V. Vasilakos, "Quantum Speedup and Mathematical Solutions of Implementing Bio-Molecular Solutions for the Independent Set Problem on IBM Quantum Computers," in *IEEE Transactions on NanoBioscience*, vol. 20, no. 3, pp. 354–376, July 2021, https://doi.org/10.1109/TNB.2021.3075733.

[20] W.-L. Chang, J.-C. Chen, W.-Y. Chung, C.-Y. Hsiao, R. Wong and A. V. Vasilakos, "Quantum Speedup and Mathematical Solutions of Implementing Bio-Molecular Solutions for the Independent Set Problem on IBM Quantum Computers," in *IEEE Transactions on NanoBioscience*, vol. 20, no. 3, pp. 354–376, July 2021, https://doi.org/10.1109/TNB.2021.3075733.

[21] Y. Zhou et al., "Quantum Computing in Power Systems," in *iEnergy*, vol. 1, no. 2, pp. 170–187, June 2022, https://doi.org/10.23919/IEN.2022.0021.

17 Advancing AI with Quantum

Quantum Machine Learning Classifiers (QML) and Transfer Learning in Neural Networks

Ch. Sandhya Rani, S. Nagini, L. Srinivasa Rao, Peyyala Balakrishna, and Akhil Dandamudi

17.1 INTRODUCTION

Since training quantum models is currently impossible due to the limitations of the quantum hardware that presently exists [1], using a pre-trained classical or quantum model accelerates learning, saves resources, and improves the performance of the model. Pre-trained models are imperative to optimizing QML applications and tapping into earlier knowledge that enhances efficiency and accuracy [2]. This is particularly effective in quantum image recognition, optimization problems, and anomaly detection where the classical pre-trained models can help extract meaningful features before the application of quantum circuits enhances computational efficiency [3].

In the near future, when pre-trained models will be the basis of scalable and high-performance QML solutions, quantum technology will mature. Hybrid quantum-classical approach: the approach makes use of the strengths of quantum computing but is stable and robust with a classically designed machine learning method. Hybrid architectures seem to be the most practical direction at present as hardware noises and scalability limitations confine full quantum models. Classical deep learning networks are known well for good feature extraction properties. High-dimensional optimization, probabilistic calculations, and even much more fall into the category of quantum circuits [4]. Taken together, they provide an efficient way of solving some of the very complex problems of finance, healthcare, and cryptography, with quite significant quantum speedups [4].

Hybrid systems, therefore, represent an important stepping stone toward the ultimate vision of complete quantum AI systems. QML is able to redefine many domains

 DOI: 10.1201/9781003538950-20

due to its application across disciplines but cannot be confined to just one domain [5]. "The huge opportunities that will soon be possible with quantum-enhanced computational power—drug discovery process, financial modeling, materials science, cybersecurity"—are mentioned. Thus, quantum models trained to solve specific problems can be adjusted for new tasks using the facilities of transfer learning techniques; hence, QML will be highly efficient across diverse fields. This cross-domain adaptability makes QML of particular importance to solve complex multidimensional challenges that classical AI finds difficult [6].

In that regard, one can note as an example in the drug discovery sector that molecular interactions can be processed very efficiently by quantum models to make drug discovery faster than ever to generate new pharmaceuticals [7]. Lastly, risk assessment and portfolio optimization are further enhanced when using QML in financial modeling by enabling quantum-enhanced probabilistic models that can process massive data more effectively [8].

It would be necessary for transitioning from theoretical research to mainstream applications for QML to change to an efficient and scalable paradigm of computing. Here, the focus is put on all current research in both these areas: decreasing noise, iterating quantum algorithms, and hardware stability-improvement for reliable large-scale deployments. The primary challenge is still scalability since resources are still limited in quantum, and classical techniques such as hybrid learning and transfer learning have to be integrated in order to improve performance without increasing computational overhead [9].

Exploiting hybrid models as well as pre-trained networks can build scalable QML architectures that cope with the challenges of the real world. Improving developments in quantum hardware and error correction techniques, new quantum software frameworks, are all expected to strongly boost the viability of practical applications of QML. Scalable QML solutions will storm industries by faster, highly accurate, and highly efficient AI-driven computations when appropriately advanced quantum processors can come into the scene [10].

17.1.1 The Threefold Objective of This Chapter

1. To explore the role of pre-trained models and transfer learning in enabling scalable QML architectures.
2. To examine hybrid quantum-classical frameworks as a near-term solution for overcoming hardware constraints.
3. To evaluate cross-domain applications—including finance, healthcare, cryptography, and drug discovery—that benefit from quantum speedups through such integration.

This chapter also highlights use cases such as drug discovery, where quantum models efficiently simulate molecular interactions, and financial modeling, where quantum-enhanced probabilistic systems offer improved risk assessment and portfolio optimization. These applications underscore the cross-disciplinary adaptability of QML and its promise for transforming industry practices.

17.1.2 Our Contributions

- A comprehensive synthesis of the current limitations of quantum model training and how pre-trained models alleviate these challenges.
- An analysis of hybrid architectures that combine classical and quantum layers for enhanced efficiency and stability.
- A discussion of the potential for transfer learning to expand the applicability of quantum models across domains.
- Identification of research frontiers, such as hardware noise reduction, quantum algorithm refinement, and the development of robust quantum software frameworks, which are critical for scaling QML solutions.

This chapter delves deeper into the fundamentals, challenges, and emerging solutions in QML. We discuss the pre-trained models, hybrid quantum-classical approaches, and cross-domain applications for the optimization of AI systems on high-performance tasks. In addition, we talk about the challenges in scalability and efficiency and how transfer learning and hybrid techniques can be promising solutions to overcome quantum hardware limitations.

17.2 APPLICATION OF TRANSFER LEARNING IN CLASSICAL MACHINE LEARNING

Transfer learning has emerged as a transformative approach in classical machine learning (ML), enabling the reuse of knowledge gained from one task to enhance learning performance in another, often with limited data or computational resources. This methodology mimics human cognitive learning behavior, where skills and knowledge acquired in one context are adapted to solve new, related problems more efficiently [11]. The study titled "Using a Novel Transfer Learning Method for Designing Thin Film Solar Cells with Enhanced Quantum Efficiencies" presents a compelling example of this concept applied in a real-world engineering context [12]. The authors define machine learning as an artificial model of the human brain's capacity to leverage past experiences to reduce the learning curve for novel tasks—such as how prior knowledge of one programming language can ease the process of learning another. In the referenced study, transfer learning is employed to optimize the design of thin-film multilayer solar cells using a surrogate modeling approach [13]. A surrogate, or metamodel, approximates the behavior of a more computationally expensive simulation model. These surrogate models are particularly useful in engineering design and materials science, where repeated simulation of physical systems is resource-intensive. The model in this case is trained on a source dataset and fine-tuned with a target dataset that shares common features or structural similarities [14]. The study demonstrates that by adapting an existing model to a related design task, significant gains in efficiency and accuracy can be achieved. Specifically, the approach reduces training data requirements by approximately 50%, while delivering prediction accuracies that are 2–3 times higher than conventional methods. This transfer learning strategy is most effective when the source and target domains exhibit substantial overlap in feature space or underlying physical properties [15].

In the case of the solar cell design, this involves datasets containing similar optical and electronic material properties. The model is initially trained on data derived from known multilayer materials and is then fine-tuned to predict the quantum efficiency of new configurations. This not only accelerates the optimization process but also improves the robustness and generalizability of the design models. Such applications underscore the broader value of transfer learning in scientific computing—particularly where data collection is expensive or limited, as in materials discovery, biomedical diagnostics, or environmental modeling. Beyond solar cell design, transfer learning has proven effective in numerous classical ML domains. In computer vision, for instance, convolutional neural networks (CNNs) pre-trained on massive image datasets like ImageNet are routinely fine-tuned for specific applications such as medical imaging or satellite image classification [16].

Similarly, in natural language processing (NLP), models like BERT and GPT, pre-trained on diverse text corpora, are fine-tuned for tasks like sentiment analysis, question answering, and document classification. These examples reveal a consistent trend: transfer learning enables researchers and practitioners to bypass the need for massive labelled datasets, making high-performing ML solutions accessible across disciplines and domains [16].

In summary, transfer learning plays a pivotal role in enabling scalable, efficient, and adaptive ML models in classical domains. Its growing relevance in scientific applications—especially when paired with metamodeling techniques—demonstrates its potential to significantly reduce computational overhead while improving model generalization. As ML continues to intersect with fields like physics, materials science, and healthcare, transfer learning will remain a cornerstone technique for knowledge reuse and accelerated innovation.

17.2.1 Quantum Computing's Historical Developments

Richard Feynman coined the phrase "quantum computing" in 1981, and it has had a long academic history since then [17]. A chronology of the significant events in this sector is shown in Table 17.1. The timeline demonstrates that current breakthroughs in the field have occurred more quickly than in the past, when there were some significantly larger gaps between occurrences. As an illustration, service providers now supply both specialized quantum computing products and quantum cloud computing services (e.g., Amazon Braket) [18]. Technology improvements and increasing funding from the public and commercial sectors have sped up the development of quantum computing. Hence, it is anticipated that quantum computing will have a substantial influence on a variety of areas such as banking healthcare and cybersecurity [19].

Recently, Google's 54-qbit machine completed a task that was expected to take a conventional computer system nearly 10,000 years to complete in less than 200 seconds [20]. It will be some years before research PCs or handhelds utilize quantum computing, which is still in its early phases of development. During the delicate process of managing quantum, any disturbance (for example, stray heat) might flip 1s or 0s, which could interfere with quantum phenomena like superposition. Significant obstacles prevent quantum computing from becoming commoditized. This demands

TABLE 17.1
History of Quantum Computing Technological Developments

Year	Development
1980	**Quantum physics might be used to computing, according to Marc Benioff.**
1981	Richard Feynman, a physicist who won the Nobel Prize, created the term "quantum computer."
1985	The quantum Turing machine is the name David Deutsch gave to his design for a quantum computer.
1992	The Deutsch-Jozsa algorithm is among the earliest instances of a quantum algorithm that is exponentially quicker than any conceivable deterministic conventional approach.
1994	The frequently used encryption formats can be broken by Shor's algorithm, which was proposed.
1996	A quantum search technique called Grover's algorithm gives a quadratic speedup over traditional computers.
2007	A business called D-Wave has shown a quantum computer gadget that it says can solve Sudoku puzzles.
2009	A two-qubit superconducting device, developed by Yale, is the first solid-state quantum processor.
2011	The first quantum computer to be sold commercially was made available by D-Wave Systems.
2012	The first specialized software firm for quantum computing, 1QB Information Technologies (1Qbit), is established.
2013	Along with NASA, Google funds a lab where D-Wave devices will be tested.
2015	NASA revealed the existence of the world's first fully functional quantum computer, the D-Wave System.
2016	IBM Research has said that it would open up quantum computing to the general public through the cloud.
2017	The 17-qubit IBM quantum computer is unveiled.
2018	Google has shown the Bristlecone, a 72-bit quantum device.
2019	The first commercial two-qubit quantum computer is unveiled by IBM (Q System 1). IBM introduces quantum computers with 53 qubits.
2020	Debut of the AWS Cloud Quantum Computing Service and Amazon Braket
2021	System Model H1 from Honeywell Quantum Solutions became the first quantum model to achieve
2023	Quantum declares accomplishment of Quantum Volume 4096.
2024	Governments around the world boosted investments in quantum computing.

complete qubit operation under unique circumstances, such as extremely low temperatures that can occasionally reach absolute zero. This also serves as justification for the study of fault-tolerant quantum computing [21].

17.2.2 Fundamental of QCA

These aspects are crucial to understanding the functioning and design of QCA technology. QCA cells are the building blocks of QCA circuits, responsible for storing and manipulating information. QCA wires, on the other hand, facilitate communication between different QCA cells, enabling the flow of data within the circuit. Additionally, QCA majority gates play a vital role in performing logical operations by determining the majority state among three input signals.

17.2.2.1 QCA Cell

QCA cells are the most fundamental building components of quantum-dot cellular automaton circuits. Each QCA cell, as shown in Figure 17.1, has four quantum dots and two free electrons at each corner. Tunnel connections separate the dots, allowing electrons to move from one spot to another. Depending on the occupation of electrons inside the dots, a QCA cell can go through different states. The QCA relies on Coulombic interactions to function. Coulombic interactions cause electrons to remain diagonally orientated, as shown in Figures 17.1a and 17.1b. This results in two polarization states: logic "0" (P = 1) and logic "1" (P = +1). P denotes the cell's polarization. Coulombic interactions allow neighboring QCA cells to communicate; the state of one influence the state of the other [22].

17.2.2.2 QCA Wire

Designers utilize normal cells (in four zones), spinning cells, cells with fixed polarization, and input/output cells in QCA in the construction of logic circuits, as shown in Figure 17.2. A binary wire is a series of cells that transport information horizontally or vertically. A QCA wire is produced by joining many cells at 90 degrees or 45 degrees side by side, as shown in Figure 17.2. As the leftmost cells are energized, the signal travels down the wire from left to right. A QCA wire formed by a line of QCA cells. A QCA wire with 45° cells divides the incoming signal into odd and even cells.

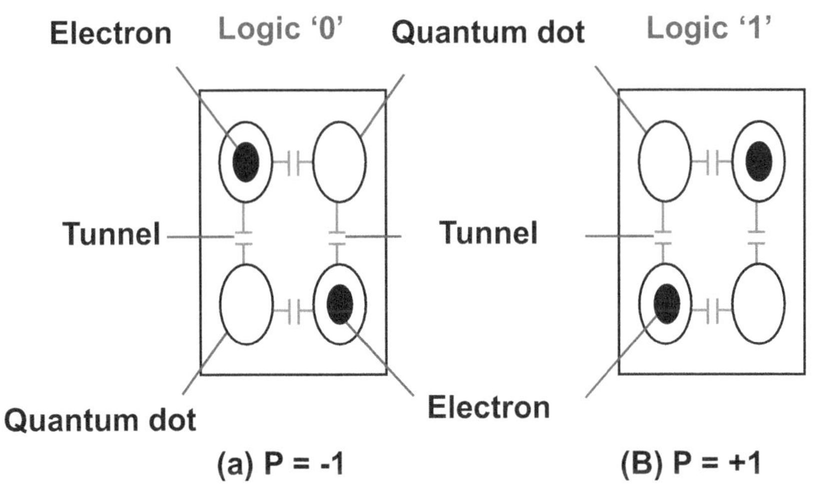

FIGURE 17.1 QCA cell polarization (a) logic "0" and (b) logic "1" [22].

FIGURE 17.2 Crosser wire of the QCA.

There are two types of wire-crossings in QCA technology: multilayer and coplanar. A coplanar wire-crossing is a wire-crossing that can be performed in one layer [22]. A QCA wire with 45-degree cells passing over a conventional. Alternatively, wires on either side of the wire-crossing should have two-phase differences. Multilayer crossovers use multilayered structures to pass QCA wires over each other.

17.2.2.3 Examples of Quantum Machine Learning

The paper "Quantum Machine Learning: A Review and Case Studies" offers a comprehensive examination of the convergence between quantum computing and machine learning, with a specific emphasis on the emerging field of QML. Targeted toward computer scientists rather than physicists, the article serves as a conceptual and technical guide for navigating the fundamental principles underlying QML. It introduces core aspects of quantum computing that are essential for understanding its applicability to machine learning, while simultaneously debunking the notion that an in-depth knowledge of quantum physics is a prerequisite [23]. The authors argue that a foundational grasp of linear algebra—especially matrix operations and vector spaces—is sufficient for engaging with quantum algorithms and their machine learning applications. The article begins by providing an overview of classical machine learning, highlighting its reliance on linear algebraic structures to manage and process large datasets through matrix manipulation. This foundational link between linear algebra and quantum mechanics is further extended by the concept of quantum bits, or *qubits*, which are capable of representing and processing exponentially larger data spaces compared to classical bits due to phenomena such as superposition and entanglement. The authors emphasize that leveraging these quantum mechanical properties enables more efficient handling of high-dimensional data, which is central to many machines learning tasks, including classification, clustering, and dimensionality reduction [24].

Furthermore, the study delves into the architectural features of quantum circuits, detailing their role in structuring QML models. Concepts such as the topology of quantum circuits, superposition, quantum entanglement, and quantum measurement are contextualized within machine learning workflows. These quantum principles are instrumental in designing quantum-enhanced versions of classical algorithms, such as quantum support vector machines (QSVMs), quantum k-means clustering, and variational quantum eigen solvers (VQEs) for optimization problems [25]. In addition, the article reviews key quantum algorithms with significant implications for machine learning. Notably, Grover's algorithm and Shor's algorithm are discussed as benchmarks of quantum advantage. Grover's algorithm demonstrates a quadratic speedup for unstructured search problems, a capability that can be exploited for searching and sampling tasks common in ML. Shor's algorithm, while primarily known for factoring large integers and compromising RSA encryption, also illustrates the computational power of quantum systems in solving classically intractable problems [26].

Collectively, these case studies and algorithmic discussions underscore the transformative potential of QML in redefining computational boundaries. They suggest that as quantum hardware matures and quantum software frameworks become more accessible, the integration of QML models into practical applications such as natural language processing, computer vision, and bioinformatics will become increasingly viable. The reviewed article not only frames QML within the broader context of scientific computing but also sets the stage for future exploration by bridging theoretical underpinnings with real-world applicability.

17.3 LEVERAGING PRE-TRAINED QUANTUM MODELS

The integration of pre-trained quantum models within machine learning workflows is emerging as a promising frontier, particularly in domains that demand high classification accuracy under constrained data or computational resources. The study "Hybrid Model of Quantum Transfer Learning to Classify Face Images with a COVID-19 Mask," by Soto-Paredes and Sulla-Torres, offers a compelling application of this approach. The research explores how quantum-enhanced transfer learning can contribute to critical real-world challenges, specifically the automatic classification of mask-wearing behaviors during the COVID-19 pandemic [27]. By leveraging a hybrid quantum-classical model architecture, the study aims to improve classification accuracy while exploring the potential advantages of quantum information processing. The hybrid architecture presented in the study combines a classical deep convolutional neural network—ResNet-18—with a quantum neural network (QNN) component implemented using the PennyLane framework. This quantum extension includes both basic entangling layers and strongly entangling layers to capture more complex data representations [27]. The ResNet-18 model, pre-trained on large-scale image datasets, serves as a feature extractor, whose output is passed into a quantum layer designed to fine-tune and optimize decision boundaries within the embedding space. This technique exemplifies quantum transfer learning, wherein a classical backbone network is adapted using a pre-trained quantum circuit for downstream classification.

The dataset used consists of 660 images representing diverse subjects (aged 18–86) and is categorized into three classes: (1) correctly worn mask, (2) incorrectly worn mask, and (3) no mask. Despite the dataset's relatively modest size, the hybrid model achieved an exceptional accuracy of 99.05%, outperforming many conventional deep learning baselines. Optimization was carried out using stochastic gradient descent with Nesterov momentum, which was found to be the most effective for the hybrid training regimen. This is particularly notable given that many quantum-enhanced models face challenges related to convergence, noise sensitivity, and limited hardware fidelity—challenges that were mitigated in this study through careful simulator-based experimentation. One of the key contributions of the study lies in its demonstration of how pre-trained classical models can be enhanced with quantum layers, offering a complementary capability to extract and process high-dimensional features. This synergy of classical and quantum architectures is particularly useful in applications with structured data and limited training samples [28]. The comparison with other mask classification methods further reinforces the novelty of the quantum-classical hybrid approach, suggesting that the incorporation of entanglement and quantum feature mapping can meaningfully improve model expressiveness. From a broader research perspective, this work highlights several important directions. First, it establishes a framework for developing hybrid quantum transfer learning models, where classical knowledge is reused and adapted through quantum circuits. Second, it suggests that pre-trained quantum models could become foundational components in more generalized quantum machine learning pipelines, especially as real quantum hardware continues to scale. Third, the study paves the way for real-time deployment of such hybrid systems in public safety domains, including surveillance, healthcare diagnostics, and smart monitoring [29].

In conclusion, the research by Soto-Paredes and Sulla-Torres illustrates not only the technical feasibility but also the societal impact of quantum-enhanced transfer learning. It underscores the promise of quantum computing when used in tandem with classical systems, advocating for deeper exploration into quantum neural architectures, transfer learning strategies, and optimization techniques that are robust under hardware limitations. As quantum computing matures, hybrid models like this one are poised to become essential tools in AI-driven decision-making frameworks.

The article "Transfer Learning in Hybrid Classical-Quantum Neural Networks," by Mari et al., surveys transfer learning in hybrid neural networks that couple classical and quantum components. For intermediate-scale quantum technologies, this is particularly timely, as it will discuss how a variational quantum circuit as an end addition to processing can enhance an already trained classical neural network. This hybrid technology handles high-dimensional data, such as pictures, first using classical networks and then incorporating key elements into a quantum processor for additional operations. This allows for more efficient handling of high-dimensional data. The study is published as a tutorial on the PennyLane website, a venue for quantum machine learning simulations.

17.4 KEY ASPECTS OF HYBRID QUANTUM-CLASSICAL TRANSFER LEARNING

The increasing maturity of quantum hardware and algorithmic frameworks has brought forth new paradigms in machine learning—particularly hybrid quantum-classical learning architectures, where transfer learning plays a crucial role. This chapter highlights significant concepts from recent advancements, specifically focusing on the integration of variational quantum circuits (VQCs) with classical deep learning models [30]. Transfer learning in this context refers to the reuse of learned representations or parameters from one domain or task to enhance learning performance on a related task. The convergence of transfer learning and QML not only addresses the challenge of limited quantum data and hardware constraints but also opens up new pathways for efficient and scalable quantum-enhanced learning systems. A foundational contribution of the reviewed study is its in-depth exploration of hybrid classical-quantum neural networks, particularly emphasizing the role of "dressed quantum circuits." These hybrid models incorporate classical pre-processing and post-processing layers that "dress" the quantum circuit, enabling more efficient handling of high-dimensional data inputs and outputs. This modular configuration enhances the expressiveness of variational quantum circuits and allows classical knowledge, such as learned embeddings from large datasets, to be transferred into quantum models for fine-tuning and domain-specific inference. The paper explains how this architectural layering facilitates the use of classical neural network weights in initializing or guiding the quantum component, creating a seamless synergy between classical and quantum computational paradigms.

Furthermore, the study classifies transfer learning in hybrid systems into four primary categories, each with unique properties and applications:

Classical-to-Classical (CC): Traditional transfer learning between classical neural networks.

Quantum-to-Classical (QC): Transfer from quantum models to classical models, often used for quantum feature extraction.

Quantum-to-Quantum (QQ): Transferring parameters or structures between quantum models operating on different datasets or tasks.

Classical-to-Quantum (CQ): The focus of this study, where knowledge from pre-trained classical models (e.g., deep CNNs) is transferred into a quantum model for fine-tuning or hybrid processing.

Among these, the CQ variant is considered particularly promising, as it leverages the scalability and pretraining capacity of classical models while allowing quantum layers to act as high-capacity learners for task-specific optimization. This approach is especially relevant for current NISQ devices, where pure quantum models may not yet be viable for large-scale tasks due to noise and decoherence limitations.

The practical implementation of these hybrid models was carried out using PennyLane, a leading quantum programming framework that supports simulation and hardware integration. The study evaluates the CQ approach through real-world use cases, such as image classification and quantum state recognition, utilizing both simulated environments and physical quantum processors. Notably, tests were conducted on IBM Quantum Experience devices, which are accessible to academic users free of charge, and Rigetti's quantum systems, which are available via AWS. These experiments highlight not only the feasibility but also the effectiveness of quantum-enhanced learning in hybrid configurations. Results from the study emphasize the efficacy of the CQ transfer learning pipeline, which successfully classified high-resolution images using real quantum hardware. The hybrid model demonstrated improvements in both convergence speed and classification accuracy compared to baseline classical-only architectures. By initializing the quantum model with insights from a classical feature extractor, the CQ approach mitigates the cold-start problem often encountered in quantum learning, where limited training data and shallow circuits hinder performance [31].

In summary, the study underscores the strategic importance of transfer learning in hybrid quantum-classical systems, particularly the classical-to-quantum direction, as a viable and forward-looking solution in modern quantum technologies. It offers compelling evidence that pre-trained classical models can be effectively adapted and extended using quantum circuits to achieve enhanced performance in complex learning tasks. As quantum computing hardware and software ecosystems evolve, such hybrid architectures are expected to form the foundation of practical, scalable quantum machine learning applications across diverse domains including healthcare, security, finance, and materials science.

17.4.1 Hybrid Approach Illustration

Bakhitov et al., in their work "Screening for COVID-19 via Acoustics using Artificial Intelligence," present a new approach to screening for COVID-19 through the use of deep learning techniques on audio data. Neither transfer learning nor quantum computing was applied in the first research, but other studies have expanded on this by combining the two. In the first hybrid model, recordings from healthy people were compared with crowdsourced audio files from those exhibiting COVID-19 symptoms. The Libros Python package was used to convert these audio recordings into log-power spectrograms (an image format), which CNNs analyzed to find patterns suggestive of the infection. The Coswara project at provided the dataset for this investigation, which consisted of audio recordings from 681 COVID-19-positive cases and 1,433 healthy people. A single person recorded nine audio files for each dataset entry, which included sounds like rapid counting, heavy breathing, and vowel pronunciations. With 70% of the data used for training, 20% for validation, and 10% for testing, the model's initial area under the receiver operating characteristics (ROC) curve (AUC) score was 85%. This study focused on the advantages of a hybrid approach combining sophisticated deep learning methods, particularly CNNs, with audio pre-processing and visual manipulation. This strategy attempted to address the problem of rapid and easy COVID-19 screening by providing a reliable and inexpensive alternative to traditional testing methods. The authors mentioned that the tests currently in use for COVID-19 often produce false negatives and that AI-driven techniques, such as the one developed in this work, would serve as a better alternative for primary screenings.

The future plans of the authors were to enhance the model by including transfer learning and quantum computing. However, these updates were not included in the first study since no additional datasets were available at the time. The study extension to this chapter incorporated quantum transfer learning to further boost the model. Specifically, a hybrid classical-quantum neural network was built from the study's initial classical neural network. This hybrid model replaced the final fully connected layer of the baseline network by replacing it with the quantum circuit, simulated through PennyLane as the platform of the quantum computation simulator. That way, in addition to supporting feature extraction initially performed using this traditional network, it can share the previously-trained weights as a contributor within this hybrid model itself. Adding that quantum circuit layer results in building this hybrid network. A transfer learning technique was implemented by adding a fresh subset of the Coswara dataset, which had not been used for training the initial model. The counting data was different from this new data subset concentrating on deep-breathing audio files. This is similar to what is found in "Designing Thin Film Solar Cells with Enhanced Quantum Efficiencies Using a Novel Transfer Learning Method." In further efforts to present useful tools for further development and research, the authors released associated code on GitHub and also presented the data model on Hugging Face platform. This extension of the pilot study demonstrates how transfer learning and quantum computing can make AI models, especially in the field of health diagnosis, better in terms of efficient and accurate analysis of complex data as presented. This chapter's study forms the foundation for the insertion of a quantum layer in the hybrid model.

The summary measurements of the data model came from the preliminary study shown in Figure 17.3. This chapter employed a minimalistic data model to illustrate both the classical and quantum transfer learning. Table 17.2 summarizes the measures for the data model that emerged from traditional transfer learning. Let us break down the computation using the provided architecture to approximate the values such as total parameters, trainable parameters, input size, forward or backward pass size, and many more. The following table's architecture can be used to obtain the values as shown here:

TABLE 17.2
Summary Measurements of the Data Model from the Traditional Transfer Learning

Layer (type)	Output Shape	Param (Original)	Param (Quantum Hybrid)
Conv2d-1	[−1, 32, 256, 256]	896	896
ReLU-2	[−1, 32, 256, 256]	0	0
MaxPool2d-3	[−1, 32, 128, 128]	0	0
Conv2d-4 (Original)/Conv2d-7 (Hybrid)	[−1, 128, 128, 128]	36,864	36,864
ReLU-5 (Original)/ReLU-8 (Hybrid)	[−1, 128, 128, 128]	0	0
MaxPool2d-6 (Original)/MaxPool2d-9 (Hybrid)	[−1, 128, 64, 64]	0	0
Conv2d-7 (Original)/Conv2d-10 (Hybrid)	[−1, 256, 64, 64]	295,168	295,168
ReLU-8 (Original)/ReLU-11 (Hybrid)	[−1, 256, 64, 64]	0	0
MaxPool2d-9 (Original)/MaxPool2d-12 (Hybrid)	[−1, 256, 32, 32]	0	0
Conv2d-4 (Original)/Conv2d-7 (Hybrid)	[−1, 128, 128, 128]	36,864	36,864
ReLU-5 (Original)/ReLU-8 (Hybrid)	[−1, 128, 128, 128]	0	0
MaxPool2d-9 (Original)/MaxPool2d-12 (Hybrid)	[−1, 256, 32, 32]	0	0
Conv2d-10 (Original)	[−1, 512, 32, 32]	1,180,160	—
ReLU-11 (Original)	[−1, 512, 32, 32]	0	—
MaxPool2d-12 (Original)	[−1, 512, 16, 16]	0	—
Linear-13	[−1, 1024]	8,388,608	8,388,608
ReLU-14	[−1, 1024]	0	0
Linear-15	[−1, 10]	10,250	10,250

17.4.2 Memory Usage in a Classical Neural Network

Understanding these components helps in optimizing the model for better performance and resource utilization. This is the input size; that is, the size of memory assigned to store fed input data to the neural network. This size is usually very small compared with other memory-consumption hungry parts of the algorithm because this is just raw input before the actual processing occurs. For instance, in the given

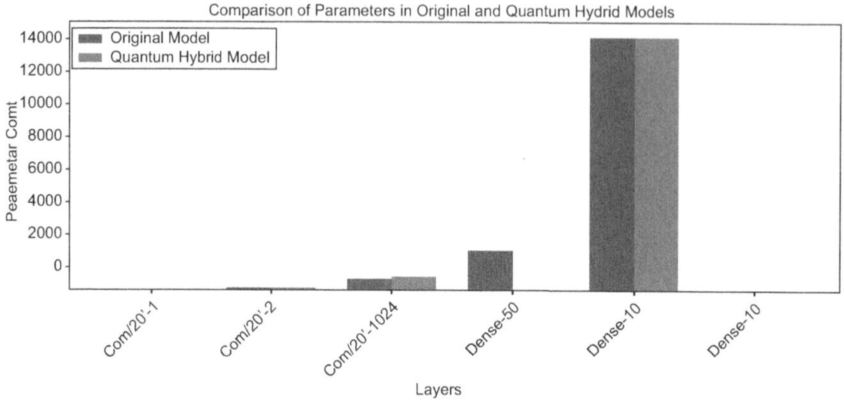

FIGURE 17.3 Summary of data measurements.

example, the input size is only 0.25 MB, which is very negligible in comparison with the overall consumption. This will take a lot of memory space because the majority of computations will be used to compute the forward and backward pass. Forward pass is the straightforward propagation of input data through layers in a network, resulting in activations and intermediate feature representations, which must be stored so gradients could be computed back to update weights in the backpropagation algorithm. A backward pass requires as much memory as, if not more than, a forward pass since extra space has to be saved to store the derivative [32].

For this model, forward and backward pass size comes at 33.76 MB—that really depicts its role in total memory allocation. Parameter size is the other major memory user. It just means that it represents the storage of trainable weights in the model. Each layer in the network has weights and biases parameters that are updated during training. The number of parameters directly relates to memory use, so the complexity of the network is defined by the number of parameters. In this experiment, the parameter size is 33.76 MB, just like the size of the forward/backward pass, which also confirms that the model weights occupy a large proportion of the memory demand. The sum of these memory components is said to bring about the total size of all of them, hence representing the total memory footprint of the neural network. The total estimated memory consumption for the model is found to be as shown in Table 17.3, 71.77 MB, comprising input, parameter storage, and training computations. Therefore, the fact that the vast number of parameters and forward and backward computations makes room for optimization regarding eliminating redundant parameters, pruning small weights, or applying efficient architecture for reduced memory usage and good performance. The ability to effectively use memory in big applications, such as deployment on limited hardware-compute models, will become vital [33].

The results of this case study show the applicability of quantum-enhanced machine learning models in practice, the benefits, and challenges that come with the inclusion of quantum circuits within conventional neural networks. This hybrid model was successfully applied by the team and accelerated quantum machine learning by providing a feasible approach to using quantum computers for augmenting traditional machine learning tasks. This research was a critical juncture in the merging of quantum and classical computing technologies because it demonstrated the model's aptness in the medical screening context as well as the overall potential of quantum computing to transform a number of sectors as depicted in Figures 17.4(a) and 17.4(b).

It has been very critical in the quantum transfer learning approach to point out the efficiency of a model in terms of the memory usage along with the pre-trained weights. The memory requirements of a quantum transfer learning model can be reasoned through the presence of several key components in such a model—namely, input size, storage for parameters, and memory required in computing operations within the training/inference phases of a model. Each of the aforementioned components relates to the eventual size of a model, thereby relating to some optimization of that model for one hardware or the other computational setup. The input size for the quantum transfer learning model was modest at 0.25 MB, which seems to actually embody the memory needed to store data input. This is because, in most deep learning models, the input data represents the features fed

TABLE 17.3
Original Classical Neural Network Without the Quantum Transfer Learning

Parameter	Value
Total Parameters	9,911,946
Trainable Parameters	9,911,946
Non-trainable Parameters	0
Input Size (MB)	0.25
Forward/Backward Pass Size (MB)	33.76
Parameter Size (MB)	33.76
Estimated Total Size (MB)	71.77

TABLE 17.4
Measurement of Quantum Transfer Learning Note the great reduction in the trainable parameters with the pre-trained models.

Parameter	Value
Total Parameters	16,876,942
Trainable Parameters	2026
Non-trainable Parameters	16,874,880
Input Size (MB)	0.25
Forward/Backward Pass Size (MB)	33.76
Parameter Size (MB)	64.38
Estimated Total Size (MB)	98.39

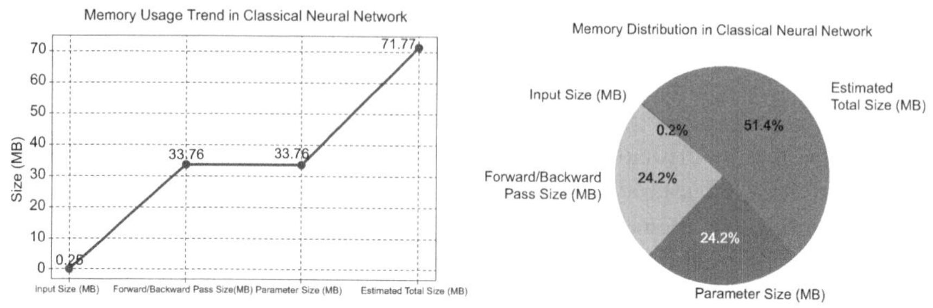

(a-b)

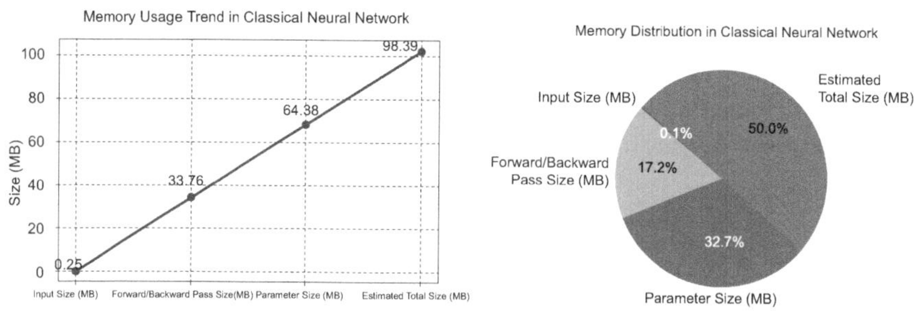

(c-d)

FIGURE 17.4 (a–b) Memory distribution in a classical neural network. (c–d) Memory usage in quantum transfer learning model.

into the network for processing, and although very important for the network, usually requires less memory than such other components as parameters or intermediate computations [33].

It follows that the larger memory footprint would be for forward and backward pass size. That is the size of the memory required for holding intermediate activations for the forward pass and gradients in backpropagation. In the quantum transfer learning model, this size is 33.76 MB, which reflects the large amount of memory required to perform these operations as shown in Table 17.4. The forward and backward pass memory consumption is independent of whether the model is pre-trained or not since it depends on the architecture of the network and the batch size. One of the most noticeable differences in quantum transfer learning is the parameter size. In a conventional model, the entire set of parameters, that is, both weights and biases, is updated during training.

However, transfer learning usually involves freezing many of the parameters. This means only a small fraction of the total parameters is changed. Here, the parameter size is 64.38 MB, which represents the total size of the model's parameters that include both the trainable and the non-trainable weights. The trainable parameters have been significantly reduced to a mere 2,062 and, in doing so, resulted in a highly dramatic reduction in comparison to the total count of parameters at 16,876,942. The rest are non-trainable parameters: 16,874,880. This implies that almost all the model's parameters have been pre-trained and are left unaltered.

The overall sum of approximated total size calculated from the sum of estimated parts, considering input, parameter, and required memory space to carry out a computation, equals to 98.39 MB. The total size would thus encompass the overall required memory for accommodating the model to perform its relevant computations. The large proportion of non-trainable parameters and the reduction in trainable parameters make the model more memory-efficient, making quantum transfer learning an attractive option for deploying complex models with limited computational resources. The graphs visually capture the distribution of memory usage across these components. The bar graph clearly indicates the way memory is broken down between input, computational operations, parameters, and the total model size [34]. It is split down to parts showing domination with non-trainable parameters along with smallish input size within the pie chart.

Lastly, a trend traced using a memory line graph follows through components indicating which elements drive up memory during quantum transfer learning. It is noted that the model of quantum transfer learning has reduced the memory usage during the training process, and this reduction is much impressive if it uses the pre-trained weights. Therefore, the model can increase its memory efficiency by freezing the majority of parameters while training just a small set of them, thus making it deployable to environments with low resources. Understanding these memory components would help in constructing optimized neural networks which can simultaneously achieve accuracy as well as balanced resource consumption, as shown in Figures 17.4(c) and 17.4(d).

17.4.3 Cross-Domain Applications

We actually present several research demonstrate this concept, though our example does not involve moving models between domains beyond the Coswara dataset. For instance, in their paper "Hybrid Model of Quantum Transfer Learning to Classify Face Images with a COVID-19 Mask" [10], Soto-Paredes and Sulla-Torres employed the classical transfer learning model, ResNet-18, along with quantum layers in the target model. The PennyLane quantum simulator was used to simulate these quantum layers, which used a simple entangler layer template for four qubits. The results were astonishingly accurate, with 99.05% accuracy in classifying face photos into three mask usage groups: no mask, mask worn incorrectly, and mask worn correctly. Moreover, the article "Transfer Learning in Hybrid Classical-Quantum Neural Networks," by Mari et al., is one of the pioneering works. Another useful source on the PennyLane site is the theory of transfer learning in hybrid classical-quantum and quantum-quantum neural networks, presented in the course material. According to the authors of the publication "Quantum Deep Transfer Learning," transfer learning can be used in many spheres of activity step-by-step.

1. Identify a relevant source domain dataset for the task.
2. Train a model using the source dataset.
3. Develop criteria for the transfer process that are tailored to the specific task.
4. Train the model on the target dataset, utilizing the knowledge transferred from the source.

"COVID-19 Detection on IBM Quantum Computer with Classical-Quantum Transfer Learning" is yet another relevant one where the authors used transfer learning to classify images of lungs for COVID-19 patients and normal people through MRI [35].

Leider et al. have also carried out studies, like "Quantum Machine Learning Classifier," which applies this method to the wine dataset using PennyLane, and "Hybrid Quantum Machine Learning Classifier with Classical Neural Network Transfer Learning," which uses the Iris dataset with the PennyLane simulator. These studies illustrate how, gradually, more and more applications of transfer learning are being used in order to amalgamate quantum computing with traditional machine learning techniques to develop further applications in the area. Therefore, the PennyLane quantum simulator is crucial in bridging the gaps of the current state of quantum computing technology, which is called the NISQ era [35]. Quantum computers are still very simple, prone to mistakes, and often produce inconsistent outputs at present time. Consequently, a significant amount of the research carried out using these machines is still largely academic. Since quantum computers are based on a probabilistic model, many runs of a quantum program are often required to determine the most likely answer, typically in "shots" of 1,000 or more.

17.4.4 Global Quantum Technology Landscape and India's Key Milestones

Quantum computing has transitioned from a largely theoretical discipline to a rapidly evolving technological domain with tangible impact on research, education, and industry. Among the platforms at the forefront of this revolution, IBM quantum computers have emerged as pivotal instruments in advancing quantum science and education globally. These platforms offer open access to quantum processors via the cloud, enabling researchers, developers, and students worldwide to explore quantum algorithms and applications. An analysis of the global distribution of IBM Quantum usage reveals a strong presence across North America, Europe, and Asia, with a particularly notable concentration in India. According to a McKinsey report, India ranks as the leading consumer of IBM Quantum services, signaling the nation's growing engagement and proficiency in quantum technologies. This development is further supported by educational indicators, as reflected in the number of graduates in quantum-relevant fields such as quantum physics, computer science, and electrical engineering. Tables 17.5 and 17.6 demonstrate a global comparison of quantum-skilled workforce readiness, where India's output of qualified professionals suggests a robust and expanding academic infrastructure poised to support next-generation quantum innovation. Beyond usage statistics, India's strides in quantum technology are also marked by institutional initiatives and national missions aimed at fostering indigenous quantum research capabilities. The National Mission on Quantum Technologies & Applications (NM-QTA), launched by the Government of India, emphasizes strategic investment in quantum computing, quantum communication, and quantum sensing, laying a strong foundation for future scientific and industrial leadership in this domain.

This section also presents a conceptual advancement at the intersection of QML and transfer learning in neural networks. QML leverages the quantum mechanical properties of qubits—such as superposition, entanglement, and quantum parallelism—to offer novel frameworks for addressing problems that are computationally intractable for classical systems. These quantum-enhanced algorithms promise significant improvements in managing and analyzing high-dimensional datasets, particularly in fields like finance, genomics, and materials science. On the other hand, transfer learning in classical deep

TABLE 17.5
Graduate Distribution in Quantum-Relevant Fields [22]

Region	Number of Graduates (2020)
European Union	115,511
India	82,110
China	57,693
United States	45,087
Russia	23,450
United Kingdom	14,601

TABLE 17.6
India's Quantum Journey: Milestones in National Quantum Initiative

Date/Timeline	Milestone	Description
2020	Announcement	The National Quantum Initiative was announced, laying the foundation for a focused quantum development strategy.
2023	Cabinet Approval	The initiative received government approval with a budget allocation of ₹6000 crores (~$750 million) to fuel its implementation.
January 20, 2024	Call for Proposals	A call for pre-proposals for establishing quantum hubs was issued, inviting various institutions to participate.
April 12, 2024	Proposal Submissions	The deadline for pre-proposal submissions, marking the first tangible step toward the initiative's implementation.
September 30, 2024	Launch of Quantum Hubs	The formal launch of quantum hubs is planned, aiming to spearhead innovation, research, and development in quantum computing and allied technologies.

learning architectures enables models pre-trained on large datasets to be repurposed for different but related tasks, significantly reducing the need for retraining while improving generalization and performance. The synergy of QML and transfer learning leads to a hybrid computational paradigm—not merely an aggregation of techniques, but a deeply integrated framework wherein quantum capabilities augment the learning efficiency and adaptability of neural networks [36].

To illustrate the practical implications of this hybrid approach, a case study on COVID-19 screening is presented. This study explores how quantum-assisted transfer learning models improve the performance of computer vision systems tasked with analyzing spectrograms of audio signals (e.g., cough sounds). The process involves encoding the spectrograms into quantum-compatible formats, applying quantum feature extraction, and using ensemble classifiers enhanced through sliding window techniques [36]. The observed gains in classification accuracy underscore the potential of quantum-inspired models in healthcare diagnostics and, more broadly, in any domain where rapid, large-scale analysis of complex data is essential. This example not only demonstrates the practical utility of quantum-classical hybrid models but also exemplifies the broader applicability of such frameworks in real-world problem-solving—an encouraging signpost for the continued evolution of quantum technologies, both globally and within India's burgeoning quantum ecosystem.

Despite the rapid global advancements in quantum computing, a comprehensive understanding of how emerging economies, particularly India, are contributing to and benefiting from this technological shift remains underexplored. While several studies have mapped the broader quantum ecosystem in developed regions such as North America and Europe, there is a noticeable research gap in examining the role of developing nations in shaping the global quantum technology landscape. This gap is particularly relevant in the context of India, a country with a growing number of quantum-trained professionals and increasing engagement with quantum infrastructure.

The objective of this section is twofold: (1) to analyze India's current positioning and participation within the global quantum computing ecosystem using empirical data on IBM Quantum usage and quantum education indicators and (2) to explore a novel computational framework that integrates QML with transfer learning to address real-world challenges—demonstrated through a practical healthcare-related case study.

The contributions of this section are threefold:

- **First**, we present a comparative analysis of global engagement with quantum computing platforms, highlighting India's emerging leadership in quantum research and education based on recent industry reports and graduate statistics (Tables 17.5 and 17.6).
- **Second**, we introduce a hybrid quantum-classical framework that synthesizes QML and transfer learning, addressing the challenge of data scalability and computational efficiency in large-scale analyses.
- **Third**, we demonstrate the real-world applicability of the proposed model through a COVID-19 screening case study, which shows enhanced accuracy in detecting disease-related audio patterns using quantum-assisted learning techniques.

By bridging global trends in quantum technology adoption with methodological innovations in quantum machine learning, this section aims to underscore both the strategic importance of India's quantum initiatives and the transformative potential of QML-augmented neural networks in practical domains.

17.5 CONCLUSION

This chapter has examined the evolving global landscape of quantum technology with a particular focus on India's emerging role as a leader in quantum research and education. Leveraging recent data on IBM Quantum system usage and graduate output in quantum-relevant disciplines, we identified India as a key contributor to the quantum ecosystem in Asia and globally. The analysis highlights a growing infrastructure supported by national initiatives such as the NM-QTA, indicating the country's strategic investment in future-ready quantum capabilities. This suggests that India is not only consuming but also actively shaping the direction of global quantum innovation. In parallel, the chapter introduced a novel hybrid computational framework that integrates QML with transfer learning. This synergistic model harnesses the computational advantages of quantum mechanics while utilizing the adaptability of classical neural networks, offering a scalable solution for complex data-driven problems. The case study on COVID-19 screening through quantum-enhanced spectrogram analysis exemplifies the practical value of this approach, demonstrating improved classification accuracy and potential for deployment in healthcare diagnostics and beyond. Looking ahead, the integration of QML with advanced machine learning paradigms presents a promising direction for future research, especially in fields requiring rapid analysis of high-dimensional data. As quantum hardware matures and becomes more accessible, the methodological insights from this chapter can serve as a foundation for building real-world applications in finance, cybersecurity, drug discovery, and smart sensing. India's strong academic pipeline and policy support position it to play a pivotal role in advancing this frontier.

REFERENCES

[1] M. Arute et al., "Quantum supremacy using a programmable superconducting processor," Nature, vol. 574, no. 7779, pp. 505–510, 2019. https://doi.org/10.1038/s41586-019-1666-5.

[2] V. Dunjko, and H. J. Briegel, "Machine learning & artificial intelligence in the quantum domain: A review of recent progress," Rep. Prog. Phys., vol. 81, no. 7, p. 075001, 2018. https://doi.org/10.1088/1361-6633/aab406.

[3] F. Flamini, N. Spagnolo, and F. Sciarrino, "Photonic quantum computing," Rep. Prog. Phys., vol. 82, no. 1, p. 016001, 2019. https://doi.org/10.1088/1361-6633/aaf285.

[4] E. Farhi, and J. Neven, "Classification with quantum neural networks on near term processors," arXiv preprint, arXiv:1802.06002, 2018. https://doi.org/10.48550/arXiv.1802.06002.

[5] S. Schuld, M. Schuld, and F. Petruccione, "The variational quantum eigensolver," arXiv preprint, arXiv:1905.10450, 2019.

[6] H. Montanaro, "Quantum algorithms: An overview," NPJ Quantum Inf., vol. 2, no. 1, p. 15023, 2016. https://doi.org/10.1038/npjqi.2015.23.

[7] A. Aspuru-Guzik et al., "Harvesting chemical energies with quantum processors," Nat. Chem., vol. 4, no. 2, pp. 103–111, 2012. https://doi.org/10.1038/nchem.1198.

[8] S. Woerner, and D. Egger, "Quantum risk analysis," arXiv preprint, arXiv:1806.00447, 2018. https://doi.org/10.48550/arXiv.1806.00447.

[9] S. Schuld et al., "Transfer learning in quantum machine learning," Quantum, vol. 4, p. 337, 2020. https://doi.org/10.22331/q-2020-10-07-337.

[10] C. Kokcu et al., "Quantum machine learning: A survey," arXiv preprint, arXiv:2310.05217, 2023. https://doi.org/10.48550/arXiv.2310.05217.

[11] S. J. Pan, and Q. Yang, "A survey on transfer learning," IEEE Trans. Knowl. Data Eng., vol. 22, no. 10, pp. 1345–1359, Oct. 2010. https://doi.org/10.1109/TKDE.2009.191.

[12] T. M. Mitchell, Machine Learning. New York, NY, USA: McGraw-Hill, 1997.

[13] A. I. J. Forrester, A. Sóbester, and A. J. Keane, Engineering Design via Surrogate Modelling: A Practical Guide. Chichester, UK: Wiley, 2008.

[14] J. T. Kwok, and W. K. Yeung, "Efficient multi-task learning by feature selection," in Proc. 24th Nat. Conf. Artif. Intell., vol. 2, pp. 875–880, 2005.

[15] T. Young et al., "Recent trends in deep learning based natural language processing," arXiv preprint, arXiv:1708.02709, 2017. https://doi.org/10.48550/arXiv.1708.02709.

[16] J. Schmidhuber, "Deep learning in neural networks: An overview," Neural Netw., vol. 61, pp. 85–117, 2015. https://doi.org/10.1016/j.neunet.2014.09.003.

[17] R. P. Feynman, "Simulating physics with computers," Int. J. Theor. Phys., vol. 21, no. 6–7, pp. 467–488, 1982. https://doi.org/10.1007/BF02650179.
[18] Amazon Web Services, "Amazon braket." [Online]. Available: https://aws.amazon.com/braket/.
[19] P. W. Shor, "Algorithms for quantum computation: Discrete logarithms and factoring," in Proc. 35th Annu. Symp. Found. Comput. Sci., pp. 124–134, 1994. https://doi.org/10.1109/SFCS.1994.365700.
[20] F. Arute et al., "Quantum supremacy using a programmable superconducting processor," Nature, vol. 574, no. 7779, pp. 505–510, 2019. https://doi.org/10.1038/s41586-019-1666-5.
[21] R. B. Patel, J. Ho, F. Ferreyrol, T. C. Ralph, and G. J. Pryde, "A quantum Fredkin gate," Sci. Adv., vol. 2, no. 3, p. e1501531, Mar. 2016. https://doi.org/10.1126/sciadv.1501531.
[22] W.-Q. Liu, H.-R. Wei, and L.-C. Kwek, "Low-cost Fredkin gate with auxiliary space," Phys. Rev. Appl., vol. 14, no. 5, p. 054057, Nov. 2020. https://doi.org/10.1103/PhysRevApplied.14.054057.
[23] A. Roohi, S. Angizi, K. Navi, and A. V. Roohi, "A symmetric quantum-dot cellular automata design for single layer wire crossing," IEEE Trans. Nanotechnol., vol. 13, no. 3, pp. 539–550, May 2014. https://doi.org/10.1109/TNANO.2014.2311818.
[24] A. Kamruzzaman, Y. Alhwaiti, A. Leider, and C. C. Tappert, "Quantum deep learning neural networks," in Adv. Inf. Commun. Process.: Proc. Future of Inf. Commun. Conf. (FICC), San Francisco, CA, USA, vol. 2, pp. 299–311, 2020.
[25] A. Zeguendry, Z. Jarir, and M. Quafafou, "Quantum machine learning: A review and case studies," Entropy, vol. 25, no. 2, p. 287, 2023. https://doi.org/10.3390/e25020287.
[26] M. Kaya, and S. Hajimirza, "Using a novel transfer learning method for designing thin film solar cells with enhanced quantum efficiencies," Sci. Rep., vol. 9, no. 1, p. 5034, 2019. https://doi.org/10.1038/s41598-019-41316-9.
[27] D. Bakhitov, R. Khemraj, J. Skorko, A. Leider, and P. Mosley, "Screening for COVID-19 via acoustics using artificial intelligence," in Proc. Future of Inf. Commun. Conf., Cham, Switzerland: Springer, pp. 630–645, 2023.
[28] M. A. Nielsen, and I. L. Chuang, Quantum Computation and Quantum Information, 10th Anniversary Ed. Cambridge, UK: Cambridge University Press, 2010.
[29] J. Clarke, and F. K. Wilhelm, "Superconducting quantum bits," Nature, vol. 453, no. 7198, pp. 1031–1042, 2008. https://doi.org/10.1038/nature07128.
[30] A. G. Fowler, M. Mariantoni, J. M. Martinis, and A. N. Cleland, "Surface codes: Towards practical large-scale quantum computation," Phys. Rev. A, vol. 86, no. 3, p. 032324, 2012. https://doi.org/10.1103/PhysRevA.86.032324.
[31] C. S. Lent, P. D. Tougaw, W. Porod, and G. H. Bernstein, "Quantum cellular automata," Nanotechnology, vol. 4, no. 1, p. 49, 1993. https://doi.org/10.1088/0957-4484/4/1/004.
[32] K. Walus, T. J. Dysart, G. A. Jullien, and R. A. Klassen, "QCADesigner: A rapid design and simulation tool for quantum-dot cellular automata," in Proc. 19th IEEE Int. Symp. Defect Fault Tolerance VLSI Syst., pp. 562–570, 2004. https://doi.org/10.1109/DFTVS.2004.1335442.
[33] P. D. Tougaw, and C. S. Lent, "Logical devices implemented using quantum cellular automata," J. Appl. Phys., vol. 75, no. 10, pp. 749–755, 1994. https://doi.org/10.1063/1.356375.
[34] W. Porod et al., "Quantum-dot cellular automata: Logic, memory, and architectures," Int. J. Electron., vol. 86, no. 5, pp. 549–590, 1999. https://doi.org/10.1080/002072199133140.
[35] C. S. Lent, and P. D. Tougaw, "Lines of interacting quantum dots: A prospective nano-electronic technology," J. Appl. Phys., vol. 74, no. 10, pp. 6211–6213, 1993. https://doi.org/10.1063/1.355007.
[36] Pauline Mosley and Avery Leider "Quantum Machine Learning Classifier and Neural Network Transfer Learning" DOI: http://dx.doi.org/10.5772/intechopen.115051.

18 Enhancing Healthcare Data Security Using Quantum Homomorphic Encryption

Sivaranjani Reddi and Jami Venkata Suman

18.1 INTRODUCTION

Healthcare data is among the most sensitive categories of information, such as medical records, diagnostic reports, and identifiers. The need to protect such data is further compounded by the increasing adoption of electronic health systems and the increasing incidence of data breaches. However, healthcare data protection needs to be weighed against enabling its secure and effective use for purposes such as research, diagnosis, and collaborative decision-making.

Traditional encryption methods provide secure protection but are likely to limit data usage, requiring decryption to process. That kind of approach leaves data exposed to vulnerabilities when being processed and can lead to privacy compromise. Moreover, adaptation to quantum computing puts longevity of classical cryptography algorithms [1] at stake; quantum-based systems are known to break the most widely implemented cryptographic protocols.

The growing use of machine learning [2] in sensitive areas such as medical diagnosis demands robust privacy-guaranteeing techniques in processing patient data. Datasets such as the Breast Cancer dataset contain valuable health information, and therefore, data processing methods with privacy preservation are needed. Traditional encryption methods typically hinder straightforward computation over encrypted data, which is a bottleneck for secure machine learning usage.

The rapid development of quantum computing has the potential to change the way we approach privacy-preserving computation in fields like medicine, where data confidentiality is retained even as it is processed. Homomorphic encryption (HE) [3] facilitates computation over encrypted data. This property is beneficial in situations where data privacy is particularly critical, for example, the analysis of medical data, in which personal details must be kept confidential even in the course of calculations.

Classical HE schemes, though, tend to have high computation overheads, which render them inefficient for huge datasets or even complex computations. Quantum computing, with its parallelism and capability to perform computations in superpositioned states, offers the possibility of optimizing the efficiency of such privacy-protecting approaches.

DOI: 10.1201/9781003538950-21

In this chapter, we integrate quantum homomorphic encryption (QHE) into the RSA encryption scheme to come up with a system that can securely run the Diabetes dataset, a well-known medical dataset, and maintain confidentiality of sensitive information. RSA [4, 5], widely used asymmetric key cryptosystem, encrypts data with large prime numbers and modular arithmetic. We simulate quantum-based RSA encryption, perform homomorphic operations [6] on encrypted data, and use quantum circuits for decryption and encryption.

We perform this on the Diabetes dataset, where the features are encrypted using RSA encryption, homomorphic addition is performed on the encrypted features, and the result is decrypted using quantum circuits. Subsequently, the decryption is compared with classical results for correctness checking of the quantum-based computation.

With assistance of quantum computer potential, we will demonstrate that QHE can be utilized in order to encrypt sensitive data but enable computationally efficient computation over encrypted data, offering a compelling solution to privacy-preserving data analysis in healthcare and beyond.

18.2 NOVELTY AND CONTRIBUTIONS

This chapter presents the novel application of QHE for securing processing of medical data, following the RSA scheme of encryption in the quantum context. Although classical HE [7, 8] facilitates computation over encrypted data, it entails heavy computational costs, which restricts its use. Quantum computing has the potential to offer much greater efficiency and scalability of encryption schemes based on quantum parallelism and entanglement.

Key aspects include:

1. Integrating Quantum Computing with Homomorphic Encryption: This chapter investigates the combination of quantum computing and traditional cryptographic methods, in this case RSA, to support privacy-preserving computations on encrypted data. It illustrates how computational power from quantum can be leveraged to support secure processing of data without disclosing confidentiality.
2. Secure Analysis of Healthcare Data: The study uses a diabetes dataset, with sensitive medical data, to demonstrate the real-world application of QHE. Through performing secure computations on encrypted data, the technique maintains patient confidentiality and enables meaningful data analysis.
3. Quantum Simulation of RSA Operations: Quantum circuits are used to emulate the RSA encryption and decryption process so that quantum-based homomorphic operations, like arithmetic addition, can be performed on encrypted integers. Decrypted results are then checked against predicted outcomes, demonstrating the applicability of quantum algorithms in cryptographic applications, even without physical quantum hardware.
4. Verification Against Classical Homomorphic Techniques: The efficiency and precision of the quantum homomorphic operations are confirmed by

comparing them to outputs from standard HE methods. The comparison guarantees that the quantum method ensures data privacy while attaining equivalent or better computational efficiency.

This method opens the door to quantum-assisted secure computations on encrypted data in a wide range of domains, such as healthcare, finance, and other privacy-critical sectors.

Objectives: The objectives of this study are:

1. Develop a Quantum Homomorphic Encryption Framework: Build an end-to-end framework that utilizes quantum computing to carry out safe homomorphic operations on encrypted information, based on the RSA encryption scheme. This comprises the development and application of quantum circuits for encryption, computation, and decryption processes.
2. Simulate RSA-Based Quantum Encryption: Use RSA encryption and decryption mechanisms via quantum circuits, where data stays encrypted and secure during computation. The circuits ought to implement basic homomorphic operations, including adding and multiplying encrypted values.
3. Implement the Framework on Real-World Data (Diabetes Dataset): Illustrate the real-world usefulness of the QHE system by using it to process the Diabetes dataset. This illustrates the ability of the system to process and handle sensitive medical information in a privacy-preserving fashion.
4. Apply Homomorphic Operations to Encrypted Data: Apply homomorphic operations, such as addition, to the encrypted dataset without decrypting. This ensures that data confidentiality is maintained during the computation process, validating the secure computing ability of the framework.
5. Check Quantum Decryption Accuracy: Validate the result of quantum decryption against that of classical homomorphic methods to verify accuracy and reliability. This step ensures that the quantum model accurately restores the original information and can serve as a secure and efficient alternative to classical methods.
6. Demonstrate the Viability of Privacy-Preserving Computation: Show the efficiency and scalability of QHE as a practical method for privacy-preserving computation on large-scale data, particularly in the sensitive areas of healthcare.

18.3 LITERATURE REVIEW

Symmetric key encryption algorithms such as the Advanced Encryption Standard (AES) are widely recognized for their computational efficiency. Symmetric encryption algorithms accommodate fast encryption and decryption and hence can be used in real-time applications like healthcare data storage and transport. Symmetric encryption has extremely hard time with key management. Since the same key is used during encryption and decryption, safe distribution and storage of keys is required, particularly in healthcare, where patient health record in confidence is disseminated between organizations like hospitals, clinics, and insurance providers. Distribution of keys safely across numerous endpoints in large systems is a complicated task. Procedures such as secure communication channels and protocols such as key distribution centers (KDCs) are required to prevent unauthorized use of encryption keys.

Though efficient, symmetric encryption is vulnerable to brute-force attack, where the attacker performs a sequential attempt at attempting all viable keys to decode the data. Symmetric encryption security is predicated on key length and randomness. Though increased keys provide larger security through exponential increases in brute-force attack processing overhead, this also introduces additional processing overhead that could impact performance in low-processing environments. In order to avoid key compromise risk, techniques such as key rotation and regular key refresh are used routinely. These comprise frequent update of encryption keys as well as immediate notification to all authorized parties when the change takes place. Through these procedures, the security system's integrity and the consequences of a compromised key are avoided as much as possible.

Homomorphic encryption, also known as homomorphic cryptography, is a mathematical approach that provides a unique benefit of encryption-enabled computations on ciphertext. This is very important in privacy-oriented fields such as healthcare, where confidentiality and privacy of patient information and medical records must be preserved. HE schemes are based on sophisticated mathematical techniques such as polynomial evaluation and lattice-based cryptography, making data processing secure without decryption. But these approaches tend to introduce heavy computational overhead, which makes them difficult for performance—particularly with time-critical tasks like electronic medical records and medical image analysis.

As a result of the recent progress made in HE, it is still hindered by the efficiency problem for practical application to healthcare, especially when handling extensive data or using it in settings with limited resources. Implementing such encryption on actual healthcare systems requires not just profound cryptographic expertise but also major development work for usability and efficiency.

Recent developments in HE and quantum cryptography have greatly improved the potential of secure computing, especially in privacy-intensive areas such as healthcare. Liu et al. [9] proposed a versatile QHE scheme tailored to efficiency and multi-role evaluators, whereas Zeuner et al. [10] illustrated an experimental demonstration of QHE, confirming its experimental viability. Based on these principles, Zhang et al. [11] introduced a better multiparty quantum private comparison protocol based on QHE, allowing secure comparison among multiple parties. In the medical field, quantum technologies are being increasingly used for secure data processing and communication. Aggarwal et al. [12] highlighted precision-based quantum computing methods in clinical applications, and Qu et al. [13] designed a quantum blockchain system for the protection of electronic medical records in the internet of medical things.

Chang et al. [14] added a dynamic QFHE scheme based on universal quantum circuits, enhancing the flexibility of encrypted quantum operations. While Abidin et al. [15] and Pulipeti and Kumar [16] surveyed the applications of quantum cryptography toward countering challenges to mobile cloud computing and healthcare security, respectively. Supportive of such technological advances, Newaz et al. [17] presented an overall survey of threats in today's healthcare system and although later withdrawn, proposed, albeit at first instance, an architecture simulation of quantum key optimization within healthcare networks by Perumal and Nadar [18]. Collectively, these works highlight the revolutionizing power of quantum-enhanced cryptographic methods for secure, privacy-protecting use in key industries.

To overcome these issues, new solutions have been put forward. One of them is the N-Crypt technique, which improves data transmission security in multi-hop wireless sensor networks by using iterative encryption and decryption processes. Simulation-based assessments show that N-Crypt performs better than conventional methods in terms of efficiency and thus can be a good alternative in constrained environments.

Similarly, innovative architectures like VBQ-Net leverage advanced machine learning techniques [19] to enhance intrusion detection in IoT networks, providing robust defenses against cyberattacks. These advances reflect the continuous evolution of encryption technology to address complicated security needs of contemporary healthcare systems.

Preliminaries:

a. Homomorphic Encryption: It is a cryptographic technique that allows computations to be performed on encrypted data without needing to decrypt it first. The result of the computation remains encrypted and can only be decrypted by owner using encryption key.

   A computation function f is considered homomorphic if it satisfies the property:

$$\mathrm{f}(m_1 + m_2) = \mathrm{f}(m_1) \oplus \mathrm{f}(m_2)$$

where:

- + represents an arithmetic operation (e.g., addition).
- $\oplus$ represents a corresponding operation in the encrypted domain.

In the context of cryptography, an encryption algorithm Enc is called a homomorphic encryption algorithm if, for any two plaintexts m_1 and m_2, following property holds:

$$\mathrm{Enc}(m_1 + m_2) = \mathrm{Enc}(m_1) \oplus \mathrm{Enc}(m_2)$$

This means that computations on encrypted data can be performed directly, without requiring decryption.

Similarly decryption ensures that:

$$\mathrm{Dec}(\mathrm{Enc}(m_1) \oplus \mathrm{Enc}(m_2)) = m_1 + m_2$$

Similarly, for multiplication in somewhat or fully homomorphic encryption schemes:

$$\mathrm{Dec}(\mathrm{Enc}(m_1) \otimes \mathrm{Enc}(m_2)) = m_1 . m_2$$

b. RSA Homomorphic Operations in Practice:
   Multiplicative Homomorphism [20]
   1. Encrypt two plaintext values: $c_1 = m_1^e (\text{mod n})$, $c_2 = m_2^e (\text{mod n})$
   2. Compute the product of ciphertexts: $c_{product} = c_1.c_2 \text{ (mod n)}$
   3. Decrypt the result: $m_{product} = c_{product}^d \text{ (mod n)} = m_1.m_2 \text{ (mod n)}$

   Simulated Addition

   Simulated homomorphic addition can be implemented as follows:
   1. Encrypt two plaintext values: $c_1 = m_1^e (\text{mod n})$, $c_2 = m_2^e (\text{mod n})$
   2. Encode the addition operation: $c_{sum} = c_1 + c_2 \text{ (mod n)}$
   3. Decrypt the result: $m_{sum} = c_{sum}^d \text{ (mod n)} \approx m_1 + m_2 \text{ (mod n)}$

c. Quantum X Gate (Pauli-X Gate)

The X gate, also known as the Pauli-X gate, is a fundamental quantum gate that performs a bit-flip operation. It is the quantum analog of the classical NOT gate.

The X gate flips the state of a qubit:

- If the qubit is in the $|0\rangle$ state, it flips to $|1\rangle$|
- If the qubit is in the $|1\rangle$ state, it flips to $|0\rangle$.

Mathematically:

$$X|0\rangle=|1\rangle, X|1\rangle=|0\rangle$$

18.4 HEALTHCARE DATA SECURITY USING QUANTUM HOMOMORPHIC ENCRYPTION

The methodology of this work revolves around implementing QHE using the RSA encryption scheme to securely process sensitive medical data (Diabetes dataset) while performing homomorphic operations without revealing the data. The approach consists of several key components, each contributing to secure encryption, homomorphic operations, and decryption. The following steps outline the methodology used in the code:

The methodology can be divided into several distinct phases to structure the process of applying QHE with RSA for secure processing of the Diabetes dataset. Each phase focuses on specific tasks, leading to encryption, secure computation, and decryption while preserving privacy, shown in Figure 18.1.

Phase 1: Data Preparation and Pre-processing:

- Dataset Selection: The Diabetes dataset is loaded from sklearn and contains various features related to diabetes and medical information.
- Scaling: To simulate integer-based encryption, each feature is scaled by multiplying by a factor (e.g., 1000). This scaling ensures that the values remain in an appropriate range for encryption.

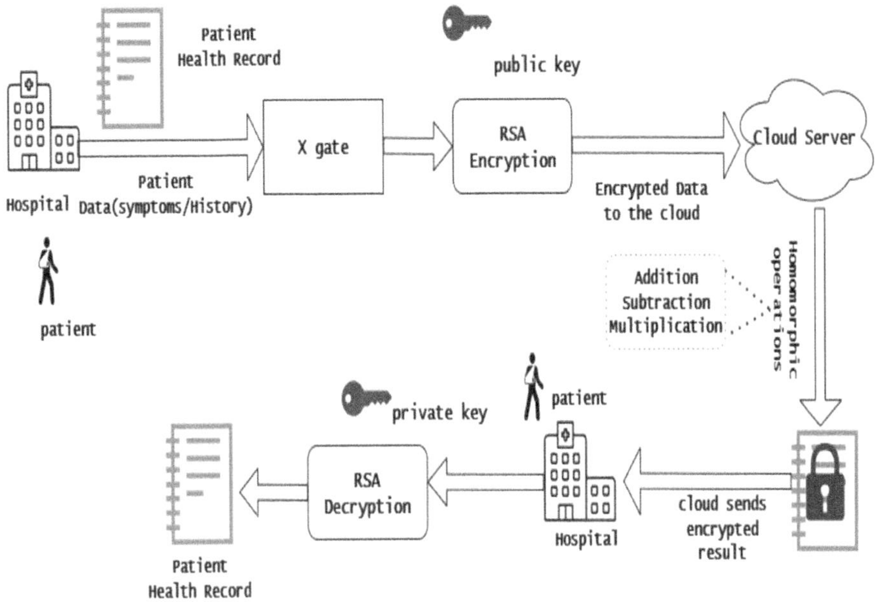

FIGURE 18.1 Architecture of the healthcare data using QHE.

- Conversion to Integers: After scaling, the feature values are converted into integers to make them compatible with the RSA encryption process, as RSA requires integer inputs. The detailed algorithm is as follows:

Algorithm: Data Pre-processing

Input:

—Dataset X: A matrix of features (rows represent samples, columns represent features).
—ScalingFactor s: A constant factor to scale the features (e.g., 1000).

Output:

—Scaled Dataset X_scaled: Scaled and integer-converted dataset.

Steps:

1. Initialize an empty list X_scaled to store the processed data.
2. For each feature x in each row of dataset X:
   a. Scale each feature by multiplying it with the scaling factor s: x_scaled = x * s.
   b. Convert x_scaled to integer (round or floor value).
3. Store each processed feature x_scaled into the list X_scaled.
4. Return the processed dataset X_scaled.

Phase 2: RSA Key Generation

- Prime Generation: Small prime numbers are selected (e.g., 17, 19, 23) for simplicity. In real-world scenarios, much larger primes would be chosen.
- Public and Private Key Generation: Using the primes, the RSA public key (n, e) and private key (d) are generated.
- Key Storage: The public key is used for encryption, while the private key is used for decryption.

Phase 3: Quantum Circuit Construction for Encryption and Decryption

- Quantum Encryption:
  - Each feature value is converted to binary and padded to fit within a quantum circuit (e.g., 10 qubits).
  - Quantum gates (specifically X gates) are applied to encode each binary bit into a qubit. The X gate flips a qubit to encode a 1 bit, while the qubit remains unchanged for a 0 bit.
  - Classical RSA encryption is then performed on the data. The encrypted message is calculated using the formula encrypted message=(m^e) % n.
  - The encryption is simulated in the quantum circuit by manipulating qubits to represent the encrypted message detailed sequences are shown in the below algorithm.

Algorithm: Quantum Encryption

Input:

—Message m: An integer to be encrypted.
—Public key (n, e): RSA public key.
—q: The number of qubits to encode the message.

Output:

—quantum_circuit: A quantum circuit containing encrypted qubits.

Steps:

1. Convert the message m to its binary representation (m_binary).
2. Initialize an empty quantum circuit with q qubits.
3. For each bit b in m_binary:
   a. If b == 1, apply an X gate to the corresponding qubit.
4. Perform classical RSA encryption: encrypted_message = (m^e) % n.
5. Encode the encrypted_message into the quantum circuit using appropriate quantum operations.
6. Return the quantum circuit containing the encrypted message.

Phase 4: Homomorphic Operations on Encrypted Data

- Homomorphic Addition:
  - Encrypted data undergoes homomorphic operations (e.g., addition). This means performing the addition of encrypted data without decrypting it.
  - Homomorphic addition is performed both on the quantum side (simulated by quantum operations) and on the classical side for validation purposes.
  - This phase allows the computation on encrypted data while ensuring that the privacy of the data is maintained throughout the process represented in the following algorithm.

Algorithm: Homomorphic Addition on Encrypted Data

Input:

—m1_encrypted: The first encrypted message (in quantum form).
—m2_encrypted: The second encrypted message (in quantum form).
—n: RSA modulus.

Output:

—m_result_encrypted: The result of the homomorphic addition, encrypted.

Steps:

1. Add the two encrypted messages modulo n:
m_result_encrypted = (m1_encrypted + m2_encrypted) % n.
2. Return the result m_result_encrypted.

Phase 5: Quantum Decryption and Result Verification

- Quantum Decryption:
  - After homomorphic operations, the encrypted qubits are measured, and the classical message is extracted.
  - The quantum decryption is based on the private key d, applying the formula decrypted message=(encrypted message^d)mod n.

The decrypted binary message is then converted back to its integer form, simulating the quantum decryption process.

- Verification:
  - The quantum homomorphic results are compared with the classical homomorphic results. This comparison ensures that the quantum homomorphic encryption and computation are valid.
  - A small tolerance is allowed due to potential minor discrepancies in floating-point calculations, but the results should match closely.
  - If the decrypted quantum results match the classical homomorphic results, the verification is successful.

Algorithm: Decryption and Verification

Input:

—m_result_encrypted: The encrypted result of homomorphic operations.
—m_classical_result: The result of homomorphic addition performed classically.
—Private key d: RSA private key.

Output:

—Verification Status: "Verification successful" or "Verification failed".

Steps:

1. Decrypt the encrypted result m_result_encrypted using quantum decryption to obtain m_result_decrypted.
2. Compare m_result_decrypted with the classical result m_classical_result:
   a. If abs(m_result_decrypted—m_classical_result) < tolerance:
   —Print "Verification successful".
   b. Else:
   —Print "Verification failed".
3. Return the verification status.

The overall methodology combines quantum and classical cryptographic techniques to secure medical data processing. Using quantum circuits to simulate RSA encryption and decryption, we can perform homomorphic operations on encrypted data. The approach ensures privacy and allows for the verification of results, making it suitable for privacy-preserving data analysis in fields like healthcare, where data confidentiality is crucial.

18.5 EXPERIMENTATION AND RESULT ANALYSIS

The suggested approach is tested using both traditional RSA deployment and quantum simulations with the Cirq framework in a virtualized environment. RSA encryption and decryption operations are performed on Google Colab with its added advantage of facilitation of easy Python-based terminal executions. For purposes of simulating actual encryption operations, the RSA algorithm is modified to accommodate different input sizes. Particularly, 20 KB, 40 KB, 60 KB, 80 KB, and 100 KB input files are used to test performance with varying volumes of data. All input files contain synthetic patient health data so that unique and relevant data is applied for every iteration of the encryption process.

To measure the computational effect of the RSA algorithm, system resource usage is tracked during the encryption and decryption phases. For every input size, the algorithm is run several times in order to get dependable and uniform performance measures. CPU and memory utilization are tracked at one-second intervals during run time, and the data gathered is saved to log files for offline analysis.

Application to the Diabetes Dataset: As a working example, the simulation platform is used on the Diabetes dataset, which includes sensitive medical features like age, body mass index (BMI), and glucose levels. The experiment consists of simulating RSA encryption through quantum circuits, executing homomorphic operations (e.g., addition) on encrypted data directly, and then decrypting the outcome—all within the quantum simulation platform. This configuration demonstrates the viability of secure data processing through quantum-assisted cryptographic methods in a healthcare scenario.

The Diabetes dataset is shown in Table 18.1, first pre-processed by scaling the features to integer values within a suitable range for encryption. This scaling is achieved by multiplying each feature by 1,000. For each feature in the dataset, RSA encryption is applied, where each feature value is encrypted using the public key (n, e). The result is an encrypted dataset (encrypted_X), which contains encrypted values simulating quantum-based encryption. Each row in this dataset represents an encrypted feature vector of a patient, where individual feature values are encrypted using RSA.

Homomorphic operations, specifically homomorphic addition, are performed on the encrypted data. In this simulated operation, the first two encrypted features from each row of the dataset are added together. For each patient (or row), the first two encrypted features are added under encryption, and the result is stored in homomorphic_encrypted_data. After completing the homomorphic addition on the encrypted values, the results are decrypted using the private key (n, d). The decrypted values are then scaled back to their original range by dividing by 1,000, as the features were

TABLE 18.1
Description of Diabetes Dataset

Feature Name	Description	Range of Values	Unit
Age	Patient age	21 to 81	Years
Sex	Patient gender (binary: male or female)	0 (female) to 1 (male)	Binary (0/1)
BMI	Body mass index (calculated as weight in kg/m²)	18.2 to 67.1	kg/m²
BloodPressure	Blood pressure (mean value of 2 hours post-challenge)	24 to 122	mm Hg
SkinThickness	Triceps skinfold thickness (a measure of body fat)	7 to 99	Mm
Insulin	2-hour serum insulin concentration (measured after a glucose tolerance test)	0 to 846	μU/ml
DiabetesPedigreeFunction	The likelihood of diabetes based on family history	0.078 to 2.42	N/A
Glucose	Plasma glucose concentration (2-hour post-challenge in oral glucose tolerance test)	0 to 199	mg/dL
Pregnancies	Number of pregnancies the patient has had	0 to 17	Count (int)
Outcome	Target variable indicating the presence or absence of diabetes (1 = diabetic, 0 = non-diabetic)	0 or 1	Binary (0/1)

previously scaled for encryption. These decrypted values correspond to the sum of the first two features of the original dataset, with the values scaled back to the original range.

In this experiment, Cirq is utilized to simulate how quantum algorithms might interact with or complement RSA in the future. For example, quantum key distribution (QKD) or hybrid encryption systems, which combine classical and quantum encryption methods, are explored. While RSA is still a classical encryption scheme, these simulations investigate how quantum advancements or the development of quantum-resistant algorithms could impact the security and performance of RSA.

The results provide a comprehensive understanding of how RSA encryption scales with different input sizes and its effect on system resource utilization, specifically CPU and memory. By measuring resource consumption during the encryption and decryption of input files of sizes 20 KB, 40 KB, 60 KB, 80 KB, and 100 KB, the experiment yields insights into how RSA handles increasing data volumes and the corresponding system impact. Table 18.2 shows a comparative analysis of key generation time in RSA vs. Paillier by varying key size; we can observe RSA is showing less than Paillier. Table 18.3 shows the comparative analysis of RSA w.r.t. Paillier encryption in terms of time complexity CPU utilization and memory utilization; we can observe that RSA time complexity is lesser than Paillier even though it is taking more CPU and memory than Paillier.

Figure 18.2(a) and (b) shows the detailed performance analysis of the proposed technique on the diabetes dataset in terms of CPU utilization and memory utilization. From the figure we can observe that, the homomorphic techniques is taking less CPU as well as the memory. In Figure 18.2(c) and (d), the scaled features distribution is shown without usage of homomorphic encryption, and using RSA homomorphic technique, it is observed that, almost, it shows the same distribution in both the images. Similarly the analysis of the proposed technique is observed in terms of decryption of the diabetes dataset using RSA and RSA-based homomorphic technique is shown in Figure 18.2(e). It is observed that, RSA-based homomorphic technique can decrypt the dataset without any deviation like RSA.

TABLE 18.2
Comparative analysis of Key Generation Time of RSA vs. Paillier

Algorithm	Key Generation Time with 256-Bit Key Size (ms)	Key Generation Time with 512-Bit Key Size (ms)	Key Generation Time with 1,024-Bit Key Size (ms)
RSA	25	289	450
Paillier	235	789	1545

TABLE 18.3
Comparative Analysis of CPU and Memory Utilization of RSA vs. Paillier

	Average Execution Time (min)		CPU Utilization (%)		Memory Utilization (MB)	
File Size (KB)	RSA	Paillier	RSA	Paillier	RSA	Paillier
20	2.1	5.5	41.4	41.3	48	45
40	4.3	11.1	41.4	41.4	49	46
60	6.4	16.3	41.7	41.6	50	48
80	8.58	22.4	41.8	41.7	51	49
100	11.3	27.2	41.8	41.9	52	51

18.6 CONCLUSION

In this chapter, we demonstrated the integration of classical RSA encryption with quantum simulation to encrypt and perform homomorphic operations on medical data, specifically the Diabetes dataset. The process involved encrypting feature values using RSA, simulating quantum-based encryption with quantum circuits, and performing homomorphic addition on encrypted data without requiring decryption.

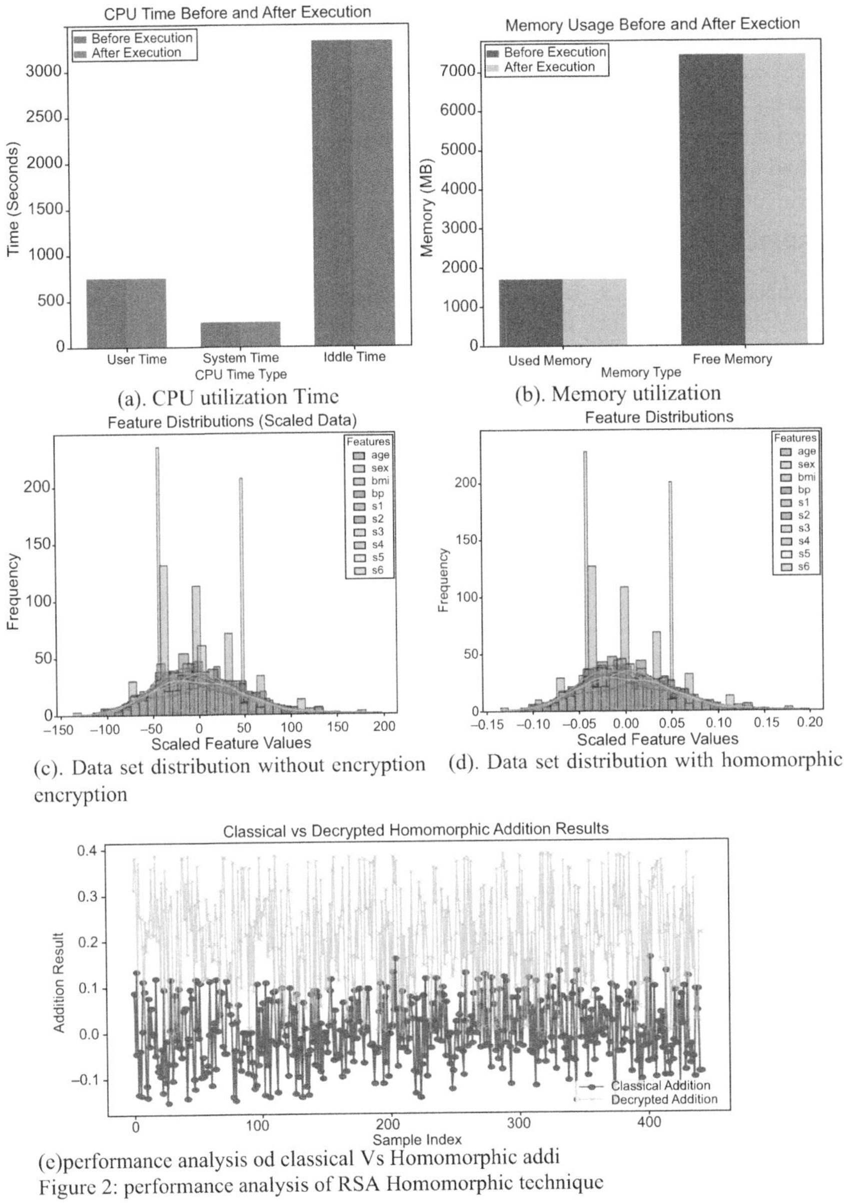

FIGURE 18.2 Performance analysis of RSA homomorphic technique.

The results showed how homomorphic encryption, although not natively supported in classical RSA, can be simulated using modular arithmetic operations like addition and multiplication. This enables privacy-preserving computations on encrypted data, which is a crucial requirement for scenarios where sensitive information, such as medical data, needs to be processed without exposing the raw values.

In conclusion, this approach showcases the power of combining classical and quantum techniques for secure data processing, with applications extending beyond medical data to areas like finance, secure communication, and privacy-preserving machine learning. However, future work could explore more efficient quantum algorithms for encryption and homomorphic operations, as well as the potential benefits of actual quantum hardware in these tasks.

REFERENCES

1. Mohammed, S. J., & Taha, D. B. (2022, March). Performance evaluation of RSA, ElGamal, and paillier partial homomorphic encryption algorithms. In 2022 International Conference on Computer Science and Software Engineering (CSASE) (pp. 89–94). IEEE.
2. Zerka, F., Barakat, S., Walsh, S., Bogowicz, M., Leijenaar, R. T., Jochems, A., . . . & Lambin, P. (2020). Systematic review of privacy-preserving distributed machine learning from federated databases in health care. JCO Clinical Cancer Informatics, 4, 184–200.
3. Munjal, K., & Bhatia, R. (2022). A systematic review of homomorphic encryption and its contributions in healthcare industry. Complex & Intelligent Systems. https://doi.org/10.1007/s40747-022-00756-z.
4. Rivest, R. L., Shamir, A., & Adleman, L. (1978). A method for obtaining digital signatures and public-key cryptosystems. Communications of the ACM, 21(2), 120–126.
5. Munjal, K., & Bhatia, R. (2022). Analysing RSA and paillier homomorphic property for security in cloud. Procedia Computer Science, 215, 240–246.
6. Hammami, H., Brahmi, H., Brahmi, I., & Ben Yahia, S. (2017, September 7–8). Using homomorphic encryption to compute privacy preserving data mining in a cloud computing environment. In Information Systems: 14th European, Mediterranean, and Middle Eastern Conference, EMCIS 2017, Coimbra, Portugal, Proceedings 14 (pp. 397–413). Springer International Publishing.
7. Mfungo, D. E., & Fu, X. (2023). Fractal-based hybrid cryptosystem: Enhancing image encryption with RSA, homomorphic encryption, and chaotic maps. Entropy, 25(11), 1478.
8. Rubia, A., & Iwendi, C. (2021). An optimised homomorphic CRT-RSA algorithm for security and efficient communication. Personal and Ubiquitous Computing. https://doi.org/10.1007/s00779-021-016,07-3.
9. Jiang Liu, Qin Li, Junyu Quan, Can Wang, Jinjing Shi & Haozhen Situ. (2022). Efficient quantum homomorphic encryption scheme with flexible evaluators and its simulation. Designs, Codes and Cryptography, 90(3), 577–591.
10. Jonas Zeuner, Ioannis Pitsios, Si-Hui Tan, Aditya N. Sharma, Joseph F. Fitzsimons, Roberto Osellame & Philip Walther. (2021). Experimental quantum homomorphic encryption. NPJ Quantum Information, 7(1), 25.
11. Jing-Wen Zhang, Gang Xu, Xiu-Bo Chen, Yan Chang, Zhi-Chao Dong. (2023). Improved multiparty quantum private comparison based on quantum homomorphic encryption. Physica A: Statistical Mechanics and Its Applications, 610, 128397.
12. Aggarwal, L., Sachdeva, S., & Goswami, P. (2023). Quantum healthcare computing using precision based granular approach. Applied Soft Computing, 144, 110458.
13. Qu, Z., Zhang, Z., & Zheng, M. (2022). A quantum blockchain-enabled framework for secure private electronic medical records in Internet of Medical Things. Information Sciences, 612, 942–958.

14. Chang, W., Li, Z. Z., You, F. C., & Pan, X. B. (2023). Dynamic quantum fully homomorphic encryption scheme based on universal quantum circuit. Journal of Information Security and Applications, 75, 103510.
15. Abidin, S., Swami, A., Ramirez-Asís, E., Alvarado-Tolentino, J., Maurya, R. K., & Hussain, N. (2022). Quantum cryptography technique: A way to improve security challenges in mobile cloud computing (MCC). Materials Today: Proceedings, 51, 508–514.
16. Newaz, A. I., Sikder, A. K., Rahman, M. A., & Uluagac, A. S. (2021). A survey on security and privacy issues in modern healthcare systems: Attacks and defenses. ACM Transactions on Computing for Healthcare, 2(3), 1–44.
17. Pulipeti, S., & Kumar, A. (2023). Secure quantum computing for healthcare sector: A short analysis. Security and Privacy, 6(5), e293.
18. Perumal, A. M., & Nadar, E. R. S. (2021). Retracted Article: Architectural framework and simulation of quantum key optimization techniques in healthcare networks for data security. Journal of Ambient Intelligence and Humanized Computing, 12(7), 7173–7180.
19. Kiratsata, H. J., & Panchal, M. (2021). A comparative analysis of machine learning models developed from homomorphic encryption based RSA and Paillier algorithm. In 2021 5th International Conference on Intelligent Computing and Control Systems (ICICCS) (pp. 1458–1465). IEEE.
20. Kamatchi, T. P., & Kumari, K. A. (2023). A hybrid homomorphic model with RSA algorithm and modified enhanced homomorphic encryption technique. In 2023 International Conference on Intelligent Systems for Communication, IoT and Security (ICISCoIS) (pp. 371–375). IEEE.

19 Quantum Communication Systems for Ensuring Secure 6G Network Infrastructure

Haranadha Reddy Busireddy Seshakagari, K. Reddy Madhavi, Nagaraj Ramrao, and Manasa Gadiraju

19.1 INTRODUCTION

History of communications technology has brought us to the era of sixth-generation (6G) network that have higher data rate, zero-latency, end-to-end communication, and enabling ubiquitous computing. All these achievements have been accompanied by an unprecedently high degree of security and data privacy problems. Current cryptographic techniques, while secure at present, are progressively under threat from the processing power of quantum computers and highly advanced cyberattacks, and they threaten the survival of integrity within the communications environment of the current era.

Quantum communication systems (QCS) provide an innovative solution for such issues through the use of principles of quantum mechanics in establishing extremely secure communication protocols. Methods such as quantum key distribution (QKD) provide unbreakable encryption via the process of entanglement and the effect of superposition at the quantum level. This enables secure key exchange and renders the process of eavesdropping nearly impossible. With the incorporation of the 6G network architecture with QCS, we can potentially create the basis of communication system that, beyond being secure in design, also becomes future-proof.

6G is the next wireless communications revolution, setting foundations upon 5G. The development of 6G will be underway by the 2030s, and it will be able to revolutionize how we communicate, interact, and utilize technology in ways we are not yet even imaging today. With 6G, the aim is to realize the true potential of ubiquitous, ultra-reliable, and high-speed connectivity beyond conventional mobile communication systems.

6G will provide super-high data speeds of up to 1 terabit per second (Tbps) to facilitate applications that require gargantuan amounts of bandwidth, including holographic communication, real-time processing of artificial intelligence (AI), and

 DOI: 10.1201/9781003538950-22

more, as well as super-immersive virtual and augmented reality experiences. Apart from speed, 6G will allow low-latency connections and super robust network infrastructure capable of handling effortlessly the huge amounts of data from the expanding internet of things (IoT).

One of the most striking aspects of 6G is its compatibility with future technologies such as artificial intelligence (AI), machine learning (ML), and quantum communication. Not only do they enhance network performance but also enable intelligent, self-configuring networks with real-time adaptability to changing situations. 6G network will also be green, with green technology support and energy efficiency as intrinsic priorities. 6G will lead to the foundation of a connected and intelligent world, fundamentally altering our life, labor, and online interactions. Emphasizing safe, fast, and reliable communication, 6G can provide innovations that will transform industries from medicine to entertainment, education to transportation and beyond.

Integrating quantum communication systems in 6G infrastructure increases its security and addresses the demand for secure, efficient, and scalable solutions for future hyper-connected ecosystems. This conversation highlights the pioneering role of quantum communication systems in making 6G network secure, focusing on their technological aspects and challenges of implementation.

19.2 LITERATURE SURVEY

Quantum communication employs underlying principles of amount mechanics, such as superposition and trap, to enable secure and effective data transmission. This check examines major developments, challenges, and practices in amount communication. QKD is an extremely advanced and most extensively studied operations of amount communication.

The role of quantum encryption in secure data distribution in multi-scale IoT installations as an inherent aspect of 6G networks [1]. Rozenman et al. (2023) highlighted the cooperative nature of 6G networks and quantum information technologies. Their premise was based on the potential that quantum repeaters and entanglement distribution would make large-scale quantum networks possible in this infrastructure [2]. Thommandru (2024) showed that QKD would be able to withstand more than 70% of cyberattacks in 6G networks, proving its effectiveness in securing networks [3].

Patel (2024) mentioned the integration of QKD into 6G networks under infrastructure expense and system complexity, highlighted incorporating QC protocols in the future 6G network infrastructure. In order to overcome potential interoperability challenges, they proposed developing hybrid systems that have a natural coexistence of classical and quantum technology. In his study, he discovered how QC uses can make the security and efficiency of 6G network stronger. They specifically mentioned benefits for autonomous systems and remote healthcare, suggesting quantum communication could make these applications more robust [4]. Studies like that conducted by Khan et al. (2022) highlights the significance of quantum encryption in enabling secure data transfer in large-scale IoT deployments, which is one of the essential features of 6G networks [5].

The BB84 protocol laid the groundwork for QKD, proposing a process for secure key exchange that can sense eavesdropping based on quantum principles. Variants include E91 protocol. Ekert, 1991) employ trap for added security [6]. Recent studies have directed efforts to expand QKD efficiency, range, and integration into traditional networks [7]. Satellite-based QKD systems, demonstrated by China's Micius satellite, highlight significant advancements in extending the range of quantum-secure communication [8].

While QKD offers physical-layer security, researchers like have explored post-quantum cryptography (PQC) to safeguard classical encryption against quantum attacks [9]. Literature highlights the complementary roles of QKD and PQC in 6G security, where QKD secures key exchange, and PQC protects data integrity and confidentiality.

6G is anticipated to utilize the THz frequency range (100 GHz to 10 THz) to achieve ultra-high-bandwidth capabilities. Research focuses on channel modeling, materials, and new antenna designs for THz frequencies [10]. AI and ML are expected to play a major role in optimizing network performance, managing resources, predicting network traffic, and enabling intelligent automation. Blockchain can provide secure, decentralized network management and improve data privacy, trust, and transparency. VLC using LED lights is being explored for high-speed communication in indoor environments, providing an alternative to RF-based communication. Quantum technology may be used for ultra-secure communications through QKD and to optimize network operations using quantum algorithms [11]. Integrated sensing and communication (ISAC) merges communication and sensing capabilities to improve both wireless communication and environmental awareness (e.g., for autonomous vehicles or industrial IoT). Applications of 6G are autonomous systems, remote healthcare and telemedicine, smart cities and IoT, extended reality (XR), ultra-high-definition media [12].

Quantum networks, which enable secure communication across multiple nodes, are a key focus for integrating quantum communication into 6G. Studies emphasize the importance of entanglement distribution and quantum repeaters in building scalable quantum networks [13]. Such networks can support global quantum communication, ensuring end-to-end security for 6G infrastructure.

The deployment of quantum communication systems in 6G faces technical challenges, such as high costs, limited range, and the need for compatible hardware [14]. Researchers examine satellite-based QKD to cross distance barriers, while others research photonic integration to minimize cost and enhance scalability [15]. Hybrid classical-quantum architectures are also being researched to address the quantum-traditional system interoperability in 6G networks.

DARPA's Quantum Network and Military Applications in the United States is focused on incorporating quantum communication into defense networks [16]. This project will look into applying quantum encryption to military communication, where security is the top priority [17]. One of the most important contributions of the DARPA Quantum Network is its research into quantum-safe cryptography and how it can be integrated into current defense infrastructure, which is still vulnerable to future breakthroughs in quantum computing [18]. By implementing QKD in a military communications system, DARPA is seeking to establish secure, tamper-proof channels of communication [19].

Although this initiative is still in its infancy, its potential impact on 6G is colossal. The creation of quantum-secured communication for defense networks will act as a proving ground for equivalent uses in strategic civilian infrastructure [20]. It also serves to highlight the importance of effective quantum key management and quantum-safe cryptography protocols that can be utilized in both the military and civilian spheres. These advancements are key to gaining an understanding of integrating quantum systems with the old infrastructure—the major challenge toward mass 6G deployment [21]. Figure 19.1 shows DARPA's quantum network for military communication:

Quantum communication networks are being customized to meet specific 6G applications, including secure IoT communication, autonomous driving, and telemedicine.

Quantum communication protocols need to be standardized for their adoption across all 6G.

Initiatives by organizations like International Telecommunication Union (ITU) and the European Telecommunications Standards Institute (ETSI) are defining quantum-secure communication standards.

19.3 DESCRIPTION

The methodology of QCS is to ensure secure 6G network infrastructure focuses on integrating quantum technologies with classical systems to address the emerging security challenges posed by the growing need for privacy, authentication, and data integrity in future communication networks. The methodology can be structured into several key phases, starting from theoretical foundations to practical implementation. Figure 19.2 represents step-by-step breakdown of how these components interact in practice to ensure secure, scalable, and high-performance communication for practical 6G applications.

19.3.1 Quantum Communication Layer

Quantum communication is a method of transmitting information using quantum states of particles, like photons, instead of classical bits. It practices concepts of quantum mechanics like entanglement and superposition for secure communication. It involves QKD system and quantum-secure encryption process. QKD used for the distribution of cryptographic keys securely makes eavesdropping interfere with the quantum states, informing the communicating parties about the potential violation. The process can be employed to ensure data integrity and privacy in 6G networks. Researchers may investigate how QKD can be integrated in current 5G and upcoming 6G infrastructures. QKD comprises QKD protocols and quantum channel. QKD protocols uses methods of securely sharing cryptographic keys on a possibly insecure communication channel by using the laws of quantum mechanics.

The most extensively researched and deployed QKD protocols are based on the intrinsic properties of quantum states, such as superposition and entanglement. Among the most significant QKD protocols are the BB84 protocol (Bennett and Brassard, 1984), E91 protocol (Ekert, 1991), B92 protocol (Bennett, 1992), six-state protocol (Gisin, 2002), continuous variable QKD (CV-QKD), and measurement-device-independent QKD (MDI-QKD). QKD protocols utilize the fundamental aspects of quantum mechanics in order to ensure that cryptographic keys are exchanged securely with the primary advantage of detecting eavesdropping. Different protocols offer different

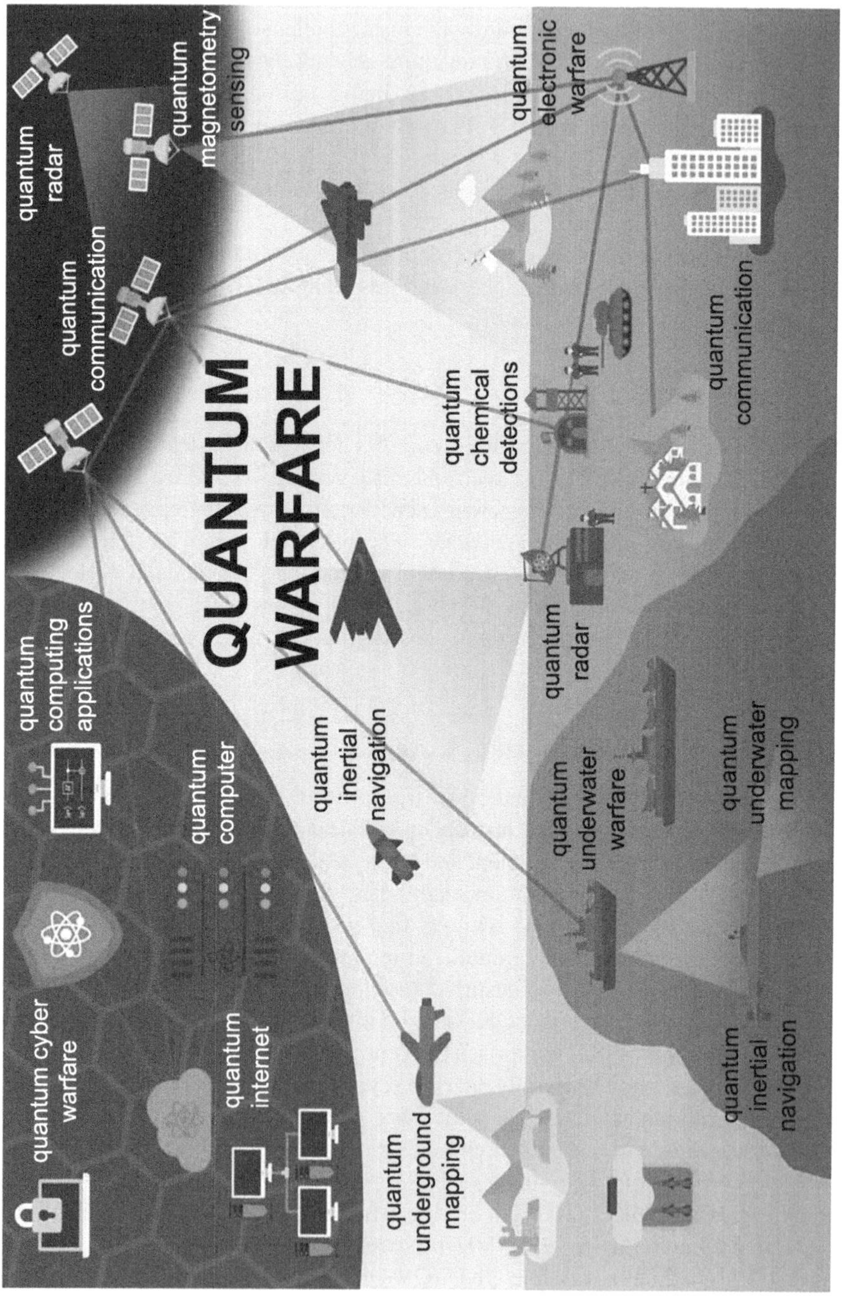

FIGURE 19.1 DARPA's quantum network for military communication.

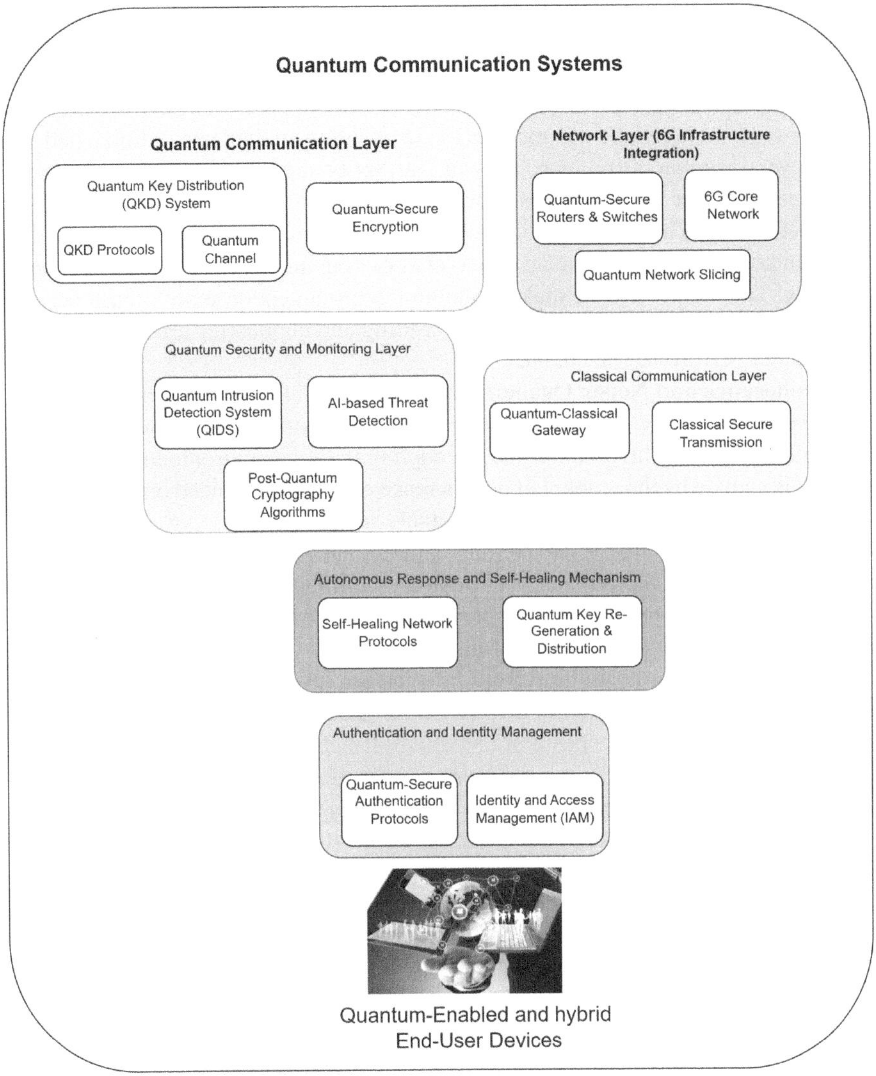

FIGURE 19.2 Overview of quantum communication systems.

levels of security, efficiency, and usability, and the technology continues to develop in order to develop more scalable and accessible quantum communication in practice.

A quantum channel is a channel over which quantum information (most commonly encoded as quantum states like qubits or photons) is communicated from one entity to another. In contrast to classical communication channels, which carry classical bits of information, a quantum channel employs the principles of quantum mechanics to send quantum bits (qubits) or quantum states. The key characteristics of a quantum channel include the following:

Quantum Superposition: A quantum channel may have quantum information transmitted in a superposition state; i.e., a qubit may have several states simultaneously until it is measured. This allows for richer information transmission than classical bits.

Quantum Entanglement: Quantum channels such as entangled photon pairs allow quantum information to be communicated via quantum entanglement. Entangled particles have a peculiar correlation, allowing instant communication between particles even separated over long distances, a property central to uses such as QKD.

Non-Cloning Theorem: The non-cloning theorem, a peculiar property of quantum channels, asserts that the arbitrary unknown quantum state cannot be copied precisely. This characteristic makes quantum communication more secure because it thwarts an eavesdropper from perfectly reading and duplicating quantum information without perturbing the channel.

Decoherence and Noise: Quantum information on its way in a quantum channel (say fiber optics or free space) is prone to decoherence (information loss of the quantum type) and noise (disturbance due to coupling with the environment). A quantum channel is gauged by the amount of decoherence or noise introduced on transmission.

Loss and Attenuation: Quantum channels suffer from loss (e.g., photon loss in optical fiber) and attenuation (weakening of the signal over long distance), which puts a limit on the range and efficiency of quantum communication. Quantum repeaters are being developed to bypass these challenges and expand the distance over which quantum information can be safely transmitted.

QC is medium to transmit quantum information, usually quantum states of photons or other quantum systems. It is based on the unusual properties of quantum mechanics, including superposition and entanglement, to facilitate secure communication. Quantum channels are, however, susceptible to issues such as noise, decoherence, and short range, with research being conducted in the effort to make them more precise and longer-range for practical application in such things as quantum cryptography and the quantum internet.

Quantum-secure encryption is an encryption method resistant to quantum computer attacks. Classic encryption algorithms, including RSA and ECC (elliptic curve cryptography), are based on the hardness of solving some mathematical problems (such as factoring big numbers or discrete logarithms) solving tasks that would take an impractically large amount of classical computers to complete. However, quantum computers could potentially solve these problems effectively, which can be dangerous to the security of current cryptographic systems.

Key concepts in quantum-secure encryption include **mutual information and error rate in QKD**, defined as the quantum key distribution error rate "e" that controls the number of information to be exchanged securely between the sender (Alice) and the receiver (Bob). The secret key rate "R" is influenced by the error rate and is calculated as:

$$R=\eta(1-H(e))$$

where R is secret key rate, η is the transmission efficiency, and e is the QC error rate.

The security of QKD comes from the fact that any eavesdropping on quantum communication will disturb the quantum states being transmitted [22], making the interception detectable. This offers a layer of security that is theoretically immune to attacks from both classical and quantum computers.

19.3.2 Network Layer–6G Infrastructure Integration

The network layer in the context of integration of 6G infrastructure is the portion of the network architecture that performs routing and data forwarding between systems and devices within a network. It is key to communication management across various and heterogeneous networks, such as terrestrial, satellite, and IoT networks, in the context of next-generation 6G infrastructure. Its role in 6G infrastructure includes the following:

Connectivity Across Diverse Networks: 6G will incorporate a high number of networks, such as terrestrial (cellular), satellite, edge, and even non-terrestrial networks (NTN), as well as IoT protocol-connected devices. The network layer will have the duty of providing end-to-end seamless data transmission between these various networks so that the communication is always efficient and smooth irrespective of the network used.

Software-Defined Networking (SDN) and **Network Function Virtualization (NFV)**: 6G will employ SDN and NFV to provide more scalable, flexible, and programmable network architectures. The network layer will have a crucial role in implementing these techniques, including dynamic reconfiguration and configuration of network resources.

End-to-End QoS (Quality of Service): In the case of mission-critical applications (e.g., self-driving cars, real-time medical care, immersive AR/VR experiences), the network layer will ensure the delivery of data packets with the requisite quality level of quality.

The 6G network layer have key technologies. 6G will need enhanced routing protocols capable of handling massive-scale, ultra-low-latency, and ultra-reliable communication, especially for use cases like autonomous driving and remote surgery. ML will be used to predict traffic routes, plan routes optimally, and change routes dynamically. 6G will bring in network slicing, where the physical network is divided virtually into several logical networks (slices) that can be tailored for various services. The network layer will manage the slices efficiently, such that each of them is optimized to meet the particular requirements of its users. AI and ML will be implemented at the network layer to forecast traffic congestion, route optimization, and real-time network performance. AI/ML models can learn to respond to varying network conditions, providing optimal utilization of resources. Edge computing, blockchain, and decentralized systems will be a component of 6G infrastructure. The network layer will be important in ensuring the decentralized systems (e.g., distributed ledger networks) seamlessly interoperate with the conventional centralized ones.

Quantum-secure routers and switches are networking appliances that are built to utilize quantum cryptography principles to enable highly secure communications. Quantum-secure routers and switches apply QKD and quantum encryption to prevent data from being intercepted or altered, allowing security theoretically immune to common hacking techniques, including those employed using future, more powerful quantum computers. Its applications are as follows:

Data Protection in Critical Infrastructure: Quantum-secure routers and switches can be applied to sectors such as finance, healthcare, and government, where strong data security is required.

Future-Proofing Networks: As quantum computing advances, current cryptographic techniques will become vulnerable at some point. Quantum-secure devices future-proof networks against quantum-enabled attacks.

Essentially, quantum-secure routers and switches are a leap ahead of constructing ultra-secure communication networks, designed to meet the challenges of the future of quantum computing.

The 6G core network is the fundamental element of the 6G wireless communication network, which will act as the hub for controlling, orchestrating, and managing communication among different devices, networks, and services in an extremely integrated, scalable, and intelligent way. It is an upgrade of the existing 5G core network but with better capabilities that will cater to the futuristic needs of 6G, such as ultra-low latency, massive connectivity, and smart service delivery.

Key Technologies in 6G Core Network:

- **AI/ML for Predictive Maintenance and Optimization**: Application of ML to forecast network problems and optimize traffic in real time.
- **Advanced 5G/6G Protocols**: New protocols optimized for increased throughput, reduced latency, and increased flexibility.
- **Terahertz Spectrum and Ultra-Wideband**: The 6G core will most probably utilize new frequency bands, such as terahertz (THz) spectrum, for ultra-high-speed communication.
- **Advanced Virtualization and Cloudification**: The core of 6G will rely extensively on the cloud with network function virtualization (NFV) and software-defined networking (SDN) for more flexibility and scalability.

Quantum network slicing is a process of partitioning a quantum network into several virtual, isolated slices—each of which is designed for different users or applications. Like 5G network slicing, it makes sharing scarce quantum resources such as entangled qubits, quantum repeaters, and quantum memory efficient. Every slice can be configured to host multiple quantum services, including QKD to enable secure data exchange, distributed quantum computing, and quantum sensing. The method enhances scalability, flexibility, and resource efficiency in future quantum internet architectures.

19.3.3 Quantum Security and Monitoring Layer

This layer provides secure communication and real-time observation of quantum network activities. It's an essential component of the quantum network framework.

Quantum networks are highly susceptible to interference, and quantum information can't be replicated (no-cloning theorem).

A **quantum intrusion detection system (QIDS)** is a next-generation cybersecurity system that uses quantum technologies to detect unauthorized access or threats in a network. Unlike traditional IDS, QIDS leverages principles like quantum entanglement, superposition, and QKD to provide faster, more secure, and more accurate threat detection. It can detect even subtle anomalies or intrusions, especially in quantum communication networks, and is designed to be resistant to attacks from quantum computers, making it crucial for future-proof cybersecurity.

AI-based threat detection uses artificial intelligence (especially machine learning and deep learning) to automatically identify and respond [23] to cybersecurity threats. It analyzes huge volumes of data—like network traffic, user behavior, or system logs—to detect anomalies, malware, or suspicious activity in real time. Unlike traditional rule-based systems, AI analyzes patterns, adapts to evolving threats, and can even anticipate attacks before they occur. It's especially useful for detecting zero-day attacks, insider threats, and advanced persistent threats (APTs).

Post-quantum cryptography (PQC) refers to cryptographic algorithms specifically designed to remain secure against attacks from both classical and quantum computers. Unlike QKD, PQC algorithms do not rely on quantum principles for key distribution but are designed to withstand the capabilities of quantum computers. Commonly proposed post-quantum algorithms include:

Lattice-Based Cryptography: These systems rely on the hardness of lattice problems, which are believed to be hard for both classical and quantum computers.

Code-Based Cryptography: This approach uses error-correcting codes, such as the McEliece cryptosystem, which has been shown to be resistant to quantum attacks.

Hash-Based Cryptography: Algorithms like Merkel signatures use hash functions to provide security against quantum attacks, though they are typically used for digital signatures rather than encryption.

Multivariate Polynomial Cryptography: This family of cryptographic schemes is based on the difficulty of solving systems of multivariate polynomial equations, which is considered a hard problem for both quantum and classical computers.

19.3.3.1 Comparison Between PQC and QKD

Quantum key distribution (QKD) and post-quantum cryptography (PQC) both aim to protect communications in a quantum computer world—yet they go about it quite differently, particularly when it comes to real-world deployment. Table 19.1 shows the comparison between PQC and QKD:

19.3.4 Classical Communication Layer

The classical communication layer is a part of a network or system that handles the transmission of traditional (non-quantum) data—like text, files, or regular internet traffic—using classical communication technologies. In quantum communication systems [24], this layer works alongside the quantum communication layer to exchange control information, authenticate users, and coordinate actions like sending or receiving quantum keys in QKD. While the quantum layer handles quantum bits (qubits), the classical communication layer manages all the supporting digital communication necessary to make the system work properly.

A quantum-classical gateway is a system or interface that enables communication and coordination between quantum systems and classical (traditional) systems. Since

TABLE 19.1
Comparison Between PQC and QKD

Feature	PQC	QKD
Based on	Math assumptions	Quantum physics laws
Hardware needed	No	Yes (specialized quantum hardware)
Scalability	High	Low
Cost	Low	High
Security	Computational	Information-theoretic
Real-world use	Emerging (standardization)	Nice

quantum devices (which use qubits) and classical devices (which use bits) operate very differently, the gateway acts as a bridge, allowing:

- Translating information between quantum and classical formats.
- Synchronizing between quantum and classical processes (e.g., in quantum key distribution).
- Controlling and monitoring quantum devices using classical systems.
- It's essential in hybrid networks or quantum communication setups, where both classical and quantum components need to work together smoothly.

Classical secure transmission is the protection of information as it moves through standard (nonquantum) communication lines. It uses encryption methods like AES, RSA, or TLS to ensure that the information stays confidential, authentic, and unchanged while in transit. The technique relies on advanced mathematical algorithms to encrypt information, and it's difficult for attackers to gain access or tamper with the data. It's the foundation for most secure communication nowadays—like online banking, emails, and VPNs.

19.3.5 Autonomous Response and Self-Healing Mechanism

It has the ability to sense, respond, and mend itself from security breaches or system crashes—naturally, with no human touch.

- Autonomous Response: AI or predetermined rules are used by the system to provide an instant reaction to threats (e.g., quarantine infected hosts, block malware IPs, or kill suspicious processes).
- Self-Healing: In case of attack or failure, the system is able to recover itself to a secure state, e.g., by repairing corrupted files, rebooting compromised services, or resetting configurations. These mechanisms prevent downtime and maintain ongoing security, particularly in high- or large-scale networks, by responding quicker than humans can. Self-healing network protocols are communication protocols that automatically detect, adapt to, and recover from network failures—without the need for human intervention. When something goes wrong (such as a node crashing, a faulty link, or a cyberattack), these protocols can reroute traffic through alternative paths, restore lost connections,

and maintain service continuity. They use techniques like dynamic routing, redundancy, and real-time monitoring to keep the network online and robust. This is especially important for critical infrastructure, IoT networks, and autonomous systems, where downtime can create severe issues. In short, self-healing protocols improve networks to be stronger, resilient, and error-tolerant.

Quantum key regeneration and distribution is a quantum cryptography process by which encryption keys are securely generated and exchanged between two parties based on the principles of quantum mechanics. It is based on QKD, which employs particles such as photons to send keys in a manner that any attempt at eavesdropping is immediately detectable. If a key is compromised or outdated, a new quantum key is regenerated and redistributed, ensuring continuous, secure communication.

19.3.6 Authentication and Identity Management

In quantum communication, authentication ensures that the parties exchanging quantum information (like keys or messages) are genuine and trusted. Since quantum systems are very sensitive, even a small interference can indicate an attack, but you still need classical [25] authentication to confirm the identities of both the sender and the recipient and prevent man-in-the-middle attacks (someone pretending to be a trusted party). Typically, classical cryptographic techniques (like hash-based message authentication codes or digital signatures) are still used alongside quantum channels for this purpose. Identity management in a quantum communication system involves securely managing and validating the identities of users, devices, or nodes in a quantum network. It includes issuing and managing quantum-safe credentials, maintaining a trusted database of users/nodes, and enforcing access controls based on verified identities.

Quantum-secure authentication protocols are security methods designed to protect identity verification (like logins or digital signatures) against attacks from quantum computers. Since quantum computers can break many traditional cryptographic systems (like RSA or ECC), quantum-secure protocols use post-quantum cryptography—algorithms based on mathematical problems that are believed to be hard even for quantum computers. These include lattice-based cryptography (e.g., Dilithium, Kyber), hash-based signatures (e.g., XMSS, SPHINCS+), and code-based cryptography (e.g., McEliece).

Identity and access management (IAM) in quantum communication is the process of securely identifying users and controlling access to quantum communication systems, using methods that are resilient to quantum threats. In quantum context, IAM must use post-quantum cryptographic methods to authenticate users securely since traditional login methods (e.g., RSA, ECC) could be broken by quantum computers. QKD enables two parties to securely exchange encryption keys by transmitting quantum particles, such as photons. IAM guarantees that only authenticated and authorized parties are allowed to take part in the key exchange process. In the future, identities may be managed using quantum-secure digital certificates, ensuring that users/devices on a quantum network are who they claim to be. IAM policies decide who can access quantum channels, control quantum devices, or retrieve quantum-generated keys. IAM in quantum communication makes sure that only trusted users can access and use highly secure quantum networks—and does so using methods that can withstand both classical and quantum attacks.

Quantum communication networks in 6G network infrastructure have various real-world applications, especially where data integrity, security, and ultra-fast transmission are crucial. There can be applications in areas like government and military, diplomacy and embassies, healthcare and telemedicine, banking and financial transactions, secure cloud and data centers, smart cities and critical infrastructure, autonomous vehicles and V2X communication, international data transfers and global enterprises, satellite communication, quantum AI and machine learning Integration, private and industrial 6G networks, blockchain and cryptocurrency, research, academia, and intellectual property protection.

19.4 CONCLUSION AND FUTURE WORK

Finally, integrating quantum communication technologies in 6G networks is a revolutionary step toward attaining unprecedented levels of security in wireless communications. With the predictive power of AI and the unbreak ability of quantum encryption, 6G architectures can be secured from emerging cyber threats. This work emphasizes the architectural adaptations, security features, and usability requirements required for such integration, as well as the disruptive nature of quantum computing to classical cryptographic infrastructure. With networks becoming increasingly sophisticated, quantum communication will become indispensable for establishing trust, privacy, and resilience in 6G systems, requiring cross-layer optimization and multidisciplinary research to achieve effective, deployable solutions. Scalable deployment mechanisms, standardization initiatives, and resolving real-world issues will be the areas of focus for future research in order to achieve full potential in quantum-secure next-generation wireless networks. Future studies will emphasize the creation of energy-efficient, lightweight quantum security protocols for edge-IoT devices, as well as massive-scale quantum repeaters with novel network control within ultra-low-latency, high-mobility 6G environments. Perhaps the greatest challenge will be seamlessly integrating quantum and classical communication frameworks into a universal, adaptive network. Intelligent networking paradigms, such as AI/ML, SDN, and NFV, will be called upon to control dynamic quantum resource allocation and assured data flows.

REFERENCES

1. Huang, T., Yang, W., Wu, J., Ma, J., Zhang, X., & Zhang, D. (2019). A survey on green 6G network: Architecture and technologies. *IEEE Access*, 7, 175758–175768.
2. Rozenman, G. G., Kundu, N. K., Liu, R., Zhang, L., Maslennikov, A., Reches, Y., & Youm, H. Y. (2023). The quantum internet: A synergy of quantum information technologies and 6G networks. *IET Quantum Communication*, 4(4), 147–166.
3. Thommandru, R. (2024). Quantum key distribution for securing 6G networks: Shaping the future of mobile communication. *Multidisciplinary Journal for Applied Research in Engineering and Technology*, 4(5), 16–20.
4. Patel, R. (2024). Exploring the viability and implications of quantum communication in 6G networks. *Recent Trends in Electronics Communication Systems*, 11(1), 1–14.
5. Rozenman, G. G., Kundu, N. K., Liu, R., Zhang, L., Maslennikov, A., Reches, Y., & Youm, H. Y. (2023). The quantum internet: A synergy of quantum information technologies and 6G networks. *IET Quantum Communication*, 4(4), 147–166.

6. Panwar, N., Sharma, S., & Singh, A. K. (2016). A survey on 5G: The next generation of mobile communication. *Physical Communication*, 18, 64–84.
7. Ding, Z., Lei, X., Karagiannidis, G. K., Schober, R., Yuan, J., & Bhargava, V. K. (2017). A survey on non-orthogonal multiple access for 5G networks: Research challenges and future trends. *IEEE Journal on Selected Areas in Communications*, 35(10), 2181–2195.
8. Sah, M. B., Bindle, A., & Gulati, T. (2022). Issues and challenges in the implementation of 5G technology. In *Computer Networks and Inventive Communication Technologies* (pp. 385–398). Singapore: Springer.
9. Painuly, S., Sharma, S., & Matta, P. (2021). Future trends and challenges in next generation smart application of 5G-IoT. In *2021 5th International Conference on Computing Methodologies and Communication (ICCMC)* (pp. 354–357). IEEE.
10. Duan, W., Gu, J., Wen, M., Zhang, G., Ji, Y., & Mumtaz, S. (2020). Emerging technologies for 5G-IoV networks: Applications, trends and opportunities. *IEEE Network*, 34(5), 283–289.
11. Lin, B.-S. P. (2021, December). Toward an AI-enabled SDN-based 5G & IoT network. *Network and Communication Technologies, Canadian Center of Science and Education*, 5(2), 1–7.
12. Ayub, M. F., Mahmood, K., Kumari, S., & Sangaiah, A. K. (2021). Lightweight authentication protocol for e-health clouds in IoT-based applications through 5G technology. *Digital Communications and Networks*, 7(2), 235–244.
13. De Alwis, C., Kalla, A., Pham, Q. V., Kumar, P., Dev, K., Hwang, W. J., & Liyanage, M. (2021). Survey on 6G frontiers: Trends, applications, requirements, technologies and future research. *IEEE Open Journal of the Communications Society*, 2, 836–886.
14. Falencik, M. I. (2021). The internet in everything: Freedom and security in a world with no off switch. *International Journal of Communication (Online)*, 1154–1157.
15. Chang, H. Y., Lin, Y. T., & Cheng, H. W. (2021). 6G wireless communications: A comprehensive survey. *IEEE Communications Surveys & Tutorials*, 23(2), 1128–1158.
16. Chiani, M., Paolini, E., & Callegati, F. (2018). Open issues and beyond 5G. *5G Italy White eBook: from Research to Market*, 1–11.
17. Simeone, O. (2018, December). A very brief introduction to machine learning with applications to communication systems. *IEEE Transactions on Cognitive Communications and Networking*, 4(4), 648–664.
18. Gyongyosi, L., & Imre, S. (2019, February). A survey on quantum computing technology. *Computer Science Review*, 31, 51–71.
19. Wilde, M. M., & Hsieh, M.-H. (2012). The quantum dynamic capacity formula of a quantum channel. *Quantum Information Processing*, 11(6), 1431–1463.
20. Izhar, M. A. M., Babar, Z., Nguyen, H. V., Botsinis, P., Alanis, D., Chandra, D., Ng, S. X., & Hanzo, L. (2018). Quantum turbo decoding for quantum channels exhibiting memory. *IEEE Access*, 6, 12369–12381.
21. Botsinis, P., Alanis, D., Feng, S., Babar, Z., Nguyen, H. V., Chandra, D., Ng, S. X., Zhang, R., & Hanzo, L. (2017). Quantum-assisted indoor localization for uplink mm-wave and downlink visible light communication systems. *IEEE Access*, 5, 23327–23351.
22. Botsinis, P., Alanis, D., Babar, Z., Ng, S. X., & Hanzo, L. (2016, July). Joint quantumassisted channel estimation and data detection. *IEEE Access*, 4, 7658–7681.
23. Dunjko, V., Taylor, J. M., & Briegel, H. J. (2016). Quantum-enhanced machine learning. *Physical Review. Letters*, 117(13), 130501–130506.
24. Ngo, H. Q., Larsson, E. G., & Marzetta, T. L. (2013, April). Energy and spectral efficiency of very large multiuser MIMO systems. *IEEE Transactions on Communications*, 61(4), 1436–1449.
25. Series, M. (2015). IMT vision–framework and overall objectives of the future development of IMT for 2020 and beyond. *Recommendation ITU*, 2083(0), 1–21.

20 Superposition in Quantum Computing—Advancements with Google's Willow Chip and IBM's Quantum Systems

Haranadha Reddy Busireddy Seshakagari, Ramesh Peramalasetty, K. Reddy Madhavi, Chinthapatla Pranay Varna, and Mannipudi Prabhu Das

20.1 INTRODUCTION

An essential principle of quantum mechanics, superposition, empowers quantum computing transformations. It differs from its classical counterpart-computing in the sense that the classical one works with either a binary digit of 0 or 1. Quantum computing uses its basic unit of operation, the quantum bit (qubit), which can exist in both the states of 0 and 1 at the same time. The principle allows quantum systems to simulate huge amounts of data in parallel, thus providing unimaginable compute power. By the implementation of superposition, qubits go beyond classical systems for encoding and manipulating information to a level of complexity in optimization and cryptography ways that were thought impossible in the pre-quantum era. Superposition has been well established, and a number of experimental tests of quantum mechanics have confirmed its existence. The existence and practical applications of this concept were known through the double-slit experiment and Schrödinger wave mechanics, which show that quantum systems could exist in different states simultaneously until an actual measurement is made, thus revolutionizing the field of computation where qubits, being the basic unit of quantum systems, were born. Unlike classical bits, qubits use superposition, and this allows them to represent and manipulate exponentially larger datasets, thereby creating new horizons in the realm of machine computation.

Since these advances in quantum hardware have made practical feasibility apparent about working in superposition, Google's Willow chip and IBM's Quantum System Two can be mentioned as working on important issues such as

DOI: 10.1201/9781003538950-23

error correction, coherence of qubit and scaling-up. The Willow has 105 qubits and has made major advances to reduce the number of errors in its computations and increased qubit retention times. The benefits enjoyed both the customers and partners opening the entire range of quantum systems to more advanced capabilities learned from the first-generation IBM Quantum System One. The utility-scale quantum applications empowered by the Quantum System Two modular architecture and scalable designs are unlocked by these breakthroughs. Superposition, in principle, shows how a computation can be parallel efficiently, such that it cannot tractably appear as classical.

Besides the hardware advancements, a further promising quantum encryption technique that can prove the issue of a layer of additional security on transmitted data by superposition is the quantum permutation pad (QPP). The QPP ensures security through superimposed states simultaneously encoding the information for quantum communication networks. Such a conclusion provides how superposition functions as twofold in the development of the quantum computer: on one hand speeding up their computation power without loss and on the other making their channel of communication fundamentally safe to break.

Superposition lies at the heart of quantum computing. This chapter covers major milestones in the field, discusses most promising approaches (contributions from Google and IBM in particular), and the potential paths forward for scalable quantum computation and secure communication. The implications of these advancements highlight the revolutionary capabilities of quantum computing and represent an inflection point in the history of computational technology.

20.2 LITERATURE REVIEW

Superposition, one of the most basic principles of quantum computing, allows qubits to be in many states at once. This unique characteristic increases computational power exponentially as quantum computers can work on multiple pieces of information simultaneously, something that is impossible for classical computers. The power of superposition is what makes solving very complex optimization problems possible, such as breaking cryptography, simulating different materials, artificial intelligence, and molecular modeling. Nevertheless, superposition faces challenges, like stability of qubits, noise and interference, and error correction, which are still active research areas. Recent breakthroughs in quantum hardware (like Google's Willow chip and IBM's quantum systems) have concentrated on exploiting superposition more efficiently, resulting in upsides for computing speed, precision, and real-world applications.

Google's Willow quantum processor, however, marks an advance in quantum error correction, one of the most critical aspects for stable superposition states throughout computations. Error correction is necessary to reduce decoherence and prevent the loss of quantum information, thereby enhancing the fidelity of quantum operations (AbuGhanem, 2024). It builds on Google's previous advances in quantum supremacy where quantum processors did calculations after just a few minutes, which would have taken the most powerful classical supercomputers thousands of years (Pasupuleti, 2024).

Live Qubit is a news aggregator that links to scientific articles about events in the quantum computing world and elsewhere. Quantum world (CW) has two modes: Mode 1 is the free mode that allows all visitors to freely browse articles. Mode 0 will collect datasets from a certain database to identify events that can provide relevant photos, videos. Mode 0 will require registration or payment to access, so you can contact them to access any event you want to. Researchers at Google Quantum AI have shown that Willow reaches error rates below the threshold for scalable quantum computation, moving us ever closer to fault-tolerant quantum computation. The chip's ability to perform random circuit sampling, a testbed problem for quantum speedup, emphasizes the power of superposition in achieving unmatched computational efficiency. Moreover, Google's research offers insights on how Willow's synergy with machine learning algorithms can optimize complex decision-making systems, paving the path for AI-driven quantum implementations.

IBM has achieved similar milestones with quantum computing, especially with the superposition for algorithmic efficiency and scalability. Utilizing superposition, IBM's 433-qubit superconducting quantum chip, Osprey, has been leveraged in various applications ranging from finance and logistics to materials science. Qubits, the building blocks of quantum computers, can have varying degrees of connectivity, coherence (how long they can maintain quantum states), and gate fidelity (how accurately quantum operations can be performed), which the system aims to enhance through other innovations. IBM plans to develop even larger processors with the Condor chip the total number of qubits in the computer exceeds 1,000, making it one of the most powerful quantum systems to ever be built.

Superposition is having a profound effect in computation-sensitive areas, as IBM's quantum algorithms, such as Shor's algorithm for the factorization of numbers and Grover's algorithm for search optimization, attest to. It surpasses state-of-the-art approaches in complexity-theoretical frameworks and free up considerable resources in the fields of computational genetics, cryptographic security, and artificial inspiration. IBM has also announced quantum cloud computing services, enabling researchers and enterprises to experiment with quantum algorithms without having direct access to quantum hardware. And although IBM's achievements in the field are promising, hurdles like noise from qubits, thermal fluctuations, and decoherence still complicate the path to building large-scale practical quantum computing.

In addition to specific improvements to quantum hardware, research on quantum has also been centered on maximizing individual qubit performance and system reliability. Research done by Google shows substantial advances in qubit noise coherence, error correction, and scalability of quantum machines for error-corrected quantum information processing applying quantum error correction with low errors utilizing this new architectures Willow's architecture is further extended by the integration of quantum neural networks (QNNs) in these AI-driven applications.

The main focus of IBM for quantum computing has been to have real-world applications, especially for pharmaceutical research, logistics, and financial modeling. Through superposition, IBM's quantum systems are progressing optimization systems applied in global supply chains and high-frequency trading algorithms.

Quantum computing systems are primarily characterized by their ability to maintain superposition, implement such operations with a high gate fidelity, and reduce quantum errors. Studies show quantum gates operating under superposition states with remarkably higher performance metrics. The accuracy of gate operations is critical to the efficiency of quantum circuits that will one day enable multi-purpose calculations across a wide range of fields. As quantum systems are highly prone to noise, quantum error correction (QEC) techniques are crucial to stabilize computations. The adoption of various forms of qubits, such as surface codes, cat qubits, and topological qubits, has been a major subject of research in recent papers, emphasizing the development of more robust and error-tolerant quantum computing.

Quantum key distribution (QKD) relies on quantum superposition to allow for provably unbreakable encryption of secure communications. Financial institutions and defense organizations are already using QKD, paying attention to the increasing dependence on quantum-secured networks. For instance, quantum computers using superposition can conduct extremely accurate analysis of molecular structures, speeding up new drug discovery and enabling protein folding predictions, which classical computers cannot manage.

AI, on the other hand, is capable of optimizing algorithms to identify the most promising solutions faster than the classical method, thereby integrating quantum computing with AI. Using quantum superposition, AI algorithms can explore multiple solutions within a single iteration, thereby increasing effectiveness in the domains of autonomous systems and inferences in finance (Bawa, 2024). Although superposition and quantum systems have progressed significantly, issues like qubit stability, noise sensitivity, and large-scale deployment are still major challenges.

20.3 SUPERPOSITION IN QUANTUM COMPUTING

Superposition happens because qubits can exist in a linear combination of the computational basis states |0⟨ and |1⟨ before measuring, which can be mathematically expressed as:

$$|\psi\rangle=\alpha|0\rangle+\beta|1\rangle$$

Here, are complex amplitudes and the squared magnitudes give the probabilities for observing |0⟨ or |1⟨. The probabilistic nature of quantum systems allows multiple computational pathways to be explored simultaneously, leading to the potential for exponential speedup in the solution of specific classes of problems (Figure 20.1).

20.3.1 Advantages of Superposition in Quantum Computing

By utilizing quantum superposition, quantum computing exerts quantum parallelism and is able to explore enormous solution spaces simultaneously and power algorithms such as Grover's searching and Shor's factorization. The fact that quantum systems can represent complex states in exponentially fewer resources than classical systems also means that this capability improves resource efficiency. In addition to that quantum cryptography operates on superposition principles of encoding

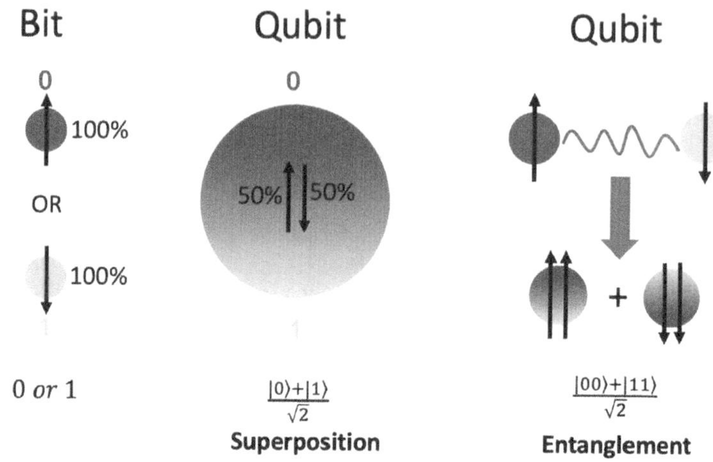

FIGURE 20.1 Superposition concept in qubits.

information securely, e.g., QPPs significantly improve the security and reliability of the communication protocols.

Superposition is one of the most important quantum properties that is the main difference between quantum computing and classical computing. It allows qubits, the basic units of quantum information, to be in many states at once, and is a very important reason that quantum computers are very powerful and efficient.

20.3.2 Understanding Superposition in Qubits

In classical computation, a bit can be either a 0 or a 1. Meanwhile, while a classical bit can unequivocally take either one of the states 0 or 1, a qubit is allowed to exist in the state of 0, in the state of 1, or in a combination of both of these states. The property of existing in states more than one at a time is termed superposition. In mathematical terms, the state of a qubit can be represented as:

$$|\psi\rangle=\alpha|0\rangle+\beta|1$$

where α and β are complex numbers denoting the probability amplitude of the qubit being in the state $|0\rangle$ or $|1\rangle$, respectively. The constraint $|\alpha|2+|\beta|2=1$ preserves the normalization of total probability.

20.3.3 Implications of Superposition

Representing a generous amount of information is the strength of superposition. For instance, with two qubits, the combined state can at the same time encode all of the four possible combinations (00, 01, 10, 11):

$$|\psi\rangle=\alpha_{00}|00\rangle+\alpha_{01}|01\rangle+\alpha_{10}|10\rangle+\alpha_{11}|11\rangle$$

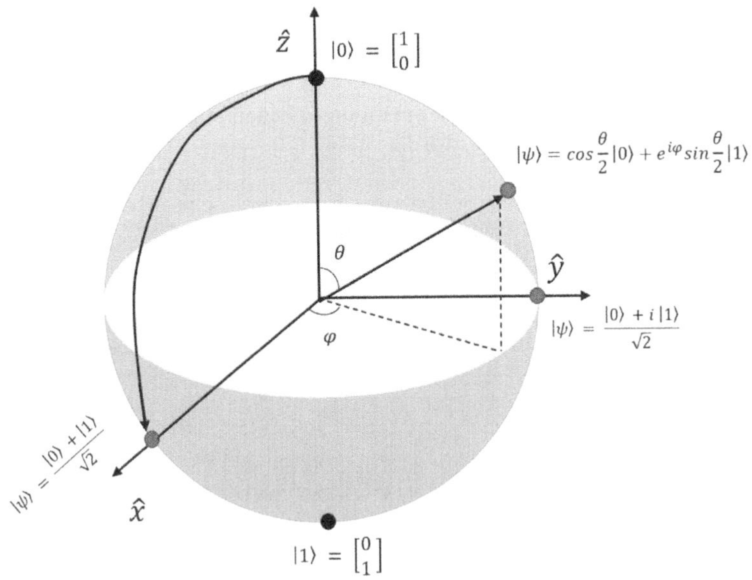

FIGURE 20.2 The Bloch sphere representation of a qubit, illustrating how quantum states exist as a linear combination of $|0\rangle$ and $|1\rangle$.

This represents an exponential increase in their representational ability, allowing quantum computers to simultaneously execute a multitude of calculations, using the principle of parallelism to solve specific types of problems much faster than classical computers.

One way to visualize superposition is with the double-slit experiment. When a beam of electrons is directed toward a barrier with two slits, interference occurs behind the slits to create an interference pattern on the screen, provided there's no one watching or observing. This pattern means that a particle goes through both slits at the same time, in superposition, until measured, when the particle collapses into one of the two possible states (going through one slit or the other).

Along with the double-slit experiment, a diagram that is a more accurate representation of superposition when delving into quantum computing is the Bloch sphere, which represents the state of a qubit in three dimensional space. In contrast to classical bits, which are either 0 or 1, qubits are not limited to these discrete states but are points on a sphere, with various points representing various responses. The Bloch sphere represents a geometric view of the quantum states $|0\rangle$ and $|1\rangle$ and how they may exist as superpositions (Figure 20.2).

Qubits can be visualized as the Bloch sphere, which is a unit sphere representing all possible states of the qubit: Pure states reside on the surface whereas the mixed ones are accommodated in between.

Key Elements

- **North Pole:** Typically represents the $|0\rangle$ state.
- **South Pole:** Typically represents the $|1\rangle$ state.

- **Equator:** Represents superposition states where both $|0\rangle$ and $|1\rangle$ have equal probabilities.

This is important for visualizing the operations of quantum gates and how quantum algorithms manipulate qubits to solve for things faster than classical systems.

20.3.4 Quantum Gates and Superposition

Quantum gates are those basic operations used in quantum computing that manipulate qubits to produce and control states of superposition. Unlike classical logic gates performing deterministic processes over bits (i.e., 0 or 1), operations at quantum gates are much more sophisticated due to the principles of superposition and entanglement.

20.3.5 Role of Quantum Gates in Creating and Manipulating Superposition

Quantum gates are unitary operators acting on qubits to implement special transformations, including the creation and manipulation of superposition states. Some of the most frequently employed quantum gates are:

1. **Hadamard Gate (H):** This flips the qubit state from a well-defined value into an even superposition of $|0\rangle$ and $|1\rangle$. Applying it to $|0\rangle$ yields

   $$H\,|\,0\rangle = \frac{1}{\sqrt{2}}\left(|0\rangle + |1\rangle\right)$$

   Such an operation is very important in many algorithms that require the parallel exploration of many possibilities.
2. **Pauli-X Gate (X):** Similar to the classical NOT gate, the Pauli-X gate flips the state of a qubit:

   $$X|0\rangle = |1\rangle \text{and}\, X|1\rangle = |0\rangle$$

   When applied to the superposition of states, it flips the probability amplitudes of the two states.
3. **Pauli-Y and Pauli-Z Gates (Y and Z):** The Y and Z gates perform rotations about the respective Y and Z axes of the Bloch sphere.
4. **Phase Shift Gates:** These gates apply a phase factor to the $|1\rangle$ part of a qubit. For instance, a Z gate applies a phase of π:

   $$Z|0\rangle = |0\rangle \text{and}\, Z|1\rangle = -|1\rangle$$

   Phase shifts are crucial for algorithms that rely on interference pattern enhancement for correct outputs.

Name	Gate(s)	Matrix	Purpose
Pauli-X (X)	X	$\begin{pmatrix} 0 & 1 \\ 1 & 0 \end{pmatrix}$	-Similar to the Classical Not -Flips the amplitudes of states 0 and 1 -Rotates the state by π around the x-axis
Pauli-Y (Y)	Y	$\begin{pmatrix} 0 & -i \\ i & 0 \end{pmatrix}$	-Rotates the state by π around the y-axis
Pauli-Z (Z)	Z	$\begin{pmatrix} 0 & 0 \\ 0 & -1 \end{pmatrix}$	-Adds a global phase of -1 to the 1 state -Rotates the state by π around the z-axis
Hadamard (H)	H	$\frac{1}{\sqrt{2}} \begin{pmatrix} 1 & 1 \\ 1 & -1 \end{pmatrix}$	-Converts between the z and x basis -Creates superposition
Phase Shift P(φ)	S	$\begin{pmatrix} 1 & 0 \\ 0 & e \end{pmatrix}$	-Adds a global phase of e to the 1 state
Controlled Not (CNOT, CX)		$\begin{pmatrix} 1 & 0 & 0 & 0 \\ 0 & 1 & 0 & 0 \\ 0 & 0 & 0 & 1 \\ 0 & 0 & 1 & 0 \end{pmatrix}$	-Performs an X gate on the target qubit if the control qubit is 1
Controlled Z (CZ)	Z	$\begin{pmatrix} 1 & 0 & 0 & 0 \\ 0 & 1 & 0 & 0 \\ 0 & 0 & 1 & 0 \\ 0 & 0 & 0 & -1 \end{pmatrix}$	-Performs a Z gate on the target qubit if the control qubit is 1
SWAP		$\begin{pmatrix} 1 & 0 & 0 & 0 \\ 0 & 0 & 1 & 0 \\ 0 & 1 & 0 & 0 \\ 0 & 0 & 0 & 1 \end{pmatrix}$	-Swaps the states of two qubits
Toffoli (CCNOT, CCX)		$\begin{pmatrix} 1 & 1 & 1 & 1 & 1 & 1 & 1 & 1 \\ 0 & 1 & 0 & 0 & 0 & 0 & 0 & 0 \\ 0 & 0 & 1 & 0 & 0 & 0 & 0 & 0 \\ 0 & 0 & 0 & 1 & 0 & 0 & 0 & 0 \\ 0 & 0 & 0 & 0 & 1 & 0 & 0 & 0 \\ 0 & 0 & 0 & 0 & 0 & 1 & 0 & 0 \\ 0 & 0 & 0 & 0 & 0 & 0 & 0 & 1 \\ 0 & 0 & 0 & 0 & 0 & 0 & 1 & 0 \end{pmatrix}$	-Performs an X gate on the target qubit if both control qubits are 1

TABLE 20.1 Common quantum gates.

5. **Controlled Gates (e.g., CNOT Gate):** These gates are multiqubit gates where one qubit termed as the target receives an operation based on the value of the control qubit. Similarly, the controlled-NOT (CNOT) gate flips the value of the target qubit if the control qubit is in state $|1\rangle$:

$$\text{CNOT}|00\rangle = |00\rangle \text{ and } \text{CNOT}|10\rangle = |11\rangle$$

Controlled gates become imperative for entangling qubits with each other at different instances for their quantum parallelism.

20.3.6 Real-World Applications of Superposition in Industries

Inside the quantum computing infrastructure, the superposition being one of its pillars finds a revolution in applications across sectors. In finance, quantum optimization is considered to be of utmost importance to portfolio optimization. Already banks, such as JPMorgan Chase and Goldman Sachs, exploit quantum computing for portfolio optimization, risk analysis, and fraud detection. Whereas classical optimization methods fail in the detail-laden financial context, quantum optimization techniques such as the quantum approximate optimization algorithm (QAOA) use superposition states to evaluate more than one investment scenario or potential return at the same time. Working with an algorithm capable of considering random variables—those in entangled states of qubit—the quantum computer can evaluate huge amounts of financial data in parallel to discover the optimal allocation of assets far more quickly than any classical model would allow. As an example, JPMorgan Chase's use of IBM's quantum processors to simulate financial market behavior is demonstrating the application of quantum computing for optimization in risk assessment and derivative pricing.

Quantum computing, right at the frontier of innovation, is transforming drug development and molecular simulation through fast-tracking atomic-scale modeling of molecular interactions, a process terribly computation-intensive for classical supercomputers, in health. Superposition entails that multiple molecular structures and interactions can be processed by quantum computers at once, meaning that models can be simulated at least by orders of magnitude faster. This ability becomes especially significant as modeling protein folding is very important for drug development against diseases like Alzheimer and cancer. Roche and other pharmaceutical companies interested in quantum simulations for drug discovery processes have teamed with Google's quantum research division to help several healthcare companies utilize superposition-based simulations to speed up drug discovery.

One big sector moving on excellent strides by the path of quantum computing is cybersecurity, with a corollary focus on quantum encryption and secure communications. Quantum cryptography thus employs QKD and QPP systems to raise the confidence level. In QKD, the property of superposition guarantees that in the event of interception of the quantum key, its state gets changed, thus making eavesdropping detectable. This ultra-secure encryption keys are being created through a method called superposition eigenstates that help ensure an ultra-secure encryption key immune to classical as well as quantum hackers. One well-known test system here has been China's Micius satellite, which successfully showed secure QKD quantum communication over a 1,200 km distance, demonstrating superposition-based encryption's potential to reinvent global cybersecurity.

This is a building block that, when combined with quantum gates which also work off superposition enables several quantum computing paradigms. More specifically, quantum parallelism enables qubits which are in a state of superposition to simultaneously evaluate each of its inputs of a function, known as the quantum parallelism trick and leading to an exponential speedup for certain problems. This given property of quantum mechanics is used by quantum gates to alter the qubit states such that the amplitude for all the undesired computational paths, interfere destructively with the amplitude of the desired computational paths, thus raising the probability of the correct outcomes. Additionally, some algorithms, such as Shor's algorithm for factoring large numbers and Grover's algorithm for database search, take advantage of superposition and carefully engineered sequences of quantum gates that outperform classical algorithms. Such applications highlight the revolutionary potential of superposition, enabling advancements in a variety of fields, including cybersecurity, healthcare, and finance.

20.4 GOOGLE'S WILLOW CHIP

Google's Willow chip, which was introduced in December 2023, represents a significant advancement in quantum hardware. With 105 qubits nearly twice as many as earlier systems Willow allows for more intricate calculations and improved error correction. Willow represents a quantum leap toward achievable quantum supremacy due to its larger radius and markedly enhanced qubit coherence and fault tolerance. Google's quest for quantum supremacy the idea that some computational tasks can be completed exponentially faster on quantum systems than on traditional supercomputers led to the development of this quantum processor.

20.4.1 Technical Innovations

Extended Qubit Coherence: Willow maintains quantum states during computations by quintupling the qubit coherence times (T1), which are close to 100 microseconds.

Error Mitigation: The reliability of quantum operations is increased by fault-tolerant error-correction protocols, which significantly reduce logical error rates.

Computational Performance: Benchmarking experiments showed that Willow achieved computational supremacy by completing tasks on classical systems that would take trillions of years.

20.4.2 Performance Metrics

Randomized benchmarking techniques are typically used to evaluate quantum processor operations errors, which are then reported as "average error." It gives a standard way to assess the quality of quantum operations. Remarkably, Chips 1 and 2 have differing T_1 (qubit coherence times) in accordance with design trade-offs. These require trade-offs between better electromagnetic shielding versus maximizing coherence; some par for the course in advanced engineering and some a challenge of physics.

Google Quantum AI's Willow chip is one of the most ambitious quantum computing chips ever built, and its performance metrics are staggering after being compared with today supercomputers.

20.4.3 Key Performance Metrics of Willow Chip

Computational Speed

Willow performed a benchmark computation in fewer than five minutes. By comparison, this would take one of the world's most advanced

TABLE 20.2
Willow Chip Performance Metrics

Willow System Metrics	Values
Number of qubits	105
Average connectivity	3.47 (4-way typical)
	Quantum Error Correction (Chip 1)
Single-qubit gate error[1]	0.035% ± 0.029%
Two-qubit gate error[1] (CZ)	0.33% ± 0.18%
Measurement error	0.77% ± 0.21%
Reset options	Multi-level reset (|1 state and above), Leakage removal (|2 state only)
T_1 time (mean)	68μs ± 13 μs[2]
Error correction cycles per second	909,000 (surface code cycle = 1.1 μs)
Application performance	$\wedge_{3, 5, 7} = 2.14 \pm 0.02$
	Random Circuit Sampling (Chip 2)
Single-qubit gate error[1]	0.036% ± 0.013%
Two-qubit gate error[1] (iSWAP)	0.14% ± 0.052%
Measurement error	0.67% ± 0.51%
Reset options	Multi-level reset (|1 state and above), Leakage removal (|2 state only)
T_1 time (mean)	98 μs ± 32 μs[2]
Circuit repetitions per second	63,000
Application performance	XEB fidelity depth 40 = 0.1%
Estimated time on Willow vs. classical supercomputer	5 minutes vs. 10^{25} years

supercomputers today around 10 septillion years (10^{25} years) to compute, showcasing an enormous speedup in quantum computing over classical computing systems.

Qubit Count and Quality

Willow uses 105 superconducting qubits, which leverage quantum mechanics, namely, superposition, to exist in multiple states at the same time. This enables them to process information at the same time, greatly improving computational efficiency over a classical bit.

Error Correction Capabilities

One of the most important methods of Willow is to exponentially decrease the error rates as more qubits are added. This means that as the system scales, the computations become more reliable, thus overcoming a long-standing challenge in quantum error-control that has been pursued by the research community for nearly three decades.

Qubit Lifetime

When looked at on average, the qubit lifetimes at Willow are fast approaching around 100 microseconds, which is about five times better than what was achieved by earlier generations of quantum chip. This may be necessary for achieving coherence during calculations.

Benchmarking Standards

Willow's performance quantification is through the random circuit sampling (RCS) benchmark, a commonly accepted measure for judging quantum processors. This benchmark measures whether or not a quantum computer outperforms a classical system for certain tasks, and Willow has consistently exceeded that threshold.

Implications and Future Potential

The Willow chip's technology advancement represents transformative possibilities for practical applications, in data science's most diverse sectors, from artificial intelligence to drug discovery. By addressing major challenges in speed and error rates, Willow enables large-scale quantum computers to solve problems that classical systems can't handle.

To facilitate fault-tolerant quantum computation, Google aspires to scale up its quantum systems. That includes improving the stability of the hardware, decreasing the residual errors, and increasing the number of qubits to tackle real-world challenges in optimization, chemistry, and machine learning.

20.5 IBM QUANTUM SYSTEMS

The Quantum System Two by IBM is an important step forward in quantum computing, leveraging infrastructure established by the earlier Quantum System One. Launched in December 2023, these platforms utilize a next-gen modular and flexible framework for a wider scale of quantum computation.

Central to Quantum System Two are three IBM Quantum Heron processors, each one with 133 fixed-frequency qubits with tuneable couplers. This design achieves three to five times the device performance gain compared to earlier systems, like the 127 qubit Eagle processors, also minimizing crosstalk between qubits. The processors are designed in a modular way that allows them to be combined into a single coherent system to boost computational power.

It is best to avoid a system overhaul, which is useful to pass through the scalability bottlenecks, while also enabling upgrading so that future generations of quantum processors may be inserted into the same framework with less friction. Quantum System Two uses quantum-safe encryption techniques such as quantum permutation pad (QPP) to ensure secure quantum functions. The techniques use physical principles from quantum mechanics, namely, superposition and entanglement, to enhance the security of data to an extent that it becomes rather impossible for unauthorized actors to decode sensitive data.

Moreover, stabilized and reliable quantum systems will experience very low temperatures: close to absolute zero. This will allow the better use of advanced cryogenic technology to maintain the environment of the qubit functioning at optimum conditions. When finally put in place, it will allow the quantum processors to optimally perform their calculation, conserving coherence and minimizing errors.

IBM Quantum System Two is the next generation of quantum technology combining a scalable modular architecture with integrated classical computing resources and state-of-the-art encryption capabilities. This architecture will allow multiple processors to interconnect, letting the system address complex workloads—the starting point for any future advances in quantum computation.

20.5.1 Key Features

Modular Design

The modularity of IBM enables several processors to be linked together to extend quantum systems for computing complex workloads. This modularity is an important step toward linking several quantum processors into a single system that can extend for computation. Together, each processor works hand in hand, sharing the load as they carry this weight even when its unreadable. Not only does this modularity help tackle the scalability issues, it also makes upgrades to the system easier. Its flexibility and extensibility enable future generations of quantum processors to integrate within the existing ecosystem, empowering long-term quantum computing infrastructures.

Quantum Utility

Instead, the goal is to produce a useful quantum machine that can be used write and run classical programs with more efficiency than a classical machine. Of course, as of October 2023, that is yet to be shown. Its approach aims at industries like pharmaceuticals, logistics, and financial modeling, where quantum systems can outperform classical computing in terms of what the industry considers "significant benefit." After all, multiple problems where the amount of data to be optimized are enormous, including supply chain management, look better if we calculate them through quantum utility. In the case of quantum utility for much larger datasets (supply chain, etc.), optimization tasks can be solved better than classical/quantum utility. So to ensure that, quantum systems go from experiments to real tools solving real problems in the industry and driving innovation in various areas.

Quantum Encryption

The platform implements quantum-safe encryption techniques. The quantum permutation pad (QPP) is used for quantum operations. Quantum encryption techniques utilize concepts from quantum physics, such as superposition and entanglement, to improve data security. QPP secures sensitive information by encoding it in superpositioned states, rendering it virtually undiscernable to unauthorized entities. In sectors such as finance and healthcare, where data fidelity and security have utmost value, this fusion is especially crucial. IBM's advancements in quantum encryption not only safeguard operations but also set a benchmark for secure communication in quantum networks.

Performance Metrics

Qubit Stability: Improved coherence time by 40%.

Scalability: Designed to contain ten processors at origin.

Performance = scale (number of qubits + quality [quantum volume] + speed [CLOPS (circuit layer operations per second)]).

Qubit Count and Quality

Current systems: 156 qubits, which are connected to each other in a heavy-hex configuration to be used to improve connectivity and crosstalk to apply a better fidelity of operations and overall performance of qubit performance.

Quantum Volume

IBM has also added quantum volume (QV) as major quantity measurement point for benchmarking a quantum system performance. QV can tell one how well a quantum computer can realize problems requiring many qubits doing complex computations. Current-generation systems are expected to reach a QV of at least 512, which indicates great improvement in error rates and gate fidelity.

Circuit Layer Operations per Second (CLOPS)

CLOPS makes the pace of quantum circuit execution a new metric—one introduced by IBM. The IBM Quantum System Two has set a new threshold of 150,000 CLOPS (cubic logical operations per second) for this concept, compared to all previous systems. This variant applies to all classical computation if included and the time that execution took by quantum circuit.

Error Rates

The IBM Quantum System Two, designed for scalability and reliability, features the lowest error rates of any IBM quantum processor released to date, with error rates per gate as low as 3.5% for CNOT operations in specific benchmarks; meanwhile, error rates can often surge in qubit gate operations when scaling quantum computers, and such low error rates represent a promising evolution of quantum computational fidelity.

Scalability and Integration

The architecture is built for scale, tying cryogenic infrastructure with classic runtime servers to enable hybrid quantum classical workflows. This modular design is intended to facilitate future advancements in quantum processors while increasing computational power.

Long-Term Vision

A decade-long roadmap for IBM's plan to solve "scalable systems with more than 100,000 qubits" using advanced error correction techniques and modular integration. This strategy allows IBM to offer quantum-centric supercomputing platforms able to solve large-scale industry problems.

IBM Quantum System Two has a roadmap for the continuous enhancement of qubit quality raising its capabilities and complexity of operation to support more advanced quantum algorithms and applications. The system is described as a core part of IBM's strategy to realize quantum-centric supercomputing, a hybrid approach that tightly integrates quantum and classical computing resources.

IBM Quantum System Two details: A new standard in performance for high-qubit counts, with improved error rates, high execution speed, and an architecture to scale as needs progress.

20.5.2 Key Achievements IBM's

Quantum System Two has reached several notable milestones, showcasing its potential:

Commercial Availability: IBM's Quantum System One was the first commercially available quantum computer, setting expectations for future systems. The Quantum System Two introduces advantages and new measures of performance.

Quantum Volume: IBM quantifies the performance of its quantum computers with quantum volume, which is defined in several ways, including the number of raw available qubits and the quality of their connectivity and error rates. The idea is to make this quantity bigger to prove that the system can perform some complicated tasks.

20.6 COMPARATIVE ANALYSIS: GOOGLE VS. IBM

The rivalry between Google and IBM in quantum computing illustrates the greater drive to achieve breakthroughs in quantum technologies. Both giants provide leadership in the field, but with very different philosophies, architectures, and goals pertaining to innovation. This section discusses a comparative evaluation of Google's Willow chip and IBM's Quantum System Two based on their philosophies on qubit count, design philosophy, error management, encryption, and long-term goals.

TABLE 20.3
Comparative Performance Metrics

Aspect	Google's Willow Chip	IBM Quantum System Two
Qubit Count	105	133 (Heron processors)
Design Philosophy	Achieving quantum supremacy	Scalability and practical utility
Error Management	Fault-tolerant error correction	Advanced modular error correction
Encryption Focus	Computational error mitigation	Quantum-safe QPP encryption
Future Vision	Scaling for fault tolerance	Utility-scale quantum systems

20.6.1 Qubit Count

The Willow chip from Google works with a count of 105 qubits, while the Quantum System Two from IBM contains Heron processors, each with a capacity to run 133 qubits. The advantage of having a higher number of qubits in the system of IBM is from scalability and computational power improvements. It is additionally the case that the system of IBM is modular; it increases qubit count through coupling multiple processors. On the contrary, Google's focus is more streamlined, targeting optimization within a single-chip framework.

These differences in qubit number demonstrate the target for each system, with that of IBM for a utility-scale quantum computer with an emphasis on adding modularity and scalability and that of Google having largely been concerned with achieving quantum supremacy that demonstrates that a quantum computer can solve certain problems significantly faster than a classical machine.

20.6.2 Design Philosophy

The principles of design of such two systems clearly state the directions they follow for the advancement of quantum technologies. Google's Willow chip, on the other hand, intends for it to be a demonstration of the great feats possible through quantum supremacy, such as the demonstration of solving problems-classical systems cannot do. This is the emphasis on following theoretical and experimental achievement.

Interestingly, on the other hand, IBM's approach has been more focused on a commercial end-use. The Quantum System Two focuses on industry-oriented scalability and ultimate utility, with studies into areas like drugs, logistics, and financial modeling. From supremacy to real-world solutions, IBM reflects the meaning of quantum utility from using an application in everyday life to an important application in the industry.

20.6.3 Error Management

Error management is very essential when it comes to quantum computing due to the delicacy of qubits. The Willow chip from Google implements fault-tolerant error correction techniques, intended to lessen the errors occurring during computation. Fault tolerance naturally means that the system stays unbolted by the errors; this feature becomes pivotal in reaching quantum supremacy.

Contrarily, IBM performs advanced modular error correction in Quantum System Two. This mode of operation places error management at the system level and utilizes the benefits of modular architecture to reduce crosstalk and improve reliability. Thus, improved advanced error correction mechanisms raise the performance of the overall system and increase the fidelity of computations on IBM's quantum processors.

20.6.4 Encryption Focus

Unlike all other forms of computing, quantum technology introduces new challenges and opportunities when it comes to encryption and data security. Although Google's approach is about mitigating errors, focusing on quantum integrity operations indirectly supports encryption. But again, that is not the primary focus on realizing a quantum-safe encryption mechanism.

An application of such quantum safe encryption methods would be using the QPP in Quantum System Two for security operations in manipulating qubit superpositions and entanglement. All these initiatives still concern the general concept of quantum-safe encryption for sensitive data in all quantum computations. It addresses potential vulnerabilities in the quantum era.

The advancement in quantum computing creates a distinct set of challenges and opportunities concerning encryption and data security. In Google's endeavors, the secure quantum operation would ensure some level of integrity on encryption, while actually, computational error mitigation is the main focus. Interestingly, the project does not deal with quantum-safe encryption algorithms.

By contrast, IBM, as part of Quantum System Two, implements quantum safe encryption techniques such as the QPP to ensure secure operations during the special processes of manipulating qubit superpositions and entanglement. Thus, quantum-safe encryption becomes critical to secure sensitive data during quantum computations from any potential vulnerabilities in the quantum era.

20.6.5 Future Vision

Fault-tolerant quantum computing is the basis of Google's vision for the long-term future. It is designed to help realize a bigger goal for Google—the ultimate self-sufficiency of quantum power—in training its quantum processors to be as error-immune as possible while increasing the number of qubit units.

On the contrary, utility-scale quantum systems are the only things that IBM seems to think about for the market. The ten-year vision that IBM has on the creation of a production-grade system with a minimum of 100,000 qubits, including advanced error correction and modular architectures, positions it squarely at the cutting edge of quantum-centric supercomputer platforms. These quantum-computing-based supercomputers purposefully blend the advantages of quantum and classical computing resources to address large-scale industrial problems.

Comparative evaluation of the Google Willow chip with the IBM Quantum System Two shows two contrary approaches that these quantum computer makers take. While on Google's part it is all about achieving—and maintaining—quantum supremacy through designs that might achieve that end and demonstrations of experiments toward that end; IBM, on the other hand, is about emphasizing practical value by making quantum computing highly accessible and applicable across industries and with economic ramifications that are positive.

Both are on a promising trajectory forward for quantum computing. While IBM builds pathways toward near-term applications, research will make future plays with design parameterization that extends practical quantum computing parameters beyond those currently in existence. As quantum technologies evolve, both types of the system will chart a fascinating future for their computation, security, and grand global problems.

20.7 CHALLENGES IN QUANTUM COMPUTING

20.7.1 Quantum Decoherence

Quantum decoherence is what happens when interactions with the environment removes from a qubits their quanta behavior and transfers them from a superposition of quantum states to a classical state. This effect ultimately limits quantum computing, as it inherently disrupts the quantum properties necessary for powerful computations. The other essential criterion for quantum processors is coherence time—the time during which their quantum state is preserved.

Challenges: Because of the inherent fragility of qubits, they are highly affected by environmental disturbances such as electromagnetic interference, thermal vibrations, and material defects. It is these disturbances that lead to computational errors and decreased reliability of the systems. Suppression of decoherence has been the objective of research aimed at isolation of qubits, error correction, and material engineering. In this regard, some newly emerging qubit candidates, such as topological qubits, show some promise due to their anticipated immunity to environmental noise and extended coherence time, which can change the face of quantum hardware design.

20.7.2 Quantum Error Correction (QEC)

With quantum error correction, we can preserve fidelity in quantum computing. It has ramifications for quantum states: being protected against most decoherences to avoid loss of information becomes painfully limited. QEC techniques make sure that whatever decoherences and other noises might happen to the quantum operations, they are detected and corrected. Hence, errors during quantum operations are by no means free from all interference.

Challenges: It takes much overhead in additional qubits to implement QEC. For example, there are surface codes, a front-running type of quantum error correction that require dozens of physical qubits to encode a single logical qubit. The way toward achieving fault-tolerant quantum computations, wherein an error is corrected before it accumulates into an error it is not possible to control, is still greatly among the aspects that attract many to the field. Advanced designs, such as concatenated codes and topological methods, are in the making to resolve this issue.

20.7.3 Scalability

Scalability in quantum computing refers to the capability to expand the number of qubits in a quantum system while maintaining high computation and low errors. This is very much a need for quantum systems to stretch these very difficult problems that classical computers cannot get to.

Challenges: With the increasing number of qubits, ensuring coherent interactions among them becomes vastly more difficult. Qubit crosstalk, thermal noise, resource allocation, and so on complicate the scaling even more. Larger quantum systems require breakthrough techniques in manufacturing, materials science, and control systems to manage the increasing complexity of their needs. Effective scalability depends on creating modular architectures to connect multiple quantum processors seamlessly, like IBM's Quantum System Two.

20.7.4 Cost and Accessibility

Financial Barriers: The field of quantum computing is still very new; therefore, the cost incurred in terms of hardware development, installation, and maintenance remains enormous. Among these costs, cryogenic cooling, precision fabrication, and error-correction of quantum processors are those factors pushing up the price. These expenditures act as a constraint on the access of quantum systems to smaller organizations or academic institutions, thereby limiting innovation to those wealthy organizations, among them.

Talent Shortage: This explains why the workforce pool in quantum technology is thin; as such, it becomes an enormous bottleneck for the promising development of technology. The interdisciplinary nature of quantum computing results in a very complicated scheme of talent grooming and retaining, where one has to know bits of quantum mechanics, computer science, engineering, and materials sciences to help push things forward. Investments into quantum education and research programs must be increased to fill this gap.

20.8 RECENT MILESTONES IN QUANTUM COMPUTING

Quantum computing has achieved rapid movement in development over the last few years with large tech companies making good strides toward practical and scalable quantum systems.

20.8.1 Amazon's "Ocelot" Quantum Chip

Amazon's chip for quantum computing, Ocelot, is making large strides in the quantum technology of computing after its unveiling. In addition to fault tolerance and scalability, the Ocelot chip can potentially increase performance in quantum error correction by 90%. For instance, it is the first breakthrough to applying cat qubits technology, which itself suppresses some forms of error, making quantum error correction much easier. However, there remains much work to be done in error reduction and scalability before quantum computers become commercially useful. Nevertheless, the introduction of Ocelot signals the tremendous strides being made in the industry, following in the footsteps of competitors like Microsoft and Google.

20.8.2 Microsoft's "Majorana 1" Quantum Processor

Topological qubits are a different approach in quantum computing, and for that, they have been relying on the Majorana zero modes for creating more stable and fault-tolerant quantum systems. In general, a qubit based on conventional superconductivity requires several error-corrected circuits. On the other hand, topological qubits' exotic quantum ground states provide them strong resistance to decoherence, unlike such conventional devices. In February 2025, Microsoft researchers announced the invention of Majorana 1, a chip designed for quantum computing using topological superconductors made up of indium arsenide and aluminum. This development takes us one step closer to Microsoft's eventual goal of developing a quantum computer using topological qubits. However, this announcement creates a stir among all the scientists because, at present, there is no public definitive evidence that Majorana 1 does behave as a Majorana zero mode.

20.8.3 Google's "Willow" Quantum Processor

Google's Quantum AI division unveiled Willow 105-qubit superconducting quantum computing chip. Willow technology is capable of below-threshold quantum error correction, which exponentially reduces the number of errors as qubits scale. Furthermore, it completed a random circuit sampling benchmark task within five minutes, whereas this accomplishment would take the most powerful current supercomputers an impractical amount of time to complete, thus demonstrating its capacity.

20.8.4 IBM's "Condor" Quantum Processor

IBM announced Condor, a superconducting quantum processor with 1,121 qubits, the first major advance in quantum hardware. Condor also adds improved qubit connectivity, coherence times, and gate fidelities, which are in line with IBM's path toward constructing a fault-tolerant quantum computer.

20.9 CONCLUSION

In fact, superposition is the foundation of quantum computing, allowing qubits to explore an extremely wide solution space through parallelism and, hence, computing capabilities otherwise unattainable by classical systems. Such has brought about progress that has been made in quantum hardware, as evidenced by Google's Willow chip and IBM's Quantum System Two. These are state-of-the-art technologies addressing some of the key challenges associated with error correction, qubit coherence, and scalability, bringing quantum computing to practical applicability.

Quantum decoherence, error management, and scalability are indeed barriers facing the impressive development of the current state of quantum technology. To penetrate these barriers, a multifaceted and integrated approach should be adopted. These include hardware advances and the developments in algorithm and software engineering. Examples of such developments are quantum cryptographic techniques like the QPP that comment, in a way, on the dual importance of computational power and security in this quantum era.

Looking further, however, quantum computing is expected to have transformative effects on several industries—from cryptography to machine learning to drug discovery to materials science. Superposition, in conjunction with cutting-edge architectures, can change the face of computation as it is known today as the commencement of a technological revolution.

REFERENCES

Abdelgaber, Nahed, Chris Nikolopoulos. (2020). Overview on Quantum Computing and Its Applications in Artificial Intelligence. IEEE Access, 17, 198–199.

AbuGhanem, M. (2024). IBM Quantum Computers: Evolution, Performance, and Future Directions. Quantum Physics. arXiv:2410.00916 [quant-ph].

Albuainain, Aminah, Jana Alansari, Samiyah Alrashidi, Wasmiyah Alqahtan, Jana Alshaya, Naya Nagy. (2022). Experimental Implementation of Shor's Quantum Algorithm to Break RSA. 2022 14th International Conference on Computational Intelligence and Communication Networks (CICN), Volume 3, 748–752.

Anwer, Sara, Ahmed Younes, Islam Elkabani, Ashraf Elsayed. (2022). Preparation of Quantum Superposition Using Partial Negation. IEEE Access, 10, 18944–18954.

Bawa, Sidak. (2024). Exploring Quantum Computing: Principles and Applications. Journal of Quantum Science and Technology, 1(3), 57–69.

Bhat, Hilal Ahmad, Farooq Ahmad Khanday, Brajesh Kumar Kaushik, Faisal Bashir, Khurshed Ahmad Shah. (2022). Quantum Computing: Fundamentals, Implementations and Applications. IEEE Open Journal of Nanotechnology, 3, 61–77.

Breuckmann, N. P., B. M. Terhal. (2016). Constructions and Noise Thresholds for Topological Quantum Codes. Quantum Information Processing, 15(11), 4331–4394.

García-Pérez, Guillermo, Matteo A. C. Rossi, Sabrina Maniscalco. (2020). IBM Q Experience as a Versatile Experimental Testbed for Simulating Open Quantum Systems. NPJ Quantum Information, 6(1).

Google Quantum AI. (2024). The Willow Quantum Processor: Advancements in Quantum Error Correction and Scalability. Retrieved from https://quantumai.google/.

Harith Akmal Zulfaizal Fadillah, Mohd, Bahari Idrus, Mohammad Khatim Hasan, Siti Munirah Mohd. (2021). Impact of various IBM Quantum Architectures with Different Properties on Grover's Algorithm. 2021 International Conference on Electrical Engineering and Informatics (ICEEI), IEEE Access, 1–6.

IBM Quantum. (2024). Quantum Computing with IBM: Osprey and beyond. Retrieved from https://quantum-computing.ibm.com/.

Kjaergaard, M., M. E. Schwartz, J. Braumüller, P. Krantz, J. I.-J. Wang, S. Gustavsson, W. D. Oliver. (2020). Superconducting Qubits: Current State and Future Directions. Annual Review of Condensed Matter Physics, 11(1), 369–395.

Kumar Das, Atanu, Saradindu Panda, Chiradeep Mukherjee, Bansibadan Maji. (2023). Assessing the Performance of Quantum Gates in Presence of Superposition State Using IBMQ Server. 2023 IEEE Fifth International Conference on Advances in Electronics, Computers and Communications (ICAECC), IEEE Access, 1–5.

Lou, Dafu, Randy Kuang, Alex He. (2021). Entropy Transformation and Expansion with Quantum Permutation Pad for 5G Secure Networks. 2021 IEEE 21st International Conference on Communication Technology (ICCT), Volume 4, 840–845.

Martinis, John, Austin Fowler, Andrew N. Cleland. (2023). High-Fidelity Qubit Readout and Quantum Error Suppression Using Surface Code. Nature Physics, 19(9), 930–944.

Microsoft Quantum. (2024). Azure Quantum: Bridging Classical and Quantum for Scalable Cloud-Based Quantum Solutions. Retrieved from https://azure.microsoft.com/en-us/products/quantum.

Montanaro, A. (2016). Quantum algorithms: An overview. NPJ Quantum Information, 2(1), 1–8.

Parmar, Sahib J., Vinitkumar R. Parmar, Jaiprakash Verma, Satyabrata Roy, Pronaya Bhattacharya. (2023). Quantum Computing: Exploring Superposition and Entanglement for Cutting-Edge Applications. 2023 16th International Conference on Security of Information and Networks (SIN), IEEE Access, 1–6.

Pasupuleti, Murali Krishna. (2024). Advancements in Quantum Computing and Information Science. International Journal of Academic and Industrial Research Innovations (IJAIRI), National Education Services, 62–107.

Riel, H. (2021). Quantum Computing Technology. 2021 IEEE International Electron Devices Meeting (IEDM), IEEE Access, 1.3.1–1.3.7.

Shafique, Muhammad Ali, Arslan Munir, Imran Latif. (2024). Quantum Computing: Circuits, Algorithms, and Applications, IEEE Access, Volume 12.

Shaw, M., N. S. Dattani, N. Chancellor, K. Bharti. (2020). A Review of Quantum Cloud Computing. Quantum Information Processing, 19(11), 378.

Sheridan, L., F. Luthi, J. S. Otterbach. (2023). Real-Time Quantum State Tomography Using Tensor Networks. IEEE Transactions on Quantum Engineering, 4, 65–79.

Toshiba Quantum Technology Division. (2024). Quantum Key Distribution and Secure Communication Protocols for Post-Quantum Era. Retrieved from https://www.toshiba.co.jp/qkd.

Yuan, Charles, Michael Carbin. (2022). Tower: Data Structures in Quantum Superposition. Proceedings of the ACM on Programming Languages, 6(134), 259–288.

Zhu, Xiaobo, Yu Xu, Shijie Hao, Luyan Sun. (2024). Superconducting Qubits: Architectures and Scaling Challenges in Next-Generation Quantum Computers. Journal of Quantum Engineering and Applications, 5(2), 101–127.

21 Quantum Internet and Its Revolutionary Implications for Modern Electronic Devices

G. Sandhyakumari, M. Bharathi, and V. Madhurima

21.1 INTRODUCTION

The quantum internet can transform how we communicate, offering a leap far beyond the capabilities of our current digital systems. The internet sends data in bits, but the quantum internet uses qubits, the building blocks of quantum computing. These qubits are part of the interesting world of quantum mechanics, utilized in algorithms, and exhibit traits like superposition, entanglement, and even quantum teleportation [1].

One of its most game-changing features is the highly secure quantum key distribution (QKD), where any attempt to intercept data is instantly detectable. It is hard to track a quantum state that keeps changing and to alert users when an infringement occurs. In a time when cyberthreats are becoming more sophisticated and frequent, this level of security could be a game-changer. But the quantum internet isn't just about keeping secrets safe. It is also applicable to quantum computing, ultra-precise sensing, and real-time scientific collaboration made possible by the capability to share quantum states across the globe. To make this happen, scientists are building a whole new kind of infrastructure, including quantum nodes, quantum repeaters, and entangled photon sources. These technologies facilitate fragile quantum links over long distances, overcoming challenges like decoherence and signal loss [2]. To smooth the transition, researchers are also working on a fusion system to combine classical and quantum networks, helping to bridge today's internet with tomorrow's.

As this technology matures, a deep mark is expected to be left on industries such as finance, healthcare, defense, and telecommunications, specifically those that rely on the fast and secure transfer of information. Imagine a future in which solving massive computational problems takes moments, not months, as data breaches are nearly impossible. The quantum internet also makes possible breakthroughs like distributed quantum computing with globally synchronized clocks. These breakthroughs could transform global information systems of today. And while much of this is still

DOI: 10.1201/9781003538950-24

developing, the progress we see now lays the groundwork toward a potential where communication is faster, smarter, and more secure than ever before.

21.2 HISTORY OF QUANTUM COMPUTING

The quantum Internet is built upon the same quantum mechanical principles that inspired quantum computing, so those same roots do also go back to the early 20th century. Quantum entanglement, also famously known as the EPR paradox, was introduced by Einstein, Podolsky, and Rosen back in 1935. Later, this initially controversial idea would become central to quantum communication.

In the 1980s, Charles Bennett and Gilles Brassard developed the BB84 protocol, marking a turning point as the first quantum cryptography method. This protocol showed that one can securely exchange cryptographic keys since the law of physics, not just math, assures it. Later decades saw researchers show necessary quantum communication feats. These feats included the quantum-teleportation- and entanglement-based messaging things. These experiments proved the likelihood for it to drive quantum information firmly. A huge step forward arrived in 2016, when China launched the Micius satellite, the first satellite built with quantum communications in mind. This made it possible to conduct QKD over thousands of kilometers of real optical fibers between cities, which had never been achieved before. The announcement in early October has since sparked waves of global interest, with countries in Europe, North America, and Asia racing to develop quantum statement networks.

While the complete emergence of a worldwide quantum internet remains in the works, the building blocks are in place. And with each advancement, we come closer to a future where secure, ultra-fast quantum communication is a reality of our world.

The quantum internet is something that will perhaps revamp industries across the board, offering higher security and performance levels that simply cannot be achieved in today's technologies. Telecommunications intend to offer the creation of ultra-secure global networks of communication. This ensures that sensitive messages, data transfers, and other defined communications will never be unsafe from interception or compromise. This built-in privacy and security is a game-changer in an ever-connected world. Hospitals and clinics will also enjoy a great deal of benefits [3]. Apart from the secure transmission of information on medical records between hospitals to clinics and research teams, quantum technology will be used in better diagnostic equipment and medical imaging to achieve superior precision and reliability.

Transactions in finance will have their data integrity elevated to an extraordinary level. Due to quantum cryptography, banking systems may in fact become fraud-proof, thereby lessening the cyber-risks associated with mobile payments or interbank transfers by huge amounts. Figure 21.1 represents the application of quantum computing. A transformation granting such trust and flexibility to the whole financial system would be unprecedented in history. Thus, other industries reliant on extreme data accuracy would find this very useful, e.g., scientific research and space exploration. In quantum-enhanced sensing and navigation, preparation about deep space missions or Earth-based climate modeling is underway. This, in turn, could alter totally the ways in which we explore, observe, and comprehend the surroundings.

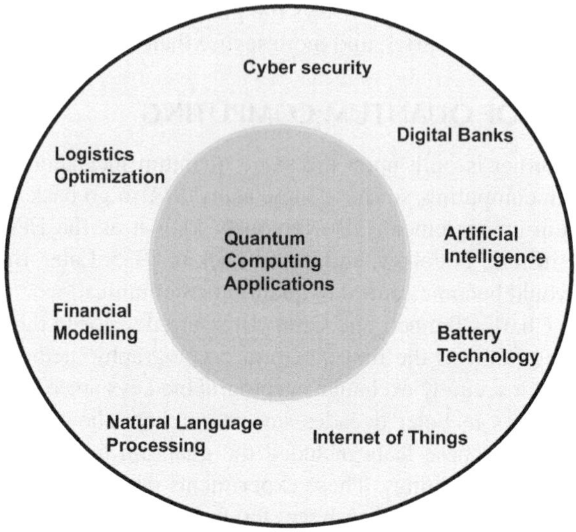

FIGURE 21.1 Applications of quantum computing.

Looking further in the future, global quantum networks' evolution could set off variables in AI and intricate problem-solving. With promising developments in distributed quantum computing, problems that are currently beyond the reach of even the most powerful supercomputers could become solvable within a practical timeframe.

21.3 CORE PRINCIPLES OF THE QUANTUM INTERNET

The quantum internet is built upon profound concepts from quantum mechanics wherein the world is witnessing a new era of protected and efficient communication. Quantum entanglement is one such founding pillar of the theory, where particles stay connected over large immense distances. This eerie connection lays the basis for quantum teleportation, in which quantum states are transmitted without physically moving the particles themselves. On the flipside of security, the quantum network gets highly secured through QKD under which codes are unbreakable. Interception attempts would instantly alter the state of the data; instead, it warns the communicating parties about an eavesdropper. Further, since quantum information cannot be imitated due to something called the no-cloning theorem, an inherent principle of quantum mechanics, the security of the system is thereby augmented.

1. ***Superposition and Parallelism:*** Distinct from standard bits, which can only symbolize a 0 or a 1 at any specified time, qubits (the building blocks of quantum computing) can exist in a superposition of both states concurrently [4]. This inimitable ability means qubits can represent multiple values at once and enable the quantum system to process enormous amount of information in parallel. As a result, quantum networks and computers offer

significantly greater computational power and efficiency compared to traditional systems [5].

Superposition, along with quantum parallelism, forms the heart of quantum electronics also and drives cutting-edge technologies like quantum computing. Classical electronics use voltage levels that represent binary states as quantum electronics manipulate superpositioned quantum states through specialized devices like quantum dots and superconducting Josephson junctions [6]. These devices harness behaviors of quantum mechanics both strange and powerful. Wave-particle duality, quantum tunneling, and interference fall under those behaviors.

Quantum parallelism acts to superposition qubits, and it operates upon many possible states at one time. Quantum systems can thus tackle optimization problems and process complex signals quickly in ways that conventional computers cannot. This parallelism can be used within devices such as quantum circuits and spintronics-based systems, as well as adiabatic quantum computers [7]. This transforms areas such as secure communication with data optimization.

Quantum circuits use quantum gates to regulate qubit interactions and change their state for carrying out calculations. The effectiveness of these circuits is affected by hardware parameters like decoherence time. A qubit will retain its quantum position for the decoherence time prior to losing information. Short decoherence times limit computational complexity.

Actual electronic devices must be integrated as an important step when theoretical quantum communication advances are changed to practical systems, notably for creating quantum routers and hybrid circuits. Recent advancements to chip-based quantum photonic circuits make high-fidelity quantum information manipulation and routing possible, and these advancements guarantee effective transmission across quantum networks [8]. To make quantum routers practical and usable in the real world, researchers are exploring hybrid designs that combine quantum photonics with classical CMOS technology. These combinations help reduce the cost, size, and power requirements of quantum devices, making them more scalable and stable, even at room temperature [9]. That's crucial for enabling real-world applications like advanced computing, high-precision sensing, and secure communication.

Interestingly, the way signals are handled in quantum systems is fundamentally different from classical systems. In traditional electronics, superposition simply means layering waveforms [10]. But in quantum systems, superposition creates probabilistic states, which open the door to entirely new possibilities. These include QKD for secure messaging, quantum sensors for ultra-sensitive measurements, and quantum memory for storing quantum information.

2. ***Entanglement:*** The transfer of quantum information while transferring particles is made possible by a mechanism called quantum teleportation. Unlike teleportation in science fiction movies, it is not about changing locations in an instant but actually reconstituting the exact quantum state of a particle at a distant particle, which requires extraordinary advanced technological devices. Information transfer in superconducting qubits and quantum dots are examples of modern quantum technologies that

facilitate teleportation through particles and classical communications [11]. Developing further, quantum teleportation commences through a splitting mechanism that separates or divides a pair of blind particles placed in different locations. Each of the particles is interacted separately, leading to a state collapse, forming new systems, as the particle splits, its quantum state is sequentially transmitted through a regular communication channel.

3. ***Quantum Key Distribution (QKD):*** QKD employs the principles of quantum physics to securely share keys for encryption. It uses the disruption of quantum states to detect potential interception. One of the best known is BB84, where the sender and receiver try to detect an eavesdropper by comparing bits of the data they share in quantum form [12]. If any interference is detected, the key is discarded. Its basis is QKD's no-cloning theorem, which states that unmeasured quantum systems cannot be duplicated because that would mean changing them. This allows the encryption to be provided with utmost integrity and security. Quantum repeaters, photonic chips, and superconducting circuits allow for long-distance secure quantum communication. Besides keeping information confidential, the no-cloning rule brings systems into conflict with assumed classical electronics that transform the traditional approaches to designing quantum information processing engines.
4. ***Quantum Repeaters:*** Quantum repeaters expand the scope of quantum communication by overcoming noise and signal loss through spreading entanglement using intermediary nodes. They accomplish long-range entanglement through techniques such as quantum error correction and entanglement swapping [13]. Stored entangled states in the quantum remembrance are kept until a persistent connection can be established. These devices enable quantum sensing, distributed quantum computing, and secure communication. To build scalable quantum networks for the quantum internet, repeaters need to sustain quantum information, making them indispensable.
5. ***Decoherence and Error Correction:*** Quantum repeaters are specialized procedures that enlarge the reach of quantum communication by distributing entangled particles across intermediate nodes [14]. They address key challenges in quantum networks, such as signal loss and environmental noise, which normally limit how far quantum information can travel.

Error correction plays a significant task in the operation of quantum repeaters. Because quantum states are sensitive and easily disrupted, repeaters use error correction to maintain fidelity and reduce the effects of noise. This enables more reliable communication over extended distances, making quantum repeaters a fundamental module of the quantum internet. They also support applications like secure key exchange, scattered quantum computing, and long-distance quantum sensing.

Decoherence and error correction are at the heart of building stable and sensible quantum systems. Decoherence occurs when a quantum system loses its delicate superposition due to interference from its surrounding environment. In electronics, this might involve qubits interacting with thermal noise or electromagnetic fields, which cause them to behave more like classical bits and lose their quantum behavior.

To counter this, quantum slip improvement techniques are used to protect quantum accuracy. These methods encode information across multiple qubits to form logical qubits. Even if a few physical qubits experience errors, the overall quantum state can still be reconstructed [15]. Techniques such as the Shor code, the Steane code, and surface codes are commonly used in electronic quantum systems to notice the proper errors without destroying the encoded quantum condition.

In systems like superconducting circuits or quantum dots, error correction is necessary for construction fault-tolerant quantum computers. It allows quantum operations to continue even when some qubits are affected by decoherence. In communication, repeaters depend on error correction to reliably transmit quantum data across vast distances, ensuring it arrives unaltered and secure. Together, decoherence and error correction define the reliability and scalability of quantum technologies. They make it possible to store, transmit, and process quantum information effectively, even in noisy and imperfect real-world environments.

6. ***Quantum Network Protocols:*** Quantum network protocols are the rulebook for how quantum information is transmitted, synchronized, and processed across a future quantum internet, ensuring efficient communication and resource optimization, much like classical internet protocols. Crucial for secure and efficient quantum communication systems and the foundation of the quantum internet, these protocols leverage quantum mechanical principles like entanglement, superposition, and teleportation to improve protection and computational competence beyond classical systems. Quantum repeater protocols combat decoherence over huge distances using entanglement transaction and quantum fault modification [16].

In distributed quantum computing, quantum processors collaborate on complex computations via quantum communication protocols, while quantum error correction (QEC) protocols protect quantum data from noise by encoding information across multiple qubits [17]. Implemented with electronic components like superconducting qubits, quantum dots, and photonic chips, these protocols enable secure quantum information transmission and manipulation, powerful advancements in communication, computing, and sense. Integration with standard network is essential for the quantum internet to coexist and interoperate with existing infrastructure, facilitating hybrid systems where classical and quantum data are exchanged seamlessly [18]. This involves using classical channels for certain tasks while quantum networks handle quantum-specific tasks like secure communication and distributed computing.

21.4 ADVANTAGES OF QUANTUM COMPUTING

Quantum computing offers quite a few important advantages in electronics, mainly its ability to out-compute any classical computer. This advantage can change industries such as cryptography, materials science, optimization, and artificial intelligence. The key advantages of quantum computing in electronics are as follows:

- **Speed:** Quantum computers are much faster than the most advanced current supercomputers. This is because qubits can exist in multiple states at the same time, analogous to a light being both on and off. This quantum parallelism allows them to explore many possibilities at the same time, enabling rapid execution of tasks such as cracking complex codes, simulating particles, and analyzing massive amounts of information [19].
- **Power:** By using entangled qubits, quantum computers can solve very complicated problems that would take classical computers forever. Algorithms like Shor's (for breaking encryption) and Grover's (for super-fast searching) show the potential to solve problems that are currently just too hard for our regular machines.
- **Mastering Optimization:** Visualize the best route for a delivery vehicle across a large city, determine the optimal mix of investments, or optimize a complex industrial process. Quantum computing could be a game-changer for these kinds of tricky optimization problems. Its ability to discover many solutions at once allow them to quickly identify the ideal answer.
- **Unbreakable Security:** While the absolute power of quantum computers could potentially crack today's typical encryption methods, it can also lead to ultra-secure communication for end-to-end technologies like QKD. Scientists are also working on quantum-safe encryption methods to make sure our information stays protected even as quantum computers become more influential [20].

In short, quantum computing in electronics isn't just about manufacture faster computers; it's about unlocking new ways to solve problems beyond our reach, with major implications for data security, material design, and smarter decision-making. Figure 21.2 illustrates the applications of quantum computing in health care.

Quantum computers are also opening up exciting new avenues in electronics beyond just raw processing power:

- **Understanding the Quantum World:** Imagine being capable of accurately depicting how particles behave in materials, chemicals, and even living things. Quantum computers can simulate these in a quantum system. This could be a major challenge for designing new materials with remarkable properties, such as better batteries or lossless conductors, discovering new medicines by accurately modeling molecular interactions, and advancing our understanding of chemistry. Things that are at present too complex for even the finest standard computers to model accurately could be simulated with quantum computers.
- **Smarter Artificial Intelligence:** Quantum computing could give a significant boost to artificial intelligence and machine learning. Certain AI algorithms that are currently slow could be sped up radically. This could lead to better image recognition, speech comprehension, and reference system.

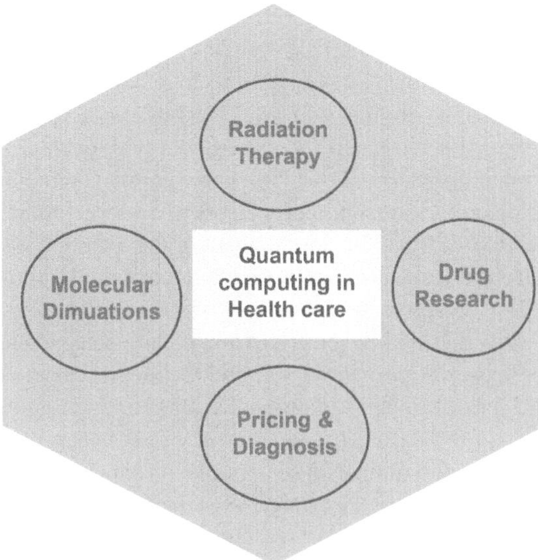

FIGURE 21.2 Quantum computing in healthcare.

- **Super-Sensitive Sensing:** The useful properties of quantum computers can also be used to produce really sensitive sensors—sensors for steering, medical imaging, or environmental monitoring that are far more precise than anything we have today [21]. This quantum-enhanced sensing could lead to breakthroughs in various fields, such as healthcare, defense, and scientific research. Superposition allows quantum computers to make several calculations in parallel. It's like having an enormous number of workers tackling different parts of a problem concurrently, doing tasks like making intricate simulations, analyzing huge datasets, and predicting patterns.
- **Designing the Future of Materials:** By being able to represent materials at the atomic level, quantum computers can help us devise utterly new and useful materials. This can possibly develop the electronics industry, and more energy-efficient electronic devices based on novel semiconductors, superconductors, and other advanced materials [22].

21.5 FUTURE TRENDS

The future of quantum computing and the quantum internet is can revolutionize various industries by harnessing the power of quantum mechanics for both advanced computing and ultra-secure communication. The key to these advancements is progress in quantum hardware, where scientists are exploring options like superconducting qubits, trapped ions, and neutral atoms to improve system stability and reduce errors. There's also a lot of hope for topological qubits, which could potentially make quantum systems more reliable and resistant to faults. Along with hardware improvement, quantum error correction is a critical focus, with techniques like surface codes and cat codes being explored to enhance error confrontation and move toward large-scale, practical quantum computing [23].

Another exciting trend is the rise of quantum cloud computing. Companies such as IBM, Google, and Amazon are now offering cloud-based access to quantum processors, opening the entry for more users to experiment with quantum capabilities. The concept of hybrid quantum-classical systems is also gaining momentum, where classical computers work alongside quantum processors to achieve optimal performance for specific tasks. At the same time, the development of the quantum internet is progressing, with QKD and entanglement-based networks promising the future of ultra-secure communications [24]. Test projects like China's Micius satellite and the US Quantum Network testbeds show that significant strides are already being made in this direction.

Breakthroughs in quantum materials and chip integration are also driving this innovation forward. For example, silicon-based quantum processors and 2D materials such as graphene are helping boost efficiency and scalability. These advancements could have a profound impact on sectors like pharmaceuticals, where quantum simulations might speed up drug discovery, and finance, where quantum algorithms could revolutionize risk analysis. Moreover, quantum-enhanced artificial intelligence and machine learning could bring about a new era in fields like pattern recognition and natural language processing [25].

While scalability is still a major challenge, both established companies and emerging startups are working hard to make quantum computing commercially viable. Over the next decade, we can expect huge progress in achieving quantum supremacy, building a fully operational quantum internet, and reshaping industries with unprecedented computational power and security capabilities.

21.6 CASE STUDIES: REAL-WORLD APPLICATIONS OF QUANTUM TECHNOLOGIES

Quantum computing and quantum communication have moved beyond theory and are now being actively applied in real-world scenarios across a range of industries. Several organizations and institutions have already demonstrated the potential of quantum technologies, showing how they can transform various sectors. One of the most prominent examples is Google's quantum supremacy experiment. In 2019, Google unveiled its 53-qubit quantum processor, Sycamore, which performed a precise task in 200 seconds, something that would obtain the world's the majority controlling supercomputer over 10,000 years. This high point confirmed the highly awaited task of quantum computing to answer multipart problems that are beyond the capabilities of classical computers [26].

The financial industry has also seen great improvement. JPMorgan Chase aligned with IBM to consider quantum algorithms for group optimization and risk analysis. By utilizing IBM's quantum computing policy, JPMorgan has been able to pick up financial modeling, ensuing in additional resourceful trade strategy and better decision-making processes [27]. In healthcare, BASF, a German pharmaceutical giant, is leveraging quantum computing to improve molecular simulations. Quantum algorithms are being used to forecast molecular relations with greater accuracy and speed up drug development, as well as decreasing research costs. This is typically helpful in the growth of novel treatments for diseases like Alzheimer's and cancer.

Quantum communication has advanced as well. China's Micius satellite stands out as an inventive idea, representing QKD over extensive distance. This quantum-encrypted communication between ground stations thousands of kilometers apart shows immense promise for cybersecurity by providing that ultra-secure data communication. In the transportation sector, Volkswagen has used quantum computing for traffic flow optimization. The company worked with D-Wave to develop quantum algorithms that simulate traffic overcrowding patterns and make suggestions to reduce travel times, increasing urban mobility.

These case studies emphasize the growth of quantum technologies across many fields. As these advancement continue, additional industries will use quantum solutions for their multifaceted issues and concerns.

21.7 LIMITATIONS

Quantum computing is developing quickly, but there are a few obstacles that prevent its widespread adoption. One major challenge is the fragile nature of qubits. These quantum bits are easily disturbed by their surroundings, leading to a loss of coherence that limits both the accuracy and the scale of computation. To direct this, researchers are developing fault-tolerant systems, but these necessitate numerous added qubits designed for error correction, and production scalability is a primary barrier.

Building large-scale quantum systems also involve overcoming engineering complexity. Maintaining the feeble environment required for quantum hardware, such as near-zero temperatures or high vacuum environments, adds to the obscurity along with cost. Different quantum platforms employ unreliable technologies, making consistency and cross-compatibility a concern.

Quantum computers offer precise executions for areas like optimization and molecular simulation. The number of practical quantum algorithms remains limited, restricting quantum systems' utility. Hybrid systems, connecting classical and quantum processing, add extra challenges and may reduce performance gains in certain applications [28]. Access to quantum computing also remains costly and limited, both because of the high expense of hardware and the specialized expertise required.

Security is another matter of concern [29]. While quantum technologies like QKD can enhance data defense, quantum algorithms such as Shor's pose a risk to standard encryption, making quantum-safe cryptographic solutions needed. Despite these limitations, steady progress continues. Advances in materials, chip design, and quantum error correction point toward promising directions. With growing investment and research, practical and scalable quantum computing solutions are moving closer to reality at an accelerating pace [30].

21.8 CONCLUSION

Quantum-enhanced technologies, such as quantum key distribution and quantum sensors, are beginning to change the security and precision of communication. As quantum technologies move toward application, they will be used with classical technologies, forming a hybrid system that is more well-organized and scalable. As we mainly focus on new devices and promote investment in quantum computing, quantum technologies may soon be part of electronics production and be incorporated in devices beyond computing. Quantum computing helps us process, protect, and make use of information.

REFERENCES

[1] H. B. Patel, S. Mishra, R. Jain and N. Kansara, "The Future of Quantum Computing and its Potential Applications," in Journal For Basic Sciences, vol. 23, no. 11, pp. 513–519, 2023.

[2] D. Ferrari, S. Carretta and M. Amoretti, "A Modular Quantum Compilation Framework for Distributed Quantum Computing," in IEEE Transactions on Quantum Engineering, vol. 4, pp. 1–13, 2023, Art no. 2500213, https://doi.org/10.1109/TQE.2023.3303935.

[3] Q. Wang, J. Guan, J. Liu, Z. Zhang and M. Ying, "New Quantum Algorithms for Computing Quantum Entropies and Distances," in IEEE Transactions on Information Theory, vol. 70, no. 8, pp. 5653–5680, Aug. 2024, https://doi.org/10.1109/TIT.2024.3399014.

[4] D. Ferrari, A. S. Cacciapuoti, M. Amoretti and M. Caleffi, "Compiler Design for Distributed Quantum Computing," in IEEE Transactions on Quantum Engineering, vol. 2, pp. 1–20, 2021, Art no. 4100720, https://doi.org/10.1109/TQE.2021.3053921.

[5] M. Rezai and J. A. Salehi, "Quantum Computation via Multiport Discretized Quantum Fourier Optical Processors," in IEEE Transactions on Quantum Engineering, vol. 5, pp. 1–11, 2024, Art no. 3100111, https://doi.org/10.1109/TQE.2023.3336514.

[6] H. C. Watanabe, R. Raymond, Y.-Y. Ohnishi, E. Kaminishi and M. Sugawara, "Optimizing Parameterized Quantum Circuits with Free-Axis Single-Qubit Gates," in IEEE Transactions on Quantum Engineering, vol. 4, pp. 1–16, 2023, Art no. 3101016, https://doi.org/10.1109/TQE.2023.3286411.

[7] M. Chakraborty, A. Mukherjee, A. Nag and S. Chandra, "Hybrid Quantum Noise Model to Compute Gaussian Quantum Channel Capacity," in IEEE Access, vol. 12, pp. 14671–14689, 2024, https://doi.org/10.1109/ACCESS.2024.3355789.

[8] M. Rezai and J. A. Salehi, "Fundamentals of Quantum Fourier Optics," in IEEE Transactions on Quantum Engineering, vol. 4, pp. 1–22, 2023, Art no. 2100122, https://doi.org/10.1109/TQE.2022.3224799.

[9] S. Otgonbaatar and D. Kranzlmüller, "Exploiting the Quantum Advantage for Satellite Image Processing: Review and Assessment," in IEEE Transactions on Quantum Engineering, vol. 5, pp. 1–9, 2024, Art no. 3100309, https://doi.org/10.1109/TQE.2023.3338970.

[10] T. G. D. Brugière, M. Baboulin, B. Valiron, S. Martiel and C. Allouche, "Reducing the Depth of Linear Reversible Quantum Circuits," in IEEE Transactions on Quantum Engineering, vol. 2, pp. 1–22, 2021, Art no. 3102422, https://doi.org/10.1109/TQE.2021.3091648.

[11] K. L. van der Enden, G. Profitiliotis and D. Croese, "Advancing a Responsible Future Quantum Internet," 2024 IEEE International Conference on Quantum Computing and Engineering (QCE), Montreal, QC, Canada, 2024, pp. 65–70, https://doi.org/10.1109/QCE60285.2024.10254.

[12] S. Sodagari, "Integrating Quantum and Satellites: A New Era of Connectivity," in IEEE Access, vol. 11, pp. 145101–145110, 2023, https://doi.org/10.1109/ACCESS.2023.3344321.

[13] T. Satoh, S. Nagayama, S. Suzuki, T. Matsuo, M. Hajdušek and R. V. Meter, "Attacking the Quantum Internet," in IEEE Transactions on Quantum Engineering, vol. 2, pp. 1–17, 2021, Art no. 4102617, https://doi.org/10.1109/TQE.2021.3094983.

[14] M. Caleffi, K. Simonov and A. S. Cacciapuoti, "Beyond Shannon Limits: Quantum Communications through Quantum Paths," in IEEE Journal on Selected Areas in Communications, vol. 41, no. 8, pp. 2707–2724, Aug. 2023, https://doi.org/10.1109/JSAC.2023.3288263.

[15] E. Pelofske, A. Bärtschi, S. Eidenbenz, B. Garcia and B. Kiefer, "Probing Quantum Telecloning on Superconducting Quantum Processors," in IEEE Transactions on Quantum Engineering, vol. 5, pp. 1–19, 2024, Art no. 3101519, https://doi.org/10.1109/TQE.2024.3391654.
[16] S. Koudia, A. S. Cacciapuoti, K. Simonov and M. Caleffi, "How Deep the Theory of Quantum Communications Goes: Superadditivity, Superactivation and Causal Activation," in IEEE Communications Surveys & Tutorials, vol. 24, no. 4, pp. 1926–1956, Fourthquarter 2022, https://doi.org/10.1109/COMST.2022.3196449.
[17] Z. Yang, M. Zolanvari and R. Jain, "A Survey of Important Issues in Quantum Computing and Communications," in IEEE Communications Surveys & Tutorials, vol. 25, no. 2, pp. 1059–1094, Secondquarter 2023, https://doi.org/10.1109/COMST.2023.3254481.
[18] J. Chung et al., "Design and Implementation of the Illinois Express Quantum Metropolitan Area Network," in IEEE Transactions on Quantum Engineering, vol. 3, pp. 1–20, 2022, Art no. 4100920, https://doi.org/10.1109/TQE.2022.3221029.
[19] A. Singh, K. Dev, H. Siljak, H. D. Joshi and M. Magarini, "Quantum Internet—Applications, Functionalities, Enabling Technologies, Challenges, and Research Directions," in IEEE Communications Surveys & Tutorials, vol. 23, no. 4, pp. 2218–2247, Fourthquarter 2021, https://doi.org/10.1109/COMST.2021.3109944.
[20] A. Tankimanova et al., "Colloidal PbS Quantum Dots for Visible-to-Near-Infrared Optical Internet of Things," in IEEE Photonics Journal, vol. 13, no. 2, pp. 1–11, Apr. 2021, Art no. 7901011, https://doi.org/10.1109/JPHOT.2021.3066521.
[21] A. Kumar et al., "Survey of Promising Technologies for Quantum Drones and Networks," in IEEE Access, vol. 9, pp. 125868–125911, 2021, https://doi.org/10.1109/ACCESS.2021.3109816.
[22] A. Kumar et al., "Survey of Promising Technologies for Quantum Drones and Networks," in IEEE Access, vol. 9, pp. 125868–125911, 2021, https://doi.org/10.1109/ACCESS.2021.3109816.
[23] S. Nagpal et al., "Quantum Computing Integrated Patterns for Real-Time Cryptography in Assorted Domains," in IEEE Access, vol. 12, pp. 132317–132331, 2024, https://doi.org/10.1109/ACCESS.2024.3401162.
[24] B. Li, T. Coopmans and D. Elkouss, "Efficient Optimization of Cutoffs in Quantum Repeater Chains," in IEEE Transactions on Quantum Engineering, vol. 2, pp. 1–15, 2021, Art no. 4103015, https://doi.org/10.1109/TQE.2021.3099003.
[25] https://www.ibm.com/quantum/technology.
[26] https://aws.amazon.com/braket/.
[27] S. Markidis, "What Is Quantum Parallelism, Anyhow?," ISC High Performance 2024 Research Paper Proceedings (39th International Conference), Hamburg, Germany, 2024, pp. 1–12, https://doi.org/10.23919/ISC.2024.10528926.
[28] Z.-Z. Sun, Y.-B. Cheng, D. Ruan, D. Pan, F.-H. Zhang and G.-L. Long, "Quantum Communication Network Routing with Circuit and Packet Switching Strategies," in IEEE Journal on Selected Areas in Communications, https://doi.org/10.1109/JSAC.2025.3543524.
[29] F. Schwierz and M. Ziegler, "Six Decades of Research on 2D Materials: Progress, Dead Ends, and New Horizons," in IEEE Journal of the Electron Devices Society, vol. 10, pp. 443–451, 2022, https://doi.org/10.1109/JEDS.2022.3144500.
[30] https://csrc.nist.gov/projects/post-quantum-cryptography

Index

Q

R

S

T

V